Size: Small (S); Medium (M); Large (L)	Consumer (C)/ Industrial (I)	Corporate Strategic Planning	Target Market Strategy	Marketing Program Positioning Strategy	Product Strategy	Distribution Strategy	Price Strategy	Promotion Strategy	Strategic Marketing Planning	Evaluating Market Performance	Marketing Research
		A	B	C	D	E	F	G	H	I	J
M	C	●	●			●			●	●	
S	C/I	●	●						●		
S	C/I	●	●		●	●			●		●
S	I	●	●	●	●				●		
L	C/I	●	●	●					●	●	
L	I	●			●					●	●
M	I	●			●					●	
S	I	●	●	●					●	●	
S	C		●		●				●	●	●
S	C		●	●			●			●	●
S	C/I		●	●			●				●
M	C/I		●	●						●	●
L	C		●	●			●	●			
L	C		●	●	●						
M	I		●	●	●				●		●
L	C		●	●	●			●			●
M	C			●		●	●	●	●		
S	C/I		●	●		●			●		
L	C/I		●	●				●	●		
S	C		●	●	●		●	●	●		
S	I		●	●	●				●		
M	C		●	●		●	●		●		
S	C		●	●				●	●		
S	C		●	●					●		
S	C		●	●					●		
L	I			●	●		●		●		
S	C	●	●			●		●	●		
S	C	●	●						●		
L	C		●	(●)	(●)				(●)		
S	I	●	●						●		
S	C/I		●	●							●
S	I		●	●							●
M	C			●							●
M	C		●								●
S	C/I		●								●
M	C			●	●						●

Strategic
Marketing
Cases and
Applications

The Irwin Series in Marketing
Consulting Editor
Gilbert A. Churchill
University of Wisconsin, Madison

DAVID W. CRAVENS

and

CHARLES W. LAMB, JR.

M. J. Neeley School of Business
Texas Christian University

Strategic Marketing Cases and Applications

1983   **RICHARD D. IRWIN, INC.**
Homewood, Illinois 60430

© RICHARD D. IRWIN, INC., 1983

ISBN 0-256-02936-9

Library of Congress Catalog Card No. 82–82880

Printed in the United States of America

1 2 3 4 5 6 7 8 9 0 MP 0 9 8 7 6 5 4 3

_To_
Eunice and James L. West
Alice S. and M. J. Neeley

Preface

The marketing profession faces an exciting new strategic challenge which has two key features. First, it calls for greater participation by marketing executives in strategic planning for the enterprise because of the market-centered focus of business strategy. Second, marketing professionals must direct more attention to strategic marketing decisions than in the past due to the impact of these decisions upon business performance. Managerial and tactical decisions are not less important than before. Instead, along with greater emphasis upon strategic decisions, they are part of the expanded responsibilities of marketing decision makers. During the past few years strategic marketing has become one of the most popular topics in business education. The topic is also being given a top-priority rating by business executives.

Strategic Marketing Applications can serve as a teaching-learning resource in several ways. It can be used with a strategic marketing book as a text and applications package in undergraduate advanced management and strategy courses and in MBA management and strategy courses. Alternatively, it can be used as the primary text for advanced or capstone marketing management and strategy courses. In addition to helping to meet the needs of instructors developing new courses in strategic marketing, the book offers instructors of marketing management courses a way to expand the strategic emphasis of these courses beyond that covered by traditional marketing management texts and casebooks. The book contains several cases that cover traditional marketing management areas.

An important part of the teaching-learning process for strategic marketing is to provide students with an opportunity to apply concepts, decision approaches, and analytical tools using cases. This casebook was developed around the strategic marketing planning process presented in the David W. Cravens *Strategic Marketing* (Richard D.

Irwin, 1982) text, but it is easily adaptable to other texts or it may be used without a supporting text. Three chapters covering a step-by-step approach to strategic marketing analysis and planning, financial analysis, and case analysis provide useful foundation materials. These chapters are particularly useful in the absence of a companion text. In addition, they provide a useful overview as a part of a text and case-book package.

As editors, we have made a comprehensive effort to obtain the best possible cases for coverage of the various parts of strategic marketing. Rather than relying only upon our experiences, various sources of cases were utilized to assure complete coverage of topics, variation by size and type of firm, consumer and industrial products and services, and other relevant characteristics. To assure strong student interest, every case was reviewed and evaluated as to interest and difficulty by a student team. We are indebted to the case authors who gave their permissions to use the cases in this book.

A comprehensive instructor's manual is available containing detailed analyses and supporting materials regarding each case. Suggestions are included for course design, and topical areas are identified for each case.

In addition to the important contributions made to the book by the authors of the cases, we want to acknowledge several others whose assistance and support were important. Gilbert A. Churchill, Jr., University of Wisconsin—Madison, as consulting editor, provided many helpful suggestions during the development of the book. Carol A. Scott of the University of California, Los Angeles, Laurence P. Feldman of the University of Illinois, Chicago Circle, and Benny Barak of City University CUNY-New York, Bernard Baruch College reviewed the manuscript and cases and offered several useful guidelines for improving the book. Our graduate assistants, Brian McCann, Christina Martin, and Elizabeth Sypien, made many essential contributions to the project. Special thanks are due Pat Townsend for typing the manuscript and for her assistance in various other aspects of the project. We are greatly appreciative of the support and encouragement provided by our dean, Edward A. Johnson, without whose help the development of the book would not have been possible. Finally, we want to thank Eunice and James L. West and Mr. and Mrs. M. J. Neeley for the endowments that help support our positions and enable us to accomplish projects like this book.

We are indebted to all of these people and to the many authors and publishers who gave us permission to use their materials. While the final result is our responsibility, the assistance provided was essential to accomplishing the project.

David W. Cravens
Charles W. Lamb, Jr.

Application grid

Case	Size*	Type†	Product/service
Part 2: Strategic Analysis and Business Strategy			
Case 2–1 The Lodge at Harvard Square, Inc.—1976	M	C	Retail apparel
Case 2–2 Bloomington Bank and Trust Company	S	C/I	Financial services
Case 2–3 KSM/Beefalo Breeding Company	S	C/I	Livestock, log homes, and restaurants
Case 2–4 TransEra, Inc.	S	I	Computer supplements
Case 2–5 American Safety Razor Company	L	C/I	Razors
Case 2–6 Norton Company	L	I	Abrasives
Case 2–7 Aero Manufacturing Company, Inc.	M	I	Farm equipment
Case 2–8 Bennett Industries	S	I	Truck tailgates
Part 3: Target Market Strategy			
Case 3–1 Pools For You, Inc.	S	C	Leisure product retailer
Case 3–2 Big Sky of Montana, Inc.	S	C	Ski resort
Case 3–3 SeaFlite	S	C/I	Water transportation
Case 3–4 United Bank (A)	M	C/I	Financial services
Case 3–5 The Gillette Company—Safety Razor Division	L	C	Shaving products
Case 3–6 Kellogg Rally Cereal	L	C	Cereal
Part 4: Marketing Program Positioning Strategy			
Case 4–1 Trus Joist Corporation (B)	M	I	Lumber products
Case 4–2 Wyler Unsweetened Soft Drink Mixes	L	C	Drink mixes
Case 4–3 Aurora Lotion	M	C	Cosmetics
Case 4–4 Gemini Oil, Ltd.	S	C/I	Distributor of oil products
Case 4–5 Easco Tools, Inc.	L	C/I	Hand tools
Case 4–6 National Beauty Supply, Ltd.	S	C	Beauty products
Case 4–7 Green Acres Seed Company	S	I	Seed corn
Case 4–8 A&W Drive-Ins (Fundy), Ltd.	M	C	Fast foods
Part 5: Strategic Marketing in Action			
Case 5–1 New Horizons Travel, Inc.	S	C	Travel services
Case 5–2 The Undercroft Montessori School	S	C	Social services
Case 5–3 Quincy Brothers Hardware	S	C	Retail hardware
Case 5–4 Bavaria Manufacturing International (BMI)	L	I	Water faucets
Case 5–5 FAFCO, Inc.	S	C	Solar heating
Case 5–6 Mirco Games	S	C	Amusement machines
Case 5–7 The Clorox Company	L	C	Household products
Case 5–8 Blueprint Building, Inc.	S	I	Buildings
Part 6: Marketing Research Planning and Analysis			
Case 6–1 TLT (A)	S	C/I	Limousine service
Case 6–2 Boltronics Corporation	S	I	Control panels
Case 6–3 Bay-Madison, Inc.	M	C	Laundry cleanser
Case 6–4 Morning Treat Coffee Bags	M	C	Coffee bags
Case 6–5 TLT (B)	S	C/I	Limousine service
Case 6–6 Pacific Coastal Federal Savings and Loan	M	C	Financial services

* S = small; M = medium; L = large.
† C = consumer; I = industrial.
Ⓧ—Primary emphasis
X—Secondary emphasis

Application areas for cases

Note: (X) denotes a circled X; X denotes a plain X.

Case	Corporate strategic planning	Target market strategy	Marketing program positioning strategy	Product strategy	Distribution strategy	Price strategy	Promotion strategy	Strategic marketing planning	Evaluating marketing performance	Marketing research
2-1	(X)	X	X		X			X	(X)	
2-2	(X)	X	X					(X)		
2-3	(X)	X		X	X			X		X
2-4	(X)	(X)	X	(X)				X		
2-5	(X)	(X)	X	X				(X)	X	
2-6	(X)	(X)		X					(X)	X
2-7	(X)			X					(X)	
2-8	(X)	X	X					(X)	(X)	
3-1	(X)			X				X	(X)	X
3-2	(X)		X			(X)			(X)	X
3-3	(X)		(X)			X				X
3-4	(X)			X					(X)	X
3-5	(X)		(X)			X	X	(X)		
3-6	(X)		(X)	(X)						X
4-1	(X)	X	X	(X)				(X)		(X)
4-2	X	X	X	(X)						X
4-3		X	X		(X)	(X)	(X)	X		
4-4	(X)		(X)					(X)		
4-5	(X)		(X)		X		(X)			
4-6	(X)		X	X	X	X		(X)		
4-7	(X)		(X)	(X)				(X)		
4-8	X		(X)		X	(X)		(X)		
5-1		(X)	(X)				X	(X)		
5-2		(X)	(X)					(X)		
5-3		X	(X)					(X)		
5-4			(X)	(X)		X		(X)		
5-5	X	(X)			(X)		(X)	(X)		
5-6	(X)	(X)						(X)		
5-7			(X)	(X)				(X)		
5-8	(X)	(X)	(X)					(X)		
6-1	(X)		(X)							(X)
6-2	(X)		(X)							(X)
6-3				X						(X)
6-4	(X)		(X)							(X)
6-5	(X)		(X)							(X)
6-6			X	(X)						(X)

Case Contributors

Jim Abell, University of Oregon
Sexton Adams, North Texas State University
Francis Aguilar, Harvard University
Viki Arbas, University of Hawaii
Jimmy D. Barnes, California State College, Bakersfield
Berry Berman, Hofstra University
Thomas M. Bertsch, James Madison University
Harper W. Boyd, University of Arkansas at Little Rock
Robert L. Byrd, University of Virginia
James J. Chrisman, Bradley University
Curtis W. Cook, San José State University
Don T. Dunn, Northeastern University
Fred L. Fry, Bradley University
T. F. Funk, University of Guelph
Christopher Gale, University of Virginia
Adelaide Griffin, Texas Woman's University
Bill Highsmith, University of Oregon
Richard Horvitz, Hofstra University
Kenneth L. Jensen, Bradley University
C. B. Johnston, University of Western Ontario
Robert B. Kaiser, Mirco Games
Bruce A. Kirchoff, University of Nebraska at Omaha
Jay E. Klompmaker, University of North Carolina
Thomas Kosnik, IMEDE
Charles M. Kummel, University of North Carolina
Peter J. LaPlaca, University of Connecticut

Andrea D. Levin, University of Virginia
Richard I. Levin, University of North Carolina
William J. Lundstrom, Virginia Commonwealth University
Paul R. MacPherson, University of Guelph
Eleanor G. May, University of Virginia
Joseph R. Mills, American Safety Razor Company
Jack Moorman, Stanford University
James E. Nelson, University of Colorado at Denver
Lonnie L. Ostrom, Arizona State University
Myron Parry, University of Oregon
Stuart Rich, University of Oregon
William E. Rief, Arizona State University
Henry E. Riggs, Stanford University
C. Richard Roberts, The University of Tulsa
D. W. Rosenthal, University of Virginia
Lawrence M. Rumble, IMEDE
Adrian B. Ryans, University of Western Ontario
Don E. Schultz, Northwestern University
Donald Sciglimpaglia, San Diego State University
Anne Senausky, Montana State University
Greg Sessler, Stanford University
Stephen A. Snow, Stanford University
Melvin J. Stanford, Brigham Young University
Stanley F. Stasch, Loyola University of Chicago
Mary Ellen Templeton, University of North Carolina
Mark Traxler, Northwestern University
Robert F. Vandell, University of Virginia
Ralph Westfall, University of Illinois at Chicago Circle

Contents

Building the plan: *The corporate strategic plan. What do we plan? Analyzing the situation.* Market target, objectives, and positioning strategy: *Setting objectives. Marketing program positioning strategy. The marketing organization.* Managing the plan: *Financial analyses and forecasts. From strategy to action.*

Analysis activities: *What do we analyze? Sales and cost information.* Financial analysis and planning methods: *Liquidity analysis. Profit analysis. Other performance measures. Budgeting and forecasting. Eliminating information gaps. Coping with inflation.*

Why cases? The case method of instruction: *Your responsibilities.* A guide to case analysis: *Step 1: Situation audit. Step 2: Problem/decision statement. Step 3: Alternatives. Step 4: Critical issues. Step 5: Analysis. Step 6: Recommendations.*
An illustration of case analysis.
Port-Marine Case, 56
Student analysis of the Port-Marine Case, 61

What is strategic planning? *Situation analysis. Mission and objectives. Composition of the business.* Business unit analysis and strategy: *Planning methods. Business unit strategy. Strategic planning guide.*

PART THREE
TARGET MARKET STRATEGY   **219**

Defining and analyzing product-markets: *Market size and growth forecasts. Customer profiles. Industry profile. Key competitors.* The target
market decision: *Niche formation. Niche description. Target market alternatives. Target market strategy.* Application Illustration.

PART FOUR
MARKETING PROGRAM POSITIONING STRATEGY   **307**

Setting objectives: *Characteristics of good objectives. Setting objectives.*
Marketing program positioning strategy: *Product/service strategy. Distribution strategy. Price strategy. Promotion strategy.*

PART FIVE
STRATEGIC MARKETING IN ACTION   **435**

The strategic marketing plan: *Some planning guidelines. Implementation.* Strategic evaluation and control.

PART SIX
MARKETING RESEARCH PLANNING AND ANALYSIS   **583**

Problem definition and information needs: *How information is used.* A case illustration. Strategies for obtaining information. Estimating costs and benefits: *Information acquisition costs. Estimating benefits.*

Part 1

Strategic Analysis, Planning, and Control

The purpose of Part 1 is to provide basic foundation materials for use in case analysis. Chapter 1, Strategic Marketing Planning, discusses the various steps that are necessary in preparing a strategic plan. The chapter provides an overview of the entire casebook, since the cases in Parts 2 through 6 cover the various topics discussed in Chapter 1. The chapter will be useful in preparing marketing plans for those cases that require such a plan. In addition, discussion regarding the various steps of the strategic plan, such as the target market decision, provides useful information for analyzing cases that focus on particular aspects of strategic marketing.

Chapter 2, Financial Analysis for Marketing Decisions, provides basic methods for performing financial analyses. The chapter reviews some of the more widely used basic financial analyses. You may find it useful to refer to Chapter 2 whenever cases include financial data for analysis. When a financial analysis has already been performed in the case, it may be useful to review the part of Chapter 2 addressing that particular topic.

Chapter 3, Guide to Case Analysis, discusses the various steps in preparing a case analysis. An actual case and a student's analysis of that case are included in the chapter. Following the student's analysis is a critique suggesting areas where the analysis could be improved. While no guide to case analysis can provide a ready-made approach suitable for use in all situations, you should find the chapter helpful as a basis for developing your own case analysis approach.

Chapters 1, 2, and 3 are not intended as a substitute for a textbook. They cover selected areas and should be useful supplements to your case analysis work. In many instances, it may be helpful for you to refer to textbooks that cover particular topics in detail. For example, you may desire or need to review textbooks or parts of textbooks that

1

Strategic marketing topics

Organization of the book	Corporate strategic planning	Target market strategy	Marketing program positioning strategy	Product strategy	Distribution strategy	Price strategy	Promotion strategy	Strategic marketing plan	Evaluating Marketing performance	Marketing research
Chapters in Part 1: Strategic Analysis, Planning, and Control.	↑	↑	↑							
1. Strategic Marketing Planning										
2. Financial Analysis for Marketing Decisions										
3. Guide to Case Analysis										
Cases in Part 2: Strategic Analysis and Business Strategy	X	X	X	X					X	X
Cases in Part 3: Target Market Strategy		X	X	X				X	X	X
Cases in Part 4: Marketing Program Positioning Strategy		X	X	X	X	X	X	X	X	X
Cases in Part 5: Strategic Marketing in Action		X	X	X	X	X	X	X	X	X
Cases in Part 6: Marketing Research Planning and Analysis		X	X	X				X	X	X

provide detailed information regarding such topics as advertising strategy, product strategy, and target market selection.

In addition to the chapters in Part 1, there is an introduction to each of the other five parts of the book. You should find the introductory materials to the various parts useful in summarizing the nature and scope of the topics covered in them. Together, the chapters in Part 1 and the part introductions in the remainder of the book offer useful foundation materials on strategic marketing.

The organization of the book is presented in the accompanying table. We have tried to key to various strategic marketing topics the chapters in Part 1 and the cases in Parts 2 through 6. This, of course, is a general overview of the topics in the book. Also, the extent of case coverage regarding a particular topic will vary. For example, the cases in Part 3, Target Market Strategy, provide a more comprehensive coverage of this topic than do the cases in other parts of the book that include a target market component.

Chapter 1

Strategic Marketing Planning[1]

One of the most satisfying experiences in business practice is to see a troubled company's management diagnose the company's problems, take corrective action, and achieve a turnaround. Sherwin-Williams, the giant paint company, appeared to be on the brink of disaster in 1977 after having attempted unsuccessfully for several years to launch a new strategic marketing plan. The problem was a combination of incomplete planning and faulty implementation. By 1980, recovery was apparent, with both sales and earnings reflecting impressive gains. Let's examine the firm's marketing strategy, the strategy's implementation, and the subsequent adjustments that were made to move the company toward profitable performance:

☐ *The strategic plan.* In the late 1960s, management decided to shift away from contractors and professional painters and instead to go after the do-it-yourself home decorating market as a primary target. This required an ambitious and costly store expansion program, but the decision offered an opportunity to reposition the paint segment of the business into the rapidly growing do-it-yourself market that other retail chains had found very attractive. Management reasoned that the main ingredient of the new strategy was a change in image that would appeal to consumers interested in home decorating and remodeling.

☐ *Implementation.* Launching the strategy involved far more changes than were anticipated. Many of the company's stores were in the wrong locations. All of the stores required major (and costly) upgrading and expansion to respond to the new home dec-

---

[1] A more comprehensive discussion of this topic can be found in David W. Cravens, *Strategic Marketing* (Homewood, Ill.: Richard D. Irwin, 1982). A condensed version was published in David W. Cravens, "How to Match Marketing Strategies with Overall Corporate Planning," *Management Review*, December 1981, pp. 12–19.

orating theme. Product lines were expanded to provide a complete offering from floor coverings to fluorescent lights. Critics observed that Sherwin-Williams did not have the retail store management experience that was needed to carry out the strategy. Performance difficulties were compounded by the decision to pull the Sherwin-Williams paint brand out of paint and hardware stores in order to avoid direct competition with company stores and to replace it with another company brand that was not supported by a strong national advertising effort. Heavy promotion would have helped pull the brand through its distribution channels. Many dealers shifted to competing brands with established brand images in order to maintain their volume.

☐ *Corrective action.* Following two years of declining earnings, Sherwin-Williams lost $8 million in 1977 and a new chairman and president, John G. Breen, was appointed. Under his leadership the company has experienced a strong turnaround. Obsolete plants and more than 100 of 1,500 retail stores have been closed. Half of the firm's top 100 managers have been replaced. Several of the new executives have extensive experience in retailing. The firm's new stores are smaller and are being located near suburban shopping malls. The firm's broad mix of decorating products is being pruned. Large increases have been made in advertising expenditures. To offer a strong brand to other retailers, Sherwin-Williams acquired the Dutch Boy trademark in 1980. Profits have been on a rapid uptrend since 1978, reaching $25 million in 1980.

The Sherwin-Williams experience illustrates some critical characteristics of successful strategic marketing plans.[2] A sound idea must be translated into a complete plan of action. And proper implementation is crucial. Few plans remain constant over time. Although the changes made by Sherwin-Williams' management were more drastic than the changes required by most strategic marketing plans, adjustment is the rule rather than the exception, thus emphasizing the ongoing nature of strategic planning. Finally, the success of a strategic marketing plan is gauged by the results it achieves, not by how elaborate and innovative it is.

During the 1970s, three forces pushed strategic planning to the center of executive attention. The first, and most important, force was the need to ensure survival of the enterprise. Strategic planning is a requirement for corporate success in these turbulent times. The second force was the recognition by many chief executive officers of the central role of markets and marketing strategies in shaping strategic plans. The third force was the need to track the rapidly changing

───────────

[2] The above illustration is drawn in part from Susan Wagner Leisner, "Cleaning Up: Sherwin-Williams Co. Is Recovering from Its Spill." *Barron's*, November 24, 1980, pp. 35–36.

business environment in order to anticipate change and to develop strategies that would take advantage of new opportunities and avoid threats in existing markets.

In this chapter we shall develop and illustrate an action-oriented approach to building a strategic marketing plan that links enterprise strategic planning and marketing planning. By following a 10-step sequence, a marketing plan can be constructed and launched. The approach has been used successfully in several different company applications. When applied in combination with management's knowledge of the firm's unique planning environment, this planning process offers a useful guide for improving marketing strategy. One of its important contributions is raising the right questions to be answered in preparing strategic plans or evaluating existing plans.

This chapter is an overview of strategic marketing planning. You should find it useful as a guide when preparing cases that require a marketing plan or when evaluating the marketing plans that are provided in particular cases. The chapter also highlights the various topics that are covered in cases throughout the book, showing how each aspect of the marketing plan fits into the planning process. Several of the topics briefly covered in this chapter are discussed further in the part introductions for Parts 2 through 6.

BUILDING THE PLAN

First, we need to define strategic marketing. It is a management process that consists of:

1. Analyzing environmental, competitive, and business factors affecting the units that make up the business, and forecasting future trends in market areas of interest to the enterprise.
2. Participating in setting objectives and formulating corporate and business unit strategies.
3. Selecting target market strategies for the product-markets in each business unit, establishing marketing objectives, and developing, implementing, and managing marketing program positioning strategies for meeting target market needs.

A *product-market* is a specific product (or line of related products) that can satisfy a particular set of needs and wants for all people or organizations that are willing and able to purchase the product. A *target market* consists of the people or organizations in a product-market toward which a company directs its *marketing program positioning strategy*. A positioning strategy is the combination of product, channel of distribution, price, and promotion strategies selected by management to position a firm against its key competitors in meeting the needs and wants of the target market.

A 10-step approach to preparing the strategic marketing plan is

Exhibit 1–1
How to prepare the strategic marketing plan

1. Understand the corporate strategic plan.
2. Select marketing planning and control units.
3. Analyze situation in product-markets.
4. Choose target market strategy.
5. Set objectives for target markets.
6. Determine marketing program positioning strategy.
7. Design the marketing organization.
8. Prepare financial analyses for marketing strategy.
9. Translate strategy into short-term plans.
10. Implement, evaluate, and update annually.

shown in Exhibit 1–1. We shall examine each step, highlighting its features and showing the requirements for completing the step.

The corporate strategic plan

Understanding the strategic plan, objectives, and business strategies of the company is the starting point for designing the strategic marketing plan (step 1). During the late 1970s, formal strategic planning of the enterprise moved from an important to a critical status on the list of the concerns of CEOs. At the heart of strategic planning is deciding the corporation's direction(s) of development. Several possible strategies for moving beyond the core business are shown in Exhibit 1–2. Some firms have followed more than one development path by, for example, expanding into both new products and new markets. Other firms have never developed beyond the core business. The corporate development strategy selected by management determines how the firm's objectives are accomplished. These objectives typi-

Exhibit 1–2
Corporate development strategies

cally include meeting growth and financial performance targets as well as meeting the firm's responsibilities to its various stakeholders (e.g., stockholders, employees).

The marketing strategist must understand the corporate game plan for four reasons. First, marketing know-how is essential in implementing many strategic analysis methods. Second, marketing decisions, such as which market niches to serve, which new product strategies to adopt, or which type of distribution strategy to use, are often key components of business strategies. Third, top-management decisions about the enterprise and its various business units guide the development of strategic marketing plans. Finally, each unit of the business is often not allocated a proportionate share of available resources. Rather, the probable winners tend to get a disproportionate share of the total, thus dictating the amount of resources available for marketing.

Steve Harrell, a strategic planner for GE's Housewares and Audio Business Division, has pointed out that the marketing manager is often the most significant functional contributor to strategic planning.[3] Using Harrell's description of business unit planning at GE, marketing management's role in strategic planning is detailed in Exhibit 1–3. Note the various strategic planning activities where marketing management is a key contributor. General Electric, a leader in management innovations, was one of the first firms to adopt formal methods of strategic analysis and planning.

What do we plan?

Unless you have a single product targeted toward one market, a basis for developing the plan is needed. Some firms plan and manage by individual products or brands. Others—for example, Quaker Chemical (industrial chemicals)—work with product lines, market targets, and specific customers. Step 2 in building the strategic marketing plan is the selection of a marketing planning unit. The plan can be developed for a specific product or brand, a line of products, or a mix of products aimed at a target market.

Several criteria are often considered in selecting the planning unit. Each planning unit should comprise a specific product, product line, or mix of products that:

☐ Serves the same or a closely related market target.
☐ Utilizes the same marketing program positioning strategy.
☐ Shares common marketing program components such as distribution channels, advertising, and sales force.

---

[3] Based on a speech by Stephen G. Harrell at the American Marketing Association's Educators' meeting in Chicago, August 5, 1980. Harrell is currently directing strategic planning at Black & Decker.

☐ Is large enough to represent a meaningful unit in strategy formulation and performance evaluation.

☐ Is small enough to facilitate planning and management.

An example will illustrate the selection of planning units. Look at the business composition of Magic Chef, Inc., shown in Exhibit 1–4. Clearly, a business segment such as major home appliances is too large for use in marketing planning. Within the segment, as indicated in the market column in Exhibit 1–4, there are at least five distinct end-user markets (replacement, private label, new homes and apartments, mobile homes, and recreational vehicles). Suppose that gas and electric ranges, microwave ovens, combination ranges, and range vent hoods are assigned to a strategic planning unit (SBU) that is responsible for the replacement and new homes and apartments markets. Assuming that different distribution channel, pricing, and pro-

Exhibit 1–3
Illustrative role of marketing management in strategic business unit (SBU) planning

Planning activity	*Marketing's role*
Mission determination	Key participant with the strategic planner and SBU manager
Environmental assessment (economic, political, customer, regulatory trends)	Primary contributor and a major beneficiary of the results
Competitive assessment (actual and potential competitors)	Primary contributor working with the strategic planner
Situation assessment (industry assessment and company position to identify strengths and weaknesses)	Major contributor working with the strategic planner
Objectives and goals	Key participant with other functional managers, including responsibility for measuring several performance indicators
Strategies	Responsible for marketing strategy and for coordination of plans with other functional strategies
Key plans	
Product/market development	Leadership role
Distribution	Primary responsibility
Business development*	Key supporting role with strategic planning and manufacturing responsible for implementation
Quality	Leading responsibility for quality
Technology	Varies according to the importance of technology to the product or service
Human resources	Responsible for functional area
Manufacturing/facilities	Typically, very limited involvement

* Decisions to expand, improve, or contract the business.

Exhibit 1–4
Business composition of Magic Chef, Inc.

Business segments	Products	Markets	Divisions and subsidiaries
Major home appliances	Gas and electric ranges Microwave ovens Combination ranges Recreational vehicle ranges Refrigerators Freezers Dishwashers Residential laundry equipment Commercial laundry equipment Trash compactors Waste disposals Range vent hoods Dehumidifiers	Replacement Private label New homes and apartments Mobile homes Recreational-vehicles	Magic Chef Division Cleveland, Tennessee Admiral Division Schaumburg, Illinois Gaffers & Sattler Division Los Angeles, California Norge Division Herrin, Illinois
Heating and air conditioning equipment	Gas, oil, and electric furnaces Central air conditioning equipment Unit heaters Heat pumps	Replacement New homes and apartments Light commercial buildings Industrial buildings	Gaffers & Sattler Division Los Angeles, California Johnson Corp. Division Columbus, Ohio
Soft drink vending equipment and dispensers	Bottle and can vendors Fountain vendors Postmix vendors Postmix and premix counter units	All major bottlers, including Coca-Cola Dr. Pepper Pepsi-Cola Royal Crown Cola Seven-Up	Dixie-Narco, Inc. Ranson, West Virginia

Geographic distribution:
The products of the Magic Chef, Admiral, Norge, and Johnson divisions and Dixie-Narco, Inc. are sold on a national basis. The Magic Chef and Admiral divisions have export operations for worldwide product distribution. The products of the Gaffers & Sattler Division are sold in the western United States.

Source: *Annual Report, 1980*, Magic Chef, Inc.

motional strategies serve the replacement and new homes and apartments markets, what are possible marketing planning units? Two could be formed to focus planning on each of these market categories (new and replacement). If marketing efforts are varied in serving the two markets, such a breakdown is appropriate. Further breakdowns could be considered.

As you can see, there are various possibilities for selecting marketing planning and control units. The criteria suggested earlier offer useful, although not final; guidelines for making the choice. In addition to product-market designations, some companies use geographic areas or functional areas (advertising, sales force) as marketing planning units.

Analyzing the situation

Step 3 consists of a situation analysis for each product-market. In order to simplify the discussion, we shall assume that we have one specific product which meets the needs of a similar group of buyers. To incorporate more than one product-market into the picture, the same kind of analysis can be conducted for the other product-markets.

Our first task is to estimate demand, determine end-user characteristics, learn about industry practices and trends, and identify key competitors for the end-user groups being considered as possible market targets for our specific product. Note that some competitors may offer the specific product that we offer, whereas others may offer a different product that meets the same set of needs that are met by our product. For example, Remington electric shavers may be competing with electric shaver brands such as Norelco, Schick, and Sunbeam as well as safety razor brands such as Gillette.

A guide to conducting a situation analysis for a specific product-market is shown in Exhibit 1–5. The guide consists of a comprehensive assessment of end-users and key competitors. It can be condensed or expanded to fit the needs of a particular firm. When completed, the situation analysis should summarize the opportunities and problems in the product-market. It will contain much of the information that management needs in selecting a target market strategy.

MARKET TARGET, OBJECTIVES, AND POSITIONING STRATEGY (STEPS 4, 5, AND 6)

Do the strategies of Ethan Allen (furniture) and Nucor Corporation (steel) have any common features? Although the firms differ in many ways, they share one strategic characteristic. Each firm has a target market strategy that contributed to its success. Instead of competing across the board with all furniture styles, Ethan Allen's management

Exhibit 1–5
Guide to conducting a marketing strategy situation analysis

Answer the following questions for each specific product-market (e.g., microwave ovens for heating foods in the home).

	Total product-market	Market niches	
Customer analysis		1	2
Estimated annual purchases (units and dollars)			
Projected annual growth rate (five years)			
Number of people/organizations in the product-market			
Demographic and socioeconomic characteristics of customers			
Extent of geographic concentration			
How do people decide what to buy?			
Reason(s) for buying (what is the need/want?)			
What information is needed (e.g., how to use the product)?			
Important sources of information			
What criteria are used to evaluate the product?			
Purchasing practices (quantity, frequency, location, time, etc.)			
What environmental factors should be monitored because of their influence on product purchases (e.g., interest rates)?			
What key competitors serve each end-user group?			

Are other products available (or under development) that are (or will be) close substitutes for this product? If so, a situation analysis should be conducted for the product-market.

	Competitor		
Key competitor analysis	A	B	C
Estimated overall business strength			
Market share (percent, rank)			
Market share trend (five years)			
Financial strengths			
Profitability			
Management			
Technology position			
Other key nonmarketing strengths/limitations (e.g., production cost advantages)			
Marketing strategy (description, assessment of key strengths and limitations)			
Target market strategy			
Program positioning strategy			
Product strategy			
Distribution strategy			
Price strategy			
Promotion strategy			

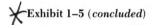Exhibit 1–5 (*concluded*)

Summary of opportunities and problems in the product-market

Prepare by major end-user group and for the total product-market.

Assumptions

Based on the situation analysis, what key assumptions regarding the next three to five years will you make in preparing the strategic plan?

Assumptions:
1.
2.
3.
.
.
.

Contingencies

For each assumption, what alternatives (contingencies) could possibly occur and how would the occurrences alter your situation analysis?

---

decided to serve the needs of households that wanted mid-to-high price and quality American traditional furniture. Nucor, a tiny firm compared to U.S. Steel and other industry giants, specializes in steel joists for construction, and it holds the number one market share position in this product category. The financial performance of both firms was impressive during the late 1970s and early 1980s.

The target market decision is the cutting edge of marketing strategy, serving as the basis for setting objectives and developing a positioning strategy. Strategy options range from using a mass strategy to

Exhibit 1–6
Illustrative analysis for product-market niche evaluation

	Niche		
	X	**Y**	**Z**
Estimated (in $ millions)			
Sales*	10	16	5
Variable costs*	4	9	3
Contribution margin*	6	7	2
Market Share†	60%	30%	10%
Total niche sales	17	53	50
Niche position			
Business strength	High	Medium	Low
Attractiveness‡	Medium	Low	High

* For a two-year period.
† Percentage of total sales in the niche.
‡ Based on a five-year projection.

serving one or more subgroups (niches or segments) of customers within a product-market. The decision to use a niche strategy is based on revenue-cost analysis and assessment of competitive position. An illustrative niche analysis is shown in Exhibit 1–6. While additional information such as key competitor evaluations is needed to make a complete assessment, Exhibit 1–6 illustrates how alternative market targets can be analyzed. How would you rank niches X, Y, and Z? Niche Z has some attractive characteristics. An important question is whether market share can be profitably increased in Z. If not, X looks like the top prospect, followed by Y and Z. Of course, management could decide to go after all three niches.

Once the target market decision has been made, the following information is often needed in building the strategic marketing plan:

- ☐ Size and growth rate of the target market.
- ☐ Description of end users that represent the target group (location and characteristics).
- ☐ Information about end users that will be helpful in selecting a program positioning strategy.
- ☐ Guidelines for developing short-term marketing plans (e.g., media habits and preferences of end users).

As an illustration, we shall use a product that is being made and marketed by a small electronics manufacturing firm. The product is a high-accuracy temperature measurement instrument with research laboratory and production temperature measurement applications. The unit uses a metal probe to measure temperatures. Electrical resistance varies proportionately to the temperature of the surface it touches. Information from the probe is transmitted to a microprocessor which transmits the temperature measurement to a visual display similar to a digital clock readout. After analyzing opportunities, costs, and competitive position in several industries and four types of temperature measurement applications (e.g., laboratory, on-line production processes, and checking and calibration of on-line measurement devices), management decided to concentrate marketing efforts in the pharmaceutical industry. An illustrative target market description is shown in Exhibit 1–7. Target market information will vary by planning situation, so the temperature measurement example should be viewed as illustrative rather than typical. Nevertheless, notice the useful guidelines that target market information provides for marketing program planning.

Setting objectives

In step 5, specific objectives are stated for each target market. Some companies prefer to set objectives that apply to all the target markets in a business unit. This practice is fine, provided that the objectives

Exhibit 1–7
An illustrative target market description and profile

Target market

Pharmaceutical companies in the United States with a need for temperature measurement devices of moderate-to-high accuracy for use in the production of intravenous or parenteral solutions which require sterilization of containers and stoppers. There are over 60 companies in this target market.

Size and growth rate

The total potential in this product-market is estimated at approximately 400 units, and its expected growth is estimated at about a 10 percent annual rate for the next five years. At an average price of $5,000 per unit, the sales potential is $2 millioin. Microprocessor penetration into the potential market has been minimal to date.

Description of end users

☐ The target market firms are concentrated in the Middle Atlantic, midwestern, and western states.

☐ The end user is an instrumentation engineer or supervisor, maintenance engineer, quality control engineer, or production manager (small plants) of the target market firms.

Marketing program positioning strategy guidelines

☐ The apparent reason for purchasing a high-accuracy instrument is to monitor the accuracy of thermocouples used in sterilizers for containers and stoppers. This need is being triggered by a pending Good Manufacturing Practice regulation which requires temperature accuracy of $\pm 0.5°$ C throughout the sterilizer heating cycle.

☐ Users' needs for information on the product include demonstrations and information on its features and performance.

☐ Important sources of information concerning temperature measurement include quality control consultants, product brochures, and technical articles in professional journals.

☐ Criteria used to evaluate alternative brands include accuracy, stability, service, price, ease of installation and operation, durability, mobility, and data-recording capabilities.

☐ The end user typically determines the need and obtains approval to purchase from the plant production manager. Given approval, the end user then selects the brand and type of product to be purchased.

☐ Competitive activity in this industry has been minimal. Only one potential key competitor exists—XYZ Corporation.

Guidelines for short-term marketing plans

☐ Direct personal selling by the manufacturer represents the most effective way of contacting end users.

☐ Price does not appear to be a major factor in the brand decision, provided that there are not substantial variations in the prices of competitive units.

☐ Advertising and sales promotion efforts should be concentrated initially upon developing product information brochures. This information can be communicated via direct mail and in conjunction with sales calls.

represent a composite of the specific objectives for each target market and that the objectives can be measured. To be useful, objectives should provide a basis for gauging performance.

Marketing affects corporate business unit performance by obtaining sales through marketing efforts and by incurring costs from the marketing activities necessary for achieving sales. By generating sales and consuming financial resources, marketing contributes to business objectives. Various operating or subobjectives are also needed to provide performance guidelines for each component of a marketing program. The accomplishment of such operating objectives should help meet sales, market share, and profit contribution objectives. For example, suppose one objective of a company's advertising strategy is to increase target market customers' awareness of a particular brand by some specified amount during a given time period. Management believes increasing brand awareness will have an effect on sales. In the case of operating objectives (e.g., increasing brand awareness), establishing a direct cause and effect relationship to sales is often difficult. Management may be convinced, based on market and competitive studies, that increasing brand awareness will increase sales but is often unable to say that an X percent increase in brand awareness will cause a Y percent increase in sales. Even though this problem exists, operating objectives should be indicated. Otherwise, there is no basis for gauging progress.

The following guidelines are suggested for placing objectives in the strategic marketing plan:

1. Indicate sales, market share, and profit contribution objectives for the total business unit and for each market target within the unit. Normally, these objectives are projected into the future year by year over the time period of the strategic plan (e.g., three to five years). The effects of inflation should be accounted for by basing projections on constant dollars or by indicating the inflation rate that is being assumed for the planning period.

2. As part of the marketing program positioning strategy (step 6), include operating objectives for product, distribution, price, advertising, and sales force strategies. These objectives should indicate what each mix component is responsible for accomplishing.

3. Break down the business unit objectives and the operating objectives into annual objectives to be included in the short-term marketing plan (step 9).

Marketing objectives cannot be fully determined until our marketing program positioning strategy has been finalized (step 6). Only then can sales forecasts be made and marketing program costs estimated.

Marketing program positioning strategy

An illustration will be useful in highlighting what must be done at step 6 of the planning process. S. C. Johnson & Son, Inc., is a successful marketer of personal care products such as Agree Creme Rinse and Agree Shampoo. Known for its waxes, polishes, and related household products, Johnson moved into personal care products in the late 1960s because of the rapid growth prospects in this market. One product, Edge shave cream, was an instant success. Several others failed because they offered no advantages over existing products and because faulty marketing programming was used. The product development and marketing strategy for Agree Creme Rinse demonstrated management's ability to learn from its failures and to formulate and implement successful marketing program positioning strategies. Agree Creme Rinse, introduced in 1977, had a 20 percent market share and was first in unit sales by 1979.

Developing product or brand positioning strategies became very popular among marketing strategists in the 1970s. We shall use the term *position* to designate how buyers in the target market perceive our marketing program relative to the marketing programs of our key competitors. In other words, how are we positioned against our competition with respect to our product offer, distribution approach, prices, advertising, and personal selling? The key issue in developing and implementing a positioning strategy is how our marketing program is perceived by the people in our target market. If our marketing program is considered identical to a competitor's, then we have the same positioning strategy as that competitor. Rarely, if ever, is this the case. In the minds of buyers, distinctions always exist among competitive offerings. Typically, the product becomes the focal point of a positioning strategy since distribution, prices, advertising, and personal selling all work toward positioning the product in the eyes of the buyer. Thus, the designation "product positioning strategy" is often used. However, since position can be achieved by using a combination of marketing program factors, product positioning is normally effected by more than just the product.

Positioning may be an attempt to differentiate a marketing strategy from a competitor's, or it may be an attempt to make a marketing strategy appear similar to that of a particular competitor. The prime consideration is deciding how to serve a target market. A positioning strategy, then, is the design of a marketing program, and it consists of the following decisions:

☐   The selection of a product or service strategy.
☐   The determination of how distribution will be accomplished.
☐   The choice of a pricing strategy.
☐   The selection of a promotional strategy.

These decisions represent a bundle of strategies. The objective is to form an integrated program, with each of the above components fulfilling its proper role in helping to position the firm in the target markets that management chooses to serve. The result often distinguishes a company product or brand from those of its competitors due to customers' perceptions of the product or brand. The product, method of distribution, price, advertising, and personal selling all help to establish these perceptions, as do the marketing program actions of competitors plus other uncontrollable factors such as government regulations. When a positioning strategy is properly selected, the needs of the people or organizations that make up the target market are satisfied. The essence of a good positioning strategy is that it delivers customer satisfaction to the firm's target market and also meets corporate and marketing objectives. Target market and positioning strategies are like two sides of the same coin. They are inseparable, with each dependent on the other.

How does management select a good positioning strategy? Typically, such a strategy is achieved by a combination of management judgment and experience, trial and error, some experimentation (e.g., test marketing), and sometimes field research. Finding the ideal positioning strategy is impossible in most situations because of the many influences that must be taken into account. Nevertheless, good strategies can be selected by following a sound analysis and evaluation process.

Strategic marketing planning activities fall into two categories. First, it is necessary to establish the major strategy guidelines for every marketing program component. For example, such guidelines may stipulate what type of distribution channel should be developed. Once these guidelines have been determined, they may not be altered for several years. For example, after Ethan Allen's management decided to use a vertically coordinated type of channel distribution and a selective distribution intensity, the company continued to follow this strategy for over a decade.[4] Second, many of the ongoing planning activities in a company consist of managing the strategies that have been adopted for each of the marketing program components. In Ethan Allen's case, distribution management involved recruiting new retailers, assisting them, and making necessary changes in strategy over time. We have indicated both categories of strategic marketing planning activities to emphasize the importance of first determining the various longer-range strategic guidelines and then managing and appraising them on a regular basis. Much of the actual content of the strategic marketing plan deals with the various management activities that fall into this second category.

The marketing organization

One basic rule in marketing organizational design (step 7) is to build the organization around the strategic marketing plan rather than

---

[4] A vertically coordinated channel is managed by one of the channel members (e.g., manufacturer, retailer), whereas a conventional channel no member manages or coordinates channel activities.

to force the plan into a predetermined organizational arrangement. These alternative approaches are used to design marketing organizations:

☐ *Functional*. Departments, groups, or individuals are responsible for functions such as advertising, pricing, sales, and marketing research.

☐ *Product*. Organizational units are formed around a product or product line. Some or all of the marketing functions are performed within each unit.

☐ *Market*. This is similar to a product-type organization except that each market target is used to form an organizational unit.

☐ *Combination*. This combines the functional and product or market approaches.

A sound organizational scheme should possess the following characteristics:

☐ It should correspond to the strategic marketing plan. For example, if the plan is structured around markets or products, then the marketing organizational structure should reflect this emphasis.

☐ Activities should be coordinated. This is essential to the successful implementation of plans, both within the marketing function and together with other company and business unit functions. The more specialized marketing functions become, the more likely it is that coordination and communications will be hampered.

☐ Marketing activities should be specialized. The specialization of marketing activities will lead to greater efficiency in performing them. As an illustration, establishing a central advertising department may be more cost efficient than establishing an advertising unit for each product category. Specialization can also provide technical depth. For example, product or application specialization in a field sales force will enable salespeople to provide consultative assistance to customers.

☐ The organization should be structured so that responsibility for results will correspond to a manager's influence on results. While this objective is often difficult to achieve fully, it should be a prime consideration in designing the marketing organization.

☐ Finally, the organization should be adaptable to changing conditions. One of the real dangers in a highly structured and complex organization is the loss of flexibility.

You may have detected a flaw in this list of desirable characteristics of a marketing organizational design. Some of the characteristics are in conflict with others. For example, specialization can be expensive if it is carried to extremes. The costs of having different sales specialists call on the same account must be weighed against the benefits obtained from the overlapping coverage. Thus, organizational design represents an assessment of priorities and a balancing of conflicting consequences.

MANAGING THE PLAN

Financial analyses and forecasts

In step 8 of the strategic marketing plan, several kinds of financial analyses and forecasts are used, including sales, profit contribution, operating margins, income, sources and uses of funds, and break-even. A typical period of analysis and projection is the past five years and a forecast five years into the future. The unit of analysis may be company business segments, divisions, strategic planning units, customer groups, product lines, or specific brands. While some of financial analyses and forecasts may not be part of the strategic marketing plan, marketing is responsible for providing information that is needed in preparing strategic financial plans. An illustrative work sheet for preparing a sales forecast for a division of a company is shown in Exhibit 1–8. The analysis shown in Exhibit 1–8 is normally prepared by the chief marketing executive and staff. We should note that such forecasts may be developed using categories other than products. For example, forecasts by major customer groups are often used. Also, breakdowns more detailed than those shown in Exhibit 1–8 may be desired, such as types of microwave ovens.

The financial analyses and forecasts that are included in the strategic marketing plan vary considerably from firm to firm. Those that are often placed in the financial analysis section of the plan include the following:

☐ Sales and market share analyses and forecasts by product, market segment, areas, and other categories.

☐ Budget projections for marketing operations.

☐ Break-even and profit contribution projections by marketing planning unit (e.g., market target, product line, and market area).

☐ Return on investment projections by marketing planning unit.

☐ Capital requirements.

The choice of the financial information to be placed in the marketing plan will depend on that plan's relationship with the corporate or business unit strategic plan. Another important consideration is the selection of performance measures to be used in gauging strategic marketing performance. Our objective is to indicate the range of possibilities and to suggest some of the more frequently used financial analyses. We shall examine financial analysis and planning in more detail in Chapter 2.

Exhibit 1–8
Illustrative work sheet for preparing a sales forecast for a division of a company

| Appliances division | 1975 | 1976 | 1977 | 1978 | 1979 | 1980* | 1981† | 1982† | 1983† | 1984† | Annual growth rate | |
											1975–1980	1980–1984
Gas ranges												
Electric ranges												
Combination ranges												
Microwave ovens												
Refrigerators												
Freezers												
Total sales												
Percentage increase												

* Estimate for current year.
† Forecast.

Completion of financial analysis is the last step (step 8) in preparing the strategic marketing plan. The remaining steps (9 and 10) are concerned with transforming the plan into short-term plans and implementing the short-term plans. We are ready now to consider these final steps in the strategic planning process.

From strategy to action

Steps 9 and 10 are concerned with the short-term programming of marketing activities and implementing the short-term plan. The strategic marketing plan guides the development of the short-term plan, which typically covers one year. The short-term plan may be included as a part of the strategic plan, or it may be prepared as a separate entity. The important consideration is to provide a specific operational plan while avoiding unnecessary paperwork and overlapping coverage with the strategic plan.

As an illustration of a short-term planning situation, suppose a new product introduction is scheduled for next year. The plan should include details and deadlines, production plans, a market introduction program, advertising and merchandising actions, employee training, and other aspects of launching the product. The plan should answer the questions what, when, where, who, how, and why for each action to be accomplished during the short-term planning period. A format for preparing the short-term marketing plan is shown in Exhibit 1–9.

Finally, in step 10, the strategic plan is implemented, progress is evaluated, and the plan is updated annually. Once in operation, marketing strategy should be evaluated and updated annually via the short-term plan. People make things happen. Plans are only mechanisms through which people convert strategies and tactics into action. Without proper implementation, plans are worthless, so implementation represents a crucial last step in strategic marketing planning. A complete discussion of implementation would cover the selection, training, motivation, and evaluation of marketing personnel. Since this is not feasible, we shall instead emphasize the importance of these activities and refer you to other sources for discussion of the people aspects of implementation. Regular evaluation of the performance of strategic plans is necessary to keep plans on track and to respond to changing conditions.

CONCLUDING NOTE

Preparation of the strategic marketing plan is one of the most demanding management responsibilities of the chief marketing executive. It requires folding together many different information gathering and analysis activities into a comprehensive and integrated plan of action. Following a step-by-step approach in building the strategic

Exhibit 1–9

Marketing planning guide

Marketing objectives

☐ ☐ ☐ ☐

Influences on marketing strategy

☐ ☐ ☐ ☐

Priority*	Market/industry/customer targets (description and objectives, including sales targets)	Products/ services	Channels	Pricing	Advertising and promotion	Sales force
		Strategy and tactics {	} { Actions Responsibilities Deadlines Estimated costs			

* A, B, C, or D (A: "must"; B: "would be a good thing"; C: "can contribute"; and D: "defer").
  Source: David W. Cravens, Gerald E. Hills, and Robert B. Woodruff, *Marketing Decision Making: Concepts and Strategy*, rev. ed. (Homewood, III.: Richard D. Irwin, 1980), p. 456.

plan is a useful way to make sure that each component of the plan is covered and that important interrelationships among the components are recognized. The starting point in the planning process is understanding the corporate strategic plan since the marketing plan is one of a bundle of functional strategies that must be combined to achieve corporate and business unit objectives.

The new challenge that marketing faces has never been greater in the history of business practice. The 1980s mark the beginning of a new era for marketing professionals, with much greater emphasis on strategic decisions and more active participation of marketing executives in corporate strategic analysis and planning. The demands of this new era are far greater than they have been in the past because of the required capabilities in corporate strategic planning and because of the need to match marketing strategies with the strategic plans for the entire company.

Chapter 2

Financial Analysis for Marketing Decisions

An understanding of the use of basic financial analysis methods is required of marketing executives in most firms. This new financial responsibility is described by David S. Hopkins of the Conference Board:

> Today's marketers are finding that strategies designed to forestall product problems often require financial considerations to be held at the forefront of their thinking and planning. Awareness that lack of profitability is so often the surest pointer to a problem means, for them, that costs, prices and profits are key elements in any product situation analysis. A few firms have established a position of marketing auditor or marketing controller who, among other duties, audits marketing costs, prices and profitability. In some other cases, firms are testing the introduction of a product-manager mutation, by making such managers *accountable* for profit to a degree somewhat beyond the looser sense of responsibility for success of the product that has traditionally been theirs. Moreover, the tendency for marketing executives to become more financially oriented is being mirrored by the rising frequency with which financial executives are finding themselves much more intimately concerned with questions of product policies and strategies than in the past.[1]

Several kinds of financial analyses are needed for marketing planning and control activities. Consider, for example, the description in Exhibit 2–1 of how advertising has been instrumental in helping Hershey Foods Corporation achieve record earnings. Note the use of sales and profit comparisons, growth rates, product sales, and advertising expenditures in discussing advertising's role in Hershey's marketing activities. Sales and costs information is used in various kinds of financial analyses for marketing management. Such analyses repre-

---

[1] David S. Hopkins, *Business Strategies for Problem Products* (New York: Conference Board, 1977), p. 42.

Exhibit 2–1
Hershey and advertising

Advertising has been a key element in the record earnings level Hershey Foods Corporation has achieved in the recent past. The improved profitability is a function of two forces, higher sales and improved productivity relating to higher sales, and advertising is one of the major reasons for the continuing growth in sales.

This is ironic because for years Hershey was the most celebrated holdout in advertising history. That situation, however, has changed dramatically in the last decade. In 1980 the corporation entered the ranks of the largest advertisers in the United States. *Advertising Age*, in a special 100 Leading Advertisers issue published in September 1981, listed Hershey as tied for 93d in this category.

Hershey spent approximately $43 million in advertising in 1980, and according to *Advertising Age*, the corporation "is increasing its ad spending faster than all but a few of the major advertisers. Its ad spending was up 40 percent last year and has increaed at a compounded rate of 34 percent in the last five years."

The publication commented that "it's no coincidence" company earnings last year were a record $62 million, up 16 percent from 1979, on record sales of $1.34 billion, and that more than 75 percent of last year's increase in chocolate and confectionery sales came from increased unit sales.

William E. C. Dearden, Hershey's vice chairman and chief executive officer, was quoted: "I think the amount of money we're putting into advertising speaks for itself. We've seen that we can sell [more of] our existing products by keeping them in the minds of the public. And when it comes to some [new] product that nobody's ever heard of, well, there's only one way to do it— mass marketing and advertising."

As an example, six of Hershey Chocolate Company's traditional products—Hershey's Milk Chocolate and Almond Bars, Hershey's Kisses, Hershey's Syrup, Hershey's Chocolate Baking Chips, and Reese's Peanut Butter Cups—had more than a 12 percent compounded growth rate in dollar sales over the last five years. Together these brands accounted for approximately half of Hershey Chocolate Company sales in 1980.

Sales of new products introduced in the last five years accounted for approximately 25 percent of total Chocolate Company sales in 1980. This has taken place in an industry which has not been known for a high rate of successful new product introductions, but rather for products with exceptionally long lives.

Other divisions of Hershey Foods Corporation have also benefited from increased marketing activity. Friendly Ice Cream Corporation has become more aggressive, as evidenced by the successful summer ice-cream promotions of 1980 and 1981, which were supported by advertising, as well as its advertising campaigns which accompany new menu introductions. San Giorgio–Skinner's long-standing advertising program has been an integral part of the marketing strategy that has made it the fastest growing company in the pasta business.

Hershey will continue to make effective use of advertising and other proven marketing tools. Commenting in *Advertising Age* about company founder Milton S. Hershey's attitude toward advertising in today's market, Mr. Dearden said he believed Mr. Hershey would have thought, "It's about time."

Source: Hershey Foods Corporation, *1981 Third Quarter Interim Report*, pp. 1 and 3.

sent an important part of your case preparation activities. In some instances, it will be necessary for you to review and interpret the financial information provided in the cases. In other instances, you may actually prepare analyses to support your recommendations.

We shall look at several financial analysis activities and methods that are used (1) to gauge how well marketing strategy is working, (2) to evaluate marketing decision alternatives, and (3) to develop plans for the future. Also, we shall discuss some special considerations that may affect marketing financial analyses. The methods covered in this chapter represent a kit of tools and techniques for use in marketing financial analysis. Throughout our discussion we are assuming that you have a basic understanding of accounting and finance fundamentals.

ANALYSIS ACTIVITIES

While many kinds of financial analyses underlie marketing operations, most of these financial analyses fall into the four categories shown in Exhibit 2–2. The *financial situation analysis* is intended to determine how well marketing activities are doing. It involves the

Exhibit 2–2
Marketing financial analysis activities

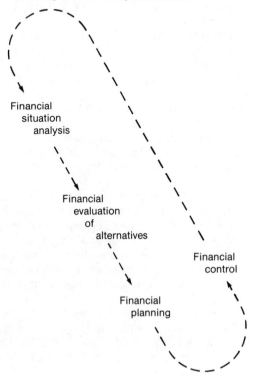

Financial
situation
analysis

Financial
evaluation
of
alternatives

Financial
control

Financial
planning

study of trends, comparative analyses, and assessments of present financial strengths and limitations for the entire business or a unit, brand, or some other component of the business. *Financial evaluation of alternatives* involves the use of financial information to evaluate such alternatives as whether to introduce a new product, expand the sales force, eliminate a mature product, or move into a new market. *Financial planning* involves projections concerning activities that marketing management has decided to undertake. For example, if it has been decided to introduce a new product on a national basis, management must prepare sales and cost forecasts, budgets, and other financial planning and control tools. Finally, in *financial control* actual results are compared to planned results. The objective is to keep the gap between actual and planned results as narrow as possible. Several illustrative financial analyses are shown in Exhibit 2–3. We

Exhibit 2–3
Illustrative financial analyses

Situation analysis
  Sales and cost analyses
  Profit contribution and net profit analyses
  Liquidity analysis

Evaluation of alternatives
  Sales and cost forecasts
  Break-even analyses
  Profit contribution and net profit projections
  Return on investment

Financial planning
  Sales and cost forecasts
  Budgets
  Pro forma income statement

Financial control
  Sales and cost analyses
  Actual results to budgets
  Profit performance

---

shall devote the remainder of the chapter to an examination of these methods of analyzing sales and cost information.

What do we analyze?

Several possible units that can be used in marketing financial analysis are shown in Exhibit 2–4. Two factors often influence the choice of a unit of analysis: (1) the purpose of the analysis and (2) the costs and availability of the information needed to perform the analysis. We

Exhibit 2–4
Alternative units for financial analysis

Market	*Product/service*	*Organization*
Total market	Industry	Company
Market niche(s)	Product mix	Segment/division/unit
Geographic area(s)	Product line	Marketing department
Customer groups	Specific product	Sales unit
Individual customers	Brand	Region
	Model	District/branch
		Office/store
		Salesperson

shall briefly examine each influence to see how it affects the choice of a unit of analysis.

In Exhibit 2–2, four types of financial analysis activities are shown. In a marketing situation analysis, more than one unit of analysis is often needed. Marketing management may be interested in examining the financial performance of several of the units shown in Exhibit 2–4. In contrast, the unit used in the financial evaluation of alternatives should represent the alternative under consideration. For example, if an expansion of the sales force is being analyzed, the salesperson is a logical unit of analysis. If a product is a candidate for elimination by a firm, an analysis should be performed to assess the revenue and cost impact of dropping the product. The analysis should include the drop candidate plus other products that would be affected. Finally, in financial planning and financial control the unit or units of analysis often correspond to products and/or organizational levels (branches, departments, business units, etc.) since budgeting and forecasting analyses are typically prepared for these units.

The most readily available sales and cost information for financial analysis is that which corresponds to the formal financial reporting practices in the given firm. Units that are used for internal reporting often include product categories, business units, and units of the sales organization (regions, districts, etc.). When the unit of analysis does not correspond to one that is included in the firm's information system, both the cost and the difficulty of obtaining information increase significantly. For example, if the cost accounting system has not tabulated costs by individual products, obtaining such information may require a substantial effort. Fortunately, the information needed for marketing financial analysis can often be estimated at accuracy levels suitable for that purpose.

Sales and cost information

The data base for marketing financial analysis is obtained by accumulating historical sales and cost data for the various units shown in

Exhibit 2–4. The data base can be used in forecasting future sales and costs for these units. In addition to the sales and cost data in the various financial analyses shown in Exhibit 2–3, marketing management often wishes to examine sales and cost trends. Among the widely used bases for the analysis of such trends are dollar and unit sales, percentage growth rates, and market share. Note, for example, the sales analysis for Long John Silver's shown in Exhibit 2–5. Sales

Exhibit 2–5
Jerrico: Long John Silver's systemwide sales analysis

With sales up, Long John Silver's has been able to increase ad expenditures. The chart illustrates the growing number of units in the A and B market groups.

	Year ended June 30			
	1981		*1980*	
Market group*	*Number of shops*	*Average annual sales†*	*Number of shops*	*Average annual sales*
A. Mature areas with good shop distribution and heavy TV media levels	412	$465,312	334	$431,820
B. Emerging markets with expanding shop distribution and moderate TV media levels	431	447,468	392	398,160
C. Underdeveloped markets with minimal number of shops, enabling low levels of TV media‡	207	388,092	241	334,488
D. Pioneer markets with no TV media . . .	75	324,000	66	268,572

* Shops are classified by markets based on actual spot TV advertising media weights experienced during each year.
† Sales of shops not open the entire year have been annualized based on the full months of operations.
‡ Markets with only a minimal level of non-prime-time TV media, previously reported as D TV markets, are included in this classification.
Source: Richard Kreisman, "Jerrico Taking Slow Approach to Fast Growth," p. 4. Reprinted with permission from the December 14, 1981 issue of *Advertising Age.* Copyright 1981 by Crain Communications, Inc.

trends can be examined for each of the four market groups (A, B, C, and D), and compared to the advertising strategy used in each group.

Cost information is not very useful for marketing financial analysis unless it is combined with revenue (sales) data to perform various kinds of profit analyses. While in some instances we can analyze historical costs such as the average cost required to close a sale, our analysis is incomplete unless we compare costs to what they have accomplished.

As we move through the discussion of financial analysis, be sure to recognize the type of costs that is being used in the analysis. Using accounting terminology, costs can be designated as *fixed* or *variable*. From basic accounting you will recall that a cost is fixed if it remains constant over a relevant range even though the volume of activity varies.[2] In contrast, a variable cost changes proportionately to changes in the volume of activity. Costs are designated as semivariable in instances when they contain both fixed and variable components.

FINANCIAL ANALYSIS AND PLANNING METHODS

Since a complete treatment of financial analysis is not feasible in a single chapter, we shall concentrate on three key areas: (1) liquidity analysis, (2) profit analysis, and (3) budgeting and forecasting. For a more extensive coverage of financial analysis, you should refer to the sources cited in the notes for the chapter.

Financial information will be more useful to management if it is prepared so that comparisons can be made. Van Horne comments upon this need:

> To evaluate a firm's financial condition and performance, the financial analyst needs certain yardsticks. The yardstick frequently used is a ratio or index, relating two pieces of financial data to each other. Analysis and interpretation of various ratios should give an experienced and skilled analyst a better understanding of the financial condition and performance of the firm than he would obtain from analysis of the financial data alone.[3]

As we examine the various financial analysis methods, note how the ratio or index provides a useful frame of reference. Typically, the ratio is used to compare historical and/or future trends within the firm or to compare a firm or business unit with an industry or specific firms.

Liquidity analysis

Marketing executives should be familiar with some of the basic measures of short- and long-term liquidity since these measures may have a bearing on new product planning, marketing budgets, and other marketing decisions. The composition of a balance sheet is shown in Exhibit 2–6. Liquidity analysis draws from the information contained in the balance sheet. You may want to refer to Exhibit 2–6 as we discuss current, quick, and debt ratios.

Current and quick ratios.   These ratios are used to gauge a firm's short-term capacity to meet its financial responsibilities. The current ratio is expressed as current assets divided by current liabilities. The more in excess of 1.0 this ratio is, the greater is a company's ability to meet its short-term financial needs. Since current assets include in-

---

[2] An excellent discussion of cost-volume relationships and other aspects of managerial accounting is provided in chap. 18 of Paul H. Walgenbach, Norman E. Dittrich, and Ernest I. Hanson, *Financial Accounting: An Introduction*, 2d ed. (New York: Harcourt Brace Jovanovich, 1977).

[3] James C. Van Horne, *Fundamentals of Financial Management*, 4th ed. (Englewood Cliffs, N.J.: Prentice-Hall, 1980), pp. 103–4.

Exhibit 2–6
Composition of the balance sheet ($000)

Cash	$ 100	Current liabilities..................	$ 75
Accounts receivable	200	Short-term debt...................	125
Inventory......................	150	Long-term debt	1,000
Total current assets	450	Total liabilities..............	1,200
Property and equipment.........	1,500		
Other assets	300	Net worth	1,050
Total assets	$2,250	Total liabilities and net worth	$2,250

ventory (which often cannot be quickly transferred into cash), another ratio that is popular with financial analysts is the quick or acid-test ratio. This is the ratio of current assets minus inventory to current liabilities.

Debt ratios. There are two ratios that can be used to measure long-term liquidity. Consider the right-hand side of the balance sheet shown in Exhibit 2–6. The first ratio consists of total debt (current liabilities, short-term debt, and long-term debt) divided by net worth. The amount of debt varies considerably across industries. Whenever the ratio is less than one, it is in a desirable range. High leverage (debt) and high sales variability can create financial problems for a firm when substantial sales declines occur.

A second ratio that is useful in evaluating debt is long-term debt divided by total capitalization (long-term debt and net worth). This ratio indicates the extent of leverage (debt) in total capitalization. There is a wide range of values for this ratio across industries and even for companies within the same industry. For example, in 1982 the Delta Airlines ratio was small compared to that of most other debt-burdened airlines. Examples of the above liquidity ratios are shown in Exhibit 2–11 for six types of wholesalers.

Profit analysis

We shall begin our discussion of profit analysis methods with break-even analysis. This is a technique for examining the relationship between sales and costs. An illustration is given in Exhibit 2–7. Using sales and cost information, you can easily see from a break-even analysis how many units of a product must be sold in order to break even. In this example 65,000 units at sales of $120,000 are equal to total costs of $120,000. Any additional units sold will produce a profit. The break-even point can be calculated in this manner:

$$\text{Break-even units} = \frac{\text{Fixed costs}}{\text{Price per unit} - \text{Variable cost per unit}}$$

Exhibit 2–7
Illustrative break-even analysis

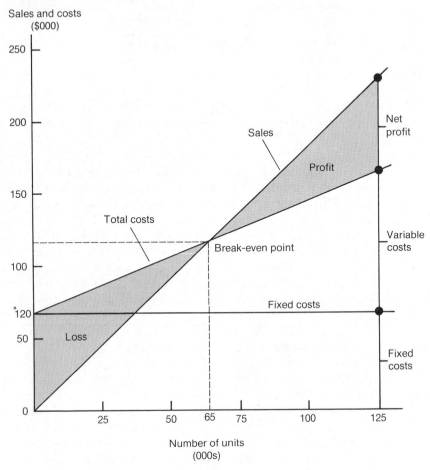

Price in the illustration shown in Exhibit 2–7 is $1.846 per unit, and variable cost is $0.769 per unit. With fixed costs of $70,000, this results in the break-even calculation:

$$\text{BE units} = \frac{\$70,000}{\$1.846 - \$0.769} = 65,000 \text{ units}$$

You should note that this analysis is not a forecast. Rather, it indicates how many units of a product at a given price and cost must be sold in order to break even. Some important assumptions that underlie the above break-even analysis should be recognized:

☐ We have assumed that fixed costs are constant and that variable costs vary at a constant rate.

☐ We have assumed that all costs are either fixed or variable.

☐ The analysis considered only one selling price. A higher price would yield a lower break-even point.

When the above assumptions do not apply, the analyst must modify the basic break-even model that we use in Exhibit 2–7. The model can be expanded to include nonlinear sales and costs as well as alternative price levels.[4]

Contribution analysis. When the performance of products, market segments, and other marketing units is being analyzed, an examination of the profit contribution generated by a unit is often useful to management. Contribution margin is equal to sales (revenue) less variable costs. Thus, contribution margin represents the amount of money available to cover fixed costs and the excess available is net income. For example, suppose a product is generating a positive contribution margin. If the product is dropped, the remaining products would have to cover fixed costs that are not directly traceable to it. An illustration of contribution margin analysis is given in Exhibit 2–8. In

Exhibit 2–8
Illustrative contribution margin analysis for product X ($000)

Sales.	$300
Less:	
Variable manufacturing costs.	100
Other variable costs traceable to product X.	50
Equals: Contribution margin	150
Less: Fixed costs directly traceable to product X	100
Equals: Product net income	$ 50

this example, if product X were eliminated, $50,000 of product net income would be lost. If the product is retained, the $50,000 can be used to contribute to other fixed costs and/or net income.

Gross and net profit margins. While contribution margin analysis is useful in examining the financial performance of products, market segments, and other marketing planning and control units, marketing executives should also be familiar with the calculation of gross and net profit margins since this information is typically used to gauge company and business unit financial performance and to budget for future operations. The profit and loss statement is also the format used to report financial performance to stockholders and to compute taxes. An illustrative profit and loss statement is shown in Exhibit 2–9.

---

[4] For an expanded discussion of break-even analysis, see J. Fred Weston and Eugene F. Brigham, *Managerial Finance*, 5th ed. (Hinsdale, Ill.: Dryden Press, 1975), chap. 3.

Exhibit 2–9
Illustrative profit and loss statement

Sales revenue	$752,000
Less: Cost of goods sold	492,000
Equals: Gross profit margin	260,000
Less: Selling and administrative expenses	140,000
Equals: Net profit before taxes	120,000
Less: Taxes	50,000
Equals: Net profit	$ 70,000

Exhibit 2–10
Financial analysis model

Profit margin		Asset turnover		Return on assets		Financial leverage		Return on net worth
↓		↓		↓		↓		↓
$\dfrac{\text{Net profits (after taxes)}}{\text{Net sales}}$	×	$\dfrac{\text{Net sales}}{\text{Total assets}}$	→	$\dfrac{\text{Net profits (after taxes)}}{\text{Total assets}}$	×	$\dfrac{\text{Total assets}}{\text{Net worth}}$	=	$\dfrac{\text{Net profits (after taxes)}}{\text{Net worth}}$

Financial analysis model. The model shown in Exhibit 2–10 provides a useful frame of reference for examining financial performance and identifying possible problem areas. The model combines several important financial ratios into one equation. Let's examine the model moving from the far right to the left. Assuming that our performance target is return on net worth, the product of return on assets and financial leverage determines performance. Increasing either ratio will increase return on net worth. This can be accomplished by increasing leverage (e.g., greater debt) or by increasing profits. Next, note that return on assets is determined by the product of profit margin and asset turnover. Thus, greater expense control or faster asset turnover (e.g., inventory turnover) can improve return on assets. The values of these ratios will vary considerably from one industry to another. In grocery wholesaling, for example, profit margins are typically very low, whereas asset turnover is very high. Through efficient management and high turnover a wholesaler can stack up impressive returns on net worth.

If you will refer to Exhibits 2–6 and 2–9, you can see how the equation incorporates the major parts of the balance sheet and the income statement. An illustration using the model ratios plus other financial ratios is provided in Exhibit 2–11. Note the variations in financial performance for the different types of wholesalers.

Exhibit 2–11
Median and upper quartile financial ratios for six types of wholesalers, 1980

Median and upper quartile financial performance by type of wholesaler

Financial ratios	Drug wholesalers		Grocery wholesalers		Hardware wholesalers		Electrical distributors		Plumbing and heating wholesalers		Industrial distributors	
	Median	Upper quartile	Median	Upper quartile	Median	Upper quartile	Median	Upper quartile	Median	Upper quartile	Median	Upper quartile
Strategic profit model ratios*												
Net profits/net sales (percent)	1.7%	3.4%	0.9%	1.5%	2.8%	4.4%	2.7%	5.1%	2.6%	4.7%	3.2%	5.0%
Net sales/total assets (times)	3.3×	3.0×	5.6×	7.3×	2.7×	3.3×	2.9×	3.0×	3.0×	3.0×	2.7×	3.2×
Net profits/total assets (percent)	5.6%	10.3%	5.0%	10.9%	7.5%	14.6%	7.9%	15.2%	7.8%	14.3%	8.6%	15.9%
Total assets/net worth (times)	2.3×	1.7×	2.1×	1.5×	1.6×	1.3×	1.9×	1.5×	1.7×	1.4×	1.7×	1.4×
Net profits/net worth (percent)	12.8%	17.5%	10.5%	16.3%	12.0%	19.0%	15.1%	22.8%	13.2%	20.0%	14.6%	22.3%
Liquidity/capital structure ratios												
Current assets/current liabilities (times)	1.9×	2.7×	2.0×	3.2×	2.7×	4.2×	2.2×	3.4×	2.5×	3.7×	2.6×	3.6×
Current liabilities/inventory (percent)	101.7%	70.5%	84.1%	51.7%	70.1%	44.0%	102.9%	64.1%	83.8%	51.1%	89.4%	56.0%
Current liabilities/net worth (percent)	103.1%	49.8%	78.4%	36.5%	50.5%	27.9%	75.2%	35.6%	59.9%	34.2%	56.4%	32.2%
Total liabilities/net worth (percent)	128.7%	67.3%	111.2%	45.9%	60.9%	33.5%	91.4%	45.4%	74.7%	37.3%	66.2%	36.4%
Productivity ratios												
Net sales/accounts receivable (times)	10.7×	17.4×	26.1×	45.6×	9.4×	12.2×	8.1×	10.1×	8.9×	11.1×	8.9×	11.1×
Collection period (days)	34.0	21.0	14.0	8.0	39.0	30.0	45.0	36.0	41.0	33.0	41.0	33.0
Net sales/inventory (times)	7.1×	9.1×	12.3×	17.6×	5.5×	8.1×	7.2×	10.3×	5.9×	8.4×	6.8×	11.5×
Working capital ratios												
Net profits/net working capital (percent)	15.2%	23.3%	11.8%	22.2%	13.5%	21.6%	17.5%	25.7%	15.4%	23.2%	18.0%	27.0%
Net sales/net working capital (times)	8.1×	14.4×	14.1×	25.4×	4.6×	7.1×	5.9×	9.2×	5.2×	7.8×	5.5×	8.0×

* The strategic profit model ratios may not multiply to the totals indicated because the ratios are median and upper quartile ratios rather than weighted averages.
Source: Dun & Bradstreet, Inc., and Distribution Research Program, University of Oklahoma.

Other performance measures

A widely used measure of productivity in retail organizations is sales per square foot of retail space. In the following discussion space productivity is used as a basis for comparing the financial performance of two bookstore chains, B. Dalton Bookseller and Waldenbooks:

> Each chain had roughly $250 million in sales in 1980 (the latest year for which comparable information is available), but Dalton sold an estimated $132 worth of books per square foot of store space to Walden's $114. A computerized inventory system installed in 1966 is what gives Dalton its edge—and is a key to why its 10 percent pretax profits are well above Walden's.[5]

Space productivity measures are also obtained for individual departments in retail stores that offer more than one line, such as department stores.

Another widely used productivity measure is inventory turnover (net sales divided by inventory). Exhibit 2–11 indicates inventory turnover for six types of wholesalers. Note, for example, the high turnover rate for grocery wholesalers.

Budgeting and forecasting

Budgets and financial forecasts represent an essential part of marketing plans. As an illustration, we have listed the pro forma financial statements and budgets prepared for product line marketing plans by a home furnishing products company:

Marketing budgets
  Field selling expense
  Advertising expense
    National
    Cooperative
    Trade
  Promotion expense
    Consumer
    Trade
  Fixturing and display expense
  Product development expense
  Market research expense
  Distribution expense
  Administrative and allocated expenses

---

[5] Jeff Blyskal[1], "Dalton, Walden, and the Amazing Money Machine," *Forbes*, January 18, 1982, p. 47.

Pro forma financial statements

Annual profit and loss statement (expense detail as shown above)

Next year pro forma by quarter

Current year budget by quarter

Last year actual by quarter

Annual revision of five-year pro forma profit and loss statement (expense detail for broad categories)[6]

A complete outline of the marketing plan from which this illustration is drawn is shown in the introduction to Part 5. The plan includes profit and marketing cost history for the product line and specific objectives for sales, market share, profit, and return on investment.

Eliminating information gaps

You will rarely find all the information that you would like to have for use in financial analysis in a case. This parallels the state of affairs in busines practice. Marketing management must often eliminate information gaps by estimating the values of information needed in an analysis. You should proceed in a similar manner when necessary (and appropriate) in performing various kinds of financial analyses for the cases in this book.

An example will be useful in illustrating how information gaps can be eliminated. Suppose you have a company with three products: A, B, and C. You want to perform a break-even analysis for product B, but the fixed-cost information provided is for the entire company. Since you have sales for each product, one way to proceed is to assume that fixed costs can be allocated to each product based on the percentage of total sales accounted for by that product. For example, if product B represents 20 percent of sales, then it would be assigned 20 percent of fixed costs. Using this fixed-cost estimate and per unit selling price and variable cost, break-even for product B can be estimated. While the fixed-cost estimate may not be exact, it is probably adequate to give a close approximation of break-even. You should note that other bases for allocating fixed costs may be appropriate in a given situation. The important consideration is that the assumptions underlying your estimating procedure be logical and, if possible, supported by facts provided in the case.

In estimating needed information, you should proceed with caution. A key requirement is that you have some basis for what you do. If you have no logical basis for estimating needed information, then you should not make unrealistic guesses about the values of the information you need. In general, a good rule to follow is to be conservative

---

[6] David S. Hopkins, *The Marketing Plan* (New York: Conference Board, 1981), p. 116.

with your estimates. It is sometimes helpful to estimate a range of values of the unknown factor. For example, if you are projecting the sales of a new product for the next three years, you might make three estimates: an optimistic estimate, a pessimistic estimate, and a most likely estimate of sales for each of the three years.

Finally, it may be helpful to determine how sensitive your analysis is to the information you are estimating. Referring again to product B, if the break-even level is not affected very much by different assumptions about how to allocate fixed costs, then any reasonable assumption about allocation should be acceptable. Alternatively, if the outcome of the financial analysis is affected significantly by small changes in the value you are estimating, then you should carefully assess the probable accuracy of your estimates.

Coping with inflation

The double-digit inflation rates of the late 1970s and early 1980s signal the importance of proper treatment of the impact of inflation on marketing financial analysis. Here is a summary of the problem:

> Persistent inflation in the American economy has led accounting rule makers to require large firms to report the effects of inflation on certain of their financial statement data. At present, these adjusted data are to be presented as supplementary disclosures under Statement of Financial Accounting Standards No. 33, "Financial Reporting and Changing Prices." One major result will be significant changes in cost estimates and asset valuations. The changes in financial accounting requirements are likely to be reflected almost immediately in managerial accounting procedures, with specific implications for marketing decisions in such areas as new product introduction, pricing strategy, and the valuation of individual customers and market segments.[7]

Conventional financial reporting using historical cost accounting suffers from two inadequacies during inflationary periods: (1) the dollar does not represent a constant or stable measuring unit over time; and (2) prior to sale, no recognition is given to changes in the prices of the assets held by a firm.[8] Some alternative methods of inflation accounting are shown in Exhibit 2–12. The challenge facing marketing decision makers in financial analysis is described by Webster, Largay, and Stickney:

> As corporate managements attempt to cope with and plan for the combined forces of inflation, tight money supply, high interest rates, and low rates of growth in the economy in general and in specific markets, they will need new criteria to evaluate marketing performance.

[7] Frederick E. Webster, Jr., James A. Largay III, and Clyde P. Stickney, "The Impact of Inflation Accounting on Marketing Decisions," *Journal of Marketing*, Fall 1980, p. 9, published by the American Marketing Association.

[8] Ibid., p. 10.

Exhibit 2–12
Alternative inflation accounting methods

	Nominal dollars*	*Constant dollars*
Historical cost	1. Method used in conventional financial reporting	2. Dollars restated to dollars of constant general purchasing power
Current cost	3. Dollar amounts reported in terms of current replacement cost of specific assets	4. Same as 3 except that all amounts in 3 are restated to a constant-dollar basis

* Actual dollars received at sale of product and expended when inventory and equipment were acquired.

Source: Adapted from Frederick E. Webster, Jr., James A. Largay III, and Clyde P. Stickney, "The Impact of Inflation Accounting in Marketing Decisions," *Journal of Marketing*, Fall 1980, pp. 9–17, published by the American Marketing Association.

Commonly used measures such as gross margin, return on sales, and changes in market share all have a shortcoming—they do not take into account the financial resources committed to a particular product, customer, sales territory, or market segment. This shortcoming can be corrected by using such measures of performance as return on investment, return on equity, and return on assets employed.

At the same time, management must be prepared to incorporate the new inflation-adjusted accounting information into these additional measures of performance. Costs must be redefined to take into account changes in prices of plant, equipment, raw materials, working capital, and the labor that have gone into inventories of finished goods and work in process. The effect will almost always be to reduce profit estimates below levels indicated by traditional accounting methods. Attractiveness of particular products, customers, sales territories, market segments, and even total businesses may be changed accordingly. The amount of the profit decrease will depend, in general terms, on the amount of capital (plant, equipment, and working capital) committed to a particular marketing unit (product, customer, territory, etc.) and specific price changes of factors such as raw materials and energy used by that marketing unit. Marketing units that look like real "winners" on the basis of traditional accounting methods and measures such as gross margin and return on sales can quickly become "losers" when inflation-adjusted costs and capital requirements are considered.[9]

Perhaps the most significant implication is the apparent emphasis by top management on the total level of asset commitment to specific products and markets. This, of course, will have its greatest impact on products and markets requiring heavy capital investments in fixed assets and working capital.[10]

The time value of money represents another influence on the evaluation of the financial performance of marketing operations. Since

---

[9] Ibid., p. 13.

[10] Ibid., p. 14.

several sources provide extensive coverage of this topic, we shall only note its importance in marketing financial analysis, particularly when dealing with uneven cash flows over long time periods.[11]

CONCLUDING NOTE

Our objective in this chapter has been to develop a foundation for marketing financial analysis. We examined the three main areas of financial concern in marketing: (1) situation analysis, (2) evaluation of alternatives, and (3) planning and control. A variety of financial analysis methods were examined. Our emphasis has been on application rather than method, since we have assumed that you already have an understanding of basic managerial accounting and finance. To supplement the coverage in the chapter, several sources are cited in the footnotes.

It is clear that marketing executives' financial analysis responsibilities are expanding rapidly, demanding a capability in using new concepts and techniques as well as interpreting financial analyses provided by others. This new orientation is described below:

> To respond to these pressures positively, marketing managers will need a better understanding of accounting and financial management than that of their predecessors. The characteristic marketing manager's emphasis in analysis and action on sales volume, gross margin, and market share must be replaced by a more general management focus on bottom-line profitability and return on investment. Top management will think increasingly in terms of total resource allocation across products and markets, assessing the total product portfolio in terms of complex trade-offs between business growth opportunities in markets requiring additional investment for future profitability versus cash generation now in markets with limited or negative investment. Heightened awareness of the impact of inflation on measures of corporate financial performance will undoubtedly sharpen management concern for this dilemma. Marketing management must adopt new attitudes, what might be called "a general management orientation," as well as make use of the sophisticated measurements, analytical techniques, and strategic planning approaches that are available to help cope with the new pressures and complexities.[12]

As you move through the analysis of the various cases, you may find it helpful to refer to this chapter when you analyze financial information or prepare your own financial analyses. Building upon the materials discussed in this chapter, in Chapter 3 we shall discuss various aspects of case analysis.

---

[11] An excellent discussion of how to handle uneven cash flows in calculating return on investment is provided in Sanford R. Simon, *Managing Marketing Profitability* (New York: American Management Association, 1969), chap. 10.

[12] Webster et al., "The Impact of Inflation Accounting," pp. 16–17.

Chapter 3

Guide to Case Analysis

A case is a factual description of a situation involving a managerial problem or issue that requires a decision. Most cases describe a variety of conditions and circumstances facing an organization at a particular point in time. This description often includes information regarding the organization's goals and objectives, its financial condition, the attitudes and beliefs of managers and employees, market conditions, competitors' activities, various environmental forces that impact upon decision making, and the organization's present and sometimes its proposed marketing strategy. Your responsibility is to carefully sift through the information provided in order to identify the opportunity, problem, or decision facing the organization; to carefully identify and evaluate alternative courses of action; and to propose a solution or decision.

This chapter provides an overview of the case method. It begins with a discussion of the role that cases play in the teaching/learning process. This is followed by a series of guidelines for case analysis. Finally, an actual case is analyzed and critiqued. After carefully reading this material, you should be prepared to tackle your first case analysis. Even if you have had previous experience with cases, this chapter will provide a useful review.

WHY CASES?

The case method differs substantially from alternative teaching/learning approaches such as lecture and discussion. Lecture- and discussion-oriented classes provide students with information *about* concepts, practices, and theories. Cases, on the other hand, give students an opportunity to *use* concepts, practices, and theories. The primary objective of a case is to provide a hands-on opportunity to apply what you have learned in your course work.

Let's consider an analogy. Suppose, for example, that you want to learn to play a musical instrument. Your instruction might begin with several classes and reading assignments about your particular instrument. This could include information about the history of the instrument and descriptions of the various parts of the instrument and their functions. Sooner or later, however, you would have to actually play the instrument. Eventually you might become an accomplished musician.

Now suppose that instead of becoming a musician, you want to become a marketing professional. You started with classes or courses that introduced you to the foundations of marketing management. Your prior studies may have also included courses in particular areas of specialization such as marketing research, buyer behavior, and promotion as well as other business disciplines such as management, finance, accounting, economics, and statistics. Before becoming an accomplished marketer, you need practice and experience. This is precisely the purpose of the case method of instruction. The cases in this book will give you opportunities to apply your knowledge of marketing and other business subjects to actual marketing situations.

Cases assist in bridging the gap between classroom learning and the so-called real world of marketing management. They provide us with an opportunity to develop, sharpen, and test our analytical skills at:

☐ Assessing situations.
☐ Sorting out and organizing key information.
☐ Asking the right questions.
☐ Defining opportunities and problems.
☐ Identifying and evaluating alternative courses of action.
☐ Interpreting data.
☐ Evaluating the results of past strategies.
☐ Developing and defending new strategies.
☐ Interacting with other managers.
☐ Making decisions under conditions of uncertainty.
☐ Critically evaluating the work of others.
☐ Responding to criticism.

In addition, cases provide exposure to a broad range of situations facing different types and sizes of organizations in a variety of industries. The decisions that you encounter in this book will range from fairly simple to quite complex. If you were the managers making these decisions, you would be risking anywhere from a few thousand to several million dollars of your firm's resources. You might well also be risking your job and your career. Consequently, your risk, or the cost of making mistakes, is much lower in the classroom environment.

A principal difference between our earlier example of learning to play a musical instrument and the practice of marketing lies in what might be called consequences. A musician's expertise is based on his or her ability to take precisely the same series of actions time after time. The outcome of perfect execution of a predetermined series of actions is the sought consequence, a beautiful melody. Marketing, on the other hand, is often described as a skillful combination of art and science. No two situations ever require exactly the same actions. Although the same skills and knowledge may be required in different situations, marketers must analyze and diagnose each situation separately and conceive and initiate unique strategies to produce sought consequences. Judgment, as opposed to rote memory and repetition, is one key to marketing success. When judgment and a basic understanding of the variables and interrelationships in marketing situations are coupled, they form the core of an analysis and problem-solving approach that can be used in any marketing decision-making situation.

THE CASE METHOD OF INSTRUCTION

The case method of instruction is different from the lecture/discussion method that you have grown accustomed to since you began your formal education 14 or more years ago. It is only natural that you are a bit anxious and apprehensive about it. The methods of study and class preparation are different, your role and responsibilities are different, and the "right" answers are much less certain. The case method is neither better nor worse than alternative methods; it's just different.

The case method is participative. You will be expected to take a more active role in learning than you have taken in the past. The case method is based on a philosophy of learning by doing as opposed to learning by listening and absorbing information. Case analysis is an applied skill. As such, it is something that you learn as opposed to something that someone teaches you. The more you practice, the more proficient you will become. The benefit that you receive from case analysis is directly proportional to what you put into it.

Your responsibilities

Your responsibilities as a case analyst include active participation, interaction, critical evaluation, and effective communication.

Active participation.   We have already noted that the case method is participative. It requires a maximum of individual participation in class discussion. Effective participation requires thorough preparation. This entails more than casually reading each case before class. The guidelines in the following section of this chapter will assist you in preparing case analyses. Also, keep in mind that there is a difference between contributing to a class discussion and just talking.

Interaction.   Interaction among students plays an important role in the case method of instruction. Effective learning results from individual preparation and thinking combined with group discussion. Whether you are assigned to work independently or in groups or teams, most instructors encourage students to discuss cases with other students. This, of course, is common practice among managers facing important business decisions. Case discussions, in and out of class, are beneficial because they provide immediate feedback regarding individual perspectives and possible solutions. Other important benefits of case discussions are the synergism and new insights produced by group brainstorming and discussion.

Critical evaluation.   One of the most difficult responsibilities of student case analysts is learning to critique their peers and to accept criticism from them. Typically students are reluctant to question or challenge their classmates or to suggest alternatives to the perspectives proposed by their classmates. Students find this difficult because they are generally inexperienced at performing these functions in the classroom. Likewise, students are not accustomed to being challenged by their peers in the classroom. However, the case method of instruction is most effective when all parties engage in an open exchange of ideas. Good cases do not have one clear-cut superior solution. Don't be shy about expressing and defending your views.

Effective communication.   Each of the three responsibilities discussed above requires effective communication. It is important that you organize your thoughts before speaking out. You will develop and refine your communication skills by making class presentations, participating in case discussions, and writing case analyses. Furthermore, the focus of the case method is developing and sharpening quantitative and qualitative analytical skills. Your analytical skills will improve as you organize information, diagnose problems, identify and evaluate alternatives, and develop solutions and action plans.

Case analysis plays an important role in your overall education. What you learn in a course that utilizes the case method may well be your best preparation for landing your first job and launching your career. If you ask a sample of recruiters to assess the students who are completing undergraduate and graduate programs in business administration today, you will probably hear that these students are extremely well trained in concepts and quantitative skills but that they lack verbal and written communication skills and decision-making skills.

A GUIDE TO CASE ANALYSIS

There is no one best way to analyze a case. Most people develop their own method after gaining some experience. As with studying, everybody does it a little bit differently. The following suggestions are intended to give you some ideas regarding how others approach cases. Try these suggestions, and make your own adjustments.

Begin by reading each case quickly. The purpose of the first reading should be to familiarize yourself with the organization, the problem or decision to be made, and the types and amount of data provided and in general to get a feel for the case. Your second reading of the case should be more careful and thorough. Many people find it helpful to underline, highlight, and make notes about symptoms, potential problems and issues, key facts, and other important information.

Now you should be in a position to investigate the tabular and numerical data included in the case. Ask yourself what each figure, table, or chart means; how it was derived; whether or not it is relevant; and whether further computations would be helpful. If calculations, comparisons, or consolidations of numerical data appear useful, take the necessary action at this time.

A large part of what you will learn from case analysis is how to define, structure, and analyze opportunities and problems. The following information is intended to provide you with a general framework for problem solving. In essence, it is the scientific method with some embellishment. If your instructor does not assign you an analytical framework that he or she prefers, it is suggested that you follow the approach shown in Exhibit 3–1. Let's examine each step in the approach.

Exhibit 3–1
An approach to case analysis

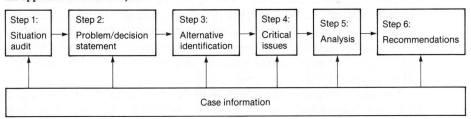

Step 1: Situation audit

The situation audit phase of the problem-solving process is basically a synopsis and evaluation of an organization's current situation, opportunities, and problems. This does not mean that you should simply restate material included in the case. The purpose of this step is to interpret and show the relevance of important case information. Thus, it is important that your situation audit be diagnostic rather than descriptive.

The breadth and depth of an appropriate situation audit are determined by the nature and scope of the case situation. In this book you will find cases that deal with both corporate and business unit decisions. Some case situations focus on major corporate strategic decisions such as the Sherwin-Williams example cited in Chapter 1. Others focus on individual marketing mix decisions at the brand level. Each case will require a situation audit that is a little different from any of the others because of the information available and the decision to be made. The following six-part format provides a useful guide in developing your situation audit.

First, if appropriate, summarize the organizational mission and objectives that are expressed or implied in the case. Mission and objective statements identify the nature and scope of a firm's operations. This information is an important basis for assessing present and future directions and decisions.

Second, assess any relevant environmental information that is available. Are there political, legal, regulatory, societal, consumer, economic, or technological forces that present significant opportunities or threats?

The third and fourth parts of this situation audit format deal with product-market and competitor analysis. These steps were addressed in Chapter 1. A guide for conducting a comprehensive assessment of end users and key competitors was provided in Exhibit 1–5. This guide identifies the key points that should be considered.

Fifth, critically assess the company's strengths and weaknesses. Are the goals and objectives realistic? Are they financially sound? Calculate appropriate ratios, make industry comparisons, determine break-even points, and make other quantitative assessments, as illustrated in Chapter 2. What are the product's strengths and weaknesses? Evaluate management's capabilities. How strong is the firm's position in the marketplace? How does the firm measure up to the competition? The criteria that you employ will be determined by the case information provided.

The final section of the situation audit deals with assumptions and opinions. Generally, enough information will be presented in each case for you to develop intelligent solutions. In some instances, however, you will be given information that is based on someone's assumptions or opinions. This information should be clearly identified as such, and its reasonableness should be evaluated. In other instances you may feel a need to make your own assumptions about the organization's objectives, competition, the environment, or something else.

Students often feel that they need more information in order to make an intelligent decision. Decision makers rarely, if ever, have all the information they would like to have prior to making important decisions. The cost and time involved in collecting more data are often prohibitive. Therefore, decision makers, like you, have to make some assumptions. There is nothing wrong with making assumptions as long as they are explicitly stated and reasonable. Be prepared to defend your assumptions as reasonable. Don't use lack of information as a crutch.

Step 2: Problem/decision statement

Identification of the main problem, opportunity, or issue in a case is crucial. To paraphrase from *Alice In Wonderland,* if you don't know where you are going, any solution will take you there. If you don't properly identify the central problem or decision in a case, the remainder of your analysis is not likely to produce recommendations necessary to solve the organization's main problem.

You may become frustrated with your early attempts at problem/ decision identification. Don't feel alone. Most students and many experienced managers have difficulty with this task. Your skill will improve with practice and direction.

A major pitfall in defining problems/decisions is confusing symptoms with problems. Such things as declining sales, low morale, high turnover, or increasing costs are symptoms that are often incorrectly identified as problems. You can often avoid incorrectly defining a symptom as a problem by thinking in terms of causes and effects. Problems are causes, and symptoms are effects. The examples cited above are the effects or manifestations of something wrong in the organization. Why are sales declining? Why is morale low? Why is turnover high? Why are costs increasing? The key question is Why? What is the cause? Sales may be declining because morale is low and turnover is high. Why is morale low, and why is turnover high? These effects may be caused by an inadequate compensation plan, which in turn may be caused by inadequate profit margins. Profit margins may be low because products have been incorrectly priced or because the distribution system is outdated. As you can see, symptoms may appear in one part of the overall marketing program and the true problem may lie elsewhere in the program. Keep asking the question why until you are satisfied that you have identified the problem (cause) and not just another symptom (effect).

Think about this analogy. You are not feeling well, so you make an appointment to see your physician. The physician will ask you to describe what is bothering you. Suppose you say that you have a headache, a sore throat, and chills and that you are running a fever. The physician will probably next take your temperature, look in your throat, and perhaps examine you in other ways. The goal, of course, is to diagnose your problem so that a remedy can be prescribed.

How does this relate to case analysis? Your headache, sore throat, chills, and fever are symptoms that something is wrong. They are signals to you to seek help. This information also assists your physician in making his or her diagnosis. These symptoms are similar to the declining sales, poor morale, high turnover, and increasing costs that we discussed earlier. They are the effects of some underlying cause. Your role, like the role of your physician, is to analyze the combination of symptoms that can be identified and then to determine the underlying problem.

Let's carry the analogy a bit further. Suppose that the physician's diagnosis is that you have a common cold. Since there is no cure for a cold, all he or she can do is prescribe medication to treat the symptoms. The cold will cure itself in a matter of days.

Now suppose that the diagnosis of the cause is incorrect. Instead of just having a common cold, you contracted malaria during a recent vacation in Southeast Asia. If the physician treats the symptoms or effects, they will be temporarily reduced or eliminated, but they will soon reappear. Each time they reappear they will be more severe until the ailment is properly diagnosed or you die. This is precisely what will happen in an organization if a symptom is incorrectly identified as a problem. Treating the symptom will temporarily reduce its dysfunctional impact on the organization, but sooner or later it will reappear. When it reappears, it will probably be more severe than it was previously. This is why it is so important to carefully identify the root problem, decision, or issue in your case analysis.

When you identify more than one major problem or decision in a case, ask yourself whether or not the problems or decisions are closely enough related to be consolidated into one problem/decision statement. You may not yet have gotten to the central problem. If, however, you have identified two or more problems that are not directly related, we recommend that you rank them in the order of their importance and address them in that order. You may find that although the problems do not appear to be closely linked, the solutions are related. One solution may solve multiple problems.

A final suggestion regarding defining problems or decisions is to state them concisely, and in the form of a question if possible. Try to write a one-sentence question that is specific enough to communicate the main concern. For example:

□ Should brand A be deleted from the product line?
□ Should General Mills implement a cents-off campaign, or should it use coupons to stimulate trial of its new cereal, Gold Rush?
□ Which two of the five candidates should be hired?
□ How should Magic Chef define its marketing planning units?
□ What is the best marketing program positioning strategy for Agree Creme Rinse?

In addition to your problem/decision statement, you may find it useful to provide a brief narrative describing the main parameters of the problem/decision. This is helpful when you have a compound problem/decision that can be subdivided into components or subproblems. This issue will be addressed further in the "Comments on the Preceding Student Analysis" section later in this chapter.

Step 3: Alternatives

Alternatives are the strategic options or actions that appear to be viable solutions to the problem or decision situation that you have posed. Often more than two seemingly good alternative actions will be available. Sometimes these will be explicitly identified in the case, and sometimes they will not.

Prepare your list of alternatives in two stages. First, prepare an initial list of alternatives which includes all the actions that you feel could be appropriate. Group brainstorming is a useful technique for generating alternatives. Be creative, keep an open mind, and build upon the ideas of others. What may sound absurd initially could become an outstanding possibility.

After you have generated your initial list of alternatives, begin refining your list and combining similar actions. Use the information that you organized in your situation audit regarding goals, objectives, and constraints to help you identify which alternatives to keep and which to eliminate. Ask yourself whether or not an alternative is feasible, given the existing financial, productive, managerial, marketing, and other constraints, and whether or not it could produce the results sought. That is, does the alternative directly address the problem or decision that you identified in step 2? If your problem/decision statement and your alternatives are inconsistent, you have erred in one step or the other. To help avoid this mistake, be explicit in showing the connections between the situation audit, the problem/decision statement, and the final set of alternatives.

Two alternatives that are often suggested by students with limited case experience are to do nothing and to collect more data. These are rarely the best alternatives available. If you have identified a problem or a decision that must be made, doing nothing probably will not help. Likewise, recommending a survey, the hiring of a consultant, or some other delay option associated with gathering more data is rarely a viable possibility. Most cases, at least those included in this book, are based on real business situations. You have the same information that was available to the decision maker when the decision was made. The major difference is that your data are already compiled and organized for you. If complete information were available, decisions would be easy. This is not the case in business situations, so you may as well get used to making decisions under conditions of uncertainty. Executives, like case analysts, must rely on assumptions and on less than perfect information.

Step 4: Critical issues

Next, you should develop a list of critical issues. These are simply the main criteria that you will use to evaluate your strategic options. By explicitly expressing the critical issues that you intend to use in evaluating alternatives, you have made clear the criteria that you intend to use in assessing and comparing the viability of your alternative courses of action.

Perhaps the best place to start in identifying critical issues is to ask yourself what factors, in general, should be considered in making a strategic decision regarding this particular problem area. For example, assume that your problem is to identify the most attractive product-market niche. Your alternatives are niches X, Y, and Z. Your question, then, would be, What criteria should be employed in assessing the alternative product-market niches? An appropriate set of criteria might include (for each niche) potential sales volume, variable costs, contribution margins, market share, total niche sales, business strength, and niche attractiveness. This will provide an evaluation relative to the market and to competition. Now return to Exhibit 1–6 in Chapter 1. This exhibit illustrates the critical issues that might be used in your subsequent analysis.

The single most important critical issue in most decisions is profitability. Since profits are a principal goal in all commercial organizations, nearly every marketing decision is influenced by monetary considerations that ultimately affect profits (or expected profits). Sometimes several profit-oriented critical issues are involved. These may include future costs and revenues, break-even points, opportunity costs, contribution margins, taxes, turnover, sales, and market share.

Many critical issues are only indirectly linked to profits. Such things as the impact of a decision on employees, the local economy, the environment, suppliers, or even customer attitudes may not be directly linked to profits. Directly or indirectly, profits are almost always the overriding critical issue.

Step 5: Analysis

Analysis entails a careful evaluation of the pros and cons of each strategic option identified. What are the advantages and disadvantages of each alternative in terms of the identified critical issues?

If you have done a thorough job in steps 1 through 4, steps 5 and 6 should be fairly easy. Let's review. First, we developed a synopsis and evaluation of the organization's current situation, opportunities, and problems. Second, we defined the major problem or decision facing management. Third, we identified the available alternative courses of action. Fourth, we specified the critical issues that we intend to employ to evaluate the alternatives. Our task now is to simply use the information developed in previous steps to select the course of action for the firm.

Some case analysts find it helpful to use an outline form to summarize their analysis. Consider using the following format:

Alternative 1: Introduce product X nationally without test marketing.

Pros:
1. Avoids costs associated with test marketing.
2. Saves time.
3. Keeps product information and marketing strategy secret.

Cons:
1. If there are product weaknesses, a recall will be very expensive.
2. If there are product weaknesses, it will be difficult to overcome initial consumer and distributor dissatisfaction.

Alternative 2: Conduct test marketing before national introduction.

Pros:
1. Will allow testing of alternative packages, prices, and advertising appeals.
2. Will assist in preparing sales forecasts.
3. Will provide information regarding who will and who will not purchase the product, repurchase frequency, and ways the product is used.
4. Will help identify any product performance weaknesses.
5. Will provide an idea of the extent to which product X cannibalizes sales of product Y.
6. Will save a lot of money if the product "bombs."

Cons:
1. Will reveal our plans to competitors.
2. Competitors may interfere with the experiment by increasing their advertising, purchasing large amounts of product X, or other activities.
3. If the results are good, some competitors may introduce similar products before our national introduction.

Although this is a fairly simple example that does not include any financial comparisons, the format can be used to evaluate any set of alternatives. Often a thorough evaluation of the advantages and disadvantages of alternative courses of action will indicate that one option is clearly superior to all others. This is particularly true if all critical issues have been identified and if a common set of criteria is used to evaluate each alternative.

The format illustrated above helps you to organize your thoughts and clearly specifies your rationale to others. Your instructor or your classmates may have selected another alternative that they felt was superior. However, if your logic is sound and your analysis is thorough, they will find it difficult to argue that your solution is not a good one.

Step 6: Recommendations

If your analysis has been thorough, the action recommendations that you propose should flow directly from it. The first part of your recommendations section addresses what specific actions should be taken and why. State the main reasons why you believe that your chosen course of action is best, but avoid rehashing the analysis section. It is important that your recommendations be specific and operational. The following example of a recommendation deals with whether a manufacturer of oil field equipment should introduce a new product line.

> The key decision that management must make is whether viscosity measurement instrumentation represents a business venture that fits into the overall mission of the firm. The preceding analysis clearly indicates that this would be a profitable endeavor. If AOS concentrates on the high-accuracy and top end of the intermediate-accuracy range of the market, sales of $500,000 appear feasible within two to four years, with an estimated contribution to overhead and profits in the $145,000 range. This is assuming that manufacturing costs can be reduced by 20 to 25 percent, that effective marketing approaches are developed, that further product development is not extensive, and that price reductions per unit do not exceed 10 percent.

The second part of your recommendations section addresses implementation. State clearly who should do what, when, and where. An implementation plan shows that your recommendations are both possible and practical. For example:

> AOS should initially offer two instruments. One should provide an accuracy of ±0.25 percent or better; the second should be in the accuracy range of ±0.1 to ±0.5 percent. Top priority should be assigned to inland and offshore drilling companies. Next in priority should be R&D laboratories in industry, government, and universities, where accuracy needs exist in the range offered by AOS. Based on experience with these markets, other promising targets should be identified and evaluated.
>
> AOS needs to move into the market rapidly, using the most cost-effective means of reaching end-user markets. By developing an OEM arrangement with General Supply to reach drilling companies and a tie-in arrangement with Newtec to reach R&D markets, immediate access to end-user markets can be achieved. If successful, these actions will buy some time for AOS to develop marketing capabilities and they should begin generating contributions from sales to cover the expenses of developing a marketing program. An essential element in the AOS marketing strategy is locating and hiring a person to manage the marketing effort. This person must have direct sales capabilities in addition to being able to perform market analysis and marketing program development, implementation, and management tasks.

The last part of your recommendations section should be a tentative budget. This is important because it illustrates that the solution is worth the cost and is within the financial capabilities of the organization. Too often, students develop grandiose plans that organizations couldn't possibly afford even if they were worth the money. Budgeting and forecasting are discussed in Chapter 2.

Your instructor realizes that the numbers you use in your tentative budget may not be as accurate as they would be if you had complete access to the records of the company. Make your best estimates, and try to get as close to the actual figures as possible. The exercise is good experience, and it shows that you have considered the cost implications.

Students often ask how long the recommendations section should be and how much detail they should go into. This question is difficult to answer because each case is different and lends itself to different treatment. In general, it is advisable to go into as much detail as possible. You may be criticized for not being specific enough in your recommendations, but you are not likely to be criticized for being too specific.

AN ILLUSTRATION OF CASE ANALYSIS

To illustrate the recommended method of case analysis we have included a sample case that is followed by an analysis prepared by a student whose undergraduate course work included consumer behavior, marketing research, and sales management as well as introductory courses in accounting, finance, and management. The case selected to illustrate the recommended method is titled "Port-Marine." This case was selected as an example because it is fairly short, reasonably complete, contains a variety of financial data, and is not particularly difficult. The case, however, is not as strategically oriented as many of the cases included in this book. It was chosen to illustrate case analysis as opposed to strategic marketing.

The student's analysis is followed by a brief critique. We suggest that you read the case and prepare your own analysis before you examine the student's work. Compare your analysis to the student's, and then review the comments on the student's analysis. This will help you prepare for tackling your first case assignment.

Port-Marine*

Port-Marine is a sailboat manufacturing company which was formed three years ago in Portland, Maine. Revenue from sales in the first full year of operation totaled $225,000. This was increased to an estimated $1,240,000 in the present year. This dramatic growth is considered to be the result of its excellent products and extensive sales promotion.

The initial product line consists of three different types of fiberglass sailboats. The P/M–17 is a small day cruiser with berths for two adults and two children and a sail area of 130 square feet; it weighs one-half ton and has an overall length of a little over 17 feet. The manufacturer's price is $3,000.

The P/M–34 is a relatively large motor sailer that sleeps seven people in three separate compartments. The main saloon contains an adjustable dining table, a complete galley, and a navigator's compartment. The main saloon is separated from the forecabin by a folding door. The aft cabin, which is entered by a separate companionway, contains a double berth, wardrobe, washbasin, and lockers. The toilet and shower are situated between the forecabin and the main saloon. The boat has a sail area of 530 square feet, weighs about five tons, and has an overall length of 33 feet 8 inches. The most significant feature of this craft, however, is that it is equipped with a full-sized diesel engine (36 or 47 horsepower). The manufacturer's price is $40,000.

The P/M–36 was designed for a different purpose. While the P/M–17 and P/M–34 are oriented toward a family approach to sailing by combining the features of safety and comfortable accommodations with reasonable sailing ability, the P/M–36 is first and foremost a sailing craft. It does have two berths, a small galley, and toilet facilities, but the emphasis is on sailing and racing rather than comfort. The boat has a sail area of 420 square feet, weighs a little less than four tons, and has an overall length of 35 feet 10 inches. The boat is also equipped with a small (7 horsepower) diesel engine for emergency power situations. The manufacturer's price for the P/M–36 is $20,000.

* From James H. Sood, *Situations in Marketing* (Plano, Tex.: Business Publications, 1976), pp. 76–80. Copyright © 1976 by Business Publications, Inc.

The hulls of all three boats are constructed of GRP (glass-reinforced plastic), and the quality of the woodwork and other finishing items is quite good.

Most of the marketing effort to date has been performed by the president of the company. During the first year of operation, a sales manager was hired; however, he resigned to take a similar position with a larger, more established boat manufacturer. Rather than trust the marketing to another new man at this critical time in the development of the company, the president assumed this responsibility himself.

In his opinion, the first priority was to establish an effective channel of distribution for the sailboats. From information obtained from friends and contacts in the industry, he compiled a list of potential pleasure boat dealers along the East Coast. He then visited these dealers in order to evaluate their showrooms, service, and marina facilities, and marketing capabilities. His next step was to persuade some of the most likely candidates to handle the products of Port-Marine. For two reasons he was quite successful in this effort. He invited each of the interested dealers to Portland to visit the factory and to evaluate the sailboats firsthand, and secondly, he offered to sell them a P/M–17 on consignment. That is, the dealers could return these boats to Port-Marine if they were unable to sell them to customers. Because of the stronger position of the dealers in the market, virtually all of the subsequent sailboats sold to the dealers were sold only after the dealers had firm orders from their customers. Thus, the dealers did not have to provide any capital to finance these sales. In addition, Port-Marine was assuming all of the marketing risk.

In order to improve the relatively weak position of the company in this channel of distribution, the president decided to try to develop another channel. His idea was to advertise and sell directly to the final customers, and thus eliminate the dealers in these transactions. His intention in this maneuver was to achieve a sufficient amount of sales in this manner and thereby use this success as a means of improving the company's bargaining position with its dealers. He selected a number of the leading newspapers in the major cities in the East and placed large, four-column ads in these papers, describing the sailboats and instructing interested buyers to contact the company directly. Although this was a relatively new approach in the sailboat industry, it achieved a fair amount of success in terms of boats sold. Approximately 25 percent of the orders received in this current year were received directly from the final customer. The negative aspects of this approach are the very large advertising expenditures and the fact that the company is not staffed to operate in this way. In addition, a number of the dealers have voiced very strong objections, since they feel that any of their customers can now purchase directly from Port-Marine and save the dealer's commission.

Port-Marine is also about to announce the introduction of a new sailboat. Whereas the present products were designed completely by relatively unknown (to the customers) people in the company, the hull of the new sailboat has been designed by an internationally known boat designer. The cost of these design services for the company was a $10,000 initial fee plus a $1,200 royalty fee for each boat produced. The new sailboat is called the P/M–29 and has an interior quite similar to that of the P/M–34. This is not unexpected, since the same Port-Marine people designed the interiors and decks of both sailboats. The new boat is a motor sailer that sleeps six people in three separate compartments, is 28 feet 9 inches long, weighs four tons, has a joined cabin space and a separate aft cabin, a small galley, toilet and shower facilities, and a 12-horsepower diesel engine. Because of a new construction technique that greatly reduces the amount of fiberglass required, the company is able to offer the boat at $20,000. The initial interest in the P/M–29 is exceedingly high, and the company is now concerned that the sales of this product might have an adverse effect on the sales of the P/M–34.

The company is in the process of preparing its production and marketing plan for the coming year in order to arrange for the financing of this plan. The president has indicated strongly that he is committed to continuing the rapid growth of the company, as shown by his proposed plan in Exhibit 1. The present balance sheet and the analysis of costs are shown in Exhibits 2 and 3, respectively.

There are three current ideas concerning the pricing of motor sailers. The predominant theory is that, most generally, price is a function of the overall length of the boat; however, a number of sailing people believe that the overall weight of the craft is a more accurate basis. The third group consists of those people who argue that neither of these ideas holds water, and that the price is a function of the special features and equipment. Exhibit 4 illustrates the present market prices for new motor sailers as a function of overall length.

Exhibit 1
Marketing results and plans

	First year			Present year			Proposed plan		
	No.	Average price	Revenue	No.	Average price	Revenue	No.	Average price*	Revenue
P/M–17	20	$ 2,500	$ 50,000	120	$ 3,000	$ 360,000	240	$ 3,300	$ 792,000
P/M–29	—	—	—	—	—	—	40	20,000	800,000
P/M–34	4	35,000	140,000	20	40,000	800,000	30	44,000	1,320,000
P/M–36	2	17,500	35,000	4	20,000	80,000	4	22,000	88,000
Total revenue			$225,000			$1,240,000			$3,000,000

* Estimated prices to cover anticipated increases in costs.

Exhibit 2

PORT-MARINE
Present Balance Sheet

Assets		Liabilities	
Cash	$ 20,000	Current liabilities	$ 620,000
Accounts receivable	380,000	Short-term debt	450,000
Inventory:		Long-term debt	950,000
Raw materials	200,000	Net worth	
Parts and equipment . . .	200,000	Common stock	
Partial and completed		(privately held)	200,000
sailboats	300,000	Retained earnings	(120,000)
Fixed assets	1,000,000	Total liabilities	
Total assets	$2,100,000	and net worth	$2,100,000

Exhibit 3

Variable-cost analysis

The variable production costs for labor, materials, and parts and equipment have been averaging 65 percent of the manufacturer's selling price for all boat types.

Fixed-cost analysis

	Present year	Estimated, next year
Production costs:		
Building expenses	$ 38,000	$ 45,000
Management salaries	30,000	62,000
Other overhead items	2,000	18,000
Total production costs	70,000	125,000
Product design costs:		
Salaries	30,000	40,000
Prototypes	65,000	70,000
Testing	25,000	30,000
Consultants	10,000	50,000
Total production design costs	130,000	190,000
Administration costs:		
Salaries	25,000	37,000
Insurance	15,000	30,000
Office expenses	5,000	8,000
Total administration costs	50,000	75,000
Marketing costs:		
Salaries	35,000	65,000
Advertising	130,000	175,000
Boat shows	45,000	60,000
Sales promotion	31,000	30,000
Travel expenses	23,000	30,000
Total marketing costs	264,000	360,000
Total fixed costs	$514,000	$750,000

Exhibit 4
Price of sailing cruisers as a function of length

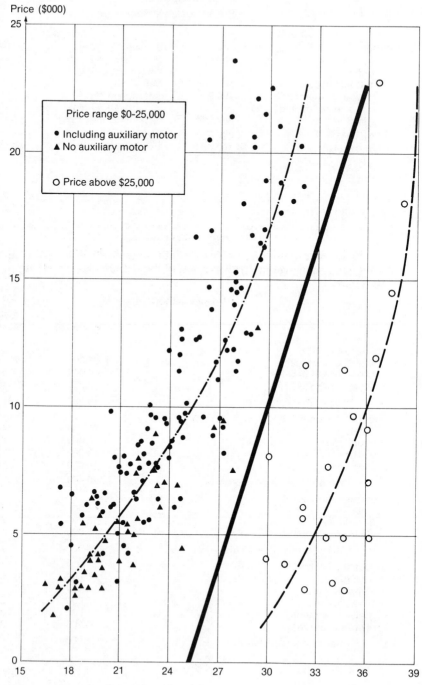

Price ($000)

Price range $0-25,000

• Including auxiliary motor
▲ No auxiliary motor

○ Price above $25,000

STUDENT ANALYSIS OF THE PORT-MARINE CASE*

STEP 1: SITUATION AUDIT

Corporate scope and objectives

Port-Marine is a small, relatively new manufacturer of three types of fiberglass sailboats with current sales totaling $1,240,000. These sailboats appeal to two target markets: consumers that purchase sailboats for family outings or pleasure trips and consumers that purchase sailboats for competitive racing purposes. The only apparent corporate objective is to continue Port-Marine's rapid growth as outlined by the president's proposed sales forecast. Port-Marine is presently preparing a production and marketing plan to arrange the necessary financing for this growth. However, its weak financial status and its poor marketing strategy make this goal unrealistic.

Financial structure

Liquidity. According to liquidity ratios, Port-Marine may not be able to meet maturing obligations. A look at a current ratio of 1.03 (1,100,000/620,000 + 450,000) shows that the firm is barely able to meet short-term debt. A quick ratio of 0.64 (400,000/620,000) shows that without inventory, which is the least liquid item, Port-Marine could not even meet short-term debt. These ratios reveal that Port-Marine is insolvent and in order to even continue current operations must acquire additional funds. Obviously, long-term obligations cannot be met.

Port-Marine's financial structure will not attract future investors. A glance at the balance sheet shows a negative balance of $120,000 in retained earnings. Currently $700,000 of assets is committed to inventory and $380,000 is tied up in accounts receivable. The inventory and accounts receivable turnover ratios, 1.77 and 3.26, respectively, are too low and reflect an inefficient use of company assets.

Further analysis shows that, in order to finance inventory and accounts receivable, Port-Marine has acquired much debt. Total debt to total assets (2,020,000/2,100,000) shows that 96 percent of the firm's financing has been supplied by creditors. Thus, creditors would be reluctant to lend Port-Marine more money. Port-Marine's management has subjected the firm to bankruptcy by allowing the company to become so highly leveraged.

Sales and costs. About 94 percent of present sales can be attributed to the sale of the pleasure sailboats, the P/M–17 and the P/M–34. The P/M–36 only represents 7 percent of sales. The first-year sales

---

* This analysis was prepared by Elizabeth Sypien, Texas Christian University.

forecast of the introduction of the P/M–29 represents 27 percent of projected total sales. This prediction is not based on any market research.

Advertising is an important cost, representing 49 percent of total marketing costs and, in turn, 25 percent of total fixed costs. Consultant costs in the present year can be directly linked to the design of the P/M–29 in the present-year data.

Net profit (loss).   Although Port-Marine has reported a significant growth in sales, the firm has not reported a new profit but rather an $80,000 loss in the current year, as shown in Exhibit 1. The forecasted

Exhibit 1

Present-Year Income Statement

Sales revenue......................................	$1,240,000
Less: Cost of goods sold (65% of sales)............	806,000
Equals: Gross profit margin........................	434,000
Less: Fixed costs.................................	514,000
Equals: Net profit before taxes	$ (80,000)

sales figure of $3 million will allow for a net profit after taxes of $180,000. The return on sales is 6 percent (180,000/3,000,000).

Marketing strategy

Competition, target markets, and objectives.   Port-Marine does not use or have pertinent data concerning its competition or target market. It seems that the main advantages of Port-Marine's competitors are that they have established distribution channels through dealers and successful pricing policies. (See "Marketing program" and "Pricing strategy)." The target market is undefined. There are no identifiable marketing objectives. This lack of data and objectives has resulted in a weak marketing program.

Marketing program.   Port-Marine products have two distinct advantages—high quality and a new construction technique. This technique has reduced expenses in the manufacturing of the P/M–29. Can this new technique be used in the construction of other P/M sailboats? The sales of the P/M–34s will decrease due to the introduction of the new P/M–29. Both are pleasure boats with nearly the same amenities, but the P/M–29 has a $24,000 price advantage and the notoriety of a well-known boat designer who consulted on its construction. Cannibalism within the product mix is inevitable unless a pricing or promotional strategy is devised to mute this effect.

Two channels of distribution are evident: One channel is through dealers on consignment, and the other is directly to the consumer induced by advertising. Dealers resent Port-Marine's attempts to bypass dealer distribution. Since both of these methods cannot exist simultaneously, which is more effective?

The prices of Port-Marine's products are not competitive. Case Exhibit 4 shows that the price of P/M–17 seems to be in line with the industry average price based on length, yet P/M–29 and P/M–36 are well below the average industry price, and P/M–34 is quite high. (See Exhibit 2.) Port-Marine's pricing policy is a weak variable in its marketing program.

Exhibit 2
Pricing audit

	Port-Marine	**Industry***
P/M–17	$ 3,300	$ 2,500– 3,500
P/M–29	20,000	27,000–30,000
P/M–34	44,000	31,000–34,000
P/M–36	22,000	35,000

*According to Exhibit 4 in Port-Marine case.

Assumptions and opinions

Assumptions.   It is assumed that the underlying marketing objective of the firm is to produce a quality product that the target market desires at competitive prices. It has also been assumed that the president has a limited background in marketing.

Opinions.   The president believes he does not need and cannot trust a new marketing person in his firm at this critical time. His first priority is to establish an effective channel of distribution.

Summary of opportunities and problems

While Port-Marine's strengths lie in its quality products and its new cost-saving construction technique, weaknesses in its financial and marketing strategies may force the company into bankruptcy. The firm's hope lies in its restructuring of these faults. Other problems arise due to the lack of a sales force and the lack of control over rising costs.

STEP 2: PROBLEM/DECISION STATEMENT

How can Port-Marine survive?

STEP 3: ALTERNATIVES

1. Port-Marine can maintain current strategies and attempt to reach the forecast sales figure.

2. Port-Marine can review its financial structure and redesign its marketing strategies.

STEP 4: CRITICAL ISSUES

1. Corporation objectives.
2. Financial status/obligations.
3. Profitability.
4. Competition.
5. Target market.
6. Product strategy.
7. Distribution channels.
8. Pricing policy.
9. Promotional strategy.
10. Marketing organization.
11. Costs of implementing alternatives.

STEP 5: ANALYSIS

Alternative 1

Sales forecast.   The proposed sales forecast supplies Port-Marine with a net profit of $180,000, as shown in Exhibit 3. However, this forecast seems to be the result of a need to increase sales to cover expenses and to report a profit rather than a reflection of market potential, competitor strength, or realistic opportunities for the introduction of a new product.

Exhibit 3

Proposed Income Statement

Sales revenue....................................	$3,000,000
Less: Cost of goods sold (65% of sales).............	1,950,000
Equals: Gross profit margin........................	1,050,000
Less: Fixed costs (estimated)......................	750,000
Equals: Net profit before taxes	300,000
Less: Taxes (assume 40% corporate)	120,000
Equals: Net profit..................................	$ 180,000

Break-even analysis.   The break-even analysis in Exhibit 4 shows that Port-Marine must sell 169 P/M–17s, 29 P/M–29s, 22 P/M–34s, and 3 P/M–36s for each product to break even. This plan would require Port-Marine to double its current sales of P/M–17s and sell 40 of the new P/M–29s. This task seems impossible. In addition, if the introduction of the P/M–29 has a cannibalistic effect on P/M–34 sales, Port-Marine would lose the contribution margin of its most profitable boat.

Exhibit 4
Break-even analysis: Port-Marine proposed plan

Product	Total revenue	Percent × Total fixed costs*	Specific product line allocated fixed costs
P/M–17	$ 792,000	26% × $750,000	$195,000
P/M–29	20,000	27 × 750,000	202,500
P/M–34	44,000	44 × 750,000	330,000
P/M–36	22,000	3 × 750,000	22,500
	$3,000,000	100%	$750,000

$$\frac{\text{BEP}}{\text{(units)}} = \frac{\text{Allocated fixed costs}}{\text{Sales price} - \text{Variable costs (65\%)}}$$

$$\frac{\text{BEP}}{\text{(P/M–17)}} = \frac{195,000}{3,300 - 2,145} = \frac{195,000}{1,155} = 169$$

$$\frac{\text{BEP}}{\text{(P/M–29)}} = \frac{202,500}{20,000 - 13,000} = \frac{202,500}{7,000} = 29$$

$$\frac{\text{BEP}}{\text{(P/M–34)}} = \frac{330,000}{44,000 - 28,600} = \frac{330,000}{15,400} = 22$$

$$\frac{\text{BEP}}{\text{(P/M–36)}} = \frac{22,500}{22,000 - 14,300} = \frac{22,500}{7,700} = 3$$

* Assume allocation of fixed costs based on the amount of sales each product represents.

For example, if P/M–34 sales fell from the projected 30 to 10, the income statement might be:

$ 2,120,000	Revenues
(1,378,000)	Variables costs (65% of sales)
(750,000)	Fixed costs
$ (8,000)	

Due to Port-Marine's financial situation it could not withstand this loss. Therefore, this alternative is eliminated and Port-Marine must review its financial structure and redesign its marketing strategies.

Alternative 2

Financial structure. In view of Port-Marine's financial structure, as discussed in the situation audit, Port-Marine is near bankruptcy. The firm must develop an immediate plan to raise additional capital to meet short-term debt and, therefore, continue the firm's existence. The firm can obtain these funds from external sources or by factoring assets.

Port-Marine's balance sheet will not attract external investors in the form of loans or the sale of stock. The potential profitability of the P/M–29 could be used to induce some investors; however, 96 percent of the firm's debt is already supported by creditors.

Port-Marine could collect its accounts receivable and reduce its inventory. A maximum of $380,000 in accounts receivable might be collected. These funds would provide Port-Marine with capital to meet some of its short-term debt and compensate for the negative retained earnings. Inventories totaling $700,000 should be reduced, especially unfinished sailboats, which represent 43 percent of inventory. Data are not available to determine the amount of inventory that represents sailboats on consignment to dealers.

Estimated fixed costs are to rise by $236,000 next year. Variable costs already represents 65 percent of the selling price. Port-Marine could attempt to reduce fixed costs by analyzing each entry to see if the expenditure is necessary. If the new construction technique used on the P/M–29 could be applied to Port-Marine's other products, these variable costs could be reduced.

Product line strategy.   Port-Marine needs to consider if it should continue including the P/M–36 in its product line. This product only represents 3 percent of total sales in the proposed forecast and is not contributing as much as it should to cover fixed cost because of its lower turnover rate. This boat is also the only product geared toward racing. If the firm eliminated this product, Port-Marine could limit its scope of operations and only appeal to the pleasure boat consumer. This would simplify Port-Marine's target market to those who buy sailboats primarily for pleasure purposes. However, the market potential of the racing segment is unknown.

With the introduction of the new P/M–29, cannibalism to the sales of the P/M–34 will occur. However, since Port-Marine is a new, small firm, this new product may establish some credibility for the firm because of the well-known designer consulting on its construction. Pricing and promotional strategies can be developed to make a notable distinction between the P/M-29 and the P/M–34 and their respective target markets.

Distribution.   Port-Marine can distribute its products through dealers or sell the products directly to the end consumers themselves. The question is, Which one is more profitable or compatible with Port-Marine?

Dealers are willing to accept these boats on consignment, and Port-Marine can choose dealers that reach the desired target market. However, in this situation Port-Marine is taking all the marketing risk by allowing dealers to sell on consignment.

Past sales produced from direct sales to the consumer represent 25 percent of total revenue. The proposed advertising expenditure totals

$175,000. Further analysis shows that last year this method lost $21,500, as shown below:

Sales revenue (25% of sales)	$310,000
Less: Cost of goods sold (65% of sales)	201,500
Equals: Gross profit margin	108,500
Less: Advertising cost	130,000
Equals: Net profit/loss.	$ (21,500)

Port-Marine's organization is not set up to handle direct distribution, and dealers object to this method because they obviously lose potential sales. If this channel were dropped, fixed marketing costs would be reduced tremendously.

Promotional strategy. If Port-Marine follows its proposed plan, advertising expenditures will increase to $175,000. This advertising may make the general audience aware of Port-Marine and its products. Apparently, it is not reaching its target market or advertising sales would have been profitable last year. Port-Marine truly cannot afford this expenditure. Eliminating direct consumer sales can reduce advertising expenditures by approximately $100,000. Further, promotion tactics should be used to build or strengthen a dealer network and advertising should be coordinated with dealers.

A main advertising message distinguishing the P/M–29 and P/M–34 should be developed to help deter cannibalism. One of the products could be considered the deluxe model, the designer boat, or the high-priced luxury P/M–34.

Marketing organization. Port-Marine's president can continue operating as the marketing head, or he can hire a marketing manager to assume these duties. Port-Marine's poor marketing strategies are the result of poor management. A professional marketing manager would realize the need to establish corporate and marketing objectives and to perform a Marketing Opportunity Analysis (MOA) to gather data concerning the target market, competitors, and potential of the sailboat market. Hiring a marketing manager would introduce additional costs.

Pricing strategy. Currently there is not an identifiable pricing strategy that Port-Marine utilizes. The present system, however, has resulted in losses. Port-Marine can develop a pricing strategy that infers high-quality products by pricing toward the upper end of industry averages. Another alternative strategy is to set lower prices compared to its competitors to enter or penetrate the market successfully. Since Port-Marine's products are of a high-quality nature and the consumer may not accept drastic changes in established high prices (assuming P/M–36 is dropped), the latter strategy would be applicable. Port-Marine should then also consider closing the gap between the new P/M–17 and P/M–34 to prevent cannibalism.

The proposed price for the P/M–17 reflects the high-price/high-quality strategy since $3,300 is near the upper range of the average. The price could even be higher.

The P/M–29's proposed price, based on the whims of Port-Marine, leaves a gap of $24,000 between the price of P/M–29 and P/M–34. Fortunately this product has not been introduced and the proposed price could easily be changed. The proposed $44,000 for the P/M–34 is still above the industry average. If P/M–29's price were based on the same price per foot as the P/M–34, the price would be approximately $34,150 ($1,188 × 28.75 feet).

STEP 6: RECOMMENDATIONS

In order to stay afloat, Port-Marine must take specific actions and change its strategy before it becomes bankrupt. Immediate steps are necessary to be able to meet short-term debt.

Since Port-Marine cannot attract new investors, it should collect accounts receivables, reduce inventory, eliminate extraneous costs, and try to apply the new construction techniques to all of its products. In the long run, the firm can attract investors by pledging inventory issuing subordinated long-term debt, and raise additional equity through the profit potential of the P/M–29. In addition, the firm may be able to permanently reduce Accounts Receivable by developing alternative sources of customer financing through dealer or local institutions.

A marketing manager should be hired despite the additional cost. An MOA is necessary in order to establish viable marketing strategies. These benefits will outweigh the costs in the long run.

Port-Marine should drop the P/M–36 because of the small portion of revenues and contribution margin it represents. This enables the firm to concentrate on pleasure sailboats at least until their operations become stabilized. Port-Marine can always reenter the racing market if research shows a potential market. It is also recommended that, in the future, Port-Marine incorporate consumer needs into the design of its products and the choice of additional products added to the product line.

Distribution through dealers is clearly the viable alternative. A Port-Marine sales force is recommended to approach dealers and maintain contact. Initially, one or two salespersons should be concentrated in the East Coast to keep costs low. Elimination of the advertising expenditures would reduce fixed costs. Promotional efforts should be concentrated on building an effective dealer network since Port-Marine's competitors have established dealers.

A pricing strategy reflecting the cost and characteristics of Port-Marine's products should be developed. This recommended strategy infers high quality through high prices and reduces the gap between P/M–29 and P/M–34.

P/M–17. $3,600. At this price, P/M–17 falls at the upper end of the industry average. Inflation and the inevitable increase in industry average prices have been taken into consideration.

P/M–29. $34,500. This represents roughly the same price per foot as the P/M–34, reduces the gap, and provides Port-Marine with a desirable profit margin it needs to survive.

P/M–34. $40,000. This is a price freeze. The industry average range is still way below this figure. Exhibit 5 is a proposed sales

Exhibit 5
Sales forecast

Unit	Number	Average price	Revenue
P/M–17	170	$ 3,600	$ 612,000
P/M–29	30	34,500	1,035,000
P/M–34	30	40,000	1,200,000
			$2,847,000

Proposed Income Statement

Sales revenue	$2,847,000
Less:	
Variable cost (55% of sales)*	1,565,850
P/M–29 royalty fees	36,000
Equals: Net contribution margin	1,245,150
Less: Fixed costs†	650,000
Equals: Net profit before taxes	$ 595,150

* Reflects a reduction in construction or materials.
† $750,000 – $100,000 of advertising expenditures.

forecast and income statement incorporating the above recommendations. This proposal reflects a return on sales of approximately 21 percent and should be viewed as a maximum outcome.

In conclusion, Port-Marine must first implement the proposed financial steps and at the same time begin to restructure its marketing strategies. If this is accomplished, Port-Marine will survive.

COMMENTS ON THE PRECEDING STUDENT ANALYSIS

Overall, the student case analyst did a reasonably good job of utilizing the case information. If you worked through the case yourself, you have probably already concluded that its length is deceptive. Although market and industry data are not given, sufficient information is provided to conclude that Port-Marine is in serious trouble. In order to reach this conclusion, however, one must analyze the data provided in the exhibits. As is often the case, the financial condition of the firm is crucial to the analysis. The following comments follow the six-step approach to case analysis suggested in the chapter and employed by the student analyst.

Step 1: Situation audit

The situation audit is generally adequate. It is diagnostic rather than descriptive, and it identifies the critical financial situation facing Port-Marine. Information regarding Port-Marine's presumed mission and objectives is assessed, as are company strengths and weaknesses. Since the case contained little environmental, product-market, or competitor information, there was not much opportunity to address these issues. Assumptions and opinions are clearly and appropriately identified.

Several specific comments regarding the situation audit are in order. The statement that Port-Marine's products appeal to two target markets illustrates an incomplete understanding of the product-markets. While it is true that the smaller sailboats appeal to the leisure/recreation market and the P/M–36 appeals to the serious sailor, the substantial differences in the sizes and prices of the P/M–17, P/M–27, and P/M–34 indicate that each of these products probably appeals to a different age, income, and lifestyle segment. For Port-Marine to succeed, proper identification of these product-markets is essential. The need for market information was clearly identified by the analyst.

The student analysis shows that the available financial data were carefully evaluated. Liquidity ratios were reported, and the calculations were shown. This is a good idea. Other relevant ratios were calculated and discussed. Some others might have also been calculated, such as inventory to working capital, current debt to inventory, current debt to net worth, fixed assets to net worth, and working capital turnover. These would have reinforced the assessment of serious financial problems and identified particular areas where problems are most evident. Another possibility would have been to compare selected ratios to industry averages. This information is available in a number of publications in most libraries for many types of businesses.[1]

The situation audit also reveals the minor contribution that the P/M–36 makes to overall sales and the relationships between advertising, total marketing, and total fixed costs. The importance of this information is revealed later in the analysis.

Several problem areas are accurately revealed, including the com-

---

[1] For example, *The Value Line Investment Survey*, published each week by Arnold Bernhard & Co., provides financial analyses of several industries and companies.

pany's failure to define target markets, the lack of product and pricing objectives, poorly conceived promotion, channel coordination problems, the apparent lack of information about competitor or industry trends, and the company's failure to explicitly define its mission and objectives. These problems are somewhat offset by the high quality of Port-Marine's products and by a new construction technique that could play a major role in Port-Marine's future.

The conclusion that the two channels of distribution now used by Port-Marine cannot exist simultaneously is probably correct in the present situation. To support this conclusion the analyst should carefully evaluate the pros and cons associated with the dual distribution strategy. Multiple channels can be effective, but Port-Marine's management probably has its hands full with one channel for now. Considering that 75 percent of sales are coming from dealers, this seems to be the best channel alternative.

Step 2: Problem/decision statement

Case analysts should not find it difficult to identify the problems facing Port-Marine. The difficulty lies in synthesizing these problem areas. The question "How can Port-Marine survive?" illustrates the case analyst's recognition that the company faces imminent disaster if major changes are not made soon. This is the central issue in the case and the major question that must be addressed. A few summary paragraphs identifying the main parameters of this issue might have been helpful. The issue will be discussed further in the following section.

Step 3: Alternatives

As we noted earlier in this chapter, a "no change" alternative is rarely a viable solution. Obviously it is not appropriate for Port-Marine. The case analyst apparently felt that it was necessary to consider this option because the company's proposed plan, if successful, would produce a net profit of $180,000. Evaluation of the proposed plan reveals that this outcome is not likely.

The second alternative suggests broad, yet unspecific, changes. This often leads to an incomplete evaluation of possible strategies to resolve a major problem/decision facing the firm. One possibility for overcoming this limitation would have been to divide the problem into its major components and consider alternatives to address each subproblem. For example, the situation audit revealed that the company needs to address or take action in each of the following areas:

☐ Mission and objectives determination.

☐ Target market definition and analysis.

☐ Liquidity.

☐   Organization.

☐   Marketing program.

Although these areas are all addressed in the evaluation of alternative 2, a more thorough assessment would have considered potential options to solve each subproblem independently.

Step 4: Critical issues

The critical issues identified are appropriate, given the problem statement and the alternatives. Had the problem been broken down into subproblems, a different set of critical issues would have been appropriate for each area.

Step 5: Analysis

Two alternatives were analyzed. The first, the company's proposed plan, was critically evaluated and rejected. This is an appropriate conclusion. Alternative 1 could have been more thoroughly evaluated in terms of the identified critical issues; however, this would have only reinforced the conclusion that this alternative is not viable.

You may have noticed that the second sentence under the break-even analysis heading is incorrect. Exhibit 4 shows that Port-Marine would have to increase sales of the P/M–17 by 41 percent (not 100 percent) and sell 29 (not 40) of the new P/M–29s to break even. This is a simple, yet noteworthy, error. Supporting details are important in case analysis. Check your calculations.

The analysis of alternative 2 illustrates the potential problem that was pointed out in the alternative identification section. The analyst is proposing solutions without exploring options. If the various subproblem areas had been individually explored, other possible strategies such as selling through manufacturer's representatives and alternatives to selling on consignment might have been revealed. The end result, of course, would have been a more specific, complete set of recommendations.

Overall, the critical issues are addressed in the evaluation of alternative 2. These include raising short-term capital, making product line decisions, minimizing the effects of P/M–29 sales on P/M–34 sales, revising the distribution structure, making promotional changes, and adding a marketing manager to analyze Port-Marine's present situation and opportunities.

Step 6: Recommendations

The recommendations section also addresses the critical issues and proposes appropriate specific actions. Issues that need to be resolved but are not addressed in the recommendations section include:

☐ Developing specific company and marketing objectives.

☐ Developing policies to guide future marketing program decisions.

☐ Incorporating P/M–29 production techniques into the P/M–34, if possible, to reduce costs.

☐ Developing a selective distribution strategy through a strong dealer network.

☐ Getting out of the consignment business.

The recommendations section might also have included additional pro forma financial statements and budgets to support the recommendations. For example, a profit and loss statement for each product and tentative budgets for each component of the marketing program might have been included. Finally, an implementation plan showing *who* will be responsible for *what* and *when* would have strengthened this section.

Summary

In sum, this student's case analysis represents a good start. Attention to several of the areas discussed above could significantly strengthen the analysis. It is much easier to critique a case analysis than to prepare one. Most of the comments on the analysis dealt with ways in which it could be strengthened by going into more detail. Since the focus of the case was on developing a strategic marketing plan for Port-Marine, the student could have strengthened the analysis by incorporating the 10-step sequence described in Chapter 1 into her recommendations. You will find that this planning approach is a useful guide for several cases in this book that deal with strategic marketing planning. The 10-steps raise the questions that need to be answered in preparing a strategic plan, and following them leads to a thorough analysis of the important issues.

Undoubtedly, additional comments about the analysis might have been made. The purpose, however, was not to provide an exhaustive set of comments but rather to highlight the key strengths and weaknesses of the analysis in order to provide you with an example and some guidelines to follow.

CONCLUDING NOTE

Our objective in this chapter has been to develop a foundation for case analysis. We examined the role of cases in the teaching/learning process, proposed a format for case analysis, and provided a sample case, analysis, and critique. You may find it helpful to refer to this chapter as you work through your first few cases. As often happens, the materials will tend to become more meaningful after you have had some experience in using them.

Part 2

Strategic Analysis and Business Strategy

Business successes and disasters often share one characteristic. Strategic planning, or the lack thereof, is often a key factor affecting business operations. And marketing strategy often plays a vital role in achieving corporate strategic goals. Contrast, for example, the impressive performance of General Mills with A&P's struggle during the 1970s to keep this once leading supermarket chain from going under. A&P's poor financial performance and loss of market position clearly indicate the dangers of faulty corporate and marketing strategies. In contrast, General Mills' management has successfully moved the company into new markets such as restaurants and specialty retailing, using the firm's core business (food processing) to generate capital for pursuing new opportunities. Underlying these moves into new business areas are carefully developed and executed strategic plans. Strategic planning for the enterprise demands perceptive insights about customers' needs and wants as well as ways of achieving customer satisfaction through the firm's marketing offer (product, distribution, price, and promotion strategies). Thus, a close working relationship between marketing strategists and executives responsible for the strategic planning of the enterprise is essential.

Strategic planning is one of the high-priority action areas of U.S. business today. And the reason is clear. The success and survival of the firm are at stake. Compare and contrast, for example, the impressive performance of Delta Airlines with that of Braniff International. Both were strong performers in the late 1970s. By 1982 Braniff was bankrupt, while Delta continued to retain a strong market position amid turbulent economic conditions and deregulation. Clearly, Delta's management recognized the forces of change and developed strategies to favorably position the airline in a competitive environment.

Unfortunately, the glamour and mystery often associated with strategic planning mask what should be viewed as a demanding yet logical process of deciding the mission and objectives of the enterprise and then devising strategies for reaching the objectives. Since many corporations have two or more business units, top management must select a strategy for each of the units. For example, General Mills operates food processing, restaurant, games and toys, fashion, and specialty retailing segments. And within each segment are several strategic business units (e.g., Red Lobster).

The 1970s brought major emphasis on strategic planning by companies. Several new planning tools were developed, including the Boston Consulting Group's portfolio analysis, General Electric's screening grid, and the Profit Impact of Market Strategy (PIMS) studies of the Strategic Planning Institute. Unfortunately, these tools are often viewed as strategic solutions rather than the diagnostic aids they were intended to be. Clearly, the emphasis should be on making sound decisions and then executing them. There is evidence of too much concern about strategic concepts:

> Long-term success does not lie in concepts. It depends on an organization's ability to pool the small incremental improvements and insights of the "antennae" of an organization—its salesmen and engineers and workers—to keep an edge on the competition.[1]

The operations of Delta Airlines provide clear evidence of the success of this hands-on approach to strategy. Every employee in the organization from pilots to maintenance people to office personnel seems to know where the firm is going, and why.

While the new planning methods are often useful in highlighting opportunities and problem areas, deciding what to do about them is top management's responsibility. Nucor Corporation is an interesting example of how a perceptive management has been able to establish a strong position for a small steel producer amid an industry dominated by giants. Nucor, if analyzed using the popular portfolio grid for market position and market attractiveness in the entire steel industry, clearly falls into the "dog" category. Yet, if we define the market as steel joists for industrial construction in the Sun Belt, Nucor is suddenly moved into a much stronger business position and a more attractive market opportunity.

In the following section we shall examine what is involved in strategic planning for a business. Next, the major strategic analysis methods are briefly described. An examination of business unit strategy follows. Finally, the nature and scope of a strategic plan for a business are discussed.

---

[1] Richard T. Pascale, "Our Curious Addiction to Corporate Grand Strategy," *Fortune*, January 25, 1982, p. 116.

WHAT IS STRATEGIC PLANNING?

Developing a strategic plan for a corporation consists of the steps shown in Exhibit 1. Starting with an objective assessment of the situation faced by the firm relative to opportunities and threats, a logical sequence of steps leads to the preparation of strategic plans for the

Exhibit 1
Strategic planning overview

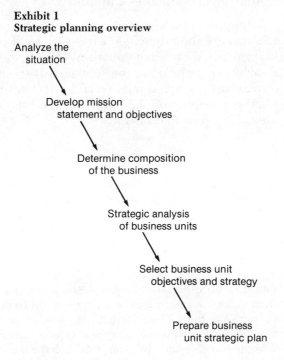

Analyze the
situation

Develop mission
statement and objectives

Determine composition
of the business

Strategic analysis
of business units

Select business unit
objectives and strategy

Prepare business
unit strategic plan

firm's business units. Each step is briefly examined on the following pages.

Situation analysis

The situation analysis provides a foundation for developing the strategic plan. The analysis should clearly describe the present situation faced by the firm. It is "an analysis of data, past, present, and future, that provides a base for pursuing the strategic planning process."[2]

A corporate situation assessment should include the following information:

☐ Analysis of external forces that are (or will) influence the corporation. These include economic, technology, social, governmental, and natural factors.

---

[2] George A. Steiner, *Strategic Planning* (New York: Free Press, 1979), p. 122.

☐ Analysis of demand, customers, industry, and distribution structure.

☐ Evaluation of key competitors.

☐ Objective assessment of corporate capabilities and limitations, highlighting key differential advantages over competition.

☐ Identification of strategic opportunities and threats.

A useful format for combining this information is a *situation assessment summary*. The summary should include a description of corporate weaknesses and strengths, threats and opportunities, and the strategic implication of each item included in the summary. It should be specific, pointing to areas that may affect mission and objectives, business composition, strategic analysis of planning units, and the other strategic planning steps shown in Exhibit 1.

Mission and objectives

Business development strategies available to the corporation were discussed in Chapter 1 (Exhibit 1–2), so our discussion will be brief. The path(s) that management chooses to follow in the development of the firm establishes key guidelines for strategic planning. The choice of mission and objectives should spell out where the company is going, and why:

> Management must initially establish the nature and scope of a firm's operations and then make whatever adjustments in these decisions that are deemed necessary over time. These strategic choices about where the firm is going in the future, taking into account company capabilities and resources and opportunities and problems, establish the mission of the enterprise.[3]

A useful means of communicating business purpose and objectives is the mission statement. The following are illustrative of the contents of the mission statement:

1. The reason for the company's existence and the responsibilities of the company to stockholders, employees, society, and various other stakeholders.
2. The customer needs and wants to be served with the firm's product or service offering (areas of product and market involvement).
3. The extent of specialization within each product-market area (e.g., deciding to offer just Tootsie Rolls rather than a variety of candies).
4. The amount and types of diversification of product-markets desired by management.

---

[3] David W. Cravens, *Strategic Marketing* (Homewood, Ill.: Richard D. Irwin, 1982), p. 42.

5. Management's performance expectations for the company.
6. Other general guidelines for overall business strategy such as the role of research and development in the corporation.[4]

You should recognize that statements containing such information are not widely available. In fact, for many of the areas covered in items 1 through 6 management is likely to be hesitant to discuss details beyond the boardroom due to the competitive nature of the information.

Composition of the business

Consider the business composition of General Mills, Inc., as shown in Exhibit 2. Note, for example, that both product and market factors

Exhibit 2
Business composition of General Mills, Inc.

Food processing	$2,800 (9%)*
Betty Crocker	
Gold Medal	
Cheerios	
Wheaties	
Restaurants	850(11%)
Red Lobster	
York Steak Houses	
Casa Gallardo	
Darryls	
The Good Earth	
Games and toys	725(11%)
Parker Brothers	
Kenners'	
Fashion group	700(16%)
Ship 'n Shore	
Kimberly	
Monet (costume jewelry)	
David Crystal (Izod/Lacoste)	
Specialty retailing	425 (5%)
Talbots (mail-order apparel)	
Wall Papers To Go	
Eddie Bauer (outdoor apparel)	

* Sales in millions (operating margin) for 1982 from *The Value Line Investment Survey*, part 3, "Ratings & Reports," Arnold Bernhard & Co.

have influenced the grouping of business activities into the five segments (e.g., restaurants). Since a segment or division may be too aggregative for use in strategic analysis and planning, it may be divided

---

[4] Ibid., p. 50.

into strategic business units (SBUs) such as Red Lobster in the restaurant segment.

Typically the SBU represents a single product-market or a grouping of product-market areas. Hall comments on the definition of the SBU:

> Ideally, an SBU should have primary responsibility and authority for managing its basic business functions: engineering, manufacturing, marketing, and distribution. In practice, however, traditions, shared facilities and distribution channels, manpower constraints, and business judgments have resulted in significant deviations from this concept of autonomy. In General Foods, for instance, strategic business units were originally defined on a product line basis, even though several products served overlapping markets, and were produced in shared facilities. Later, these product-oriented SBUs were redefined into menu segments, with SBUs like breakfast food, beverage, main meal, dessert, and pet foods targeted toward specific markets, even though these, too, shared common manufacturing and distribution resources.[5]

An SBU consists of as a single product or brand, a line of products, or a mix of products that meets a common market need or a group of related market needs, and the unit's management is responsible for all (or most) of the business functions.[6]

BUSINESS UNIT ANALYSIS AND STRATEGY

Once the composition of the business has been determined, each SBU should be analyzed to determine its role in the corporate portfolio. Let's examine some of the more popular methods used by strategic planners to diagnose SBU position and to guide future strategy.

Planning methods[7]

Business unit evaluation consists of gauging how performance has been in the past, determining the present position, and forecasting the future attractiveness of the product-markets in which the business unit participates. Using this information, management must determine the future strategy of the business unit, considering the unit's opportunities, threats, strengths, and limitations and then compare it to other units in the corporation.

Several methods of strategic analysis have been developed over the past 30 years. The most popular approaches are briefly described:

☐   *Product-market grids.* Using this approach, each business unit or specific product-market is positioned on a two-way grid according

---

[5] William K. Hall, "SBUs: Hot New Topic in the Management of Diversification," *Business Horizons*, February 1978, p. 19.

[6] Cravens, *Strategic Marketing*, p. 54.

[7] This discussion is drawn from ibid., pp. 63–64.

to the attractiveness of the product-market(s) and the unit's business strength compared to competition. Depending on where a unit is located on the grid, alternative strategies are indicated. Several versions of grid analysis exist, the most popular being the Boston Consulting Group portfolio approach and General Electric's screening method.

☐ *Profit impact of marketing strategy (PIMS)*. Using a large data bank, the Strategic Planning Institute in Cambridge, Massachusetts, can analyze various strategic factors (e.g., market share) that are related to profit performance and can compare a company or business unit to other firms and units in the data bank. These computerized analyses provide various diagnostic comparisons and also indicate promising strategic actions based on the results of the analyses.

☐ *Other analysis methods*. A wide variety of other methods are available, including strategic checklists, product life cycle analysis, and strategic guidelines. These methods are less formal than the grid and PIMS methods, depending more heavily on management judgment and experience.

The above approaches are listed in the general order of their popularity with strategic planners. Companies may utilize two or more of the methods, gaining certain benefits from each.

Strategic analysis is concerned with two vital activities: (1) diagnosis of the enterprise's strengths and limitations and (2) prescription of strategic actions for maintaining or improving performance. Management must decide what priority to place upon each business area regarding resource allocation and then choose the strategic actions necessary to meet the objectives established for the business unit. The choice of an approach to strategic analysis rests then upon how well it serves management in diagnosing the business and prescribing appropriate strategic actions. None of the methods is complete in meeting these needs. Each demands a considerable amount of judgment and experience in applying it in a particular firm.

Business unit strategy

After completing the analysis of an SBU, the following questions should be answered:

☐ What is the strategic situation of the business unit in terms of product and market maturity?

☐ How has the business unit performed during the past three to five years?

☐ How attractive will the product-market opportunities be in the next three to five years?

- ☐ How strong is our business unit position compared to that of competition?
- ☐ What should be the future strategy of the business unit over the next three to five years?[8]

The use of a three–five-year time span will vary among firms, depending on the planning horizon used. The decision will depend on the rate of change in markets, competition, and other external factors.

The strategy options for an SBU range from an aggressive growth strategy to maintaining market position to exit from the business area. In a multi-unit corporation, the strategies for SBUs will normally be determined as a part of the corporation's total portfolio strategy.

Exhibit 3
Illustrative business composition

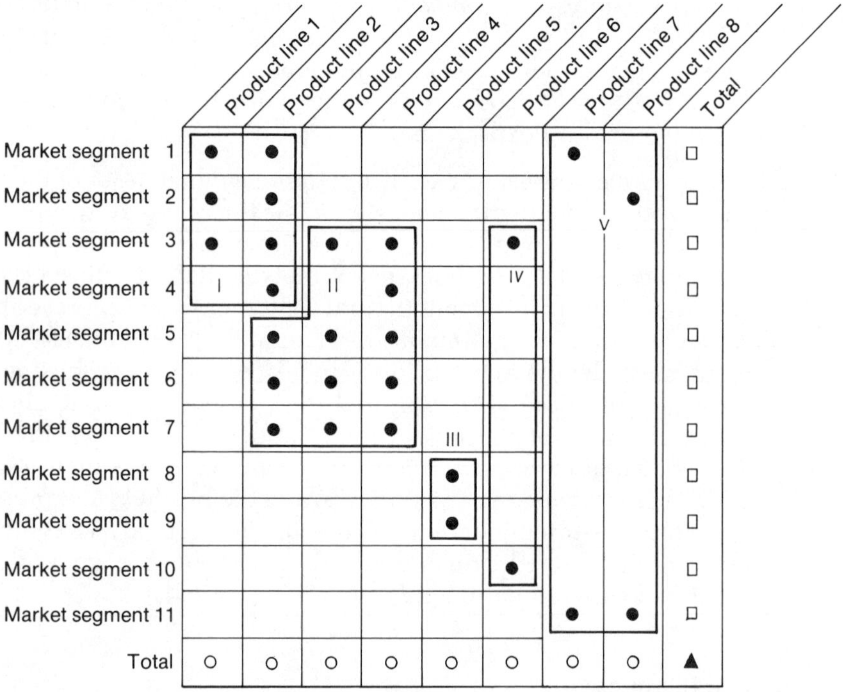

● Product/market segment totals

○ Product line totals

☐ Market totals

▲ Company totals

Source: Reprinted, by permission of the publisher, from *Management for the 1980s,* rev. ed., by William F. Christopher, © 1980 by AMACOM, a division of American Management Associations, p. 48. All rights reserved.

---

[8] Ibid., p. 107.

Exhibit 4
Strategic planning guide

Business mission/objectives/capabilities
Business mission definition and description.
Objectives*
Summary of business position (strengths and limitations)*

Complete the following for each unit of the business and each major product-market within the unit.

Situation analysis
Product-market analysis
Market size and growth.
Describe existing/potential customers.
How do customers decide what to buy?
What factors influence buying?
Industry/distribution analysis
Industry characteristics and trends.
Operating practices in the industry.
Competition from other industries.
Analysis of key competitors
Estimated overall business strength.
Market position.
Financial strengths and performance.
Management capabilities (and limitations).
Technical and operating advantages.
Marketing strategy evaluation.
Other key strengths/limitations.
Analysis of our strengths/limitations
Same factors as for key competitors.
Summary of strategic opportunities and threats in the product-market
Key assumptions underlying our strategic plan
Major contingencies to be considered in the strategic plan

Target market(s) description
The target market decision is the choice of the people or organizations in a product-market toward which a firm will air its marketing program strategy.
Describe each major customer/prospect group toward which a specific marketing strategy will be directed.
Indicate priority for each target market.

Strategic plan for business unit
Objectives
Strategies for achieving objectives
Key plans
Business development.
Marketing strategy.
Operations.
Finance.
Human resources.
Other.

Financial analysis and summary

Contingency plans

---

* Determined after completion of the situation analysis.

Strategic planning guide

The business competition shown in Exhibit 3 (p. 82) consists of five (I–V) SBUs, with two or more product-market segments in each SBU. Suppose you are assigned the responsibility for developing a strategic plan for SBU–II. What should be included in your plan? While the actual composition of a strategic plan will vary by individual firm, the strategic planning guide shown in Exhibit 4 (p. 83) contains the areas that are often included in such a plan.

CONCLUDING NOTE

This introduction offers an overview of corporate and business unit planning. The cases that follow involve various aspects of strategic analysis and business strategy. They will provide an opportunity to examine actual business situations in the following areas:

☐   Performing a corporate situation analysis.

☐   Examining the mission statement and objectives.

☐   Analyzing the composition of businesses.

☐   Strategically analyzing business unit opportunities and threats.

☐   Recommending business unit objectives and strategies.

You may also find the strategic planning guide in Exhibit 4 useful as a checklist of strategic planning activities.

Case 2-1

The Lodge at Harvard Square, Inc.—1976

The first Lodge was opened in Harvard Square in 1969 in Cambridge, Massachusetts. By spring 1976 the number of units had grown to 11. This growth had far outpaced the expectations of its founder and chairman of the board of directors, William Silverman. Sales, only $815,000 in fiscal 1971, had continuously increased until they were nearly $4 million in the 12 months ending August 21, 1975. (See Exhibit 1.) Even with this remarkable growth, the company had produced profits in every year, thus increasing net worth to over half a million dollars. (See Exhibit 2.)

Since the strength had come principally through adding new stores and thereby expanding the trading area to encompass a larger number of consumers, Mr. Silverman was focusing on the question of whether the expansion should be continued and if so whether the pace should be faster or slower. Also he was concerned about future locations, that is, not only specifically where he might locate new stores, but also what The Lodge's policy should be toward entering new market areas.

TOP MANAGEMENT'S ROLE IN THE LODGE

The top management of The Lodge consisted of two men: Mr. Silverman, the chairman of the board, and Kent Spellman, the president. (The organization chart is shown in Exhibit 3.) Kent Spellman had joined the company as controller in 1970, one year after the inception of The Lodge. Mr. Spellman's ability in solving start-up problems of The Lodge earned the confidence of Mr. Silverman, resulting in his promotion to president and a share of the equity. By 1975, Kent Spellman was the principal manager of the company's operations, even though Mr. Silverman retained the title of chief executive officer.

This case was prepared by Robert L. Byrd under the supervision of Professor Robert F. Vandell, and revised by Associate Professor Eleanor G. May. Copyright © 1976 by the University of Virginia The Colgate Darden Graduate School Sponsors.

Exhibit 1

THE LODGE AT HARVARD SQUARE, INC.
Income Statements
Fiscal Years Ending August 31
(in $000s)

	1971	1972	1973	1974	1975	1976*
Sales	$814.9	$1,312.4	$2,228.6	$3,247.1	$3,890.2	$3,720.0
Cost of sales	465.2	755.0	1,257.1	1,862.5	2,154.4	2,075.2
Gross margin	349.7	557.4	971.5	1,384.6	1,735.8	1,644.8
Expenses	319.3	466.8	806.0	1,080.6	1,344.7	1,332.5
Operating income	30.4	90.6	164.5	304.0	391.1	312.3
Other income	(6.0)	(4.1)	6.7	(20.0)	4.8	22.3
Income before income taxes	24.4	86.5	171.2	284.0	395.9	334.6
Federal and state income taxes	8.1	41.5	84.1	147.8	186.0	167.3
Net income	$ 16.3	$ 45.0	$ 87.1	$ 136.2	$ 209.9	$ 167.3

* Nine months ending May 29, 1976.
Source: Company annual reports for all data except cost of sales, gross margin, and expenses, which have been disguised to protect confidentiality.

Exhibit 2

THE LODGE AT HARVARD SQUARE, INC.
Balance Sheets
Fiscal Years Ending August 31
(in $000s)

	1972	1973	1974	1975	1976*
Assets					
Cash	$ 97.7	$119.8	$ 243.2	$ 266.7	$ 146.7
Merchandise (lower of cost or market, retail method)	277.9	328.6	472.5	682.4	708.8
Prepaid expenses and other	13.6	26.0	30.0	30.3	70.6
Total current assets	389.2	474.4	745.7	979.4	926.1
Improvements, furniture, and fixtures	197.9	255.7	302.7	457.9	552.9
Depreciation	38.9	68.3	78.2	107.0	184.0
Net improvements, furniture, and fixtures	159.0	187.4	224.5	350.9	368.9
Other assets	4.8	14.8	33.7	47.2	67.2
Total assets	$553.0	$676.6	$1,003.9	$1,377.5	$1,362.2
Liabilities and Net Worth					
Accounts payable	$262.7	$242.2	$ 378.9	$ 510.1	$ 358.4
Accrued expenses and other	38.7	38.8	34.5	40.7	41.9
Income taxes payable	35.8	44.6	64.4	40.6	36.2
Other	22.0	34.6	–0–	–0–	–0–
Total spontaneous current	359.2	360.2	477.8	591.4	436.5
Due to stockholders	—	17.3	17.3	17.3	17.3
Current maturities—long-term debt	24.0	42.0	30.0	36.7	32.2
Total current liabilities	383.2	419.5	525.1	645.4	486.0
Long-term debt (noncurrent)	44.5	44.5	120.0	163.3	140.1
Net worth	125.3	212.6	358.8	568.8	736.1
Total liabilities and net worth	$553.0	$676.6	$1,003.9	$1,377.5	$1,362.2

* Nine months ending May 29, 1976.
Source: Company annual reports.

Exhibit 3
Organization chart

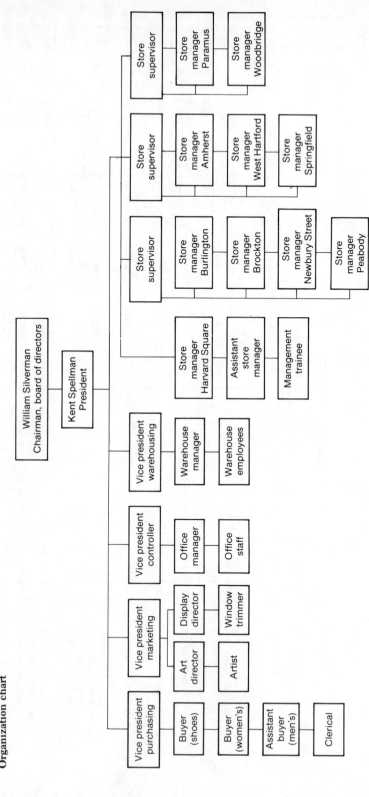

THE COMPANY

The Lodge was a unique specialty retail chain which sold a wide selection of inexpensive casual attire for the "young in spirit." The merchandise included jeans, casual slacks, shirts, jackets, shoes, and accessories. (See Exhibit 4 for a listing and description of the mer-

Exhibit 4
Merchandise categories and descriptions

Category	Description	Percent of sales*
Shoes	Western and hiking boots, work shoes, sneakers, Swedish clogs, sandals, and stylish casual footwear for both men and women. Brand names include Frye, Bass, Dunham, Clark's, Bort Carlton, and Sperry.	15%
Children's clothing	Denim overalls, jeans, and jackets; corduroy pants; T-shirts; tops; and sweaters. (There is a "Little Lodgers" corner in every store.)	7
Accessories	Belts, bandanas, handbags, and socks.	2
Skirts and dresses	Basic denim and corduroy skirts; casual dresses of fabrics such as denim, corduroy, and cotton.	5
Outerwear	Denim and corduroy short jackets; stylish over-coats; leather and suede coats and jackets.	3
Blue jeans	All current blue jean styles, featuring such brand names as Levi, Lee, Landlubber, and Wrangler. Sales in the blue jean category were up nearly 25 percent in 1975 over 1974. (The demand for prewashed blue jeans was greater than the suppliers could meet; therefore, The Lodge did its own prewashing.)	21
Casual slacks	Everything from basic corduroy jeans to men's and women's dress slacks.	20
Tops	Fashion-oriented, medium-priced women's tops; both basic and fashion knit men's tops. (Women's tops outsold men's by two to one.)	14
Shirts	Dress, work, flannel, and western shirts. A heavier concentration on men's than women's, but more fashion orientation in women's.	13
		100%

* These data have been disguised to protect confidentiality.

chandise carried at The Lodge.) Classifying The Lodge as a family-oriented business, including merchandise for children in each of its stores, Mr. Spellman said that the majority of The Lodge's customers were between the ages of 15 and 35. An extensive effort by all company personnel to make older people feel comfortable shopping in the sotres had resulted in a significant amount of business with parents shopping for clothes and gifts for children. Many of the older customers also bought such items as jeans or flannel shirts for themselves.

The Lodge attempted to appeal to all ages and types of people who enjoyed wearing casual clothes, by maintaining a large inventory of basic items along with what were considered to be fashion merchandise for both men and women. The Lodge's sales were roughly 50 percent women's wear, 40 percent men's wear, with less than 10 percent in children's attire.

Kent Spellman noted:

> We sell it all, but there is not one like us. Everything we sell in one of our mall stores can be found in four other stores in the mall. The key is that we offer a wide selection of quality casual attire at a medium, competitive price in a warm, unique, creative atmosphere with friendly, low-key sales service.

Prominently posted in Mr. Spellman's office and in all stores was a placard which echoed this statement:

> Tradition is what The Lodge is all about: an established tradition of quality casual clothing, fair prices, and the friendliest of service.

Through large inventories and wide selections, in 1975 The Lodge achieved an average of $242 in sales per square foot of floor space in its stores. Mr. Spellman said that the average for most other retail outlets was "around $100 per square foot."

The merchandise sold was purchased from a large number of manufacturers but consisted primarily of nationally advertised lines. The Lodge had neither long-term nor exclusive purchase commitments or arrangements with any manufacturer. No one supplier's goods accounted for more than 10 percent of the total purchases.

The Lodge's policy was to offer quality merchandise competitively priced. Mr. Silverman said that this policy was made possible by cost-conscious buying, limited markdowns and shrinkage, and the high sales per square foot ratio.

MERCHANDISING AND INVENTORY CONTROL

Buying was conducted by the vice president—purchasing, two buyers (shoes and women's), and an assistant buyer for men's. The buyers and assistant buyer reported to the vice president, who had responsibility for buying men's clothing. This staff was located at the company headquarters in Newton, Massachusetts, where there was close contact with Mr. Spellman and Mr. Silverman. The vice president and buyers were responsible for making certain that merchandise was properly presented by the stores.

The headquarters staff was informed of inventory and sales by store through inventory unit reports which were prepared weekly through a computerized system. All merchandise, except shoes, was marked with Kimball tickets; the stubs were sent to a service bureau which prepared the unit data and had it in the Newton offices by Wednesday of the following week. Clericals posted the data from the printouts, as well as purchase and distribution data, to the records for the vice president's and buyers' use.

The company merchandised each of its stores differently. The Lodge management felt that buying patterns and popularity of styles varied among the market areas of each of its stores and, therefore, each store must be stocked individually. It was believed that this gave The Lodge an advantage over larger, less flexible retailers. Also the inventory reports allowed the company to respond to trends, while avoiding the risk of fad-oriented buying.

The company's philosophy was to price its merchandise at the manufacturer's suggested retail price (about a 50 percent markup); its cost of goods sold averaged 57 percent of sales. Even so, the customers reported that they found The Lodge an economical place to shop as well as a convenient place to assemble a wardrobe of compatible casual wear.

Because The Lodge sold a mixture of staples and high-volume, moderate-price, fashion casual wear, it was not as vulnerable to the markdowns experienced by higher-price, fashion-oriented, specialty stores. Prices were cut quickly on slower-moving lines to clean them out before they became larger markdowns. The management believed that by following this policy The Lodge was effective in speedily adapting its merchandise mix to the latest trends.

Although many retail clothing stores lease their shoe departments, The Lodge operated its shoe business, with a separate shoe buyer and special salespeople in each store. The shoe inventory was controlled manually on a unit basis by store.

STORE DESIGN AND ADVERTISING POLICY

Just as The Lodge sought broad appeal through its merchandising, it also sought to achieve public acceptance through its store design, advertising, and promotion. The interiors of all the stores were clean, well lit, and bright. All merchandise was displayed in depth on counters or racks. Window and in-store displays were key elements of merchandising strategy. Display props, such as lobster traps, driftwood, school desks, and canoes, were used to give the windows special themes. The interiors of all stores were rough pine, with movable hanging racks and tables of natural wood. The interior store layouts were redone on a regular basis to maintain a fresh, clean look and to meet the changing demands of effective merchandising.

The vice president—marketing selected and scheduled the advertising media. Both newspapers and radio were used, as well as mall tabloids and occasionally local area promotions. All the company's copy and layout were prepared by the art director and artist. The advertising expenditures were about 2 percent of sales, after inclusion of manufacturer's cooperative advertising allowances. Advertising for special and seasonal promotions was coordinated with window and in-store display.

The Lodge's management had an aggressive policy in price promotions. When possible, special purchases of merchandise, advertised in cooperation with the supplier, were offered at special prices. The company believed this practice enhanced customer relations by offering first-quality goods at substantial savings. A large proportion of the advertising budget went to the promotion of such merchandise.

The Lodge frequently became involved with special promotions which the management believed gave the customer something extra for shopping at its stores; for example, a gift of a houseplant in a pot decorated with The Lodge logo, with each purchase over $10. In another instance, The Lodge joined with the Boston Museum of Fine Arts in a special program; the museum utilized window and in-store display space at the five Boston-area stores, and The Lodge gave customers passes to the museum. The company had had similar promotions with a ski resort in New Hampshire and with Boston-area theaters. The management reported that the consumers' reactions to these special events had been excellent.

In its merchandising, advertising, and promotion, The Lodge sought to project an image of straightforwardness with uniqueness; a company whose stores were pleasant to be in but whose main concern was customer satisfaction.

STORE LOCATIONS

The company had 11 stores in operation by April 1976. (Descriptive data, sales histories, and income and operating statements for the nine months ending May 1976 are shown in Exhibits 5, 6, and 7.) All store premises were leased. The company also leased a combination warehouse and office building in Newton, Massachusetts, which served as a merchandise receiving, marking, and distribution location, as well as management headquarters.

The company's stores were in several different types of locations. Based on the operating and sales results in this variety of locations, the company's later expansion policy had been solely in shopping center locations, although downtown sites, if they appeared to be unique, would still be considered.

Mr. Spellman cited three criteria that he and Mr. Silverman had used in recent expansion: (1) the size of and sales potential in the total market area and whether the area could support a Lodge store; (2) the mall itself and the characteristics of its specific market area; and (3) the location within the mall. Mr. Spellman spent considerable time personally searching for and investigating malls, and engaging in the subsequent lease negotiations with mall owners. Most of The Lodge

Exhibit 5
Store locations and descriptions

Store	Location	Square feet of space	Opening date
Harvard Square, Cambridge, Mass.	Downtown	2,000	August 1969
Newbury Street, Boston, Mass.	Downtown	1,300	May 1970
Brockton, Mass.	Freestanding unit	1,900	March 1971
Lawrence, Mass.*	Downtown	1,800	April 1972
West Hartford, Conn.	Regional shopping mall	2,800	August 1972
Peabody, Mass.	Regional shopping mall	940	August 1972
Springfield, Mass.	Regional enclosed shopping mall	1,340	August 1973
Paramus, N.J.	Regional enclosed shopping mall	2,200	March 1974
Amherst, Mass.	Freestanding unit	1,800	April 1974
Woodbridge, N.J.	Regional enclosed shopping mall	2,500	August 1975
Burlington, Mass.	Regional enclosed shopping mall	1,500	August 1975
Plymouth Meeting, Pa.	Regional enclosed shopping mall	2,200	April 1976

* Lawrence store was closed September 1975.
Source: Company records.

Exhibit 6
Sales per store, fiscal years ending August 31 ($000)

Store	1971	1972	1973	1974	1975	1976*
Harvard Square, Cambridge, Mass.	$504	$ 617	$ 764	$1,022	$1,029	$ 790
Newbury Street, Boston, Mass.	180	301	403	482	503	393
Brockton, Mass.	131	277	345	361	425	357
Lawrence, Mass.	—	76	181	171	135	73†
West Hartford, Conn.	—	25	303	317	326	230
Peabody, Mass.	—	16	203	257	288	245
Springfield, Mass.	—	—	30	302	315	264
Paramus, N.J.	—	—	—	250	530	507
Amherst, Mass.	—	—	—	85	259	223
Woodbridge, N.J.	—	—	—	—	40	297
Burlington, Mass.	—	—	—	—	40	338
Plymouth Meeting, Penn.	—	—	—	—	—	65
Totals	$815	$1,312	$2,229	$3,247	$3,890	$3,722

Note: These data have been disguised to protect confidentiality.
* Nine months ending May 29, 1976.
† Closed September 1975.

leases were of the type where varying percentages of sales were paid, over a minimum base rent, after a specified sales rate was attained.

The size of the total market area was important to The Lodge because management believed that to operate efficiently a market area must be able to support three to five Lodges. Also each store had to do at least $275,000 in sales per year to attain the company's profit goals

Exhibit 7

THE LODGE AT HARVARD SQUARE, INC.
Store Income and Expense Statements
Nine Months Ending May 29, 1976

	Harvard Square	Newbury Street	Brockton	Lawrence*	West Hartford
Sales:					
Clothing and accessories.....	$101,678	$ 59,918	$ 47,285	$ 2,062	$ 31,378
Shoes....................	212,863	82,596	10,283	0	71,726
Corduroy	118,765	42,727	74,600	1,943	32,748
Denim....................	49,196	24,220	24,869	869	8,161
Tops.....................	100,060	73,415	55,340	2,473	36,417
Dress clothing.............	64,252	38,304	46,233	583	14,731
Blue jeans	143,863	71,952	99,524	5,355	34,386
Returns and allowances......	387	378	972	23	769
Net sales	790,290	392,754	357,162	13,262	228,778
Opening inventory	76,435	60,273	46,831	15,520	59,022
Purchases:					
Clothing and accessories.....	72,927	38,595	36,104	(1,534)	23,768
Shoes....................	102,808	43,788	6,491	(30)	36,196
Corduroy	60,683	16,861	36,361	(2,491)	9,680
Denim....................	35,934	18,547	20,902	(603)	8,546
Tops.....................	55,416	42,423	32,501	(1,713)	24,152
Dress clothing.............	36,511	16,279	30,092	(342)	7,292
Blue jeans	75,918	35,401	51,857	(1,197)	16,007
Purchase discounts	9,845	4,184	3,520	0	2,584
Incoming freight.............	5,427	2,550	2,138	0	1,533
Closing inventory	90,863	63,876	56,012	0	49,876
Total cost of sales.......	421,351	206,657	203,745	7,610	133,736
Gross margin	368,939	186,097	153,417	5,652	95,042
Expenses:					
Salaries	63,039	34,446	27,367	2,530	25,260
Advertising and promotion ...	10,130	4,317	4,134	0	6,301
Depreciation	8,652	4,162	4,317	0	3,163
Maintenance	953	824	860	80	480
Payroll taxes	6,373	3,471	3,250	246	3,567
Rent	35,136	16,071	9,718	8,750	16,750
Utilities...................	4,137	3,013	3,920	485	2,212
Bad debts.................	621	298	150	0	43
Cash (over) or short........	473	202	263	30	(15)
Other store expenses........	17,370	4,621	2,301	155	2,306
Central office and warehouse charge	122,446	60,841	55,146	2,122	36,851
Total expenses..........	269,330	132,266	111,426	14,398	96,918
Operating income............	$ 99,609	$ 53,831	$ 41,991	$ (8,746)	$ (1,876)

and to carry sufficient inventory to project The Lodge's image. Lodge stores ranged in size from 940 to 2,800 square feet, but the company's policy in 1976 was to open only when a space was available which was between 1,350 and 2,300 square feet, with at least 20 "front feet."

In early 1976, the company was concentrating efforts and inquiries

Peabody	Springfield	Paramus	Amherst	Woodbridge	Burlington	Plymouth Meeting
$ 29,765	$ 22,641	$ 60,425	$ 37,891	$ 34,168	$ 45,821	$ 14,450
48,174	40,173	181,978	14,111	92,091	43,929	9,518
53,562	73,430	38,580	38,436	22,669	59,191	662
10,261	9,694	26,746	13,354	18,471	18,898	8,742
34,694	41,883	72,340	49,761	42,583	62,490	13,318
17,077	22,857	32,977	27,143	23,685	32,349	4,282
52,229	54,251	93,999	42,294	64,329	75,514	14,195
979	1,596	208	373	1,000	63	92
244,783	263,333	506,837	222,617	296,996	338,129	65,075
43,369	41,666	59,079	43,206	63,899	53,751	0
20,576	18,931	44,698	34,312	25,908	36,616	20,506
22,850	19,791	99,263	6,207	51,410	19,808	15,498
22,751	35,314	18,328	18,031	5,267	26,436	2,334
9,236	7,165	13,815	9,889	12,242	16,206	8,320
21,120	26,865	44,348	34,298	25,761	39,338	17,285
7,032	10,934	15,742	16,099	12,263	15,633	7,613
26,856	28,592	45,523	23,988	28,443	39,739	17,490
2,726	3,052	5,889	2,415	3,513	3,923	759
1,645	1,797	3,532	1,426	1,975	2,207	418
40,296	41,731	61,855	49,053	54,791	40,831	51,717
132,413	146,272	276,584	135,988	168,864	204,990	36,988
112,370	117,061	230,253	86,629	128,132	133,139	28,087
26,051	24,135	33,617	22,073	26,399	29,281	9,190
3,291	4,314	1,760	7,533	5,367	4,329	4,962
968	1,436	6,733	4,933	14,633	10,020	2,316
832	1,201	4,168	375	5,165	2,611	651
2,781	2,369	3,127	2,169	2,701	3,016	906
14,020	13,620	29,844	11,275	19,216	19,882	3,698
1,933	1,206	3,409	2,916	4,862	969	1,713
123	98	78	15	56	61	0
11	21	92	43	102	44	187
1,233	563	862	1,267	2,321	1,655	2,136
37,165	40,290	73,094	35,619	48,521	49,101	9,412
88,408	89,253	156,784	88,218	129,343	120,969	35,171
$ 23,962	$ 27,808	$ 73,469	$ (1,589)	$ (1,211)	$ 12,170	$ (7,084)

Note: These data have been disguised to protect confidentiality.
* Closed September 1975.

on large metropolitan areas, especially Philadelphia, where The Lodge believed potential for stores in several suburban malls existed as well as in one or two downtown locations. A cluster of stores made all aspects of doing business more economical: merchandising, control, and management as well as advertising and promotion.

The Lodge was most interested in enclosed regional shopping malls. In a mall, the company liked to have at least two strong major retailers plus a good mix of specialty stores. Also The Lodge was interested in malls whose promotion office and merchants' association continually worked at attracting people to the center. Within the market area, besides the population and income necessary to sustain a regional mall, The Lodge wanted to have a cross-section of people: blue- and white-collar workers, high school and college students, and so forth.

Mr. Silverman said, "Location is a vital factor in successful specialty retail chain operations." He found, however, that the best spaces in the better shopping malls were difficult to obtain, but that a specialty store like The Lodge, with a proven record of sales, had an edge in obtaining a lease. The Lodge's record was one which was attractive to mall developers and mall operators. He said that, as a result, the newer Lodges were generating more total revenue and more revenue per square foot than were the older stores. Also The Lodge was favored by shopping center managements because of its good sales record and resulting "overages" paid to the lessor. Waiting lists typically existed for sites in the better malls, with the result that since only a few stores could obtain leases, the mall managements could be very selective in the new stores allowed to open in the mall. "The Burlington Mall is a good example," explained Mr. Spellman. "Four hundred firms had applications on file for a location in the Burlington Mall when we were accepted."

Within each mall, The Lodge was interested only in what Mr. Silverman called "prime" locations, which he said could not be defined in general because what was considered to be prime could not be determined except through inspecting the individual mall. Mr. Silverman said he did not care about his location relative to other retailers in the center. He believed that The Lodge was not in direct competition with any one other retailer and, so long as there was good foot traffic in front of The Lodge, it could do a profitable business, no matter where other stores were located in the mall.

Management believed that a Lodge store was an asset to any regional mall. The Lodge had proven it could meet optimistic sales projections; in all its mall locations the company was paying overages on its leases. Management also believed that the success of a new store was a direct result of the amount of attention received at opening and in the immediately subsequent period before it was absorbed into the daily operations of the company.

In the past, the company had made a determined effort to expand slowly. Three stores had been opened in 1972, but only one store in 1973, two in 1974, two in 1975, and one so far in 1976. Mr. Silverman said that the best time of year to open a store was in March–April or August–September in order that they could take advantage of a full season of sales.

FINANCIAL POSTURE

The Lodge's fiscal year ended on August 31, which tended to distort the financial position of the company because of heavy fall inventories. Even with high inventories at the end of August, however, the company's cash position usually exceeded its bank loans.

Bank loans were not utilized by the company except to finance furniture and fixtures for new stores. The loans carried an interest rate of 1½ percent over prime and were repaid over four years. Until 1975, Mr. Silverman had been required personally to endorse the loans to the company. In 1975, however, the bank had agreed to make loans for furniture and fixtures without his endorsement.

Return on equity, which had run consistently around 60 percent, provided the means for internal growth. Except for a loan from an officer, and a modest increase in bank debt, all growth has been financed internally.

PERSONNEL POLICY

Mr. Silverman and Mr. Spellman believed that one of the most important reasons for The Lodge's success had been their ability to acquire, train, and retain good people in the stores who could and would project a strong image of the company. Managers received on-the-job training and were promoted after showing ability to run a store effectively and capacity to deal with customers cheerfully. The company took pride in having outgoing, amiable salespeople, casually yet attractively dressed, who appeared to project naturally a feeling of friendliness while making sure that all customers were attended to. When hiring salespeople, the quality most sought after was the individual's ability to relate well and act at ease with all types and ages of people. Sales personnel were selling goods that most of them used by preference, to customers whose needs and interests often were similar to their own. This itself facilitated attracting and retaining the right kind of people for the job.

Salespeople were required to study a 16-page manual that instructed them in the way The Lodge stores were run, gave them useful information about the clothing they were selling, and instilled in them a sense of pride about The Lodge and its successful dealings with customers. Salespeople who worked for The Lodge had to be able to contribute to a pleasant atmosphere that the customers could remember as unique. "Current but wholesome" was a well-worn phrase around The Lodge, but one whose meaning was the backbone of the sales force selection as well as the selection of the merchandising principals. Most of the people in the stores were attuned to the interests of the customers. This helped in spotting trends and provided a flow of ideas to the buyers and the vice president—purchasing.

Three store supervisors were in charge of the operation of a "cluster" or group of two to four stores. (The Harvard Square store was not included in a cluster; the store manager there reported directly to Mr. Spellman.) The store supervisors were all college graduates who previously had been store managers of one of The Lodge stores. Mr. Spellman characterized the store supervisors as "good both with people and with details." The store supervisors, all in their 20s, each managed up to four stores. Store supervisors were paid a straight salary of about $15,000 or $16,000 yearly. Mr. Spellman considered good store supervisors "hard to find. . . . I have only three."

The store supervisors had offices in the company headquarters. Their duties were to coordinate paperwork, shipments of goods, and advertising among the stores and headquarters and to handle other related problems. Mr. Spellman measured the performance of these managers through sales, payrolls (projected payrolls for each store were submitted weekly for Mr. Spellman's review) and shortages in each of the stores in their cluster.

Store managers were young college graduates who had been hired originally by Mr. Spellman as management trainees. After a short period of time as a management trainee, usually less than a month, successful people were promoted to assistant to the store manager, next assistant store manager, then store manager as they showed ability and openings occurred. The typical store manager had been with The Lodge for somewhere between four and nine months when this position had been attained. Store managers were paid straight salaries of between $9,000 and $14,000 per year. Performance measurement of store managers was the same as that of store supervisors. All training was done on the job.

No written management policy existed in the corporation, although one was in the process of being written by the vice president—marketing.

MANAGEMENT

Kent Spellman, age 27, started at The Lodge in 1970, after receiving a B.A. in Accounting from Babson College, when the company had only two stores. At that time the company was experiencing problems with shortages, apparently from poor buying, and inadequate store management. Kent became involved in many facets of the business while solving these problems and "learned the retail business from the ground up."

Mr. Spellman worked a long, hard week, his hours generally being 9:00 A.M. to 7:30 or 8:00 P.M. Monday through Friday and Saturday from 10:00 A.M. until 4:00 P.M. He was both interested and involved in the day-to-day store operations, as well as devoting much of his time to investigating and arranging for future store openings. He described his typical day as spending time "mostly working with my people in financial, budgeting, buying, and control decisions." Mr. Spellman's energy and desire to maximize the use of his time were evident in that, during the interview with the casewriter, he was planning the size and quantity distribution to the stores of a newly arrived shipment of merchandise.

Kent talked daily, either in person (usually two or three times per week) or by telephone, with his store supervisors to determine the status of their stores and discuss any problems or decisions to be made. In addition, Kent stated, "since I like to keep close contact," he talked daily with each store manager concerning the day's activities, problems, progress, and decisions.

The stores were set up and operated so that no expenditure decisions had to be made by store supervisors or managers. Mr. Spellman talked daily with Mr. Silverman as a matter of course, at which time expenditures of significance were discussed. Kent could not define "significance," but said he felt comfortable making expenditures alone "depending on what it is, but Bill Silverman's business advice is invaluable."

Discussing the future growth of the company, Kent saw money as no obstacle to growth. He said that the company did not seek more debt to expand faster, because "it would be risky." Mr. Spellman said that they did not need outside equity because "money is not the problem; getting good people is. Quality control of our operations is imperative. Should we expand too fast and not maintain our good record, it will impact our ability to command premium store locations in much-sought-after malls."

In discussing future growth, Mr. Spellman said he felt that The Lodge could comfortably add at most four stores per year. For planning purposes, the company had developed two basic store prototypes. Exhibits 8 and 9 show financial requirements and projects expected by Mr. Spellman for these two 2,200- and 1,400-square-foot prototypes.

Mr. Spellman in summarizing the company's philosophy said, "We just want to stick to what we know how to do. We are not interested, for example, in manufacturing, buying our own private label merchandise, opening different types of stores, or using another store name, although all might be profitable. The key to our success is high sales volume, the result, first, of our concept and, secondly, of having good people working for the company."

Although Bill Silverman, as chairman of the board of The Lodge, was involved in all major decisions, he said he was attempting to phase himself out of the company's business and spend much of his time operating a small successful ladies' wear store owned by him and his wife. At 52 years of age, Mr. Silverman's goal was to retire in three years. An economics graduate from Harvard in 1946, Bill, prior to

Exhibit 8

THE LODGE AT HARVARD SQUARE, INC.
Projected Income Statement for 2,200-Square-Foot Prototype Store
($000)

	Year				
	1	2	3	4	5
Sales	$500.0	$600.0	$672.0	$740.0	$810.0
Cost of sales.....................	275.0	330.0	370.0	410.0	445.0
Gross margin	255.0	270.0	302.0	330.0	365.0
Expenses:					
Salaries	40.0	48.0	54.0	59.0	65.0
Depreciation	14.0	14.0	14.0	14.0	14.0
Advertising	3.5	3.8	4.1	4.5	4.9
Common area charge and real					
estate taxes	7.0	7.0	7.0	7.0	7.0
Rent	30.0	36.0	40.3	44.4	48.6
Utilities.......................	4.0	4.2	4.4	4.6	4.8
Payroll taxes	3.8	4.6	5.2	5.7	6.2
Other expenses..................	58.4	70.0	78.4	86.4	94.5
Prorated expenses	10.0	11.0	12.0	13.0	14.0
Total expenses..............	170.7	198.6	219.4	238.6	259.0
Operating profit	$ 54.3	$ 71.4	$ 82.6	$ 91.4	$106.0
Store opening costs:					
Construction and fixtures	$ 67.0				
Other equipment.................	3.0				
Inventory (at cost)...............	70.0				
Opening advertising expenses	3.0				
Total	$143.0				

opening the first Lodge, had been president for 12 years of a national candy manufacturing firm, a position he left "to work for himself" as a result of a stockholders' fight over control of the company.

Mr. Silverman started The Lodge with modest expectations. He commented that The Lodge was "not to be this big so that we could avoid the headaches of bigness. We certainly had no thoughts of going national."

Mr. Silverman classified himself as an "idea" man. It was apparent from the unique format of the stores that he was extremely creative and possessed a considerable amount of merchandising skill. "I come up with the big ideas but am not as strong or as interested in details, which Kent is good at, and so I leave them to him," commented Mr. Silverman.

In spite of the fact that Mr. Silverman was trying to remove himself from the business, his enthusiasm caused him to call his managers often. A store opening would inspire Bill to spend considerable time in the first few weeks at the new location talking with customers and seeing that operations were getting off to a good start. Mr. Silverman

Exhibit 9

THE LODGE AT HARVARD SQUARE, INC.
Projected Income Statement for 1,400-Square-Foot Prototype Store
($000)

	Year				
	1	*2*	*3*	*4*	*5*
Sales	$325.0	$390.0	$437.0	$481.0	$529.0
Cost of sales	179.0	215.0	240.0	265.0	291.0
Gross profit	$146.0	$175.0	$197.0	$216.0	$238.0
Expenses:					
Salaries	$ 26.0	$ 31.0	$ 35.0	$ 38.5	$ 42.0
Depreciation	10.0	10.0	10.0	10.0	10.0
Advertising	2.0	2.0	2.4	2.6	2.8
Common area charge and real estate taxes	5.0	5.0	5.0	5.0	5.0
Rent	19.5	23.4	26.2	28.9	31.7
Utilities	3.0	3.2	3.4	3.6	3.8
Payroll taxes	2.3	2.8	3.2	3.4	3.8
Other expenses	37.9	45.5	41.0	56.1	61.7
Prorated expenses	6.0	6.5	7.0	7.5	8.0
Total expenses	111.7	129.4	143.2	155.6	168.8
Operating profit	$ 34.3	$ 45.6	$ 53.8	$ 60.4	$ 69.2

Store opening costs:	
Construction and fixtures	$ 47.0
Other equipment	3.0
Inventory (at cost)	60.0
Opening advertising expenses	2.5
Total	$112.5

was viewed by the company personnel as a great motivator who was good with a "pep talk." After several weeks, when operations had become more routine, Mr. Silverman would become less involved with the individual stores.

Mr. Silverman attributed the firm's success to "control of inventory and control of people." He emphasized his belief in building a good management team and expressed an attitude similar to that of Mr. Spellman concerning the ability to find good people. Mr. Silverman said that he would not want to accelerate the growth in number of stores opened per year because "I wouldn't feel comfortable borrowing money (long-term debt) to expand. Besides, as I mentioned before, I'm worried about getting good people. We need more good people. I know Kent has to work too hard."

FUTURE GROWTH

The year-to-date results in spring 1976 were showing continued improvement for The Lodge. Volume was running way ahead of the prior year, due largely to the success of the three most recently opened stores, Woodbridge, Burlington, and Plymouth Meeting, but also all stores were exceeding their previous year's volumes. Another new store was scheduled to open in an enclosed mall in early fall 1976 in New Jersey.

Opportunity for continued growth abounded. Preliminary investigation of locations for store openings in the areas alread served by the company (expansion of the clusters) looked attractive. There was also the almost unlimited opportunity of expanding geographically to other major metropolitan areas such as Washington, Pittsburgh, Cleveland, Chicago, Indianapolis, and Atlanta.

Case 2-2

Bloomington Bank and Trust Company

Bloomington Bank and Trust (BBT hereafter) is a state-chartered commercial bank located in an affluent eastern state. The bank's assets currently stand at approximately $35 million, a figure which ranks the bank as medium-sized in comparison to the other commercial banking institutions of the state. At the close of 1975 BBT found itself in better shape than ever, at least in pure numbers. Demand deposits had increased 14.6 percent during 1975 (55 percent since 1970); likewise, time deposits had grown 10 percent in the past year and 75.4 percent in the recent five-year period. Also, total assets had risen 62.3 percent and total capital had grown 43.5 percent since 1970.

The bank's market had also grown geographically in recent years as branches had opened in three area towns, and plans were being formulated for the creation of two more. Formerly bank management had been hesitant about expanding into new towns, fearing that the bank would lose its close identification with Bloomington residents. However, at the same time, larger commercial banks were not hesitating to install branches of their own in Bloomington, and as a result, BBT had gradually been losing market share. BBT's first branch opening was experimental in nature, but its resulting success encouraged bank officers to plan for more in the future.

Now that BBT had established itself as a highly successful bank not only in its base town but in the state's most competitive banking region as well, its president, Jim McGowan, felt it an opportune time to retire. He announced his plans in June 1975, and a search for his

Copyright 1977 by Peter J. LaPlaca, University of Connecticut. Special thanks are given to research assistant Michael Noles.

successor, who would take office at the start of 1976, was immediately initiated.

On January 2, 1976, McGowan's successor, Brian McQuade, began his stewardship as president of BBT. McQuade had been a vice president of the state's largest commercial bank before accepting his new post and possessed an exceptional financial background, developed from previous executive positions at banking institutions throughout the East. The bank's board of directors was extremely satisfied with its selection, and McQuade felt confident that he would continue where Jim McGowan left off.

The new president's first task involved an investigation of BBT's past and present strategies. He studied all memos left to him by the bank's former president and analyzed the programs employed by the insitution, but still, after weeks of painstaking research, McQuade felt his efforts were wasted. Upon accepting his executive role, McQuade had pledged to the board of directors that he would continue to lead BBT toward highly successful operation, that he would continue to strive for goals toward which the bank had progressed under the leadership of Jim McGowan. Unfortunately McQuade could not determine what these goals were. Nowhere had the former president explicitly stated any formal goals or objectives by or toward which the bank would operate. In fact, the only material that McQuade could proceed on was a list, compiled by himself, of various strategies BBT had undertaken in the last 15 years. This list, however, was an inadequate basis from which to plan future programs.

Next, McQuade conferred with four of the bank's top executives in hope that they might clarify the problem. He found that all were top-flight and knowledgeable concerning strategies they were responsible for, and information gathered from these meetings was helpful to McQuade in determining the commercial and consumer markets toward which BBT concentrated activity. Nevertheless, McQuade still could not uncover a list of specific goals of objectives around which past strategies were planned or toward which future strategies might be geared.

Finally, the new president decided to meet with Jim McGowan himself. The meeting lasted approximately three hours, and McQuade left the McGowan home with a clearer picture of the past administration's planning process; however, planning for the future was as vague a concept as ever. In his conference with BBT's former chief executive, McQuade confirmed what he had suspected; that is, all programs had been initiated *instinctively* by McGowan. Whenever McGowan had felt that a new program was "right" for the bank, he had ordered it implemented. Perhaps McGowan had acted toward some type of long-term goals subconsciously, but they were not formal or written objectives. Moreover, McGowan himself could not articulate these subconscious goals for McQuade.

Now McQuade knew that the greater part of his first year as BBT's president would have to be spent formulating goals and objectives by which the bank would operate. He felt that BBT, especially now that it was expanding significantly each year, could no longer be operated according to an executive's intuition. What the bank needed now was a written operating plan. If such a plan could be drawn up, he felt, new strategies could be implemented as part of the plan. Also, any proposed strategy would be considered by management only if that strategy were consistent with the goals set forth in the plan. Conceptually, the idea seemed perfect, but McQuade knew that it could fail in actual practice. In fact, McQuade's former bank had attempted to utilize an operating plan. In theory, that plan was still in existence; in practicality, it was all but useless. Still, McQuade felt that the situation was different in Bloomington. BBT was but 1/60 the size of the other bank (by assets), and interests here were not as diverse and uncontrollable as those in the larger bank. McQuade knew that an operating plan could work at BBT if it were wisely and efficiently conceived.

McQuade also knew that he wouldn't be able to draw up the plan himself. Consequently, he informed his four top aides of his plans and asked them to think about the bank's operations: where they presently stood and where they should head in the future. McQuade also realized his limitations as a professional planner; therefore, he called an outside consultant, Dr. Richard Baker, whom he knew to be an expert in business planning.

On May 4, 1976, McQuade and Baker met in McQuade's office. The bank president explained the situation to Baker, stressing the need for an operating plan that would be specific enough to establish direction toward predetermined goals, yet flexible enough to encompass innovative strategies. Baker responded favorably to the idea and felt confident that a written operating plan was a viable system for management of BBT. He immediately suggested that a schedule be drawn up for the completion of the various stages involved in creating the plan and that every effort be made to follow the timetable. The two men spent the remainder of the evening developing the schedule (Exhibit 1). As the meeting ended, Baker suggested to McQuade that work begin on accomplishing task 1 as soon as possible.

The suggestion was actually unnecessary, as Brian McQuade had already planned to confer with his department heads the very next morning. McQuade was now firmly committed to the planning idea, and made this known to his officers when he arrived at the bank on May 5. A meeting was arranged for May 18 at which Baker and McQuade would meet with McQuade's four top aides: Jim Carlson (Commercial and Mortgage Lending, Marketing), Bob Delaney (Operations, Personnel), John Erickson (Trust, Portfolio Investments), and Ted Fredericks (Consumer Lending, Credit and Debit Cards).

Exhibit 1
Bloomington Bank and Trust Company planning milestones

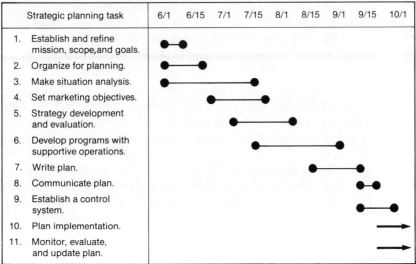

Strategic planning task	6/1	6/15	7/1	7/15	8/1	8/15	9/1	9/15	10/1
1. Establish and refine mission, scope, and goals.	●━●								
2. Organize for planning.	●━━━●								
3. Make situation analysis.	●━━━━━━━━━●								
4. Set marketing objectives.			●━━━━━●						
5. Strategy development and evaluation.				●━━━●					
6. Develop programs with supportive operations.					●━━━━━●				
7. Write plan.						●━━━●			
8. Communicate plan.							●━●		
9. Establish a control system.							●━━━●		
10. Plan implementation.								→→→	
11. Monitor, evaluate, and update plan.								→→→	

That meeting opened as McQuade introduced Baker to the executives and explained the nature of the meeting:

McQuade: Gentlemen, today we're to lay the groundwork for an operating plan which I hope will serve as a management guide for all of us. By November, it is hoped that a strategic operating plan for the year 1977 will have been developed. But the development of a short-term plan necessitates reference to longer-term strategic goals. Therefore, today, through a brainstorming session of sorts, we will attempt to devise BBT's mission and its goals. Later, we'll attempt to build strategies that can be used to attain those goals. Before we begin, are there any questions that you would care to ask either Dr. Baker or myself?

Delaney: I'm a little confused. Many concepts that are considered to be goals are but means toward achieving more generally defined goals. Are we distinguishing between the two?

Baker: That's very true, Bob, but today we're just trying to assemble a list of any objectives for the operation of BBT. After we've compiled the list, we might separate the goals into separate groups; for instance, *ends* goals and *means* goals. But again, the separation can be done some other time. Today we want to get all of the objectives down on paper.

McQuade: OK; I guess we're all set now. Let fly with any concepts which you feel best describe what we're trying to achieve here at BBT. I'll be taking the minutes of the meeting.

Erickson: Well, for starters, I feel that one of our main objectives is to provide a full range of banking services to the markets in which we're located.

McQuade: Good! In fact, that may even be our mission here.

Carlson: Another goal might be to increase profits substantially.

Baker: Can we make it more specific than that? To be effective, the goal should contain a fairly exact range to strive toward.

Carlson: I see. Well, how does 8–10 percent sound? Increasing profits after taxes 8–10 percent compounded annually.

McQuade: Much better. Some more ideas . . . ?

The meeting continued for three hours as goals of the institution were established and a division of responsibility in the planning process was discussed. As the men became more involved, possible strategies to be used in 1977 were discussed, but it soon became apparent that an exhaustive inventory of possible strategies could not be accomplished in just one evening. Therefore, McQuade cut short the session and suggested that all concerned deliberate for a few weeks upon further proposals. On June 1 he issued the following memo, a recapitulation of the thoughts that were expressed on May 18.

Memo

June 1, 1976

To: James Carlson
      Robert Delaney
      John Erickson
      Ted Fredericks

From: Brian J. McQuade

Subject: Planning

Here is a first stab at outlining the goals, objectives, and strategies we have been discussing. During the next several months, we will be working to develop a marketing plan for late 1976 and 1977, a 1977 budget, and the foundation for a longer-term strategic plan. Your suggestions and comments are essential.

1. *BBT goals*
   A. Provide full range of banking services to market in which located.
   B. Increase profits after taxes 8–10 percent compounded annually.
   C. Build and retain capital to maintain capital to deposit ratio of 1 : 12–15.
   D. Increase a stock value steadily over time.
   E. Provide a "stimulating" and financially rewarding work atmosphere for employees.
   F. Maintain and build an image of BBT as a quality, imaginative, service-oriented and "professional" institution.
   G. Maintain size and profitability advantage over other banks in town.

H.   Build toward a profit goal of 1 percent plus of assets (reduced by check deposit float).
I.   Specifically develop the capacity of BBT to meet the operational, investment, and lending needs of commercial and professional customers and prospects in our marketing area.
J.   Increase demand deposits 8–12 percent *plus* annually.
K.   Increase time deposits 10–15 percent *plus* annually.
L.   Build from the present 50 percent plus loan to deposit ratio to one of 65–70 percent by 1980.

2. *Planning*
   A.   The overall bank planning shall be directly the responsibility of the president.
   B.   Primary assistance will come from four department heads:

James Carlson	Branch administration
	Commercial and mortgage lending
	Marketing
Bob Delaney	Operations
	Personnel
John Erickson	Trust
	Portfolio investments
Ted Fredericks	Consumer lending
	Credit and debit cards

   C.   All officers and key supervisory personnel will be encouraged to participate in the planning function through submission and reaction to ideas and periodic meetings.

3. *Strategies*
   A.   Intensify BBT commercial/professional exposure.
      a.   Direct call program.
      b.   Direct mail program.
      c.   Educational forums/seminars.
   B.   Activate statement savings d/d–d/w.
   C.   Issue debit card to DDA and savings customers.
   D.   Telephone transfers including non-BBT/DDA a/cs.
   E.   Alter NOW charges—perhaps full-analysis basis (?).
   F.   Offer personal reconciliations via serialized checks onto statement.
   G.   Make Master Charge picture card optional.
   H.   Install a personal/commercial revolving credit service.
   I.   Install equipment for competitive check clearing service.
   J.   Institute "Working Trust" service.
   K.   Extend drive-in hours for commercial activity.
   L.   Institute accounts receivable financing service.
   M.   Branch into more commercially developed areas such as East Harrington, Jackson, and Westfield.
   N.   Open Cookston Branch on Sunday.
   O.   Eliminate 78 method on installment loans—go to simple interest.
   P.   Intensify bill-paying services.
   Q.   Offer account reconciliation services.
   R.   Provide lockbox service.
   S.   Intensify and formalize government securities facilities, including perhaps repurchase agreement handling.

We have a Planning Meeting scheduled for 2 P.M. on Thursday, June 3. Please be prepared to comment on the items in this memo and to add your own suggestions. Particularly as relates to your area of responsibility, let's get all ideas "out on the table" regardless of what you feel might be their final disposition after more thorough study.

(Signed)
Brian J. McQuade

On June 3 all six men met again in order to complete the file of possible projects to be implemented in 1977. Once again, the president of BBT displayed his commitment to the operating plan by recording the minutes of the meeting.

McQuade: Gentlemen, today we're going to go through another brainstorming session. Our meeting of May 18 was highly successful; still, it was only a beginning. Today I want to hear your ideas concerning possible programs that might contribute to our objectives. We won't be discussing the viability of the various programs today; therefore, I want to hear of any ideas that come to mind. Assessment of their significance or workability can wait until later. To keep some semblance of order, Dr. Baker has suggested that we divide our ideas among four categories: loan service–oriented programs, deposit/operations service–oriented programs, public relations–oriented programs, and other or multiple service–oriented programs. I think that we can start with those projects that are loan oriented. Of course, Jim and Ted, since these are your areas of responsibility, we may be looking to you for many suggestions. However, we're looking for recommendations from the entire group; therefore, I hope, Bob and John, that you won't hesitate to contribute whenever an idea comes to mind. OK, I guess we're ready now. Please feel free to start.

Delaney: How about if we develop contractor and dealer business in the home improvement and construction areas?

McQuade: Got it. Anybody else?

Fredericks: I think that our commercial customers would benefit if we provided financial analysis programs for them. We might be able to do this through time-sharing facilities.

McQuade: Definitely something to investigate. Some more ideas . . . ?

The session went on for five hours, and when the six men broke up that night, they had compiled no fewer than 113 possible programs. The president took the list home with him that night and reviewed it with mixed emotions. He was extremely pleased with the production of the meeting. Nevertheless, he now faced a fresh problem, that is, deciding upon the priority of the various programs. Certainly, it was impossible to implement each of the suggestions, but choosing the more viable alternatives was not an easy task. The next morning he called Dr. Baker and informed him of his dilemma. The consultant didn't appear surprised by the problem and suggested that some type of collaborative rating system be used. He recommended that the president and his department heads rank each of the programs on a scale in terms of meeting the goals of the institution. McQuade accepted the advice and drafted the following memo. The complete list of programs was attached and appears as Exhibit 2.

Memo

Date: June 15, 1976

To: Department Heads

From: Brian J. McQuade

Subject: Planning

Based on our 6/3 meeting and my 6/1 memo, we broadly defined BBT goals as meeting specifics to do with:

1. Increased profits.
2. Improved employee effectiveness.
3. Meeting of growth objectives.
4. Meeting of market share objectives.
5. Meeting of service objectives.

We came up with 113 possible ideas that might contribute to these objectives. Please review the attached list,[1] and rate each idea on a scale of 1 (low) to 10 (high) in terms of meeting the broad goals outlined above. Obviously, your rating will be based on less than full understanding of each idea, but give it a try.

I would appreciate your giving your copy to Jean by 9 A.M. Wednesday. You should be able to complete this in 30 to 60 minutes.

(Signed)
Brian J. McQuade

On June 17 McQuade sent the final compilation of the ratings to his department heads and Dr. Baker. On that same day a meeting between the six men was scheduled for the purpose of making preliminary decisions concerning projects to be undertaken. The memo is followed by Exhibit 2, the rating results of the various proposals.

---

[1] List is shown in Exhibit 2 after the four department heads had ranked each item. The highest possible score is 50. The top 25 items are so indicated in the right-hand column.

Exhibit 2
Ranking of program proposals

	Points received	Rank
A. Loan service–oriented programs		
1. Make Master Charge picture card optional	38	24
2. Install a personal/commercial revolving credit service	40	12
3. Institute an accounts receivable financing service	24	
4. Eliminate 78 method on installment loans—go to simple interest computations	23	
5. Develop contractors/dealers business in home improvement and construction areas	38	25
6. Provide financial analysis programs for commercial customers—perhaps via time-sharing facilities	30	
7. Install a lease financing program	21	
8. Utilize Master Charge for under $500 loans	36	
9. Computerize commercial loan function	37	
10. Institute short term-line of credit facility for both individuals and businesses	38	
11. Intensify sales effort for large-dollar direct installment loans	44	1
12. Develop a second-mortgage loan program	41	11
13. Develop a formalized house-to-house loan program	35	
14. Develop a MGIC and other low-down-payment mortgage program	26	
15. Expand dealer financing on selective basis	32	
16. Develop a mortgage product with ascending amount payments	26	
17. Formalize a skip payment installment loan program	33	
18. Install a variable-rate mortgage program	33	
19. Extend new car installment loans to 48 months	36	
20. Institute a balloon payment installment loan program	22	
21. Give rate breaks on Master Charge finance charges to employees and preferred customers	27	
22. Provide coupon books for mortgage payments	33	
23. Activate automatic installment loan and mortgage payments	29	
24. Institute a private label credit card program using Master Charge facilities	32	
25. Add BancAmericard to present Master Charge program	28	
26. Install American Express Gold Card program	27	
B. *Deposit/operations service–oriented programs*		
27. Activate statement savings d/d–d/w	40	13
28. Issue debit card to DDA and savings customers	42	6
29. Install telephone transfer service, including facilities for non-BBT, DDA customers	38	
30. Alter NOW charges—perhaps to full-analysis basis	31	
31. Offer personal reconciliations via serialized checks on the statement	32	
32. Install equipment for competitive check clearing service	40	14
33. Extend drive-in hours for commercial activity	38	
34. Intensify bill-paying services	33	
35. Offer account reconciliation services for commercial DDA customers	32	
36. Provide a lockbox service	29	

Exhibit 2 (*continued*)

		Points received	Rank
37.	Institute a "goal" savings account program	28	
38.	Make packages of foreign currency available for sale	20	
39.	Institute a courier deposit pickup service for commercial businesses	40	15
40.	Intensify bank by mail program	26	
41.	Institute an emergency 24-hour, wide-area money transfer facility using outside sources	24	
42.	Institute an automatic savings program for BBT customers with and without our checking accounts	32	
43.	Institute GIRO bill payments product	27	
44.	Expand automated tellers to other offices	19	
45.	Install complete in-house computer facilities	32	
46.	Install lobby depositories and/or automated tellers	27	
47.	Install minimax checking account	30	
48.	Provide facsimile transmission among our offices	21	
49.	Institute a prepaid interest program using dollars or premiums	27	
50.	Expand branch courier service	28	
51.	Install outgoing WATS line	20	
52.	Institute service charges for checking accounts	30	

C. *Other or multiple service–oriented programs*

		Points received	Rank
53.	Intensify commercial/professional direct call program	44	2
54.	Intensify commercial/professional direct mail program	40	16
55.	Institute "Working Trust" service	26	
56.	Branch into more commercially developed areas such as East Harrington, Jackson, and Westfield	42	7
57.	Open Cookston Branch on Sunday	22	
58.	Intensify/formalize government securities service	30	
59.	Provide a commercial service information kit	38	
60.	Provide a more formalized municipal finance assistance program		
61.	Create and staff a new marketing department	28	
62.	Expand East Harrington Branch with safe deposit facilities, etc.	31	
63.	Provide more service "breaks" for senior citizens	23	
64.	Simplify paperwork on a bank-wide basis	26	
65.	Develop a more formalized advertising program	44	3
66.	Create a consumer advisory service	30	
67.	Create and staff a new business development sales force	43	4
68.	Expand through acquisition of other banks	32	
69.	Develop a physical facilities plan	36	
70.	Institute a 24-hour telephone transfer service	31	
71.	Improve customer forms bank-wide	36	
72.	Provide MICR encoded coupons for all customer transactions possible	31	
73.	Increase use of premiums	27	
74.	Install free incoming WATS line	22	
75.	Install closed-circuit TV facilities between offices	16	
76.	Purchase Texas Instruments high-powered calculator	40	17
77.	Expand Cookston parking facilities through property acquisition	31	

Exhibit 2 (*concluded*)

	Points received	Rank
D. *Public relations–oriented programs*		
78. Intensify commercial/professional educational forums/seminars	40	18
79. Play music on telephone holds	21	
80. Acquire jai alai passes for and with customers	20	
81. Provide service starter kits for individuals	37	
82. Intensify local school education program	28	
83. Institute merchants relationship program	35	
84. Institute new apartment dwellers call program	29	
85. Institute a home consulting program	27	
86. Institute a business consulting program	37	
87. Institute a consumer information program	34	
88. Run a photo contest for a BBT calendar	42	8
89. Make available a BBT "24-hour" T-shirt	25	
90. Install coffee bars in branches for customers	18	
91. Renovate main office stairway	25	
92. Redecorate East Harrington Branch	32	
93. Construct a children's waiting facility at main office	32	
94. Procure benches and/or fountains, birdbaths, etc., for main office outside	21	
95. Improve outside lighting for main office	30	
96. Provide customer service area in Operations Department	32	
97. Utilize more exhibits in main office	34	
98. Acquire season tickets for pro hockey games for and with customers	40	19
99. Acquire Pro Am slot at Greater Columbia Open	26	
E. *Employee effectiveness–oriented programs*		
100. Provide customer contact employees with uniforms	20	
101. Enlarge employee lunchroom	40	20
102. Constitute an employees' club for discounts, joint activities, etc.	36	
103. Improve employee job descriptions, salary ranges, etc.	43	5
104. Eliminate cash payday for employees	36	
105. Provide payroll deduction facilities for employees	39	22
106. Institute an employees' sales incentive program	42	9
107. Activate a formalized employee training and education program	40	21
108. Conduct thorough staffing evaluation survey throughout the bank	42	10
109. Institute a profit center accounting system	35	
110. Institute an officer bonus/incentive program	39	23
111. Eliminate employee Christmas bonus with base pay increases	34	
112. Conduct off-premises and nonworkday educational program for employees	30	
113. Conduct off-premises and nonworkday educational program for board of directors	35	

Memo

June 17, 1976

To: Department Heads

From: Brian J. McQuade

Subject: Planning

Attached is a résumé of the responses to my memo of June 15 on ranking the ideas generated on June 3. The highest-rated 25 items have been so annotated to the right of the total weight column. Also attached is a sheet showing the distribution of responses for the entire 113 ideas submitted.

We will be discussing this further at our session this afternoon. The results of this survey should be viewed simply as advisory and one of a number of inputs that will go into a specific action plan.

(Signed)
Brian J. McQuade

On June 28 another meeting was held, at which 62 of the 113 proposals were designated as workable for the year 1977. Each of the officers was assigned responsibilities for the implementation of programs covered by his department. The projects to be effected and those responsible for the systematic planning of their implementation were presented to all officers. Items were designated as the sole responsibility of one officer, the joint responsibility of two or more officers, or delegated to other employees. Also several programs needed review by Bob Delaney prior to receiving a go-ahead. All officers were expected to have completed all planning reports by August 9, when another meeting was scheduled.

On August 9 BBT's officers met in order to submit final planning reports concerning strategies from their respective departments. Each of these department heads had spent a considerable amount of time constructing schedules and plans for the projects' implementations, and their resultant work was top-rate. Excerpts from two of the officers' final reports appear below.

Selected portions of planning report of John Erickson, vice president and trust officer

Project 36—The "Working Trust"

Brian McQuade has proposed the establishment of a new service which he has labeled the "Working Trust." He is recommending that we consider the establishment of this service to provide investment advice to the relatively small investor who does not have the time, is not interested, or does not have the expertise needed to make economical and intelligent decisions regarding the investment of liquid funds. There are many items to be considered in regard to this matter, such as:

a.   Other alternatives available to the customer.
b.   Charges to be assessed.
c.   Demand use of BBT savings.
d.   Bookkeeping reports required and costs thereof.
e.   Computer capability of handling.
f.   Estimated demand for the service.
g.   Proper pricing.
h.   Legality of pooling funds.
i.   Possible use of money market funds.
j.   Profitability to bank.

These items, in addition to many others, must be thoroughly addressed before the "Working Trust" may be proposed to the Board of Directors. I will take the responsibility for investigating this project during 1977, with the intention of presenting a recommendation to Brian McQuade and the Board of Directors no later than March 30, 1977, regarding the possible inception of a new service entitled "The Working Trust."

Selected portions of planning report of Ted Fredericks, Assistant vice president (consumer lending, credit and debit cards)

I.   Issue debit card to DDA/savings account customers
  A.   *Goals:* To increase customer awareness and usage of automated teller service, thereby reducing transaction costs. *Control:* (*a*) increase cardholder base by 400 percent (to 8,000 cardholders) by June 1977; (*b*) increase total usage/week as percent to base to 8–10 percent by June 1977.
  B.   *Steps*
    1.   Determine eligibility criteria—usage per day, availability of credit line, and geographic considerations (by August 1976).
    2.   Design appropriate art work for card. Determine promotional and distribution strategies. Use ad agency (by September 1976).
    3.   Order plastics from manufacturer—8–10 weeks lead time (in house by October 1976).
    4.   Emboss and encode cards—distribute to customers. If credit line offered, cards cannot be mass-mailed (time ?).
    5.   Institute promotional campaign to stimulate usage—establish personal demonstration program (ad agency to decide timing).
  C.   *Resources/costs/regulatory problems*
    1.   Approximate cost per thousand cards issued will be $250 (includes embossing).
    2.   As transactions increase, more work time required to process paper—need feasibility study on on-line versus off-line.
    3.   Have experience in operating debit card program.

II. Related project: Install lobby depositories and automated tellers
 A. *Goals:* To reduce lobby congestion, to offer unlimited banking hours, to expedite customer transaction time, to enhance innovative image.
 B. *Steps*
 1. Determine feasibility of lobby depositories and need for automated teller services at branch locations. For lobby depository, simple queuing theory formulas can be utilized.
 2. If feasible, lobby depositories would have to be procured and promoted. In the case of the ATMs (automated teller machines) a decision would have to be made with regard to manufacturer.
 3. ATM installation schedule would have to be prepared.
 4. ATM promotion at branch location would have to be planned and coordinated with debit card promotion.
 5. Balancing and credit procedures would have to be established.
 C. *Resources*
 1. State U MBA student doing queuing theory study at East Harrington Branch.
 2. ATM scheduled to be installed at Westfield Office.
 3. Plans to expand debit card base in process.

For the next month, McQuade reviewed the minutes of the meetings of the past four months and gradually completed a preliminary draft of a 1977 Operating Plan. To do so, he, along with Dr. Baker, first reexamined the list of goals which had been prepared at their May 18 meeting. A further subdivision was made as approximately one half of the objectives were categorized as general goals while the remainder, "means goals," were included as a plan to meet the more general goals. The two men also reviewed the reports that had been submitted by the department heads and incorporated ideas under appropriate headings. The preliminary plan was submitted to each of the department heads on September 6 to make certain that their findings had not been distorted in any manner, and finally, after minor revisions, the finalized plan was submitted to BBT's board of directors for final approval on September 22. Budgets for each of the programs were prepared, and the plan began operation in November 1976, two months ahead of schedule.

After six months of painstaking work by all involved, Bloomington Bank and Trust was operating according to a formal written plan for the first time in its history, and its president, Brian J. McQuade, felt confident his bank was headed toward even greater success.

Memorandum

To: Board of Directors and Officers

From: Brian J. McQuade

Subject: 1977 Operating Plan

September 22, 1976

This plan has been developed over the last several months through input, discussion, and suggestions from customers, employees, and directors. To plan for one year necessitates reference to longer-term strategic goals. We have just begun to formalize a strategic plan and have done enough to construct the shorter-term operating plan. This plan is intended as a guide, a summary, and a reference point. It should be studied in detail by all officers.

Mission of BBT: To provide to our market a full range of conveniently delivered banking services of high quality at competitive prices and at the same time to develop a record of growth and profitability which will be financially rewarding to our stockholders.

A. *Goals*
   1. Increase profits after taxes 10–15 percent compounded annually.
   2. Build toward a profit goal of 1 percent return on assets (less check-float-created due from balances).
   3. Build toward realizing a return on invested capital of 10–12 percent.
   4. Build and retain capital to maintain capital to deposit ratios of 1 : 12–15.
   5. Increase stock value steadily.
   6. Maintain and build BBT as an imaginative, service-oriented, and professionally operated institution.
   7. Provide a stimulating and financially rewarding work environment for employees.

B. *General plan to meet goals*
   1. Increase demand deposits 8–12 percent annually.
   2. Increase savings and time deposits 10–15 percent annually.
   3. Build from the present 50 percent plus loan to deposit ratio to one of 65–70 percent by 1980.
   4. Adopt a posture of more aggressive sales through a combination of more rapid product enhancement and development, improved and intensified advertising, improved development and communications, intensified calling on the business community, and a progressive branching program.
   5. Specifically develop the capacity of BBT to meet the operational, investment, and lending needs of professional and commercial customers in our marketing area.

6. Increase market penetration in towns having branches, with particular emphasis on Bloomington. Intensify efforts to penetrate more fully towns contiguous to those in which branches are located.

7. Intensify efforts to improve the profitability of that part of the investment portfolio which prudently need not be considered primary reserves.

C. *Prime 1977 programs*

Some of the 1977 programs may be implemented during the remainder of 1976 but are included here to solidify this initial written operating plan. Quantitative details will be developed during a budgeting process to be conducted in the fourth quarter.

1. *Organizational structure*
   a. President—will be responsible for overall results and management, including planning. His role will include a major public relations effort, sales initiatives with selected prominent prospective customers, and contact with current major customers. He will be assisted by three department heads, each reporting directly to him.
   b. Department heads
      (1) James Carlson
         (a) Banking services, including commercial lending.
         (b) Branch administration.
         (c) Marketing.
      (2) Bob Delaney
         (a) Operations.
         (b) Financial reporting.
         (c) Personnel administration.
      (3) John Erickson
         (a) Trust marketing and operations.
         (b) Investment services.
         (c) Investment portfolio management.

2. *Intensify lending activities*
   a. Install a personal/commercial revolving credit service (in addition to Master Charge).
   b. Institute a short-term line of credit facility for both individuals and businesses.
   c. Intensify installment lending activity
      (1) Formalize a deferred/tailored installment loan program.
      (2) Develop contractor/dealer business in home improvement areas.
      (3) Intensify efforts to develop a more competitive pricing posture consistent with BBT goals.
      (4) Develop a second-mortgage loan program.
   d. Implement a formalized house-to-house loan program.
   e. Computerize the commercial loan function.
   f. Make Master Charge picture card optional.

3. *Intensify overall marketing effort on a wide basis*
   a. Hire an advertising agency.
   b. Institute a formal officer call program.

    c. Initiate a program of business/professional seminars/forums.

    d. Intensify social program for selected major customers and prospects.

    e. Add to staff a business development officer to concentrate on noncustomers in Bloomington and selected parts of East Harrington in 1977.

4. *Improve and intensify nonlending product lines and sales effort*

    a. Institute d/d–d/w statement savings.

    b. Institute serialized check service.

    c. Issue a debit (noncredit) card for automated teller activation.

    d. Institute a telephone transfer service.

    e. Investigate and implement, if feasible, a deposit pickup service for businesses.

    f. Investigate and implement, if feasible, a minimax checking account service.

    g. Revise NOW account service charges to present more competitive product.

    h. Implement a formalized government security service.

    i. Investigate and implement, if feasible, the "Working Trust" service.

    j. Develop operational service "starter kits" for individuals and businesses.

    k. Review service pricing schedules, and revise to increase revenues where possible.

    l. Build customer service conference area outside Bookkeeping Department.

5. Open Westfield Branch in early 1977.

6. Open Four Corners and/or Buckingham branches in late 1977 or early 1978.

7. *Improve internal operations*

    a. Accounting.

      (1) Install remote entry data processing equipment.

      (2) Place all loan accounting functions in one centralized "back office" operation.

    b. Financial reporting.

      (1) Automatic investment portfolio accounting.

      (2) Eliminate cash basis accounting, and install a full accrual system (while retaining cash basis tax reporting while advisable).

      (3) Progress toward a profit center accounting system.

    c. Formalize a facilities plan and an ongoing facilities plan procedure for action to be taken in 1978 and beyond.

    d. Develop formalized job descriptions (and possibly salary ranges).

    e. Develop a more formalized officer evaluation program.

    f. Evaluate and implement better performance-oriented compensation programs for officers.

    g. Intensify communications between Board of Directors and Cookston Advisory Board and bank management.

8. Investigate and where possible implement changes in trust services and charges consistent with overall BBT goals.
9. Complete Main Office banking floor renovations.

D. *Five-year financial scenario*

Tables 1–9 describe a course that could develop based on tentative longer-range goals and the continuation of the overall philosophy of business being developed in this plan. From our current vantage point, the 1976 and 1977 net income projections may be difficult to achieve. Hopefully near-term deficiencies may be overcome during the period 1978–81.

E. *Conclusion*

The planning process is a continuing one, involving all personnel in management positions. I believe that the meetings, memos, studies, discussions, and surveys that have gone into this initial plan have already proven beneficial to the individuals involved and the bank. Bloomington Bank is a solid and respected institution—it has performed well in its marketplace and for its stockholders. We have the opportunity to create an even more interesting and exciting institution—one that can serve its present and an expanded marketplace better than it has. We have the opportunity to create a more dynamic work environment for all employees and to obtain better financial results for stockholders and employees. The task is not an easy one. The business of banking shares with other businesses the pressures of regulation, increasing costs and the resultant squeeze on profits, and increasing competition.

I suggest that we view our challenge as opportunities to grow personally and as an institution. Better management in its broadest sense, and including all levels, is the greatest need in banking today—I believe we can learn together to manage better.

1977 will be an exciting and interesting year for Bloomington Bank. Much of what we have planned is basic and simply position us better vis-à-vis our competition. In the planning process we have deferred for 1977 some of the more creative steps that we may have wished to take. Experience confirms the wisdom of learning to walk before running. We have chosen to walk more quickly—we may or may not ultimately decide to run.

I seek both your support and cooperation and in turn offer you mine.

(Signed)
Brian J. McQuade

Approved by Board of Directors
on September 22, 1976

Table 1
Demand deposits

Historical:

	Demand	Percent increase
1970	$ 7,185,000	
1971	7,937,000	8.0%
1972	8,901,000	12.1
1973	8,893,000	(0.1)
1974	9,713,000	9.2
1975	11,136,000	14.6

Five-year: 55%.

Projection:

	8 percent growth projection	12 percent growth projection
1976	$10,500,000*	$10,500,000*
1977	11,340,000	11,760,000
1978	12,247,200	13,171,200
1979	13,226,976	14,751,744
1980	14,285,134	16,521,953
1981	15,427,944	18,504,587

* 1976 estimate down from 1975.

Table 2
Time/savings deposits

Historical:

	Time/savings deposits	Percent increase
1970	$10,620,000	
1971	11,985,000	12.8%
1972	13,181,000	10.0
1973	14,413,000	9.3
1974	16,933,000	17.5
1975	18,631,000	10.0

Five-year: 75.4%.

Projection:

	10 percent growth projection	15 percent growth projection
1976	$20,460,000	$21,390,000
1977	22,506,000	24,598,500
1978	24,756,600	28,288,275
1979	27,232,260	32,531,516
1980	29,955,468	37,411,243
1981	32,951,014	43,022,929

Table 3
Total deposits

Historical:

	Total deposits	Percent increase
1970	$17,805,000	
1971	19,923,000	11.9%
1972	22,082,000	10.8
1973	23,304,000	5.5
1974	26,646,000	14.3
1975	27,818,000	4.4

Five-year: 56.2%.

Projection:

	Low-growth projection	High-growth projection
1976	$30,960,000	$31,890,000
1977	33,846,000	36,358,500
1978	37,003,800	41,459,475
1979	40,459,236	47,283,260
1980	44,240,602	53,933,196
1981	48,378,958	61,527,516

Table 4
Total Loans

Historical:

	Total loans	Deposit to loan ratios
1970	$ 8,708,000	1 : .489
1971	10,073,000	.506
1972	11,927,000	.540
1973	13,271,000	.569
1974	14,372,000	.529
1975	15,118,000	.507

Five-year: 73.6%.

Projection:

	Low-growth projection	High-growth projection	Projected loan to deposit ratio
1976	$16,718,400	$17,220,600	.54
1977	19,292,220	20,724,345	.57
1978	22,202,280	24,875,685	.60
1979	25,489,318	29,788,453	.63
1980	29,198,797	35,595,909	.66
1981	33,865,270	43,069,261	.70

Table 5
Net income

Historical:

	Net income	Percent increase
1970	$160,000	
1971	174,500	9.1%
1972	135,100	(22.6)
1973	216,200	60.0
1974	245,000	13.3
1975	230,000	(6.1)

Projection:

	10 percent growth projection	15 percent growth projection
1976	$236,500	$247,250
1977	260,150	284,337
1978	286,165	326,988
1979	314,781	376,036
1980	346,259	432,411
1981	380,885	497,308

Table 6
Dividends

Historical:

		Dividend*	Percent increase
1970	$70,000	$0.70	
1971	70,000	0.70	–0–
1972	72,500	0.725	3.5%
1973	75,000	0.75	3.4
1974	80,000	0.80	6.6
1975	85,000	0.85	6.2

* Adjusted for 5/20/74 100 percent stock dividend.

Projection:

	Low	High
1976	$ 85,000	$ 85,000
1977	94,600	98,900
1978	104,060	113,735
1979	114,466	150,415
1980	138,504	172,977
1981	152,354	198,923

40 percent of earnings used for all projections 1977–81.

Table 7
Capital

Historical:

	Capital	Percent increase
1970	$1,761,000	
1971	1,874,000	6.4%
1972	1,951,000	4.1
1973	2,163,000	10.9
1974	2,381,000	10.1
1975	2,527,000	6.1

Five-year: 43.5%.

Projection:

	Low	High
1976	$2,641,900	$2,662,250
1977	2,797,990	2,847,687
1978	2,969,689	3,060,940
1979	3,170,004	3,286,562
1980	3,377,760	3,546,027
1981	3,606,291	3,844,412

Table 8
Ratio deposits to capital ($000s)

Historical:

	Total capital	Deposits	Deposits to capital ratio
1970	$1,761.1	$17,805.2	10.1
1971	1,874.1	19,923.1	10.6
1972	1,951.5	22,082.5	11.3
1973	2,163.1	23,304.1	10.8
1974	2,382.6	26,646.6	11.2
1975	2,527.6	29,818.1	11.8

Projection:

	Low	High
1976	11.7	12.0
1977	12.1	12.8
1978	12.5	13.5
1979	12.8	14.4
1980	13.1	15.2
1981	13.4	16.0

Table 9
Percent return on capital

Historical:

	Percent
1970	9.1%
1971	9.3
1972	6.9
1973	10.0
1974	10.3
1975	9.1

Projection:

	Low percent	High percent
1976	8.95%	9.29%
1977	9.30	9.98
1978	9.64	10.68
1979	9.93	11.44
1980	10.25	12.20
1981	10.56	12.94

Case 2–3

KSM/Beefalo Breeding Company

"It seems that every week brings a new dimension to our business," mused George Schweiger, president of KSM Enterprises. "I wonder where we will be a year from now." Schweiger sat reflectively at his desk, gazing out the window of the log home that served as the sales office for the Beaver Log Home distributorship that KSM acquired late in the summer of 1977. He was looking across a snow-covered pasture toward the barns and livestock pens of the Clarence Korte farm. It was on this Illinois farm that Schweiger and Korte launched the Beefalo Breeding Company in April 1977 with the importation of 40 head of half-blood beefalo from California. After less than a year of operation in their two businesses, the management team of Schweiger and Korte were considering diversification into yet another distinct enterprise—fast-food restaurants.

EVENTS LEADING TO THE NEW BUSINESSES

The business experience of George Schweiger, which spans 30 years, has been primarily that of a salesman, promoter, and entrepre-

---

This case was prepared by Curtis W. Cook of San José State University.

neur. For 13 years he was in the insurance business, for 7 years in the construction business, part of which involved site location/acquisition, contractor negotiations, and equipment installations for the Bonanza Steak House chain of restaurants in the Seattle region. About 11 years ago he relocated in Illinois as the national marketing director for a new firm specializing in outdoor lighting systems. From this position he spun off a new firm involved in custom plastic packaging. Eventually this enterprise diversified toward end products by manufacturing nonprescription pharmaceuticals and cosmetics. Schweiger's function in the above two businesses was in *sales management*. Five years ago he switched into brokerage consulting, specializing in diamonds and bulk Scotch whisky. After two years in the brokerage business he organized a company to develop an organic fertilizer produced from a bacteria blend of decomposing sawdust. It was through this agricultural venture that he developed a working relationship with Clarence Korte, an experienced organic farmer and dairy rancher.

Clarence Korte, after retiring from military service in 1956, joined his brother Ralph to start the Korte Construction Company. Currently this construction firm is one of the largest in southern Illinois with several multimillion-dollar contracts for industrial and commercial buildings. However, in 1962 Clarence decided to leave management involvement in Korte Construction and return to his family's tradition in farming. In partnership with his brother, Clarence developed a large Holstein dairy herd and converted to all-organic farming on the 520-acre farm near Pocahontas, about 40 miles east of St. Louis. In November 1976 fire destroyed most of the physical plant of the dairy operation, causing an estimated $350,000 loss. Rather than rebuild for dairy production, the Kortes liquidated all dairy assets in February 1977. Clarence was intrigued by the economic and nutritional superiorities of beefalo (a bison-bovine hybrid) over conventional beef cattle. In conjunction with George Schweiger, the Kortes decided to venture into this new breed of livestock. Thus, Beefalo Breeding Company was formed as the start of a herd buildup begun in spring of 1977.

While the calamity of a fire provided the circumstances that cleared the way for entry into beefalo production, the log home business began more as a marketing outgrowth of another product line sold through KSM Enterprises. KSM was also established in 1977 when Schweiger, who has a penchant for novel products, brought to the new firm the distributorship for a European-produced, low-temperature radiant heating system. The product is a system conductive foil sealed in sheet plastic that is stapled to ceiling framing prior to installation of drywall, plasterboard, or acoutical tile. Out of a desire to have a means of displaying and demonstrating the product, the possibility of selling and/or constructing homes was considered. Management quickly narrowed the search to becoming a distributor for some manufacturer of precut log homes, and Beaver Log Homes of Grand Island, Nebraska, was selected.

Thus, by the end of their first year of investment/management association, Schweiger and Korte had established their two principal businesses as log home sales and beefalo breeding/production. Yet serious challenges remained as to the desired direction and rate of future growth, with capital availability a chronic constraint.

MANAGERIAL ROLES

In seeking to define alternatives relative to these challenges, the two principals in these joint enterprises have informally evolved specialized roles. Clarence Korte, with experience in construction and livestock/farming management, concentrates on production-related tasks. This involves not only management of the livestock operation but also supervision of erecting log structures and constructing whatever finishing touches are desired by the purchaser of a log home or barn.

George Schweiger tends to the sales and financial side of the business. Included in his role are direct selling/merchandising of both log homes and beefalo as well as promoting investments in beefalo under a variety of tax-sheltered programs. Schweiger acknowledges that he is a dreamer and a promotor of ideas and novel concepts:

> Probably the greatest problem I have is going from one thing to another. I am looking for the new products, the different ideas. I have always maintained that talent is the cheapest commodity that can be obtained. Sure, good talent is expensive, but in relationship to its performance it is a value. My feeling has always been that if I can get it together, so to speak, then I'll find somebody else more qualified than I to manage it. . . . So I tend to be a dreamer. If a potential product is there, it can be made to work, given the proper infusion of capital and management expertise. If I have any expertise at all, I think it is in the field of taking ideas and converting them into different types of presentations for development of a business.

KSM ENTERPRISES AND THE BEAVER LOG HOME CONTRACT

KSM Enterprises, Inc., was incorporated on March 1, 1977, with 300,000 no-par shares authorized (although franchise taxes were paid on only 100,000 shares). An initial equity capitalization of approximately $87,000 was obtained with investments from Korte equal to 29.2 percent of the total, Schweiger with 26.5 percent, one silent investor with 32 percent, and six others totaling 12.3 percent. As of December 31, 1977, book value was 87 cents per share. During its formative period, KSM relied on borrowed funds to provide partial financing of physical facilities and periodically to supply working capital. One year from the date of incorporation, debt financing totaled approximately $35,000.

Schweiger brought to KSM the radiant heating system with which he had been involved for about eight months prior to incorporation. In deciding to expand the product line to include the home in which the heating system could be installed, he did not want the newly established KSM to compete directly with more experienced companies. Speaking in February 1978, Schweiger explained:

> We just didn't want to go out and start building stick-built homes, so we started to explore the log home market and found that everything indicated that it was probably the fastest growing segment of the building market. We felt that there was an opportunity here. Three years ago, there probably wasn't a log home—other than Abe Lincoln's cabin up at Salem—within a 50-mile radius of here. Today there are probably a dozen.

With a determination to enter into a distinctly different segment of the construction industry, after researching the product, production methods, and financial capabilities of 15 log home manufacturers, management decided to negotiate with Beaver Log Homes. When asked why Beaver Log Homes was selected over other manufacturers, Schweiger stated:

> Principally, because our studies of other companies indicated to us that both from the standpoint of the finished product as well as the overall financial strength and capabilities of the firm, Beaver offered to us and to the consumer the best log home on the market today for the price. There is a superior log home to Beaver, cut from Michigan White Cedar, but it is not the home for the average buyer. So we just felt that Beaver was by far the best company to deal with.

The contract gave KSM dealership rights to all of southern Illinois, including the right for KSM to contract for subdealers in communities throughout that part of the state. One contract provision required KSM to build either a log home or a log office building to serve as a demonstration model. Since the Korte farmland was adjacent to I–70 (a major interstate connecting the St. Louis metropolitan region to points east), management decided to erect a log office facility adjacent to the interstate where it would be clearly visible from both directions, even though exits and the closest commercial activities are approximately two miles from the site. The nearest community with light industrial firms is Highland, about five miles to the southwest.

Under terms of the contract with Beaver, KSM will receive a 27.5 percent discount from list price if it equals or exceeds the purchase of 50,000 lineal feet of logs annually. Additionally, quarterly quotas are to be met or the margin will be reduced. For each quarter that quotas are met, an additional 2 percent production bonus (beyond 27.5 percent) is awarded.

MARKETING OF LOG HOMES

Beaver sells log homes principally on the basis of logs precut for several types of basic floor plans, both one- and two-story homes. The design of an average-sized Beaver Log Home requires 2,050 lineal feet of logs, suggested retail price for logs about $8,300. Custom design is possible as log construction is not limited to size or shape of floor design, although height is limited without cross-tie structural support. Clarence Korte, for example, built and custom-designed a 3,100-square-foot home for his family. Logs are cut and number-coded (to match blueprint designs) at the mill in Claremore, Oklahoma, and transported by truck to the building site.

KSM sells on a cash basis, with 30 percent down payment required either from the individual purchaser or the subdealer at the time the contract is signed. The remainder is due at the time logs are delivered. KSM will help prospective customers work with local banks or S&Ls to arrange mortgage financing. For individuals purchasing within about a 100-mile radius of Highland, Illinois, KSM will erect the log home shell on the owner's foundation if the owner/builder so desires. Clarence Korte assembles and supervises a crew of laborers for this purpose on an as-needed basis. KSM will also provide whatever finishing the customer desires. Once a contract is signed, the normal delivery schedule is 45 days for delivery, with 15 days' variance according to the mill's cutting schedule.

KSM engages in little newspaper advertising. The parent does advertise in some trade magazines and popular home-related magazines (i.e., *Better Homes and Gardens*). KSM relies primarily on local home shows as a means of achieving exposure and creating interest. For such purposes, an 8-foot by 10-foot display booth (constructed of Beaver logs) is erected at the show site. The principal costs of such promotional activity are the show promotional fee and the labor cost of someone to work at the booth distributing free brochures, talking to those who pass by, and selling to interested parties a $3 book of Beaver plans and specifications for standard model homes. Promotional fees are for advertising of the home show, typically for radio spots which might run from $280–$560 for 40 to 120 spots that promote both the show and the sponsorer (in this case KSM's Beaver Homes).

Because of the vastness of the franchised sales territory, KSM management intends to sell primarily through contracts with builders/dealers who represent one to three county areas. KSM will discount logs to subdealers or contract builders from 5 percent to 22.5 percent off list price, depending on expected sales volume of the dealer. Such a practice would reduce the pressures on Schweiger to personally be responsible for direct selling to individual homeowners.

For KSM to qualify for the 27.5 percent operating margin discount, approximately 24 average-size homes of 2,050 lineal feet need to be sold annually, with about 20 per year necessary to break even. Such an average size (based on Beaver sales statistics) represents a value of $7,000–8,000 each. Logs represent 18–25 percent of the total cost of the house, with 20 percent considered a rule of thumb. Other cost factors include foundation or basement, plumbing, heating systems, electrical, doors and windows, and so on.

After the first six months of the Beaver dealership, KSM had sold three homes. By February 1979 (after 1½ years), a total of 18 log buildings had been sold, and bids were out on 15 additional plans.

BEEFALO AS A NEW MEAT SOURCE

Beefalo are a hybrid bison/bovine cross-developed to impart the growth advantages of bison (buffalo) into meat production animals that would have color, confirmation (shape), and edible characteristics similar to beef cattle. A successful breed was first announced in 1973 by developer D. C. "Bud" Basolo, after years of experimentation and breeding up to arrive at a pureblood sire. A pureblood beefalo is defined as three eighths American Bison and five eighths domestic bovine (typically three eighths Charolais and two eighths Hereford). Several production advantages are claimed for beefalo over beef.

1. Beefalo calves are smaller at birth (approximately 45–65 pounds compared to 80–105 pounds for cattle). Thus, less assistance and care are necessary at birth, resulting in lower losses (deaths), especially on open ranges.

2. Beefalo are believed heartier than cattle, able to withstand greater temperature extremes and less prone to sickness. Historically buffalo herds roamed from Canada to Mexico and prior to man, their principal adversary was the predator (wolves, coyotes, etc.). Calves are able to run approximately four hours after birth regardless of weather conditions.

3. Beefalo mature more quickly than beef. Animals mature to a slaughter weight (approximately 1,000–1,100 pounds) in about 12 months compared to about 18 months for beef.

4. Beefalo convert feed to flesh more efficiently than beef and require less grain for finishing. A test conducted by Dr. Gary C. Smith at Texas A&M University in 1976 statistically confirmed the superior productive efficiency of 486 head of beefalo compared to bovine control groups. Among Dr. Smith's findings, one pen of cattle on a feed ration of 14 percent roughage and 86 percent concentrate (corn, rolled oats, soy meal, etc.), over a 120-day period for finishing prior to slaugh-

ter, gained an average 2.55 pounds per day at a feed cost of 47 cents per pound. Beefalo which were on a 26 percent roughage ration averaged a gain of 2.71 pounds per day at the same 47 cents cost. Those beefalo on a 36 percent roughage produced an average daily gain of 0.5 to 0.7 of a pound more (3.21 to 3.41) at a cost of 37 cents per pound.

5. Beefalo yield a proportionately higher percentage of meat to live weight. This results from more energy being converted into muscle tissue rather than fat. In the A&M study, all beefalo carcasses were federally graded in yield grade 2, the most favored yield grade of producers since excess fat is minimal yet the meat tissue is bright in color and well conformed (blocky rather than thin and rangy). As a percentage of dressed carcass to live weight, the beefalo averaged 63 percent compared to a typical 59–61 percent yield for steers or English-bred cattle. Dr. Smith commented, "Based on my experience of 15 years' work in this field, they [beefalo] have remarkable dressing percentages, and it is due to the fact that they are muscular, extremely muscular in relation to other cattle."

Considered as food for human consumption, beefalo test out favorably in terms of nutritional value relative to beef. The following data from Certified Labs, Inc., 19 Hudson Street, New York (USDA Certified Laboratory #3677), are representative of comparative analysis of beefalo (ground) and ground beef as purchased in supermarkets:

	Lot Dec 484 ground beefalo	Lot Dec 483 ground beef
Protein	20.35%	16.67%
Fat	3.65%	24.80%
Calories	32.4/ounce	82.4/ounce
Cholesterol	5.19 mg./ounce	150.5 mg./ounce

BEEFALO BREEDING COMPANY'S PRODUCTION OPERATIONS

Within one year of its inception, Beefalo Breeding Company developed the largest herd of beefalo in the Midwest. Most of the 520 acres on the Korte brothers farm are devoted to organic farming of feed grains for feed fattening and finishing of livestock. Since 1970 the farm has been entirely organic, eliminating the use of chemical fertilizers, herbicides, and pesticides. The farm carries organic certification and is one of two selected by Dr. Barry Commoner of Washington University for comparative studies between chemical and ecological farming. This farm has a capacity for producing grain and alfalfa capable of finishing approximately 800 head per year on the basis of a quarterly turnover (90-day finishing). The Korte farm itself is not intended for extensive grazing, as all but about 65 acres is cultivated farmland.

Currently there are four grain storage tanks adjacent to the feedlot, each capable of holding approximately 65 tons of feed.

The company is incorporated separately from KSM, with Schweiger and the Korte brothers as the stockholders. It is a member of both the World Beefalo Association (California) and the American Beefalo Association (Kentucky), organizations concerned with registering breeders and developing performance data on the various beefalo bloodlines. Beefalo Breeding Company is under a management/feeding contract with the Korte farm for the feeding and care of the herd. Under terms of the arrangement, the corporation pays Korte 27.5 cents per pound of weight gain, which provides an adequate return to the Korte farm. If Holsteins or Herefords were being fattened instead of beefalo, a fee of at least 35 cents per pound would be necessary for the farm to obtain a similar return. This difference is because of the genetic advantage of beefalo, which have the same digestive track as buffalo, a more efficient converter of feed.

Beefalo Breeding Company prefers to place 800- to 850-pound beefalo (after grass feeding) into the feedlot for 60–90 days. A 12- to 15-bushel hot feed ration (of rolled oats, corn, crushed wheat, soy meal, etc.) will produce white marbling and exterior fat suitable to yield a choice quality grade (the most-used grade in major supermarkets) and a quantity-yield grade of 2.

To accommodate grassland feeding, Beefalo Breeding Company bought a 670-acre ranch located in south-central Missouri, near Salem (valued at $300,000). The 540 acres of pastureland in this ranch, once improved, will be capable of supporting a 300–350-head beefalo cow-calf operation. While the first year of business saw a buildup to 135 animals at the Illinois facility, in April 1978 the first 124 head were delivered to the Missouri ranch. This herd was purchased from a breeder in Pauls Valley, Oklahoma, at a cost of $38,000 delivered, financed through an open-end bank note.

MARKETING BEEFALO

While beefalo is subject to the same grading process as beef, in February 1978 the meat division of the USDA issued basic guidelines to its field graders that would certify beefalo as a class of animals separate from beef. Having this classification enables beefalo to be marketed as distinct from beef, although in practice it can be sold through supermarkets as beef since the consumer would not discern the difference.

Since beefalo are a relatively new breed of livestock, on a national basis herd sizes remain small. To build up herds, most breeders retain heifers for calf production and sell off as slaughter animals young bulls/bullocks (most breeding is through artificial insemination from registered pureblood bulls). This scarcity of slaughter animals enables beefalo producers generally to command a premium price for their meat, usually about 10 cents per pound over comparable beef carcass grades. Organically produced and certified meat of any kind also usually commands a higher price because of presumed health advantages.

By late March 1978, Beefalo Breeding Company had 30 head ready for slaughter (1,100–1,200 pounds each), the first in any quantity for retail sale. At this time the Chicago Board of Trade price quote for choice beef was in the $46–48 range, live weight basis. Schweiger and Korte both expressed disillusion with conventional meat distribution systems, since the producer essentially is a price taker. For this reason they explored alternative marketing approaches. Schweiger remarked:

> We are not in accord with the current marketing methods of the agricultural industry. We think they are controlled too much by speculators. If we can control our production cost and go directly to the consumer with the finished product, we can reap the profits currently enjoyed by the speculators as opposed to the producers.

Since Beefalo Breeding had not previously slaughtered more than one or two animals at a time, it had no regular clientele or distribution procedures. Several alternatives were thus explored. Schweiger phoned Nelson Name Service in Minneapolis to see if it could compile lists of all the health food stores and Weight Watchers clubs in Illinois. Packages of frozen select retail cuts (i.e., steaks, roasts, ground beefalo) could be sold to health food stores. To Weight Watchers the intent would be to sell halves or quarters of beefalo, either in fresh carcass form or cut and frozen. Beefalo Breeding Company also was contacted by a New York beefalo firm asking if it would be possible to purchase slaughter-ready livestock. Although the New York firm was smaller in actual numbers of beefalo, it had an established promotional and distribution system (selling direct to consumers in halves and quarters).

Schweiger also contacted area supermarket chains to explore the feasibility of a special beefalo promotion. In talking with the manager of meat operations with the National Supermarket chain (which had a large share of market in the St. Louis area), the idea was readily acceptable. However, to be able to use beefalo as a promotional item, National would require at least 300 head since it followed a policy of uniform advertising within a metropolitan market.

Another option was to have approximately 80 percent of the carcass ground into hamburger patties to build up a supply pending the opening of Beefalo barns restaurants (details noted in future section). The remaining 20 percent (steaks only) would be packaged in 10-pound units, frozen, and sold through local promotion.

However, because these animals had to go to slaughter (additional feeding would result in minimal salable weight gain), Schweiger in

April made arrangements to supply five IGA markets (local independents) in Peoria, Illinois, with 14 head for a special sale. The price was 10 cents per pound dressed weight over choice beef. Additionally, in a reciprocal arrangement with a Springfield, Illinois, radio station, Beefalo Breeding Company sold livestock directly to a Springfield packer, with the radio station advertising the availability of beefalo halves and quarters. The advertising was at no direct cost to the company since Clarence Korte had supplied an electrical power generator to the radio station when an ice storm in late March knocked out its power source and forced it off the air. Schweiger saw these market sources more as temporary, although he recognized residual value in (*a*) exposing the public to beefalo, (*b*) possibly attracting some wealthy investors into tax-sheltered partnerships of herds under management contract to Beefalo Breeding Company, or (*c*) attracting potential investors to the fast-foods concept of Beefalo Barns.

THE NEED FOR OUTSIDE CAPITAL

While developing markets (at a premium price) for fattened livestock consumed part of Schweiger's time, most of his energy during 1978 was devoted to developing a variety of prospectuses for attracting equity investors or debt capital. Additional capital was desired for three purposes: (*a*) to build up herd size to fully utilize the feedlot capacity and/or provide adequate meat supply to six restaurants; (*b*) to launch a fast-food restaurant operation through general partnerships, franchising, and/or stock placement; and (*c*) to lease and/or purchase additional pastureland where beefalo would graze until reaching an appropriate feedlot weight.

Schweiger worked with two firms that might be able to attract investors interested in the tax-sheltering prospects of livestock. He held several meetings during 1978 with the St. Louis office senior tax partner of Peat, Marwick, and Mitchell and with a principal in the Investment Planning Group of Clayton, Missouri. The intent of working with these firms was to pull together a group of investors with sufficient capital for one or more large herds of beefalo. Schweiger explained the basics of one of his proposals:

> If we had a 100 per herd, we would sell an absentee owner group the animals and manage the herd under the contract. With this arrangement we would not need anyone's money [for working capital]. We would have all our own. The basic annual fee would be $350 per year per cow. There would be a $300 maintenance cost on the cow plus a $50 breeding fee. We would maintain the cow with her calf until the calf was weaned, and then prorate the remaining number of months [to anniversary date of contract] against the $300 maintenance fee for the offspring. We would assume all feeding costs and charge outside veterinarian fees. If the investing group wanted insurance, it would be their responsibil-

ity. The annual management-maintenance fees would be paid in advance.

A 100-head partnership program would require a total capital investment of $204,000. If we had one partner in a 40–50 percent tax bracket, let's say with a 5 percent participation, he would initially invest $10,200. In the first year he would write off 85 percent of his capital contribution against his income tax [for paper losses since there is no revenue inflow]. In the second year against his cash contribution he will write off 188 percent against his taxes; the fourth year, 444 percent; and from the fourth year on, the partnership is actually in an income-producing position. But from an investor's viewpoint, the front-end years provide a tremendous write-off against personal income tax. The net result of a seven-year program, based on current prices of animals, would be a net cash accumulation in excess of $2 million if the herd is liquidated. Although programmed to terminate at the end of the seventh year, in reality there would be no good reason to liquidate unless the limited partners wanted their capital to invest in another program that would have an accelerated depreciation schedule.

Finding it difficult to put together tax-sheltered partnerships in the magnitude mentioned above, Schweiger toward year-end 1978 began promoting smaller programs, based on a minimum of 10 head. Such programs would involve a first-year cash outlay of approximately $11,000 for 10 beefalo heifers (females). This proposal included many of the features of previous ones (i.e., describing beefalo, the principle of breeding up, advantages of starting with half-blood heifers, risk factors, and management), although in less detail. Exhibits 1A–1D present some of the agreement forms and financial projections for this type of program.

Exhibit 1A
Sample pages of tax-shelter beefalo proposal

Beefalo Purchase Agreement

THIS AGREEMENT made and entered into on the _____ day of
_____ , 197_____ , by and between Clarence A. Korte and George D. Schweiger, d/b/a Beefalo Breeding Company ("Seller"), R.R. #1, Pocahontas, Illinois, 62275, and _____ ("Buyer"), whose mailing address is _____

WITNESSETH:

In consideration of the mutual covenants, terms and conditions contained herein, the parties hereto do hereby agree as follows:

1.   Seller agrees to sell to Buyer _____ head of one-half (½) blood registered Beefalo Breeding cattle (hereinafter referred to as the Breeding Herd), which animals are more particularly described in Exhibit A at-

---

Exhibit 1A (*continued*)

tached hereto and made a part hereof. All animals purchased shall be subject to the approval of Buyer at the time of delivery.

2.   Buyer and Seller are entering into a certain Management and Marketing Agreement of even date herewith, relating to the management, maintenance and breeding of the Breeding Herd and all progeny resulting therefrom.

3.   The animals in the Breeding Herd are represented and warranted to be breeders capable of being registered in either or both the World Beefalo Association (WBA) or the American Beefalo Association (ABA) and, at the option of Buyer, shall be registered in the association elected by Buyer.

4.   Seller shall successfully breed each female in the Breeding Herd with semen from a pureblood Beefalo bull; should any animal fail, after a reasonable time, to settle, Seller shall replace it with a comparable animal. Any replacement or substitution of animals in the Breeding Herd shall carry the same warranties as set forth herein.

5.   Buyer agrees to pay a total purchase price of one thousand five hundred ($1,500) dollars for each female in the Breeding Herd for a total purchase price of $_____ .

   a.   The sum of six hundred ($600) dollars per female in the Breeding Herd shall be paid on the date hereof:

   b.   The balance of nine hundred ($900) dollars per female in the Breeding Herd shall be paid on or before January 1, 197____ , provided, however, that Buyer may have the option, in lieu of making such payment, to execute and deliver to Seller a Promissory Note in the form attached hereto as Exhibit ____ in the principal amount of such balance. The Promissory Note, until the balance of the purchase price is paid, shall accrue interest at the rate of nine (9%) percent per annum, and such principal shall be paid upon the earlier of:

   (1)   Sale, with the consent of Buyer, of female animals (except culls) from Buyer's herd, which are the animals purchased hereunder or their progeny (or sale of any animals in liquidation of the herd), such payment to be limited to the proceeds of such sale.

   (2)   Seven years from date of the execution hereof.

6.   The outstanding balance of principal and interest thereon shall be secured by a security interest in all animals purchased hereunder and their progeny. Buyer agrees to execute from time to time such Financing Statements or other documents as Seller may request a perfect such security interest in the State of Illinois, Missouri and elsewhere; including, without limitation, any Uniform Commercial Code Financing Statements or renewals thereof. Buyer appoints Seller as Buyer's attorney-in-fact to execute and file any such documents.

7.   In the event Seller shall default under the Management and Marketing Agreement and as a result of such default Buyer as Owner terminates said Agreement, Buyer shall nevertheless remain obligated to satisfy the Note.

Exhibit 1A (*concluded*)

8. In the event that Buyer terminates this Agreement during the first three calendar years, he will pay to the Company 50% of the progeny value as additional fees. Determination of the value of the progeny shall be made by an independent third party selected and mutually agreed upon by both parties hereto.

9. All representations, conditions, warranties and agreements set forth herein shall survive delivery of title, and Buyer acknowledges that there have been no representations, expressed or implied, except as set forth herein.

10. This Purchase Agreement, the Management and Marketing Agreement, the Security Agreement and the Note constitute the entire understanding between the parties hereto with respect to the subject matter hereof. Any changes, amendments or deletions must be in writing and signed by the parties to this Agreement.

This Agreement shall be interpreted in accordance with the laws of the State of Illinois.

IN WITNESS WHEREOF the parties have set their hands and seals this _____ day of _____ 197_____ .

Buyer _____   Seller _____

Exhibit 1B

Management and Marketing Agreement

THIS AGREEMENT is made and entered into on this _____ day of _____, 197_____ , by and between Clarence A. Korte and George D. Schweiger, d/b/a Beefalo Breeding Company, hereinafter referred to as "Company," and _____ , whose mailing address is _____ , hereinafter referred to as "Owner."

WITNESSETH:

WHEREAS, Owner is the sole owner and operator of the Beefalo breeding livestock, hereinafter referred to as "livestock" or "animals," described in Exhibit A, which is attached hereto and made a part hereof, and,

WHEREAS, Company is presently operating Beefalo breeding ranches in Illinois and Missouri and is experienced in the breeding management and marketing of Beefalo livestock, and,

WHEREAS, Owner desires Company to manage, breed and sell said Livestock under the terms and conditions of this Management and Marketing Agreement.

Exhibit 1B (*continued*)

NOW THEREFORE in consideration of the mutual promises and covenants contained herein, the parties agree as follows:

1.   Owner represents that he is the sole owner of the Livestock (Exh. A), subject only to the terms of the Beefalo Purchase Agreement, and a Promissory Note and Security Agreement referred to therein.

2.   Company shall provide all management and shall maintain, care for, feed and take whatever other steps are reasonably necessary for the well-being of the Livestock and their progeny. The maintenance of the Livestock under this Agreement shall include the breeding, feeding, calving, normal veterinarian services, raising and growing out of progeny, and the keeping of breeding and identification records in connection with the Livestock. Company agrees to maintain, care for and breed the Livestock in accordance with the standard practices for a purebred Beefalo operation and in accordance with the instruction of Owner.

3.   Company shall furnish Owner semiannual reports regarding the status of the Livestock subject to this Agreement. In addition, Company will furnish Owner, as soon as reasonably possible, data concerning any accident, illness, or sickness causing the death of any of the Livestock, and a postmortem report with regard to such animal.

4.   At the option of Owner and at Owner expense, Company will prepare applications for registration in Owner's name of all progeny complying with the regulations covering said registration in either or both the World Beefalo Association (WBA) or the American Beefalo Association (ABA) and shall use its best efforts to obtain a lifetime membership in the Association of Owner's choosing. Fees for membership or the registration of progeny shall be paid by Owner and are not included in the fee due Company described in paragraph 8.

5.   In order to assist Owner in its operation of its Livestock, Company shall be available periodically to consult with Owner in connection with the maintenance, care and growth of the animals subject to this Agreement. Such advice and counsel shall be in connection with the general and special maintenance of the Livestock, the sale of progeny, the retention of progeny, the selling, culling and replacement of Livestock in the Herd, and such other matters which are incident to the husbandry of Beefalo Livestock.

6.   All Livestock subject to this Agreement shall be kept and maintained at such place or places as Company determines in its sole discretion, and during the term of this Agreement, Company shall, at all times, maintain control and jurisdiction over said animals; provided Company shall advise Owner of the location thereof and they shall be available for Owner's inspection at reasonable times.

7.   Company shall not be responsible or liable for any loss or damage to any of the Beefalo Livestock subject to this Agreement, on account of any accident, disease or death, or by reason of any acts of any employee,

Exhibit 1B (*continued*)

servant or agent of the Company, except in the event of gross negligence or willful misconduct by Company or its employees, servants or agents. However, Company shall have the right to replace or substitute any animal lost for any reason from the original Beefalo Breeding Herd, said replacement or substitution to be of comparable quality to animal(s) replaced or substituted.

8.   In consideration of the Company's responsibilities, obligations and warranties hereunder, as a fee for the management of the Breeding Herd, Owner agrees to pay the Company as follows:

(1)   The sum of four hundred ($400) dollars for each breeding female in the herd, said sum payable upon the date first set forth above.

(2)   The sum of four hundred ($400) dollars for each breeding female in the herd, said sum payable on the date of the first anniversary of this Agreement.

(3)   The sum of four hundred ($400) dollars for each breeding female in the herd, said sum payable on the date of the second anniversary of this Agreement.

(4)   In addition to the fees set forth above [para. 8 one, two & three], the Company shall receive fifty (50%) percent of all net proceeds (gross sales less expenses) derived from the sale of any animals or other income from Owner's Herd during the term of this Agreement and the Beefalo Purchase Agreement as full payment for management, maintenance, breeding and other services provided by the Company.

Company and Owner agree that the net proceeds realized from the sale of animals from the Herd, income from semen sales or other income, shall be distributed between the parties as set forth below:

a.   Company shall receive fifty (50%) percent of all net income as provided in paragraph 8, Art. 4 above.

b.   Owner shall receive fifty (50%) percent of all net income, provided, however, that from such amount Owner shall pay to Company any interest due on the Note for the current or prior years.

9.   The Company may collect and sell semen obtained from bulls in the Owner's Breeding Herd. Bulls and semen from Owner's Breeding Herd may be used by Company on all cattle owned or managed by Company at no cost to Company.

10.   This Management Agreement shall be effective commencing the date of execution and shall continue for a period of seven years from said date, provided however, that this Agreement shall be renewed at then prevailing rates being charged new Herd owners and, otherwise, on the same terms and conditions for one additional seven-year period from and after such termination date unless either party notifies the other, in writing prior to 90 days preceding the termination date, of its intent to terminate this Agreement. Notwithstanding the foregoing, Owner may at any time cancel this contract by 90 days' written notice to Company. Upon termination of this Agreement for any reason, all amounts owing to either party in

Exhibit 1B (*concluded*)

accordance with the terms of this Agreement shall be paid on the same basis as if the Agreement were continued to the end of the quarter following the quarter in which notice is given. Owner shall be responsible for the removal of the Livestock from the place or places in which they are maintained as of the effective date of the termination, and as of such date Company shall have no further responsibility in connection with such Livestock.

11. All notices required or permitted under the terms of this Agreement shall be delivered in person or by certified mail, postage prepaid, addressed as follows:

If to Company:

BEEFALO BREEDING COMPANY
R.R. 1
Pocahontas, Illinois 62275

If to Owner:

_____

_____

12. This Agreement shall be binding upon the parties hereto, their heirs, executors and administrators.

13. Any insurance with regard to the Livestock subject to this Agreement shall be paid by Owner, provided, however, the Company shall use its best efforts to secure such coverage as requested by Owner.

14. The obligations of Owner under this Agreement are secured by a Security Agreement of even date herewith, and a default hereunder shall constitute a default under the Security Agreement.

15. Company shall not be required to advance any sums on behalf of Owner, but if it does, Owner shall repay the same promptly on demand and repayment thereof shall be secured by the security interest in the Livestock.

16. Owner is fully aware of the speculative nature of purchasing and managing breeding cattle and represents that his or its financial circumstances are consistent with this investment and that he or it is a sophisticated investor and by reason of his or its business and financial experience, he or it has the capacity to protect his or its own interests in connection with his or its investment.

17. This Agreement constitutes the entire agreement of the parties hereto.

IN WITNESS WHEREOF, the parties hereto have set their hands on the date and year first above written.

OWNER(S)   BEEFALO BREEDING COMPANY

By _____   By _____

Exhibit 1C
Three-year cash investment

Purchase of 10 beefalo breeding heifers:		
Down payment..		$ 6,000.00
Management expense...............................		4,000.00
Interest (prepaid).....................................		810.00
Cash paid out 197_...................................		$10,810.00
Tax effect:		
Depreciation (seven-year life—half year)...............	$2,142.90	
Management expense...............................	4,000.00	
Interest expense.....................................	810.00	
Investment tax credit (10%)*.........................	3,000.00	
Total equivalent deductions..........................		$10,252.90
Second year:		
Management expense...............................	$4,000.00	
Interest expense.....................................	810.00	
Cash paid out 197_...................................		$ 4,810.00
Tax effect:		
Depreciation†..	$3,673.50	
Management expense...............................	4,000.00	
Interest expense.....................................	810.00	
Total deductions.....................................		$ 8,483.50
Third year:‡		
Management expense...............................		$ 7,000.00
Interest expense.....................................		810.00
		$ 7,810.00
Income (estimated sales $6,000 ÷ 50%)...............		3,000.00
Cash paid out 197_...................................		$ 4,810.00
Tax effect:		
Depreciation...	$2,623.90	
Management expense...............................	4,000.00	
Interest expense.....................................	810.00	
Total deductions.....................................		$ 7,633.90

    * Investment tax credit assumes a 50 percent tax bracket and a tax credit equivalent to $3,000 of standard deductions.
    † Balance of depreciation is $6,559.70.
    ‡ No direct cash investment after third year.

THE BEEFALO BARNS (FAST-FOOD) CONCEPT

Most of the conventional marketing alternatives available to Beefalo Breeding Company represent variations of the beef distribution system. The company is committed to breed and produce beefalo, but seeks a market outlet that preserves the identity of beefalo and provides a premium price. When asked if his proposed development

Exhibit 1D
Economic projection of seven-year program*

	Ordinary income	Capital gains	Total
Total sales	$90,000	$136,800	$226,800
Expenses:			
Cost of herd.	15,000		15,000
Management and marketing			
Original fees.	14,000		14,000
50 percent of sales	45,000	68,400	113,400
Interest	5,670		5,670
Total.	79,670	68,400	148,070
Net profit before taxes	10,330	68,400	78,730
Net tax liability (below)†.			17,345
Net aftertax profit			$ 61,385
Taxes:			
Net profit before tax	10,330	68,400	78,730
60 percent capital gains exclusion		41,040	41,040
Total taxable.	$10,330	$ 27,360	$ 37,690
Tax on above at 50 percent			18,845
Investment tax credit			1,500
Net tax libilitity (above)			$ 17,345

* Assumptions:
1. An expected 100 percent live calf crop in the first year and an 80 percent calf crop thereafter. That 50 percent are male and 50 percent are female and all females are bred and calve annually.
2. That the original herd increases to 126 head, the average price is $1,800 per head, and herd liquidation takes place at the end of seven years.
3. That 40 percent of sales is ordinary income and 60 percent is capital gains.
† For the purposes of this computation it has been assumed that the 50 percent management fee would be deducted against the proceeds to which it relates. Accordingly, a substantial portion ($68,400) has been deducted against capital gains income. Had this instead been reflected as an ordinary deduction, the net tax liability of $17,345 would have been a net refund of $3,175 or additional net aftertax profits of $20,520.
The analysis of economic benefits is based on assumptions concerning future events and present tax laws (which may be changed). Some assumptions may not occur which could have substantial effect. Therefore, the actual results obtained may vary considerably from the projections.

of a new fast-food chain was viewed as a means of controlling disposition of the end product, Schweiger responded:

No, I see the restaurant alternative as a completely separate program with beefalo and catalyst for a restaurant chain—for a franchised chain—as opposed to setting up one or two restaurants just to get into the restaurant business. The ultimate limitation with the restaurant concept is that it cannot enjoy the accelerated growth that potentially might be there because there simply are not the animals to support it. This year we wouldn't assemble more than 50,000 head of beefalo even if we contacted every breeder in the country. But we can put together a sufficient number of animals to supply six restaurants over the next 12–18 months.

The concept that Schweiger began exploring early in 1978 was to develop distinctiveness in fast foods through both product and building design. His idea was to extend the log home concept into a restaurant building structure constructed of Beaver logs. The menu would feature beefalo burgers in several sizes as a means of achieving product differentiation. The integration of the product and the structure would build promotion and furnishings around a western theme. Schweiger did not, however, foresee thrusting a marketing appeal to specific segments, such as the health-conscious consumer. He commented, "Anyone who stops at a fast-food restaurant is a market for us. We're not after only the teenage market, the older age market, the after-hours disco crowd, or anything like that." However, he later noted that the health aspects of beefalo might be a major selling point. "This is the message we want to get to the American people. If you're going to eat red meat, then why not eat something that's good for you."

To identify his project, Schweiger initially used the name Beefalo Inns, then changed that to Beefalo Barns. He spoke of the need to approach the naming of the restaurant from a scientific view but suggested that tentatively the barn concept captured the architectural style with its gabled roof atop the log structure. He was further thinking about freeway locations for the first Beefalo Barns in order to quickly expose people to the idea. "If we use freeway locations, people are adventuresome, so they're going to try it. The type of building housing our restaurant is a totally new concept in fast-food buildings. We also have a meat product that probably 99 percent of the American public still have not tasted. But it is being more widely known and advertised every day."

The principal feature of Beefalo Barns would be a variety of burgers. Schweiger would prefer to use all fresh meat, to achieve further product distinctiveness similar to Wendy's. He would use the Burger Chef concept of a condiment bar to allow customers to add what they like. Steaks might possibly be offered; if so, the selections probably would be a 6-ounce ground beefalo steak and an 8-ounce rib eye. Prices would be competitive, but probably 10 percent over McDonald's or Burger Chef. "Basically what we want to shoot for is a $1.70 average ticket covering patties, fries, drink, and apple turnover."

Schweiger estimated that at least two restaurants would be necessary to test the feasibility of continued expansion. Although the first facility probably would be wholly owned, he projected moving quickly to joint venturing or franchising. "I would see getting into the fast-food business as a vehicle for a national franchise. To me, who needs the hassle of operating simply one restaurant?" Six facilities were seen as a feasible target for the first year, with additional facilities limited only by the number of animals available for slaughter. He thought that one way of assuring adequate meat supply would be to involve other breeders as limited partners, stockholders, or franchisees. Schweiger noted that there were approximately 50 beefalo breeders in Kentucky and Tennessee, so that might be a natural area in which to expand. Nationally, there are breeders in the 48 continental states. (Two pages of a 10-page proposal circulated to interested breeders and parties are reproduced as Exhibits 2A and 2B, which include the introduction and pro forma income statement.)

Exhibit 2A
Sample pages of Beefalo Barn proposal

Introduction

Beefalo Barns offers a new and exciting approach to the fast-food industry. The serving of beefalo exclusively in the atmosphere of early American log buildings offers a unique dining experience for the consumer.

The format of the Beefalo Barns will combine the features of several fast-food-type restaurants and will offer both eat-in and carry-out service.

The success of the so-called fast-food industry and the forecast for future growth are a phenomenon in the business world. When one considers that in 1960, just 18 years ago, there were virtually no fast-food chains, it is difficult to realize the tremendous impact these outlets have had and the amount of the consumers' food dollar that is going into their cash registers.

Most people are familiar with the golden arch of McDonald's or the goatee of Colonel Sanders, but few realize the true magnitude of their operations. McDonald's alone uses the hamburger from 20,000 head of cattle per week; Kentucky Fried Chicken uses about 7 percent of our total poultry production; and these are but two of a long and growing list of chains—Wendy's, A&W, French's, Taco Bell, Zantigo, Burger Chef, Dairy Queen, Burger King, Pizza Hut, etc.

Combined annual sales of the fast-food industry today exceed $20 billion and represent about 35 percent of all food dollars.

We at Beefalo Barns strongly believe that there is room for one more, one that is built around a new meat called beefalo. We hope that as you evaluate the balance of the material in this brochure that you will come to the same conclusion and will join with us in this new venture.

During 1978 Schweiger entered into negotiations with property holders of several potential sites. (See map in Exhibit 3.) One site was at the Pocahontas exit off I–70, about two miles from the KSM sales office and the Korte farm. Preliminary studies indicated a year-round average traffic count under the interstate overpass at 11,000 cars per day in 1976, with a summer average of 13,900. The exit traffic (coming off the interstate) was 4,000 cars per day, of which 20 percent was considered to be local traffic. The year-round passenger count per vehicle was 1.7, while during the months of May through September it was 2.5. Based on these figures, Schweiger calculated that roughly

Exhibit 2B

BEEFALO BARN
Pro Forma Income and Expense
($000)

	%		%		%	
Gross sales	100%	$200,000		$300,000		$400,000
Food costs	32	64,000		96,000		128,000
Gross profit	68	136,000		204,000		272,000
Operating expenses:						
Labor	22.0%	44,000	21.0%	63,000	20.0%	80,000
Employee taxes, benefits	3.0	6,000	3.0	9,000	3.0	12,000
Paper goods	4.0	8,000	4.0	12,000	4.0	16,000
Utilities	2.0	4,000	2.2	6,600	2.5	10,000
Laundry	.5	1,000	.6	1,800	.7	2,800
Advertising	1.5	3,000	1.8	5,400	2.0	8,000
Office supplies	.3	600	.4	1,200	.5	2,000
Telephone	.6	1,200	.6	1,800	.6	2,400
Legal and accounting	.5	1,000	.8	2,400	.7	2,800
Insurance	1.5	3,000	1.5	4,500	1.5	6,000
Maintenance and repairs	1.0	2,000	1.0	3,000	1.0	4,000
Miscellaneous	1.0	2,000	1.0	3,000	1.0	4,000
Total operating expenses	38.4	75,000	37.9	113,700	37.5	160,000
Fixed costs:						
Land and building		16,000		16,000		16,000
Equipment and fixtures		14,000		14,000		14,000
Total fixed costs	15.0	30,000	10.0	30,000	7.5	30,000
Total costs	85.4	169,000	79.9	239,700	77.0	318,000
Net income	14.6%	$ 31,000	20.1%	$ 60,300	23.0%	$ 82,000

Note: Land and building costs can vary substantially from unit to unit. Equipment and fixtures are assuming five-year lease.

3,700 persons per day might be looking for food or other services such as gasoline. He commented: "If we can tap 15 percent of the potential traffic May through September, we can pay all of our bills, gross $150,000, and lock up the place for six months if need be [the non-tourist season]."

Negotiations were entered into for a second site, also adjacent to I–70, but several miles to the west at the Illinois 143 exit. This property is owned by King Oil Company, which operates a truck stop at the off-ramp location (the only commercial establishment at the exit). The oil company tentatively would be willing to construct the building with site improvements (exclusive of interior equipment) and lease the facility to Beefalo Barns for a 10 percent return to King (lease payments estimated $6,000–7,000 annually). Schweiger thought such terms to be advantageous:

I don't see how we can go wrong in putting in the equipment and opening this location because it certainly reduces the sales volume necessary to meet the lease obligation. The other advantage obviously is that it eliminates a lot of front-end cash requirements on our part. Where

Exhibit 3
Proposed Beefalo Barn locations

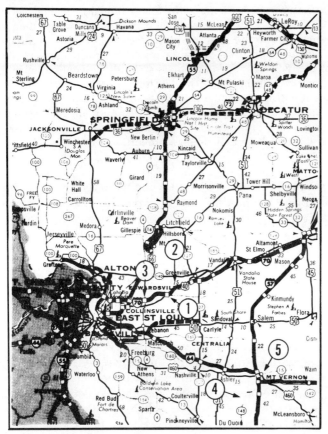

we were nominally looking at probably $60,000–100,000 cash up front, we are probably looking at $25,000–40,000 maximum with this type of arrangement. As a pilot program, obviously the lower you can keep your cash requirement, the better off you are going to be.

The King Oil site probably would be operated year-round because of the steady flow of trucks and cars that normally stop for refueling. Among other sites where investor contact had been made was one in conjunction with a sports complex at Rend Lake (seasonal resort area) and a downtown location in Mt. Vernon (year-round). Schweiger indicated that a group of Illinois and St. Louis investors had expressed an interest in owning the Beefalo Barn at the Mt. Vernon site:

> Tentatively we would set up ownership on a limited partnership basis, and we [Beefalo Barns, Inc.] would be the general partners. We would probably establish 50 units at $2,100 per unit, with a two-unit

minimum to comply with Illinois security statutes of limiting the partnership to 25 or fewer investors. Of the $105,000 we would raise, $100,000 would be applied to the partnership capital account and $5,000 would cover organizational expenses. We would then as a partnership acquire the land, build the facility, lease the equipment, and provide the operating capital. With such an arrangement, we would probably go in as general partners at 30–40 percent participation, with no capital contributions. The limited partners would pick up 60–70 percent with their capital contribution. As general partners, we would not participate in any partnership profits until all limited partners had received back their capital contributions. Once they have 100 percent return, then we participate on a proportional basis.

Management believes it would be unable to require large franchise fees, should this be the direction of expansion. In the absence of an established record, it is considering not charging a franchise fee per se but charging a predetermined fee based on franchise performance. A tentative front-end fee of $5,000 was discussed to cover Beefalo Barn's expenses for assistance in site location, building design, equipment lineup, etc. The franchisee would have the total obligation for purchasing equipment, land, and building. Beefalo Barns would then charge a royalty fee based on dollar sales of beefalo purchased through the parent firm.

The Beefalo Barn restaurant would use a 36-foot by 48-foot Beaver log building, with seating capacity for 66 people (see Exhibit 4). Decor would be in a western motif, with wooden tables, wagon wheel light fixtures, cattle brand displays, etc. Service equipment would use standard models (not customized), with a gas-fired fry grill used for cooking. Schweiger anticipated relying heavily on experienced managers (or formally trained food service managers from one of the special schools in Dallas, Las Vegas, or Purdue) for operation of the restaurants. Some standards would be established regarding personnel, sanitation, and food storage/preparation. But largely, individual restaurant managers would have responsibility and authority to manage their operation in response to local conditions. For example, deciding whether to open for breakfast and the specification of breakfast menu items would be the manager's prerogative.

Schweiger emphasized that quality control was the primary factor on which success was dependent:

> To me, the most critical factor in the whole thing is the movement of meat from the feedlot, through the slaughterhouse, to the retail outlet. To start out, we're only going to have one to three stores and we're going to be starting from scratch. So we've got two things to worry about initially—to control the quality of that meat and keep spoilage down, and yet to maintain adequate supplies at the restaurant, because the last thing you need to do is to run out.

Exhibit 4
Beefalo Barn restaurant layout (seating = 66)

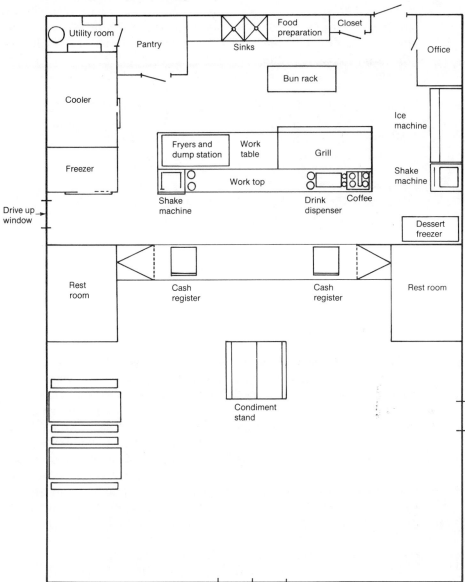

THE FUTURE

By early 1979, the future direction for KSM and Beefalo Breeding Company remained uncertain. During mid-1978, the Beefalo Barns idea was very central to the thinking of Schweiger. It presented not only an outlet for beefalo in which maximum value could be added to the product but also an opportunity to branch out into another business. Six months later, however, no commitments had been made to start the first restaurant. In the interim, Schweiger had been closely involved with a group of investors in southern California who were considering not only the tax-sheltering possibilities of beefalo but who also expressed interest in the concept of marketing beefalo through restaurants (tentatively located in either California or Colorado). This group could assemble a multimillion-dollar capital investment fund with 72 hours. Their major reservation to date about starting a restaurant chain was concern over the availability of a guaranteed supply of beefalo. They estimated that at least 1,000 cows producing calves for meat would be necessary to sustain the scale of operations that this group felt necessary to make a major investment attractive.

In the first year in which beefalo were available for meat production, about $50,000 was generated through red meat sales. The most recent sale involved 4,200 pounds of ground beefalo to an Oklahoma public school system for institutional feeding (cafeterias). By February 1979, Beefalo Breeding Company was caring for approximately 500 head of beefalo, about two thirds of which involved herd management contracts for outside investors. Seventy-five head had recently arrived at the Missouri ranch from a prominent California beefalo producer. It was expected that a management contract for a 250-head herd would be finalized within 60 days. In anticipation of herd expansion, on February 15 Schweiger was meeting with representatives of property east of Jefferson City, Missouri, to work out terms for a 15-year lease of 600–880 acres of pastureland capable of supporting 400 head.

Schweiger continued to feel himself stretched thin in terms of being able to devote ample time to his various programs. Much of his time was involved in negotiating and in attempting to interest various individuals and groups in one or more facets of his existing or proposed businesses. He talked at one time of taking on an assistant, but finding a relatively young person who could function as a jack-of-all-trades with high tolerance for uncertainty was difficult. Hiring such a person at this time also was complicated by limited cash flow, since herd buildup required keeping cows out of the marketing stream for breeding purposes.

In discussing his dilemma with a class of MBA students, Schweiger remarked:

> I'm not reasonably sure at this time which of our business activities ought to be emphasized. Which way do I go? Should I spend most of my time raising capital for buying beefalo herds and in finding high-paying outlets for carcass beefalo? If so, what would be my best approach to marketing? What do I do with Beefalo Barns idea, or with Beaver Homes? What are the trade-offs and payoffs? I'm open to your suggestions?

Case 2–4

TransEra, Inc.

COMPANY HISTORY

In December 1976 a Tektronix salesman in the western United States approached Ronald Wilson about the possibility of developing a floppy disk compatible with the Tektronix 4051 graphic system. Because of the high demand for such a product and the apparent potential for long-range sales, it was decided to take on the project. A partnership was organized for this purpose, the original partners being Ronald Wilson, Ralph Wilson, and another person who was a recent physics graduate. After some initial development efforts, it was found to be no longer profitable to continue development since Tektronix had begun manufacturing a disk of its own.

During this same time, Dr. Dennis Leavitt, a medical physicist, had developed some programs on the 4051 for calculating dose levels in radiation therapy. After finishing the programs, he found that they were much too slow. To increase the calculation speed, he asked Tektronix for help in developing machine code versions of his BASIC language programs. This project was referred to the three partners. In the course of converting the BASIC programs to machine-coded routines, it was discovered that the Read Only Memory (ROM) interface necessary for implementing machine code was a powerful way to implement a variety of special-purpose routines and interfaces requiring high speed and direct processor control.

After the partnership began work on the ROM interface, it was dissolved and TransEra Corporation was formed on July 1, 1977. The name "TransEra" came from the words *trans* and *era* to give a meaning of "spanning the ages," which became one of the corporate objectives. The name was also intended to be identified with the word *transistor* to help in associating the company with its electronic emphasis.

Besides continuing support of the radiation therapy project, the corporation began developing a line of products based on the ROM pack interface. The first product developed was a real time clock. After this came the development of some products for the data acquisition market. These included analog to digital converters and a digital to analog converter. The principal buyers of these products were government, industry, and university institutions. In addition to a general product line, several specialized ROM packs were developed for such customers as the Navy, which purchased a large number of the Tektronix computers for installation in ships.

PERSONNEL

TransEra's staff in 1980 consisted principally of members of two families, the Wilsons and the Waites. The third original partner left TransEra in 1978, after negotiating a sale of his one-third stock ownership to the company for $20,000 ($2,000 cash and a note for $18,000). Some differences of opinion about management had arisen between him and the Wilson brothers, whom he saw as bright, creative and hardworking but spread too thin and in need of some business help.

Ronald Wilson, the president of TransEra, graduated from college in April 1977 with a degree in electrical engineering. He specialized in solid-state electronics. During his undergraduate years he was employed at Megadiamond Corporation, where he designed and developed electronic control systems for its synthetic diamond process. After graduation he had a part-time university position as research associate. In this capacity he was responsible for designing the electronic controls and diagnostics for the Topolotron project in the fusion reactor field. He also completed his thesis work on a solar energy cell for a master's degree in electrical engineering in 1979. His expertise in electronic hardware design was considered a valuable asset to TransEra.

Ralph Wilson graduated from college in April 1977 with a degree in electrical engineering, having specialized in computers and digital electronics. He was instrumental in developing the ROM programs, which were a part of every product manufactured by TransEra. Because of his general involvement with each of the products, he assumed the role of product manager.

Roger Wilson, a younger brother of Ron and Ralph, joined TransEra in 1979 as business manager after graduating from college in finance. Barbara and Elaine Wilson, sisters of the three Wilson brothers, also worked at TransEra. Barbara was a full-time secretary-receptionist, and Elaine worked part time with Barbara while attending college. All five members of the Wilson family lived together in a house they owned near TransEra. Their parents lived in another city.

Randy Waite, vice president of TransEra, graduated from college in April 1975. His specialty was in communications circuits. He spent the next two years working on a master's degree before accepting a position with Hewlett-Packard in Colorado. After one year of experience there, he returned to TransEra.

Bill Waite joined TransEra in 1979 as controller after graduating

Exhibit 2
652–ADC, 752–ADC

12-bit 16-channel data acquisition system—Analog to digital converter ROM pack compatible with 4050 series graphic system.

Whether you use the Model 652–ADC with the 4051 or the Model 752–ADC with the 4052, the resulting combination provides unequaled data acquisition, analysis, and display capabilities.

The direct analog input feature provided by the A/D ROM pack transforms the 4050 graphic system into a powerful new tool with applications ranging from monitoring medical instruments to digitizing music or speech.

This data acquisition system will be at home in the laboratory or the classroom. The scientist as well as the student will find it a friendly system to work with.

Data acquisition has never been so easy. the TransEra A/D ROM pack combines fast machine-coded ROM programs with analog to digital converter circuitry in one small package that outperforms other larger, more expensive, and hard-to-use data acquisition devices. The A/D ROM pack also overcomes the problem of getting the data into the computer with its direct memory access capability. The data is always ready for analysis or display.

You can get into the exciting "real world" of analog signal processing with the TransEra A/D converter ROM pack.

A/D ROM pack features

Completely self-contained—just plug in.
12 powerful ROM routines for data gathering, conversion, and display.
High speed: 32,000 samples/second.
High resolution: 12 or 8 bits.
Direct memory access.
True differential inputs.
Auto ranging and averaging.
Auto scanning.
Automatic conversion to engineering units.

A/D ROM pack applications

Data acquisition.
Physiological readings.
Digitize speech and music.
Monitor temperature, pressure, etc.
Laboratory testing.
Shock and environmental testing.
Industrial controls.
Signal analysis.
Digitize photo detector signals.
Data logging.

Exhibit 3

Micro Disk—8-inch Winchester-type hard disk compatible with 4050 graphic system

Fed up with tapes and flexible disks? The TransEra Micro Disk will end your mass storage problems for good. No more clutter of tapes and discettes. No more lost programs and data files. The Micro Disk in its 10-megabyte version is the equivalent of over 35 tapes and over 17 discettes in storage capacity and yet takes up less room than a flexible disk drive.

Put it all together in one package. No more fumbling for the right floppy or tape. With named files and multiple library levels you can end the headaches of finding the right tape and remembering where you saved the program or data file you need now. From the time you power up you have instant access to all program and data files. The high-speed seek and transfer rates will leave you no time for thumb-twiddling.

The Micro Disk has its own real time clock to keep you up-to-date on when files were last accessed. This is a feature that will be appreciated in many ways.

The Micro Disk has its own intelligent controller that takes care of all data formatting and transfer protocol. A high-level command structure has also been provided that makes programming easy for the novice as well as flexible for the experienced programmer.

Don't miss out on the most powerful accessory yet offered for the 4050 graphic system. The TransEra Micro Disk will put you at the top in interactive computing capabilities.

Hard disk features

10–40 megabyte capacity.
Write protectable surfaces.
20K byte/second transfer rate via ROM pack interface.
High-level disk operating system.
Named files.
Multilevel library.
Dynamic file expansion.
Real time clock.
Daisy chain up to 16 drives.
Compact size and lowest cost/bit.
Optionally supports up to four computer systems.

Custom product work (not shown on the price list) made up about one third of TransEra's business. TransEra engineers liked to do custom work because of the challenges involved. Although they realized it was not especially profitable, they believed it would enhance their skill and reputation.

Pricing was generally done on a rough rule of thumb of a selling price of three times materials costs and direct labor. Since most of TransEra's products were made by no one else, there was no market price to use for a comparison. Tektronix had come out with a real time clock and had priced it the same as TransEra's at $500.

FINANCIAL MATTERS

TransEra showed a loss of $5,082 in 1977 (its first year), a profit of $31,155 in 1978, and a loss of $10,950 in 1979 (see Exhibit 4). There would have been a profit in 1979 except for the stock repurchase, which was expensed to salaries.

Exhibit 4

TRANSERA CORPORATION
Condensed Comparative Income Statements
For the Years Ended December 31

	1979	1978	1977
Revenue:			
Sales	$163,337	$99,465	$ 7,790
Less sales discounts	274	270	—
Net sales	163,063	99,195	7,790
Cost of goods sold	80,236	31,930	6,558
Gross profit on sales	82,827	67,265	1,232
Operating expenses:			
Selling	5,553	111	285
General and administrative	75,701	26,196	3,460
Depreciation	9,840	4,026	2,080
Total operating expenses	91,094	30,333	5,825
Income from operations	(8,266)	36,932	(4,593)
Other income:			
Interest revenue	133	—	—
Other expenses:			
Interest expense	2,817	1,225	489
Income from continuing operations before income taxes	(10,950)	35,707	(5,082)
Income tax	—	4,552	—
Net income	$ (10,950)	$31,155	$(5,082)

Current assets consisted mostly of accounts receivable. TransEra did not carry a large inventory of parts or supplies. Payables were reasonably current. The majority of loans (see Exhibit 5) had been obtained from Robert Wilson and Willis Waite (father of Randy and Bill Waite).

Expenses were kept relatively low for a small company by means of low compensation for the Wilsons and the Waites, who took out salaries of only about one fourth of the amounts they could expect to get if working for another company. They were able to live on such modest pay because of their family living arrangements. It was their intent to raise salaries to a competitive level and to distribute bonuses as soon

Exhibit 5

TRANSERA CORPORATION
Condensed Comparative Balance Sheet
December 31

	1979	1978	1977
Assets			
Current assets............................	$ 64,626	$47,030	$ 4,953
Funds and investments	3,260	250	—
Fixed assets—tangible (net) .:..............	35,353	10,835	5,144
Fixed assets—intangible (net)	174	240	306
Total assets..............................	103,413	58,355	10,403
Liabilities			
Current liabilities	36,237	20,311	3,130
Long-term liabilities:			
Thrift leasing, 18%	3,342		
Robert Wilson, 12%	7,402	9,522	9,410
Robert Wilson, 14%	4,000		
Willis Waite, 14%	10,000		
Beau Vest Financial, 12%	9,202		
Stock repurchase note, 10%................	18,000	—	—
IBM.....................................	309	651	—
Total long-term liabilities	52,255	10,173	9,410
Total liabilities............................	88,492	30,484	12,540
Owners' Equity			
Common stock............................	3,000	3,000	3,000
Treasury stock	(2,000)	—	—
Retained earnings	13,921	24,871	(5,137)
Total owners' equity......................	14,921	27,871	(2,137)
Total liabilities and owners' equity..............	$103,413	$58,355	$10,403

as profits and cash flow would permit. Ronald Wilson planned to get married and establish his own home later in the spring of 1980, so his salary would have to be increased at that time. The wages paid to the part-time help were competitive with other hourly rates for similar work and amounted to about half of the total payroll.

Sales for 1980 had been projected at $480,000, not including disk sales, with profits before taxes (and before any salary increases) estimated by Bill Waite at 35 percent of sales. Actual sales for the first three months of 1980 were $92,811, and Bill and others anticipated an increasing rate of sales later in the year in response to some product demonstration meetings. Order backlog on April 1, 1980, was about $45,000 plus one disk.

MARKETING

Most of TransEra's sales came through Tektronix salesmen, who often could improve a customer's use of Tektronix equipment by means of a TransEra product. As TransEra's reputation for quality and performance was spread by word of mouth, some orders and inquiries came directly, especially for custom work.

Some larger potential sales opportunities, such as government contracts, were brought to TransEra's attention by Tektronix salesmen, and then Ronald or Ralph Wilson would follow up on the lead. There was no one person at TransEra responsible specifically for marketing. Advertising had been limited to the mailing of brochures. However, disk and other product demonstration meetings in large U.S. cities were planned to begin in the summer of 1980.

Inquiries to represent TransEra had been received from firms in several foreign countries. Replies to these inquiries were usually handled by Bill Waite, the controller. Exclusive representation agreements had been signed with a man in the Netherlands and a firm in South Africa. The agreements had been drafted by Bill Waite, following the pattern of some other legal contracts he had seen.

Potential orders requiring any kind of technical relationship with a customer were often handled by Ralph Wilson. Routine customer questions were usually answered by Bill Waite or Barbara Wilson. Bill also did most of the purchasing of parts and supplies. TransEra's manufacturing consisted of assembly of component parts which were purchased from a variety of sources in the electronics industry.

OBJECTIVES AND CONCERNS

In the back of the minds of Ron and Ralph Wilson was a desire to build TransEra to a resource level where it could engage in more advanced technology. One prominent mathematician who had done some work with them saw Ron Wilson as having a potential like that of Seymour Cray, a renowned designer and manufacturer of supercomputers. Ralph expressed the idea that they could make a very good living working for someone else if they wanted to, so he did not feel that just making a living was the reason they were in business.

Although the Wilson brothers felt an inclination to control their own business, they were concerned about how to manage the growth of the company. Ron and Ralph especially wanted to spend a lot of time with the technical side of the business—but without giving up the management.

Roger Wilson saw problems in growth, facilities, the need for more people, and possibly the need for more capital. If the new disk really got moving in the marketplace, as was hoped and expected, it could bring some rapid growth to TransEra. Existing office and laboratory space of 3,000 square feet in a new suburban professional plaza was adequate for the present volume of sales and research. TransEra held a five-year lease on its facilities and had been in them less than a year, after operating from inception in the Wilsons' garage and house. It was estimated that up to about 50 disks per month could be assembled in the present facilities, allowing also for storage of components and finished units awaiting testing and shipping. Beyond that number, larger facilities would be required, although Ron Wilson believed that TransEra would prefer to keep the offices in the present building during the term of the lease. Plant space in the vicinity of TransEra's office was fairly abundant at reasonable cost. But it would take time to locate, lease, and set it up if needed. Who would do it? More people would also be needed, but TransEra did not yet have the cash flow even to pay its present full-time staff competitive salaries. The company was beginning to establish a sound credit rating, however, and was negotiating for an operating line of credit for at least $40,000 at a local bank.

Ralph Wilson believed that there were about 8,000 Tektronix 4050 series systems in use and that the number might rise to about 10,000 by the time Tektronix came out with the new 4060 line planned for market sometime in 1981. Each user of a Tektronix 4050 series was considered to be a potential customer of a TransEra disk. Tektronix had given TransEra access to its 4050 series documentation, which enabled TransEra to build its ROM packs and disk, but Ralph did not know whether he could get the same information for the 4060 series. He and Ron had learned that Tektronix was doing some developmental work on a disk of its own, to relate primarily to its new 4060 line of graphic computers. Tektronix was a large company (see financial summary, Exhibit 6), and the Wilsons didn't think it would go into a new

Exhibit 6
Financial Summary of Tektronix, Inc.

	1979	*1978*	*1977*	*1976*	*1975*	*1974*
Sales ($000)	786,936	598,886	454,958	366,645	336,645	271,428
Assets ($000)	642,906	491,130	415,328	344,860	306,616	251,061
Net income ($000)	77,151	56,846	43,971	30,089	26,329	21,353
Equity ($000).	402,799	326,696	274,122	232,003	202,321	175,488
Long-term debt ($000).	67,800	40,900	42,800	38,600	29,800	600
Employees	21,291	19,147	14,637	12,970	12,664	12,693
Profit/sales (%).	9.8	9.5	9.7	8.2	7.8	7.9
Profit/equity (%).	19.2	17.4	16.0	13.0	13.0	12.2
Profit/capital (%)	16.7	16.0	14.4	11.7	11.7	12.1
Equity/assets (%)	63	67	66	67	66	70

Common stock: 18,257,000 shares, 7,305 shareholders, 87 percent of capital.
Source: SEC 10K Reports of Tektronix, Inc., Beaverton, Oregon.

product unless it saw a large market for it. There was a lot of software complexity which made it difficult to produce a good disk. Ralph saw the prospective Tektronix disk as being more generally adaptable than the specialized TransEra disk, but from the data he had on

Tektronix development he concluded that the latter's disk would be slower, substantially more expensive, and physically larger and heavier than TransEra's disk. Thus, he and Ron hoped that not only could TransEra look to the 4050 series market without significant interference from Tektronix's disk but that the TransEra disk could be further developed to interface with a majority of computer equipment in general. Other competitors made small, hard disks but focused on storage and low cost (some under $5,000), but Ralph described them as having far less software, speed, and flexibility than TransEra's disk. Hewlett-Packard and Texas Instruments had graphic computers with disk drives, but they were priced much higher than Tektronix equipment. Large disk drives produced by such industry leaders as IBM and Digital Equipment Corporation were even more expensive and not economically feasible for use with a small graphic computer such as Tektronix made. The Wilsons believed that TransEra's disk would offer much more for the money than any competing disk.

Ronald and Ralph Wilson were the sole stockholders of TransEra. Some stock had been promised to the Waite brothers to make up for their working for low pay with the Wilsons, but no amount or timing had been determined. Ron was introduced to a partner in a prominent law firm by a trusted family friend. After some initial discussion about the stock situation, a more general conversation about TransEra's entire situation ensued. The lawyer observed that TransEra could benefit from some management help.

Ron Wilson was interested in several lines of technology besides those in which TransEra was already engaged. One of the most promising, it seemed to him, was photovoltaic cells to produce electrical energy direct from solar radiation. Although TransEra presently had no capital to develop photovoltaic technology, Ron had a friend who worked in computer-controlled manufacturing in the aircraft industry in southern California. The two of them had in mind a new approach to photovoltaics which, with automated production, they believed could be more cost effective than the conventional photovoltaic methods—which were still very expensive. Industry publications indicated that R&D spending (both public and private) in the photovoltaic area would be around $200 million in 1980.

Could TransEra continue to bootstrap its own growth? Ron wondered. What should they do about the disk if demand were great when it was finished? How should they handle the problems of growth? Ron was also concerned about what kind of strategy to develop for TransEra.

Case 2–5 ———————————————————————

American Safety Razor Company

American Safety Razor Company's fight for survival was one of Virginia's biggest business news stories in 1977. Philip Morris, the parent company of American Safety Razor (ASR), had been seeking a buyer for the troubled subsidiary. However, sale was not easy because profits of ASR had declined each of the previous three years (see Exhibit 1). Philip Morris also insisted that prospective buyers guaran-

Exhibit 1

AMERICAN SAFETY RAZOR COMPANY
Five-Year Comparative Income Statement
($000)

	1973	1974	1975	1976	1977*
Net sales	$22,909	$26,089	$28,008	$27,917	$30,286
Royalties and other revenues . . .	24	27	94	75	51
Total operating revenues .	22,933	26,116	28,102	27,992	30,337
Less:					
Variable cost	8,768	9,692	9,924	9,965	11,225
Shipping expense	630	618	579	653	794
Fixed manufacturing	4,001	4,602	4,767	4,086	4,278
Available contribution margin . .	9,534	11,204	12,832	13,288	14,040
Operating expenses:					
Advertising	1,616	1,601	1,744	1,882	1,324
Sales force and promotion	4,503	5,571	7,451	8,070	8,462
Marketing research/marketing					
administration	379	449	453	417	346
General and administrative	1,290	1,320	1,720	1,397	1,479
Research and development	506	547	599	702	627
Total operating expenses .	8,294	9,488	11,967	12,468	12,238
Operating profit	1,240	1,716	865	820	1,802
Interest expense	0	0	0	0	0
Other expenses	245	432	24	118	723
Profit before taxes	$ 995	$ 1,284	$ 841	$ 702	$ 1,079

* Amounts projected prior to management purchase in September.

tee to retain all 870 ASR employees. The Bic Pen Company had agreed to buy ASR; however, the Federal Trade Commission blocked the sale and claimed that such an agreement would be in restraint of competition.

———————
This case was prepared by Joseph R. Mills, customer service manager of American Safety Razor Company, and Thomas M. Bertsch, associate professor of marketing at James Madison University. Confidential information has been disguised.

Since no other purchase offers were considered acceptable, Philip Morris decided to close ASR. Manpower was reduced drastically as part of Philip Morris' liquidation plan. In operations alone, one third of the work force was laid off. The national sales force was cut from 80 people to 30. Then, in September 1977, ASR's president, John R. Baker, and eight other company executives finalized an agreement to purchase ASR from Philip Morris. The executives paid $600,000 of their own money and $15 million which they had borrowed from two banks and a federal aid program.

COMPANY STRATEGY

Baker's initial marketing strategy after acquisition of ASR was to offer lower prices than Gillette and Schick and to expand ASR's share of the existing female market with the unique woman's razor, Flicker. From 1960 to 1976, ASR had focused on increased advertising expenditures, expansion of the sales force, greater consistency in product quality, competitive pricing, and development of new products. However, the new owners could not afford expensive, high-risk marketing strategies because of the financial strain of purchase and the need to pay off company debts that amounted to over $1 million a year in interest alone.

Baker expected ASR to "bounce back" and grow. He believed that ASR had an advantage over competition because the new owners were the company's managers and the existing work force was determined to succeed. However, management continued to search for ways to speed the improvement of company profits and market share.

COMPANY SALES COMPOSITION

As indicated in Exhibit 1, ASR's sales were approximately $28 million for the year prior to management purchase of the firm. Seventy percent of company sales were in the "wet shave" consumer market. Its own brands provided more than three fourths of the dollars obtained by ASR from that market segment.

Industrial products provided the next largest portion of ASR sales revenue. Twenty-seven percent of company business was in the industrial market segment. Sales growth since 1967 was attributed largely to the efforts of ASR to serve industrial consumers, regardless of how unique the product might be.

The surgical blade market segment accounted for less than 5 percent of ASR's sales. Although the demand was not large, surgical blade sales were consistent in volume.

The remainder of company sales revenue came from foreign markets. By 1977 ASR's international sales had almost reached $2 million. Shaving blade products accounted for approximately 60 percent of the sales dollars from exports, and industrial products accounted for the rest.

BLADE MARKETS

Domestic consumer market

In 1977 the U.S. "wet shave" market was estimated by the health and beauty aid industry to be $400 million per year at the retail level. That year, Gillette was holding 55 percent of the shaving blade market. Schick claimed 22 percent, and ASR held 11 percent. The remainder of the wet shave market was divided between Bic and Wilkinson.

Little market growth was expected for at least the next 10 years because of the slow rate of population growth. Opportunities were increasing in the women's market segment because teenage girls were shaving at an earlier age and more frequently than they did during the early 1970s. However, males were shaving less frequently. Beards were more widely accepted in the late 1970s than they were in the early 1970s, and the popularity of the "bearded" look had increased. Very few electric razor users switch to blades, so that market segment did not represent a significant area of possible growth for ASR. Firms in the blade industry expected most new domestic consumer business to come from either increasing market share of their company or opening up new markets.

Industrial blade market

The industrial blade market in the United States was estimated by industry leaders to be in the $40 million to $50 million range. ASR held about 20 percent of that market, which made it one of the largest manufacturers of industrial blades in the United States. Ardell Industries, Crescent Manufacturing, and Winsor Manufacturing had 10 percent, 5 percent, and 2 percent, respectively, of the industrial blade market. Exacto and Durham, which offered a limited product line, each had gross sales in the $5 million to $6 million range. Of the four major producers of shaving blades, only ASR competed in the industrial market.

Surgical market

The surgical blade market was estimated at only $6 million. Bard-Parker was the sales leader, with a 59 percent share of the market; ASR was a distant second, with 29 percent, followed by Beaver, with 8 percent. Proper, a foreign company that exports large quantities of blades to the United States, was next, with 2 percent of the market. The surgical blade market was very small compared to the wet shave consumer market.

International market

The sales potential of foreign wet shaving markets was estimated by one industry leader to be 10 times the actual dollar sales to the U.S. market. In 1977 Gillette accounted for between 80 and 90 percent of the foreign sales of U.S. blades. Schick, Wilkinson, and ASR also competed in the overseas market, but Gillette had taken the lead in teaching people to shave.

ASR has had mixed results from its efforts to penetrate foreign markets. The company had approximately half of the shaving blade market in Puerto Rico. However, high labor costs forced closing of its production facility in Scotland, and its efforts in Brazil to provide technical assistance for blade manufacturing did not meet expectations. Even though setbacks were encountered in several foreign markets, the new owners of ASR still believed that some international markets could be highly profitable for ASR.

PRODUCT STRATEGY

ASR offers over 500 different versions of packaged shaving, industrial, and surgical blade products. See Exhibit 2 for a list of product line changes made by ASR.

Products by Gillette have become the industry standards for comparison. Therefore, ASR's shaving blade products are judged against Gillette's products and are designed to meet those standards. However, ASR's shaving systems, such as Flicker and Double II, are designed to be distinctive in appearance.

Exhibit 2
Major product line changes of ASR

Year introduced	Product	Status as of 1977
1875	Star Safety Razor	Replaced with Gem Razor
1889	Gem Safety Razor	Continued, with modification
1915	Ever-Ready Shaving Brush	Continued
1919	Gem, Star, and Ever-Ready shaving blades	Continued
1933	Lightfoot soap	Discontinued in 1973
1934	Electric shaver	Discontinued in 1934
1935	Pile Wire-Carpet	Discontinued in 1977
1935	Surgical blades and handles	Continued
1947	Double-edge shaving blade	Continued
1948	Injector shaving blade	Continued
1963	Stainless steel coated blade	Continued
1969	Face Guard shaving blade	Continued
1970	Personna tungsten steel blades	Continued
1971	Flicker	Continued
1973	Personna Double II shaving system	Continued
1974	Personna Injector II blade	Continued
1975	Double Edge II	Discontinued in 1976
1975	Lady	Continued
1977	Single II shaving system	Continued

Typically, major competitors in the blade industry denied that they developed products in response to the introduction of a new product by a competitor. Company representatives usually stressed that they were responding to consumer needs, not actions of competitors. The industry practice, though, was for major producers to quickly follow a competitor's innovative product with a competing product. When Wilkinson introduced its stainless steel blade in the early 1960s, all major competitors followed with similar products. In 1969 Gillette introduced its Platinum Plus blade and competitors followed with versions of the platinum-chromium blade. Eighteen months after ASR introduced Flicker to the women's wet shaving market, Gillette introduced Daisy. The time between introduction of a new type of product and introduction of a similar product by a major competitor is now only 10 to 12 months.

New product introductions are one way for a firm to increase market share. However, a new, better shaving blade product may not gain much market share. This fact became painfully clear to ASR soon after the introduction of twin-blade systems in 1971. Gillette's introduction in this product category was the Trac II. Schick called its introduction Super II. ASR decided that it had one of three choices: make no introduction, make the same design as Gillette and offer it under a different name, or make a slightly different product. ASR's management decided it had to make an introduction because of the large market potential involved. The ASR version came out eight months later and was called Double II.

Since ASR was late in entering this new consumer market segment, management chose to try a modified twin-blade system. The new version was a double-edge bonded blade system, which offered twice as many shaves as the Trac II and Super II. The shaving system uniquely featured a gap between the bonded blades that permitted the cut hair to be washed away. With discounts offered, the consumer could buy the ASR system at the same price as Trac II. ASR's new product was a good one, according to consumer tests, but Double II did not pick up the 16 percent market share expected (see Exhibit 3).

The major marketing emphasis in the industry since the middle 1960s has been directed toward the marketing of "shaving systems"

Exhibit 3
Market performance of twin-blade systems

Product	Date of introduction	1971–1973 advertising ($ millions)	January 1974 share of total razor blade market	1973 sales ($ millions)
Trac II (Gillette)	1971	$117	23.2%	$10.9
Super II (Schick)	1972	4	6.3	2.5
Double II (ASR)	1973	3	1.3	0.6

versus razors and blades. One of the newest systems to be introduced is the disposable razor. Some market analysts estimated that the disposable razor category could build into a 20 percent segment of the estimated $400 million blade market. By 1978 Wilkinson and Schick had followed Bic and Gillette into the low-priced disposable razor market with their own versions of a disposable razor.

ASR offered industrial blades for the carpet industry, utility knife blades, and specialty blades for the food, textile and electronic industries. There was also an industrial line of injector, single-edge, and double-edge blades. The company had been able to convince its industrial customers that disposable blades mean a quality product and a reduction of machine downtime. The strategy of ASR was to find new industrial users for disposable blades, but the market was specialized, so customized orders were common.

ASR offers a full line of surgical blades and handles. Since competitors have not made any recent introduction of new products for this market, ASR has devoted its efforts to technological and quality improvements. Consistent processing effort is expended to improve the sharpness and durability of its surgical blades.

Although standard brand shaving blade products and industrial blades were sold in the international market, many products were especially prepared for each market. For instance, in South America many double-edge blades are sold one at a time; therefore, ASR individually wrapped and packaged each blade for that market. Package labels for Europe were printed in four languages: English, French, Portuguese, and German. In the Far East, a single-edge blade with an extra-thick back for easier handling was sold instead of the standard single-edge blade. Customized orders were accepted in the hope of building repeat business.

DISTRIBUTION STRATEGY

Most razors and razor blades in the United States were sold in retail groceries and drugstores. New retail accounts were solicited directly on the basis of their expected volume. ASR had decided to concentrate on large accounts. Therefore, it used distributors to serve small accounts, but it sold direct to large accounts. Much of the industry was dominated by large accounts, such as chain drugstores and supermarkets.

The company was hesitant to reject requests for dealer labels. Management felt that ASR could not compete unless its product offerings were in a dominant position on the shelf. This was particularly true of wholesalers and retailers, who were willing to push their own brand considerably more than a manufacturer's brand.

In general, demand for manufacturers' brands of blades was not growing significantly. However, ASR saw an opportunity to increase its market share in the dealer brand segment of the market. A product was considered eligible for dealer labels if it had at least 8 to 10 percent of the branded market. All dealer label accounts were handled by a small corporate department which performed the necessary marketing functions. ASR held 75 percent of this growing market segment.

ASR sold its surgical blades through a national hospital supply company, which acted as exclusive distributor for the blades. The distributor was permitted by contract to ship to any location in the world. The 1976 contract between the two firms also included renewal clauses.

ASR's industrial products were sold to both users and distributors. Brokers were used to sell less than 20 percent of the products. ASR's industrial sales force concentrated its efforts on the large-volume customers and distributors. Many of the direct customers were manufacturers in the electronics, textile, and food industries.

The International Marketing Division utilized distributors in most countries because ASR did not employ an international sales force. ASR preferred to sell to many distributors within a country in order to obtain wide distribution and to avoid dependence on a single distributor; however, many foreign distributors had exclusive selling rights in their country. The most active accounts were in Latin America, Canada, and Japan.

PRICING STRATEGY

ASR's prices for unique products, such as Flicker and single-edge blades, were competitive with the prices of other shaving products in the market. If a retailer did any local promotion of ASR's brands of products, then cooperative advertising was arranged. ASR's double-edge, injector, and Double II products were priced less to retailers than similar items offered by competitors.

ASR was the price leader for industrial blades. Since dealer promotions and national advertising were not used for industrial blades, this market segment was a consistent contributor to profitability.

The company's surgical products were priced low in relation to competition. The national distributor established the resale prices, and the wholesale prices were renegotiated annually.

ASR's products were sold in foreign wholesale markets for approximately one third less than they were sold for in the United States. Price quotes on export orders did not include shipping costs, although domestic prices included shipping charges.

PROMOTION STRATEGY

The amount spent by ASR on national advertising varied according to the newness of the product. Established products, such as single-edge blades, were not advertised. However, a product such as Flicker did receive attention. Flicker was both a relatively new product and one which was dominant in the market. Therefore, ASR allocated $1 million for promotion of its Flicker ladies' shaving system in 1977.

Razors and razor blades were typically marketed with large expenditures for promotion. Gillette, for example, spent $6 million on promoting its new Good News shaver in 1977. Gillette also planned to support its new Atra (automatic tracking razor) with a $7.7 million advertising campaign in 1977. Major competitors of ASR had spent large sums of money on consumer-directed advertising and promotion to maintain strong national brand preference.

The Bic Pen Company, which had been blocked from buying ASR, decided in 1976 to compete in the American branded blade market. It planned a large and expensive introductory marketing program for 1977, budgeting $9 million for sales and promotion of its single-blade, lightweight razor, which is completely disposable. Part of the promotional strategy was to give away a disposable razor and blade to 40 percent of the U.S. households.

Promotional methods used by major producers of blades included giveaways, rebates, cents-off programs, couponing, cooperative advertising with retailers, special displays, and volume discounts. The industry relied heavily on the use of TV advertising. However, several other advertising media were used, including full-page magazine ads and Sunday newspaper supplement ads.

MARKETING ORGANIZATION

Prior to the planned liquidation of ASR by Philip Morris, the marketing group consisted of brand managers, assistant brand managers, a marketing administrator, a single marketing researcher, and an assistant researcher. By 1978 the group had been reduced to the vice president of marketing, the director of product management, and the director of international marketing (see Exhibit 4). ASR's top management felt that the smaller marketing team could handle the reduced advertising budget and the target market segments.

Both the sales group and the marketing group were based in Staunton, Virginia. The vice president of sales reported to the company president. The directors of field sales, industrial products, and national accounts reported to the vice president of sales. Three field sales managers reported to the director of field sales. Twenty-four regional managers reported to the field sales managers. ASR had four selling divisions: Branded Products, Private Label Products, Industrial and Surgical Products, and International Marketing.

The sales force represented the only link between the company and large retail accounts, such as chain drugstores and supermarkets. Chain stores were very important since they represented the key strategic approach of the ASR shaving blade business. Each regional sales

Exhibit 4
Marketing-sales organization

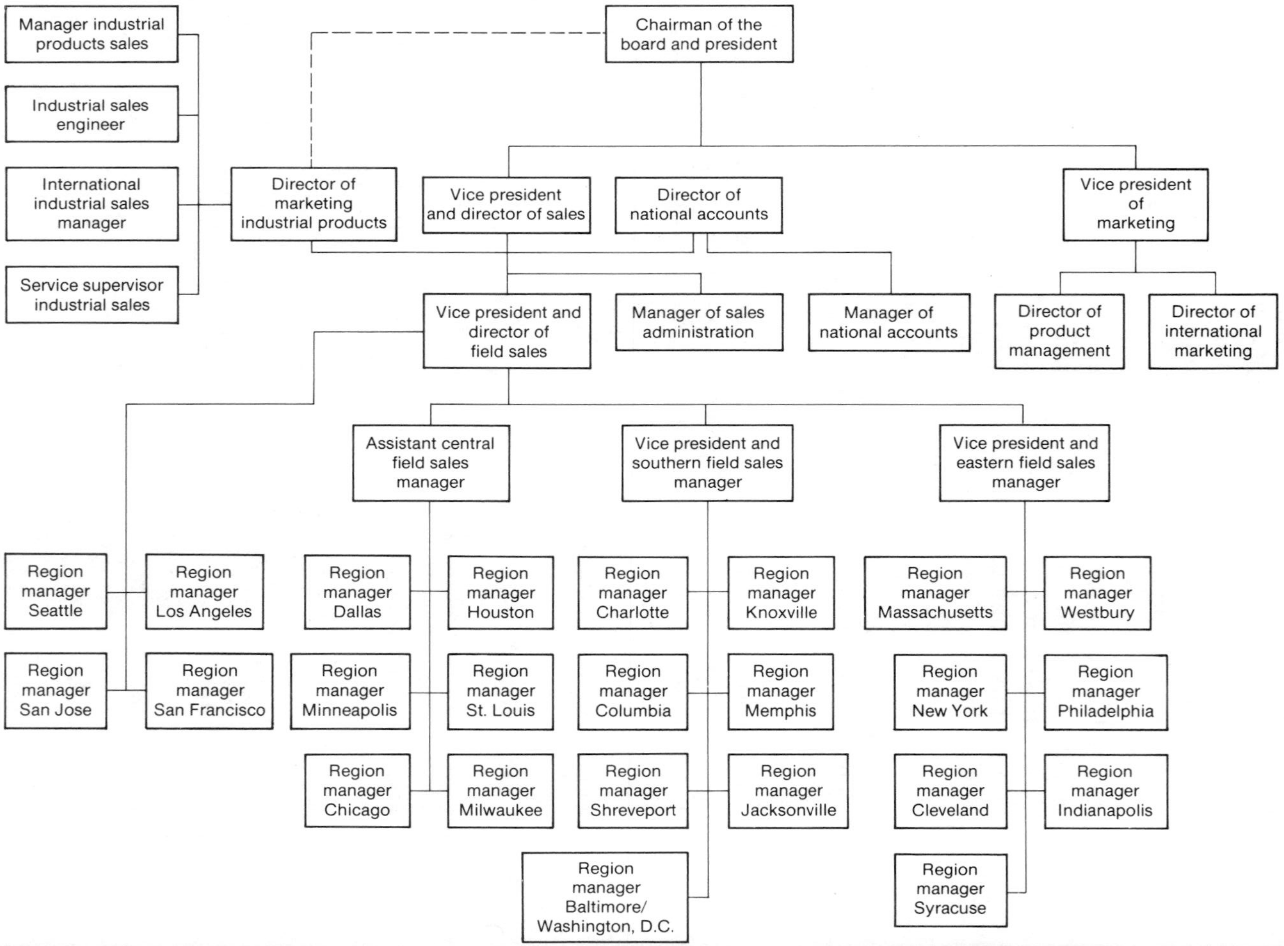

manager was expected to spend much of his time in developing sales to the big chains.

Until late 1974, ASR's field sales people received a compensation package composed of straight salary plus fringe benefits. Then, in 1975, an incentive system was introduced which included a monthly commission, a semiannual incentive for participation in company promotional programs, and annual compensation opportunities related to regional profitability. The new compensation package was introduced to help both the sales managers and the salespersons. By 1978 the sales managers felt that ASR was attracting better quality, experienced salespersons and that the sales personnel liked the new incentive rewards.

Case 2–6

Norton Company

Subject to the business cycle swings of the capital goods industry, Norton Company experienced the usual drop in sales during the economic downturn of 1975. What was unusual for Norton was its ability on this occasion to sustain profits compared to the customary plunge in earnings whenever the economy dipped. Robert Cushman, president and chief executive officer of Norton Company, saw this performance as evidence of the growing effectiveness of Norton's strategic planning.

As of 1976, five years' efforts had gone into developing planning activities that specifically could help top management shape strategies for the firm's diversified business operations. Mr. Cushman was pleased with the results of these efforts:

> Our strategic planning has made a tremendous difference in the way the company is now managed. It gives us a much-needed handle to evaluate strategies for each of our many businesses.

One of the difficult strategic planning decisions faced by top management in 1976 concerned a reevaluation of the long-term strategy for the coated abrasives business operations in the United States. This situation is described following a general explanation of the strategic planning process at Norton Company and how it came to be.

This case was prepared by Professor Francis Aguilar with the assistance of Norton Company to serve as a basis for class discussion rather than to illustrate either effective or ineffective handling of an administrative situation. Copyright © 1979 by the President and Fellows of Harvard College.

The company

Norton Company, headquartered in Worcester, Massachusetts, was a multinational industrial manufacturer with 85 plant locations in 21 countries. The firm employed almost 19,000 persons.

As the world's largest abrasives manufacturer, Norton produced both abrasive grain raw materials and finished products. The latter included such items as sandpaper and grinding wheels. The company also produced a wide range of other industrial products, including industrial ceramics, sealants, catalyst carriers and tower packings for the chemical process industries, engineered plastic components, tubing and related products for medical applications and for food processing, and industrial safety products. In 1975, these other products accounted for about 27 percent of the reported total sales of $548 million.[1] Exhibit 1 contains a five-year summary of financial results.

Organization

Norton Company was organized into "low growth" and "high growth" product groups. This organizational structure reflected two basic corporate objectives. The first was to remain the worldwide leader in abrasives. The second was to improve profitability through "a limited number of diversified product lines and without conglomeration."[2]

When introducing this structure in 1971, Cushman had remarked:

> As you look at Norton Co. you see two major areas of business: our traditional abrasives products, which are good-cash generators but have low growth, and our newer nonabrasive lines, which need cash but have high growth potential. We need a different type of manager to run each area.

Harry Duane, age 45, headed the abrasives group. His job was characterized as that of "running a large, cyclical-prone, slow-growth business with stiff competition in many different markets." Successful performance in this business was said to depend on careful cost control, keeping products up to date, and holding established markets. Duane had had experience in the abrasives business abroad as well as in the United States since joining Norton in 1957.

---

[1] On September 9, 1976, Norton Company announced an agreement in principle to merge with Christensen, Inc., for stock valued at $100 million. Christensen, with 1975 sales of $118 million and net income of $9.5 million, manufactured diamond-drilling bits and coring bits for the petroleum and mining industries. With Christensen, nonabrasive products would account for about 40 percent of total sales.

[2] The *Norton Company Annual Report* for 1975 also highlighted three other corporate objectives: (1) to maintain responsible corporate citizenship, which at times means accepting lower profits; (2) to maintain a superior employee working environment; and (3) to enhance the value of Norton stock.

[3] *Business Week*, August 7, 1971, p. 80. Reprinted by special permission. © 1971 by McGraw-Hill, Inc., New York, N.Y. 10020. All rights reserved.

Exhibit 1

NORTON COMPANY
Five-Year Financial Summary
($ millions)

	1971	*1972*	*1973*	*1974*	*1975*
Net sales	346	374	475	558	548
Net income*...........................	11.4	14.5	25.4	21.6	20.9
Net income, excluding effect of foreign currency exchange rate changes*......	10.3	15.0	21.3	25.1	24.8
By line of business:					
Abrasives					
Sales (%).........................	70	75	75	75	73
Net income (%)	85	87	89	76	70
Diversified products					
Sales (%).........................	30	25	25	25	27
Net income (%)	15	13	11	24	30
By subsidiaries outside the United States:					
Sales (%)	41	41	42	45	49
Net income (%)	39	33	56	56	40
Working capital.......................	148	151	155	159	200
Total debt...........................	69	65	66	102	112
Shareholders' equity..................	211	218	232	244	255
Operating and financial ratios:					
Net income as percentage of sales.......	3.3	3.9	5.3	3.9	3.8
Net income as percentage of equity......	5.4	6.7	10.9	8.8	8.2
Current ratio	3.7	3.6	2.9	2.3	3.3
Percent total debt to equity............	33	30	29	42	44
Per share statistics†					
Net income*.........................	2.12	2.70	4.70	4.02	3.85
Net income, excluding effect of foreign currency exchange rate changes*....	1.92	2.80	3.94	4.68	4.57
Dividends...........................	1.50	1.50	1.50	1.575	1.70
Stock price (NYSE)..................	27–37	32–39	23–36	19–29	21–29

* Exchange gains and losses resulting from the translation of foreign currency financial statements were included for the first time in the 1975 annual report in determining net income in accordance with a new procedure recommended by the Financial Accounting Standards Board (FASB). The net income results excluding foreign currency effects conform to prior reporting practices at Norton and generally throughout industry.

† The average number of shares of common stock outstanding varied between 5.37 million and 5.67 million during this period.

Source: Annual reports and *Moody's Industrial Manual*, 1975.

Donald R. Melville, age 50, headed Norton's diversified products business group. He had joined the company in 1967 as vice president of marketing after having served in various marketing capacities with Continental Can Company, Scott Paper Company, and Dunlop Tire & Rubber. As reported in *Business Week:*

> Melville's management style relies on creating an entrepreneurial atmosphere that will allow people to operate where they are not bogged down by a formal line-management reporting system. "In the case of abrasives," says Melville, "you compensate your people on the basis of

whether or not they make that month's budget. In diversified products, you don't care as much about a month's budget—you try to double your sales in 12 months."[4]

The 1976 company organization structure is shown in Exhibit 2.

Concepts for strategic planning

In 1967, as executive vice president in charge of company-wide operations, Cushman faced the problem of assessing the role each of some 75 product lines was to play in Norton's future. The conventional corporate long-range planning then in use at Norton was found wanting for this task. Mr. Cushman consequently began to search for more appropriate ways to plan multibusiness operations. He later remarked:

> During the early 60s, Peter Drucker, widely known spokesman, critic, and analyst to business, began to describe business in terms of certain variables which seemed to determine a company's future. But it was Fred Borch, marketing vice president of the highly diversified General Electric, who in 1960 asked the key question and then assigned two members of his staff, Jack McKitterick and Dr. Sidney Schoeffler, to find the answer. "Why is it," he said, "that through the years some of our businesses fail while others succeed? There must be certain decisions, strategies, or factors which lead to certain results. With hundreds of products ranging from electric pencil sharpeners to diesel engines and nuclear plants, it is difficult to do an effective job of planning. It is, in fact, impossible for management to have a direct, personal feeling and knowledge about so many business environments. We need better guidelines."

In 1967, Dr. Schoeffler was invited to Norton to describe the results of GE's "profitability optimization" study. Based on sophisticated multiple regression analyses covering 10 years' experience for 150 product lines at General Electric, Dr. Schoeffler had been able to identify some 37 factors which accounted for more than 80 percent of the variations in profit results. The findings showed how profitability varied with respect to such factors as market share, market growth rate, and the level of investments required. The findings also showed how profitability varied with respect to policies on such matters as research and development as a percentage of sales, marketing expenditures, product quality, and pricing.[4] Mr. Cushman was struck with the relevance and concreteness of the resulting guidelines.

In his search for better guidelines, Mr. Cushman also became interested in the work of Bruce Henderson, founder and president of the Boston Consulting Group. Based on the premise that costs decreased

---

[4] Ibid.

[5] Examples of profit determinants would include: (1) high marketing expenditures damage profitability when product quality is low; (2) high R&D spending hurts profitability when market share is small but increases ROI when market share is high; and (3) high marketing expenditures hurt ROI in investment-intensive businesses.

Exhibit 2
Partial organization chart, June 1976

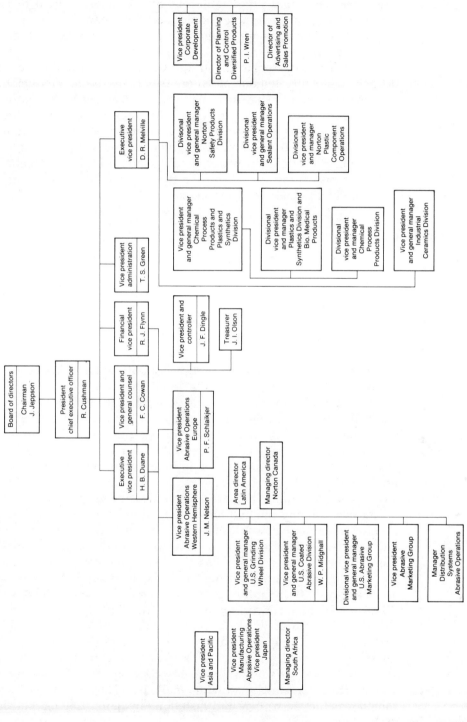

with experience in a predictable manner, Henderson held that the firm with the greatest volume should have the lowest costs for a given product line. Market share served as a measure of relative volume for planning purposes.

The cash flows associated with growth and mature industries constituted a second element of Henderson's approach. Product lines with leading market shares in mature industries were generators of surplus cash; those in growth industries represented the potential cash generators for future years. For diversified business operations, Henderson urged that attention be given in strategic planning to the creation of a portfolio in which some product lines could generate sufficient cash throw-off to nourish the development and growth of other product lines in growing markets.

Strategic planning at Norton

The basic building block for planning continued to be the strategy analysis for individual product lines. This analysis considered a wide range of business factors such as competitive conditions, technology, and future trends, and concluded with a proposed course of action over time. Each strategy was prepared by the manager holding profit responsibility for the product line and was evaluated by group and corporate line management. The customary analysis and review of strategy were extended to include two additional tests based on the somewhat related sets of concepts described above.

One of these additional tests concerned the intrinsic profit potential for a business. Based on experiential data for a wide range of businesses (such as had been generated for General Electric), Norton was able to ascertain a measure of the profit level appropriate for a business as it existed. It was also able to ascertain the extent to which profits and cash flows might be increased under alternative strategies. These financial norms helped management to evaluate how well a business was being run and how much additional potential it had.

A business strategy was also evaluated in the context of total corporate cash flows. The strategy had to conform to the overall availabilities of or needs for cash. For this purpose, market share performance served as a major controlling device. In broad terms, businesses were assigned the task of building, holding, or harvesting market share. "Building strategies" were based on active efforts to increase market share by means of new product introductions, added marketing programs, etc. Such strategies customarily called for cash inputs. "Holding strategies" were aimed at maintaining the existing level of market share. Net cash flows might be negative for rapidly growing markets and positive for slowly growing markets. "Harvesting strategies" sought to achieve earnings and cash flows by permitting market share to decline.

In line with this approach, Norton's operations had been divided into some 60 businesses whose characteristics were sufficiently different to warrant the development of individual business strategies. These subdivisions were known as substrategic business units. Combinations of these substrategic business units were grouped into about 30 strategic business units for purposes of top-management review.

Strategy Guidance Committee

In April 1972, Cushman formed a top-management committee to assist in the evaluation of these business strategies. As Cushman later reported to the Norton Board:

> The function of the Strategy Guidance Committee is to review at appropriate levels the strategy of each business unit, to make certain it does fit corporate objectives, and to monitor how effectively its strategy is being carried out. It provides the executive, regional, and division manager an opportunity for an "outside" peer group to examine and advise.
>
> The committee totals 12: the president, the executive vice president, the regional vice presidents, the financial vice president, the controller, the vice president of corporate development, and Graham Wren as secretary. Depending on the circumstances, business units are reviewed on a two-year cycle. Well-documented strategies along standard lines are sent to members for review before meetings.

Each strategic business unit was responsible for preparing a strategy book for review. Copies of this book were distributed to members of the Strategy Guidance Committee at least one week prior to the scheduled review. To focus attention on the critical issues, Cushman had set the following ground rules for the review session:

> No formal presentation is required at the meeting because each committee member is expected to have thoroughly studied the strategy book.
>
> Discussion during the meeting will generally center around these questions:
>
> 1. Questions of facts, trends, and assumptions as presented in the strategy book.
> 2. Questions as to the appropriateness of the mission of the business in terms of Build, Maintain, or Harvest.
> 3. Questions as to the appropriateness of the strategy in the context of the facts and mission.
> 4. Questions suggested by PIMS analysis.
> 5. How does the business unit and its strategy fit and relate to similar businesses within Norton (e.g., coated abrasives Europe versus coated abrasives worldwide)?
> 6. How does the business unit and its strategy fit within the corporate portfolio and strategy?

Involvement of line managers

The involvement of key line managers in the Strategy Guidance Committee and the methodology used in generating the strategy books gave a distinct line orientation to planning at Norton. Management for each business unit had to take a position concerning its mission, strengths and weaknesses, likely competitive developments, trends, and finally its strategy. The analysis and recommendations had to stand the test of critical evaluation by an experienced and involved top management.

Although Cushman was pleased with the planning tools Norton had developed, he felt that the deep involvement of line managers in both the formulation and review of strategies served to prevent a mechanical or otherwise undue reliance on the planning tools themselves. He believed it highly desirable that an operating manager's "gut feel" remain an important input to strategic planning.

Other elements related to strategic planning

In 1976 detailed cash flow models which could be used to support and extend the analysis described above were being completed. Several Norton managers remarked that these models would contribute importantly to the strategic planning efforts.

Also, Norton's incentive system was designed to motivate managers in carrying out their assigned strategic moves—whether to build, maintain, or harvest their business. Cushman reported the use of over 50 different custom-tailored plans for this purpose.

Finally, Cushman's deep-seated involvement in the strategic planning process and the respect he commanded from other senior-level managers at Norton undoubtedly influenced this process in major ways.

COATED ABRASIVES DOMESTIC[6]

One of the difficult cases for consideration by the Strategy Guidance Committee in 1976 concerned a reevaluation of the strategy to be followed for the U.S. coated abrasives business. Coated Abrasives Domestic (CAD), one of Norton's larger operating divisions, had had a recent history of declining market share and profitability.

In 1974 Norton management had decided to stem further loss of market share by a major restructuring of the CAD division. During the ensuing two years, market share and profitability continued to decline. These unfavorable results raised important questions about the merits of the earlier decision. The case for holding market share (the

---

[6] Numbers for the remainder of the case are disguised.

current strategy) was further challenged by the recommendations resulting from the PIMS regression analysis. The PIMS report had concluded that the CAD business should be moderately harvested (market share permitted to decline) for its cash throw-off.

The remainder of this case presents excerpts from information presented to the Strategy Guidance Committee or otherwise known by its members concerning CAD.

The abrasives market

Abrasive finished products were generally classified as bonded or coated. Bonded abrasives were basic tools used in almost every industry where shaping, cutting, or finishing of materials was required. Some of the major uses were in foundries and steel mills for rough grinding of castings and surface conditioning of steels and alloys, in metal fabrication for such products as automobiles and household appliances, in tool and die shops, in the manufacture of bearings, and in the paper and pulp industry. Norton produced more than 250,000 types and sizes of grinding wheels and other bonded abrasive products.

Coated abrasives (popularly referred to as sandpaper) were widely used throughout the metalworking and woodworking industries, in tanneries, and in service industries such as floor surfacing and automobile refinishing. Norton produced more than 38,000 different items in the form of sheets, belts, rolls, discs, and specialties. The most common form of coated abrasives was the endless belt, some major applications of which included the grinding and finishing of automobiles and appliance parts, the precision grinding and polishing of stainless and alloy steel, and the sanding of furniture, plywood, and particle board.

The overlap of customers' requirements for bonded and coated abrasives varied from industry to industry. For example, the woodworking industry used coated abrasives almost exclusively. In contrast, the auto industry purchased large quantities of both bonded abrasives (e.g., for grinding engine parts) and coated abrasives (e.g., for finishing bodies). Industrial distributors, which accounted for a large portion of Norton's abrasive sales, usually carried both bonded and coated abrasive products. Both Norton and Carborundum offered full lines of bonded and coated abrasive products; 3M competed only in coated abrasives.

In management's opinion, the principal factors which contributed to a favorable market position in this industry included quality and reliability of product, completeness of product line, nonpatented technological "know-how," substantial capital investment, length of experience in the business, familiarity and reputation of name, strength of marketing network, technical service, delivery reliability, and price.

In 1975 no single customer, including the U.S. government, accounted for as much as 5 percent of Norton's net sales.

CAD in the corporate context

As was customary, the meeting of the Strategy Guidance Committee to review the CAD strategy was opened by Mr. Graham Wren, secretary of the committee, with a short presentation showing where the product line in question fitted in the Norton portfolio of businesses. The first chart he presented contained an overview of the market share strategies for 31 strategic business units, as summarized in Figure 1.

Figure 1
Summary of market share strategies for the Norton portfolio of businesses

Market share strategy	Sales ($ millions)	Abrasive operations	Diversified products
Build	96	In the actual presentation, each strategic business was listed under its appropriate category. For example, CAD and 15 other business units were listed in the abrasives column for the maintain strategy.	
Build/maintain	135		
Maintain	257		
Maintain/harvest	60		
Harvest	0		
Total	548	400	148

Separate charts showed the ranking of all business units with respect to return on net assets (RONA), return on sales (ROS), and asset turnover ratio for 1974 and 1975, and the average for the two years. CAD placed in the ranking as follows:

Coated abrasives domestic

	Rank among 31	Value for 1974–1975 average	Norton average operations
RONA	27	6.0	10
ROS	26	3.5	6
Asset turnover	23	1.7	1.9

A growth share matrix showed CAD to lie well in the undesirable low-growth/smaller-than-competitor quadrant (see Exhibit 3). A product experiencing both low growth and low market share (relative to the industry leader) would likely be a net user of cash with little promise for future payoff.

Exhibit 3
**Norton portfolio of businesses on growth share matrix (balloon areas
proportional to sales)**

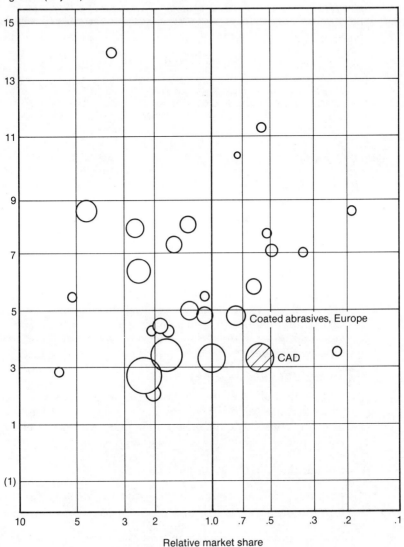

Real market
growth (%/year)

Relative market share

Finally, the committee's cash generations versus market share corporate test was applied to the CAD proposed strategy. As shown in
Figure 2, the combination of maintaining market share at its present
level and generating cash was acceptable.

Figure 2
The cash generation/market share strategy test

Cash generation	Market share strategy		
	Build	Maintain	Harvest
Uses cash	A/?	U	U
Provides own cash	A/?	U	U
Disengages cash	A	Ⓐ ↙ CAD	A

A = The combination is an acceptable strategy.
? = The combination is a questionable strategy.
U = The combination is an unacceptable strategy.

CAD STRATEGY PLAN

Paul Midghall, vice president and general manager for Norton's U.S. Coated Abrasives Division, was the principal architect of the strategic plan to maintain market share. His reasoning as laid out in the 1976 strategy book for CAD began with a statement of the division's role and strategy:

Mission: Cash Generation

Norton's long-term objective is to allocate resources to high-growth opportunities while maintaining total world abrasives leadership. CAD's role within that corporate objective is: to be a long-term cash generator; to act as the technical focal point for coated abrasives operations worldwide.

Strategy: Restructure and Maintain

To meet that objective, CAD has in the last two years radically restructured its operations. Its strategy now is to complete the restructuring; to consolidate the organization into a confident, coherent team; and to pursue market segmentation based on the strengths which have emerged from restructuring. To understand how this strategy evolved, one must turn to CAD's history.

The strategy report went on to identify the reasons for the earlier deterioration of market share and profitability. These included:

1. Inadequate reinvestment in the basic coated abrasives business in favor of investments which attempted to build allied businesses.[7]
2. High wage rates and fringe benefits coupled with low productivity and poor work conditions.

---

[7] According to Mr. Duane, coated abrasives and the other allied businesses had been organized in a single profit center at that time. The focus of attention had been on the total unit's overall performance. With the current approach to strategy analysis, each major product line was examined separately.

3. High overheads.
4. Premium pricing without compensating benefits to the customer.
5. A labor strike in 1966.

Serious attempts to reverse the negative trends for CAD had proved unsuccessful, and in late 1973 management decided a major change had to be made to the business. The current strategy report reviewed the alternative strategies that had been considered earlier:

> By late 1973, CAD's condition demanded positive action; share had dropped to 26 percent and RONA to 7.5 percent. A fundamental change had to occur. The principal options were:
>
> 1. Sell, liquidate, or harvest. These alternatives were eliminated because: (*a*) a viable coated abrasives business was deemed important to worldwide coated abrasives business; (*b*) a viable coated abrasives business was judged important to U.S. bonded abrasives business.
> 2. Attempt to regain lost share and with it volume to cover fixed expenses. In a mature industry, with the major competitors financially secure and firmly entrenched, such a strategy was judged too expensive.
> 3. Greater price realization. We already maintained a high overall price level, and 3M was the price leader in the industry. In later 1974, Norton tried to lead prices up dramatically to restore profitability but the rest of the industry did not follow.

Alternative: Comprehensive Cost Reduction

> A new cost structure was the only reasonable choice for a radical change. We had to scale down to a cost level consistent with our volume and our position in the industry.

In 1974 a decision to restructure the CAD business by making major cost reductions was made by Norton's Executive Committee and approved by its Board of Directors. This move was intended to make CAD more competitive so that it could prevent further erosion of its market share.

Restructuring

The strategy review of 1974 had identified many areas for cost reduction. These touched on almost every segment of operations and included: moving labor-intensive manufacturing operations from New York to Texas; combining the coated abrasives sales force with that for bonded abrasives (e.g., grinding wheels); and reducing fixed assets. The product line was also to be reduced. Earlier about 4,000 product items out of some 20,000 (that is, 20 percent) had accounted for 87 percent of sales.

During the two-year period 1974–75, over $2 million had been invested to implement the restructuring. The changes were eventually expected to result in over $9 million annual direct recurring savings, raising RONA by about 8 percentage points to a total of 14 percent.[8] The number of employees for CAD had declined from 2,000 to 1,300 by 1976.

CAD's future environment

The U.S. coated abrasives industry was expected to experience low growth and gradual changes as a rule. The strategy book forecast long-term growth at 2.5 percent per annum. Industrial markets, which constituted 75 percent of Norton's CAD business, were to grow even more slowly. Because of the depressed level of business operations in early 1976, annual growth for industrial markets was forecast to spurt to about 7% until 1980.[9]

Product technology was expected to change slowly, but in important ways. The strategy book noted:

> The advent of Norzon grain, new resin bonds, and synthetic backings illustrates the fact that although coated abrasives may be a mature product, it is not a commodity product. Technological evolution is slow but continuous, and a competitor who fails to keep abreast cannot survive.
>
> While product development exhibits highly visible evolution, process development is inconspicuous. No major changes have occurred, or are expected, in manufacturing technology.
>
> Capacity in all segments of manufacturing will be adequate to fill demand well into the 1980s.

The U.S. coated abrasives market was said to have "healthy, strong, rational competition." With the exception of 3M, the return of most

---

[8] It was estimated that 3M had a RONA of 17 percent of 20 percent in coated abrasives.

[9] An investment advisory report issued by Loeb Rhoades some months later (August 1976) had this to say about future prospects for the industry as a whole (bonded and coated products):

> We have believed for some time that there were fair prospects for higher profitability in abrasives on a secular and not just a cyclical basis, merely because profitability had been poor for a long enough (seven to nine years) time. In a product that is basic to economic activity and that is capital intensive, and where no unusual reason can be discerned for the poor return on investment, such as foreign competition or technological change, etc., a lengthy period of poor profitability generally will lead to changes by industry factors designed to improve returns. . . . At some point supply and demand come into a better balance, which then supports firmer pricing. And in fact . . . pricing had improved significantly since late 1974 despite declining demand in real terms.

Figure 3
U.S. coated abrasives market share estimates

	1975 sales ($ millions)	Total market share	
		1975	1973
3M	99	34%	32%
Norton	76	26	27
Carborundum	40	14	15
Armak	23	8	8
Other U.S. manufacturers	35	12	12
Foreign	21	7	7
Total industry	294	100%	100%

	Market segment		
	Metal working*	Wood working	General trade†
Market potential, 1975 ($ millions)	130	36	81
Estimated market share, 1975			
3M	30%	27%	65%
Norton	29	26	20
Carborundum	22	10	11

* Includes primary metals, fabricated metals, and transportation equipment (autos, aircraft) industries.
  † Includes hardware retail and automobile finishing businesses.

competitors was thought to be below the U.S. industrial average. Figure 3 shows sales and market shares for the principal competitors.

CAD strategy for 1976

The proposed strategy for CAD contained two principal elements. One element was a continuation of the restructuring and cost cutting that had begun in 1974. CAD management estimated that about 75 percent of this program had been put into effect and that two more years would be required to complete the steps under way.

The second element of the strategy was to focus on those market segments where Norton had competitive advantage. Detailed share/growth balloon charts, such as shown in Exhibit 4, were used to identify specific sectors for attention.

To foster product innovation, the 1976 plan had introduced a recommendation to expand R&D efforts. Twenty-two men had been assigned to CAD product development in 1975.

These strategic moves were predicted to produce favorable results.

Exhibit 4
CAD growth share matrices (balloon areas proportional to Norton's sales)

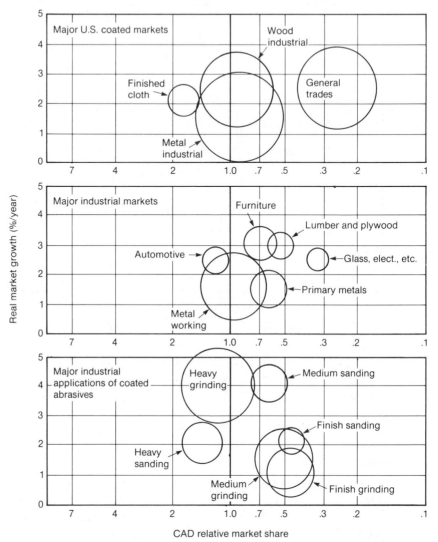

CAD relative market share

The CAD report identified the units' future strengths to include: variable costs to be among the lowest in the industry; distribution channel relations to be among the best, especially with the close tie between coated and bonded abrasives; and a technological edge on new products (e.g., Norzon). The ultimate result, the report forecast, would be the generation of more than $7 million cash during 1977–80. Excerpts from the summary of financial results are shown in Figure 4.

Figure 4
Summary of financial results (numbers disguised)

	Actual					Expected*				
	1971	1972	1973	1974	1975	1976	1977	1978	1979	1980
a. Market share (%)	29	28	27	26	25.5	26	27	27.5	27.5	27.5
b. Net sales (index)	77	90	107	120	100	108	128	150	160	180
c. Net income (index)	215	220	310	230	100	140	480	760	810	950
d. Percent return on sales (c/b)	4.4	3.9	4.6	3.0	1.6	2.0	6.0	8.0	8.0	8.0
e. Percent RONA	8	8	7.5	7	5	4.5	8	13	13	13
f. Funds generated ($ millions)						(4.7)	0.5	2.5	3.4	1.3

* 7 percent inflation per annum assumed.

The PIMS report[10]

The PIMS analysis for CAD had resulted in a recommendation at variance with that made by Mr. Midghall. A summary of these findings was included in the strategy book submitted to the Strategy Guidance Committee. The remainder of this section presents excerpts from the PIMS analysis:

> The 1975 PAR report[11] indicates that the Coated U.S. business is a below-average business in a weak strategic position with a *pretax* PAR-ROI of 12.0 percent. The business' operating performance has been very close to PAR with a 1973–75 average *pretax* actual ROI of 12.2 percent.
>
> The major factors impacting on PAR-ROI and their individual impacts are listed below.[12]

Major negative factors	Major positive factors
(1.5) Marketing only expense/sales	1.8 Sales direct to end users
(1.7) Capacity utilization	
(4.1) Effective use of investments	

> During the three-year period, the *marketing less sales force expenses/sales* ratio averaged 6 percent compared to the 4.1 percent PIMS average. PIMS findings acknowledge that high marketing expenses hurt profitability when relative product quality is low; i.e., it doesn't pay to market heavily a product with equivalent or inferior product quality. The average relative product quality for the business over the three years was estimated as follows: 10 percent superior, 75 percent equivalent, and 15 percent inferior.
>
> For the Coated-U.S. business, the positive impact indicates that selling through distributors instead of direct should lower customer service costs.
>
> Whether the Coated-U.S. business objective is to optimize cash flow or ROI over the long term, the Strategy Sensitivity Report (SSR) suggests a *moderate harvest* strategy. The SSR is based upon how other participating businesses with similar business characteristics have acted to achieve their objectives.
>
> The SSR suggests that the following strategy should be pursued to optimize either cash flow or ROI over the long term.

---

[10] As a subscriber to the services of the Strategic Planning Institute, Norton received on a regular basis analysis reports for several of its major businesses. These reports were circulated to divisional and corporate managers concerned with the business in question.

[11] The PAR report specified the return on investment that was normal for a business, given the characteristics of its market, competition, technology, and cost structure.

[12] The figures represent the impact of that factor on PAR-ROI. For example, the higher marketing (excluding sales force) expenses/sales ratio noted in the following paragraph when comparing CAD to all PIMS businesses was said to have an effect of reducing the PAR-ROI by 1.5 percent. In contrast, by selling directly to the end users, PAR-ROI was increased by 1.8 percent compared to all PIMS businesses.

1. *Prices.* Prices relative to competition should be maintained.
2. *Working capital/sales.* The SSR suggests that this ratio be lowered significantly to about 25 percent through primarily reduced inventory levels.
3. *Vertical integration.* Over the long term, the degree of vertical integration should be reduced.
4. *Fixed capital.* Don't add large segments of capacity, and maintain capacity utilization at the 80 percent level.
5. *R&D marketing expenses.* The SSR recommends that R&D expenditures should be reduced; and consequently, the relative product quality remains inferior. Also, the products should be marketed less energetically during the implementation phase.

The results from this strategy are (1) a gradual loss of market share from 26 percent to 21 percent; (2) an average ROI of 24 percent versus the current PAR-ROI of 12 percent; and (3) a 10-year discounted cash flow value of $2.33 million.

A study was undertaken to compare the PAR-ROI of this business in its steady-state environment (after the recommended strategy has been implemented—1978–80) with the 1973–75 PAR-ROI. The results indicate that the strategy is successful in moving this business into a much better strategic position. The pretax PAR-ROI increases from 12 percent to 24 percent.

The major factors that had a significant impact on the improved PAR-ROI are *relative pay scale* and *use of investments.* These two factors account for a majority of the 12 percentage point increase in PAR-ROI.

The general message from the SSR for the *restructured* Coated U.S. business is the same as for the *current* business; i.e., if the objective is to manage the business for cash flow or ROI, a *moderate harvest strategy* is recommended by PIMS.

Management considerations

Norton's top managers recognized how difficult it was for them to remain objective when deciding the fate of a core part of the company's traditional business. As Mr. John Nelson, vice president abrasive operations western hemisphere, remarked:

> There is no question that this decision has been an emotional one for me and probably for others as well. It would be difficult to turn our backs on CAD. Yet, if the business cannot produce the target return on net assets, I think we are prepared to take the appropriate actions.
>
> I do not think that we are likely to close shop on U.S. coated abrasives. It is too important to other parts of our business to go that far. For example, coated abrasives strengthens our sales of bonded abrasives and is a plus to our distribution system in the United States. It also provides us with a bigger base for R&D on coated abrasives. This benefits our overseas coated abrasives operations. Nonetheless, whether to stay with our earlier decision to maintain market share or to harvest the business was and still is very much at issue.

Both Mr. Duane and Mr. Nelson remarked that the choice of strategy in 1973–74 had been predicated on the belief that the industry could support a profitable number two and that Norton could play that role with its existing market share. The continued loss of market share was a cause of concern to them and to other members of the Strategy Guidance Committee. As noted in the minutes for the CAD review session of June 7, 1976:

> In the shorter-term period of late 1973 to the first quarter 1976, CAD market share dropped from 27 percent to 25 percent. Some of this drop was due to intentional de-emphasis of the general trades segment. However, there was also an unintentional loss in the industrial segment. The key question is whether this short-term market share decline in the industrial area can be stopped and reversed.

The PIMS recommendations for an alternative strategy also served to raise questions about the soundness of the present approach. One Norton executive put in context the relative impact of PIMS with the following observation: "We are still learning how to use PIMS. At present, we consider it a useful input, among many, to our thinking. We would not reverse divisional management's position on the basis of PIMS alone."

Mr. Donald Melville, executive vice president, diversified products, made the following comment about the CAD issue:

> You have to consider the dynamics of Norton's situation in 1976. We have done a lot to restructure the company, and the results in 1975—a bad recession year for abrasives—show our progress. But we are not yet in a position where we can harvest a major segment of our abrasives business, because that is the major guts of our company.
>
> By the early 80s our restructuring should be complete and we will not be so dependent on abrasives. If we were faced with the decision in, say, 1982, instead of 1976, we could and probably should be willing to harvest CAD. In the meantime, we might as well repair CAD, because if we succeed, then we won't have to harvest it in the 80s. And if we fail, we will have lost very little.

A relative newcomer to the top management ranks at Norton, Mr. Richard Flynn, financial vice president, made the following comments about Norton's approach to strategic planning:[13]

> However the Strategy Guidance Committee finally decides on this matter, I think they are at least addressing the right issues, and that itself is something.

---

[13] Richard J. Flynn joined Norton Company in January 1974, as financial vice president and as a member of the Board of Directors and the Executive Committee. He had been president of the Riley Stoker Corporation, a subsidiary of the Riley Company, manufacturers of steam generating and fuel burning equipment. He previously held executive positions with Ling-Temco Vought and Collins Radio.

The wide use of profit centers in large U.S. corporations has often led to bad analysis when different products were lumped together. Corporate-wide planning did not help the situation. Looking at a single product line family, as we are doing for U.S. coated abrasives, gives management much more meaningful data to work with.

The other thing I like about Norton's strategic planning is that we are doing it repeatedly during the year. This means that we are always called on to think strategy. Looking at different businesses at different times enables us to take on different perspectives to our strategic thinking. This sometimes helps us to gain new insights for other businesses.

All in all, the strategic planning sessions have been very effective in helping top management to think about and to deal with business strategies.

Case 2–7

Aero Manufacturing Company, Inc.

On March 15, 1975, Gerald Giles, president of the Aero Manufacturing Company, Inc., called a meeting of his staff to discuss the position of the firm. Giles had just received from Jochim, the financial manager, the annual report for the year ending February 28, 1975. While gross sales had increased to $4,369,568, net income after taxes had declined to $313,788. It was Giles's desire to locate the problem areas, review appropriate solutions proposed by the staff, and implement the necessary changes to return the Aero Manufacturing Company to the rapid growth of sales and earnings which was its pattern in the past.

HISTORY OF AERO MANUFACTURING

The Aero Manufacturing Company, a closely held corporation, produces a highly diversified line of products for use in the agricultural industry. The products, which include grain-drying and -handling equipment, rolled steel tubing, and, until very recently, golf carts and minibikes, have traditionally been marketed throughout the Midwest. The firm markets its grain equipment to dealers via distributors in Iowa, Nebraska, Missouri, Illinois, Minnesota, North Dakota, South Dakota, Kansas, and Colorado.

Initially, Giles had established an electric motor service in Wayne, Iowa, in 1955. In 1958, he expanded that service to a second outlet in

This case was prepared under the direction of Bruce A. Kirchoff of the University of Nebraska–Omaha.

the Pisgah Industrial Park, Pisgah, Iowa. He named the new firm Midland Electric Motor Service. This company specialized in electric motor rewinding and repair. His background in electrical maintenance and servicing of grain-drying equipment led to his desire to design drying equipment to function with less specialized supervision. In due course, Aero Manufacturing was founded by Giles in May 1964. This company was an outgrowth of companies he had previously established. The initial capital of this firm was $9,900. Giles developed his first crop dryer in 1966, and adopted the trade name Grain-Air. The trade name was registered with the U.S. Patent Office.

Growth of the company had been rapid in terms of sales, product line, and expanded facilities since 1964. As development of the crop dryers progressed and they became widely accepted in the field, the company rapidly expanded the product line to include other component accessories related to grain drying and handling. Additional product offerings included perforated plank-type drying floors, steel substructures, grain spreaders, bin ladders, unloading sumps and augers, sweep augers, and a full line of aeration fans and aeration systems. Aero decided not to produce grain bins, since management thought Aero could not be competitive.

The first building for Aero Manufacturing measured 50 feet by 100 feet and was erected in 1965. Gross sales reached $35,372, and profit after taxes reached $5,460 in 1965. Building space was doubled in size the next year, and in 1967 another 4,000 square feet was added to the building. That same year, Aero Manufacturing acquired a plant at Ames to house the perforated-floor machine and the steel-tube mill. Sales had risen by this time to $169,086.

It was Giles's aim to develop one or more new products each year. In line with this goal, a tube mill was built in 1969 to roll six-inch pipe from 14- to 16-gauge galvanized steel and to produce black steel pipe for general farm use. Aero's spectacular growth continued unabated through 1969, with sales topping $397,000 and net income after taxes climbing to $29,363.

The rate of sales growth for Aero Manufacturing slowed during 1971, with sales increasing by only $29,905 over 1970. Short-term debt tripled from the previous year to $41,500 (see balance sheet in Exhibit 1). In addition, increased capital of $44,600 was obtained through the issuance of common stock.

In April 1972, anticipating continued sales increases and in need of additional space for production and storage, Aero purchased a 150,000-square-foot factory building in Pisgah, Iowa. The company obtained a Small Business Administration loan of $365,000 to acquire the new facility, which had formerly housed the Monastersky Manufacturing Company of Pisgah, Iowa.

Through the period ending February 28, 1974, sales increased to $3,876,101, while net income after taxes increased to $424,909. No

Exhibit 1

AERO MANUFACTURING COMPANY, INC.
Balance Sheet
For Years Ending February 28, 1965–1975

	1975	1974	1973	1972	1971	1970	1969	1968	1967	1966	1965
Assets											
Current assets:											
Cash	$ 24,435	$ 40,827	$ 23,050	$ 48,867	0	$ 15,293	$ 14,800	$ 34,110	$ 8,742	$10,082	$ 5,227
Certificates of deposit	0	125,573	100,391	85,750	0	0	0	0	0	0	0
Accounts receivable—trade	253,648	419,992	258,108	106,241	58,091	63,722	43,031	30,741	9,565	2,342	3,336
Accounts receivable—other	1,215	63,875	13,975	1,215	1,786	5,280	19,480	48,304	0	0	775
Inventory at cost	1,905,000	990,946	406,581	221,032	162,683	113,419	106,321	0	49,762	2,000	
Other assets:											
Investments (at cost)	7,500	7,500	7,500	7,500	9,417	38,417	2,500	8,169	0	0	0
Loans to employees	2,115	0	0	7,472	2,298	2,207	2,755	970	152	297	0
Other assets—prepaid taxes	395,449	0	0	985	0	0	0	0	259	1,549	485
Fixed assets:											
Buildings and land	363,364	377,687	377,687	376,723	180,613	59,234	50,262	40,001	28,665	25,983	13,853
Furniture and equipment	589,769	454,546	278,017	148,925	0	0	0	0	0	0	0
Less accumulated depreciation	(284,306)	(199,390)	(127,608)	(72,480)	(39,387)	(23,778)	(17,562)	(12,417)	(8,510)	(4,730)	(1,860)
Total assets	$3,258,189	$2,281,486	$1,337,701	$932,230	$375,501	$273,794	$221,587	$149,878	$88,635	$37,523	$21,816
Liabilities and Stockholders' Equity											
Current liabilities:											
Accounts payable	$ 564,172	$ 510,457	$ 223,645	$112,471	$ 44,253	$ 51,666	$ 52,783	$ 24,880	$11,126	$ 8,834	$ 5,781
Customer deposits	0	45,167	0	0	0	0	0	0	0	0	0
Accrued expenses	108,045	139,704	22,154	4,601	1,790	10,677	12,182	16,806	1,192	0	0
Accrued income—taxes payable	283,536	210,284	142,400	76,659	18,785	16,062	16,642	12,424	7,604	1,423	635
Current portion—mortgage payable	32,000	32,000	30,681	55,486	0	0	0	0	0	0	0
Current portion—contracts payable	14,600	7,088	4,958	5,566	0	0	2,745	2,618	0	0	0
Cash in bank—overdraft	0	0	0	0	6,711	0	0	0	0	0	0
Notes payable—current portion	600,000	0	0	0	41,500	15,000	0	0	3,490	0	0
Notes payable—officers	27,261	0	0	0	0	195	0	0	0	0	39
Long-term liabilities:											
Notes and contracts payable	49,719	41,098	7,820	0	0	0	0	0	0	0	0
Mortgage payable	241,363	271,285	304,380	307,888	0	0	0	0	0	0	0
Total liabilities	1,920,696	1,257,781	736,038	562,671	113,039	93,600	84,352	56,728	23,412	10,257	6,455
Stockholders' equity:											
Common stock	106,100	106,100	106,100	101,000	100,000	55,400	43,700	28,900	28,900	12,900	9,900
Paid-in surplus	18,800	18,800	18,800	0	0	0	0	0	0	0	0
Retained earnings	1,212,593	898,805	476,763	268,559	162,462	124,794	93,535	64,250	36,323	14,366	5,461
Total stockholders' equity	1,337,493	1,023,705	601,663	369,559	262,462	180,194	137,235	93,150	65,223	27,266	15,361
Total liabilities and stockholders' equity	$3,258,189	$2,281,486	$1,337,701	$932,230	$375,501	$273,794	$221,587	$149,878	$88,635	$37,523	$21,816

further expansion of Aero Manufacturing facilities occurred until the company announced plans in late 1974 to locate a branch in Akron, Iowa.

AERO MANUFACTURING'S CURRENT POSITION

The firm experienced difficulties in several areas during the year ending February 28, 1975. A majority of these could be directly traced to the economic recession the nation was experiencing during the latter part of 1974 and into early 1975. The overall result was that farmers were reluctant to make new purchases, and the result was a much poorer year than was anticipated by Giles for Aero Manufacturing.

Marketing

Gross sales increased during 1974 to $4,369,568. This was an increase of 12 percent over the previous year, but it was significantly lower than the $6 million which had been projected. Net income after taxes decreased to $313,788. A schedule of income statements is presented in Exhibit 2. Gross sales by product line are presented in Exhibit 3.

Giles hoped to expand his sales territories, although he had no specific goal in regard to market share, nor had he adequately defined his market. In this regard, Giles hired a marketing manager in February 1975 to revamp and implement current and future marketing strategy. While no change was contemplated in the company's present pricing policy, Giles had been seriously considering increasing the number of dealers.

Aero's present competitors in the grain-drying field are Chicago Eastern and Farm Fans. The firm's main competitor in the tubing area is Valmont. Other competitors include Midwest Equipment, Square D, and Wigman. Major manufacturers have not been in direct competition since Aero has sold its product for 15 to 25 percent less.

Even though the company wished to introduce one or two new products every year, the products designated for 1975 were still in the research stages as of February 28, 1975.

Aero is presently advertising in *Iowa Farmer, Farm Journal,* and other regional farm magazines.

Finance

Inventories climbed throughout 1974 to reach a level of $1,905,000 as of February 28, 1975, the company's fiscal year-end. This amounted to an increase of 92 percent over the previous year. The inventory accumulation resulted in approximately 3 times too much in raw materials, and 2½ times too much in finished goods. The majority of the inventory was being stored at the Pisgah plant. Approximately 75,000

Exhibit 2

AERO MANUFACTURING COMPANY, INC.
Income Statement
For Years Ending February 28, 1965–1975

	1975	1974	1973	1972	1971	1970	1969	1968	1967	1966	1965
Gross sales	$4,369,568	$3,876,101	$1,998,279	$1,116,716	$496,845	$466,940	$397,612	$267,452	$169,086	$67,201	$35,372
Sales returns and allowances	(158,835)	(116,649)	(59,556)	(54,381)	(26,225)	(29,226)	(12,509)	(20,048)	0	(1,553)	0
Discounts	(35,797)	(32,604)	(16,422)	0	0	0	0	0	0	0	0
Net sales	4,174,936	3,726,848	1,922,301	1,062,335	470,620	437,714	385,103	247,404	169,086	65,648	35,372
Cost of goods sold:											
Beginning inventory	990,946	406,581	221,032	162,683	113,419	106,321	48,304	49,762	2,000	775	0
Raw material purchased	2,967,638	2,449,820	1,088,830	560,957	238,980	214,005	272,265	122,335	128,765	30,924	12,781
Production labor	412,270	263,410	148,158	87,399	83,587	74,651	51,097	38,283	24,419	12,354	11,667
Supplies	51,826	7,698	10,606	20,567	21,865	18,838	9,173	4,618	5,416	1,947	1,337
Freight	34,600	32,469	14,874	15,564	8,956	4,671	5,350	0	0	0	0
Total goods available:	4,457,280	3,160,008	1,483,500	847,170	466,807	418,486	386,189	214,998	160,600	46,000	25,785
Ending inventory	(1,905,000)	(990,946)	(406,581)	(221,032)	(162,683)	(113,419)	(106,321)	48,304	(49,762)	(2,000)	(775)
Cost of goods sold	2,552,280	2,169,062	1,076,919	626,138	304,124	305,067	279,868	166,694	110,838	44,000	25,010
Gross profit on sales	1,622,656	1,557,786	845,382	436,197	166,496	132,647	105,235	80,710	58,248	21,648	10,362
Operating expense	1,066,217	810,310	510,725	287,368	104,212	80,525	58,400	40,358	28,687	11,319	4,267
Net profit from operations	556,439	747,476	334,657	148,829	62,284	52,122	46,835	40,352	29,561	10,329	6,095
Other income:											
Rental income	3,550	36,219	49,861	42,514	0	0	0	0	0	0	0
Interest and other	37,335	38,347	5,686	1,492	0	0	20	0	0	0	0
Total other income	40,885	74,566	55,547	44,006	0	0	20	0	0	0	0
Net profit before state and federal taxes	597,324	822,042	390,204	192,835	62,284	52,122	46,855	40,352	29,561	10,329	6,095
State and federal income taxes	283,536	397,133	10,630	86,739	24,617	20,862	17,492	12,424	7,604	1,423	635
Net profit after taxes	313,788	424,909	209,574	106,096	37,667	31,260	29,363	27,928	21,957	8,906	5,460
Net income per share	$ 295.74	$ 400.47	$ 197.52	$ 105.04	$ 37.67	$ 56.42	$ 67.19	$ 96.63	$ 75.97	$ 69.03	$ 55.15

Exhibit 3
Gross sales by products by month for fiscal 1975

	March	April	May	June	July	August	September	October	November	December	January	February	Total
Aeration fans	$ 36,920	$ 72,144	$ 67,582	$121,162	$ 83,023	$ 44,247	$ 72,483	$ 32,438	$ 43,156	$ 14,203	$19,450	$ 1,393	$ 608,201
Aeration accessories	2,912	9,390	19,802	18,183	15,154	22,974	13,954	22,942	14,557	4,358	2,737	5,798	152,761
Vent fans	2,684	11,323	9,816	11,422	13,357	4,536	5,042	7,376	20,101	2,372	3,061	965	92,055
Vent fan accessories	788	3,218	1,554	8,088	5,585	3,088	4,368	3,751	3,753	1,154	1,168	722	37,237
Drying fans	58,788	39,303	15,605	54,380	30,909	51,990	56,887	36,839	44,466	14,222	(2,863)	355	400,881
Drying burners	6,535	7,448	5,517	20,082	12,834	9,394	17,209	13,471	10,227	9,370	(20)	(4)	112,063
Drying accessories	2,822	8,990	5,710	8,115	10,514	9,120	6,578	10,627	19,663	2,246	2,276	418	87,079
Vaporizers	0	0	0	0	0	0	394	2,600	3,515	66	(66)	(241)	6,268
Centrifugal fans	28,264	20,358	27,249	27,087	31,855	53,770	45,809	52,485	44,713	7,127	2,013	9,193	349,923
Centrifugal fan accessories	4,200	3,891	3,083	5,648	6,447	29,223	10,509	21,407	9,102	1,664	1,997	3,234	100,405
Electric humidity controllers	11,066	31,507	16,618	25,381	22,574	25,020	33,260	16,450	22,234	2,412	(353)	81	206,250
Johnson products	993	0	0	0	297	330	2,114	524	524	567	1,700	0	7,049
Zelbarth products		0	0	0	0	858	238	879	238	0	0	0	2,213
Bin liners	255	560	0	68	2,056	609	1,325	4,138	757	0	0	0	9,768
A & V aerators	0	13		0	165	1,198	87	521	358	44	87	165	2,638
Irrigation pump crib				2,216	752	523	609	1,492	413	0	0	0	6,005
Golf carts and minibikes	674	46		17	30	257	667	226	175	0	0	48	2,140
Electric motors	7,307	11,621	23,194	4,515	13,209	3,724	3,747	7,404	21,555	2,174	1,535	374	100,359
Miscellaneous	1,805	3,159	2,899	676	3,954	9,743	2,315	2,130	4,512	372	3,075	36,531	71,171
Augers	4,477	8,290	15,431	8,297	27,978	34,482	22,453	19,970	15,401	1,658	2,717	1,591	162,745
Hofard augers			7,826	18,225	8,307	4,479	10,541	15,823	7,595	674	(217)	0	73,253
Spreaders 20-24-30	648	349	6,337	616	842	941	1,004	4,902	1,305	0	14	52	17,010
Fibers	16,364	21,594	24,252	15,805	48,291	37,891	32,991	12,991	8,486	1,608	1,746	1,575	223,594
Channels	6,436	4,910	7,458	2,843	12,884	13,968	3,809	5,909	3,162	960	367	420	63,126
Supports	2,587	19,166	10,206	3,982	16,706	19,408	8,580	6,858	4,733	1,247	294	342	94,109
Floor parts		591	4,312	453	3,690	242	837	5,720	1,645	159	61	635	18,345
Aeration flush	891	2,588	7,574	4,284	2,680	1,736	1,028	3,888	299	311	505	0	25,784
Moisture testers	2,331	1,797	3,225	0	1,787	2,322	734	2,356	2,238	750	0	140	17,680
Mufflers	55	0	0	30	0	0	127	37	0	24	0	42	315
Motor repair stand	639	0	633	0	0	1,462	0	0	657	0	0	62	3,453
Probe meter	0	110	0	0	62	28	80	279	110	736	783	0	2,188
Hog sorting gate	0	0	0	0	0	0	93	0	0	0	0	0	93
Pipe 6" and 8"	81,362	97,918	149,834	109,412	108,528	229,287	70,369	77,269	60,246	52,162	18,584	35,368	1,090,339
Power outlets	0	0	0	0	0	0	0	0	0	0	0	1,503	1,503
Total	$281,803	$380,284	$435,717	$470,987	$484,470	$616,850	$430,241	$393,702	$369,896	$122,640	$60,651	$100,762	$4,148,003

Exhibit 4
Schedule of operating expenses for fiscal years indicated, year ending February 28

	1975	1974	1973	1972	1971	1970	1969	1968	1967	1966	1965
Commissions and selling expenses	$ 198,169	$158,808	$ 80,018	$ 60,813	$ 11,630	$13,613	$ 8,526	$ 2,637	$10,564	$ 2,181	$ 657
Depreciation and amortization	84,916	71,782	60,269	34,718	15,609	6,216	5,195	3,957	3,830	2,919	1,910
Bad debt expense	138,000	78,775	46,075	12,305	2,380	1,939	0	0	0	0	0
Administrative salaries	107,063	85,696	42,500	56,691	20,000	20,000	18,000	18,000	6,000	0	0
Employee benefits	41,933	42,089	31,728	4,620	483	2,096	808	339	267	0	0
Interest	48,927	29,788	31,660	27,968	2,986	2,141	1,467	514	616	719	417
Office salaries and wages	74,388	58,177	31,294	0	0	0	0	0	0	0	0
Truck and auto expense	63,479	31,473	26,139	2,026	6,035	2,201	1,945	606	0	69	0
Utilities	28,565	22,358	23,585	21,395	2,709	2,410	2,111	1,658	1,058	287	357
Insurance	34,503	28,045	17,510	21,167	6,605	3,155	1,212	2,025	1,008	355	116
Truck drivers' wages	30,521	26,516	17,057	0	0	0	0	0	0	0	0
Telephone	17,070	20,096	15,166	5,833	3,432	2,143	598	0	0	0	0
Real estate taxes	8,028	9,451	10,518	0	0	0	0	0	0	0	0
Advertising	17,433	13,856	8,486	8,142	7,974	3,414	4,182	1,412	1,019	471	9
Personal property taxes	12,504	6,698	8,450	3,560	3,330	3,737	2,193	1,519	466	189	0
Repairs and maintenance	15,460	14,626	7,901	0	0	0	0	1,125	455	45	107
Legal and accounting	17,323	9,472	7,105	8,106	2,370	1,779	1,803	1,199	425	275	0
Office supplies	18,741	11,386	6,879	4,883	2,116	2,692	1,225	677	479	330	263
Contributions	4,147	9,077	6,643	1,225	556	100	412	232	0	0	0
Travel	4,401	3,975	5,428	0	1,607	0	0	0	138	0	0
Miscellaneous expense	508	1,910	5,011	1,598	965	330	1,180	156	158	476	57
Licenses and permits	6,709	7,204	4,871	0	0	0	0	0	0	0	0
Machine shop wages	10,949	13,734	4,840	0	0	0	0	0	0	0	0
Shop supplies	10,003	7,036	4,748	5,541	2,439	1,812	605	0	0	1,803	274
Rent	4,740	1,527	3,027	1,719	8,885	8,424	4,800	2,400	1,800	1,200	100
Sales tax	1,032	1,562	2,286	4,058	1,101	1,323	0	0	0	0	0
Directors' fees	1,000	1,000	1,000	1,000	1,000	1,000	1,000	1,300	0	0	0
Dues and subscriptions	661	534	531	0	0	0	414	173	0	0	0
Tool and die wages	42,021	30,111	0	0	0	0	0	0	0	0	0
Freight out	15,256	11,080	0	0	0	0	0	0	0	0	0
Entertainment	2,562	1,217	0	0	0	0	0	0	0	0	0
Collection forms	1,928	1,251	0	0	0	0	0	0	0	0	0
Leased equipment	0	0	0	0	0	0	724	429	404	0	0
Research and development	3,277	0	0	0	0	0	0	0	0	0	0
Total	$1,066,217	$810,310	$510,725	$287,368	$104,212	$80,525	$58,400	$40,358	$28,687	$11,319	$4,267

Exhibit 5
Total pay by department for fiscal year 1975

	Shipping	Tool and die	Truck drivers	Machine shop	Salesmen	Production
March	$ 2,886.11	$ 1,802.22	$ 2,810.77	$ 1,059.11	$ 5,100.00	$ 26,906.82
April	2,623.02	1,878.97	2,868.01	959.65	3,040.00	21,744.55
May	2,979.62	2,103.10	2,363.14	953.62	11,302.07	22,633.16
June	3,794.56	2,085.85	2,626.31	874.64	4,240.00	29,428.00
July	4,403.17	3,116.60	2,331.83	1,091.06	14,090.00	39,450.79
August	3,642.67	2,928.02	2,171.67	885.86	4,215.00	28,147.93
September	4,194.98	3,049.55	2,783.76	852.12	3,040.00	24,761.90
October	6,026.78	4,314.05	3,274.65	528.66	15,300.00	30,931.49
November	3,992.72	4,334.76	2,260.55	864.47	13,040.00	19,812.43
December	2,737.98	6,201.59	2,306.72	923.65	33,240.20	21,516.53
January	2,565.94	5,168.69	2,280.39	946.17	14,106.00	21,301.80
February	3,079.32	5,030.94	2,442.86	1,019.35	19,701.00	22,025.92
Total	$42,925.87	$42,014.34	$30,520.66	$10,948.36	$140,414.27	$308,661.32

additional square feet was added within the building by constructing a second floor which was used to store the excessive inventory. Giles stated that the main reason for this inventory buildup, besides the recession, was that the firm had experienced great difficulty in obtaining raw steel products in earlier years of peak demand and Giles did not want to jeopardize relations with suppliers by canceling orders. He also stated that a similar buildup on a much smaller scale had occurred in 1971.

The increase of raw materials and finished goods inventory, coupled with the reduced sales, was making it difficult for the firm to reduce its short-term debt. As a result of this and of a new law requiring prepayment of corporate income taxes, Aero Manufacturing was unable to liquidate $600,000 worth of short-term debt by the end of the 1974 fiscal year. This was the first time in its history, according to Giles, that the corporation was unable to eliminate its short-term debt by the end of the fiscal year. Although the line of credit extended by the bank was $1,250,000, the short-term debt and the cash flow situation were causing deep concern among the firm's management. A schedule of operating expenses is presented in Exhibit 4.

Aero offered credit terms of 2/10, net 30 to its dealers. The firm also had an early discount policy of allowing 55 to 10 percent if the dealer would pay 25 percent down at the time of purchase.

Aero Manufacturing currently employs between 50 and 60 people. Even though the economic climate was deteriorating in 1974, Giles continued to produce finished goods because he felt it was Aero's social responsibility to keep its people employed. It was also difficult to obtain, retain, and house technically skilled people in a small town. Pisgah's population is 15,000. Nevertheless, approximately 30 percent of the work force had been laid off in late 1974 as the company continued to experience a sales slowdown. Total wages by department are

St. Thomas	Main- tenance	Service	Office	Electrical Division	Akron	Special account	Total
$ 0	$ 0	$ 0	$ 4,340.66	$ 0	$ 0	$ 8,575.74	$ 53,481
0	0	0	4,861.52	0	0	4,000.00	41,965
1,129.60	0	0	5,982.32	0	0	4,000.00	53,446
300.25	0	0	4,987.24	0	0	4,067.50	52,404
560.16	0	0	6,582.08	0	0	6,179.56	77,805
1,475.34	0	0	5,352.75	0	0	5,834.56	54,653
2,027.91	0	0	5,387.31	0	0	6,514.56	52,612
2,668.16	646.52	0	6,908.00	0	0	8,143.20	78,741
1,945.42	944.86	664.40	5,527.29	148.50	0	6,514.56	60,048
1,923.62	672.80	1,720.24	10,538.40	267.51	0	7,041.05	89,090
2,257.45	729.60	1,492.66	6,961.65	358.20	0	10,943.20	69,111
2,317.65	1,038.07	1,610.87	6,957.87	497.42	273.01	10,249.34	76,243
$16,605.56	$4,031.85	$5,488.17	$74,387.09	$1,271.63	$273.01	$82,063.27	$759,605

presented as Exhibit 5. The organizational chart as of February 28, 1975, is presented as Exhibit 6.

Production/facilities

The Akron facility was leased in January 1975. It consisted of 10,000 square feet, 30 percent being office space. As of February 28, 1975, two people were employed at the site and production consisted

Exhibit 6
Organization chart, February 8, 1975

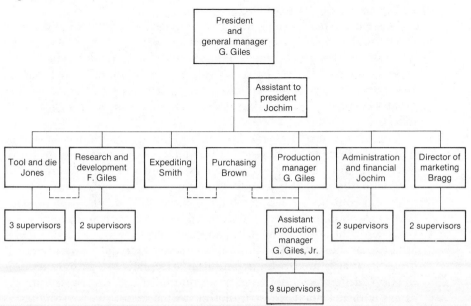

of one gravity grain box per day. Aero has also had an aluminum foundry at St. Thomas, Iowa.

Production is currently at 50 percent of capacity at the Pisgah site. The plant is full of inventory that has accumulated during the past year, and its storage capacity is quite strained. Giles estimates that 40 percent of the Pisgah plant floor area is for production; the remainder is for storage. A sales turnaround is expected, but as of March 1975 it had not yet materialized.

THE FUTURE AT AERO MANUFACTURING

Looking toward the immediate future, Giles plans to have his company back to full production within three months. He bases this plan on the assumption that the economy will be back to normal by that time. Giles has read that the consensus among the nation's leading economists is that the economy will bottom out by September 1975 and the recovery will not really be felt until early 1976.

In fiscal 1976, the company is forecasting gross sales of $8 million, with a 20 percent profit before taxes. The sales forecast was revised down from an earlier projection of $10 million. If this new forecast is attained, Aero Manufacturing will have doubled its sales of $4 million in 1975. Also, the firm intends to reduce its short-term debt to zero by the end of fiscal 1976.

Giles plans to rely heavily upon his two new assistants, Bragg and Jochim. Bragg, the new marketing assistant, has had vast experience in marketing and sales with other similar agribusiness companies. Jochim is a CPA who used to conduct the annual audit for Aero Manufacturing. Both of these men will be responsible for developing plans and goals for their respective areas.

In regard to marketing strategy, Bragg has already decided that it is in the best interest of the firm to obtain more dealers. He is in the process of setting up direct channels with more dealers via factory representatives. He is also venturing into new markets in Montana and Texas in an attempt to obtain new business. Bragg has stated that greater emphasis upon dealers will provide the firm with higher profit margins.

Concerning products, the firm still plans to come out with one or two new products every year. Giles plans to continue the firm's production of replacement auto mufflers because there is a strong demand for them. If the federal government relaxes its standards on emission controls (as appears likely) to the 1974 level, Giles thought that Aero would be able to sell its mufflers as original equipment since they meet the 1974 standards. Management believes that it will be able to sell these mufflers throughout the continental United States if these standards are lowered. The firm also plans to continue its production of new, technologically unique auto and tractor engine oil filters with the hope of obtaining bigger markets.

The firm has been directing its advertising toward the individual farmer, but recently it has changed its emphasis from the farmer to the dealer.

In regard to acquisitions, Aero is and will continually be looking for opportunities. Firms that are in a financial bind and manufacture farm implements and machinery are prime prospects. Giles says, however, that he would rather buy the assets than the firm itself. He also believes that good bargains can be obtained in this manner and that it opens up new markets for Aero's existing products.

As an overall policy, Aero plans to tighten its administrative internal control and develop a managerial planning mechanism by instituting a management by objectives program. This, it feels, will provide better guidance to the various managers and thus more efficiently utilize managerial talents.

Case 2–8

Bennett Industries

In April 1981 Mr. Mark Bennett, president and founder of Bennett Industries, met with his associates, Mr. Jim Stone and Mr. Andy Breckenridge, to discuss the progress that had been made in the last several months concerning the formation of his new business. Though still little more than a concept, Bennett Industries appeared nearly ready to enter the mechanical tailgate market. Several obstacles still existed, however, and Mr. Stone, in particular, was concerned about the long- and short-term feasibility of the proposed venture. Mr. Stone was especially worried about Bennett's ability to meet delivery schedules and the possible reactions of its formidable competitor, Tyson Tailgate Company, to the entry of a new firm into the market.

BACKGROUND

Mr. Bennett had been involved in the tailgate industry for more than two years as a sales representative for Tyson Tailgate Company. Bennett was quite successful in the tailgate business, and during his tenure at Tyson he accounted for almost one third of the company's total sales. Because of personal conflict with the owner, Charles Tyson, Bennett resigned in May 1980 and began the task of organizing a firm to compete with his former employer. Bennett's animosity toward Tyson was shared by many in the industry, and he felt that his firm would be welcomed into the market with open arms.

Prepared by Professors James J. Chrisman and Fred L. Fry, Bradley University.

Young, bright, and eternally optimistic, Mark Bennett possessed all of the traits associated with sales success. After several frustrating months of preparation, some of Bennett's initial optimism began to wear off and he realized that it would be necessary to seek assistance in such areas as marketing, finance, management, and engineering. Bennett saw no problem in selling his tailgate, frequently commenting, "If I didn't believe this thing would sell, I wouldn't be getting into the business."

The first person Bennett recruited for his business was his brother-in-law, Andy Breckenridge. Mr. Breckenridge was an excellent mechanical engineer, besides being knowledgeable about the mechanical tailgate. Breckenridge agreed to participate in the organization of the business, despite the fact that Bennett could not afford to pay him until the business was more stable. Andy was to be responsible for the design and installation of the tailgate, and Bennett agreed to pay him on a commission basis for this service. Breckenridge was to receive $200 for each design and $500 for installations. It also was agreed that he should receive a small share of the business after it began to make a profit. Because of his close involvement with the beginning of the business, Breckenridge was often in conflict with Bennett about the correct course of action that should be taken. At times, their relationship seemed strained.

Jim Stone was beginning his final semester of graduate study at a midwestern university when he first was introduced to Bennett. Both were impressed by their initial conversation, and Bennett was able to convince Stone to assist him in the formulation of his business plans and strategies. Stone saw his involvement with Bennett as an opportunity to gain business experience as well as the possibility of future employment. Stone agreed to work with Bennett until graduation, free of charge. After Stone graduated, Bennett offered to employ him at a salary of $25,000 per year plus a small interest in the business. Stone was instrumental in the development of the marketing and financial strategies that Bennett Industries proposed to use in the future.

THE TAILGATE INDUSTRY

The mechanical tailgate is manufactured for use on off-highway mining and construction trucks. Exhibits 1 and 2 provide illustrations of the mechanical tailgate as it appears before and after it is installed. Tailgates have several applications in the mining and construction industries. Tailgates are ideal for transporting such loose or soupy materials as coal slag. Stone quarries frequently install gates in their trucks to enable them to carry more material per load and to reduce spillage. Tailgates facilitate loading. Because the load will not slip off the back, fewer passes are needed to fill the truck and less material is lost in transportation. When the material involved consists of large

Exhibit 1

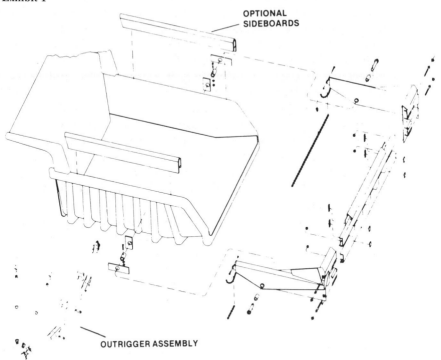

OPTIONAL
SIDEBOARDS

OUTRIGGER ASSEMBLY

The outrigger assembly is mounted and held by clamps
(1 per side) and support tubes (2 per side) welded to the
frame.

Exhibit 2

STANDARD
CLEARANCE

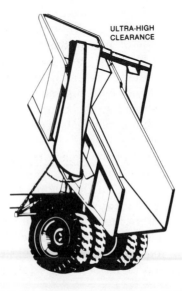

ULTRA-HIGH
CLEARANCE

stone, spillage on the haul road can be very costly because of the serious damage to tires caused when the trucks run over the rocks. Since tire replacement can be quite expensive (about $4,000 per tire), many firms are forced to use bulldozers to clear the haul roads after each trip. Tailgates can eliminate this problem.

Because of the way tailgates are employed by end users, truck manufacturers look with disfavor upon the product. Their position is that tailgates reduce the life of the truck by encouraging end users to overload their equipment. Because tailgates can also cause an uneven weight distribution when the truck is loaded, adding a tailgate increases the chance of a breakdown. Since the manufacturer bears the brunt of criticism and sometimes the cost of repair, it is not surprising that none of the truck manufacturing firms include tailgates in their product lines.

Because manufacturers refuse to become involved with mechanical tailgates, most are sold either through distributors or directly to the end user. Some distributors refuse to market tailgates for the same reasons that truck manufacturers discourage their use. Despite this fact, many dealers are quite willing to sell this product and account for many of the tailgates sold for new trucks. Most of the tailgates sold for trucks already in use are purchased directly by end users. The former channel requires less selling effort than the latter, but the discounts allowed to the dealer segment of the market are greater. Selling directly to the end user permits higher markups but also involves more customer contact and follow-up effort.

All of the tailgates available in the market are similar in design, but several factors make it impossible to mass-produce this product. Given a specific capacity, substantial differences exist among the various truck designs used by the individual manufacturers. Another problem in making tailgates is that each truck has several different body designs, reflecting the density of the material to be hauled. The body of a truck that carries iron ore will have to be smaller than the body of the same truck if it is used to haul fly ash, because the latter substance is much lighter per cubic foot and thus requires a larger body to hold the recommended capacity. Further consideration must be given to the clearance needed for dumping. Trucks hauling larger-volume materials will need more dump clearance than ones carrying finer materials.

All of these factors must be incorporated into the design of each individual tailgate. Because of these unique characteristics, tailgates must be made to order. This prevents tailgate manufacturers from carrying any inventory except for the necessary raw materials. Fortunately, once the tailgate has been designed and the necessary raw materials acquired, assembly is a relatively simple process. A tailgate requires about two weeks for assembly, and except for some welding and metal-bending equipment, a tailgate could be assembled in the basement of a private home. In fact, this is the way Tyson Tailgate got started. Because of the simplicity of the product, many end users have been inclined to build and install their own makeshift tailgate rather than purchase one on the market.

TYSON TAILGATE COMPANY

Tyson Tailgate Company, located in Lincoln, Illinois, is the only current manufacturer of the mechanical tailgate. Founded in 1969, the company has grown steadily and presently boasts sales of over $3 million. Besides the tailgate, which accounts for the majority of Tyson's activity, the firm is engaged in the production of a growing line of related products, such as coal bodies, liners, sideboards, and top covers.

Tyson makes two basic types of gates, the Standard and the Extra-High. The Extra-High model is designed for trucks that carry materials needing greater dump clearance. Though the Standard model is less costly and acounts for the majority of Tyson's sales, the Extra-High model is the more profitable of the two.

Tyson's sales are geared mainly to end users, though many tailgates are sold through distributors. Tyson emphasizes end-user sales because of the higher profit margins and because of its experienced installation crew. Partially because of this strategy, and partially because of the business tactics of Charles Tyson, the company has never enjoyed favorable relationships with distributors.

Exhibits 3 and 4 summarize the current activities of Tyson and provide estimates of the breakdowns of the markets presently served by Tyson. Most of this information was compiled by Jim Stone through conversations with Mark Bennett and through outside research.

BUSINESS PREPARATION

In preparing to enter the tailgate market, the first obstacle to be overcome was finding an acceptable manufacturer for the product. Bennett was not interested in manufacturing the tailgate himself. His belief, which was shared by all concerned, was that they could contract with another firm to take care of production. Once again, family ties proved the answer to the problem. Breckenridge happened to be related to the owner of a small metal fabricating firm in Mattoon, Illinois, known as Deacon Manufacturing. After several conferences in which the details of the arrangement were worked out, Deacon agreed to make the tailgates for Bennett Industries provided that a signed purchase order could be produced. Bennett consented to this condition and soon provided Deacon's management with specifications for several tailgate designs that had been prepared by Breck-

Exhibit 3
Competitor analysis—Tyson Tailgate Company (as
estimated by Jim Stone)

Year	Units sold	Yearly sales and income (estimated)	
		Average price	Revenues
1977	200	$5,400	$1,080,000
1978	275	6,000	1,650,000
1979	335	6,775	2,270,000
1980	370	7,300	2,700,000
Projected:			
1981	400	7,800	3,120,000
1982	440	8,500	3,740,000
1983	480	9,300	4,464,000

Sales breakdown by state (estimated)

West Virginia	15%	North and South Carolina	10%
Pennsylvania	12	Texas	7
Virginia	10	Indiana	5
Georgia	10	Illinois	5
Florida	10	Other	6
Ohio	10		

Sales breakdown by month (estimated)

Month	Percent	Month	Percent
January	3%	July	12%
February	5	August	17
March	8	September	12
April	8	October	7
May	8	November	5
June	12	December	3

enridge. Deacon stated that they could provide Bennett with up to 10
gates per month and that an individual gate would take approximately
two to three weeks to complete. This corresponded to the time it took
Tyson to make a similar gate. Deacon also provided Bennett with
price quotations based on the number of identical tailgates ordered
(see Exhibit 5). Mark Bennett believed that Deacon's prices were
close enough to his own estimate of Tyson's manufacturing costs that
Bennett Industries would not be vulnerable to competitive price reactions by Tyson. In fact, Bennett believed that the best way to attack
Tyson was through price. Stone questioned this strategy, but Bennett
stood firm in his convictions.

In order to get a reasonable estimation of demand, Stone and Bennett prepared a market survey that was sent to various off-highway
truck dealers throughout the country. Exhibits 6 through 8 show the
results of the survey.

Exhibit 4
Competitor analysis—Tyson Tailgate Company (as estimated by Jim Stone)

Approximate sales breakdown by customer

Coal	50%
Quarry	25
Construction	15
Special applications	10

Pricing and discount structure

Standard	$ 8,900	
Extra-high	$10,700	
Standard discount		15%
Cash payment		2
Follow-up performance report		5
New trucks		5
Installed with qualified mechanic		5
Promotional participation		5
Total discount possible		37%

Manufacturing costs (estimate)

Standard	$2,900
Extra-high	$3,500

Distribution

Dealers	50%	75% new trucks	25% used trucks
End users (direct sales)	50%	25% new trucks	75% used trucks

Exhibit 5
Price quotes from Deacon Manufacturing

One gate	$5,400 each
Two gates (same size and type)	4,800 each
Five gates (same size and type)	3,800 each

The results of the survey were satisfactory for the most part, although Stone expressed some dissatisfaction with a few of the questions that Bennett had included. The survey pointed out several states that seemed especially promising. The majority of dealers appeared to be responsive to the idea of a new manufacturer serving the industry, but surprisingly (at least to Bennett), few were dissatisfied with current price levels. The survey also pointed out the need for a direct sales force in certain geographic areas, such as Pennsylvania. It also confirmed Bennett's belief that the tailgate market was concentrated in the mideastern, Atlantic coast, and Sun Belt regions.

After finishing their analysis of the market survey, both Bennett and Stone came to the conclusion that another survey, directed at the end

Exhibit 6
Number of dealers responding to survey,
by state

Alabama	1	New Mexico	2
Arizona	2	New York	1
Arkansas	1	North Carolina	3
California	7	North Dakota	2
Colorado	1	Ohio	4
Florida	3	Oklahoma	1
Georgia	3	Oregon	2
Illinois	2	Pennsylvania	6
Indiana	2	South Carolina	1
Iowa	2	South Dakota	2
Kansas	1	Tennessee	3
Kentucky	3	Texas	3
Maine	2	Utah	1
Michigan	4	Virginia	1
Minnesota	3	Washington	1
Mississippi	1	West Virginia	3
Nevada	1	Wisconsin	2

Note: Total number of surveys mailed—230;
total responses—77.

Exhibit 7
Summary of truck dealers' responses, by target states

	Tailgate sales	Prices	Attitude toward alternative supplier
Florida	Very high	Reasonable	Favorable
Georgia	Low	Reasonable	Favorable
Illinois	Low	High	Favorable
Indiana	Low	Reasonable	Unfavorable
Iowa	Low	High	Favorable
Kentucky	High	Reasonable	Favorable
Michigan	Low	Reasonable	Unfavorable
North Carolina	Low	Reasonable	Undecided
Ohio	High	Reasonable	Favorable
Pennsylvania	Very high	Reasonable	Unfavorable
Tennessee	Low	Reasonable	Undecided
Texas	Average	Reasonable	Favorable
Virginia	Low	Reasonable	Favorable
West Virginia	Average	Reasonable	Favorable

users in the mining and construction industry, was needed. The two
men resolved that this survey would be prepared more carefully and
that it would be restricted to end users in the target markets identified
as the most promising.

GENERAL MARKET ANALYSIS

To supplement the information obtained in the first market survey,
Stone further analyzed the past performance and future growth projec-

Exhibit 8
Survey form and frequency of responses

1. Approximately how many mechanical tailgates are sold in your defined dealership territory annually? (Check one.)
   74% 0–5 15% 6–10 9% 11 or more 2% No response

2. Of the off-highway trucks sold, what is their capacity size?
   8% Less than 30 tons 38% 35–40 tons 30% 55–55 tons
   14% 85 tons 6% 120 tons 2% More than 120 tons

3. Via dealership sales, mechanical tailgates are primarily sold for which of the following?
   29% Fine or fluidic material 5% Special construction
   47% Overburden or crushing 16% Other (specify)
   3% No response

4. How many days does a mechanical tailgate take to install at the dealership or in the field with a service engineer and two dealership service people?
   20% One day 47% Two days 11% Three days
   3% Over three days

5. Adequate availability for mechanical tailgates is?
   24% Less than three weeks 19% Three weeks
   29% Four weeks 11% Five weeks 7% More than five weeks
   10% No response

6. Of the existing mechanical tailgates on the market, please comment on their prices.
   58% Reasonable 30% Too high 12% No response

7. With every mechanical tailgate sold through the dealership, assuming there would be a supervising field engineer available, should the engineer's fee for service be included in the list price, or should it be separate?
   49% Included 37% Separate 14% No response

8. Would you consider a complete tailgate installation service offered by the manufacturer as opposed to installation by your service department?
   24% Yes 38% No 29% Need more information
   14% No response

9. What would you recommend to the manufacturer of mechanical tailgates concerning the color of the tailgate?
   66% Standard truck color 2% Standard tailgate color
   19% Primed only 6% No preference 7% No response

10. What options are included in the purchase of a mechanical tailgate?

    How successful are they?

11. Would the construction and mining industry benefit from the addition of another manufacturer of tailgates for off-highway trucks?
    36% Yes 40% No 24% No response

12. As a machinery dealer, what are your overall thoughts and comments regarding mechanical tailgates and their concepts?

Thank you very much. Your cooperation has been greatly appreciated.

tions of the mining, construction, and off-highway truck industries. The results of this analysis appear below. Additional information concerning the off-highway truck market is presented in Exhibits 9 through 12.

Mining industry

The mining industry has been hurt in the last several years because of sagging demand (due to recession) and rapidly inflated costs. The projected real growth rate for the mining industry is estimated to be about 2 percent per year. One area that appears promising in the future is coal mining. The energy shortage the world has faced over the past decade has encouraged coal producers to increase production dramatically. Coal has become the most important single market for the off-highway truck industry.

Unfortunately, several factors exist that could hurt the coal industry in the short run. Despite the increasing need for coal as an alternative energy source, demand has not kept pace with the rapid increase in supply. Presently, the industry is able to produce roughly 10 to 15 percent more coal than can be consumed. This has resulted in downward pressure on prices and low profit margins for coal producers. Another factor contributing to the industry's low profitability is a decline in the productivity of labor. This has been attributed to an influx of new, inexperienced miners, prohibitive governmental regulations, and bad union-management relations. The productivity downturn is expected to reverse itself in the future, however, because of improved mining techniques and equipment.

Perhaps the most serious short-term problem facing the coal mining industry is the threat of an extended labor strike. If this situation occurs, the performance of the coal industry as well as that of the off-highway truck manufacturers will be impaired. This could also have a major influence on the entry of Bennett Industries into the tailgate market.

Construction industry

According to the Department of Commerce, the value of new construction in 1980 declined approximately 10.5 percent after adjustments for inflation. Perhaps no other industry in the country was hurt more by the recent economic downturn. Except for certain areas in the Southwest, the exorbitant interest rates and skyrocketing inflation caused the outlook for the construction industry in 1981 to appear sluggish at best. Another factor that made the near future even less attractive, especially as it concerned the off-highway truck market, was the near completion of the interstate highway system. Historically, a significant portion of the demand for off-highway equipment came from this segment of the construction market.

Exhibit 9
Market breakdown by customer type

	1977		1979	
	35–50 tons	Over 70 tons	35–50 tons	Over 70 tons
Coal*	53%	37%	30%	50%
Quarry	12	6	12	—
Construction	17	—	40	—
Copper and iron	—	41	—	31
Other mining	18	16	18	19

* Before 1972, about 5 percent.

Exhibit 10
Industry truck sales—North America

	1978	1979
35–50–60 tons	1,700	1,200
75–85 tons	240	240
More than 100 tons	210	260

Exhibit 11
Total truck populations—North America

20–30 tons	35 tons	50 tons	75–80 tons	100–150 tons	More than 150 tons
3,000	8,000	6,0000	2,100	1,700	900

Exhibit 12
Truck sales by major target states

	1979			1980		
	35 tons	50 tons	85 tons	35 tons	50 tons	85 tons
Kentucky	45	80	36	30	39	33
Pennsylvania	35	54	10	9	12	n.a.
Ohio	16	23	n.a.	9	22	n.a.
Illinois	23	6	n.a.	8	4	n.a.
Indiana	n.a.	23	n.a.	16	7	n.a.
Virginia	31	24	10	4	23	6
West Virginia	25	69	21	15	27	12
Tennessee	24	21	0	8	1	0
Michigan	n.a.	n.a.	9	n.a.	n.a.	11
Total U.S.A. sales	499	543	142	287	292	120

n.a.—information not available.

Though the short-term possibilities in this industry seem bleak, the expected recovery of the economy after 1981 should improve the future outlook for this industry, and demand for construction equipment could pick up over the next three to five years.

Off-highway truck industry

The off-highway truck market basically consists of the two industries previously described, mining and construction. As long as current conditions persist in these industries, growth in the off-highway truck market will be slow. The estimated compound real-growth rates for off-highway truck sales to the mining and construction industries (according to *U.S. Industrial Outlook, 1980*) are 3.6 percent and 2.8 percent, respectively, through 1984. As Exhibits 9 through 12 indicate, sales of the 35- to 85-ton trucks declined in 1978 and 1979. By the beginning of 1981, this trend had reversed, but labor problems in the coal industry made the outlook for the remainder of the year uncertain.

If the economy can recover from the recession in the near future, several factors could improve the growth potential for the off-highway truck market. Experts predicted that strip mining could double in the early 1980s due to demand for coal as an alternative energy source and to new federal strip mining regulations. Though these regulations are strict, they are much clearer than those in the past. This removed a lot of the uncertainties that previously discouraged strip mining. The outlook for the future could be further stimulated by an increasing need to replace the depleted supply of high-grade ores with lower-quality minerals. Because these lower-grade ores are harder to extract, truck demand for these types of operations should improve.

Overall outlook for tailgate demand

Though the picture that emerged from analyzing the three industries did not appear optimistic, both Bennett and Stone realized that there were other factors to be dealt with before any definite conclusions concerning the potential of the tailgate market could be reached. While the recession might restrict demand in the new truck segment of the market, there could be an opposite effect on tailgate demand for used trucks. High interest rates (which discourage capital investment) combined with rapidly escalating costs could motivate end users to search for ways to improve equipment utilization. This could make such accessories as tailgates much more attractive purchases. Distributors might also find tailgates a desirable addition to their product lines. If truck sales remained low, dealers could be expected to turn to products that would help compensate for the slack sales.

Finally, consideration had to be given to the potential competitive reaction of Tyson Tailgate. In spite of the fact that any price reduction on the part of Tyson could reduce its revenues and despite Bennett's ability, through Deacon Manufacturing, to compete on a cost basis, the possibility of a price war could not be discounted. It seemed unlikely that Mr. Tyson would sit back and let Bennett capture a share of the tailgate market without retaliating in some manner—especially given the hard feelings that existed between Mr. Tyson and Mark Bennett. The entry of Bennett Industries into the mechanical tailgate market as a direct competitor of Tyson would certainly not improve this relationship. Therefore, any course of action chosen had to be made with the competitive implications in mind.

THE APRIL 1981 MEETING

Bennett opened the April 1981 meeting with several brief comments before Stone presented the results of the market analysis provided earlier:

> I think that we all agree that the tailgate market looks pretty good. What I want to do today is put all the information we have been accumulating into some concrete strategies and plans. I am anxious to get things going. The longer we wait, the more sales we lose. Jim, why don't you fill us in on what you have been doing the last several months. I'm sure you've got a lot to tell us.

Stone began his presentation with a short explanation about the methods and sources he used to prepare his analysis of the market. After completing his report, Stone concluded with some questions directed at Breckenridge as well as Bennett.

Jim: Andy, what I'd like to know from you is exactly how many different tailgate designs have you been able to finish?

Andy: Well, Jim, actually I've only completed two up till now, but we have the information we need from the various parts manufacturers for the rest of them. Besides, it only takes a few days to make them up. They aren't that complicated, you know.

Jim: Sure, they are not that complicated, but what I'm worried about is our ability to provide Deacon with specs as soon as we get an order. I'm also concerned with material lead times that could delay production. How much material does Deacon keep in stock? Can we realistically expect them to be able to meet our needs? Remember, we don't have anything down in writing.

Mark: Jim, I think you're worried about nothing. Deacon's just adding on a second shift, and they will jump at any business we can give them. Besides, Tyson usually takes three to five weeks to actually deliver their tailgates. I know we can match that.

Further discussion ensued of the market analysis as well as the result of the survey that Bennett and Stone had prepared. Everyone agreed that the prospects for the tailgate looked good overall and that the most promising markets were in the mideastern, Atlantic coast, and southern states. As the discussion began to wane, Mark Bennett dropped a bombshell:

> Gentlemen, what I'm about to present to you is so exciting I've been saving it as a surprise. In the past couple of weeks I've been on the phone with a few of my old contacts in the industry. As a result, I was able to line up a few potential customers. I know we probably won't get all these orders, but I'm pretty sure that we can sell at least 75 percent of these people [see Exhibit 13].

Exhibit 13
Potential customers—Bennett Industries 4/1/81

Customers	Potential orders	Truck size	Location
Potter Stone	2	50-ton	Illinois
Milton Martin	1	35-ton	West Virginia
Stork Stone Company	1	40-ton	Pennsylvania
Omar Corporation	1	33-ton	Illinois
Captain Quarries	2	22-ton	Iowa
Lake Products	2	50-ton	Iowa
Golleta Brothers	2	50-ton	West Virginia
Canary Mining	6	50-ton	West Virginia
Bison Coal Company	2	85-ton	West Virginia
American Trucking	4	40-ton	Virginia
Mann Quarries	3	35-ton	New Jersey
White Rock Contractors	2	55-ton	West Virginia

Needless to say, both Stone and Breckenridge were impressed. The three men briefly discussed the probability of actually getting these orders and, after everyone was satisfied, it was decided that the next task to complete was preparing some pro forma financial statements to see what the business looked like on paper. Bennett and Breckenridge provided most of the cost estimates used to compute the operating expenses for the remainder of 1981 and 1982, while Stone handled the paperwork. Exhibit 14 is the projected operating schedule for the last seven months of 1981. The pro forma income statements and balance sheets for both years as well as the cash flow schedule that are displayed in Exhibits 15 through 19 are based on these assumptions.

Exhibit 14
Projected operations schedule—1981 (in units)

	June	July	August	September	October	November	December
Sales	4	8	8	10	4	3	3
Production	4	8	8	10	4	3	3
Delivery	0	4	8	8	10	4	3
Receipts	0	2	6	8	9	7	3½
Payments	0	2	6	8	9	7	3½

Notes: Production completed one month after sales order. Product delivered within one week of production. Receipts and payments—50 percent month of delivery, 50 percent next month.

Exhibit 15
Projected cash flow schedule—Bennett Industries—6/1/81–12/31/81

	June	July	August	September	October	November	December	Total
Receipts	$ 0	$15,200	$45,600	$60,800	$68,400	$53,200	$26,600	$269,800
Cost of goods sold	0	9,600	28,800	38,400	43,200	33,600	16,800	170,400
Cash inflows	0	5,600	16,800	22,400	25,200	19,600	9,800	99,400
Expenditures:								
Telephone	150	150	150	150	150	150	150	1,050
Wages and salaries	1,000	2,400	5,200	6,600	7,300	5,900	7,450	35,850
Office equipment	200	200	200	200	200	200	200	1,400
Advertising	100	2,100	700	700	700	700	700	5,700
Freight	0	600	1,200	1,200	1,500	600	450	5,550
Travel	0	1,200	2,400	2,400	3,000	1,200	900	11,100
Insurance	210	210	210	210	210	210	210	1,470
Taxes	0	0	0	0	8,850	0	0	8,850
Miscellaneous	1,250	1,000	1,000	1,000	1,000	1,000	1,000	7,250
Cash outflows	2,910	7,860	11,060	12,460	22,910	9,960	11,060	78,220
Net cash flow	(2,910)	(2,260)	5,740	9,940	2,290	9,640	(1,260)	21,180
Beginning balance	10,000	7,090	4,830	10,570	20,510	22,800	32,440	10,000
Ending balance	7,900	4,830	10,570	20,510	22,800	32,440	31,180	31,180

Note: All sales prices computed at $7,600 per truck. Cost of goods sold computed at $4,800 per truck. (These figures are used in Exhibits 15–19.)

Exhibit 16

BENNETT INDUSTRIES
Projected Income Statement
6/1/81–12/31/81

Sales		$304,000
Cost of goods sold.		192,000
Gross margin		112,000
Operating expenses:		
Wages and salaries.	$39,000	
Office equipment	1,400	
Telephone	1,050	
Insurance.	1,470	
Freight	5,550	
Advertising.	5,700	
Travel	11,100	
Miscellaneous	7,250	
Total operating expenses.		72,520
Income before taxes		39,480
Taxes		11,800
Income after taxes		$ 27,680

Exhibit 17

BENNETT INDUSTRIES
Projected Balance Sheet
12/31/81

Assets		*Liabilities*	
Cash.	$31,180	Accounts payable.	$21,600
Accounts receivable.	34,200	Wages payable	3,150
		Taxes payable.	2,950
Total assets.	$65,380	Total liabilities	27,700
		Equity	
		Owner's equity	10,000
		Retained earnings	27,680
		Total equity	37,680
		Total liabilities and equity.	$65,380

Sales were projected at 60 tailgates for 1982, or 5 per month. Sales revenue was projected based on an average price of $7,600, and average cost was computed at $4,800 per unit.

Bennett was quite pleased with the bottom lines that the statements showed, although he had expected them to be somewhat higher. It was agreed that Bennett would put up $10,000 to provide the business with the working capital that was needed to take care of the negative cash flows anticipated in the first few months. Neither Breckenridge nor Stone offered to sink any of his own money into the venture, but it was agreed that no more than $10,000 would probably be needed.

Exhibit 18

BENNETT INDUSTRIES
Projected Income Statement
For 1982

Sales		$456,000
Cost of goods sold..........................		288,000
Gross margin		168,000
Operating expenses:		
Wages and salaries........................	$67,000	
Office equipment	2,400	
Telephone	1,800	
Insurance................................	2,520	
Freight	8,700	
Advertising...............................	8,400	
Travel	16,500	
Miscellaneous	12,000	
Total operating expenses...............		120,220
Income before taxes		47,780
Taxes......................................		19,100
Income after taxes (net income)..............		$ 28,680

Note: Based on sales of 60 units; all figures based on 1981 dollars.

Exhibit 19

BENNETT INDUSTRIES
Projected Balance Sheet
12/31/82

Assets		*Liabilities*	
Cash......................	$ 20,135	Accounts payable...........	$ 48,000
Marketable securities........	30,000	Wages payable	7,000
Accounts receivable.........	76,000	Taxes payable..............	4,775
Total assets................	$126,135	Total liabilities	59,775
		Equity	
		Owner's equity	10,000
		Retained earnings	56,360
		Total equity	66,360
		Total liabilities and equity....	$126,135

Note: Based on sales of 60 units; all figures are in 1981 dollars.

BENNETT'S STRATEGIES

It was not until May 1, 1981, that Bennett and Stone met for the final time to prepare their strategic plans. Exhibit 20 illustrates the marketing strategies that Bennett Industries proposed to use as a result of that meeting. Bennett finally conceded to Stone's previous contention that Bennett Industries should not attempt to compete on a price basis. However, a discount structure was agreed upon that would encourage rapid payment by its customers.

Exhibit 20
Preliminary market strategies

Product	One basic model (similar to Tyson's Extra-High model), reduces engineering requirements
Promotion	Pamphlets—informational Inside sales force—telephone contact with dealers reduces selling expenditures Personal service—to take advantage of Tyson's bad customer relations Direct sales—to complement inside sales force
Distribution	75 percent dealer—to take advantage of dealer's sales force 25 percent direct sales to end users
Pricing	Prices based on Tyson's Skimming strategy to minimize competitive reactions Market study indicates price not major buying influence Discounts to make dealers' profits more attractive
Pricing schedule	Suggested dealer resale price $10,700 Full price 8,900 10 percent dealer discount 8,000
Terms	Cash payment—10 percent discount $ 7,200 10-day payment—5 percent discount 7,600 30-day payment—net price 8,000
Markets	Primary target markets—states east of the Mississippi Emphasis on tailgates for 35- to 85-ton trucks, which account for the majority of truck sales in the United States Major end users targeted—coal mining and quarries (stone producers).

Bennett believed that his contacts in the industry would enable the company to conduct much of its selling activity over the telephone. Stone was not convinced that this would be possible, but he agreed that it would be much less expensive and decided it was worth a try. This selling method also fitted in well with Bennett's strategy to concentrate on dealers.

A critical element in the strategic plan was the decision to limit investment to the initial sum that would be used to supply working capital. This low commitment of funds reflected the limited resources available to the company and also represented a desire to have the option of a speedy exit from the market should the venture prove unsuccessful. Accordingly, the two decided to use Bennett's home residence as their temporary place of business.

The long-range objective of Bennett was to milk whatever profits were available in the market and to get out before competition became too intense. One of Stone's jobs was to be exploration of new opportunities for investment. It was agreed that in order to have any long-term chance for sales growth to exceed 100 units per year, the company would need a more permanent facility. Neither thought that this was an attractive idea.

LINGERING DOUBTS

After Stone left the meeting with Bennett, he began to brood over the events that had taken place during the previous few months. He had several lingering doubts about the feasibility of the venture in which he had become involved. Stone wondered whether or not the information Bennett had provided was accurate. He knew that Bennett was experienced at selling and was afraid Bennett might have exaggerated the true potential of the market. Stone also questioned his own work and wondered if he had collected enough information. Finally, he wondered if the conclusions that had been reached were correct. Was this market really that attractive? Could the company really compete head to head against Tyson? Only time would tell, but Stone wished he could be more confident about the future.

Part 3

Target Market Strategy

Deciding what people or organizations to serve in the marketplace is one of management's most important and demanding strategic decisions. All operations of the firm revolve around the target market decision. Target market alternatives range from serving all (or most) buyers using a mass strategy to serving one or more niches (segments) using a differentiated strategy in each niche.

There are clear indications that market niching will become the dominant strategy of successful firms in the 1980s—particularly those that are not market leaders. This is because high market share is often linked to strong business performance. Serving a niche or segment of a product-market is often the only feasible way for a firm to gain and hold market share. While the niche decision alone will not guarantee high performance, it can be the first step in building a high-performance marketing strategy. For example, the Profit Impact of Market Strategies (PIMS) program continues to signal a key link between market share position and business success:

> Some of the most dramatic and well-publicized strategic successes of recent years have been based on the principle of segment focus that we advocate. For example, Philip Morris steadily improved its share of the cigarette market throughout the 1970s. Part of the company's success has been due to its heavy support for Merit, a low-tar brand that apparently had special appeal for health-conscious smokers.[1]

Two major activities underlie the target market decision: (1) defining and analyzing product-markets to gauge present opportunity and growth potential; and (2) deciding *what* people/organizations to serve and *how* to target the firm's marketing efforts in each product-market of interest to it. We shall briefly examine each of these activities.

---

[1] Robert D. Buzzell and Frederik D. Wiersema, "Successful Share-Building Strategies," *Harvard Business Review*, January–February 1981, p. 144.

The cases in Part 3 focus on market opportunity analysis, forecasting, and the selection of market targets. The discussion included in this introduction should be particularly useful in (1) showing what information is needed in market analysis and forecasting and (2) indicating what criteria should be taken into account in selecting a target market strategy. The discussion is introductory and thus does not provide a complete coverage of these topics.

DEFINING AND ANALYZING PRODUCT-MARKETS

Market opportunity analysis serves two useful purposes. It enables the firm to understand markets before deciding *whether* and *how* to serve them. Equally important, it enables the firm to track product-market trends so as to determine when shifts in targeted customers or adjustments in marketing efforts are needed. The Limited Stores, Inc., a successful retailer of medium-priced women's fashion apparel, illustrates both uses of market information. During the 1970s management targeted its marketing efforts toward the rapidly expanding 16–35 age group. Projected changes in age group composition that will occur during the 1980s have resulted in an alteration of the firm's target market:

> During the 1980's the number of women 15 to 24 will decline, while the 25 to 34 year old market will increase by 13 percent. In order to capitalize on this opportunity, we are carefully and gradually positioning the business to appeal to fashion conscious women in the 20 to 40 year old age category . . . in other words, the growth market of the 1980's. Among other things, this involves upgrading the quality and taste level of our merchandise and placing more emphasis on those merchandise classifications that appeal to these women. The strategy appears to be working.[2]

Limited's target market strategy is apparently to follow into the next stage in the life cycle the large age group category that responded so well to the firm's marketing efforts during the 1970s.

The first task in market opportunity analysis is to establish the boundaries of the product-market to be analyzed. Since markets are groups of people (or organizations) that have the *ability* and *willingness* to buy *something* for end-use purposes, ability and willingness represent demand for a product or service.[3] People with needs and wants buy product or service benefits. Thus, a product-market is a matching of people with needs that lead to demand and certain product benefits that satisfy those needs. Unless product benefits are available, only people with needs exist, not markets. Likewise, unless

---

[2] The Limited Stores, Inc., *First Quarter Report, 1982*, November 12, 1981.

[3] The following discussion is based on suggestions offered by Robert B. Woodruff of the University of Tennessee, Knoxville.

people (or organizations) have demands for what products can do, there cannot be product benefits of value.

Often we find that a subgroup of brands within a specific product category (color television) compete with one another. Typically, all brands of a specific category do not compete with all others. For example, K mart brand TVs and Curtis Mathes are not directly competing for the same end users. An additional factor is that different products can sometimes satisfy the same need. Steel competes with aluminum, plastics, and other materials. Closed-circuit television competes with air travel for conferences and meetings. Thus, defining the competitive arena for a brand should include all products/brands that can satisfy a particular need or want.

Once the product-market has been defined, several types of information are needed to analyze the opportunity present in the market. To simplify the discussion, assume that all brands competing with our brand are from the same specific product category (e.g., color television). Often it is helpful to analyze a product-market at the levels shown in Exhibit 1. Note that the generic level contains all of the specific product (or service) categories that satisfy the same generic need (e.g., home entertainment). The information needed for product-market analysis is shown in Exhibit 1. Let's briefly examine each category.

Market size and growth forecasts

We are interested in the size of the market (generic, specific, and brand) and how it is changing. Is the market expected to grow or decline over the next three–five years? What is the annual compounded rate of change in the market? For example, personal computer sales were approaching 2 million units in 1982 and were expected to double by 1984 or 1985.[4] Apple and Tandy/Radio Shack, with about equal market shares, represented nearly half of the market, followed by Commodore, with a 10 percent share. Note that to obtain market size information at the generic level it is necessary to sum all of the specific product category forecasts. At the brand level we are interested in the sales forecast for our brand.

Customer profiles

It is important to learn as much as possible about the people/organizations that are comprised by each market level. Who are they, what are their needs, what are their socioeconomic and demographic characteristics, and how do they choose among alternative brands? As we move from the generic to the brand level, customer profiles should

---

[4] Kathleen K. Wiegner, "Tomorrow Has Arrived," *Forbes*, February 15, 1982, p. 113.

Exhibit 1
Product-market levels and information needs

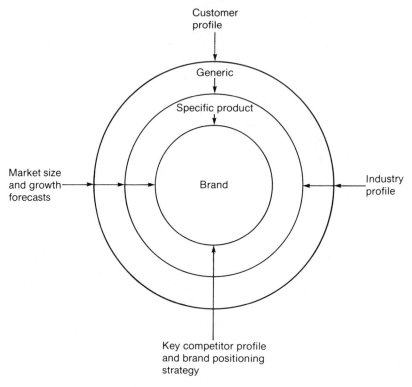

become more specific and detailed. Attempting to gain an understanding of *why* people buy can be quite useful in target market selection and marketing program design. For example, General Mills, to stay abreast of customer needs and wants for its restaurant units (e.g., Red Lobster), uses intensive marketing research to guide site selection, menu modification, and development of consumer profiles.

Industry profile

This information should include industry characteristics such as size, number of firms, growth rates, distribution practices, and other descriptive guidelines. The industry analysis provides a broad overview description of the firms that make up the generic and specific product-markets. Industry trade publications are good sources of information for constructing an industry profile. Also, government publications such as the *U.S. Industrial Outlook*, published each year by the Department of Commerce, provide useful industry analyses and projections.

Key competitors

The detailed analysis of firms viewed as direct (or potential) competitors should include their overall strengths, market share, financial strengths, management strengths (and shortcomings), technical and operating advantages, and marketing strategy features and limitations. The key competitor analysis should also supply guidelines for the firm's brand positioning strategy.

THE TARGET MARKET DECISION

A firm is more likely to use a mass market strategy in a new market than in an established market. With only a few competitors and with end users whose needs and wants are similar, mass strategies may be appropriate early in the product-market life cycle. Intense competition, differentiated products, and variations in customer needs and wants create both a need and an opportunity for market niching.

While mass market strategies are used by some firms, many others have chosen to serve one or more customer groups within the total market. Regional banks, for example, are looking for market niches that will enable them to position their banks in the highly competitive financial services area created by deregulation. Some illustrative niche strategies include:

> Hawkeye Bancorp, Des Moines, Iowa, long a big agricultural lender, has turned to managing farms for absentee owners. . . .
>
> Bank One, Columbus, Ohio, has become a leader in specialized services. It hired out to competition and now processes cash-management accounts for nine brokerage firms, which are prevented from issuing checks. . . .
>
> In Missouri, Mark Twain Bankshares Inc.'s financial consultants sell their expertise in business problems as diverse as cash flow and strategic planning.[5]

Even firms considering mass strategies may find analysis at the market niche level useful in deciding how to position themselves against competition. Because of this we shall assume that the target market decision involves niche formation and analysis, regardless of the target market ultimately chosen by management. These are the steps in selecting a target market strategy: ,

1. Decide how to form niches in the product market.
2. Describe the people/organizations in each niche.

---

[5] John Helyar, "Regional Banks Search for a Niche in Face of New Rules, Competition," *The Wall Street Journal,* February 4, 1982, p. 25.

3. Evaluate target market alternatives.
4. Select a target market strategy.[6]

Niche formation

Niches can be identified through experience and judgment, analysis of existing information, or marketing research studies. The objective is to divide the product-market into two or more subgroups, such that each group differs in its responsiveness to a particular marketing effort (product offer, distribution approach, price, and promotional strategy). Identifying niches may be difficult without the aid of customer research. In some instances historical sales by customer category can be analyzed to help identify customer groups with similar needs and wants. An interesting discussion of how Kraft, Inc., identified market niches for its ice-cream brands is included at the end of this overview of target market strategy.

Niche description

Much of the information obtained from product-market analysis can be used in describing market niches. Exhibit 1–5 in Chapter 1 is a useful guide to the types of information needed in describing the people/organizations that constitute market niches. The starting point in describing niches is the definition and analysis of the product-market (customer profiles) that were discussed earlier. The objective is to identify key characteristics that will be useful in distinguishing one niche from another.

Target market alternatives

Unless management decides to serve the entire product-market using a single marketing program positioning strategy, it must evaluate alternative niches to determine which to select as target markets. Recall that Exhibit 1–6 in Chapter 1 illustrated how alternative targets can be evaluated. Such evaluation should include an assessment of the market demand in each niche, the competitive situation, the costs of a marketing mix to serve the niche, and the estimated profit contribution.

Target market strategy

The choice of what people/organizations to serve in a product-market involves consideration of the following factors:

☐   Needs/wants of end users.
☐   Product-market size and structure.

---

[6] David W. Cravens, *Strategic Marketing* (Homewood, Ill.: Richard D. Irwin, 1982), p. 167.

- ☐ Company/brand market share.
- ☐ Company resources/capabilities.
- ☐ Intensity of competition.
- ☐ Production/marketing scale economies.[7]

While the ultimate decision will depend on management's preferences, evaluation of these factors will indicate the feasible options. For example, if the needs and wants of all end users are very similar, a market niche strategy may not be feasible. The target market decision establishes key guidelines for selecting a marketing program positioning strategy.

Niching or segmentation may be difficult in new product-markets, and limited competition may make niching unnecessary. In new markets there is often not enough information about buyers to enable grouping those with similar needs and wants. In contrast, as product-markets mature, niche strategies may become essential for all firms except, possibly, the market leaders.

The niche strategy used by Kraft for the firm's ice-cream brands is described in the following application illustration by Samuel R. Gardner, vice president of marketing—Retail Food Group.

Application Illustration[8]

Like many other businesses, the dairy business represents a far different marketing climate than it did only some 10 to 20 years ago. In those earlier days, success was pretty much based on the ability of the many local processors to establish strong distribution franchises in their own trading areas. Consumer demand was traditionally quite strong and stable, and federal and local regulations were basically protectionist. Food retailers, for the most part, had not yet decided to invest heavily in processing their own milk and related by-products.

By the 1960s, a lot of this had changed. Major food retailers, capitalizing on the mass demand and high turnover of these products, had started moving into the dairy business. And through networks of centralized, controlled distribution, they were able to market their own labels more efficiently than could many of the local or regional suppliers.

The consumer climate was changing, too. Dietary concern, new lifestyles, and the explosion of new products—along with the rising

---

[7] Ibid., pp. 188–92.

[8] This case example whose author is Samuel R. Gardner, vice president–marketing, Retail Food Group of Kraft Inc., is reproduced by permission from Earl L. Bailey, ed., *Product-Line Strategies* (New York: Conference Board, 1982) pp. 40–42.

consumer demand for other beverages and snacks—all tended to have a depressing effect on per capita consumption of milk and ice cream.

Ironically, the very regulatory climate that earlier had helped to maintain the franchise of the independent brand producers now acted as a deterrent to the kind of marketing innovation that was called for to combat the new competitive situation. Ice cream is a typical example, since it is a product category where most of the ingredients and methods of processing have been standardized by the Food and Drug Administration for many years. Until the 1960s, the marketing strategies and product positionings of most ice-cream marketers had developed along the lines of either a pricing incentive of one form or another or some kind of inflated claim of superior quality.

By the late 1960s, Kraft realized that the alternative of competing primarily on a price appeal was not an acceptable strategy for long-term growth and profitability in this business. The company also realized that something more was needed than simply an overall quality umbrella based on the traditional reputation of a product's brand name and on its distribution network. To be successful, Kraft knew that somehow it would have to convince the retail trade that its profitability in ice cream would be maximized by offering the consumer a *mix* of premium-priced brands along with their own lower-priced private labels. Of course, this whole mix argument rested upon one critical assumption: That we could, in fact, develop and successfully market the kind of products that would generate consumer demand for reasons not related primarily to a low price.

Someone familiar with successful packaged goods marketing techniques may find nothing especially startling in this approach. But 10 years ago—and even today to a large degree—this approach was a revolutionary departure from the marketing philosophy that existed for a long time in the dairy industry.

THE BREYERS STORY

In the late 1960s, Kraft was marketing an ice cream called Breyers in the New York, Philadelphia, and Baltimore-Washington areas. It has always been a fine product, made virtually in the same way for more than 100 years. Like most other well-known local brands, Breyers ice cream had always been positioned very generally as a premium quality product, with the reputation of its brand name offering the primary difference from other brands. But in the 1960s, a significant difference in the way Breyers ice cream was formulated became the focus for a new positioning strategy.

As spelled out in a pledge of purity that appears on every carton, Breyers ice cream does not contain *any* kind of artificial flavoring, nor does it contain any added coloring. And, more significantly, it does not contain any stabilizers or emulsifiers which tend to provide a degree of creaminess that is just not possible without their aid.

The nonstabilized formulation of Breyers provides what we in the business call a better "flavor release" and distinctive "mouth-feel." This basic product difference triggered a whole new approach to promoting ice cream. For instance, in Breyers peach ice cream, only four simple ingredients are used: milk, cream, sugar, and peaches. Nothing else is added—a product attribute that did not have much meaning or exposure only a decade or so ago.

In those days, the consumers' interest in natural foods was just beginning to emerge as a positioning consideration; and very few, if any, marketers were making much noise about it. An advertising campaign was developed that targeted the Breyers product as *"The* All-Natural Ice Cream." This positioning was deliberately designed to be more of an ingredient story than to have a health or ecological appeal. Copy reported on the quantity as well as the quality of the ingredients (e.g., Breyers takes more than a pound of peaches to make a half gallon of peach ice cream).

This new Breyers positioning caught on quickly, and in three years sales in its traditional marketing areas had doubled. It was then realized that this strategy could be an effective means of introducing the brand into new markets where the all-natural positioning had not yet been used to its fullest. This was a great idea, but how could we face up to the challenge of attempting to justify the introduction of a new premium ice cream, Breyers, when we were already well represented in these markets by Sealtest, another premium quality brand? Why would the trade want to make room for both of our premium ice creams, especially when they were already having trouble accepting the rationale for allowing even one of them to compete with their own label?

And what about the consumer? If we sell the consumer on the merits of Breyers as being the best quality product, what do we say about Sealtest? That it is almost as good? Might we really be only competing with ourselves for the same customer? And possibly even confusing the consumer about which one is really the better?

In coming to grips with these and other somewhat difficult strategic questions, a solution evolved that led to the creation of what was called "The Premium Ice Cream Program." Basically, this is a three-brand marketing strategy that recognizes several key consumer purchase and demand considerations that are important to the ice-cream business.

First of all, we knew that the success of the Breyers "all-natural" appeal was not just limited to consumers with higher incomes, who could afford to pay a premium price. Our experience in New York and Philadelphia indicated that this particular all-natural product positioning was effective among all demographic groups. But what about the considerable number of ice-cream consumers who could care less about the appeal of naturalness but who want something they feel is special in an ice cream?

THE SEALTEST STORY

To appreciate the development of Kraft's Sealtest positioning, it is important to know that many Americans have come to believe that ice cream from an ice-cream parlor is somehow superior in quality to products distributed in supermarkets. Right or wrong, this perception persists for many; and, in fact, it has been flourishing lately with the increasing number of retail ice-cream parlors opened during the past years. It was also interesting to us that, during this period, total sales of ice cream sold through supermarkets had been declining, while that sold through ice-cream parlors was increasing. It was not all in the form of cones either.

The well-entrenched, top-quality image of the ice-cream parlors' ice cream has been responsible, no doubt, for the fact that a surprisingly high tonnage of it has been sold to consumers in the form of packaged half gallons, usually at a price of up to two, and sometimes three, times higher than supermarket-distributed half gallons, including Sealtest ice cream. Since blind product testing confirmed that Sealtest compared favorably on taste with "ice-cream-parlor" ice creams, and since this meant that we could then have a potentially meaningful price-value advantage over these products (which were competing directly against our customers, the supermarkets), an exciting positioning strategy presented itself for the Sealtest brand.

So Sealtest became "The Supermarket Ice Cream with That Ice Cream Parlor Taste." This positioning now gave us a strong sales argument for the trade, as well as a powerful consumer appeal that, we hoped, would be compelling for its own merits, yet would not necessarily conflict with the natural ingredient appeal developed for Breyers.

To execute the Sealtest taste strategy, we created dramatic TV advertising featuring hidden-camera interviews with real people who, after testing both products, could not tell the difference. This advertising, as well as quality packaging, helped to build the believability of this positioning. It had really worked, thanks mainly, in the final analysis, to the performance of the product.

AN ICE MILK BRAND

Finally, our Premium Ice Cream Program recognizes the relatively small, but still very meaningful, opportunity to attract consumers of ice milk, who buy this product either because they cannot or do not want to pay the price for fine ice cream. The problem is that, as a category, ice milk traditionally has not been formulated to measure up to ice cream. The ice milks are cold and sweet; and they are a lot less expensive than ice cream. But, by and large, that's it! So-so flavor and so-so texture. A very unexciting product category from a marketing development standpoint.

We saw an opportunity to capitalize on this situation by developing a premium ice milk brand with a lot of the texture and taste qualities typical of ice cream. Such a product would be targeted directly at the existing ice milk user but, strategically, would also become a viable alternative for consumers of lower-priced, lower-quality ice creams. Since this positioning called for a superior tasting ice milk, premium pricing was required, even though it would still be established below the pricing of both Breyers and Sealtest ice creams.

Such a product was developed and marketed under the Light n' Lively name, which was nicely suited for this brand since all ice milk, by law, is required to have less butterfat than ice cream. The minimum for ice cream is 10 percent; for ice milk, it is between 2 and 7 percent. Light n' Lively has been formulated to support a claim of "Less than Half the Fat of Ice Cream."

Also, with the Light n' Lively name came the added advantage of being able to benefit from any synergistic effect of the promotion and awareness of what is happening with all of the other low-fat products bearing the Light n' Lively name—such as fluid milk, process cheese, low-fat yogurt, and cottage cheese. Advertising stressed an "ice creamy ice milk" texture claim, since research had told us that, after price, this is the single best motivating claim area for ice milk users. It also happens to be the positioning that is most likely to be able to justify a premium price.

NOW, A COMPLETE LINE

With the addition of the two ice-cream products, Kraft would have a line of packaged frozen dessert brands that could maximize profitable sales both to the consumer and to the trade. Each would have its own distinctive niche in the marketplace; and, in total, Kraft could now provide a more complete marketing program, since the three brands would be not so much *competitive* as *compatible* with each other. For us, this has been the magic of this three-brand positioning strategy.

Since the early 1970s, ice-cream consumption in the United States has been relatively flat. In the five years following the inception of the program, total sales of packaged ice cream increased about 5 percent. During this same period, Breyers sales increased over 50 percent overall, with a 17 percent increase in the markets where Breyers ice cream had been a well-established brand for many, many years. And on top of this, Sealtest sales jumped another 23 percent. As for the ice milk situation, this business has also remained relatively flat. However, Light n' Lively, as an integral part of the Premium Ice Cream Program, jumped 45 percent during the same five years.

The program worked in an extremely difficult marketing climate, but the positioning for these three brands was right. I am happy to add that, while some of our competitors have attempted to emulate our positioning to one degree or another, the total impact of the Kraft program is still relatively unusual and highly successful in this business.

A CARRY-OVER TO COTTAGE CHEESE

We are now in the process of using the same basic positioning concepts that have worked so well on frozen desserts to other selected dairy product categories with which Kraft is involved. For instance, in cottage cheese, another large-tonnage market like ice cream, with sales around $1 billion a year, Kraft has developed what we call "The Premium Cottage Cheese Program."

The primary consumer appeal in this food category has always been diet—the desire for lower-calorie food alternatives at mealtime. It is a fact that all cottage cheese can satisfy this desire to one degree or another, but the Light n' Lively brand has been deliberately targeted right at this important hard-core diet appeal, since it is specially formulated as a 1 percent low-fat product. The so-called regular cottage cheeses are standardized by law to contain a minimum of 4 percent fat—four times greater than Light n' Lively cottage cheese.

Today, Light n' Lively is the leading brand among low-fat cottage cheeses. So our Premium Cottage Cheese Program is well represented as far as a specific diet positioning is concerned. But while this diet appeal may be the prime purchase motivation for most users, the market for the so-called low-fat cottage cheeses still amounts to only about 15 percent of total category sales, even though it is growing faster than that for the regular type.

As with many food products, there tends to be a range of taste or flavor appeals beyond price that offer possibilities to segment consumer demand. In the case of cottage cheese, product characteristics such as creaminess, freshness, texture, and curd size can all be important purchase considerations. So in addition to the Light n' Lively diet-oriented product offering, this program features two other brands which are positioned to satisfy a particular taste appeal that is meaningful for this category. Our Sealtest brand is a "regular" (or 4 percent butterfat) type of cottage cheese that is specially formulated with a sweet cream dressing in both small- and large-curd varieties, as well as some flavors (which tend to be a minor factor in total demand).

In all of these forms, the brand is deliberately positioned to appeal to the widest segment of potential buyers since it is a relatively fresh and sweet-tasting product whose flavor is, we feel, so pronounced that it is able to stand out from all the other foods that research tells us are usually eaten along with cottage cheese. This is a product appeal that certainly should be meaningful to most category users, particularly those who are not really crazy about cottage cheese and tend to be using it only for diet-related reasons.

A third product in our program is Breakstone's cottage cheese, which is deliberately formulated to be somewhat drier and more tangy than the Sealtest brand. It is also a 4 percent fat type of cottage cheese which is marketed in both small- and large-curd styles. Breakstone's brand is also positioned as a premium-priced brand, and it is especially popular in the East, where a number of Breakstone's products have had a large following going back, like Breyers ice cream, for more than 100 years. It tends to appeal more to the people who want a very distinctive product—what we refer to as a "traditional" type of cottage cheese. And unlike our other two brands, Breakstone's is formulated to be completely natural.

Thus, here again, a multibranded, segmented positioning approach has been able to maximize Kraft's opportunity within the total category—in this case, cottage cheese. In all of this positioning, the key has been to identify or, sometimes, to create meaningful and distinctive consumer appeals that can be well satisfied by products that can deliver value regardless of the required pricing.

Case 3-1

Pools For You, Inc.

INTRODUCTION

Pools For You, Inc., is a six-store leisure goods retailer selling primarily aboveground swimming pools, pool tables, artificial Christmas trees, and gas grills. The firm started in 1953; as of 1980, it had six stores, all of which were located within a 70-mile radius of Emory, a northeastern metropolitan city. Pools For You is currently the largest pool retailer in its trading area.

The predecessor of Pools For You, Inc., was a card and gift shop which was started in 1953 by three brothers: John, Bill, and Murray Wright. In 1957, after four successful years at their location, the brothers faced a difficult decision. The shopping center's management required a significant rental increase as a condition for the store's obtaining a lease renewal. If the brothers agreed to the rental increase, the store's profits would be greatly reduced; if they refused, they would have to not only close the store but also be unable to sell the business as a going concern.

Their decision to close the store served as an important lesson to the Wright brothers. In 1957 they founded Wright Realty, Inc., whose main purpose was to purchase real estate to house their retail business. While property ownership tied up much of the Wright brothers' capital, it prevented a recurrence of the 1953 situation. According to John Wright, Wright Realty served four functions for the retail entrepreneurs. "One, it eliminated the risk associated with a landlord charging exorbitant rent increases at lease renewal time. Two, it shielded the retail operation from the concern that a landlord might refuse to renew a lease. Three, if the retail business had a particularly disastrous year, the realty operation could forgive rental payments. (In 1972 Wright Realty forgave rental payments on two locations.) Four, rental income from other tenants in adjacent stores provided the brothers with an additional source of income."

Through 1967 the brothers continued to operate stores which sold

---

This case was prepared by Professor Barry Berman, Hofstra University, and Richard Horvitz, a student at Hofstra University. Copyright © 1980 by Barry Berman.

greeting cards, gifts, and toys. In 1967 they owned three stores within a 20-mile radius. While each store was profitable, the brothers were concerned that the present stores were too small to stock a broad selection of gift and toy items. According to Bill Wright, greeting cards don't require much space, and one's trading area will not increase substantially by having a selection greater than that of the average candy store. The situation for gift items and toys is totally different. At least 30,000 to 40,000 square feet is required to operate a gift and toy store with maximum efficiency. Since more of the Wright brothers' stores in 1967 were of that size, John, Bill, and Murray also felt that it was a logical time to rethink their product line strategy.

After exploring a series of product categories, the brothers decided to shift their product lines to aboveground pools and artificial Christmas trees. Several factors influenced their decision.

1.   Both products were perceived to be at the introductory stage of their product life cycles. While some retailers were concerned that "both" products would be fads, the Wright brothers saw them as fulfilling an enduring purpose.

2.   Both products offer excellent long-term value to the consumer. In-ground pools typically cost 6 to 10 times as much as aboveground pools, not counting required landscaping costs, building permits, or increased real estate taxes for an in-ground pool.

While an artificial Christmas tree may be two to four times as expensive as a natural tree, the artificial tree has the following advantages:

1.   It is made from fire-retardant materials.
2.   The cost represents a one-time investment. An artificial tree has an estimated 8- to 12-year life.
3.   There are no problems with disposing of the artificial tree.
4.   The needles do not fall off and create a mess in one's home.
5.   Christmas trees would help to counteract the extreme seasonality of the aboveground pool business.

Special expertise is required in selling, installing, and servicing aboveground pools. The brothers felt that because of this special expertise, the degree of competition from department and discount stores would continue to be low.

As of 1980, Wright Realty, Inc., owned four of the six Pools For You locations. Pools For You, Inc., is organized as a closed corporation held by four brothers: John, Bill, and Murray, who work at Pools For You full time; and Joe, who has an unrelated job but does most of the management work for Wright Realty.

Exhibit 1 shows net income and total sales for Pools For You from 1967 to 1977. Exhibits 2 and 3 show important data relating to the size of the swimming pool market.

Exhibit 1
Net income and total sales
1967-1977

Year	Net income	Total sales
1967	$ 8,497	$ 283,233
1968	20,537	387,491
1969	32,637	604,389
1970	19,739	616,844
1971	29,841	828,917
1972	n.a.	1,100,077
1973	14,606	1,327,818
1974	27,887	1,640,412
1975	26,018	1,858,429
1976	36,767	2,297,938
1977	28,830	2,930,846

Exhibit 2
Number of residential swimming pools,
1948-1979 (selected years)*

	Cumulative totals	Pools built during preceding year
1948	2,500	
1958	87,500	
1968	575,700	61,600
1970	713,900	69,200
1972	851,300	73,600
1974	1,021,500	86,700
1975	1,097,100	75,600
1976	1,163,500	66,400
1977	1,241,200	77,700
1978	1,328,600	87,400
1979	1,424,900	96,300

* Built for private use by not more than two families and their guests. Includes pools of all construction types. The total number of aboveground pools sold in the United States in 1979 was well below 100,000 pools.

Source: "Swimming Pool Industry Market Report for 1978," *Swimming Pool Weekly* (Fort Lauderdale, Fla.: 1979), p. 7.

MARKETING STRATEGY

Pools For You operates stores in three counties surrounding a major northeastern metropolitan area. Four of its six stores are within the boundaries of a major city; the other two are located in adjacent cities, Oliver and Rider.

Oliver is an old industrial city which had its most vigorous economic development 70 years ago. In contrast, the Rider area is largely

Exhibit 3
Number of swimming pools, northeastern United States and total United States, 1958–1979 (selected years)

	Northeastern United States		Total United States	
	Cumulative Totals	Pools built during preceding year	Cumulative totals	Pools built during preceding year
1958	17,700	—	133,000	—
1968	156,350	21,400	804,200	78,600
1970	203,600	24,250	982,900	91,000
1972	247,500	22,700	1,155,300	89,900
1974	296,100	25,400	1,361,800	104,700
1975	318,600	22,500	1,453,300	91,500
1976	335,500	16,900	1,530,400	77,100
1977	349,700	14,200	1,614,600	84,200
1978	362,895	13,195	1,708,600	94,000
1979	375,295	12,400	1,812,700	104,100

Source: "Swimming Pool Industry Market Report for 1978," Swimming Pool Weekly (Fort Lauderdale, Fla.: 1979), p. 7.

Exhibit 4
Sales before cancellations, by location ($000)

	May 1979	June 1979	July 1979
Emory area			
Store 1	$92	$74	$52
Store 2	53	66	40
Store 3	4*	60	36
Store 4	74	85	30
Total Emory area	$223	$285	$158
Oliver†	90	76	22
Rider	31	43	17
Total Pools For You, Inc.	$344	$404	$197

* Not meaningful—store 3 was open for only one week in May. This store had a major facelift and did not have a sign for most of the pool-buying season.
† First season for Oliver.

Exhibit 5
Average gross profit per pool sale and average pool sale by location

	May 1979		June 1979		July 1979	
	Average gross profit per pool	Average pool sale	Average gross profit per pool	Average pool sale	Average gross profit per pool	Average pool sale
Emory area						
Store 1	$527	$1,142	$543	$1,120	$570	$1,215
Store 2	686	1,444	534	1,140	525	1,140
Store 3	N.M.*	N.M.	608	1,246	631	1,323
Store 4	626	1,319	588	1,216	602	1,279
Oliver†	636	1,318	765	1,118	631	1,323
Rider	608	1,354	562	1,214	666	1,384

* N.M.—not meaningful. Store 3 was open for only one week in May.
† First season for Oliver.

Exhibit 6
Selected data on three counties

	Emory	Oliver	Rider
1979 population	510,000	290,000	420,000
Total 1979 retail sales ($ millions)	2,173.6	734.2	880.8
1979 effective buying income*			
($ millions)	2,682.7	1,334.9	1,872.3
Number of households	201,250	99,590	144,440
Percentage of households with			
$15,000 and over effective buying			
incomes	38.1	43.2	38.4
General merchandise sales ($ millions)	499.9	110.1	123.3
Firm-household appliance sales			
($ millions)	108.7	38.2	47.6
Buying power index†	.27	.13	.008
Store data—Pools For You, Inc.			
Number of stores	4	1	1
Average square feet per store	38,000	30,000	40,000
Estimated market share of			
Pools For You, Inc. (%)	50	40	30

   * Effective buying income is personal income (wages, salaries, interest, dividends, profits and property revenues) minus federal, state, and local taxes. This is roughly equivalent to disposable personal income.
   † Buying power index = .05 (the area's percentage of U.S. effective buying income)
            + .03 (the area's percentage of U.S. retail sales)
            + .02 (the area's percentage of U.S. population).

agricultural. However, it is beginning to develop a strong industrial base due to the presence of a good work force, industrial tax incentives, and its nearness to important consumer markets.

Exhibit 4 summarizes sales for the six locations for May, June, and July 1979. Exhibit 5 provides data on the average gross profit per pool sale and the average pool sales by store location.

The marketing strategy of Pools For You can be summarized as follows:

1. The retailer sells primarily exclusive lines of pools. This enables Pools For You to advertise its pools without concern about fostering price competition from other retailers. This also allows Pools For You to develop a strong relationship with pool manufacturers.

2. The sales program is geared to selling packages consisting of a pool, a filter, a ladder, and chemicals. Three different packages (in terms of size and quality) are offered with each pool. The packages serve several purposes. One, they make the selection process less complicated for the customer. Two, they reduce the time required to close a sale. Three, they increase related-item selling.

3. A well-stocked central warehouse allows for a high proportion of orders to be filled from stock on hand. This is particularly important if the weather is hot, humid, and sunny for an extended time period. It is important to note that a critical decision factor in store choice is

delivery and installation speed. While delivery can generally be made within five business days, installation lead time can be extended to as much as three weeks.

4.   Pools For You is open 12 months per year. This is in strong contrast to competing firms which close between five and seven months per year. To Pools For You, the additional money which would have to be spent in training a new staff each year (plus the cost of lost sales and inefficiency due to inexperience) is greater than the cost of keeping the stores open all year. Two other factors have influenced the brothers' decision to stay open the year round. First, the retail firm has a sense of permanence to consumers. Second, customers who have off-season problems with pool parts (such as pool covers and pumps for pool covers) or defective installations know that the store is open. This serves as an important competitive advantage for many buyers.

5.   Pricing is conducted on a negotiated basis. Salesmen have flexibility within tight limits to reduce the price on a package to close a sale. While prices are clearly posted on each item and pool packages are advertised with prices featured in the advertisements, buyers know that if they purchase additional items (such as deck-type ladders or winterizing equipment) with their pool, they can "strike a deal" with the salesperson. Installation costs, which differ depending upon pool size and type, required leveling, and the access to the pool area, are also frequently negotiated.

The negotiated nature of pricing has had a small effect on Pools For You profits. In 1979 the gross margin averaged 47 percent, with few regular sales (excluding floor models, as-is units, or end-of-season merchandise) outside the 45–50 percent gross margin range.

6.   Installation work is subcontracted—80 percent of all pools retailing over $350 are installed through Pools For You. Defects in manufacture or installation occurring within one year of the date of purchase will be repaired or replaced free of charge.

7.   Pools For You also sells pool tables, artificial Christmas trees, and gas grills. The selling of other merchandise by pool retailers is common. A research study of retail pool stores showed that in 1978 43.0 percent of the pool stores surveyed sold outdoor furniture, 8.3 percent sold Christmas trees and decorations, 1.9 percent sold skis, 1.2 percent sold ice rinks, 1.6 percent sold paddle tennis and platform tennis supplies, and 43.0 percent sold "other products."[1]

AREAS REQUIRING FURTHER STUDY

The brothers are concerned with two areas of Pools For You operation: seasonality and installation.

---

[1] "Swimming Pool Industry Market Report for 1978," *Swimming Pool Weekly* (Fort Lauderdale, Fla.: 1979), p. 5.

Seasonality

Pools For You makes 75 percent of its yearly sales within a five-month period: Swimming pools are sold primarily from May through July; pool tables and Christmas trees, in November and December. Exhibit 7 shows the sales distribution of Pools For You for 1973

Exhibit 7
Sales distribution, 1973–1978

Year	Percent of total yearly sales, May–July	Percent of total yearly sales, November–December
1973	44	28
1974	43	28
1975	43	35
1976	38	32
1977	45	32
1978	43	35

through 1978. The product mix seasonality affects both personal utilization and cash flow budgeting.

As a result of seasonality and the year-round opening strategy of Pools For You, store managers have a very small labor crew when the sales emphasis shifts from pools and gas grills to pool tables and Christmas trees, and vice versa. During this time period, the entire store must be transformed from an extensive backyard vacation theme to a winter wonderland one. Likewise, warehouse employees are under extreme pressure during the five busiest months. This pressure may result in costly errors; that is, the wrong merchandise or noticeably defective merchandise may be accepted from vendors and/or delivered to customers.

Cash inflows during the seven slow months have been insufficient to cover even a skeleton staff of full-time employees in addition to utility and lease payments. The negative cash flow during this time period is compounded by the relatively high financial leverage of the firm (see Exhibit 8).

Installation

Pools For You provides each pool customer installation service for an additional fee, if desired. Installation is viewed by both the retail firm and the pool buyer as a critical part of the sale. An improperly installed pool could collapse. Physical harm to the occupants, the destruction of the pool's retaining walks, and water damage to adjacent homes are very real dangers.

While few pools have collapsed, pool leaks due to liner tears, the buckling of retainer walks due to improper grading or settling, and

Exhibit 8
Selected financial data, 1974–1979

	Liquidity measures			*Leverage measures*	
	Working capital ($000)*	*Current ratio†*	*Acid test‡*	*Debt ratio§*	*Debt to equity ratio‖*
1974	150	1.32	0.43	0.98	3.70
1975	120	1.37	0.60	0.90	1.90
1976	80	1.14	0.17	0.87	0.82
1977	190	1.26	0.23	0.82	1.34
1978	95	1.19	0.34	0.90	0.92
1979	280	1.23	0.32	0.80	0.41

* Working capital = Current assets – Current liabilities.
† Current ratio = Current assets ÷ Current liabilities.
‡ Acid test = (Current assets – Inventory) ÷ Current liabilities.
§ Debt ratio = Total debt ÷ Total assets.
‖ Debt to equity ratio = Total debt ÷ Equity.

nonfunctioning pumps are common occurrences. The fact that a district manager (who was hired to ensure that chain operations and policies were uniform) spends much of his time at customers' homes underscores the installation problems.

In the past, Pools For You subcontracted pool installation work and charged the customer its installation cost. Pools For You used a strategy for controlling installation quality that should have worked:

1. Pools For You threatened to hold back new work to installers who installed pools improperly and who did not complete repairs satisfactorily.
2. Pools For You held back a given percentage of installation fees to ensure that installers would correct problems.

This strategy was unsuccessful since installers typically would state that the problem was caused by a manufacturing defect. It was difficult to determine whether the cause of a problem was improper manufacture, improper handling by Pools For You, or improper installation by subcontractors. While vendors would replace defective parts, they refused to reimburse Pools For You or its installers for labor costs attributable to defects in the product. Installers billed Pools For You for this additional labor. Furthermore, in some cases, vendors attributed the defects in the merchandise to improper handling or installation and refused to fully reimburse Pools For You for materials. In a recent year, Pools For You spent over $30,000 in nonreimbursable labor and materials expenses to satisfy customer complaints. While this problem was an important one to the firm, no records were available on installation defects by installer, pool manufacturer, and pool model.

As of summer 1980, Pools For You planned to hire its own installation crews and foreman and to purchase the required installation equipment. While this will increase the cost of installation to pool buyers and will have an adverse effect on the retailer's cash flow, the Wright brothers feel that the increased quality control will make the increased costs and investment worthwhile.

Case 3–2 ———————————————————————
Big Sky of Montana, Inc.

INTRODUCTION

Karen Tracy could feel the pressure on her as she sat at her desk late that April afternoon. Two weeks from today she would be called on to present her recommendations concerning next year's winter season pricing policies for Big Sky of Montana, Inc.—room rates for the resort's accommodation facilities as well as decisions in the skiing and food services areas. The presentation would be made to a top management team from the parent company, Boyne USA, which operated out of Michigan.

"As sales and public relations manager, Karen, your accuracy in decision making is extremely important," her boss had said in his usual tone. "Because we spend most of our time in Michigan, we'll need a well-based and involved opinion."

"It'll be the shortest two weeks of my life," she thought.

BACKGROUND: BIG SKY AND BOYNE USA

Big Sky of Montana, Inc., was a medium-sized destination resort located in southwestern Montana, 45 miles south of Bozeman and 43 miles north of the west entrance to Yellowstone National Park.[1] Big Sky was conceived in the early 1970's and had begun operation in November 1974.

The 11,000-acre, 2,000-bed resort was separated into two main areas: Meadow and Mountain villages. Meadow Village (elevation 6,300 feet) was located two miles east of the resort's main entrance on U.S. 191 and seven miles from the ski area. Meadow Village had an 800-bed capacity in the form of four condominium complexes (ranging

---

This case was prepared by Anne Senausky and Professor James E. Nelson. Copyright © 1978 by the Endowment and Research Foundation at Montana State University.

[1] Destination resorts were characterized by on-the-hill lodging and eating facilities, a national market, and national advertising.

from studios to three-bedroom units) and a 40-room hostel for economy lodging. Additional facilities included an 18-hole golf course, six tennis courts, a restaurant, a post office, a convention center with meeting space for up to 200 people, and a small lodge serving as a pro shop for the golf course in the summer and cross-country skiing in the winter.

Mountain Village (elevation 7,500 feet) was the center of winter activity, located at the base of the ski area. In this complex was the 204-room Huntley Lodge, offering hotel accommodations, three condominium complexes (unit size ranged from studio to three-bedroom), and an 88-room hostel, for a total of 1,200 beds. The Mountain Mall was also located here, next to the Huntley Lodge and within a five-minute walk of two of the three condominium complexes in Mountain Village. It housed ticket sales, an equipment rental shop, a skier's cafeteria, two large meeting rooms with a maximum occupancy of 700 persons (regularly used as sack lunch areas for skiers), two offices, a ski school desk, and a ski patrol room, all of which were operated by Boyne. Also in this building were a delicatessen, a drugstore/gift shop, a sporting goods store/rental shop, a restaurant, an outdoor clothing store, a jewelry shop, a T-shirt shop, two bars, and a child day-care center. Each of these independent operations held a lease that was due to expire in one to three years.

The closest airport to Big Sky was located just outside Bozeman. It was served by Northwest Orient and Frontier Airlines with connections to other major airlines out of Denver and Salt Lake City. Greyhound and Amtrak also operated bus and train service into Bozeman. Yellowstone Park Lines provided Big Sky with three buses daily to and from the airport and Bozeman bus station (the cost was $4.40 one-way, $8.40 round trip) as well as an hourly shuttle around the two Big Sky villages. Avis, Hertz, National, and Budget offered rent-a-car service in Bozeman with a drop-off service available at Big Sky.

In July 1976, Boyne USA, a privately owned, Michigan-based operation, purchased the Huntley Lodge, Mountain Mall, ski lifts and terrain, golf course, and tennis courts for approximately $8 million. The company subsequently invested an additional $3 million in Big Sky. Boyne also owned and operated four Michigan resort ski areas.

Big Sky's top management consisted of a lodge manager (in charge of operations within the Huntley Lodge), a sales and public relations manager (Karen), a food and beverage manager, and an area manager (overseeing operations external to the Lodge, including the Mall and all recreational facilities). These four positions were occupied by persons trained with the parent company; a fifth manager, the comptroller, had worked for pre-Boyne ownership.

Business figures were reported to the company's home office on a daily basis, and major decisions concerning Big Sky operations were discussed and approved by "Michigan." Boyne's top management visited Big Sky an average of five times annually, and all major decisions, such as pricing and advertising, were approved by the parent for all operations.

THE SKIING

Big Sky's winter season usually began in late November and continued until the middle of April, with a yearly snowfall of approximately 450 inches. The area had 18 slopes between elevations of 7,500 and 9,900 feet. The terrain breakdown was as follows: 25 percent novice, 55 percent intermediate, and 20 percent advanced. (Although opinions varied, industry guidelines recommended a terrain breakdown of 20 percent, 60 percent, and 20 percent for novice, intermediate, and advanced skiers, respectively.) The longest run was approximately three miles in length; the temperatures (highs) ranged from 15 to 30 degrees Fahrenheit throughout the season.

Lift facilities at Big Sky included two double chair lifts, a triple chair, and a four-passenger gondola. Lift capacity was estimated at 4,000 skiers per day. This figure was considered adequate by the area manager, at least until the 1980–81 season.

Karen felt that the facilities, snow conditions, and grooming compared favorably with those of other destination resorts of the Rockies. "In fact, our only real drawback right now," she thought, "is our position in the national market. We need more skiers who are sold on Big Sky. And that is in the making."

THE CONSUMERS

Karen knew from previous dealings that Big Sky, like most destination areas, attracted three distinct skier segments: local day skiers (living within driving distance and not utilizing lodging in the area); individual destination skiers (living out of state and using accommodations in the Big Sky area); and groups of destination skiers (clubs, professional organizations, etc.).

The first category typically comprised Montana residents, with a relatively small number from Wyoming and Idaho. (Distances from selected population centers to Big Sky are presented in Exhibit 1) A 1973 study of four Montana ski areas, performed by the Advertising Unit of the Montana Department of Highways, characterized Montana skiers as:

1. In their early 20s and males (60 percent).
2. Living within 75 miles of a ski area.
3. From a household with two skiers in it.
4. Averaging $13,000 in household income.
5. Intermediate to advanced in ability.

Exhibit 1

Proximity of population centers to Big Sky

City	Distance from Big Sky (miles)	Population (U.S. 1970 census)
Bozeman, Montana	45	18,670
Butte, Montana	126	23,368
Helena, Montana	144	22,730
Billings, Montana	174	61,581
Great Falls, Montana	225	60,091
Missoula, Montana	243	29,497
Pocatello, Idaho	186	40,036
Idaho Falls, Idaho	148	35,776

Approximate distance of selected major U.S. population centers to Big Sky

City	Distance to Big Sky* (in air miles)
Chicago	1,275
Minneapolis	975
Fargo	750
Salt Lake City	375
Dallas	1,500
Houston	1,725
Los Angeles	975
San Francisco	925
New York	2,025
Atlanta	1,950
New Orleans	1,750
Denver	750

---

* Per passenger air fare could be approximated at 20 cents per mile (round trip, coach rates).

6.   Skiing five hours per ski day, 20 days per season locally.
7.   Skiing four days away from local areas.
8.   Taking no lessons in the past five years.

Karen was also aware that a significant number of day skiers, particularly on the weekends, were college students.

Destination, or nonresident, skiers were labeled in the same study as typically:

1.   At least in their mid-20s and males (55 percent).
2.   Living in a household of three or more skiers.
3.   Averaging near $19,000 in household income.
4.   More intermediate in ability.
5.   Spending about six hours per day skiing.
6.   Skiing 11–14 days per season, with 3–8 days away from home.
7.   Taking ski school lessons.

Through data taken from reservation records, Karen learned that individual destination skiers accounted for half of last year's usage based on skier days.[2] Geographic segments were approximately as follows:

Upper Midwest (Minnesota, Michigan, North Dakota)	30%
Florida	20
California	17
Washington, Oregon, Montana	15
Texas, Oklahoma	8
Other	10

Reservation records indicated that the average length of stay for individual destination skiers was about six or seven days.

It was the individual destination skier who was most likely to buy a lodging/lift package; 30 percent made commitments for these advertised packages when making reservations for 1977–78. Even though there was no discount involved in this manner of buying lift tickets, Karen knew that it was fairly popular because it saved the purchaser a trip to the ticket window every morning. Approximately half of the individual business came through travel agents, who received a 10 percent commission.

The third skier segment, the destination group, accounted for a substantial 20 percent of Big Sky's skier day usage. The larger portion of the group business came through medical and other professional organizations holding meetings at the resort, as this was a way to "combine business with pleasure." These groups were typically comprised of couples and individuals between the ages of 30 and 50. Ski clubs made up the remainder, with a number coming from the southern states of Florida, Texas, and Georgia. During the 1977–78 season, Big Sky drew 30 ski clubs with memberships averaging 55 skiers. The average length of stay for all group destination skiers was about four or five days.

A portion of these group bookings was made through travel agents, but the majority dealt directly with Karen. The coordinator of the professional meetings or the president of the ski club typically contacted the Big Sky sales office to make initial reservation dates, negotiate prices, and work out the details of the stay.

THE COMPETITION

In Karen's mind, Big Sky faced two types of competition, that for local day skiers and that for out-of-state (i.e., destination) skiers.

Bridger Bowl was virtually the only area competing for local day skiers. Bridger was a "nonfrills," nonprofit, and smaller ski area located some 16 miles northeast of Bozeman. It received the majority of local skiers, including students at Montana State University, which

---

[2] A skier day is defined as one skier using the facility for one day of operation.

was located in Bozeman. The area was labeled as having terrain more difficult than that of Big Sky and was thus more appealing to the local expert skiers. However, it also had much longer lift lines than Big Sky and had recently lost some of its weekend business to Big Sky.

Karen had found through experience that most Bridger skiers usually "tried" Big Sky once or twice a season. Season passes for the two areas were mutually honored at the half-day rate for an all-day ticket, and Big Sky occasionally ran newspaper ads offering discounts on lifts to obtain more Bozeman business.

For out-of-state skiers, Big Sky considered its competition to be mainly the destination resorts of Colorado, Utah, and Wyoming. (Selected data on competing resorts are presented in Exhibit 2.) Because

Exhibit 2
Competitors' 1977–1978 package plan rates,* number of lifts, and lift rates

	Lodge double (2)†	Two-bedroom condo (4)	Three-bedroom condo (6)	Number of lifts	Daily lift rates
Aspen, Colorado	$242	$242	$220	19	$13
Steamboat, Colorado	230	230	198	15	12
Jackson, Wyoming	230	242	210	5	14
Vail, Colorado	230	242	220	15	14
Snowbird, Utah	208	none	none	6	11
Bridger Bowl, Montana	No lodging available at Bridger Bowl			3	8

* Package plan rates are per person and include seven nights' lodging, six lift tickets (high-season rates).
† Number in parentheses denotes occupancy of unit on which price is based.

Big Sky was smaller and newer than the majority of these areas, Karen reasoned, it was necessary to follow an aggressive strategy aimed at increasing its national market share.

PRESENT POLICIES

Lift rates

It was common knowledge that there existed some local resentment concerning Big Sky's lift rate policy. Although comparable to rates at Vail or Aspen, an all-day lift ticket was $4 higher than the ticket offered at nearby Bridger Bowl. In an attempt to alleviate this situation, management at Big Sky instituted a $9 "chair pass" for the 1977–78 season, entitling the holder to unlimited use of the three chairs plus two rides per day on the gondola, to be taken between specified time periods. Because the gondola served primarily intermediate terrain, it was reasoned that the chair pass would appeal to the local, more expert skiers. A triple chair serving the bowl area was located at the top of the gondola, and two rides on the gondola would allow those skiers to take ample advantage of the advanced terrain up there. Otherwise, all advanced terrain was served by another chair.

However, if Big Sky was to establish itself as a successful, nationally prominent destination area, Karen felt that the attitudes and opinions of all skiers must be carefully weighed. Throughout the season she had made a special effort to grasp the general feeling toward rates. A $12 ticket, she discovered, was thought to be very reasonable by destination skiers, primarily because Big Sky was predominantly an intermediate area and the average destination skier was of intermediate ability but also because Big Sky was noted for its relative lack of lift lines, giving the skier more actual skiing time for the money. "Perhaps we should keep the price the same," she thought. "We do need more business. Other destination areas are likely to raise their prices, and we should look good in comparison."

Also discussed was the possible abolition of the $9 chair pass. The question in Karen's mind was whether its elimination would severely hurt local business or would sell an all-lift $12 ticket to the skier who had previously bought only a chair pass. The issue was compounded by an unknown number of destination skiers who opted for the cheaper chair pass too.

Season pass pricing was also an issue. Prices for the 1977–78 all-lift season pass had remained the same as last year, but a season chair pass had been introduced which was the counterpart of the daily chair lift pass. Karen did not like the number of season chair passes purchased in relation to the number of all-lift passes and considered recommending the abolition of the season pass as well as an increase in the price of the all-lift pass. "I'm going to have to think this one out carefully," she thought, "because skiing accounted for about 40 percent of our total revenue this past season. I'll have to be able to justify my decision not only to Michigan but also to the Forest Service."

Price changes were not solely at the discretion of Big Sky management. As the case with most larger western ski areas, the U.S. government owned part of the land on which Big Sky operated. Control of this land was the responsibility of the U.S. Forest Service, which annually approved all lift pricing policies. For the 1976–77 ski season, Forest Service action kept most lift rate increases to the national inflation rate. For the 1977–78 season, larger price increases were allowed for ski areas which had competing areas near by; Big Sky was considered to be such an area. No one knew what the Forest Service position would be for the upcoming 1978–79 season.

To help Karen in her decision, an assistant had prepared a summary of lift rates and usage for the past two seasons (Exhibit 3).

Exhibit 3
Lift rates and usage summary

Ticket	Consumer cost	Skier days*	Number season passes sold
1977–78 (136 days' operation)			
Adult all-day all-lift	$ 12	53,400	
Adult all-day chair	9	20,200	
Adult half-day	8	9,400	
Child all-day all-lift	8	8,500	
Child all-day chair	5	3,700	
Child half-day	6	1,200	
Hotel passes†	12/day	23,400	
Complimentary	0	1,100	
Adult all-lift season pass	220	4,300	140
Adult chair season pass	135	4,200	165
Child all-lift season pass	130	590	30
Child chair season pass	75	340	15
Employee all-lift season pass	100	3,000	91
Employee chair season pass	35	1,100	37
1976–77 (122 days' operation)			
Adult all-day	$ 10	52,500	
Adult half-day	6.50	9,000	
Child all-day	6	10,400	
Child half-day	4	1,400	
Hotel passes†	10/day	30,500	
Complimentary	0	480	
Adult season pass	220	4,200	84
Child season pass	130	300	15
Employee season pass	100	2,300	70

* A skier day is defined as one skier using the facility for one day of operation.
† Hotel passes refers to passes included in the lodging/lift packages.

Room rates

This area of pricing was particularly important because lodging accounted for about one third of the past season's total revenue. It was also difficult because of the variety of accommodations (Exhibit 4) and the difficulty in accurately forecasting next season's demand. For example, the season of 1976–77 had been unique in that a good portion of the Rockies was without snow for the initial months of the winter, including Christmas. Big Sky was fortunate in receiving as much snow as it had, and consequently many groups and individuals who were originally headed for Vail or Aspen booked in with Big Sky.

Pricing for the 1977–78 season had been made on the premise that there would be a good amount of repeat business. This came true in part but not to the extent that had been hoped. Occupancy experience had also been summarized for the past two seasons to help Karen make her final decision (Exhibit 5).

As was customary in the hospitality industry, January was a slow period and it was necessary to price accordingly. Low season pricing was extremely important because many groups took advantage of

Exhibit 4
Nightly room rates*

	Low-season range	High-season range	Maximum occupancy
1977–78			
Huntley Lodge			
Standard	$ 42–62	$ 50–70	4
Loft	52–92	60–100	6
Stillwater Condo			
Studio	40–60	45–65	4
One-bedroom	55–75	60–80	4
Bedroom with loft	80–100	90–110	6
Deer Lodge Condo			
One-bedroom	74–84	80–90	4
Two-bedroom	93–103	100–110	6
Three-bedroom	112–122	120–130	8
Hill Condo			
Studio	30–40	35–45	4
Studio with loft	50–70	55–75	6
1976–77			
Huntley Lodge			
Standard	$ 32–47	$ 35–50	4
Loft	47–67	50–70	6
Stillwater Condo			
Studio	39–54	37–52	4
One-bedroom	52–62	50–60	4
Bedroom with loft	60–80	65–85	6
Deer Lodge Condo			
One-bedroom	51–66	55–70	4
Two-bedroom	74–94	80–100	6
Three-bedroom	93–123	100–130	8
Hill Condo			
Studio	28–43	30–45	4
Studio with loft	42–62	45–65	6

* Rates determined by number of persons in room or condominium unit and do not include lift tickets. Maximum for each rate range apply at maximum occupancy.

these rates. On top of that, groups were often offered discounts in the neighborhood of 10 percent. Considering this, Karen could not price too high, with the risk of losing individual destination skiers, or too low, such that an unacceptable profit would be made from group business in this period.

Food service

Under some discussion was the feasibility of converting all destination skiers to the American plan, under which policy each guest in the Huntley Lodge would be placed on a package to include three meals daily in a Big Sky–controlled facility. There was a feeling both for and against this idea. The parent company had been successfully utilizing

Exhibit 5
Lodge-condominium occupancy

In room-nights (1977–78)*

	December (26 days' operation)	January	February	March	April (8 days' operation)
Huntley Lodge	1,830	2,250	3,650	4,650	438
Condominiums†	775	930	1,350	100	90

In room-nights (1976–77)

	December (16 days' operation)	January	February	March	April (16 days' operation)
Huntley Lodge	1,700	3,080	4,525	4,300	1,525
Condominiums‡	600	1,000	1,600	1,650	480

In person-nights§

December 1977 (1976)	January 1978 (1977)	February 1978 (1977)	March 1978 (1977)	April 1978 (1977)
7,850 (6,775)	9,200 (13,000)	13,150 (17,225)	17,900 (17,500)	1,450 (4,725)

* A room-night is defined as one room (or condominium) rented for one night. Lodging experience is based on 124 days of operation for 1977–78, while Exhibit 3 shows the skiing facilities operating 136 days. Both numbers are correct.

† Big Sky had 92 condominiums available during the 1977–78 season.

‡ Big Sky had 85 condominiums available during the 1976–77 season.

§ A person-night refers to one person using the facility for one night.

this plan for years at its destination areas in northern Michigan. Extending the policy to Big Sky should find similar success.

Karen was not so sure. For one thing, the Michigan resorts were primarily self-contained and alternative eateries were few. For another, the whole idea of extending standardized policies from Michigan to Montana was suspect. As an example, Karen painfully recalled a day in January when Big Sky "tried on" another successful Michigan policy of accepting only cash or check payments for lift tickets. The reactions of credit card–carrying skiers could be described as ranging from annoyed to irate.

If an American plan were proposed for next year, it would probably include both the Huntley Lodge Dining Room and Lookout Cafeteria. Less clear, however, were the prices to be charged. There certainly would have to be consideration for both adults and children and for the two independently operated eating places in the Mountain Mall (see Exhibit 6 for an identification of eating places in the Big Sky area). Beyond these considerations, there was little else other than an expectation of a profit to guide Karen in her analysis.

Exhibit 6
Eating places in the Big Sky area

Establishment	Type of service	Meals served	Current prices	Seating	Location
Lodge Dining Room*	A la carte	Breakfast	$2–5	250	Huntley Lodge
		Lunch	2–5		
		Dinner	7–15		
Steak House*	Steak/lobster	Dinner only	6–12	150	Huntley Lodge
Fondue Stube*	Fondue	Dinner only	6–10	25	Huntley Lodge
Ore House†	A la carte	Lunch	0.80–4	150	Mountain Mall
		Dinner	5–12		
Ernie's Deli†	Deli/restaurant	Breakfast	1–3	25	Mountain Mall
		Lunch	2–5		
Lookout Cafeteria*	Cafeteria	Breakfast	1.50–3	175	Mountain Mall
		Lunch	2–4		
		Dinner	3–6		
Yellow Mule†	A la carte	Breakfast	2–4	75	Meadow Village
		Lunch	2–5		
		Dinner	4–8		
Buck's T–4†	Road house restaurant/bar	Dinner only	2–9	60	Gallatin Canyon (two miles south of Big Sky entrance)
Karst Ranch†	Road house restaurant/bar	Breakfast	2–4	50	Gallatin Canyon (Seven miles north of Big Sky entrance)
		Lunch	2–5		
		Dinner	3–8		
Corral†	Road house restaurant/bar	Breakfast	2–4	30	Gallatin Canyon (Five miles south of Big Sky entrance)
		Lunch	2–4		
		Dinner	3–5		

* Owned and operated by Big Sky of Montana, Inc.
† Independently operated.

THE TELEPHONE CALL

"Profits in the food area might be hard to come by," Karen thought. "Last year it appears we lost money on everything we sold." (See Exhibit 7.) Just then the telephone rang. It was Rick Thompson, her

Exhibit 7
Ski season income data (percent)

	Skiing	Lodging	Food and beverage
Revenue	100.0%	100.0%	100.0%
Cost of sales:			
Merchandise	0.0	0.0	30.0
Labor	15.0	15.9	19.7
Maintenance	3.1	5.2	2.4
Supplies	1.5	4.8	5.9
Miscellaneous	2.3	0.6	0.6
Total cost of sales	21.9	26.5	58.6
Operating expenses	66.2	66.4	66.7
Net profit (loss) before taxes	11.9%	7.0%	(25.2)%

counterpart at Boyne Mountain Lodge in Michigan. "How are your pricing recommendations coming?" he asked. "I'm about done with mine and thought we should compare notes."

"Good idea, Rick—only I'm just getting started out here. Do you have any hot ideas?"

"Only one," he responded. "I just got off the phone with a guy in Denver. He told me all of the major Colorado areas are upping their lift prices one or two dollars next year."

"Is that right, Rick? Are you sure?"

"Well, you know nobody knows for sure what's going to happen, but I think it's pretty good information. He heard it from his sister-in-law who works in Vail. I think he said she read it in the local paper or something."

"That doesn't seem like very solid information," said Karen. "Let me know if you hear anything more, will you?"

"Certainly. You know, we really should compare our recommendations before we stick our necks out too far on this pricing thing. Can you call me later in the week?" he asked.

"Sure, I'll talk to you the day after tomorrow; I should be about done by then. Anything else?"

"Nope—gotta run. Talk to you then. Bye"—and he was gone.

"At least I've got some information," Karen thought, "and a new deadline!"

Case 3–3

SeaFlite

SeaFlite first graced Hawaii's ocean waters on June 15, 1975. That day marked the first return to a water transport system in Hawaii since the last ferry had carried passengers in 1948. In this case, three Boeing jetfoil ships had been introduced to provide the service.

In 2½ years, the jetfoils ceased operating in Hawaii and were sold to a Hong Kong company. Technical difficulties and unfulfilled marketing projections had caused sizable operating losses. There remained great statewide interest in retaining the only waterway transport system; however, new financial backers did not immediately materialize.

A former architect and current owner of a Waikiki hotel announced the purchase of one Boeing jetfoil ship for $10.8 million by mid-1979. He further announced that the new ship would be transporting passengers between the islands of Oahu and Maui by mid-1981. An additional $3 million was to be spent on accessories for the ship. It was estimated that the capital investment would total $18 million by 1981.

The dimensions of the new jetfoil were to remain the same, however, with upgraded propulsion features and an improved design. The new ship would accommodate 270 passengers, where 190 were accommodated in the prior design. It was estimated that the new ship would have to run at 48 percent capacity for two trips per day to achieve profitability. Fares were to remain in line with airline fares. One year from the beginning of operations, a new jetfoil was to be purchased if warranted by demand.

It was estimated that a total of 60 employees would be hired, including a crew of 13 for the ship.

The Public Utilities Commission transferred the operating licenses to the new owner. The State Department of Transportation signed over the leases for the existing harbors on Honolulu and Maalaea in Maui.

It was a promise for a new, more modest beginning of private industry implementing a waterway system between the Hawaiian islands. The question was whether the company could achieve long-range survival where the prior company could not. Following is an overview of the history of operations of Pacific Sea Transportation, Ltd., which had run the SeaFlite system.

This case was prepared by Professor Jimmy D. Barnes, Ph.D., and Viki Arbas, MBA.

INTRASTATE TRANSPORTATION IN HAWAII

The state

The major industry of the state of Hawaii is tourism. The number of visitors who stayed overnight or longer in Hawaii are:

1975	*1976*	*1977*
2,830,000	3,220,000	3,434,000

Interisland airport passenger counts are shown in Exhibit 1. Visitors constituted about half of those traveling between islands.

Oahu, home of the State Capitol of Honolulu and the famed resort of Waikiki, was the most heavily populated and traveled island. Traffic congestion was a problem in the higher-density areas, particularly

Exhibit 1

Statewide airport system interisland passengers (arrivals, departures, through)

Year	Passengers	Growth percent
1967	4,235,114	
1968	4,695,898	10.8%
1969	5,449,244	16.0
1970	5,985,554	9.8
1971	6,760,062	12.9
1972	8,186,676	21.1
1973	9,618,194	17.4
1974	10,349,828	7.6
1975	10,648,170	2.8
1976	11,746,276	10.3
1977	12,827,694	9.2

Interisland by airport, 1977

	In	*Out*
Honolulu	2,586,533	2,601,860
Hilo	585,382	540,260
Upolu	1,512	1,297
Waimea	13,381	12,189
Ke-ahole	545,990	560,267
Kahalui	1,400,385	1,420,339
Hana	10,685	10,945
Kaanapali	46,935	47,708
Molokai	99,016	96,268
Kalaupapa	4,163	4,449
Lanai	23,814	23,324
Lihue	1,095,060	1,093,606
Other	991	1,335
Total	6,413,847	6,413,847

Source: Myra Tamanaha, research statistician, Hawaii Department of Transportation, Air Transportation Facilities Division, *State of Hawaii Airport Statistics, 1978*, pp. 3 and 47.

between the airport and Waikiki as well as between the downtown business district and the residential suburb of Hawaii Kai.

Air traffic to and from Honolulu had also been increasing over the years. Kentron Hawaii, Ltd., had conducted a study of the entire state-wide airports system and had acted as consultant for the Oahu General Aviation Master Plan. The intent was to find a method of dispersing general aviation facilities away from the congested air traffic areas of Oahu.

Oahu's neighbor islands were basically agricultural, and population and per capita income were declining. The island of Maui had the largest-growing resort destination traffic, and tourism contributed some revenues and jobs on the other islands.

A state goal was stimulating travel to the neighbor islands in order to ensure growth in the tourist industry, reduce Oahu's congestion, and ease the flow of goods and services throughout the state.

A marine highway

The director of the Department of Transportation had developed a proposal for a marine highway for the state, linking the neighbor islands and heavily traveled destination points on Oahu.

Jetfoils were first investigated for providing a shuttle service on Oahu. Problems immediately presented themselves:

1. The harbor at Waikiki was dominated by pleasure yachts and boats, and it was determined unfeasible for use as a loading station.
2. Loading and unloading baggage speedily and efficiently proved troublesome.
3. Finding what to do during off-peak hours with the vessels that were needed at peak departure and arrival times at the airport. This problem led to the investigation of the use of jetfoils traveling between islands.

A number of feasibility studies of water navigation systems had been conducted by the state since the 1950s. The concept researched most frequently was that of a ferry system which would transport passengers, their autos, and other cargo between islands. The quantitative data and demand forecasts from these earlier studies had been heavily criticized. The qualitative data from these studies did provide some relevant information regarding travel by water. Among the findings were that:

1. The public indicated enthusiasm for water travel, but intentions to ride on the ferry semed to be based more on wishful thinking than on a potential for actual usage.

2. There was debate as to whether the ferry system could be handled by private enterprise with no government subsidies.
3. The Kirkpatrick study indicated that breakdowns could cancel the service altogether.
4. The Tuttle study found a strong preference for air travel by local residents.
5. The Schipper study indicated that success hinged on low fares and a fast, comfortable ride.
6. The Guralnick study stated that travel by air had the advantage of speed but that high costs precluded its ever becoming the prime mover of people to the outer islands. Thus, the need for a ferry system was self-evident.
7. The Dymsza study indicated that demand for travel was price inelastic. Continued patronage of a ferry system would depend on a seasickness factor. The traffic would be seasonal. Passenger and cargo transport were not a good mix.
8. A 1967 Kentron study concluded that the most important consideration in marine transport was sea conditions. Passengers should be separated from cargo.
9. A Meller study found opposition to the ferry by the public because of the long travel time involved.

THE COMPANIES

L.T.V. Corporation

The L.T.V. Corporation, formerly known as Ling-Temco-Vaught, was a multibillion-dollar, Dallas-based conglomerate.

L.T.V.'s main industries were steel, meat-packing, and aerospace. In 1970, the company was on the edge of bankruptcy. The company had been known for its policy of rapid expansion and at that time had been investing in tourist-oriented activities, including a hotel in Mexico and a ski resort in Colorado.

Kentron Hawaii, Ltd., was a subsidiary of the Aerospace Division. This division also did business with Boeing Corporation.

Kentron Hawaii, Ltd.

Kentron's operations, in terms of revenues and profits, were largely government support services, with L.T.V. offering technical and logistic support to various U.S. government agencies, spread from Newfoundland to Korea. These agencies included the U.S. Departments of the Army, Navy, Air Force, and Transportation; the U.S. National Aeronautics and Space Administration and European application satellite systems; and the U.S. Federal Aviation Administration.

Kentron's other operations could be classified as commercial services, primarily oriented to Hawaii tourists.

The president of Kentron, an ex-Navy captain, had begun investigating the use of the British Hovercraft ship, which blew up its own cushion of air to ride upon the waters. The ship was determined to be unable to effectively withstand the unpredictable currents of Hawaii's waters. Furthermore, it was excessively noisy.

From 1969 to 1971, Kentron was perfecting a system to meet the State Transportation Department's specifications for an Airport-Waikiki oceangoing shuttle service. Kentron stated that it would put up some $30 million to implement this service without state aid. The service was projected to shuttle passengers and provide baggage handling service for $4 per person. The project was dropped when no adequate harbor terminal could be obtained in Waikiki.

Another ex-Navy man with Kentron was selected as president for the newly formed subsidiary, Pacific Sea Transportation, Ltd. He, too, had served as a member of the Department of Transportation Marine Highway Task Force. It had been his search of off-peak utilization of the ships in the Airport-Waikiki shuttle that had led to prospects of interisland service.

Two U.S. companies, Grumman and Boeing, had been developing commercial models of hydrofoil ships which had originally been designed for military service. Versions of the hydrofoil models had been operating some 20 years outside the United States, including between Hong Kong and Macao and across the English Channel from London to Ostend, Belgium. Some were operated on inland waterways in the Soviet Union. Safety was a key factor of these models.

Not a single fatality had occurred over some 2 billion passenger-miles. Very infrequent mishaps had occurred, even when taking into consideration that the waterways upon which the hydrofoils traveled had provided little test of their true stability. Hawaii's waters between islands, particularly through the Molokai channel, would prove to be the toughest test of the hydrofoil's technical capabilities.

Kentron's president became interested in Boeing's design of a passenger ship fashioned from a 60-ton hydrofoil gunboat which had seen service in Vietnam. Boeing had sold two of these to the Far East Hydrofoil Company for the Hong Kong route and was investigating further potential markets. Hawaii was to be a showcase for Boeing's jetfoils.

Kentron's subsidiaries

Pacific Sea Transportation, Ltd. Pacific Sea Transportation, Ltd., owned 75 percent by Kentron and 25 percent by Boeing, was established to be the operator of SeaFlite. This name was coined for the new hydrofoil ships, purchased from Boeing at $4.8 million each in

February 1973. The SeaFlite venture was entered into with the encouragement and support of the administration and legislature.

From 1973 to June 15, 1975, the development of facilities was undertaken and the SeaFlite operations were promoted. Because of the
need to coordinate facilities with vehicle availability, PSTL elected to
develop its own facilities. Terminals were built or upgraded on four
islands: Pier 8, downtown Honolulu on Oahu; Nawiliwili on Kauai;
Maalaea on Maui; and Kawaihae on Hawaii. The cost of these facilities was $2.8 million.

The terminals had facilities for ticketing, waiting, and rest rooms.
They were designed to handle passengers' boarding and unloading.

On June 15, 1975, the first hydrofoil ship began service between
islands, followed by the second in August and the third in October.
The three ships were named after kings of the Hawaiian monarchy:
Kamehameha, Kalakaua, and Kuhio. By this date, an additional $6
million over the purchase price of the ships had been allocated to the
program.

SeaFlite was totally financed with private capital. The only indirect
support was that provided by the Seventh Legislature, which excluded use tax on the import of the three hydrofoils, and by the use of
Title XI Maritime Administration Insurance on the bonds which were
sold by Pacific Sea Transportation. By 1976, SeaFlite was actively
supporting having the state take over SeaFlite facilities. The move
would have put SeaFlite in the same category as other marine transportation using state harbor facilities and airlines using airport facilities.

The company's projections were:

1.   To appeal to half the current interisland air travel market.
2.   To develop greater demand for travel by promoting a mixed mode
     of travel—by surface and air—thus offsetting any passenger losses
     by the airlines.
3.   To show a profit by 1977.
4.   To service additional areas such as Molokai, Kahalui on Maui,
     Hilo on the big island of Hawaii, and Lanai, expanding the service
     to 18 boats by 1995.
5.   To develop waterways connecting Oahu destination points.

A plan which was developed in 1975 and seriously considered was
that of dredging near Hawaii Kai on Oahu to open a channel for
SeaFlite connecting with downtown. Since nonpeak hours of interisland service were in the morning and late afternoon, a commuter
service was planned for these hours.

This idea called for the state to purchase the ships, now priced at $7
million each, and for PSTL to lease them for operating the runs.
Moonlight rides could also be added for additional revenues. Some 80
percent of the dredging costs could have been financed by federal

Exhibit 2
SeaFlite organization chart

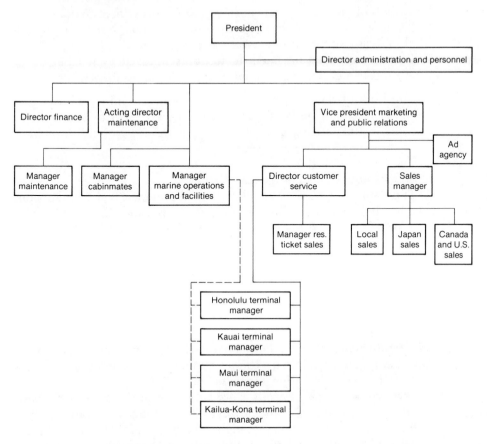

highway funds in conjunction with the marine highway proposal. This operation did not materialize.

For a time, PSTL had also thought it feasible to coordinate services with Young Brothers, a local cargo-carrying marine transport system between islands. The plan was to jointly transport passengers and their autos. This plan also did not materialize during PSTL's short life.

In 1976, PSTL was given a permit to construct a landing pier near the Aloha Stadium on Oahu, to provide commuter services for sports fans. PSTL was not able to accomplish this construction either.

The interisland SeaFlite service was a viable proposition, and PSTL employed some 190 people for this operation (see Exhibit 2).

The Sea Transit. From 1972 to 1978, the Sea Transit provided a commuter service carrying workers between Pearl Harbor, Hickam, and Iroquois Point. The marketing mix and fees charged were as follows:

1. A shuttle run, much like a marine bus service, at 50 cents per passenger.
2. A tour of Pearl Harbor, boarding at Kewalo Basin, at $5 per person. This was a service for the tourist market, though many comparable, less expensive tours were also available.
3. A trip from Kewalo Basin to Iroquois Point at $1 per person. A round-trip cruise was available at $2 for the tourists.

The bulk of the passengers rode between the military bases and Iroquois Point for 50 cents. This service was nevertheless lucky to draw even 100 passengers per day. No advertising expenditures were ever budgeted for this company.

The company lost $50,000 per year for the six years of service and closed its operations on May 20, 1978.

The Paradise Cruise.   This boat cruise provided lavish and expensive excursions during the day. At night, it became a floating restaurant for a 2½-hour dinner cruise. On Saturdays, at 9:00 P.M., the boat would leave Kewalo Basin for a "disco rock boogie party."

This subsidiary was sold March 1978.

Boeing Corporation

Boeing was facing decreasing demand for military vehicles following the Vietnam War. The B-52 bomber was successfully converted to the 707 airplane. Boeing then converted a 60-ton hydrofoil gunboat, the Tucumcari model, to a 110-ton, 90-foot by 31-foot jetfoil, capable of traveling 48 to 52 miles per hour (42 to 45 knots).

Surface-piercing hydrofoils were in use from the Florida Keys to the Bahamas. These models, however, had a tendency to roll over in waters with waves over six feet high. A submerged hydrofoil was then developed which would not begin to roll until the waves were over 10 feet high from trough to crest. Waters around the Hawaiian islands exceeded 10 feet no more than 10 percent of the time year round.

These ships were propelled by an inboard system of gas turbines which did to water what the jet plane did to air. Thus, it was named the Jetfoil. The forward speed caused the vessel to lift several feet above the surface, minimizing water resistance. The ships were able to turn in short distances like banking aircraft.

The interior configuration allowed seating up to 250 passengers. A model seating 190 was selected for SeaFlite operations.

Sales of jetfoils were being negotiated in Hawaii, Venezuela, Japan, England, and Hong Kong.

Delivery of the new jetfoils to Hawaii was scheduled for November 1974, after testing at Puget Sound at Lake Washington and, following that, in the ocean at the Oregon coast. The delivery was first delayed until January 1975. An accident at the Boeing plant caused further delay until May 1975.

HYDROFOIL OPERATIONS IN HAWAII

Costs

The first year of operation, SeaFlite's vessels experienced 20–30 percent downtime. A mere 3½ days downtime had been caused by bad weather. The downtime was mainly due to mechanical problems.

Two weeks after the maiden voyage, on a busy Fourth of July weekend, the ship's two large turbines failed. Air had hit a vent in the center strut of the after foils. As the ship skimmed over choppy water, its body lifted six or seven feet above the water. The interruption of the flow of water caused a cutoff device to automatically shut down. The system, which had been designed to ensure a safe, smooth ride, backfired. The boat plopped in the water and tossed about in the waves.

SeaFlite's mechanical reliability factor was 91 percent, where 98 percent was considered standard. The major reasons were:

1. Breakdown in the gearboxes at a cost of $200,000 each. The expected life of the gearboxes was three years. SeaFlite went through 20 gearboxes in its first year of operations.
2. Shutdown of the propulsion system in the foils when air was gulped rather than water.
3. The need to maintain a third vessel for backup. Other mishaps included a later fire which put one jetfoil out of service and some damages caused by high waves.

Break-even had been calculated at a 54 percent load factor for 10 scheduled trips per day between islands. This schedule entailed the necessity of using all three jetfoils daily since average turnaround time was about five hours.

Passenger statistics were:

1975	1976	1977
69,000	195,000	260,000

The load factor in 1977 was 38–40 percent.

Boeing flew technicians to Hawaii to redesign some of the most troublesome engine parts. It picked up on all of its warranties on parts. Warranties on parts built by some of the subcontractors were not all honored. The charge was that usage had been harder than had been originally specified.

SeaFlite ships in dry dock became a common sight for passing motorists on the main highway between the airport and downtown Honolulu.

Employment figures went beyond the originally projected numbers. In 1972 dollars, employment costs had been projected as:

| 68 full time, 12 part time on Oahu | $750,000 |
| 2 full time, 3 part time on all other islands | 27,000 |

By the second year of operations, the actual employment figures were as follows:

41 full time, 32 part time on Oahu
7 full time, 21 part time on Maui
2 full time   on Hawaii
2 full time, 15 part time on Kauai

The crew on each ship consisted of a captain, first officer, and four cabin attendants. Each future addition of a ship would require the addition of these employees.

In 1978, PSTL's president stated that during its operation PSTL had employed 265 full-time employees and 48 part-time employees. The company had spent $17,978,000 for material, services, and labor in connection with its boat operations.

The cost of renting state land and facilities was some $252,918, paid to the State Department of Transportation.

A public service tax of 4 percent on all revenues was assessed during the period of operations.

Diesel oil consumption had been projected at 420 gallons ($200) per hour. The actual needs proved to be some 560 gallons per hour.

A hand-done reservations posting system was set up by the company. This was cost effective by some $20,000–$30,000 per month over a computer system.

Operational *losses* were as follows:

1973	1974	1975	1976	1977	Total
$209,000	$424,000	$1,990,000	$3,950,000	$4,494,000	$11,077,000

The consumers

The SeaFlite passenger mix was 70 percent tourists and 30 percent local residents by the last year of operations. The airlines carried a mix of 50 percent tourists and 50 percent residents interisland.

Hawaii's visitors: Types of westbound travelers to the state

Year	Visitors	Intended residents	Returning residents
1967	754,910	44,117	130,995
1968	869,116	42,236	140,592
1969	1,008,802	41,162	152,404
1970	1,127,950	40,073	173,252
1971	1,207,898	41,562	162,967
1972	1,540,268	44,388	171,772
1973	1,815,443	36,886	194,974
1974	1,899,632	37,007	154,154
1975	1,935,396	39,233	178,040
1976	2,245,252	40,690	186,684
1977	2,453,541	43,617	179,298

Types of travel—percentage distribution

	1977	1976	1975	1974
Organized tour group/incentive trip	42.1	46.2	45.1	47.2
Individual basis	57.5	53.4	54.6	52.3
Government-military	0.4	0.4	0.3	0.5

Westbound visitor profile by percentage

Family income	1973	1974	1975	1976
Under $5,000	2.5%	1.7%	1.5%	1.5%
$5,000–$7,499	5.4	4.2	3.6	2.8
$7,500–$9,999	8.5	6.9	6.1	4.6
$10,000–$14,999	21.8	19.5	18.1	16.8
$15,000–$24,999	33.3	35.0	33.3	35.5
$25,000 and over	28.5	32.8	37.4	38.8
Median income (dollars)	$18,600	$20,100	$21,200	$21,800
College graduates	47.3%	48.6%	47.9%	47.9%
Using travel agent	73.0	76.8	77.9	82.9
Arrangements for outer island travel:				
Made before arrival	79.7	81.4	82.3	81.7
Made after arrival	20.3	18.6	17.7	18.3

Of all westbound visitors, 21 percent remained on the island of Oahu exclusively.

Number of trips to Hawaii by westbound visitor party heads by percentage

	1977	1976	1975	1974
First trip	58.9	61.3	60.3	62.7
Second trip	17.5	16.9	17.1	16.2
Third trip	7.4	7.0	7.2	6.7
Fourth trip and over	16.2	14.8	15.4	14.4

Eastbound visitor profile

Year	Numbers
1967	231,715
1968	298,727
1969	345,983
1970	420,835
1971	388,619
1972	461,640
1973	563,091
1974	601,869
1975	621,688
1976	668,550
1977	670,355

Intended length of stay:

1 to 6 days	90.7%
7 to 12 days	7.2
13 days and over	2.0

Median stay: 5 days, 4 nights

Type of travel:

Organized tour group	87.9%
Other	12.1

Neighbor islands are usually visited in a one-day tour. Few remain overnight.

Westbound visitors to the neighbor islands

Year	Maui	Percent of state total	Hawaii	Percent of state total	Kauai	Percent of state total
1967	304,437	34.1	286,590	32.1	275,461	30.8
1968	364,364	35.9	369,509	36.4	327,813	32.3
1969	396,145	33.5	410,967	34.8	363,759	30.8
1970	447,985	33.8	445,401	33.6	410,075	30.9
1971	554,799	38.8	522,166	36.5	472,663	33.0
1972	710,050	39.8	637,562	35.8	565,386	31.7
1973	766,791	37.1	694,170	33.6	590,575	28.6
1974	852,204	39.0	742,839	34.0	601,703	27.5
1975	931,863	42.2	769,779	34.9	632,821	28.7
1976	1,110,726	43.5	816,514	32.0	699,275	27.4
1977	1,257,142	45.5	839,008	30.4	740,501	26.8

Percentage of westbound visitors by their intended length of stay in the states who traveled to the respective islands, 1977

Length of stay	Maui	Hawaii	Kauai
1 to 6 days	3.6	4.2	2.8
7 to 12 days	56.1	51.8	51.4
13 to 18 days	33.9	38.3	39.6
19 to 24 days	4.3	3.8	4.3
25 to 30 days	1.2	1.1	1.1
31 to 60 days	0.7	0.6	0.6
60 days and over	0.1	*	*
Median (days)	(11.5)	(11.8)	(12.0)

* Less than 0.05 percent.

Percentage of westbound visitors by type of travel arrangements to the state, 1977

Traveler status	Maui	Hawaii	Kauai
Organized tour group	42.2	49.6	46.5
Individually arranged	57.7	50.3	53.4
Military	0.1	0.1	0.1

Residence of westbound visitors by percentage

Area of residency	State	Maui	Hawaii	Kauai
Pacific coast	37.6	38.2	33.9	39.4
Mountain	5.9	6.5	7.3	7.7
West North Central	6.6	6.5	6.7	6.5
West South Central	5.7	5.8	7.1	6.0
East North Central	15.7	17.3	18.1	17.1
East South Central	2.1	1.7	2.2	1.6
New England	3.3	2.9	2.9	2.7
Mid-Atlantic	10.4	9.6	10.2	8.7
South Atlantic	6.6	5.7	7.4	6.2
Canada*	4.9	4.9	3.1	3.1
Other foreign	1.3	0.9	1.0	1.0

* The only Canadians included in this survey are those arriving from American ports or on American carriers. The percentages can be assumed to be a good approximation.

The local residents

A survey of local interisland travelers was conducted by the *Honolulu Star-Bulletin*. The newspaper reported its findings to the Marine Highway Task Force in December 1975. The findings were:

96 percent of local travelers had used the plane for their most recent business trip.

93.9 percent had used the plane for their most recent nonbusiness trip.

6.2 percent had traveled on SeaFlite.

The Hawaii Chamber of Commerce published the following findings in 1976:

33.3 percent of local travelers go to the outer islands for business purposes.

30.0 percent take pleasure trips to the outer islands for three days or less.

50.0 percent take pleasure trips to the outer islands for six days or less.

Numbers of resident enplanements by island, 1975

Island	Enplanements	Population	Ratio
Oahu	416,000	705,000	0.5900
Hawaii	341,000	75,300	4.5290
Maui	254,000	47,500	5.3470
Kauai	197,000	32,700	6.025
Molokai	113,000	5,400	20.926
Lanai	16,500	2,100	7.857

THE MARKETING OF SEAFLITE

The schedule of departure and arrival times is shown in Exhibit 3. The actual schedule of arrivals and departures varied considerably over time, due to continued mechanical problems. The original forecast had called for 10 trips per day by November 1975. However, only eight trips were running in November. By January 1976, the Kona trip had been canceled. For a time, only six trips were running per day. In mid-1976, eight trips per day were again scheduled.

Proximity to the harbors did, in part, determine resident travel patterns. Advertising had been done to the business community in Honolulu, for example, to promote people walking from their offices to the terminal. Driving was necessary to reach the airport areas, a ride of some 15–20 minutes. Actual business travel by SeaFlite was slight, however.

On the Big Island of Hawaii, the SeaFlite harbor at Kawaihae was 30 miles from Kailua, Kona, a popular destination area. The Ke-ahole

Exhibit 3

Schedule of one-way fares

		Nawiliwili, Kauai	*Maalaea, Maui*	*Kailua-Kona, Hawaii*
Honolulu, Oahu	FF	$22	$22	$28
	MF	19	19	25
	YGF	11	11	14
Maalaea, Maui	FF			22
	MF			19
	YGF			11

Children 2 through 11 years old pay one-half adult fare.
Round-trip fare twice one-way full fare.
FF = full-fare adult.
MF = military standby fare (active duty)
YGF = youth group fare (passengers under 20 years of age traveling as group of 10 or more accompanied by an adult-fare passenger over 20 years of age).

Ask about our hourly charter rates for special cruises, either local or interisland.

Baggage

Three normal-size bags per passenger	Free
Additional bags	$3
Surfboards	4
Bicycles	4

Seaflite schedule commencing 5/28/76

Eastbound		*Daily* 215	*Daily* 225	*Daily ex. Sunday* 245	*Daily* 142	*Sunday only* 226
Nawiliwili, Kauai	Lv				4:10 P.M.	
Honolulu	Ar				6:50 P.M.	
Honolulu	Lv	7:30 A.M.	8:00 A.M.	1:50 P.M.		
Maalaea, Maui	Ar	10:00 A.M.	10:30 A.M.	4:20 P.M.		
Maalaea, Maui	Lv					11:00 A.M.
Kailua-Kona	Ar					1:00 P.M.

Westbound		*Daily* 502	*Daily ex. Sunday* 512	*Daily* 522	*Daily* 241	*Sunday only* 622
Kailua-Kona	Lv					2:00 P.M.
Maalaea, Maui	Ar					4:00 P.M.
Maalaea, Maui	Lv	10:20 A.M.	10:55 A.M.	4:40 P.M.		
Honolulu	Ar	12:45 P.M.	1:20 P.M.	7:05 P.M.		
Honolulu	Lv				1:10 P.M.	
Nawiliwili, Kauai	Ar				3:50 P.M.	

Exhibit 3 (*concluded*)

Ground transportation to major resort and business centers available at all SeaFlite terminals:

Tropical and Avis Rent-A-Car
Grayline shuttle bus
Taxis

For reservation and information call:

Oahu   (808) 521-7841
Kauai   (808) 245-3925
Maui   (808) 244-3915
Hawaii   (808) 329-1466

Pacific Sea Transportation, Ltd.
Pier 8
155 Ala Moana Blvd.
Honolulu, Hawaii 96813

Airport was seven miles from Kona. South Kona had approximately 6 percent of the island's population and North Kona, about 9 percent, in 1976. The areas closest to the SeaFlite terminal were Kohala and Waimea, which contained some 4 percent of the island's population. Another airport was in Hilo, a popular destination point located on the opposite side of the island.

On Maui the SeaFlite terminal was at Maalaea, closest to the Lahaina area, which contained some 16 percent of that island's population. The Wailuku-Kahalui-Makawao areas had about 82 percent of the island's population jointly. Distances to various resident destination points were:

	Wailuku	Pukalani	Makawao	Paia	Kahalui
Miles to:					
Kahalui Airport	2	8	6	4	1 or 2
SeaFlite, Maalaea Harbor	6	13	11	9	6 or 7

Pricing

SeaFlite operated as a common carrier, regulated by law by the State Public Utilities Commission. The rate structure was based on a rate of return on investment.

The Civil Aeronautics Board regulated airline fares. The major airlines offered a common fare for travel to the neighbor islands of Oahu with the purchase of a round-trip ticket to Hawaii from the mainland United States. The common fare plan allowed for the purchase of tickets to neighbor islands at $13 each stopover. A one-way trip on SeaFlite cost $22. However, the common fare would not apply unless all such stopovers were made by airline. A trip to one of the other islands with a return to Honolulu cost $39 by air on the common fare plan. Incorporating SeaFlite in the trip meant a cost of $44 or $45.

It was not until early 1977 that SeaFlite was included in the common fare plan by the CAB. The trip by SeaFlite still cost $22, but any other portion of the trip made by air could be applied to common fare.

Essentially, SeaFlite fares were set at $1 lower than a comparable trip by air.

The repeat traveler was able to purchase a membership for $5 annually, which allowed for a 15 percent discount on regular fares.

Military standby tickets and youth fare were half the regular fare. Children under three years of age rode free. Under the group plan, every 15th passenger rode free.

Commissions to travel agents were 7–11 percent of the sales price. Higher commissions were paid for group bookings of several hundred passengers. The commission structure employed by SeaFlite was comparable to the one paid by the airlines.

Sales, advertising, and promotion

Sales to the visitor market were accomplished through mainland airline booking agents, tour operators who packaged group tours, and travel agents who sold the tours.

Marshall-Williams International of Redondo Beach, California, was responsible for all travel industry and interline sales throughout southern California, Arizona and Colorado. Travel Industry Marketing of Burbank, California, wholesaled tour options for retail agents to sell, such as one-day tours to the neighbor islands, including one leg of the trip by SeaFlite.

	1975	*1976*	*1977*
Number of passengers	69,000	195,000	260,000
Sales ($ millions)	$2.3	$4.8	
Operating losses ($ millions)	$1.2	$2.2	$4.5

SeaFlite began advertising in Hawaii's print and broadcast media to build recognition. The consumer appeal factors which were stressed were novelty and scenic offerings. Advertising appeared by July 1975.

The advertising budget was projected at 3 percent of the company's revenues, after an initial sales push. The budget was to be spent in proportion to the estimated visitor and resident markets.

Hawaii's navigational history was portrayed in the tourist media, and souvenir books on this topic were also sold by SeaFlite. In all advertising, SeaFlite was compared to flying. It was compared to a jet flying over water; its leave-takings were called takeoffs; and the journeys were described as flights.

Promotions included providing environmental organizations with free rides on a space-available basis, and special "flights" were arranged for charity or educational organizations. SeaFlite was provided for filming the "Hawaii 5-0" television series in order to build recognition of the product.

THE COMPETITION

Hawaiian Airlines and Aloha Airlines were the two major interisland carriers. They were regulated by the Public Utilities Commission and the Federal Aviation Administration. At the time of SeaFlite's operations, Hawaiian and Aloha were the only airlines operating without any federal subsidy. They had been operating successfully for 25 years.

Service to all the islands, excepting Niihau, was provided. Each airline had 28 flights per day between Kauai and Honolulu. Each airline had 40 flights per day between Maui and Honolulu.

Hawaiian flew DC–9 twin jets carrying 138 passengers each. Aloha flew Boeing 737 tri-jets carrying 118 passengers each.

Hawaiian and Aloha Airlines	*1975*	*1976*	*1977*
Total revenue passengers	4,767,000	5,263,000	5,724,000
Combined operating profits		$2,318,300	$2,193,500
Load factor	65.3%	64.3%	65.8%
Break-even factor	65.1	61.1	65.6

	1976	*1977*
Hawaiian Airlines		
Promotion and sales expense	$10,792,066	$12,185,998
Passenger revenues	57,243,393	61,718,255
Aloha Airlines		
Promotion and sales expense	8,388,827	9,421,091
Passenger revenues	44,177,172	47,851,442

Some small commuter-type airplanes also operated between islands. Some provided simple carrier service. One offered an aerial one-day sight-seeing tour of all the Hawaiian islands, including landings on the islands. Helicopters also offered sight-seeing and charter flights.

Both of the major airlines charged the same fares. Children flew at half the adult fare. In 1976, both airlines introduced travel clubs. These clubs made it possible for residents to get the same rate structure as was charged the tourists by the common fare plan.

The travel clubs required a $5 annual membership fee. The membership allowed the bearer a 20 percent fare reduction when flying between 12:01 P.M. and 7:59 A.M. A 50 percent fare reduction was allowed for Honolulu departures either between 12:01 A.M. and 6:30 A.M. or between 8:00 P.M. and 12:00 P.M.

Passengers traveling in groups of 10 or more were allowed a 20 percent fare reduction.

A 5 percent increase or decrease in passenger traffic made the difference between the airlines showing a profit or a loss.

COMPANY POSITION IN 1978

On January 16, 1978, L.T.V. Corporation divested itself of all tourism-related activities. The stockholders of PSTL determined that they would no longer bear the costs of trying to reestablish SeaFlite. Since a buyer for the company had not materialized by the end of 1977, the three jetfoils were sold to the Far East Hydrofoil Company for $5 million each. To date, those ships remain in operation between Hong Kong and Macao.

PSTL continued rental payments to the state for the terminal facilities. Default of such payments would have authorized the state's takeover of those facilities. Restrictive terms in the original lease precluded the subrental of facilities by PSTL.

The PUC service tax obligation for PSTL facilities was in arrears $392,913 for 1976 and 1977. By August 1978, the billing was $453,038. At that time, PSTL proposed that the state forgive the tax in exchange for the facilities.

The future value of the facilities for the state depended on use by a similar hydrofoil craft since the facilities had been so specifically designed. The state did not have funds to alter the premises, and the harbors were not essential to state harbor operations.

At the public hearing of the PUC relative to the request of PSTL to suspend operations and sell its three jetfoils, the state administration through the Public Utilities Division and the governor's advisers on marine affairs had opposed that request. The opposition premised on the importance of this service to the state of Hawaii. The PUC ultimately granted PSTL's request and extended the license for one year but asked that efforts continue to locate a suitable operator. Thus, PSTL retained some key personnel and kept machinery and equipment in place throughout 1978. An active search for buyers of the company continued.

The capital investment of over $20 million was recovered by the company.

In 1978, the state appropriated a small budget to the Hawaii Visitors Bureau for an advertising campaign promoting travel to the neighbor islands of Oahu. Extensive cooperative advertising was launched, primarily in conjunction with the major airline carriers, including United Airlines. United provided $625,000 to the HVB's $125,000.

Big Island of Hawaii promotions appeared in the March 1978 issues of *National Geographic, People, Travel and Leisure,* and *Smithsonian.* The ads also appeared in selected midwestern and East Coast issues of *Time, Newsweek,* and *Better Homes and Gardens.*

Versions of these ads with emphasis on all islands were run in April through August 1978 in *National Geographic, People, Travel and Leisure,* and *Smithsonian* magazines.

The state continued its efforts to reestablish and maintain an alternative mode of interisland travel and to stimulate travel to the neighbor islands.

Case 3–4

United Bank (A)

In the early spring of 1978, the board of directors of United Bank decided that the building in which the bank was presently located was too small to serve its existing customers. Mr. John Lynn, chairman of the board, then obtained an option to lease the adjacent building, but was unsure whether to move next door or out of the downtown area altogether. He felt that he should have additional information about his current customers and the general market in the city prior to finalizing the relocation decision. Therefore, he decided that the bank should evaluate its present position and its future, with specific emphasis on whether or not United Bank should appeal to commercial accounts as opposed to retail (individual household) accounts. Because of business and personal reasons, Mr. Lynn wanted the study to be limited to published data and bank records.

UNITED'S POSITION

United Bank was founded in 1970 and was located in the central business district (CBD) of a southwestern metropolitan area. It was the smallest of three downtown banks with regard to deposits and loans. In addition to the three CBD banks, there were seven others located within the city but out of the downtown area. These non-CBD banks were considered to be suburban banks simply because of location (out of the downtown business district).

United Bank was one of the 11 banks belonging to a bank holding company and the only one currently operating in the city. Branch banking was allowed in the state, but only under highly restrictive conditions. A bank could have a branch, but it had to be located within 2,000 feet of the main bank and have a physical connection (a pneumatic tube was sufficient). Each bank belonging to the parent company was designated as United Bank—City (in which it was located).

This case was prepared by Professor Kenneth L. Jensen of Bradley University. The name was changed to protect the confidentiality of the bank.

Therefore, since the parent company had already announced that a new bank was to be opened in a community just outside the city, United's primary market would be those accounts within the city.

The present building which housed United Bank was a one-story affair which, in Mr. Lynn's opinion, offered little or no visibility. The adjacent building, on which Mr. Lynn had a lease option, had six floors—more than enough space to handle United's customers. The current location had adequate parking but was difficult to get to because of the one-way street patterns. The lease-option building would also have the same access.

MARKET SITUATION

In recent years, banks had been facing stiffer competition for retail customers from a variety of sources, primarily from savings associations, credit unions, and retail department stores. The city had six savings and loan associations, three of which had downtown offices. In addition, there were 12 suburban offices or branches in the city. Several of these associations were aggressively seeking customer deposits through various promotions and advertising.[1]

Five credit unions had offices in or near the CBD; six had suburban offices. Most were already offering share drafts—essentially interest-bearing checking accounts. Several were also competing in the home mortgage market, and most offered rebates on loans after they were paid off. All paid higher interest rates on deposits and charged lower rates on loans.

The three major national department store chains had stores in the city. A large regional department store also had a store there. Only one of these four stores was located near the CBD. None accepted credit cards other than their own, thus being in competition with bank credit cards. In addition, there were several other local stores of the department store type, two of which had CBD stores in addition to their suburban stores.

The major shopping areas of the city had shifted to non-CBD locations in recent years. Many retailers in the CBD had moved to suburban areas following the changed consumer shopping patterns. As a consequence, the CBD was in a state of decline. However, there existed a very strong movement to revitalize the downtown area that was meeting with success. Several buildings had been remodeled, and a new civic center was nearing completion. A major hotel chain had recently announced that a new hotel would be built in the downtown area. In addition, the city was in the process of constructing a pedestrian shopping mall in the downtown area.

---

[1] Six-month money market certificates were not yet available.

UNITED'S CUSTOMER BASE

Prior to starting a new investigation by the bank's staff into United's future, Mr. Lynn called the senior vice president of the bank, Mr. Johnson, to see what information the bank had already compiled concerning its customers. Mr. Johnson had just completed an account analysis with the following results.

United had just over 3,500 accounts, of which 569 (15.2 percent) were classified as commercial, 2,161 were retail (61.5 percent), and the remaining 782 were unclassified. These unclassified accounts generally consisted of loans made to individuals or businesses that did not have a deposit at United. Regarding deposit accounts, most (1,794) were demand deposits, 836 were savings accounts, and 206 were CDs. The remaining 676 accounts were unclassified as to deposit category.

Most of United's accounts were located within the city—2,678 of 3,512 (76.4 percent). No other area had a large proportion of accounts. Only since 1974 had United Bank attracted more new accounts each year other than the year it opened. United's best year to date was 1977, with 465 new accounts. As of the year the study was made, in 1978, United was keeping about the same pace with regard to new accounts as in 1977.

The median value of a deposit was $463 in 1978, while loans had a median value of $3,420. Most of the loans were installment loans, this classification accounting for 71.9 percent of the loans outstanding. Only 133 (10.3 percent) of the loan accounts had two or more loans in the last year with United. Altogether, 1,285 (36.6 percent) of United's accounts had loans outstanding.

Most of United's accounts (70.3 percent) had just one account. Only 24.5 percent had multiple deposits; 4.4 percent had multiple loans; and just 0.8 percent had more than one of both deposits and loans.

The commercial accounts were generally demand deposits (492 of 569); only 56 had savings deposits, and a minuscule 21 had CDs. In contrast, the bulk of savings and CDs were retail accounts, with 858 savings deposits. Regarding the proportion of new commercial accounts to the total of new accounts added, United experienced a declining proportion from 1970 to 1974, going from 30.5 percent to 18.4 percent. Beginning in 1975, the ratio of new commercial to total new accounts grew, reaching 32.0 percent in 1976; but then it fell again, to 18.3 percent in 1978. The average annual growth rate of new commercial accounts was 5.6 percent from 1970 to 1977; the equivalent rate for retail accounts was 9.9 percent.

As expected, the median deposit value of a commercial account was higher than that of a retail account—$1,319 to $409. The same relationship held with regard to loan value—$8,333 to $3,455.

These results mildly surprised Mr. Lynn, for he had thought of United Bank as a heavy commercial oriented bank. That is, its location had led to the impression that commercial accounts accounted for most of its business. Now he knew that he needed more information before he and the board could make a decision to move. He then directed Mr. Johnson to conduct a study concerned with United's competitive position in the banking community, the population and income characteristics of the city, and local business conditions. He and the board of directors would then meet to interpret and discuss the data presented by Mr. Johnson.

APPENDIX: INFORMATION COLLECTED BY MR. JOHNSON

Exhibit 1
Bank deposits, 1970–1977 ($ millions)*

Bank†	1970	1971	1972	1973	1974	1975	1976	1977
United	$ 3.6	$ 5.5	$ 6.5	$ 8.1	$ 9.7	$ 14.1	$ 16.5	$ 17.8
A	98.9	112.5	116.1	125.4	142.0	157.2	170.2	187.6
B	138.8	155.1	180.0	179.3	181.0	185.3	191.8	216.4
C	22.4	25.2	29.0	31.6	36.0	41.6	48.0	57.2
D	7.3	7.9	9.1	10.1	11.4	14.1	17.2	19.6
E	11.0	12.5	13.5	13.5	15.2	14.4	15.9	18.5
F	9.7	11.2	12.3	15.0	17.1	17.2	20.6	23.5
G	9.8	10.7	11.9	12.4	14.1	16.0	17.8	20.8
H	—	—	—	1.5	5.3	9.0	11.0	12.5
I	—	3.1	4.1	5.5	7.4	10.3	14.9	20.4
Total	$301.5	$343.7	$382.5	$402.4	$439.2	$479.2	$523.9	$594.6

Note: Bank H opened in 1973; bank I, in 1971.
* As of December 31 statements.
† United and banks A and B are CBD banks; C–I are suburban banks.
Sources: Bank records and the local newspaper.

Exhibit 2
Bank loans, 1970–1977 ($ millions)*

Bank	1970	1971	1972	1973	1974	1975	1976	1977
United	$ 3.5	$ 4.1	$ 4.9	$ 5.7	$ 7.1	$ 8.4	$ 12.2	$ 11.6
A	55.0	60.1	65.1	75.2	83.5	96.7	100.1	112.6
B	83.1	88.5	94.9	105.9	106.4	103.4	108.1	127.3
C	13.7	16.3	17.2	18.9	21.9	26.2	29.3	35.2
D	4.7	5.2	5.5	7.0	8.1	9.7	12.5	13.1
E	6.3	8.4	8.4	8.2	9.8	9.1	10.4	13.3
F	6.1	7.0	8.7	9.3	9.4	9.6	11.0	11.0
G	6.3	8.1	9.8	9.8	10.0	11.0	12.3	13.4
H	—	—	—	.5	2.7	6.2	5.5	5.7
I	—	2.7	3.7	4.3	5.7	6.7	9.8	13.5
Total	$178.7	$200.4	$218.2	$244.8	$264.6	$287.0	$311.2	$356.7

* As of December 31 statements.
Sources: Bank records and the local newspaper.

Exhibit 3
Population and income, 1970–1976

Year	Population (000s)	Household (000s)	Effective buying income (000s)	Per capita EBI	Per household EBI
1970	117.0	37.4	$371,181	$3,172	$ 9,925
1971	116.7	37.4	393,111	3,369	10,511
1972	116.9	38.8	425,924	3,643	10,977
1973	116.5	39.2	459,734	3,946	11,728
1974	116.7	39.4	509,073	4,362	12,921
1975	111.0	38.6	534,846	4,818	13,856
1976	111.5	38.8	622,864	5,586	16,053

Source: "Survey of Buying Power," *Sales and Marketing Management*, 1971 to 1977 issues.

Exhibit 4
Income distribution of households, 1970–1976

Income class	1970	1971	1972	1973	1974	1975	1976
$ 8,000– 9,999	14.9%	14.7%	14.6%	13.9%	8.8%	8.1%	6.9%
10,000–14,999	31.2	20.2	20.7	21.5	21.4	20.2	17.9
15,000–24,999	—	14.0	15.5	20.4	33.3	26.8	28.6
25,000 or greater	—	—	—	—	—	10.6	16.7

Note: In those cells represented by a —, the last number in the column for each year represents the proportion *over* the lower limit of that income class.
Source: "Survey of Buying Power," *Sales and Marketing Management*, 1971 to 1977 issues.

Exhibit 5
Total retail sales, 1970–1976 ($000)

Year	Total retail sales	Retail sales/household
1970	$238,531	$ 6,378
1971	255,968	6,844
1972	291,919	7,524
1973	366,018	9,337
1974	464,409	11.787
1975	487,921	12,640
1976	526,825	13,587

Source: "Survey of Buying Power," *Sales and Marketing Management*, 1971 to 1977 issues.

Exhibit 6
Building permits issued, 1970–1977

Year	Housing*	Commercial†	Total
Number of permits			
1970	2,047	713	2,760
1971	2,256	877	3,133
1972	2,749	1,000	3,749
1973	2,431	1,262	3,693
1974	2,276	933	3,209
1975	2,863	1,122	3,985
1976	2,723	1,231	3,954
1977	2,349	1,424	3,773
Value of permits (000s)			
1970	$ 8,320.1	$ 5,528.3	$13,848.3‡
1971	14,355.3	9,044.6	23,399.9
1972	19,878.9	12,599.0	32,478.0
1973	19,102.4	20,916.0	40,019.3
1974	18.295.8	17,615.6	35,911.3
1975	29,538.8	16,871.2	46,410.0
1976	41,103.1	21,379.2	62,482.4
1977	51,629.5	30,412.2	82,041.7

* Includes new single-family dwellings, apartments, residential additions and renovations, and house moving permits.
† Includes all others, primarily retail store and other forms of industrial and business construction.
‡ Totals may var due to rounding.
Source: Building Inspection Department, City.

Exhibit 7
Distribution of account type by deposit type

Account type	Deposit type			
	Demand	Savings	CD	Total*
Commercial	492	56	21	567
Retail	1,302	767	91	2,160
Total	1,794	823	112	2,729

* Unclassified accounts are not represented in the total.
Source: Bank records.

Exhibit 8
Number of accounts opened, 1970–1978

Account type	Year opened								
	1970	1971	1972	1973	1974	1975	1976	1977	1978*
Commercial	79	31	36	51	52	62	94	116	31
Retail	180	96	113	203	231	199	199	348	138
Total	259	127	149	254	283	261	293	464	169

* As of the end of April 1978.
Source: Bank records.

Exhibit 9
Distribution of accounts by deposit value

	Account type	
Value class	Commercial	Retail
$ 0– 500	206	1,301
501– 1,500	91	456
1,501– 3,000	55	146
3,001– 6,000	63	104
6,001– 10,000	44	37
10,001– 20,000	38	42
20,001– 50,000	33	24
50,001–100,000	16	8
Over $100,000	15	9

Source: Bank records.

Exhibit 10
Distribution of accounts by loan value

	Account type	
Loan class	Commercial	Retail
$ 0– 500	5	40
501– 1,500	5	82
1,501– 3,000	14	56
3,001– 6,000	30	99
6,001– 10,000	18	65
10,001– 20,000	14	28
20,001– 50,000	20	15
50,001–100,000	8	1
Over $100,000	15	0

Source: Bank records.

Exhibit 11
Distribution of deposits by value

	Deposit type		
Deposit value	Demand	Savings	CD
$ 0– 500	1,031	480	5
501– 1,500	374	155	32
1,501– 3,000	118	74	23
3,001– 6,000	96	50	39
6,001– 10,000	49	23	19
10,001– 20,000	45	19	35
20,001– 50,000	32	12	22
50,001–100,000	14	1	12
Over $100,000	10	5	18

Source: Bank records.

Case 3–5

The Gillette Company— Safety Razor Division

In July 1978, Mike Edwards, brand manger for TRAC II®[1], is beginning to prepare his marketing plans for the following year. In preparing for the marketing plan approval process, he has to wrestle with some major funding questions.

The most recent sales figures show that TRAC II has continued to maintain its share of the blade and razor market. This has occurred even though the Safety Razor Division (SRD) has introduced a new product to its line, Atra. The company believes that Atra will be the shaving system of the future and, therefore, is devoting increasing amounts of marketing support to this brand. Atra was launched in 1977 with a $7 million advertising campaign and over 50 million $2 rebate coupons. In less than a year, the brand achieved a 7 percent share of the blade market and about one third of the dollar razor market. Thus, the company will be spending heavily on Atra, possibly at the expense of TRAC II, still the number one shaving system in America.

Edwards is faced with a difficult situation, for he believes that TRAC II still can make substantial profits for the division, provided the company continues to support the brand. In preparing for 1979, the division is faced with two major issues:

1. What is the future potential of TRAC II and Atra?
2. Most important of all, can SRD afford to support two brands heavily? Even if it can, is it sound marketing policy to do so?

COMPANY BACKGROUND

The Gillette Company was founded in 1903 by King C. Gillette, a 40-year-old inventor, utopian writer and bottle-cap salesman, in Boston, Massachusetts. Since marketing its first safety razor and blades, the Gillette Company, the parent of the Safety Razor Division, has been the leader in the shaving industry.

The Gillette safety razor was the first system to provide a dispos-

Sales, market share, advertising data, and other cost figures used in this case were taken from published and unpublished sources and are to be considered as estimates only. These data provide a representative picture of the situation discussed in the case. This case was made possible by the cooperation of the Gillette Company.

This case was prepare by Charles M. Kummel, research assistant, under the supervision of Associate Professor Jay E. Klompmaker, The University of North Carolina at Chapel Hill, School of Business Administration.

[1] TRAC II® is a registered trademark of the Gillette Company.

able blade which could be replaced at low cost and provided a good inexpensive shave. The early ads focused on a shave-yourself theme: "If the time, money, energy and brainpower which are wasted [shaving] in the barbershops of America were applied in direct effort, the Panama Canal could be dug in four hours."

The pre–World War II years

With the benefit of a 17-year patent, Gillette was in a very advantageous position. However, it wasn't until World War I that the safety razor began to gain wide consumer acceptance. One day in 1917 King Gillette came into the office with a visionary idea: present a Gillette razor to every soldier, sailor, and marine. Other executives modified this idea such that the government would do the presenting. In this way, millions just entering the shaving age would give the nation the self-shaving habit. In World War I, the government bought 4,180,000 Gillette razors as well as smaller quantities of competitive models.

The daily shaving development

While World War I gave impetus to self-shaving, World War II popularized frequent shaving—12 million American servicemen shaved daily. Thus, there were two results: (1) Gillette was able to gain consumer acceptance of personal shaving, and (2) the company was able to develop an important market to build for the future.

The post–World War II years

After 1948, the company began to diversify through the acquisition of three companies which gave Gillette entry into new markets. In 1948, the acquisition of the Toni Company extended the company into the women's grooming aid market. Papermate, a leading maker of writing instruments, was bought in 1954, and the Sterilon Corporation, a manufacturer of disposable supplies for hospitals, was acquired in 1962.

Diversification also occurred through internal product development propelled by a detailed marketing survey conducted in the late 1950s. The survey found that the public associated the company with personal grooming as much as or more than with cutlery and related products. Gillette's response was to broaden its personal care line. As a result, Gillette now markets such well-known brands as Adorn hairspray, Tame cream rinse, Right Guard antiperspirant, Dry Look hairspray for men, Foamy shaving cream, Earth Borne and Ultra Max shampoo, Cricket lighters, and Pro Max hairdryers as well as Papermate, Erasermate and Flair pens.

Table 1
Sales and contributions to profits of Gillette business segments, 1973–1977

The approximate percentages of consolidated net sales and contributions to profits during the last five years for the company's business segments or product lines are set forth below.

Year	Blades and razors		Toiletries and grooming aids		Writing instruments		Braun products		Other	
	Net sales	Contributions to profits	Net sales	Contributions to profits	Net sales	Contributions to profits	Net sales	Contributions to profits	Net sales	Contributions to profits
1977	31%	75%	26%	13%	8%	6%	23%	13%	12%	(7)%
1976	29	71	28	15	7	6	21	10	15	(2)
1975	30	73	30	15	7	5	20	8	13	(1)
1974	30	69	31	17	7	6	20	5	12	3
1973	31	64	32	20	7	5	22	10	8	1

Source: 1977 Gillette Company annual report, p. 28.

Gillette today

Gillette is divided into four principal operating groups (North America, International, Braun AG, Diversified Companies) and five product lines. As Table 1 indicates, the importance of blades and razors to company profits is immense. In just about all the 200 countries where its blades and razors are sold, Gillette remains the industry leader.

In 1977, Gillette reported increasd worldwide sales of $1,587.2 million, with income after taxes of $79.7 million (see Exhibit 1). Of

Exhibit 1
Gillette Company annual income statements, 1963–1977 ($000)

Year	Net sales	Gross profit	Profit from operations	Income before taxes	Federal and foreign income taxes	Net income
1977	$1,578,209	$834,786	$202,911	$158,820	$79,100	$79,720
1976	1,491,506	782,510	190,939	149,257	71,700	77,557
1975	1,406,906	737,310	184,368	146,954	67,000	79,954
1974	1,246,422	667,395	171,179	147,295	62,300	84,995
1973	1,064,427	600,805	155,949	154,365	63,300	91,065
1972	870,532	505,297	140,283	134,618	59,600	75,018
1971	729,687	436,756	121,532	110,699	48,300	62,399
1970	672,669	417,575	120,966	117,475	51,400	66,075
1969	609,557	390,858	122,416	119,632	54,100	65,532
1968	553,174	358,322	126,016	124,478	62,200	62,278
1967	428,357	291,916	101,153	103,815	47,200	56,615
1966	396,190	264,674	90,967	91,666	41,800	49,866
1965	339,064	224,995	75,010	75,330	33,000	42,330
1964	298,956	205,884	72,594	73,173	35,500	37,673
1963	295,700	207,552	85,316	85,945	44,400	41,545

total sales, $720.9 million were domestic and $866.3 million were international, with profit contributions of $109 million and $105.6 million, respectively. The company employs 31,700 people worldwide, with 8,600 employees in the United States.

Statement of corporate objectives and goals

At a recent stockholders' meeting, the chairman of the board outlined the company's strategy for the future:

> The goal of the Gillette Company is sustained growth. To achieve this, the company concentrates on two major objectives: to maintain the strength of existing product lines and to develop at least two new significant businesses or product lines that can make important contributions to the growth of the company in the early 1980s.
> In existing product lines, the company broadens its opportunities for growth by utilizing corporate technology to create new products. In

other areas, growth is accomplished through either internal development or the acquisition of new businesses.

The company uses a number of guidelines to evaluate growth opportunities. Potential products or services must fulfill a useful function and provide value for the price paid; offer distinct advantages easily perceived by consumers; be based on technology available within, or readily accessible outside, the company; meet established quality and safety standards; and offer an acceptable level of profitability and attractive growth potential.

THE SAFETY RAZOR DIVISION

The Safety Razor Division has long been regarded as the leader in shaving technology. Building upon King Gillette's principle of using razors as a vehicle for blade sales, and of associating the name "Gillette" with premium shaving, the division has been able to maintain its number one position in the U.S. market.

Share of market

Market share is important in the shaving industry. The standard is that each share point is equivalent to approximately $1 million in pretax profits. Over recent history, Gillette has held approximately 60 percent of the total dollar market. However, the division has put more emphasis on increasing its share from its static level.

Product line

During the course of its existence, Gillette has introduced many new blades and razors. In the last 15 years, the shaving market has evolved from a double-edged emphasis to twin-bladed systems (see Exhibit 2). Besides Atra and TRAC II, Gillette markets Good News! disposables, Daisy for women, and double-edge, injector, carbon, and Techmatic band systems (see Exhibit 3). Within their individual markets, Gillette makes 65 percent of all premium double-edge blade sales, 12 percent of injector sales, and almost all of the carbon and band sales.

Marketing approach and past traditions

During 1977, the Gillette Company spent $207.9 million to promote all its products throughout the world, of which $133.1 million was spent for advertising, including couponing and sampling, and $74.8 million for sales promotion. In terms of the domestic operation, the Safety Razor Division uses an eight-cycle promotional schedule, whereby every six weeks a new program is initiated. During any one cycle, some but not all products and their packages are sold on promo-

Exhibit 2
Long-term summary of Gillette razor blades: Percent consumer blade sales—food/drug total,
United States (estimated market share)

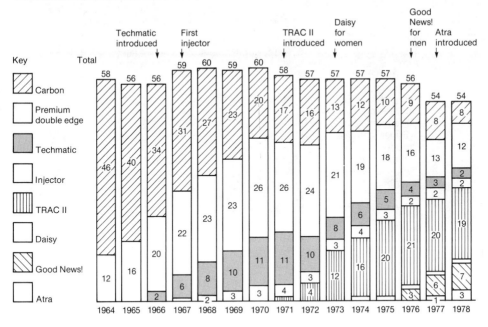

tion. Usually one of the TRAC II packages is sold on promotion during each of these cycles.

> Gillette advertising is designed to provide information to consumers and motivate them to buy the Company's products. Sales promotion ensures that these products are readily available, well located and attractively displayed in retail stores. Special promotion at the point of purchase offers consumers an extra incentive to buy Gillette products.[2]

In the past the company has concentrated its advertising and promotion on its newest shaving product, reducing support for its other established lines. The theory is that growth must come at the expense of other brands. For example, when TRAC II was introduced, the advertising budget for other brands was cut such that the double-edge portion decreased from 47 percent in 1971 to 11 percent in 1972, while TRAC II received 61 percent of the division budget (see Exhibit 4).

A long-standing tradition has been that razors are used as a means for selling blades. Thus, with razors the emphasis is to induce the consumer to try the product by offering coupon discounts, mail samples, and heavy informational advertising. Blade strategy has been to emphasize a variety of sales devices—such as discounts, displays, and

---

[2] Source: 1977 Gillette company annual report, p. 14.

Exhibit 3
Safety Razor Division product lines, June 1978

	Package sizes	Manufacturer's suggested retail price (dollars)
Blades		
TRAC II	5, 9, 14, Adjustable 4	$1.60, 2.80, 3.89, 1.50
Atra	5, 10	1.70, 3.40
Good News!	2	0.60
Daisy	2	1.00
Techmatic	5, 10, 15	1.50, 2.80, 3.50
Double-edge		
Platinum plus	5, 10, 15	1.40, 2.69, 3.50
Super-stainless	5, 10, 15	1.20, 2.30, 3.10
Carbon		
Super blue	10, 15	1.50, 2.15
Regular blue	5, 10	0.70, 1.25
Injector		
Regular	7, 11	1.95, 2.60
Twin-injector	5, 8	1.40, 2.20
Razors		
TRAC II	Regular	3.50
	Lady	3.50
	Adjustable	3.50
	Deluxe	3.50
Atra		4.95
Double-edge		
Super-adjustable		3.50
Lady Gillette		3.50
Super speed		1.95
Twin-injector		2.95
Techmatic	Regular	3.50
		3.95
Three-piece		4.50
Knack		1.95
Cricket lighters		
Regular		1.49
Super		1.98
Keeper		4.49

sweepstakes at pharmacies, convenience stores, and supermarkets—
to encourage point of purchase sales. In spite of this tradition, razor
sales are a very significant portion of division sales and profits.

At the center of this marketing strategy has been the company's
identification with sports. The Gillette "Cavalcade of Sports" began
with Gillette's radio sponsorship of the 1939 world series and continues today with the world series, Super Bowl, professional and
NCAA basketball, and boxing. During the 1950s and 60s, Gillette
spent 60 percent of its ad dollar on sports programming. Influenced by
research that showed prime-time entertainment offered superior audience potential, in the early 1970s the company switched to a prime-

Exhibit 4
Approximate Gillette historical advertising expenditures, 1965–1978

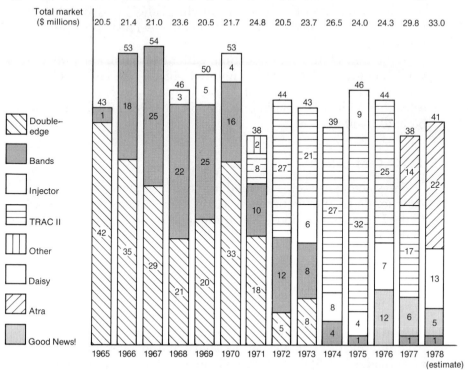

time emphasis. However, in the last two years Gillette has returned to its sports formula.

Marketing research

Research has been a cornerstone to the success of the company, for it has been the means to remain superior to its competitors. For example, Gillette was faced in 1917 with the expiration of its basic patents and the eventual flood of competitive models. Six months before the impending expiration, the company came out with new razor models, including one for a dollar. As a result, the company made more money than ever before. In fact, throughout the history of shaving Gillette has introduced most of the improvements in shaving technology. The major exceptions are the injector, which was introduced by Schick, and the stainless steel double-edge blade, introduced by Wilkinson.

The company spends $37 million annually on research and development for new products, product improvements, and consumer testing. In addition to Atra, a recent development is a new sharpening process called "Microsmooth" which improves the closeness of the shave and the consistency of the blade. This improvement is to be introduced on all of the company's twin blades by early 1979. Mike Edwards believes that this will help to ensure TRAC II's retention of its market.

At the time of Atra's introduction, Gillette research found that users would come from TRAC II and non-twin-blade systems. This loss was estimated to be 60 percent of TRAC II users. Recent research indicates that with heavy marketing support in 1978, TRAC II's loss will be held to 40 percent.

THE SHAVING MARKET

The shaving market is divided into two segments: wet shavers and electric. Today, the wet shavers account for 75 percent of the market. In the United States alone, 1.9 billion blades and 23 million razors are sold annually.

Market factors

There are a number of factors at work within the market: (1) the adult shaving population has increased in the past 15 years to 74.6 million men and 68.2 million women; (2) technological improvements have improved the quality of the shave and increased the life of the razor blade; and (3) the volume of blades and razors has begun to level off after a period of declining and then increasing sales (see Exhibit 5).

While the shaving market has increased slightly, there are more competitors. Yet Gillette has been able to maintain its share of the market—approximately two thirds of the dollar razor market and a little over half of the dollar blade market.

Market categories

The market is segmented into seven components: new systems, disposables, and injector, premium double-edge, carbon double-edge, continuous band, and single-edge systems. In the early 1900s the shaving market was primarily straight-edge. During the past 70 years, the market has evolved away from its single- then double-edge emphasis to the present market of 60 percent bonded systems (all systems where the blade is encased in plastic). Exhibit 6 shows the recent trends within the market categories.

Competitors

Gillette's major competitors are Warner-Lambert's Schick, Colgate-Palmolive's Wilkinson, American Safety Razor's Personna, and BIC.

Exhibit 5
Razor and blade sales volume, 1963–1979

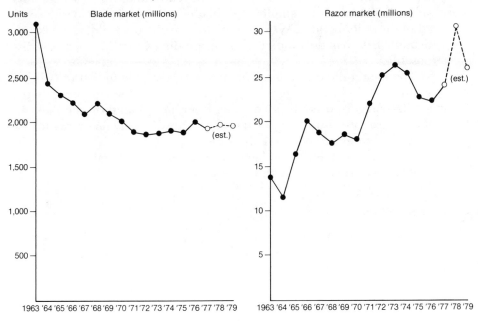

Exhibit 6
Recent system share trends

	1972	1973	1974	1975	1976	1977	First half, 1978
Volume							
New systems	8.8%	20.6%	28.8%	36.2%	39.9%	40.8%	43.8%
Injector	20.2	17.6	17.1	16.3	15.7	14.2	12.8
Double-edge							
premium	39.4	34.9	30.8	27.4	24.5	21.1	19.0
carbon	12.0	10.6	9.4	8.1	7.3	7.6	6.6
Bands	13.1	10.3	8.0	6.4	4.7	3.7	2.7
Disposables	—	—	—	—	2.5	6.9	9.7
Single-edge	6.5	6.0	5.9	5.6	5.4	5.7	5.4
Total market	100.0%	100.0%	100.0%	100.0%	100.0%	100.0%	100.0%
Dollars							
New systems	11.8%	26.9%	36.9%	46.0%	50.1%	50.1%	52.1%
Injector	21.8	18.6	17.8	16.4	15.0	13.8	12.5
Double-edge							
premium	41.5	34.2	28.7	24.0	20.8	18.1	16.1
carbon	6.1	5.4	4.7	4.2	4.0	4.1	3.5
Bands	15.4	11.8	8.7	6.5	4.8	3.6	2.8
Disposables	—	—	—	—	2.8	7.5	10.5
Single-edge	3.4	3.1	3.2	2.9	2.5	2.8	2.5
Total market	100.0%	100.0%	100.0%	100.0%	100.0%	100.0%	100.0%

Each has its own strongholds. Schick, which introduced the injector system, now controls 80 percent of that market. ASR's Personna sells almost all of the single-edge blades on the market. Wilkinson's strength is its bonded system, which appeals to an older, wealthier market. BIC has developed a strong product in its inexpensive disposable.

The competitive pricing structure is comparable to that of Gillette within the different system categories. While all the companies have similar suggested retail prices, the differences found on the racks in the market are a function of the companies' off-invoice rates to the trade and their promotional allowances.

While it is not much of a factor at this time, private label covers the range of systems, and continues to grow.

Market segmentation

The success of Gillette's technological innovation can be seen by its effect on the total shaving market. While other factors are at play in the market, new product introductions have contributed significantly to market expansion, as Table 2 indicates.

Table 2
New product introductions and their effects on the market, 1959–1977

Year	Product segment	Sales blade/razor market ($ millions)	Change (percent)
1959	Carbon	$122.4	Base
1960	Super blue	144.1	+17.7 over 1959
1963	Stainless	189.3	+31.3 over 1960
1965	Super-stainless	201.2	+6.3 over 1963
1966	Banded system	212.1	+5.4 over 1965
1969	Injector	246.8	+16.3 over 1966
1972	Twin blades	326.5	+32.2 over 1969
1975	Disposable	384.0	+17.6 over 1972
1977	Pivoting head	444.9	+15.9 over 1975

THE TWIN-BLADE MARKET

Research played a key role in the development of twin blades. Gillette had two variations—the current one, where the blades were in tandem; the other, where the blade edges faced each other and required an up-and-down scrubbing motion. From a marketing standpoint and the fact that the Atra swivel system had problems in testing development, TRAC II was launched first. The research department played a major role in the positioning of the product when it discovered hysteresis, the phenomenon of whiskers being lifted out and after a time receding into the follicle. Thus, the TRAC II effect was that the second blade cut the whisker before it receded.

Since its introduction in 1971, the twin-blade market has grown to account for almost 60 percent of all blade sales. The twin-blade market is defined as all bonded razors and blades (e.g., new systems: Atra and TRAC II; disposables: Good News! and BIC).

Table 3 shows the trends in the twin-blade market.

Table 3
The twin-blade market, 1972–1978 (in $ millions)

	1972	1973	1974	1975	1976	1977	1978 (est.)	1979 (est.)
Razors	29.5	32.1	31.4	31.3	31.5	39.7	53.8	
Disposables	—	—	—	—	14.5	41.5	64.9	
Blades	31.6	72.0	105.7	147.5	176.3	183.7	209.2	
Total twin	61.1	104.1	137.1	176.2	222.3	264.9	327.9	
Total market	326.5	332.6	342.5	384.0	422.2	444.9	491.0	500.0

During this period, many products have been introduced. They include: 1971—Sure Touch; 1972—Deluxe TRAC II and Schick Super II; 1973—Lady TRAC II, Personna Double II, and Wilkinson Bonded; 1974—Personna Flicker, Good News!, and BIC Disposable; 1975—Personna Lady Double II; and 1976—Adjustable TRAC II and Schick Super II.

Advertising

In the race for market share, the role of advertising is extremely important in the shaving industry. Of all the media expenditures, television is the primary vehicle in the twin-blade market. For Gillette, this means an emphasis on maximum exposure and sponsorship of sports events. The company's policy for the use of television advertising is based on the conviction that television is essentially a family medium and that programs should be suitable for family viewing. Gillette tries to avoid programs that unduly emphasize sex or violence.

As the industry leader, TRAC II receives a great deal of competitive pressure in the form of aggressive advertising from competitors and other Gillette twin-blade brands (see Exhibit 7). For example, the theme of recent Schick commercials was the "Schick challenge," while BIC emphasized its low-cost and comparable clean shave in relation to other twin-blade brands. However, competitive media expenditures are such that their cost per share point is substantially higher than that of TRAC II.

Despite competitive pressures, TRAC II aggressively advertises too. As a premium product, it does not respond directly to competitive challenges or shifts in its own media; rather, it follows a standard principle of emphasizing TRAC II's strengths.

Exhibit 7
Estimated Media Expenditures ($00)

	1976	First half, 1977	Second half, 1977	Total 1977	First half, 1978	Total 1978 (est.)
Gillette	$10,800	$ 4,800	$ 6,400	$11,200	$ 8,100	$13,800
Schick	7,600	3,700	4,300	8,000	4,300	8,900
Wilkinson	2,700	1,400	2,200	3,600	1,400	2,200
ASR	2,600	700	200	900	200	800
BIC	600*	4,300	1,800	6,100	4,000	7,300
Total market	$24,300	$14,900	$14,900	$29,800	$18,000	$33,000
Brands						
Trac II	$ 6,000	$ 3,300	$ 1,700	$ 5,000	$ 2,400	$ 4,000
Atra	—	—	4,000*	4,000	4,500	7,500
Good News!	1,900	1,200	600	1,800	700	1,600
Super II	2,600	1,400	2,600	4,000	3,000	4,600

* Product introduction.

Exhibit 8
1976, 1977 TRAC II media plan

	Quarter				
	1 JFM	2 AMJ	3 JAS	4 OND	Total
1976					
Prime	$ 835	$ 575	$1,200	$ 550	$3,160
Sports	545	305	450	1,040	2,440
Network	1,480	880	1,650	1,590	5,650
Other	80	85	70	165	400
Total	$1,560	$ 965	$1,720	$1,755	$6,000
1977					
Prime	$1,300	$ 900	$ 300	—	$2,500
Sports	500	400	400	400	1,700
Network	1,800	1,300	700	400	4,200
Print	—	—	200	200	400
Black	75	75	75	75	300
Military, miscellaneous	25	25	25	25	100
Total	$1,900	$1,400	$1,000	$ 700	$5,000

As Exhibits 8 and 9 indicate, the TRAC II media plan emphasizes diversity with a heavy emphasis on advertising using prime-time television and on sports programs. In addition, TRAC II is continuously promoted to retain its market share.

For 1978, the division budgeted $18 million for advertising, with Atra and TRAC II receiving the major portion of the division budget (see Exhibit 10). The traditional Gillette approach has the newest brand receiving the bulk of the advertising dollars (see Exhibit 4).

1978 TRAC II media plan

Media flowchart

	Jan.	Feb.	March	April	May	June	July	Aug.	Sept.	Oct.	Nov.	Dec.	Totals
Prime TV*		$1,055M — 15 weeks →							$115M — World series promo →				$1,170M
Baseball†				$1,278M — 19 weeks + All Star, playoffs, and world series →									1,278M
Miscellaneous sports†	$1,062M — 52 weeks →												1,062M
Spot TV											$230M — 4 weeks →		230M
Black, military Sunday newspaper, miscellaneous			$260M — 40 weeks →										260M
													$4,000M

Note: M = $1,000.

Prime-time TV advertising:

KAZ
ABC Friday Movie
Tuesday Big Event
ABC Sunday Movie
Roots Two
Love Boat
Different Strokes
Real People
Duke
Rockford Files

† *Sports TV advertising:*

Wide World of Sports, Saturday
College Basketball
NBA All Star Game
International Teen Boxing
Wide World of Sports, Sunday
NBA Basketball
History of Baseball
Game of the Week Day
This Week Baseball

Exhibit 10
1978 division marketing budget

	Atra line	TRAC II line	Good News!	Double-edge blades	Double-edge razors	Techmatic line	Daisy	Injector line	Twin injector	Total blade/razor
Marketing expenses										
Promotion*	42.3%	69.4%	65.2%	92.2%	75.4%	52.7%	58.4%	77.5%	48.3%	60.7%
Advertising†	55.6	28.8	31.2	4.6	—	—	39.0	—	26.3	36.5
Other	2.1	1.8	3.6	3.2	24.6	47.3	2.6	22.5	25.4	2.8
Total	100.0%	100.0%	100.0%	100.0%	100.0%	100.0%	100.0%	100.0%	100.0%	100.0%
Percent line/total direct marketing	34.1%	38.4%	14.9%	7.6%	0.4%	0.3%	3.4%	0.2%	0.7%	100.0%
Percent line/total full-revenue sales	20.5	41.8	13.4	16.8	1.4	2.1	2.2	0.6	1.2	100.0

* Defined as off-invoice allowances, wholesale push money, cooperative advertising, excess cost, premiums, and contests and prizes.
† Defined as media, sampling, couponing, production, and costs.

Therefore, it is certain that Atra will receive a substantial increase in advertising for 1979; whether the division will increase or decrease TRAC II's budget as well as whether the division will increase the total ad budget for 1979 is unknown at this time.

TRAC II

The 1971 introduction of TRAC II was the largest in shaving history. Influenced by the discovery of the hysteresis process, by the development of a clog-free dual-blade cartridge, and by consumer testing data which showed 9 to 1 preference for TRAC II over panelists' current razors, Gillette raced to get the product to market. Because the introduction involved so many people and was so critical to reversing a leveling of corporate profits (see Exhibit 1), the division president personally assumed the role of product development manager and lived with the project day and night through its development and introduction.[3]

Launched during the 1971 world series promotion, TRAC II was the most frequently advertised shaving system in America during its introductory period. Supported by $10 million in advertising and promotion, the TRAC II results were impressive: 1.7 million razors and 5 million cartridges were sold in October; and during the first year, the introductory campaign made 2 billion impressions and reached 80 percent of all homes an average of 4.7 times per week. In addition, a multimillion-unit sampling campaign was implemented in 1972 which was the largest of its kind.

For five years TRAC II was clearly the fastest-growing product on the market, and it helped to shape the switch to twin blades. Its users are predominantly men who are young, college-educated, metropolitan, suburban, and upper income.

The brand reached its peak in 1976, when it sold 485 million blades and 7 million razors. In comparison, projected TRAC II sales for 1978 are 433 million blades and 4.2 million razors. During the period, TRAC II brand contribution decreased 10 percent (see Exhibit 11).

Competitors' responsive strategies seem to be effective. The growth of Super II during the last two years is attributed to certain advantages that it has over TRAC II. Super II has higher trade allowances (20 percent versus 15 percent), has gained valuable distribution, has increased media expenditures, and has generally lower everyday prices.

In preparing the 1979 marketing plans, the objective for TRAC II was to retain its consumer franchise despite strong competitive chal-

---

[3] For an excellent account of the TRAC II introduction, by the president of Gillette North America, see William G. Salatich, "Gillette's TRAC II: The Steps to Success," *Marketing Communications*, January 1972.

Exhibit 11
TRAC II line income statement, 1972–1978

	1972*	1973	1974	1975	1976 (base)	1977	1978 (est.)
Full-revenue sales (FRS)							
Promotional	28%	41%	71%	100%	100%	110%	112%
Nonpromotional	38	91	89	83	100	80	65
Total	32	60	78	93	100	99	95
Direct cost of sales							
Manufacturing	63	77	93	111	100	88	83
Freight	51	80	91	106	100	82	80
Total	62	77	93	111	100	88	83
Standard profit contribution	26	56	75	89	100	101	97
Marketing expenses							
Promotional expenses							
Lost revenue	26	39	72	100	100	114	126
Wholesale push money	455	631	572	565	100	562	331
Cooperative advertising	27	36	58	71	100	115	133
Excess cost	25	50	59	83	100	63	92
Premiums	3	29	16	28	100	78	217
Contests and prizes	7	21	110	115	100	215	109
Total	26	40	67	90	100	112	129

Advertising							
Media	90	83	110	119	100	96	75
Production	96	128	130	104	100	196	162
Couponing and sampling	470	344	177	112	100	166	131
Other	19	120	68	78	100	54	54
Total	124	110	108	117	100	96	78
Other marketing expenses	108	120	847	617	100	242	86
Marketing research	122	65	47	34	100	134	91
Total assignable marketing expenses	67	69	87	102	100	106	108
Net contribution	14	53	81	85	100	100	94
Percent promotional FRS/total FRS	56	43	58	76	163	70	74
Percent promotional expenses/promotional FRS	15	16	16	15	11	17	20
Percent promotional expenses/total FRS	9	7	9	10	11	12	15
Percent advertising expenses/total FRS	28	13	10	9	7	7	6
Percent media expenses/total FRS	17	8	8	8	6	6	5

* Each year's data are shown as a percentage of 1976's line item. For example, 1972 sales were 32 percent of 1976 sales.

lenges through consumer-oriented promotions and to market the brand aggressively year round. Specifically, TRAC II was:

1. To obtain a 20 percent share of the cartridge and razor market.
2. To deliver 43 percent of the division's profit.
3. To retain its valuable pegboard space at the checkout counters in convenience, food, and drug stores as well as supermarkets.

In 1978, Mike Edwards launched a new economy-size blade package (14 blades) and a heavy spending campaign to retain TRAC II's market share. He employed strong trade and consumer promotion incentives supported by (1) new improved product claim of Microsmooth; (2) new graphics, and (3) a revised version of the highly successful "Sold Out" advertising campaign.

Midyear results indicate that TRAC II's performance exceeded division expectations as it retained 21.6 percent of the blade market and contribution exceeded budget by $2 million.

ATRA

Origin

Research for the product began in Gillette's United Kingdom Research and Development Lab in 1970. The purpose was to improve the high standards of performance of twin-blade shaving and, specifically, to enhance the TRAC II effect. The company's scientists discovered that instead of moving the hand and face to produce the best shaving angle for the blade, the razor head itself could produce a better shave if the razor head could "pivot" in such a way as to maintain the most effective twin-blade shaving angle. Once the pivoting head was shown to produce a better shave, test after test, research continued in the Boston headquarters on product design, redesigning, and consumer testing.

The name "Atra" came from two years of intensive consumer testing of the various names which could be identified with this advanced razor. The choice was based on its easiness to remember and on its communication of technology, uniqueness, and the feeling of the future. Atra stands for *Automatic Tracking Razor Action*.

Introduction

Atra was first introduced in mid-1977. The introduction stressed the new shaving system and was supplemented by heavy advertising coupled with $2 razor rebate coupons to induce trial and 50-cent coupons toward Atra blades to induce brand loyalty.

During its first year on the national market, Atra was expected to sell 9 million razors, although 85 percent of all sales were made on a discount basis. Early results showed that Atra sold at a faster level than Gillette's previously most successful introduction, TRAC II.

The Atra razor retails for $4.95. Blade packages are sold in 5 and 10 sizes. TRAC II and Atra blades are not interchangeable. Because of Gillette's excellent distribution system, it hasn't had much problem gaining valuable pegboard space.

CURRENT TRENDS AND COMPETITIVE RESPONSES IN THE TWIN-BLADE MARKET

There has been quite a bit of activity in the shaving market during the first half of 1978. Atra has increased total Gillette share in the razor and blade market. During the June period, Atra razors have continued to exceed TRAC II as the leading selling razor while the Atra blades share was approximately 8 percent, accounting for most of Gillette's 4 percent share growth since June 1977. Thus, the growth of Atra has put more competitive pressure on TRAC II.

In addition, the disposable segment due to BIC and Good News! has increased by five share points to a hefty 12 percent dollar share of the blade market. Combined with TRAC II's resiliency in maintaining share, competitive brands have lost share: Schick Super II, ASR, and Wilkinson were all down two points since June 1977.

In response to these recent trends, the TRAC II team expects competition to institute some changes. In an effort to recover its sagging share, Edwards expects the Schick muscular dystrophy promotion in October to help bolster Super II with its special offer. The pressure may already be appearing with Schick's highly successful introduction of Personal Touch for women this year, currently about 10 percent of the razor market, which has to draw TRAC II female shavers. In addition, it appears inevitable that Schick will bring out an Atra-type razor. This will remove Atra's competitive advantage but increase pressure on TRAC II with the addition of a second pivoting head competitor.

Continuing its recent trends, it appears that the disposable segment of the market will continue to expand. The first sign of this is the BIC ads which offer 12 BIC disposables for $1. Good News! will receive additional advertising support in the latter half of the year as well as the introduction of a new package size.

One of Edwards' major objectives is to emphasize the importance of TRAC II to upper management. Besides the Microsmooth introduction, a price increase on TRAC II products will be implemented soon. It is unclear whether the price change will have an adverse effect on brand sales.

In preparing the 1979 TRAC II marketing plan, Edwards realizes that Atra will be given a larger share of the advertising dollars following a strong year and that the disposable market will continue to grow.

TRAC II share remains questionable and is dependent upon the level of marketing support it receives. Whether TRAC II will be able to continue its heavy spending program and generate large revenues for the division remains to be seen. All of these factors as well as the company's support of Atra make 1979 a potentially tough year for Mike Edwards and TRAC II.

1979 MARKETING PLAN PREPARATION

Edwards recently received the following memorandum from the vice president of marketing:

Memo to: Brand Group

From: P. Meyers

Date: July 7, 1978

Subject: 1979 Marketing Plans

In preparation for the marketing plan approval process and in developing the division strategy for 1979, I would like a preliminary plan from each brand group by the end of the month. Please submit statements of objective, corresponding strategy, and levels of dollar support requested for the following:

1.   Overall brand strategy*—target market.
2.   Blade and razor volume and share goals.
3.   Sales promotion.
4.   Advertising.
5.   Couponing and sampling.
6.   Miscellaneous—new packaging, additional marketing research, marketing cost-saving ideas, etc.

See you at the weekly meeting on Wednesday.

In developing the TRAC II marketing plan, Edwards has to wrestle with some strategy decisions. To get significant funding, how should he position TRAC II? Can he enhance the likelihood of retaining current spending levels for TRAC II with the proper positioning strategy?

In addition, where do disposables fit into Gillette's overall marketing strategy? Are they a distinct segment? How does he convince the vice president that dollars are more effective on TRAC II than on Good News!? What is Atra's current positioning strategy, and does he anticipate changes? Given the strategies of TRAC II, Atra, and disposables, what problems will this create for the consumer and for the trade?

---

* Brand strategy means positioning the brand in such a way that it appeals to a distinguishable target market.

Case 3–6

Kellogg Rally Cereal

In early 1978, Mr. A. B. Smith sat in his office in Battle Creek, Michigan, evaluating the nutritional portion of the ready-to-eat cereal market. He was particularly concerned about several trade reports he had seen recently about the success of the Quaker Oats Company's Life cereal commercial titled "Mikey." The commercial was being touted as one of the best-remembered commercials on the air.

Mr. Smith was also concerned about the recent trends in the ready-to-eat (RTE) cereal category such as the success of the bran-type products and the declining interest in the so-called natural cereals. The growth in the nutritional RTE category had been strong. Kellogg's product entries in this category, however, had not shown the same growth as the market leader, Life. In addition, Life, through the "Mikey" commercial, had strengthened its position as a "nutritional cereal the whole family will like." Kellogg's two nutritional products, Product 19 and Special K, had both been strongly positioned against the adult market.

In the early 1970s, Kellogg had successfully market-tested a new product which was directly competitive to Life under the name of Rally. With the growth of the category, the established position of the present Kellogg brands in the nutritional area, and the present consumer concern about sugar content in RTE cereals, Mr. Smith was reviewing Kellogg's position in the category prior to making a recommendation to management for 1979. Launching a new brand of RTE cereal was a major undertaking involving several million dollars. In addition, Mr. Smith was concerned about the potential cannibalization of Kellogg's Special K and Product 19 if another product were introduced.

If Life's "all-family" appeal was being communicated through the "Mikey" commercial, was that an area Kellogg was missing?

Rally had been market-tested in the early 1970s. Was that test still valid? Could the results of that test be used as a basis for a new product introduction in 1979? All of these questions and more were crossing Mr. Smith's mind as he pondered the problem.

KELLOGG COMPANY

Kellogg Company had grown out of the Western Health Reform Institute, a 19th-century health clinic in Battle Creek, Michigan, affili-

---

This case was prepared by Professor Don E. Schultz and Mr. Mark Traxler of Northwestern University.

ated with the Seventh-Day Adventist movement. Dr. John Harvey Kellogg had become head of the institute in 1876. With his younger brother Will, Kellogg became interested in whole-grain cereal products for patients at the clinic. C. W. Post, who had been a patient at the clinic, had the same idea and had developed and promoted some of the foods served at the clinic into successful products.

By 1906, Will Kellogg began producing cereal products developed at the clinic under the Battle Creek Toasted Corn Flake Company name. As the company grew and the cereals were widely accepted, the name was changed to Kellogg Company in 1922.

Kellogg quickly became the market leader in RTE cereals and presently enjoys an approximate 42 percent share of business, followed by General Mills with 19 percent, General Foods Post Division with 16 percent, and Quaker Oats with 8 percent. Kellogg markets some 15 different brands of RTE cereal, including such famous names as Rice Krispies, Corn Flakes, Sugar Frosted Flakes, Fruit Loops, and Raisin Bran. Kellogg cereal sales totaled $726 million out of total corporate sales of $1.385 billion in 1976. In addition, Kellogg has expanded into other food categories primarily through acquisition of such companies as Salada Foods, Mrs. Smith's Pie Company, and Fearn International.

THE BREAKFAST CEREAL MARKET

In 1977, the RTE cereal industry continued its upward climb in total pound and dollar sales. RTE cereals are now the fifth-fastest-growing consumer product category, averaging nearly a 5 percent annual increase, according to the U.S. Department of Commerce. Sales for the past four years were:

Year	Pounds (billion)	Percentage change
1974	1.63	—
1975	1.69	+4%
1976	1.81	+7
1977	1.85	+2

Retail sales in 1976 amounted to $1.48 billion, which is approximately 1 percent of all retail food store sales. Per capita consumption of RTE cereal is increasing also. Between 1972 and 1973, consumption of RTE cereals increased from six to eight pounds per person. The Cereal Institute estimates "cold cereal" consumption by age as follows:

Age	Pounds/ person/ year
1–2	7.2
3–5	9.4
6–8	12.0
9–11	9.8
12–14	9.8
15–19	5.9
20–54	3.6
55+	5.9

Since 1974, cereal prices have been steadily increasing.

Year	RTE average retail price per pound	Change
1974	$0.908	—
1975	0.933	+3%
1976	0.951	+2
1977	1.022	+7

Usage of RTE cereals is spread fairly evenly across the country, with nearly 80 percent of all persons using them. Target Group Index (TGI) defines "heavy users" as those consuming six or more individual portions of RTE cereal per week. These "heavy users" comprise nearly 38 percent of all RTE cereal users. There is a slight geographic variance in RTE heavy users. The Mid-Atlantic (110) and East Central (107) areas index the highest, while the South East (88) and South West (84) areas are the lowest (index average = 100). There is also a slight seasonal sales skew, ranging from a high of 110 in July and September to a low of 88 in November (index average = 100).

The cereal category is broken down into seven categories by Selling-Marketing Areas, Inc. (SAMI). These categories and their approximate percentage of the total are:

Category	Share
Children's	24%
All family	46
Highly fortified	9
Bran	7
Granola	4
Variety pack	3
Other	5
Granola bars	2

TGI separates RTE cereal into three categories—presweetened, natural, and regular. Based on research data, it appears that consumers are even less discriminating, preferring to lump RTE cereals into either presweetened or regular. In spite of this generalization, there is consumer recognition of the various types of products available, with some five to seven "acceptable brands" on most shoppers' lists.

Changes in manufacturer's list prices for RTE cereals are relatively infrequent. The normal retail margin is approximately 18 percent.

There are few middlemen in the RTE cereal channels. Orders flow from the grocery chain buyer or food broker to the sales force to the factory. The goods are shipped to the grocer's warehouse and from there directly to the retail outlet. RTE cereals are fast-moving products, with about one box purchased per family per week. Typical RTE promotion to consumers includes cents-off coupons and self-liquidating premiums. The package is used as a breakfast-time entertainment medium by printing interesting information or games on the back and/ or side panels.

While there are certain anticipated trade deals for new products, established brands rely more heavily on consumer advertising and promotion than on promotional programs.

Because of the large number of brands marketed, there is no one dominant brand. Kellogg Corn Flakes is the largest selling brand, with an approximate 7 percent, share followed by Cheerios, with approximately 5.6 percent. Others range downward, with most in the 1.00 percent to 1.5 percent share area.

NUTRITIONAL RTE CEREALS

The "nutritional" segment constitutes about 15 percent of the total RTE market when several "all-family" entries are added to the SAMI "adult highly fortified" category. The "adult highly fortified" brands are Life, Product 19, Special K, Buc*Wheats, Golden Grahams, and Total. Other all-family RTE which appear to be directly competitive are Cheerios, Chex (Rice, Corn, Wheat), Wheaties, Shredded Wheat, and Team. Most of the brands in this segment are long established, with few recent additions. Total RTE brand share ranges from a low of approximately 0.27 percent for Fortified Oat Flakes to approximately 5.6 percent for Cheerios. Kellogg's two entries in this category are Special K, with 2.2 percent share, and Product 19, with 1.2 percent share. The Special K share has been declining slightly over the past two years, while Product 19 has remained steady.

The growth rate of the nutritional segment is much faster than the growth rate of the total RTE cereal market. The following table demonstrates.

Year	Nutritional increase	RTE increase
1974	6%	N.A.
1975	13	4%
1976	14	7
1977	16	2

When new cereals are priced, prices of directly competing products are an important consideration. Typical out-of-store (OOS) pricing for brands in the competitive segment are as follows:

Brand	Size (oz.)	Price
Buc*Wheats	15	$1.11
Cheerios	10	0.83
Life	15	0.93
Product 19	12	1.03
Special K	15	1.21
Total	12	1.05

Note that Product 19 and Total, which are in direct competition, are priced accordingly.

Due to the number of brands offered to the consumer, sales volume requires frequent assessment by grocery chain buyers of which brands to reorder. The decision is based on SAMI and Nielsen data to define the best-selling brands, the grocery's own historical sales data, and in the case of new products, the national advertising and promotional plans. New products are usually given a six-month trial period by most grocery retailers. However, gaining the necessary two shelf facings to launch the new brand requires several decisions. It is common for the RTE cereal aisle to be set proportionately to the grocer's sales for each brand.

Sales forces in the RTE category are highly trained and motivated. Since cereal is an established category, the sales force is usually a key determinant in a successful new product introduction.

Brands in the high-nutrition segment invested an average of $6.35 million in measured media in 1977 according to the Leading National Advertisers (LNA) annual summary. In 1976, investments in the directly competitive market ranged from less than $1.9 million for Buc*Wheats to over $10 million for Cheerios. Life expenditures in 1976 were estimated to be approximately $6.4 million compared to the Special K investment of $6.2 million and the Product 19 budget of $2.9 million. With the success of the "Mikey" commercial, Life was expected to increase its advertising expenditures in 1978.

As a rule of thumb, advertisers in the high-nutrition and all-family cereals invested 60 percent of their funds in network television, 33 percent in spot television, and approximately 7 percent in print.

The messages of the major competitors are summarized below.

Special K   An adult cereal with high-protein and -nutrition campaign stressing weight control and fitness. Copy focuses on the "Special K Breakfast" of less than 240 calories.

Wheaties   Advertising features Bruce Jenner, a current sports celebrity who included Wheaties as part of his winning diet. The brand is known as the "Breakfast of Champions."

Total   Campaign stresses vitamin and nutrition content compared against that of other leading cereal brands. Good taste is a secondary message to reassure the consumer.

Cheerios   A long-running family-oriented campaign which says, "Get a powerful good feeling with Cheerios."

Product 19   Campaign aimed at adults focusing on good nutrition. The copy asks, "Did you forget your vitamins today?"

Life   Uses "Mikey" (described below) as product hero in its long-running campaign.

The essence of the "Mikey" commercial for Life is as follows: The commercial shows two skeptical older children and a younger child, Mikey, in a kitchen setting. Because the older children already know that Life is supposed to be "good for you," implying that Life could not possibly taste good, they use Mikey as a guinea pig to taste Life cereal. Mikey innocently eats it while the other two eagerly watch for his reaction. Mikey smiles. Amid shouts of "He likes it!" and "He's eating it!" the two skeptics conclude that Life *must* taste good for Mikey to like it.

Life cereal has used trial-size sampling to stimulate interest in the product. The packages included three one-ounce servings of Life and sold for 10 cents in chain grocery outlets. Sales improved slightly as a result.

The heavy media dollars and promotional efforts described above are aimed at the primary purchasers of high-protein/high-nutrition cereals. They are profiled as women 18–49 for products like Life, Cheerios, and Wheaties and as slightly older women (25–54) for Special K, Product 19, Buc*Wheats, and Total. They live in SMSAs, most have at least a high school education, and annual household income is in excess of $10,000. They are married, with three or more individuals in the household, and children 6–11 years old, according to TGI.

THE PRODUCT

Kellogg's new product development department describes Rally as a delicately presweetened high-protein cereal for younger adults and children. The actual appearance is a square puffy pillow shape much like that of Ralston-Purina's Chex cereals. Since Rally is a rice-based product, it stays crisper in milk than oat- or wheat-based cereals. Rally's delicate presweetening translates into 18 percent sugar by volume as compared to less than 10 percent for nonsweetened brands. Nutritionally, RALLY has 20 percent of the U.S. recommended daily allowance (RDA) of protein with milk and is enriched to 25 percent RDA with eight essential vitamins and iron. Quaker's Life is the only other product with such a high protein level, light presweetening, and a comparable vitamin and mineral content. Rally contains 33 percent of the RDA for vitamins B_1 and B_2, niacin, and iron, compared to Life's 25 percent.

In choosing a package size for Rally, Kellogg looked at the brand's direct competitor, Life cereal. Life markets two sizes, 15 ounces and 20 ounces. The 15-ounce box retails for 93 cents. To compete with Life in the same price range, the largest size Kellogg could offer would be a 13-ounce box at 97 cents because of a difference in the cost of goods. Rally was tested in a 7-ounce box priced at 75 cents in the 1970 market test.

Rally's test market package design showed the red Kellogg logo, a black sticker stating "High protein," and the name Rally in big black letters at the top. The bottom portion showed a bowl full of cereal. In the midsection was a set of pennants waving above the bowl as if it were a stadium.

CONSUMER TEST

The 1970 consumer panel results for Rally among women and children were very encouraging.

	Preferred Rally	Preferred Life	No preference
General appearance	76%	14%	10%
Shape	54	19	27
Taste	62	20	18
Texture "just right"	83	16	

From the consumer test, the major advantage of Rally over Life appears to be based on the comment, "Life gets soggy too soon."

Rally was preferred 3 to 1 over Life by a consumer panel of children and was rated superior in taste, texture, and sweetness level. Against four leading nutritional brands (Life, Total, Product 19, and Special K), women showed a significant preference for Rally. Consumers also rated Rally as better than the cereals they were presently using.

MARKET TEST

Rally was market-tested in two eastern cities in the early 1970s. It was positioned as an "all-family nutritional cereal with better taste" directed to children and young adults. Rally was able to generate and maintain a sales rate equaling a 1 percent share of the total RTE market pound sales in these tests.

The introductory sell-in used Kellogg's own sales force to acquaint grocery clients with Rally and offered a 75 cent–$1 per dozen introductory case allowance to help defray warehousing and stocking expenses. The media plan included network children's and prime-time programming and spot children's and daytime programming for the 17-week introductory period.

SUMMARY

In reviewing the Rally test case, Mr. Smith was still undecided about a recommendation to introduce Rally nationally. On the positive side, consumer response seven years ago was good. Unlike many presweetened cereals, Rally's sugar content would not stir consumer concern. Every day in the papers consumers read about the importance of good nutrition, and high protein was certainly an important part of nutrition. And finally, Rally seemed to overcome the consumer problem of Life, getting soggy in milk too soon.

However, there were problems to be considered, not the least of which was the product name. Should it still be called Rally? Was Kellogg's target market—young adults and children—correct during the test market? As a new product, could Rally compete with Life in gaining both segments of the target? After 17 years, Life had only recently acquired a strong children's following with the "Mikey" commercial. Are the test market results still valid for a new product introduction in 1979? What about cannibalization of Kellogg's existing brands?

Finally, if Mr. Smith should make the recommendation to introduce Rally before giving his final recommendation to management, he would have to answer such questions as the following: What package and pricing changes would be necessary; what improvements in the distribution system would be required; and what sort of advertising strategy and promotion should be used to make Rally a viable competitor against Life and its "Mikey" commercial?

Part 4

Marketing Program Positioning Strategy

An overview of the integration of corporate and marketing strategies is shown in Exhibit 1. Note that a marketing strategy consists of:

☐ Choosing a strategy for each target market to be served by the business unit.

☐ Setting objectives for each target market.

☐ Designing a marketing program positioning strategy for each target market.

☐ Implementing and managing the marketing strategy.

We examined target market strategy in Part 3. Part 4 is concerned with setting objectives and with marketing program design. In Part 5 we shall consider implementing and managing marketing strategy.

An illustration will help to place in perspective the marketing programming task. Ask almost anyone what brand name first comes to mind for coloring crayons, and the reply will probably be "Crayola." Few people know that Binney & Smith, Inc., produces and markets Crayola crayons. Binney & Smith has about 80 percent of the U.S. Market for crayons.[1] From 1967 to 1980 the firm's sales and profit performance was modest. Today, the company has become an aggressive marketer:

> Binney & Smith is beginning to reap the benefits of a marketing program designed to gain sales outside its traditional crayon business. It has taken eight years to implement, but now Binney & Smith is plastering the green and yellow Crayola trademark on dozens of products that formerly carried other brands names. The strategy is beginning to pay off. Sales of watercolors, formerly sold under the Artista label, are up 20 percent in units.

[1] The follow illustration is drawn in part from Steven Flax, "The Greening of Crayola," *Forbes*, April 12, 1982, pp. 190 and 192.

Exhibit 1
Integrating corporate and marketing strategies

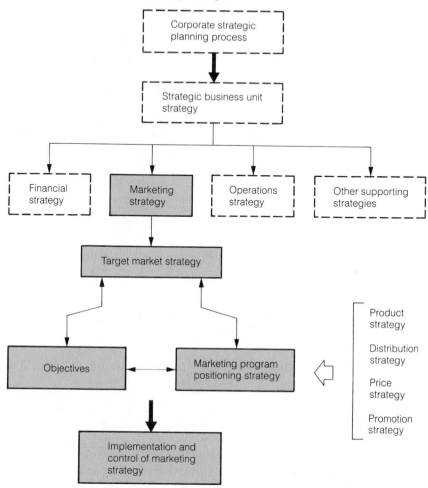

Source: David W. Cravens, *Strategic Marketing.* (Homewood, Ill.: Richard D. Irwin, 1982), p. 201.

More important, Binney & Smith has developed a host of new products to put that trademark on.[2]

A marketing program positioning strategy consists of more than a product, or even a line of products. Distribution, price, and promotion strategies must be combined with product strategy to form an integrated marketing mix. In 1975 a consultant advised Binney & Smith's management to strengthen its marketing approach. New people were added to the marketing team, new product priorities were set, distri-

---

[2] Ibid., pp. 190 and 192.

bution channels were changed, and advertising and personal selling efforts were aimed at promising market niches.

SETTING OBJECTIVES

An objective indicates something that marketing management wants to accomplish, such as increasing market share in target market A from 21 percent last year to 28 percent during the next three years. Objectives should cover various areas such as sales, expenses, profit contribution, and human resources. Each objective should indicate a desired level of performance, how the performance will be measured, and who will be responsible for meeting the objective. We shall examine some characteristics of good objectives and then discuss how to set objectives.

Characteristics of good objectives

There are several characteristics that should be reflected in a good set of objectives:

☐ Is each objective relevant to overall results? For example, if market share gain is an objective, will increasing advertising awareness contribute to the market share objective?

☐ Is each objective consistent with the other marketing objectives and with nonmarketing objectives as well? An inconsistent objective may work against another objective.

☐ Does each objective provide a clear guide to accomplishment? An objective will be of minimal value unless, when compared to actual results, management can determine the extent to which the objective has been achieved. Has the objective been quantified and a time frame specified?

☐ Is the objective realistic? Is there a reasonable chance of meeting the objective? Objectives should represent achievable results.

☐ Is *responsibility* for each objective assigned to someone? Are joint responsibilities indicated?

Setting good objectives is one of management's prime responsibilities. The task is demanding, and it requires close coordination among the people in the marketing organization to assure that all objectives correspond to the marketing mission.

Setting objectives

Since several guidelines for setting objectives were discussed in Chapter 1, our treatment here will be brief. There are essentially two kinds of objectives: (1) those that specify end results (e.g., profit contribution); and (2) those that, if accomplished, will (or should) help to achieve end results (e.g., add 10 new retail outlets by January 1, 1984). Objectives should cover market position, productivity, resources, profitability, and other important end results.

Among the troublesome problems encountered in setting objectives are the interrelationships among objectives and the shared responsibility for achieving objectives. Each objective does not fit neatly into an isolated box. Thus, considerable skill is required in determining a balanced set of objectives for different organizational levels and across different functional areas (e.g., advertising and personal selling).

Marketing objectives are normally set at the following levels:

☐   The entire marketing organization within a particular company or business unit in a diversified firm.

☐   Each market target served by the company or business unit.

☐   The major marketing functional areas such as product planning, distribution, pricing, and promotion.

☐   Subunits within particular functional areas (e.g., individual salespeople).

The extent to which the above levels are relevant in a particular firm will depend on the size and complexity of the organization.

MARKETING PROGRAM POSITIONING STRATEGY

As we noted in Chapter 1, the marketing program positioning strategy is how marketing objectives are accomplished in a firm's target markets. Product, distribution, price, and promotion strategies represent an integrated bundle of actions aimed at customers/prospects in the target market. An overview of the decisions that make up a positioning strategy is shown in Exhibit 2. We shall briefly examine each program area, beginning with product/service strategy.

Product/service strategy

The role of product strategy is described below:

Product strategy is the core of strategic planning for the enterprise and it plays a pivotal role in shaping marketing strategy. Management's strategic decisions about the products to be offered are among the most important of those affecting the future of a company. No other strategic decision has such widespread impact, cutting across every functional area and affecting all levels of an organization. This key strategic role should not come as a surprise since meeting people's needs and wants with goods and services is what business is all about.[3]

[3] David W. Cravens, *Strategic Marketing* (Homewood, Ill.: Richard D. Irwin, 1982), p. 229.

Exhibit 2
Positioning strategy overview

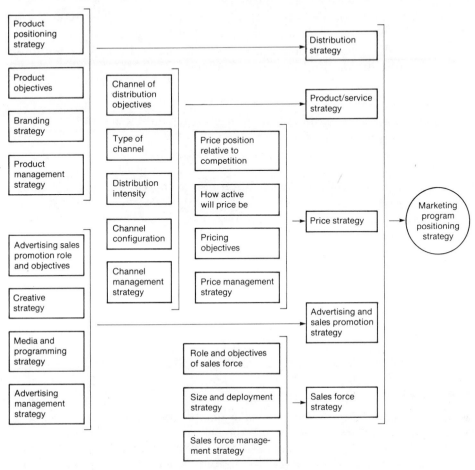

Source: David W. Cravens, *Strategic Marketing* (Homewood, Ill.: Richard D. Irwin, 1982), p. 378.

The major components of a product strategy are highlighted in Exhibit 2. We shall briefly examine each component.

Product positioning and objectives. Product positioning consists of deciding how to compete with a product or line of products against key competitors in the market targets selected by management. Key decisions about quality, price, and features establish guidelines for product development and product improvement activities. Closely associated with positioning decisions are the strategic objectives for the product strategy. Illustrative objectives are market penetration, profit contribution, and establishing a reputation for quality.

Branding strategy. The major alternatives in the branding decision of a manufacturer are:

☐ Make no attempt to establish brand identify, and instead rely on intermediaries to establish brand reputation.

☐ Produce products which have the private brands of retailers on them.

☐ Utilize the corporate name (e.g., Deere & Co.) as an umbrella identity for all of the firm's products.

☐ Establish brand names for lines of products, as with Sears' Craftsman tools.

☐ Build a strong brand identification for individual products, as in the case of Procter & Gamble.

☐ Use a combination of the above strategies.[4]

Marketing intermediaries often utilize the company and/or brand identity of manufacturers. Alternatively, if they have the resources, retailers and other intermediaries may choose to establish private brand identities.

Product planning and management.   Firms are continually faced with the management of their product portfolios. Decisions include new product development, product improvement, product repositioning, and product elimination. Increasingly, firms are formalizing their product planning and management activities to more closely link product strategies will corporate, business unit, and marketing strategies.

Distribution strategy

From the point of view of a manufacturer, distribution strategy consists of first deciding whether to go direct to end users using a company sales force or, instead, to work through marketing intermediaries such as wholesalers, distributors, dealers, and retailers. Choice of the latter strategy requires additional decisions such as the type of channel of distribution to be used, the intensity of distribution, and the types and number of intermediaries to include at each level in the channel.

The channel decision rests heavily upon the role of the manufacturer in the channel. If the firm has a strong market position and adequate resources, then management may decide to manage the channel. Ethan Allen, in furniture, has built a strong network of independent retailers. These dealers have been instrumental to the success of the company. Small firms with limited resources may be restricted to finding distribution channels to which they can gain access.

---

[4] David W. Cravens, Gerald E. Hills, and Robert B. Woodruff, *Marketing Decision Making: Concepts and Strategy*, rev. ed. (Homewood, Ill.: Richard D. Irwin, 1980), pp. 235–36.

Price strategy

It is unfortunate that a few highly publicized instances of the use of price as a survival strategy overshadow many other logical uses of price as a strategic element in firms' marketing program positioning strategies. Price was a central feature in A&P's struggle to regain market position in the supermarket industry in the mid-1970s. The strategy did not work. Braniff resorted to price competition in 1981–82. The firm went bankrupt.

The major elements of a price strategy are shown in Exhibit 2. Two of these decisions, the decision on price position relative to competition and the decision on how active price will be in the marketing program, establish the nature and scope of price strategy. The first decision is closely linked to several other aspects of marketing program positioning strategy, including product quality, distribution strategy, and advertising and personal selling programs. The second decision establishes, for example, how price will be utilized in advertising and personal selling efforts. Once these two decisions are made, guidelines can be established for price objectives and for the management of pricing activities.

Promotion strategy

Advertising, personal selling, publicity, and sales promotion activities represent communications efforts to inform and persuade buyers and others involved in the purchase decision. Each communications medium has certain assets and limitations. Management's task is to shape a promotion mix using the available communications elements. A key issue is selecting the role and objectives of advertising and personal selling in the marketing program. Once this issue has been resolved, the remaining decisions in advertising and sales force strategies consist of those shown in Exhibit 2.

CONCLUDING NOTE

The purpose of this introduction to Part 4 is to briefly describe the nature and scope of marketing program positioning strategy. The positioning strategy overview shown in Exhibit 2 identifies the key decisions for each component of the marketing program. As you work on the cases in Part 4, you may find it useful to refer to this exhibit. The cases have been selected to provide you with an opportunity to examine and develop overall marketing program positioning strategies as well as strategies for each of the program components, including product or service, distribution, price, and promotion. Several of the cases involve more than one component of the marketing mix.

Case 4–1

Trus Joist Corporation (B)

Mr. Mike Kalish, salesman for the Micro=Lam® Division of Trus Joist Corporation, had just received another moderately sized order for the product Micro=Lam laminated veneer lumber; however, the order held particular interest for him. The unique feature of the order was that the material Micro=Lam was to be used as a truck trailer bedding material. This represented the second-largest order ever processed for that function.

Earlier in the fall of 1978, Mr. Kalish had spent some time in contacting prospective customers for truck trailer flooring in the Northwest and Midwest; however, the response from manufacturers had been disappointing. Despite this reception, smaller local builders of truck trailers were interested and placed several small orders for Micro=Lam laminated veneer lumber. The order Mr. Kalish had just received was from one of the midwestern companies he had contacted earlier, thus renewing his belief that the trailer manufacturing industry held great potential for Micro=Lam laminated veneer lumber as a flooring material.

COMPANY BACKGROUND

The Trus Joist Corporation, headquartered in Boise, Idaho, is a manufacturer of structural wood products with plants located in the Pacific Northwest, Midwest, Southeast, and Southwest. Annual sales, which totaled over $78 million in 1978, were broken down into three major product categories: the Micro=Lam Division, contributing 7 percent of sales (the majority of Micro=Lam sales were internal); the Commercial Divisions, with 82 percent of sales; and the Residential Sales Program, with 11 percent of sales.

In the late 1950s, Art Troutner and Harold Thomas developed a unique concept in joist design, implemented a manufacturing process

---

This case is produced with the permission of its author, Dr. Stuart U. Rich, Professor of Marketing and Director, Forest Industries Management Center, College of Business Administration, University of Oregon, Eugene, Oregon.

for the design, and then founded the Trus Joint Corporation. By 1978, the company employed over 1,000 people, of whom about 180 were sales personnel. The majority of salesmen were assigned to the regional Commercial Division sales offices; four outside salesmen were assigned to the Micro=Lam Division. The functions of selling and manufacturing were performed at each of the five geographically organized Commercial Divisions; therefore, the salesmen concentrated on geographic selling. The Micro=Lam Division was more centralized in nature, conducting all nationwide sales and manufacturing activities from Eugene, Oregon.

In 1971, Trus Joist first introduced and patented Micro=Lam laminated veneer lumber. The product is made of thin $\frac{1}{10}'$ or $\frac{1}{8}'$-thick veneer sheets of Douglas fir glued together by a waterproof phenol formaldehyde adhesive. Under exact and specified conditions, the glued sheets are heated and pressed together. The Micro=Lam lumber, or billet,[1] is "extruded" from specially made equipment in 80' lengths and 24' widths. The billets can be cut to any customer-desired length or width within those limiting dimensions. The billets come in several thicknesses ranging from $\frac{3}{4}"$ to $2\frac{1}{2}"$; however, $1\frac{1}{2}"$ and $1\frac{3}{4}"$ are the two sizes produced regularly in volume.

MARKETING MICRO = Lam

When Micro=Lam was first introduced, Trus Joint executives asked an independent research group to perform a study indicating possible industrial applications for the product. The first application for Micro=Lam was to replace the high-quality solid sawn lumber 2" × 4" trus chords[2] in its open web joist designs and the solid sawn lumber flanges[3] on its wooden I-beam joist (TJI). Into the fall of 1978, this still represented the majority of Micro=Lam production. The findings of the research report suggested that Micro=Lam could be used as scaffold planking, mobile home trus chords, and housing components. These products accounted for about 25 percent of the Micro-=Lam production. Mr. Kalish had also begun to develop new markets for Micro=Lam, including ladder rails and framing material for office partitions.

When marketing Micro=Lam to potential customers, Trus Joist emphasized the superior structural qualities of the product over conventional lumber. Micro=Lam did not possess the undesirable character-

---

[1] Micro=Lam is manufactured in units called billets, and the basic unit is one billet foot. The actual dimensions of a billet foot are 1' × 2' × 1½", and one billet is 80' × 24' × 1½'.

[2] Trus chords are the top and bottom components in an open web trus incorporating wood chords and tubular steel webs.

[3] Flanges are the top and bottom components in an all-wood I-beam. Refer to Exhibit 1.

Exhibit 1
End view of an all-wood I-beam (TJI)

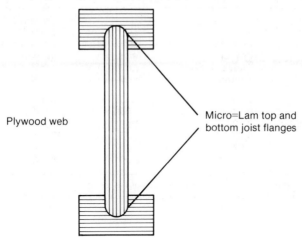

Plywood web

Micro=Lam top and
bottom joist flanges

istics of warping, checking, and twisting; yet it did show greater bending strength and more structural stability. (One ad claimed, "Testing proves Micro=Lam to be approximately 30% stiffer than #1 dense select structural Douglas fir.") In some applications, Micro=Lam offered distinct price advantages over its competing wood alternatives and this factor always proved to be a good selling point. Manufacturers were often concerned about the lead/delivery time involved in ordering Micro=Lam. Trus Joist promised to deliver within one to three weeks of an order, which was often a full two weeks to two months ahead of other wood manufacturers.

The industrial application report had also suggested using Micro=Lam as a decking material for truck trailers. This use became a reality when Sherman Brothers Trucking, a local trucking firm that frequently transported Micro=Lam, made a request for Micro=Lam to redeck some of its worn-out trailers. To increase the durability of the flooring surface, the manufacturing department of Trus Joist replaced the top two veneer sheets of Douglas fir with apitong. Apitong was a Southeast Asian wood known for its strength, durability, and high specific gravity. This foreign hardwood had been used in the United States for several years because of the diminishing supplies of domestic hardwoods. (See Exhibit 2.)

The pioneer advertisement for Micro=Lam as a trailer deck material had consisted of one ad in a national trade journal and had depicted the Micro=Lam cut so that the edges were used as the top surface. (See Exhibit 3.) The response from this ad had been dismal and had resulted in only one or two orders. The latest advertisement depicting Micro=Lam as it was currently being used (with apitong as

Exhibit 2
Mechanical properties of wood used for trailer decking

Common name of species	Specific gravity (percent moisture content)	Modulus of elasticity (million psi)	Compression parallel to grain and fiber strength maximum crush strength (psi)
Apitong	0.59	2.35	8,540
Douglas fir	0.48	1.95	7,240
Alaska yellow cedar	0.42	1.59	6,640
White oak	0.68	1.78	7,440
Northern red oak	0.63	1.82	6,760
Micro=Lam*	0.55	2.20	8,200

* Micro=Lam using Douglas fir as the veneer faces of the lumber.
   Source: *Wood Handbook: Wood as an Engineering Material*, USDA Handbook no. 72, rev. ed., 1974; U.S. Forest Products Laboratory.

Exhibit 3
End view of *remanufactured* Micro = Lam

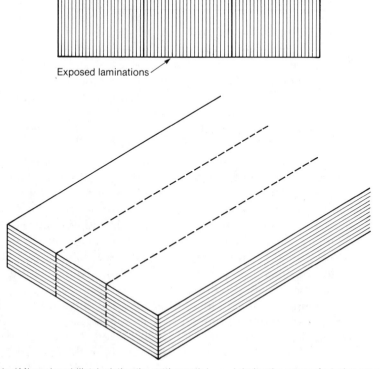

Exposed laminations

Original Micro=Lam billet depicting the cutting path (-------) during the remanufacturing process

the top veneer layers) had better results. This ad, sent to every major truck or trailer manufacturing journal as a news release on a new product, resulted in 30 to 50 inquiries which turned into 10 to 15 orders. Approximately 15 decks were sold as a result of the promotion.

Everyone at Trus Joist believed that the current price on Micro=Lam was the absolute rock bottom price possible. In fact, most people believed that Micro=Lam was underpriced. The current price of Micro=Lam included a gross margin of 20 percent. The price of 1¼″ thick and 1½″ thick Micro=Lam was based on the costs of a 1½″ billet. The total variable costs of 1½″ material were multiplied by ⅚ to estimate the same costs of 1¼″ material. There had recently been some discussion over the appropriateness of this ratio. Some of the marketing personnel believed that a more appropriate estimate of the variable costs for the 1¼″ Micro=Lam would be the ratio of the number of veneers in a 1¼″ billet to the number of veneers in a 1½″ billet, or ¹⁴⁄₁₆. At the present time, the costs of veneer represented 55 percent of the selling price. Glue cost was approximately 13 cents/square foot; fixed overhead represented 14 cents/square foot; and other variable costs amounted to approximately 12½ cents/square foot. The total variable costs were divided by 0.80 to cover all selling and administrative expenses and to secure a profit.[4]

In 1977, truck trailer manufacturers ordered and used 46 million square feet for installation in new truck trailer construction. This figure was understated because redecking or replacement of worn-out floors of trailers had not been incorporated, and there was little organized information to determine what this potential could be. As of 1975, 236 truck trailer manufacturers produced $646.7 million worth of trailers. (See Exhibits 4 and 5.)

Exhibit 4
Truck trailer shipments and dollar value (by calendar year)

	1975	1974	1973	1972	1971
Complete trailers and chassis	67,888	191,262	167,201	141,143	103,784
Value	$613,702,000	$1,198,520,000	$956,708,000	$795,500,000	$585,264,000
Containers	4,183*	10,108*	18,626	18,166	8,734
Value	$18,071,000	$27,343,000	$60,159,000	$51,527,000	$26,514,000
Container chassis	2,936	12,883	12,790	15,498	9,775
Value	$14,898,000	$42,076,000	$33,143,000	$39,028,000	$24,999,000
Total units	75,007	214,253	198,617	174,807	122,293
Value	$646,671,000	$1,267,939,000	$1,050,010,000	$886,055,000	$636,777,000

Author: Truck Trailer Manufacturers Association. Data for 1975 preliminary and subject to slight possible change.
* Containers not reported June–October 1974 and January–March 1975.
Source: *Ward's Automotive Yearbook, 1978*, p. 91.

---

[4] All cost figures have been disguised.

Exhibit 5
Truck trailer manufacturers

Allentown Brake & Wheel Service, Inc., Allentown, Pa.
Allied Products Corp., Chicago, Ill.
Aluminum Body Corp., Montebello, Calif.
American Body & Equipment Co., Grand Prairie, Tex.
American Trailers, Inc., Oklahoma City, Okla.
Anthony Co., Streator, Ill.
Atlantic International Corp., Baltimore, Md.
Atlantic International Marketing Corp., Baltimore, Md.
Atlantic Manufacturing Corp., Baltimore, Md.
Atlantic Mobile Corp., Cockeysville, Md.
Atlas Hoist & Body, Inc., Montreal, Que., Can.
Bartlett Trailer Corp., Chicago, Ill.
Bethlehem Fabricators, Inc., Bethlehem, Pa.
Adam Black & Sons, Inc., Jersey City, N.J.
Black Diamond Enterprises, Inc., Bristol, Va.
Herman Born & Sons, Inc., Baltimore, Md.
Budd Co., Troy, Mich.
Centennial Industries Division, Columbus, Ga.
Copco Trailer Division, South Bend, Ind.
Custom Trailers, Inc., Springfield, Mo.
Delta Truck Trailer Co., Inc., Camden, Ark.
Distribution International Corp., Ft. Washington, Pa.
Dorsey Corp., Chattanooga, Tenn.
Dorsey Trailers, Inc., Elba, Ala.
Dura Corp., Southfield, Mich.
Durobilt Mfg. Co., El Monte, Calif.
Eight Point Trailer Corp., Los Angeles, Calif.
Essick Mfg. Co., Los Angeles, Calif.
Evans Products, Portland, Ore.
Expediter Systems, Inc., Birmingham, Ala.
Firmers Lumber & Supply Co., Sioux City, Iowa
Ford Motor Co., Dearborn, Mich.
Ford Motor Co. of Canada Ltd., Oakville, Ont., Can.
Fruehauf Corp., Detroit, Mich.
Fruehauf Trailer Co. of Canada Ltd., Dixie, Ont., Can.
General Body Mfg. Co., Inc., Kansas City, Mo.
Gerstenslager Co., Wooster, Ohio
Great Dane Trailers, Inc., Savannah, Ga.
Hawker Siddeley Canada Ltd., Toronto, Ont., Can.
Hendrickson Mfg. Co., Lyons, Ill.
Hercules Mfg. Co., Henderson, Ky.
Hesse Corp., Kansas City, Mo.
Highway Trailers of Canada Ltd., Cooksville, Ont., Can.
Hobbs Trailers, Fort Worth, Tex.
Hyster Co., Portland, Ore.
Leland Equipment Co., Tulsa, Okla.
Lodestar Corp., Niles, Ohio

Exhibit 5 (*concluded*)

McCade-Powers Body Co., St. Louis, Mo.
McQuerry Trailer Co., Fort Worth, Tex.
Meyers Industries, Inc., Tecumseh, Mich.
Mindustrial Corp., Ltd., Toronto, Ont., Can.
Mitsubishi Electric Corp., Chiyoda-ku, Tokyo, 100, Japan
Moline Body Co., Moline, Ill.
Montone Mfg. Co., Hazelton, Pa.
Nabors Trailers, Inc., West Palm Beach, Fla.
Noble Division (Waterloo Plant), Waterloo, Iowa
OMC-Lincoln, Lincoln, Neb.
Ohio Body Mfg. Co., New London, Ohio
Olson Trailer & Body Builders Co., Green Bay, Wis.
Pike Trailer Co., Los Angeles, Calif.
Pointer Truck Trailer Co., Renton, Wash.
Polar Manufacturing Co., Holdingford, Minn.
Pullman, Inc., Chicago, Ill.
Pullman Trailmobile, Chicago, Ill.
Ravens-Metal Products, North Parkersburg, W.Va.
Reliance Trailer Manufacturing, Cotati, Calif.
Remke, Inc., Roseville, Mich.
Rogers Bros. Corp., Albion, Pa.
Shetky Equipment Corp., Portland, Ore.
Southwest Truck Body Company, St. Louis, Mo.
Starcraft Corp., Goshen, Ind.
Sterling Precision Corp., West Palm Beach, Fla.
Thiele, Inc., Windber, Pa.
Timpte, Inc., Denver, Colo.
Timpte Industries, Inc., Denver, Colo.
Trailco, Hummels Wharf, Pa.
Transport Trailers, Cedar Rapids, Iowa
Troyler Corp., Scranton, Pa.
Utility Tool & Body Co., Clintonville, Wis.
Valley Tow-Rite, Lodi, Calif.
Peter Wendel & Sons, Inc., Irvington, N.J.
Whitehead & Kales Co., River Rouge, Mich.
Williamsen Truck Equipment Corp., Salt Lake City, Utah

Source: *Poor's Register.*

The problem Mr. Kalish saw with this aggregate data was that it was not broken down into the various segments of trailer builders. For example, not all of the 236 manufacturers produced trailers which used wooden floors. Among those not using wooden floors were tankers and logging trailers. Mr. Kalish believed that the real key to selling Micro=Lam in this industry would be to determine the segment of the trailer industry on which he should concentrate his selling efforts. Mr. Kalish also knew that he somehow had to determine trailer manufacturers' requirements for trailer decking. The Eugene-Portland, Oregon, area offered what he thought to be a good cross section of the type of trailer manufacturers that might be interested in Micro=Lam. He had already contacted some of those firms about buying Micro=Lam.

GENERAL TRAILER COMPANY

Mr. Jim Walline had been the purchasing agent for General Trailer Company of Springfield, Oregon, for the past 2½ years. He stated, "The engineering department makes the decisions on what materials to buy. I place the orders after the requisition has been placed on my desk."

General Trailer Company was a manufacturer of several different types of trailers: low-boys, chip trailers, log trailers, and flatbeds. In 1977, General manufactured five flatbeds and redecked five flatbeds. General did most of its business with the local timber industry; however, it sold three flatbeds in 1977 to local firms in the steel industry.

The flatbeds General Trailer manufactured were 40' to 45' long and approximately 7' wide. Log trailers were approximately 20' to 25' long.

General Trailer manufactured trailers primarily for the West Coast market, although it had sold a few trailers to users in Alaska. On the West Coast, General's major competitors were Peerless, Fruehauf, and Trailmobile, all large-scale manufacturers of truck trailers. Even though General was comparatively small in size, it did not feel threatened, because "we build a top-quality trailer which is not mass-produced," as Mr. Walline put it.

General had been using apitong as a trailer decking material until customers complained of its weight and its expansion/contraction characteristics when exposed to weather. At that time, Mr. Schmidt, the general manager and head of the engineering department, made the decision to switch from apitong to laminated fir.

Laminated fir (consisting of solid sawn lumber strips glued together) was currently being used as the material for decking flatbeds, and Pacific Laminated Company of Vancouver, Washington, supplied all of General's fir decking, so General would only order material when a customer bought a new trailer or needed to have a trailer redecked. Mr. Walline was disappointed with the two- to three-week delivery time, since it often meant that much more time before the customer's trailer was ready.

Laminated fir in 40' lengths, 11¾" widths, and 1¼" thickness was used by General. General paid approximately $2 to $3 per square foot for this decking.

Even though Pacific Laminated could provide customer-cut and -edged pieces with no additional lead time, General preferred shiplapped fir in the previously noted dimensions, with the top two layers treated with a waterproof coating.

The different types of trailers General manufactured required different decking materials. Low-boys required material 2¼″ thick and General used 3″ × 12″ rough-cut fir lumber. Chip trailers required ⅝″ -thick MDO (medium density overlay) plywood with a slick surface.

Mr. Walline said General had used Micro=Lam on one trailer; however, the customer had not been expecting it and was very displeased with the job.[5] Therefore, the current policy was to use only laminated fir for the local market unless a customer specifically ordered a different decking material. Trailers headed for Alaska were decked with laminated oak, supplied by a vendor other than Pacific Laminated.

Mr. Walline said that if he wanted to make a recommendation to change decking materials, he would need to know price advantages, lead times, moisture content, availability, and industry experience with the material.

SHERMAN BROTHERS TRUCKING

"We already use Micro=Lam on our trailers," was the response of Mr. Sherman, president of Mayflower Moving and Storage Company, when asked about the trailer decking material his company used. He went on to say, "In fact, we had hauled several shipments for Trus Joist when we initiated a call to them asking if they could make a decking material for us."

Mayflower Moving and Storage owned 60 trailers (flatbeds) which it used to haul heavy equipment and machinery. It had been in a dilemma for eight years about the types of materials used to replace the original decks. Nothing seemed to be satisfactory. Solid apitong was tough, but it was too heavy and it did not weather very well. Plywood did not provide adequate weight distribution and had too many joints. Often the small wheels of the forklifts would break through the decking, or heavy equipment with steel legs would punch a hole through the decks. Laminated fir was too expensive.

Mayflower Moving and Storage was currently redecking a trailer per week. It usually patched the decks until the whole bed fell apart; then the trailer would sit in the yard waiting for a major overhaul. By this time the trailers needed to have the crossbeams repaired and new bearings as well as a new deck.

---

[5] After purchasing Micro=Lam, General Trailer modified the material by ripping the billets into 1½″ widths and then relaminating these strips back into 12″- or 24″-wide pieces of lumber. This remanufacturing added substantial costs. Also, the laminations were now directly exposed to the weather. Moisture could more easily seep into cracks or voids, causing swells and buckling. (See Exhibit 3.)

Mr. Sherman went on to say, "The shop mechanic just loves Micro-=Lam. This is because it used to take the mechanic and one other employee two days to redeck a trailer, and now it just takes the shop mechanic one day to do the same job." Advantages (over plywood and apitong) of the 2' × 40' Micro=Lam pieces were ease of installation, excellent weight distribution due to the reduced number of seams, and reduced total weight of the bed.

Mr. Sherman explained that Mayflower Moving and Storage usually purchased four or five decks at a time, and warehoused some of the materials until a trailer needed redecking.

Mr. Sherman thought the original decking on flatbeds was some type of hardwood, probably oak, which could last up to five years; however, a similar decking material had not been found for a reasonable price. The plywood and fir decks used in the past 8 to 10 years had lasted anywhere from 1 to 2 years, and some had worn out in as little as six months. After using Micro=Lam for six months, Mr. Sherman expected the decking to last up to three to five years.

When asked about the type of flooring used in the company's moving vans, Mr. Sherman emphasized the top care that those floors received. "We sand, buff, and wax them just like a household floor; in fact, we take such good care of these floors they will occasionally outlast the trailer." The original floors in moving vans were made out of a laminated oak and had to be kept extremely smooth, allowing freight to slide freely without the possibility of damaging items of freight with legs. The local company purchased all of its moving vans through Mayflower Moving Vans. The only problem with floors in moving vans was that the jointed floors would occasionally buckle because of swelling.

The fact that Micro=Lam protruded ⅛" above the metal lip[6] which edged the flatbed trailers posed no problem for Sherman Brothers. "All we had to do was plane the edge at 40 degrees. In fact, the best fit will have the decking protrude a hair above the metal edge," Mr. Sherman said. Just prior to this, Mr. Sherman had recounted an experience which occurred with the first shipment of Micro=Lam. Because the deck was too thick, Mayflower Moving and Storage had about ⅛" planed from one side of the decking material. However, the company shaved off the apitong veneer, exposing the fir. Mr. Sherman said that he laughed about it now, but at the time he wasn't too pleased.

PEERLESS TRUCKING COMPANY

"Sure, I've heard of Micro=Lam. They [Trus Joist salesmen] have been in here, . . . but we don't need that good a material." This was

---

[6] Refer to Exhibit 6.

Exhibit 6
Cross-sectional end view of trailer decking (tongue and groove)

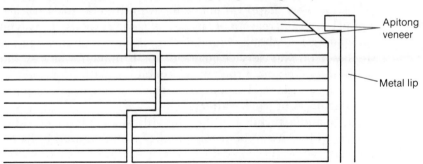

Apitong
veneer

Metal lip

the response of Mel Rogers, head of Peerless' Purchasing Department, Tualatin, Oregon, when asked about the use of Micro=Lam as a truck decking material. Mr. Rogers, a 30-year veteran of the trailer manufacturing industry, seemed very skeptical of all laminated decking materials.

The primary products manufactured by Peerless (in Tualatin) required bedding materials very different from Micro=Lam. Chip trailers and rail car dumpers required metal beds to facilitate unloading. Low-boys required a heavy decking material (usually 2″ × 12″ or 3″ × 12″ rough planking) as Caterpillar tractors were frequently driven on them. Logging trailers had no beds.

Approximately 60 decks per year were required by Peerless in the manufacture of flatbeds and in redecking jobs. Micro=Lam could have been used in these applications, but fir planking was used exclusively, except for some special overseas jobs. Fir planking was available in full trailer lengths, requiring eight man-hours to install on new equipment. Usually, five or six decks were stocked at a time. The estimated life of a new deck was two to three years.

Fir planking was selected for decking applications on the basis of price and durability. Peerless purchased fir planking for $1,000 per MBF. Tradition supported fir planking in durability, as it was a well-known product.

Decking material thickness was critical, according to Mr. Rogers, as any deviation from the industry standard of 1⅜″ required extensive retooling.

Any new decking materials for use in original equipment manufacture had to be approved by the Peerless engineering department. Alternative decking materials could have been used locally if specified by the customer.

Mr. Rogers was certainly going to be a hard person to sell on the use of Micro=Lam, Mr. Kalish felt. "Why use Micro=Lam when I can buy fir planking for less?" Rogers had said.

FRUEHAUF TRUCKING COMPANY

"I'd be very happy if someone would come up with a durable [trailer] deck at a reasonable price," was the response of Wayne Peterson when asked about Fruehauf's experience with decking materials. Mr. Peterson was service manager for Fruehauf's factory branch in Milwaukie, Oregon. Fruehauf Corporation, with its principal manufacturing facilities in Detroit, Michigan, was one of the nation's largest manufacturers of truck trailers.

The manufacturing facilities in Milwaukie produced 40-ton low-beds as well as assembled truck bodies manufactured in Detroit. The low-beds were subjected to heavy use, often with forklifts, which required a decking material of extreme strength and durability. Laminated decking materials then available were therefore excluded from this application.

The decking materials used in the truck bodies were specified by the sales department in Detroit, based on customer input. Generally, apitong or laminated oak was installed at the factory. Any new product to be used in original equipment manufacture had to be approved by Fruehauf's well-developed factory engineering department.

The Milwaukie operation also did about 15 redecking jobs per year. The decking material was specified by the customer on the basis of price and weathering characteristics. The materials used were laminated oak (11½″ W × 40′), apitong (7″ × ⅟₃₈″—random lengths), Alaska yellow cedar (2″ × 6″ T&G), fir planking (2″ × 6″ T&G), and laminated fir (24″ W × 40′). Alaska yellow cedar was priced below all other decking materials, followed (in order) by fir planking, laminated fir, laminated oak, and apitong.

Fruehauf's suppliers of decking materials were as follows: laminated fir—Pacific Laminating, Vancouver, Washington; Alaska yellow cedar—Al Disdero Lumber Company, Portland, Oregon; and apitong—Builterials, Portland, Oregon. There were no specific suppliers for the other materials.

A minimum inventory of decking materials was kept on hand to allow for immediate repair needs only. Orders were placed for complete decks as needed.

A redecking job typically required 30 man-hours per 7′ × 40′ trailer, including the removal of the old deck and installation of the new one. Decking materials that were available in full trailer lengths were preferred, as they greatly reduced installation time, improved weight distribution, and had fewer joints along which failure could occur.

The use of alternative products, such as composition flooring of wood and aluminum, was not under consideration.

Alaska yellow cedar and fir planking had the best weathering characteristics, while apitong and laminated oak weathered poorly. Oak and apitong did, however, have a hard, nonscratching surface that was desirable in enclosed use. When asked about the weathering characteristics of laminated flooring in general, Mr. Peterson responded, "It's all right for the dry states, but not around here."

COMPETITION

There were a large number of materials with which Micro=Lam competed in the trailer flooring market, ranging from fir plywood to aluminum floors. Trus Joist felt that the greatest obstacles to Micro=Lam's success would be from the old standard products like laminated fir and oak, which had a great deal of industry respect. For years, oak had been the premier flooring material; recently, however, supplies had been short and delivery times long (two months in some cases), and prices were becoming prohibitive. (See Exhibit 7.)

Exhibit 7
Decking material prices, November 1978

Product	Price	Form
Alaska yellow cedar	$650/MBF	2″ × 6″ T&B 15′ lengths
Apitong	$1.30–$2/lineal foot*	1⅜″ × 7″ random lengths
Fir planking	$1/bd. ft.	2″ × 6″ T&G random lengths
Fir, laminated	$2.50/sq. ft.	1¼″ × 11¾″ × 40′
Micro=Lam	$1.30/sq. ft.	1¼″ × 24″ × 40′
	$1.50/sq. ft.	1½″ × 24″ × 40′
Oak, laminated	$2.20/sq. ft.	1⅜″ × 1½′ × 40′

* Lineal foot = price per unit length of the product.
Sources: Al Disdero Lumber Company, Portland, Oregon; Builterials, Portland, Oregon

Mr. Kalish had found that in the Northwest Pacific Laminated Company was one of the major flooring suppliers to local manufacturers. Pacific Laminated produced a Douglas fir laminated product that was highly popular; however, like oak, it was relatively high-priced. Despite the price, Pacific Laminated could cut the product to dimensions up to 2′ wide and 40′ long. Delivery time was excellent for its customers, even with special milling for shiplapped or tongue and groove edges and manufacturing to user thickness.

CONCLUSION

Although Mr. Kalish had had limited success marketing Micro=Lam to truck trailer manufacturers, he was concerned with the marketing program for his product. Several trailer manufacturers had raised important questions concerning the price and durability of Micro=Lam compared to alternative decking materials. He knew Micro=Lam had some strong attributes, yet he was hesitant to expand beyond the local market. Mr. Kalish was also wondering about the action he should eventually take in order to determine the additional information he would need to successfully introduce Micro=Lam nationally as a trailer decking material. One thought that crossed his mind was to define the company's marketing strategy for this product. Meanwhile, small orders continued to trickle in.

Case 4–2

Wyler Unsweetened Soft Drink Mixes

As Mr. Kenneth Otte sat in his office in Northbrook, Illinois, in early August 1977, he felt a bit like Jack, in the children's story "Jack and the Beanstalk." He was facing a major challenge against a dominant foe, General Foods' Kool-Aid powdered soft drink mix, the giant of the unsweetened drink mix category.

The question Mr. Otte was considering was whether or not to recommend a major national introduction of Wyler's Unsweetened Soft Drink Mix against Kool-Aid in 1978. He knew RJR Foods' Hawaiian Punch was considering such a move, and because of Kool-Aid's dominant position in the market, a 92 percent share and virtually unchallenged in its 50-year existence, he questioned whether there was room for more than one additional brand in the market. If he waited another year, it might be too late. If, however, Wyler's introduced an additional brand in 1978 and Hawaiian Punch did, too, perhaps neither brand would achieve its goals.

The question was more complex than just whether or not to introduce. Wyler's Unsweetened Soft Drink Mix had just completed the second year of testing under Mr. Otte's direction with somewhat mixed results. There was certainly time to make changes and adjustments in the program, but the question was, What changes should he investigate or recommend prior to a January meeting with the Wyler sales and broker force?

Management had requested a review of the situation and Mr. Otte's recommendations by October 1, 1977. Since a national introduction in 1978 would require substantial investment spending, Mr. Otte had several questions facing him. Should he recommend a national program for 1978? If not, what recommendation should he make? More

This case was prepared by Assistant Professor Don E. Schultz and Mr. Mark Traxler of Northwestern University.

test markets? A fine-tuning of his present program? Major changes? What?

If he did recommend a national program, what, if any, changes should be made in the recently completed test program? He wondered about such questions as advertising, promotion, and distribution. He still had time to investigate and test new ideas, but exactly what did the results of the test markets mean?

As Mr. Otte prepared to develop his recommendation, he reviewed the entire situation of the category, the product, competition, and test market results. Did he have enough ammunition to challenge the Kool-Aid giant?

COMPANY HISTORY

Wyler Foods is a Chicago-based company manufacturing several products. Its line includes instant soups, bouillon powders and cubes, and powdered soft drink mixes.

The original company was organized in the late 1920s, and in 1930 it introduced Cold Kup soft drink mix, a presweetened mix in a pouch. Cold Kup was available in four flavors. About the same time, Peskin Company introduced Kool-Aid, an unsweetened soft drink mix. Peskin was later acquired by General Foods, and Wyler was purchased by Borden. Wyler continued to concentrate on the presweetened soft drink mix market. In 1954, it introduced a powdered lemonade mix very successfully. By 1977, lemonade flavor accounted for approximately 40 percent of all Wyler soft drink mix sales.

Wyler and Kool-Aid continue to do battle in the soft drink mix market, with Wyler dominant in the presweetened market and Kool-Aid in the unsweetened market. In the early 1960s, Kool-Aid entered the presweetened market with an artificially sweetened product using cyclamates. This sweetener was banned by the federal government in 1969, and Wyler, with its sugar sweetening, rapidly gained ground in the mix market. As a result of the ban, Wyler moved up to a 20 percent share of the presweetened market. In 1972, Wyler introduced an industry "first" by packaging presweetened soft drink mixes in canisters of 10 to 15 quarts. With this innovation, Wyler's share of the presweetened market increased to over 40 percent. Its share has declined slightly from this level as increased competitive pressures have segmented the market. Wyler did not have an unsweetened entry until it initiated a test in 1976.

SOFT DRINK MARKET

The liquid refreshment market, comprising hot, cold, and alcoholic beverages, is limited in growth by the "Share of Belly" concept, which suggests that human beings can consume just so much liquid in a given year. All entries in the soft drink mix market are competing with all other potable refreshments for some space in an unexpandable belly. Under the Share of Belly concept, the level of per capita liquid consumption is tied to the U.S. population growth rate and/or changing consumer preferences.

In 1977, soft drink mix quart sales increased 9 percent over the previous year. During that same period, single-strength drinks remained unchanged, while carbonated beverage sales increased 7 percent. Mr. Otte predicts that soft drink mix tonnage will increase by 5 percent in 1978. Carbonated soft drinks will continue to grow, but less dramatically; canned fruit drinks will decline by 10–15 percent; and iced tea mixes will grow between 5 and 7 percent.

POWDERED SOFT DRINK MIXES

The soft drink mix business, the 12th largest dry grocery product category, accounts for about 10 percent of all soft drink sales. It has increased in both quart and dollar sales each year since 1970. This growth is due to a greater demand for more product convenience, a wider assortment of flavors, and a more economical cold beverage alternative to carbonated drinks and single-strength canned drinks. In 1977, the segment is expected to produce sales of $503 million and 4,195 million quarts. Mr. Otte predicts that with a 5 percent growth in 1978, soft drink mixes will generate sales of $565 million and 4,405 million quarts.

The division of the powdered drink mix market is somewhat confusing. In terms of quart-equivalent tonnage, the market is divided 52.4 percent presweetened and 47.6 percent unsweetened. In terms of dollar sales, the split is 74.6 percent presweetened and 25.4 percent unsweetened. The major difference is the cost per quart of the sweetened product versus the unsweetened. More families purchase presweetened soft drink mixes than unsweetened; however, the buyer of unsweetened mixes appears to be a much heavier consumer (or purchaser at least). The presweetened buyer purchases the product an average of every 56.5 days compared to the more frequent purchase pattern of the unsweetened buyer, who purchases every 46.7 days. Consumer panel data show that both unsweetened and presweetened purchasers pick up an average of six pouches on each shopping occasion.

In comparison with other beverage categories, soft drink mixes are inexpensive, with unsweetened mixes the least expensive of all. Mixes cost less than half as much as carbonated beverages and single-strength canned drinks. Unsweetened mixes are least expensive due to the economy of adding one's own sugar. The following table of costs per 4-ounce serving emphasizes this point.

Beverage	Price
Unsweetened powdered mix	3.0¢
Presweetened powdered mix	4.7
Iced-tea mix	5.0
Frozen orange juice	10.2
Single-strength drinks	10.4
Carbonated soft drinks	11.7
Chilled orange juice	11.7

Source: A. C. Nielsen Food Index, May 1977.

The buyer profile for powdered soft drink mix users shows that soft drink mixes are purchased by about two thirds of all U.S. households. The primary purchaser is the female homemaker between the ages of 18 and 44, with the heaviest concentration in the 25–34 age range. She is unemployed and has a high school education. Her husband is a blue-collar worker, clerk, or salesman with an annual household income between $10,000 and $20,000. The family has three or more individuals in it, including children under age 18. All users and heavy users who consume at least five glasses per day are concentrated in the North Central and South regions, as evidenced by the table for 1977 from Target Group Index (TGI) shown on p. 332.

Soft drink mix sales are highly seasonal. Sales peak during the summer months and drop off almost entirely during the winter months. Many grocers, particularly in the northern climates, do not stock powdered soft drink mixes during the winter months after the summer inventory is sold. An attempt to overcome this extreme seasonality was initiated in 1976 by Wyler's. Its "second season" promotion strategy, which promotes to both the consumer and the trade, was designed to encourage year-round product use.

UNSWEETENED POWDERED SOFT DRINK MIXES

The basic ingredients of a powdered soft drink mix are citric acid, artificial flavors, ascorbic acid (vitamin C), artificial color, and, depending on whether the mix is sweetened or unsweetened, some sugar. Kool-Aid and Wyler's are packaged in 2-quart foil pouches. Hawaiian Punch is expected to follow that precedent. The directions for mixing a single package are as follows: Empty contents into a large plastic or glass pitcher. Add one cup of sugar and the quantity of ice water needed to make 2 quarts. Stir.

A comparison of the available and most popular flavors shows that the "red" flavors and grape are by far the fastest selling. The following table lists the available flavors for Wyler's and, in the case of Kool-Aid, the 6 out of 16 flavors that constitute 73 percent of its unsweetened

	All users				Heavy users			
	A (000)	B percent down	C percent across	D index	A (000)	B percent down	C percent across	D index
North East	5,976	18.8	40.5	81	2,206	21.7	15.0	94
North Central	10,484	33.0	59.5	119	3,220	31.7	18.3	114
South	10,128	31.9	49.4	99	3,353	33.0	16.3	102
West	5,209	16.4	48.0	96	1,393	13.7	12.8	80

volume. The flavors listed for Hawaiian Punch are those that it has offered in its presweetened line.

Kool-Aid	Wyler's	Hawaiian Punch
Strawberry	Strawberry	Strawberry
Cherry	Cherry	Cherry
Fruit punch	Fruit punch	Red punch
Grape	Grape	Grape
Orange	Orange	Orange
Lemonade	Lemonade	Lemonade
		Raspberry

The unsweetened market is divided up as follows:

	Share
Kool-Aid	92%
Private label	4 (A&P's Cheri-Aid and Kroger's Flavor-Aid)
Others	4 (Wyler's in test market)

The unit cost for the major competitors is 9.4 cents per pouch. The wholesale case cost for Wyler's and Kool-Aid is $26.95. Although the out-of-store price per pouch ranges from 10 to 13 cents, the suggested retail is 12 cents. This reflects a 21.7 percent profit margin. The following table shows the profit margin for the common out-of-store prices.

Price	Profit margin
10¢	6.0%
11	14.5
12	21.7
13	27.7

In the grocery aisle, the unsweetened category is normally placed next to the presweetened powdered soft drink mix section. The product is displayed on trays containing 72 pouches with three shelf facings. Wyler's and Kool-Aid cases contain four 72-pouch trays. Hawaiian Punch has announced that it will offer trays containing 36 pouches with two shelf facings, two trays per case.

Wyler's has instructed its food broker salespeople to position Wyler's unsweetened next to the same Kool-Aid flavor, to stack no more than two trays high, and to avoid stacking one flavor on top of another. Floor display racks are offered by both Wyler's and Kool-Aid to increase brand awareness and stimulate trial. The Wyler's rack holds 15 cases and provides secondary distribution. Store managers are reluctant to use racks because they clutter the aisles.

| | All users | | | Heavy users | | | | |
	A (000)	B percent down	C percent across	D index	A (000)	B percent down	C percent across	D index
North East	4,109	17.0	27.8	73	2,441	23.2	16.5	100
North Central	7,660	31.6	43.4	114	4,298	40.9	24.4	148
South	8,372	34.6	40.8	107	2,490	23.7	12.1	74
West	4,073	16.8	37.5	99	1,288	12.2	11.9	72

INTRODUCING WYLER'S UNSWEETENED

In 1977, Wyler's Unsweetened was introduced into 33 broker areas representing 28 percent of the U.S. population and 40 percent of total sales in the unsweetened category. Only 25 of the 33 areas had achieved adequate distribution by mid-1977. The 25 successful areas comprised 17.2 percent of the U.S. population and 33.7 percent of total volume in the unsweetened category. The unsweetened case volume achieved 6 percent share during the peak months of June and July 1977 and declined to its present share of 5 percent in October. Projected for the whole nation, the product's share in the peak was 3.2 percent and its share on a continuing basis was 2.5 percent.

According to the 1977 TGI, the strongest concentration of Kool-Aid, both presweetened and unsweetened, was in the South and North Central regions. Wyler's strength, primarily based on presweetened sales, was centered in the North Central region. Possible reasons for this skew are that powdered soft drink mixes started and have remained popular in the North Central region and that Kool-Aid has many more users in each region than Wyler's, with only 33 measured broker areas. The table from TGI on p. 334 shows the regional concentration.

The target market selected for Wyler's introduction differed slightly from the one selected by Kool-Aid. The notable differences were the household head's occupation and the market size. The following table summarizes the target demographics.

	Wyler's	Kool-Aid
Income	$15,000–19,999	$15,000–19,999
Household size	3 or more	3 or more
Age of female head	Under 45	Under 45
Age of children	12 & under	Any under 18
Occupation of household head	White collar	Blue collar
Market size	500,000–2,500,000	Non-SMSA

The prime users were children 2–12, who were thought to have little influence on the purchase decision. The female homemaker bought the products she thought best for her family. Hence, most Wyler advertising was directed at mothers.

Wyler entered the market with two main copy themes in advertising: "Double Economy" stressed Wyler's as an unsweetened drink for the entire family which was economical because you added your own sugar and the entire family enjoyed it; Wyler's claimed that its unique flavor boosters (salt and other flavor enhancers) made Wyler's taste better. Both executions emphasized the red flavors and vitamin C content and soft-pedaled lemonade. Although the two campaigns were used in the test, they were both considered interim efforts.

Based on the test, a different claim set placing even more emphasis on flavors was being considered. This involved using Roy Clark, the television personality, as spokesperson, and having him stress the good taste of Wyler's. Spot television was the major medium used in the market tests, but it was backed by print media used as coupon carriers.

Kool-Aid's advertising came in three varieties with separate messages for general brand awareness, economy of use, and children appeal. The general brand awareness execution was a nostalgia appeal to mothers which said, "You loved it as a kid. You trust it as a mother." The economy of use execution showed children's preferences for Kool-Aid's flavor over single-strength beverages and the economy of adding one's own sugar. The execution with child appeal showed the Kool-Aid "Smiling Pitcher" saving the day by foiling some dastardly deed. Most advertising was placed in television—70 percent network and 30 percent spot evenly divided between day and night.

It is anticipated that Hawaiian Punch will use its character "Punchy" to introduce the new unsweetened powdered mix since he has been used extensively before.

For the 1977 test, Wyler had divided the media budget into a peak and second season push. A total of $1,010,000 was to be invested in spot television in the 33 broker areas which made up the test. From mid-April to mid-August, Wyler had purchased spot TV in prime, day, and early fringe time. For the second season, the schedule was to be composed of day and early and late fringe time from September until Christmas and from late January into late March. Already Mr. Otte had received a suggestion from the agency and his assistant that if the test were continued in 1978, media weight tests should probably be undertaken, since a level spending pattern had been used in the 1977 test markets.

Compared to Wyler's test program, Kool-Aid was spending approximately $18 million in measured media in 1977. It was spending $6 million against presweetened, $6 million against unsweetened, and $6 million against the Kool-Aid brand. Two thirds of the network budget was being used on weekdays and was directed toward women. The remainder was being spent on Saturday/Sunday rotation directed at kids. Spot TV funds were being allocated almost evenly between day (36 percent), night/late night (34 percent), and early fringe (30 percent). During the peak season, Kool-Aid planned to spend $13,405,000, divided into $6.58 million in the second quarter and $6.825 million in the third quarter. The second season expenditure was $4.59 million, divided into $2.57 million in the first quarter and $2.025 million in the fourth quarter. Kool-Aid was expected to spend about $20 million in 1978 for consumer advertising.

Mr. Otte anticipates that if Hawaiian Punch introduces, it would spend $4.7 million in a 1978 introduction. Two thirds would probably be used in network (33.5 percent each for day and prime) and 33 percent for spot. Advance information indicated that this budget would break down to $3.2 million for network ($1.6 million in prime and day time and $1.5 million for spot).

In addition to the heavy consumer advertising, Wyler's planned to invest $827,670 in consumer promotions during the tests to generate trial and awareness. These included samples and various coupon drops. Coupons and samples were being delivered by several print media, such as Sunday supplements and best food day newspaper sections. It was still too early to determine the results of these promotions for this year.

Trade promotions in 1977 were budgeted at $292,330. All were in case allowances to encourage retailers to stock Wyler's unsweetened. No matter how much money Wyler's spent on consumer advertising and promotion, it appeared from tests that the trade would not stock another powdered soft drink mix without sizable case allowances to sweeten the deal since most of the powdered drink mix inventory traditionally had been sold to retailers on trade deals. Whether Wyler's unsweetened entered additional tests or went national in 1978, Mr. Otte felt that to ensure successful distribution a case allowance of $3.60 between the end of February and the end of April would be needed. This case allowance would be the highest ever offered in the unsweetened drink mix category.

Mr. Otte had conducted research testing consumer reactions to both the product and the advertising. The product quality of Kool-Aid and Wyler's unsweetened was essentially the same. However, in-depth taste tests revealed that Kool-Aid's grape and strawberry flavors rated higher than Wyler's. This was a matter of substantial concern since these two flavors were the two most popular in the unsweetened category.

Wyler's "Double Economy" commercial was evaluated by Burke in 1977 and by McCollum/Spielman in July–August 1976. By Burke norms, Wyler's did very well. For the target market of women 25–34, 35 percent recalled the commercial in "day after" testing. The norm was 27 percent. The McCollum/Spielman indicated strong awareness of the brand name but low specific recall of Wyler's unsweetened.

The situation, as Mr. Otte saw it, was that heavy advertising and consumer promotion were necessary to combat the consumer's neutral attitude toward unsweetened powdered soft drink mixes. Awareness of unsweetened brands was much lower than that of presweetened mixes. However, Kool-Aid had extremely high brand awareness. Mr. Otte felt that the Wyler's name was associated with powdered soft drink mixes in the consumer's mind, though there was no consumer research to back this up. Also, heavy trade promotion was necessary to get the product on the shelves.

If he decided on another test plan in 1978, Mr. Otte estimated that he would need a minimum investment of $4 million for Wyler's unsweetened. The plan would involve $2.2 million in media advertising and $1.8 million in consumer promotions. If he decided to introduce nationally, he of course would need a substantially larger budget than that. Just what he should plan was one of the unknowns that would have to be determined once a decision was made.

What to do? Should he risk another test and perhaps lose the opportunity to go national to Hawaiian Punch, or should he develop a plan to invade Kool-Aid's territory in 1978 on a national basis? The risks and the rewards were great either way.

Case 4–3

Aurora Lotion

John Fairchild frowned as he hung up the telephone. He had just finished another conversation with Urs Brunner, the general manager of Produits Pour Femmes, SA (PPF), on a subject that had become increasingly troublesome over the last three years: how to respond to the problem of parallel importing of Aurora Lotion into Switzerland. Fairchild was the general manager of the Overseas Division of Smythe-Dabney International, Ltd., a British company which marketed Aurora and other women's cosmetics. A large portion of his job was devoted to offering information and recommendations to the managers of the subsidiary companies which made up the division.

The management of PPF, the Swiss subsidiary, had reported a growing rash of price cutting on Aurora Lotion, one of its most important products, by a group of independent distributors who were buying Aurora in England and bringing it to Switzerland themselves. This practice, which had been dubbed "parallel importing" or "black importing" in the trade, had put PPF's gross margins under pressure and squeezed the company's return on sales. The situation had reached the point that Urs Brunner had asked John Fairchild to intervene and recommend a strategy to counter the threat, including a substantial reduction of PPF's selling price for Aurora, if necessary.

SMYTHE-DABNEY INTERNATIONAL, LTD.

The parent company for PPF was Smythe-Dabney International, Ltd. (SDI), with headquarters outside London. In 1977, SDI's sales were £25.8 million and its trading profits were £2.6 million. In the last

This case was prepared by Thomas Kosnik, research associate, under the direction of Professor Christopher Gale. Copyright © 1978 by l'Institut pour l'Étude des Méthodes de Direction de l'Entreprise (IMEDE), Lausanne, Switzerland. Reproduced by permission.

10 years, earnings per share had increased at the compound rate of 20 percent a year. Sir Anthony Carburton, the chairman of SDI, felt that the impressive record was the result of several factors, including the quality of the company's products, the energies and talents of a close-knit management team, and the ability to stay a step ahead of competitors in the marketplace.

From the earliest days with the introduction of Aurora Lotion, SDI had marketed only products of high quality and had stressed that theme in advertising and promotion campaigns. As a result, the various SDI cosmetics, under the Aurora name and in several other well-known brand families, enjoyed widespread brand recognition and consumer loyalty.

A keen sensitivity to the needs of both the channels of distribution and consumers caused the company's directors to search continually for ways to make their products and services more competitive. They had defined the market they served as the women's beauty care market, and had acquired a wide line of products that complemented each other and ensured efficient utilization of the sales force and marketing staff. They quickly learned that the ability to supply the trade was critical and earned a reputation for having the company's products in stock in a timely fashion, providing a valuable service for their distributors. They used extensive television advertising to stimulate demand, and point of purchase displays in retail outlets to make it easier for consumers to select the products they needed.

The objectives of the company for the next three years were to increase sales and EPS 20 percent a year and to maintain a pretax income/sales ratio of 10 percent. The basic guidelines the corporate management had drafted to reach those objectives were to:

1. Increase unit volume of sales in all product lines.
2. Maintain historic direct (gross) margins.
3. Keep corporate overhead expenses low by maintaining a lean home office staff.
4. Give management of subsidiary companies decision-making authority on all tactical matters, with consultation with corporate management on strategic issues.

THE OVERSEAS DIVISION

SDI was composed of the UK Division and the Overseas Division. In 1977, the Overseas Division sold £10.8 million worth of women's beauty products in continental Europe, North America, and the Far East. In Europe, SDI had company-owned subsidiaries in France, Germany, and Switzerland and marketed its products in other countries through independent wholesale distributors.

Both Fairchild and Carburton shared the view that the most promising markets for future growth were in Europe and North America. In 1977, much of the 20 percent growth in sales and profits projected for the company as a whole was expected to come from the Overseas Division.

PRODUITS POUR FEMMES, SA

PPF was responsible for the marketing of Aurora and other SDI products in Switzerland. Its reporting relationship in the Overseas Division is shown in Exhibit 1. The organization was small, with 14

Exhibit 1
Smythe-Dabney International Ltd.—Overseas Division organization chart

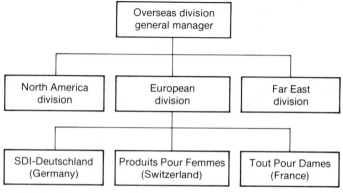

Source: SDI company records.

people in all, comprising a sales force, marketing department, accounting department, and warehouse crew.

Sales of the company in 1977 were SFr. 4.3 million, up 22 percent from the year before. Exhibit 2 shows PPF's income statement for 1976 and 1977.

Urs Brunner had recently taken over as general manager. He and his marketing manager were the key decision makers in day-to-day activities; John Fairchild and Dustin Cushman, the general manager for Europe, involved themselves with PPF only on matters of strategic importance.

THE PRODUCT

Aurora Lotion was a high-quality, all-purpose lotion for women. It was applied by being spread lightly over the skin of the face, arms, legs, and other parts of the body and then rubbing gently until the lotion was completely absorbed into the skin. The company stressed in its advertising that Aurora relieved dryness due to sun, wind, water,

Exhibit 2

PRODUITS POUR FEMMES, SA DIVISION
Income Statement
1976 and 1977
(000 Swiss francs)

	1976	*1977*
Sales	3,525	4,300
Less: Cost of goods sold	1,160	1,720
Direct margin	2,365	2,580
Less:		
Advertising	405	430
Distribution	240	330
Promotion*	175	230
Other expenses†	55	70
Brand contribution	1,490	1,520
Less:		
Sales force expenses	410	430
General and administration	670	610
Trading profit (before tax)	410	480

  * Does not include trade discounts on Aurora Lotion.
  † Other expenses included marketing research, product research, public relations, depreciation, and inventory losses through obsolescence, damage, etc.
  Source: SDI company records (disguised).

or detergents and made skin feel soft, clean, and gentle to the touch. It also stated that the effects of the lotion were longer lasting than those of many similar products. A single application of Aurora before bedtime each evening kept the skin "soft and beautiful," while it was necessary to apply other lotions as often as three or four times a day to get the same protection. The secret of Aurora's long-lasting effectiveness was a unique formula which allowed the lotion to penetrate the skin more completely than competing brands.

Aurora Lotion was the brand leader in a growing line of beauty products which included hand lotion, moisturizers, and bath preparations. Exhibit 3 contains the Aurora product line's brand contribution statement to PPF. The company also marketed the full line of SDI products under other brands, including facial cosmetics, eye cosmetics, hair preparations, nail polish, and deodorants. In 1977, Aurora Lotion sales accounted for 20 percent of the total sales of PPF.

Over the years, Aurora Lotion had become increasingly familiar to women in many European countries. In fact, parallel importers capitalized on this brand recognition and easily sold Aurora Lotion in Switzerland that had been shipped directly from Britain, even though the directions for use of the lotion were in English. Fairchild and Brunner estimated that 120,000 bottles of Aurora were parallel-imported into Switzerland in 1977, compared with PPF sales of 200,000 bottles in the same period.

Exhibit 3

AURORA PRODUCT GROUP PPF
Brand Contribution Statement
1976 and 1977
(000 Swiss francs)

	1976	*1977*
Sales.	850	1,140
Less: Cost of goods sold	290	526
Direct margin	560	614
Less:		
Advertising	94	106
Distribution expenses	50	55
Promotion*	74	150
Other expenses†	15	12
Brand contribution	327	291

    * Does not include trade discounts on Aurora Lotion.
    † Other expenses included marketing research, product research, public relations, depreciation, and inventory losses.
    Source: SDI company records (disguised).

COMPETITIVE PRODUCTS

All-purpose lotions for women were available in great variety and a wide range of price and quality. However, they tended to cluster in three main groups.

1. *High-priced products.* These lotions were most often produced by companies making fashionable women's perfumes. They had the same scents as popular women's fragrances, so the consumer could use the lotion along with her favorite cologne or perfume. These lotions were sold for SFr. 20 to SFr. 50 in retail outlets, for bottles of 100 to 200 centiliters (cl). Some packages were annotated in grams rather than centiliters.

2. *Medium-price lotions.* Many of these lotions were imported to Switzerland from France and England. They were attractively packaged, and often made claims to characteristics that differentiated them from other lotions. Some were made by perfume houses to match less expensive fragrances. They sold for between SFr. 7.50 and SFr. 15, and the most common bottle size was 200 cl.

3. *Low-price lotions.* These products were the simple, functional answer to the everyday problems of dry, rough skin due to water, weather, and housework. Prices ranged from SFr. 3 to SFr. 6 for a plastic container of 240 cl to 450 cl.

Exhibit 4 provides examples of all-purpose lotions in the three price ranges. Aurora Lotion, with a suggested retail price of SFr. 15 for 200 cl, was positioned near the top of the middle range of lotions.

Consumers cited several problems that sometimes arose when us-

Exhibit 4
Sample of all-purpose lotions available in Switzerland

Product	Size of selling unit	Retail selling price per selling unit
High price		
Caron	120 cl	SFr. 28.00
Chanel	80 g	24.50
Je Reviens	100 cl	22.50
Amnioderm	200 cl	30.00
Medium price		
Aurora Lotion	200 cl	SFr. 15.00
Bea Kasser	150 cl	14.50
Janine D	200 cl	13.50
4711	200 cl	9.50
Ma Garde	125 cl	7.50
Oil of Olay	200 cl	7.50
Fenjal	250 cl	7.50
Winston's	300 cl	8.40
Low price		
Rose Milk	240 cl	SFr. 5.90
Nivea	250 cl	4.95
Kaloderma	300 cl	4.50
Jana Lait de Toilette (Migros)	430 cl	3.50

Source: Field research at retail outlets, Lausanne, Switzerland.

ing an all-purpose lotion. These related to the fragrance of the lotion and its ability to penetrate the skin. Some products had a heavy, sweet, or powerful scent that could potentially clash with or mask the fragrance of perfume. Some lotions left the skin felling slippery, greasy, or wet after application, while others were not absorbed into the skin and washed off immediately upon contact with water. In the former case, the lotion might stain clothing or furniture. In the latter case, it was necessary to apply the lotion several times a day, after bathing, doing dishes, or returning from out-of-doors. The popularity of Aurora Lotion was due in large part to the fact that it had a light, clean scent that did not clash with perfumes and also that it penetrated deeply, without leaving the skin slick or greasy.

THE BEAUTY CARE MARKET IN SWITZERLAND

Switzerland was a small, topographically rugged country in the center of Western Europe. The Swiss enjoyed a relatively high standard of living; the per capita GNP in 1975 was SFr. 22,500, the highest in Europe. The population was 6.4 million people, and the diversity of the Swiss was reflected in the fact that there were four official languages, as follows:

First language	Percentage of population
German	65%
French	18
Italian	12
Romansch	1
Other	4
Total	100%

Source: Market Research Report, Swiss Federal Railway.

There were 3.28 million women in Switzerland, who were distributed among the following age groups:

Age group	Number of women (000)
0–14	700
15–19	240
20–29	510
30–39	450
40–49	400
50–59	340
Over 60	640
Total	3,280

Source: *Consumer Europe 1977.*

Retail sales of all beauty products in Switzerland were SFr. 535.3 million in 1975. The per capita expenditure for the Swiss adult woman was nearly SFr. 210. The women's cosmetic market comprised several segments, which in 1975 accounted for the following percentages of the total retail sales:

Product category	Percentage of beauty product sales
Face cosmetics	12%
Eye cosmetics	4
Hair preparations	22
Skin preparations	18
Fragrances	18
Deodorants	8
Bath preparations	4
Other	14
Total	100%

Source: *Consumer Europe 1977.*

Total sales of beauty products increased 12.6 percent form 1974 to 1975 in Switzerland. There were also changes in the structure of the market. Sales of fragrances and skin preparations, which included all-purpose lotions, rose sharply, while there was a decline in the volume of face and eye cosmetics and bath preparations.

According to some experts, the potential for the skin preparations market varied significantly among European countries. Sales levels depended not only upon the predominant skin types in a country but also upon the affluence of the women. Partly because of the standard of living in Switzerland and the fact that a relatively large proportion of the women were fair-skinned, the expenditure per adult woman on skin preparations was higher than in every other Western European country but Germany. In 1973, the "average" Swiss woman spent about SFr. 37 on skin lotions of various types. Exhibit 5 gives a break-

Exhibit 5
Swiss market for skin preparations, 1975

	Retail sales (SFr. million)	Unit sales (packs)	Usership (million women)	Percent of usership
Hand cream/lotion	22.8	7.8	1.85	72
Body cream/lotion	12.2	2.5	0.98	38
Moisturizers	7.5	1.2	0.73	29
All-purpose lotions	34.0	6.4	1.74	67
Others	18.8	+	+	+
	95.3			

Source: *Consumer Europe 1977.*

down of sales and usership of various categories of skin preparations, including all-purpose lotions.

CHANNELS AND PRICING

Smythe-Dabney products reached the buying public through a variety of channels of distribution, each with its own pricing arrangement. Aurora Lotion was manufactured in England and then sold in the United Kingdom to independent wholesalers or large retail chains. In countries with an SDI subsidiary, such as Switzerland, Aurora was sold to the affiliated company, which then resold it to wholesalers and retail stores. SDI billed all customers in pounds sterling. Company-owned subsidiaries were charged a transfer price, which was the standard manufacturing cost of the product, including:

Raw materials.
Direct labor.
Factory overhead.
Handling and warehousing.

The senior management of SDI adopted this transfer pricing arrangement in order to give the managers of each subsidiary maximum discretion over margins and profits. The reasons for this strategy were:

1. The majority of marketing costs were, in fact, incurred in the country where the product was sold.
2. Advertising, price promotions, and sales force management decisions were under the control of the subsidiary's management.
3. The practice reinforced the SDI concept of division autonomy on day-to-day decisions and fostered good relationships between subsidiary managers and corporate officers.

SDI's price to independent customers in Britain was standard manufacturing cost plus a percentage of the cost for contribution to overhead and profit. All customers paid freight charges from factory to their warehouses.

SDI gave independent distributors in the United Kingdom a 3¾ percent discount for cash purchases and up to 6 percent volume rebate for purchases of large amounts of any product. In addition, each month the company ran price promotions for groups of products in order to encourage British distributors to increase the volume of products they carried.

In England, wholesalers' markups on cosmetics were usually between 15 percent and 25 percent; retail margins were 35 percent to 45 percent of the selling price to the consumer. On the other hand, wholesale margins for beauty products in Switzerland were between 40 percent and 55 percent of the selling price to retail outlets, and retail margins were 42 percent to 50 percent. In Switzerland, Aurora Lotion and other PPF products were sold at the retail level in a wide variety of outlets. Exhibit 6 shows the percentage of total sales of beauty care products that were sold through various outlets in 1975. While the data were incomplete, there was evidence of a rapid increase in the portion of total sales that were accounted for by hypermarkets in the last few years.

PARALLEL IMPORTS

Perhaps the biggest single problem that confronted the management of PPF was the parallel importing of Aurora Lotion. The difference in the wholesale price in Britain and Switzerland made it profitable for a distributor to send a buyer to England, purchase the product at the British wholesale price, and ship it to Switzerland for eventual resale to retail outlets. The process had become increasingly common in the last several years, and the management of PPF counted several large distributors who parallel-imported Aurora Lotion among their main competitors in the marketplace. Although parallel importing was

Exhibit 6
Percentage of retail sales of women's beauty care products sold through various outlets in Switzerland

Outlet	Description	Percent of total sales
Department and cosmetics stores	Cosmetic departments of large department stores and small shops and "parfume-ries" specializing in cosmetics	20%
Drugstores and pharmacies	Drugstores sold cleaning compounds, preparations, and parapharmaceuticals; pharmacies sold prescription drugs and other products	40
Multiple stores/hypermarkets	Large chains selling food items as well as many nonfood products, from clothing to hardware to beauty products, often at discount prices (e.g., Migros and Carre-four)	25
Direct sales	Door-to-door salespersons.	3
Supermarkets/food outlets	Small and medium-size retail stores selling mainly food, with some nonfood lines	9
Others		3
Total		100%

Source: *Consumer Europe 1977.*

irritating to the sales force and management of PPF, it was not illegal and it was impossible to monitor.

There were three main reasons that the wholesale price of Aurora Lotion was lower in England than in Switzerland. First, retail prices were higher on the Continent than in Britain, reflecting a higher cost of living. Second, SDI conducted aggressive promotions in the United Kingdom each month, and the resulting average level of wholesale prices was lower than in Europe, where such promotions occurred less frequently. Finally, from 1972 through 1978 there had been a substantial decline in the value of the British pound against other currencies, including the Swiss franc. As a result of this trend, Swiss distributors had not had to increase the price of Aurora Lotion to the retail trade in five years, although SDI had hiked prices in Britain by as much as 25 percent a year in the same period. Since SDI billed its customers in pounds sterling, the fall of the pound against the Swiss franc had offset the British price increase.

Table 1 contains a hypothetical example of the landed cost per bottle of parallel-imported Aurora Lotion.

A large British wholesaler purchased Aurora Lotion at £10.55 per case of 12 bottles. Normally the distributor was expected to take a 3.75 percent cash discount and to be eligible for a volume rebate of 6 percent on his net purchases. When reselling these goods in large volume, he was content to receive a 15 percent markup.

A wholesale distributor or large retailer doing business in Switzerland sent a representative across the English Channel to buy from the

Table 1
**Hypothetical example of parallel importer's
cost per bottle of Aurora Lotion***

SDI price/case	£10.55
SDI price/bottle	0.88
Less: 3.75% cash discount	0.04
Net purchase	0.84
Less: 6% volume rebate	0.05
British distributor's cost	0.79
Add: 15% markup	0.14
Wholesale price	0.93
Add: transport cost at 6%	0.06
Landed cost/bottle	£ 0.99
Landed cost/bottle†	SFr. 3.70

* Figures have been rounded.
† Assumes 3.75 SFr./pound.
Source: Discussions with SDI directors.

British supplier. He paid £0.93 for each bottle, and incurred additional freight charges at 4 percent to 8 percent of the cost of goods, depending upon the volume shipped to Switzerland. Assuming at the time of the transaction an exchange rate of 3.75 Swiss francs per pound, his cost for a 200 cl bottle of Aurora Lotion landed in Switzerland was SFr. 3.70. The price list for PPF recommended the following price structure for the 200 cl bottle of Aurora:

PPF suggested prices for Aurora Lotion (including freight)

PPF suggested list price to distributors	SFr. 5.00
Distributor's suggested list price to retail outlets	8.70
Retailer's suggested list price to consumers	15.00

According to Urs Brunner, the retail price of Aurora Lotion had not declined in the last few years, despite the parallel imports. Since the consumer was paying the same price, the channels were apparently enjoying higher margins.

It was difficult to assess the impact of parallel importing on PPF or SDI as a whole. On the one hand, the average price of Aurora Lotion sold by PPF to the trade had declined over 20 percent in the past three years. Although PPF's list price for the product had not been reduced, the company had run a series of trade promotions which gave discounts to distributors, aimed at countering the competition from parallel imports. Exhibit 7 provides details in the trend of PPF's selling price for Aurora.

Sales of Aurora Lotion had increased in units and in Swiss francs, and Fairchild was not sure whether the increases were in spite of the parallel imports or because of them. Probable effects of the activity had been higher market penetration of the product and increased

Exhibit 7
Trends in average selling price and landed cost of Aurora Lotion (200 cl)
by Produits Pour Femmes, SA, 1975–1978

	1975	*1976*	*1977*	*1978**
Average selling price per bottle (SFr.)†	5.00	4.70	4.30	4.00
Average landed cost per bottle (pounds)	0.35	0.40	0.45	0.50
Average exchange rate (SFr./£)‡	5.40	4.05	3.95	3.75

* 1978 is average for the first quarter of the year.
† "Average price" is list price less discounts given in trade promotions.
‡ Average rate during fourth quarter, 1975–77; during first quarter, 1978.
Source: SDI company records (disguised).

brand recognition, both of which were beneficial to PPF. Besides, from SDI's point of view, the sales of Aurora parallel imported from England benefited the parent company by the contribution from the SDI sales to the British wholesalers.

Even if the practice had mixed results, Fairchild knew that he could not shrug off the situation. It was clear from his conversation with Brunner that it had resulted in low morale in the Swiss subsidiary's sales force. Salespersons were rewarded for units sold and wanted to cut the price of Aurora to make them more competitive with the parallel importers.

ALTERNATIVES

John Fairchild reviewed the possible responses he had considered to the problem at hand. One alternative was to lower PPF's recommended selling price for Aurora Lotion to distributors. He was concerned about the possible financial consequences of such a price cut, both for PPF and for SDI. Moreover, he wondered what steps he should take to ensure that trading profits would not be sacrificed. He believed that related options included cutting the subsidiary's advertising budget, trimming the sales force, and raising the prices of other products.

On the other hand, he wondered whether PPF could simply adhere to the policy that had been followed in the past. Such a strategy would continue to consist of three elements:

1. Avoid direct competition in published list prices.
2. Use trade promotions such as price-off discounts or "buy two, get one free" to respond to competitive pricing.
3. Stress the advantages provided by PPF to the trade, such as continuity of supply, advertising to stimulate demand, and a full line of related products.

Although the problem of what to do about the price of Aurora Lotion demanded action in the short run, it also had implications for the future of the subsidiary over the long term. Fairchild wondered whether the independent Swiss wholesalers would begin to parallel-import more SDI products across the Channel. Aurora Lotion, which accounted for 20 percent of PPF sales, might only be the first of a growing number of products on which the subsidiary would face increasing price competition.

Perhaps the existence of parallel importers was a signal that PPF was not an efficient channel of distribution. SDI might be better off to conduct its business directly with the independent distributors in Switzerland. This issue took on added significance because of SDI's plans to expand abroad in the future. The corporate directors would be faced with the decision of whether to set up a company subsidiary or to sell SDI products through existing independent wholesalers each time they entered a market in a new country or region.

A meeting with Sir Anthony Carburton and the other SDI directors was scheduled soon. Fairchild decided that this would be the best time to present his views on the situation at PPF and make his recommendations to the group.

Case 4–4

Gemini Oil, Ltd.

On the morning of January 9, 1978, Mr. Tom Wood, president of Gemini Oil Limited, asked his marketing manager, Mr. Bill Robinson, to step into his office.

"Bill, as you know, I was in Detroit last week, and while I was there I discovered a product made by Atlas Chemicals, Ltd., which may prove to be financially rewarding to Gemini, if we handle it properly. It's a paint sealant for automobiles. Here, take this information and sample I've got, check the feasibility of us marketing it, and report back to me with your findings next week."

GEMINI OIL LIMITED

Gemini Oil, Ltd., was a local independent company founded by Tom Wood in 1967. Gemini had grown substantially due to hard work and a skilled management team. With its head office located in Kitchener, Ontario, Gemini currently operated several gas stations in the Kitchener-Waterloo-Guelph area. Exhibit 1 outlines the organizational structure.

This case was prepared and copyrighted by Professor Paul R. MacPherson of the University of Guelph, Guelph, Ontario, Canada. Copyright © 1980.

Exhibit 1
Organizational structure of Gemini Oil, Ltd.

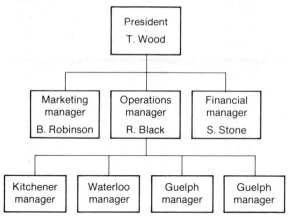

Tom Wood had been involved in the oil industry for a great number of years, first as a salesman, then as a territory manager for a multinational corporation. Believing that an independent discount gas station would be economically viable in the golden triangle area, he had resigned his position in 1967 and opened the first Gemini station in Kitchener, followed by another in Waterloo in 1969 and two in Guelph in 1972 and 1976. He was the sole shareholder of Gemini.

Bill Robinson was also quite familiar with the oil industry, for he too had worked for a major oil company in the marketing department. Bill had joined Gemini in 1975.

Gemini's operations manager, Richard Black, was highly qualified for his job, having been a former Imperial Oil, Ltd. (Esso), agent. Richard had been employed by Gemini since 1971.

Sam Stone came to the organization with an extensive background in accounting and finance, acquired through working several years in retail businesses as a controller. The station managers were local employees who were responsible for the daily upkeep and management of their respective stations.

SEARCH FOR NEW OPPORTUNITIES

Recent trends in the gasoline industry, such as the advent of self-service gasoline stations and increasing price competition from the major oil companies, had sent the management team of Gemini searching for new diversification projects. It was for this reason that Tom Wood had traveled to Detroit the previous week.

Bill Robinson took the information (Exhibit 2) and sample back to his office and studied them. At first glance, the product seemed too good to be true. The product claimed to eliminate the need for con-

Product	Automotive paint sealant series 60.
Use	Seals and protects all types of lacquer and enamel paints used by automotive manufacturers and body repair shops after one application.
	Suitable for new and used cars.
Properties of Series 60 paint sealants	Liquid—white in color, contains *no* wax.
	Tailored to individual specifications by altering chemical additives at source.
	Extremely low surface tension allows glaze to penetrate paint surface and encircle individual molecules, which strengthens paint and thereby reduces chipping.
	Chemicals seal out environmental fallout, repel water, and *inhibit surface* rust caused by salt.
	Ultraviolet ray absorbers prevent fading and bleaching of paint.
	Paint oxidization is prevented due to sealing characteristics.
	Enhances paint luster and brilliance provided by cleaner wax.
	Allows paint to breathe.
Durability	Repeated testing under actual and simulated conditions reveals lasting protection and brilliance for four years.
Application method	*Step 1.* A good quality cleaner wax must be applied to the automobile's finish, either by hand or by buffer, to clean and shine the surface. Allow to dry and wipe off.
	Step 2. Any of series 60 paint sealants are now applied by hand using a soft cloth to the entire vehicle's surface (paint and chrome). Allow 20 minutes to dry to a white haze, then buff off, using a clean, dry cloth. Total application time approximately three hours.
	Note. The product should be sprayed around grilles, nameplates, etc., to allow *rust-inhibiting* properties to seep behind these areas.
	Note. Paint must be dry before application begins (six weeks minimum).
Care of surface	Tunnel car washes will not "wash off" the sealant once it has been properly applied. Luster and durability will not be affected by spray waxes.
	Wax of any kind should not be applied by hand over the sealant, as dulling and streaking may occur due to buildup.
	Periodic wiping with a soft, dry cloth will enhance the shine after vehicle has been thoroughly cleaned and dried.
Recommended application	One 8-ounce (Canadian) application.
Container size	45 gallons (Canadian).
	Note. Must not be applied in the sun.

Exhibit 2 (*concluded*)

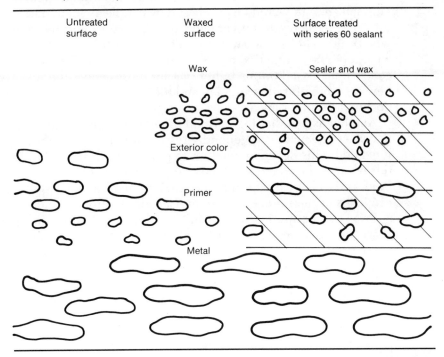

| Untreated surface | Waxed surface | Surface treated with series 60 sealant |

stant waxing of an automobile's exterior finish; one application should "last a lifetime." This sharply contrasted with Bill's own experience with automobile waxing. Bill constantly waxed his red 1974 sports car in order to keep it shiny and looking new. In fact, he knew that a person should clean and wax a car every three to four months to remove the old wax that had yellowed and the oxidized paint that caused a car's finish to appear dull and faded.

That night Bill cleaned his car and applied the sealer as outlined in the instructions. He was very impressed with the ease of application and the results, as were others of the management team the next morning. Clearly, this was a product that warranted study.

THE MARKET

In an effort to obtain information about potential consumers of the sealant, Bill interviewed a friend of his who was a local automotive dealer, since Bill perceived this to be an automobile accessory product. After discussing the properties of the sealant, his friend stated that the product would be purchased primarily by persons who were ordering a new car, had just obtained possession of a new car, or owned a car that was no more than one year old. Bill's friend thought that a minimal amount would be purchased by people about to trade in their car, so as to increase the vehicle's trade-in value, and by individuals who could not afford a paint job on their old car but might see this as an acceptable alternative to restore the car's finish. He came to these conclusions based on his belief that for most people the novelty of a new car wore off rather quickly and the desire for a shiny automobile declined in importance.

Another aspect that Bill's friend thought was important was the fact that since the male was generally responsible for automobile upkeep, it would be his decision whether to purchase this type of product. At this point in the conversation his friend turned to his desk drawer and produced a chart containing some 1977 automobile sales statistics and estimates of the number of cars in Canada (Exhibits 3 and 4).

Prior to meeting his friend, Bill had learned that for the past few years Canadians were keeping their cars longer, the average car now being resold approximately 36 months after being purchased new. He asked his friend why.

"This may be attributed to the fact that the consumer price index for automobiles has been increasing for the last several years, combined with the economic slowdown in the nation." His friend went on to say, "Car prices are expected to continue to increase at about 6.5 percent per year for the foreseeable future. At least, that's what the head office tells me".

Bill's friend told him that the majority of customers didn't know what they wanted in the way of a car until they stepped on the lot. It was the job of the salesman to find out their needs and wants and maneuver them from purchasing a stripped-down model to purchasing a vehicle with more options. Salesmen generally received a 10 percent commission on the purchase price of an automobile.

His friend went on to say, "Automobile manufacturers target different models to various types of consumers whose likes and needs are similar." The Honda automobile was one example: its manufacturer appeared to have the female buying public as a particular area of focus.

As Bill was about to leave, his friend gave him a list of the number of auto dealers in Canada (Exhibit 5) and mentioned that Gemini's new product might best be sold at the dealership level, since the customer was already predisposed to purchasing when he ordered his new vehicle.

He said, "We're selling rustproofing to about 75 percent of our new car customers. I think your product would receive a similar response . . . if the price is right!"

Exhibit 3
Retail sales of new motor vehicles in units, by type of vehicle, by province, 1977

Month	Canada	Newfound-land	Prince Edward Island	Nova Scotia	New Brunswick	Quebec	Ontario	Manitoba	Saskat-chewan	Alberta	British Columbia*
All vehicles											
Total	1,344,959	21,768	5,470	42,124	35,195	333,617	497,155	58,040	54,213	151,927	145,450
January	93,760	1,229	387	2,740	2,058	20,900	36,865	4,195	3,975	11,238	10,519
February	97,389	1,388	360	2,932	2,382	21,371	35,665	4,204	4,261	12,564	12,262
March	128,528	2,230	456	3,955	3,408	34,240	45,010	5,305	5,550	14,405	13,969
April	127,314	2,233	508	4,070	3,664	35,383	46,662	5,156	4,478	13,001	12,159
May	139,916	2,353	634	4,461	4,123	37,413	50,462	5,887	4,810	15,461	14,312
June	135,445	2,338	598	4,382	3,915	34,048	51,689	5,855	4,905	13,961	13,754
July	108,760	1,936	496	3,534	2,910	27,736	39,674	4,896	4,367	11,607	11,604
August	107,668	1,826	373	3,584	2,668	26,626	38,775	5,019	4,645	11,835	12,317
September	87,443	1,464	341	2,706	2,195	20,419	32,120	3,693	3,740	10,037	10,728
October	131,677	1,937	595	3,747	3,242	34,048	48,429	6,017	5,496	15,457	12,709
November	107,291	1,794	422	3,529	2,797	24,828	40,695	4,335	4,664	12,467	11,760
December	79,768	1,040	300	2,484	1,833	16,605	31,455	3,478	3,322	9,894	9,357
Passenger cars											
Total	991,398	14,937	4,084	31,910	25,308	272,538	388,568	39,686	32,876	86,682	94,809
January	68,426	811	265	2,024	1,429	16,607	28,611	2,889	2,286	6,474	7,030
February	71,022	970	256	2,172	1,736	17,273	27,733	2,775	2,518	7,168	8,421
March	94,144	1,633	345	2,981	2,442	28,149	34,682	3,598	3,368	8,026	8,920
April	96,467	1,649	377	3,109	2,786	29,956	36,802	3,601	2,819	7,335	8,033
May	104,740	1,730	481	3,427	3,067	31,072	39,686	4,077	3,061	8,983	9,156
June	101,434	1,673	471	3,477	2,901	28,044	40,810	4,092	3,164	8,025	8,777
July	79,562	1,390	369	2,751	2,123	22,313	30,664	3,386	2,823	6,590	7,153
August	78,093	1,170	295	2,706	1,856	21,340	29,765	3,369	2,841	7,000	7,751
September	63,470	946	253	1,989	1,546	16,139	24,827	2,583	2,292	5,886	7,009
October	97,826	1,232	435	2,749	2,207	28,243	38,258	4,179	3,280	8,925	8,318
November	79,052	1,125	323	2,705	1,973	20,114	32,324	2,883	2,710	6,914	7,981
December	57,162	608	214	1,820	1,242	13,288	24,406	2,254	1,714	5,356	6,260
Commercial vehicles											
Total	353,561	6,831	1,386	10,214	9,887	61,079	108,587	18,354	21,337	65,245	50,641
January	25,334	418	122	716	629	4,293	7,908	1,306	1,689	4,764	3,489
February	26,367	418	104	760	646	4,098	7,932	1,429	1,743	5,396	3,841
March	34,384	597	111	974	966	6,091	10,328	1,707	2,182	6,379	5,049
April	30,847	584	131	961	878	5,427	9,860	1,555	1,659	5,666	4,126
May	35,176	623	153	1,034	1,056	6,341	10,776	1,810	1,749	6,478	5,156
June	34,011	665	127	905	1,014	6,004	10,879	1,763	1,741	5,936	4,977
July	29,198	546	127	783	787	5,423	9,010	1,510	1,544	5,017	4,451
August	29,575	656	78	878	812	5,286	9,010	1,650	1,804	4,835	4,566
September	23,973	518	88	717	649	4,280	7,293	1,110	1,448	4,151	3,719
October	33,851	705	160	998	1,035	5,805	10,171	1,838	2,216	6,532	4,391
November	28,239	669	99	824	824	4,714	8,371	1,452	1,954	5,553	3,779
December	22,606	432	86	664	591	3,317	7,049	1,224	1,608	4,538	3,097

* Includes Yukon and Northwest Territories.
Source: *Statistics Canada*.

Exhibit 4
Automobiles, by number and percentage distribution of households, by province, 1974, 1975, and 1976

	Households with automobiles								Households without automobiles (000)	Percentage of households
Province	Total households (000)	Percentage of households	One automobile (000)	Percentage of households	Two automobiles (000)	Percentage of households	Three or more automobiles (000)	Percentage of households		
Canada										
1974	6,493	100.0	3,663	56.4	1,177	18.1	225	3.5	1,429	22.0
1975	6,703	100.0	3,745	55.9	1,294	19.3	247	3.7	1,416	21.1
1976	6,918	100.0	3,803	55.0	1,388	20.1	300	4.3	1,427	20.6
1976/1975 (%)	+3.2		+1.5		+7.3		+21.5		+0.8	
Newfoundland										
1974	118	100.0	63	53.4	13	11.0	—	—	38	32.2
1975	125	100.0	68	54.4	17	13.6	—	—	37	29.6
1976	130	100.0	71	54.6	17	13.1	5	3.8	38	29.2
1976/1975 (%)	+4.0		+4.4		—		—		+2.7	
Prince Edward Island										
1974	29	100.0	18	62.1	5	17.2	—	—	5	17.2
1975	30	100.0	18	60.0	6	20.0	—	—	6	20.0
1976	32	100.0	18	56.2	7	21.9	—	—	5	15.6
1976/1975 (%)	+6.7		—		+16.7		—		-16.7	
Nova Scotia										
1974	219	100.0	130	59.4	32	14.6	5	2.3	52	23.7
1975	222	100.0	125	56.3	36	16.2	6	2.7	55	24.8
1976	227	100.0	127	55.9	41	18.1	8	3.5	51	22.5
1976/1975 (%)	+2.3		+1.6		+13.9		+33.3		-7.3	
New Brunswick										
1974	165	100.0	101	61.2	23	13.9	5	3.0	37	22.4
1975	169	100.0	101	59.8	29	17.2	6	3.6	32	18.9
1976	172	100.0	102	59.3	29	16.9	6	3.5	35	20.3
1976/1975 (%)	+1.8		+1.0		—		—		+9.4	

	Total	%		%		%		%		%
Quebec										
1974	1,721	100.0	1,014	58.9	209	12.1	32	1.9	466	27.1
1975	1,764	100.0	1,061	60.1	220	12.5	38	2.2	445	25.2
1976	1,832	100.0	1,091	59.6	231	12.6	45	2.5	465	25.4
1976/1975 (%)	+3.9		+2.8		+5.0		+18.4		+4.5	
Ontario										
1974	2,453	100.0	1,380	56.3	499	20.3	89	3.6	484	19.7
1975	2,540	100.0	1,410	55.5	542	21.3	86	3.4	502	19.8
1976	2,622	100.0	1,439	54.9	574	21.9	107	4.1	501	19.1
1976/1975 (%)	+3.2		+2.1		+5.9		+24.4		-0.2	
Manitoba										
1974	306	100.0	177	57.8	47	15.4	8	2.6	74	24.2
1975	311	100.0	181	58.2	53	17.0	10	3.2	67	21.5
1976	314	100.0	170	54.1	61	19.4	11	3.5	72	22.9
1976/1975 (%)	+1.0		-6.1		+15.1		+10.0		+7.5	
Saskatchewan										
1974	264	100.0	160	60.6	42	15.9	12	4.5	50	18.9
1975	273	100.0	152	55.7	54	19.8	17	6.2	50	18.3
1976	279	100.0	137	49.1	75	26.9	26	9.3	41	14.7
1976/1975 (%)	+2.2		-9.9		+38.9		+52.9		-18.0	
Alberta										
1974	497	100.0	272	54.7	106	21.3	24	4.8	95	19.1
1975	519	100.0	266	51.3	128	24.7	33	6.4	92	17.7
1976	542	100.0	276	50.9	135	24.9	42	7.7	89	16.4
1976/1975 (%)	+4.4		+3.8		+5.5		+27.3		-3.3	
British Columbia										
1974	722	100.0	349	48.3	200	27.7	45	6.2	128	17.7
1975	749	100.0	362	48.3	210	28.0	47	6.3	129	17.2
1976	767	100.0	371	48.4	217	28.3	48	6.3	130	16.9
1976/1975 (%)	+2.4		+2.5		+3.3		+2.1		+0.8	

Source: *Statistics Canada.*

Exhibit 5

	Auto agents and dealers (new and used)	Auto agents and dealers (new only)	Auto agents and dealers (used only)
Newfoundland and Maritimes	575	442	271
Quebec (total)	1,309	1,060	512
Montreal and suburbs	415	314	232
Ontario (total)	2,317	1,381	1,529
Toronto and suburbs	378	203	267
Western Provinces	2,216	1,965	809
Canada (total)	7,210	5,365	3,620

DISTRIBUTION

Back in his office Bill reflected on his friend's advice. Bill was of the opinion that there were two types of potential consumers of the sealant: (1) those in the "do-it-yourself market," who would buy the product and apply it much like wax; and (2) those who would pay to have the product professionally applied, as in a "simonize" treatment.

Clearly, different distribution paths would be required to tap these markets. This idea was reinforced when Bill read several articles dealing with automobile care. Another area of concern focused on the geographic area which should be penetrated initially.

PRODUCT

The product segment of the marketing strategy posed several questions. Although the product from Atlas was a sealer, should a cleaner/ wax be sold along with it? Second, in light of Atlas' testing, Bill was considering that a guarantee might be included to foster credibility, as he knew that warranty claims averaged only 3-5 percent of sales for automotive products. On the other hand, guarantees were not popular with automotive dealers. Many dealers had been "burned" by rustproofing claims made by disgruntled car owners. Dealers had to stand behind the rustproofer's guarantee even though they had only sold and applied the rustproofing. The company manufacturing and selling the rustproofing to the dealership was often no longer in existence or was bankrupt. Furthermore, the Ministry of Consumer and Commercial Relations (a branch of the Ontario provincial government) was investigating guarantees quite carefully at the present time.

Bill was also considering the idea of a new "total product concept" which would involve supplying dealers with the necessary sealant chemicals, cooperative advertising, and management assistance, since he knew that such an approach had been highly successful in the food industry.

PRICING

An appropriate pricing policy was also an important consideration because Bill knew that as time went on, the pricing strategy would probably have to be altered at both the retail and wholesale levels. Bill compiled the wax prices that are found in Exhibit 6, and after

Exhibit 6
Competitive wax prices

Shiny Wax—liquid 18 oz.	$ 2.69
Body Shine—18 oz.	1.69
Mister Wax—18 oz.	1.99
Regal Paste—24 oz.	4.95
Silicone Paste Wax—24 oz.	5.95
All Year Wax/Cleaner—liquid 24 oz.	2.79
Trend Paste—18 oz.	4.95
Wax treatment (professionally applied)	45.00

obtaining quotes from various suppliers, he drew up an estimated cost sheet illustrating the various costs relevant to the alternative distribution strategies. These figures are shown in Exhibit 7.

In talking with wholesalers, Bill found that a 50 percent markup on selling price would ensure their support, while a retailer would ex-

Exhibit 7
Relevant costs of paint sealant project

Advertising	$15,000.00
Atlas sealant (can gallon) (includes freight and duty)	25.00
Cleaner/wax per car	0.45
Filling machinery—10-year life	8,000.00
Heat, light (year)	960.00
Instruction sheet	0.05
Kit boxes (each)	0.20
Miscellaneous expenses	2,000.00
Packing case (24 kits/case)	1.20
Postage and handling (kits)	1.30
Rent (year)	4,800.00
Salesman's salary (each)	12,000.00
Sealer bottle and cap	0.10
Travel	5,000.00
Wages (filler)	8,000.00
Wax bottle and cap	0.10
Window sticker (each)	0.05

pect a markup of 60 percent on selling price if he sold the product over the counter and 80 percent on selling price if he applied it professionally. The approximate application time of three hours was considered to be realistic. This would amount to $9.75 at prevailing labor rates.

Bill targeted Gemini's markup at 40 percent on selling price since the product was new to Canada.

PROMOTION

Bill reasoned that promotion would play a major role in the overall financial success of the sealant since consumers would need to be educated on the various benefits of the sealant. He set aside $15,000 for this but was concerned about how and when it should be allocated so as to achieve the best possible return. To further the decision-making process, Bill prepared a list of various promotional costs (Exhibit 8) and made a copy of new automobile sales figures (Exhibit 9). Bill also wanted to develop a promotional theme for this new product which would identify it in the minds of consumers.

Exhibit 8
Selected promotional costs

Radio—30-second spots

Time classifications	AA	A	B	C
London	$50.50	$42.35	$31.75	$20.25
Toronto	$90.10	$75.00	$50.00	$40.75
Kitchener	$42.50	$31.75	$22.00	$14.00

Television (London)

Time classifications	AA	A	B	C
60 seconds	$500.00	$400.00	$225.00	$90.00
30 seconds	$275.00	$225.00	$155.00	$70.00
10 seconds	$175.00	$150.00	$115.00	$35.00

Newspaper (southwestern Ontario)

Rates	
Full page (black and white)	$2,500
Half page (black and white)	1,250
Quarter page (black and white)	625
Extras	
Black and one color	$400
Black and two colors	850
Brochures—two colors + black	
0–10,000	$30/1,000
10,000–20,000	25/1,000
20,000–50,000	22/1,000
50,000 +	19/1,000

Retail sales of new motor vehicles in units, by type of vehicle, by province, 1963–1977

Year	Canada	Newfoundland	Prince Edward Island	Nova Scotia	New Brunswick	Quebec	Ontario	Manitoba	Saskatchewan	Alberta	British Columbia*
All vehicles											
1963	654,989	9,458	3,252	21,410	17,191	165,925	260,771	30,157	34,520	54,958	57,347
1964	725,879	10,536	3,300	24,671	19,637	182,053	286,945	32,974	39,126	60,131	66,506
1965	830,995	12,638	3,912	26,273	22,661	205,338	336,665	33,421	43,519	66,904	79,664
1966	827,431	14,392	3,785	27,013	23,182	200,747	326,550	38,288	44,511	70,678	78,285
1967	815,307	14,564	3,457	27,100	19,845	199,056	319,272	40,487	43,713	71,976	75,837
1968	889,453	14,005	3,838	30,791	22,847	218,738	357,732	37,602	39,919	78,066	85,915
1969	917,505	12,643	3,458	27,795	22,935	225,935	372,237	37,223	33,814	83,851	97,664
1970	774,241	12,147	3,192	24,650	19,987	198,604	309,950	31,824	26,582	66,271	81,034
1971	940,332	16,333	3,978	29,997	27,191	236,464	379,144	37,031	34,110	78,751	97,333
1972	1,065,621	21,065	4,495	32,897	30,088	270,871	415,053	43,579	42,073	93,365	112,135
1973	1,226,698	24,160	5,139	40,019	33,912	316,430	469,190	52,218	49,363	106,320	129,947
1974	1,249,304	23,066	5,359	42,175	35,073	317,346	453,106	56,511	60,851	120,795	135,022
1975	1,316,629	22,075	5,148	41,448	35,019	323,703	510,633	55,922	61,647	128,287	132,747
1976	1,291,463	20,343	5,336	41,403	35,005	336,347	456,610	59,028	61,192	145,547	130,652
1977	1,344,959	21,768	5,470	42,124	35,195	333,617	497,155	58,040	54,213	151,927	145,450
Passenger cars											
1963	557,787	7,499	2,595	18,100	14,314	144,761	229,668	25,652	26,477	40,835	47,886
1964	616,759	8,384	2,652	20,928	16,180	160,397	251,297	27,948	29,519	44,849	54,605
1965	708,716	10,169	3,143	22,544	18,876	182,719	297,465	27,817	31,622	49,502	64,859
1966	694,820	11,752	2,989	23,041	19,444	177,881	283,730	31,170	31,374	50,896	62,543
1967	679,435	12,128	2,759	22,909	16,181	176,140	274,291	32,398	30,327	51,715	60,587
1968	741,915	11,453	3,004	25,534	18,692	195,423	307,017	30,029	28,408	55,867	66,488
1969	760,803	10,560	2,781	23,263	18,445	201,169	319,084	29,629	23,559	59,265	73,048
1970	640,360	9,945	2,541	20,454	15,765	176,578	265,009	24,935	18,187	46,750	60,196
1971	780,762	13,105	3,168	25,413	22,205	209,366	325,755	29,462	23,612	55,811	72,865
1972	858,959	16,835	3,567	26,889	24,183	235,884	346,819	33,837	28,157	62,834	79,954
1973	970,828	18,781	4,001	32,412	26,652	272,919	387,309	39,039	32,200	67,035	90,480
1974	942,797	16,923	3,972	32,581	26,108	264,829	359,427	39,866	36,279	72,060	90,752
1975	989,280	15,584	3,809	31,397	25,746	269,011	409,198	37,742	33,705	73,931	89,166
1976	946,488	14,042	3,990	31,318	25,535	276,239	351,523	40,433	34,810	84,103	84,495
1977	991,398	14,937	4,084	31,910	25,308	272,538	388,568	39,686	32,876	86,682	94,809
Commercial vehicles											
1963	97,202	1,959	657	3,310	2,877	21,164	31,103	4,505	8,043	14,123	9,461
1964	109,120	2,152	648	3,743	3,457	21,656	35,648	5,026	9,607	15,282	11,901
1965	122,279	2,469	769	3,729	3,785	22,619	39,200	5,604	11,897	17,402	14,805
1966	132,611	2,640	796	3,972	3,738	22,866	42,820	7,118	13,137	19,782	15,742
1967	135,872	2,436	698	4,191	3,664	22,916	44,981	8,089	13,386	20,261	15,250
1968	147,588	2,552	834	5,257	4,155	23,315	50,715	7,573	11,511	22,199	19,467
1969	156,702	2,083	677	4,532	4,440	24,766	53,153	7,594	10,255	24,586	24,616
1970	133,881	2,202	651	4,196	4,222	22,026	44,941	6,889	8,395	19,521	20,838
1971	159,570	3,228	810	4,584	4,986	27,098	53,389	7,569	10,498	22,940	24,468
1972	206,662	4,230	928	6,008	5,905	34,987	68,234	9,742	13,916	30,531	32,181
1973	255,870	5,379	1,138	7,607	7,260	43,511	81,881	13,179	17,163	39,285	39,467
1974	306,507	6,143	1,387	9,594	8,963	52,517	93,679	16,645	24,572	48,735	44,270
1975	327,349	6,491	1,339	10,051	9,273	54,692	101,444	18,180	27,942	54,356	43,581
1976	344,975	6,301	1,346	10,085	9,470	60,108	105,087	18,595	26,382	61,444	46,157
1977	353,561	6,831	1,386	10,214	9,887	61,079	108,587	18,354	21,337	65,245	50,641

* Includes Yukon and Northwest Territories.
Source: *Statistics Canada.*

OTHER CONCERNS

When talking to Mr. Wood a few days after his initial meeting, Bill became concerned about the fact that the chemical formulation of the series 60 sealants (the sealant with which Bill was involved) was based upon each customer's durability and luster specifications and that Atlas could produce a similar but not identical product by merely altering certain additives. Any exclusive license or distributorship that Gemini could acquire from Atlas would be subject to Atlas merely altering the formulation of the sealant and distributing it under a different trade name. Bill wondered how this risk could be reduced.

Bill also recognized that government authorities were considering a rust code or warranty regarding new automobiles that the manufacturers would be obliged to honor. In addition, both new and used car dealers were viewed by the buying public with a general air of suspicion and mistrust.

Bill also wondered whether the large automotive wax manufacturers would retaliate, and if so, in what maner. Finally, he had to reconcile the fact that this would be a totally new market for Gemini and hence new problems would have to be solved by management.

With these questions in mind, Bill set out to address two main questions in his written report. First, should Gemini enter the market, and second, assuming that the decision was affirmative, how would the product be marketed?

Case 4–5

Easco Tools, Inc.

In May 1975, Thomas Dillard, director of marketing for Easco Tools, Inc., was attempting to develop an advertising strategy which would best enable him to accomplish the introduction of the Easco brand name into the hand tools market.

The question was a complex one. Easco was a new brand name under which the product lines of several established hand tool companies were being consolidated. Each company had had its own distribution and brand name, some better known than others. Mr. Dillard was attempting to market the consolidated lines under one new brand name without losing the positive elements of past marketing efforts.

This case was prepared by Christopher Gale and D. W. Rosenthal, The Colgate Darden Graduate School of Business Administration, the University of Virginia. Copyright 1976 by the Sponsors of The Colgate Darden Graduate School of Business Administration, the University of Virginia.

Mr. Dillard was uncertain as to the specific role he should expect advertising to play in the introduction of the Easco brand. He wanted to establish explicit objectives for advertising but was unsure how to approach the question. Additionally, Dillard found it difficult to know what elements he should include in his consideration of advertising strategy. Dillard had just received a report from Easco Tool's advertising agency, Mason, Nagel & Osborne, which identified and described the major hand tools markets, but he was uncertain as to the report's implications for an advertising strategy. (For information on the hand tool industry, see Appendix A.)

Dillard knew that his decisions as to objectives and strategy would be reflected in the budget proposal which was to be made shortly to the parent corporation. Dillard was convinced that upper management was strongly committed to the success of the new consolidated line, but he was unsure as to how far this commitment went in terms of advertising dollars. He expected the budget to be in the $100,000 to $200,000 range, and he was certain, therefore, that wide-scale consumer advertising was beyond his means. Further, he tried to keep in mind that this was but the first year in a long-term commitment and that previous advertising expenditures by the hand tools group had been negligible.

Dillard was convinced that once the basic issues such as target audience and objectives had been decided, his subordinates, with the help of the agency, could handle the specifics of the advertising program's implementation. Dillard wanted to arrive at a suitable strategy as soon as possible in order to provide enough lead time to introduce Easco at the hardware show in August.

BACKGROUND

The name "Easco" was a contraction of the old company name, Eastern Stainless Steel Company. Through acquisitions and mergers, etc., Easco Corporation had become a diversified manufacturing company with yearly sales of roughly $200 million. The corporation was divided into four major groups: hand tools, aluminum products, industrial products, and engineering services. The original stainless steel businesses had been spun off, and by 1972 Easco consisted entirely of acquired companies. (For financial data, see Exhibits 1 and 2.)

Hand tools represented Easco's largest and principal business segment. The company was the supplier of all wrenches, ratchets, and socket sets marketed by Sears, Roebuck & Co. under the "Craftsman" trade name. Recently the company had consolidated its other hand tool lines, including hammers, hacksaw frames, axes, and trowels, into a unified line of proprietary tools sold under the Easco label by Easco Tools, Inc. The creation of a new line of sockets and wrenches to be sold under the Easco label was in the planning stages.

Exhibit 1

EASCO TOOLS, INC.
Financial Data

	1974*	1973	1972	1971	1970
Summary of operations (for the year)					
Net sales.................................	$194,368	$159,929	$133,230	$112,130	$96,880
Gross profit exclusive of depreciation	36,594	33,706	28,944	24,053	19,227
Selling, general, and administrative expense	17,894	16,676	15,274	13,331	10,760
Depreciation of properties	3,206	2,930	2,612	2,435	2,097
Interest expense	3,214	1,978	1,363	1,692	1,268
Income before taxes thereon	12,280	12,122	9,695	6,595	5,102
Federal and state income taxes, before investment tax credit	6,370	6,445	5,145	3,336	2,661
Investment tax credit	362	248	207	112	216
Income before extraordinary item†	6,272	5,925	4,757	3,371	2,657
Preferred dividend requirements...........	558	559	570	572	591
Income applicable to common stock†	5,714	5,366	4,187	2,799	2,066
Financial position (at December 31)					
Cash	$ 1,665	$ 1,752	$ 1,290	$ 1,300	$ 2,867
Receivables (net)	26,869	24,203	22,050	17,023	13,954
Inventories............................	41,448	30,980	25,398	20,907	20,761
Prepaid expenses	1,452	1,107	787	758	464
Total current assets	71,434	58,042	49,525	39,988	38,046
Total current liabilities..................	29,287	36,618	25,980	19,026	19,560

Working capital (current assets less current liabilities)	42,147	21,424	23,545	20,962	18,486
Land, buildings, and equipment, net	32,188	29,520	24,337	24,676	24,042
Other assets	1,137	1,301	1,098	1,081	1,098
Total capital employed (total assets less current liabilities)	75,472	52,245	48,980	46,719	43,626
Deduct: Long-term debt, less portion due in one year	33,153	14,771	15,319	16,345	17,300
Deferred federal and state income taxes	1,789	1,555	1,237	811	591
Shareholders' equity (net worth)	$ 40,530	$ 35,919	$ 32,424	$ 29,563	$25,735

Statistics

Per share of common stock:					
Income before extraordinary item—primary, assuming no dilution†	$2.20	$2.08	$1.59	$1.06	$.79
Cash dividends declared	$0.425	$0.32	‡	‡	‡
Shareholders' equity (book value)	$10.87	$9.09	$7.87	$6.72	$5.14
Common shares outstanding at year-end	2,594,087	2,593,409	2,534,075	2,523,193	2,526,419
Average common shares used in earnings per share data	2,593,843	2,583,729	2,626,634	2,634,439	2,607,936
Number of common shareholders at year-end	7,099	7,014	7,024	7,229	7,377
Number of employees at year-end	5,044	4,836	4,834	4,325	3,997
Capital expenditures (gross)	$5,852	$7,559	$3,347	$4,715	$4,354

Ratios

Income from operations as a percentage of:					
Net sales	3.2%	3.7%	3.6%	3.0%	2.7%
Shareholders' equity§	16.4%	17.3%	15.3%	12.2%	10.7%
Working capital (ratio of current assets to current liabilities)	2.4 to 1	1.6 to 1	1.9 to 1	2.1 to 1	1.9 to 1
Long-term debt as a percentage of total capital employed	44%	28%	31%	35%	40%

Note: Dollar amounts are expressed in thousands; debt figures are given on a per share basis
*Reflects change to LIFO method of inventory valuation.
†Excludes an extraordinary charge of $407,000 or $0.16 per share for reorganization expenses in 1972.
‡Not comparative in years prior to reorganization of November 8, 1972. Actual historical amounts were $0.50 in 1972, $0.78 in 1971, and $0.88 in 1970.
§Based on average of beginning and ending of year balances.
Source: 1974 annual report.

Exhibit 2

EASCO TOOLS, INC.
Summary of Operations by Business Activity

Net sales

	1974		1973		1972		1971		1970	
Operating group										
Hand tools	$ 82,687	42%	$ 66,976	42%	$ 57,478	43%	$ 45,366	41%	$40,654	42%
Aluminum products	65,314	34	55,978	35	41,688	31	34,365	31	26,632	28
Industrial products	37,342	19	27,044	17	24,194	19	21,861	19	20,134	21
Engineering services	10,002	5	10,563	6	9,593	7	9,860	9	8,823	9
Operating totals†	195,345	100%	160,561	100%	132,953	100%	111,452	100%	96,243	100%
Discontinued operations	—		—		1,010		1,520		1,493	
Intergroup sales eliminated in										
consolidation	(977)		(632)		(733)		(842)		(856)	
Total net sales	$194,368		$159,929		$133,230		$112,130		$96,880	

Operating pretax profits

Operating group	1974*		1973		1972		1971		1970	
Hand tools	$ 8,876	51%	$ 7,575	48%	$ 6,605	52%	$ 4,778	48%	$ 3,634	48%
Aluminum products	6,577	38	5,047	32	3,331	26	2,243	22	1,150	15
Industrial products	1,262	7	2,421	15	1,161	9	1,014	10	886	12
Engineering services	620	4	708	5	1,624	13	2,042	20	1,893	25
Operating totals†	17,335	100%	15,751	100%	12,721	100%	10,077	100%	7,563	100%
Discontinued operations	—		—		(205)		(218)		(317)	
Interest expense, net	(3,214)		(1,978)		(1,363)		(1,692)		(1,268)	
Corporate items, net	(1,841)		(1,651)		(1,458)		(1,572)		(876)	
Pretax Income	$ 12,280		$ 12,122		$ 9,695		$ 6,595		$ 5,102	

Return on sales (%)

Operating group	1974*	1973	1972	1971	1970
Hand tools	10.7	11.3	11.5	10.5	8.9
Aluminum products	10.1	9.0	8.0	6.5	4.3
Industrial products	3.4	9.0	4.8	4.6	4.4
Engineering services	6.2	6.7	16.9	20.7	21.5
Operating totals†	8.9	9.8	9.5	9.0	7.8
Pretax Income	6.3	7.6	7.3	5.9	5.3

Note: All dollar amounts are expressed in thousands.
*Reflects change to LIFO method of inventory valuation.
†Sales are before deducting intergroup sales, and operating pretax profits are before interest, unallocated corporate administration expenses, and an extraordinary item in 1972.
Source: 1974 annual report.

The *Easco Aluminum Products Group* was one of the nation's largest independent extruders of aluminum. Easco was engaged in the production of billets and extruded shapes and components for use in the building products, furniture, transportation, appliance, electronics, and leisure equipment industries.

The *Easco Industrial Products Group* manufactured metal gratings, specialty fasteners, precision springs, and marine products. The major product, gratings, was used as floorings, walkways, and stairs primarily in plants of the electrical-generating, petroleum, petrochemical, chemical, and water- and waste-treating industries.

The *Engineering Services Group* was Easco's smallest business segment, representing roughly 5 percent of net sales. The unit conducted environmental analyses and performed a wide variety of engineering and architectural services of a planning, design, technical management, and supervisory nature. Its services included the design of airports and terminals, mass transit systems, fixed and movable bridges, highways and urban expressways, tunnels, port facilities, sewage and disposal systems, and other environmental-ecological systems.

Each of these major business segments was directed by a corporate officer responsible for planning, manufacturing, and marketing in response to the needs and opportunities of designated markets, with accountability for profit and capital employed. Within these major business segments were individual operating units, each headed by its own management team.

THE HAND TOOL GROUP

The Easco Hand Tool Group was divided into two parts, the Moore Company and Easco Tools, Inc. The Moore Company manufactured all of the ratchets, sockets, and wrenches marketed by Sears under its Craftsman name. Moore contributed almost $70 million in sales in 1974.

Easco Tools, Inc., comprised three operating companies with combined sales of over $10 million in 1974. The three operating companies were: Ennis Manufacturing Company, maker of striking tools (hammers, etc.), cement tools, trowels, and axes; Dreier Manufacturing Company, maker of quality hacksaw frames; and Hillsboro Manufacturing Company, manufacturer of high-quality stampings, automobile parts, and pinch bars. (For an organization chart of Easco Tools, Inc., see Exhibit 3.)

The consolidation of the three component companies of Easco Tools, Inc., had taken place in 1974, just one year ago. The purpose of the consolidation was to complement Easco's capabilities and expertise in tool production and design by developing programs in the fields of marketing and distribution. In order to provide a framework

Exhibit 3
Organization chart

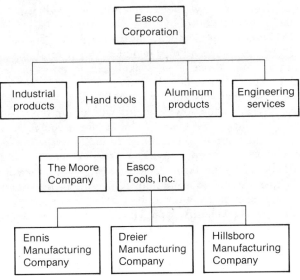

Source: Company Records.

for administrative and marketing direction, the new company was formed.

Prior to the consolidation, the three component companies had each been responsible for its own marketing efforts. The tools manufactured by the companies had been marketed under several brand names to retail markets, professional mechanics, and industrial markets. In 1975 the various tool lines were culled and consolidated, and one brand name, Easco, was established over all products. In addition, a reorganization of the sales force was begun on a national basis, such that each sales representative would handle the full Easco line.

IMAGE

Dillard felt that a major portion of his marketing problems was due to the different natures of the operating companies making up Easco Tools. Not only had the companies manufactured different products under different brand names, but their quality, distribution, corporate images, and whole "personalities" were different. According to Dillard,

> Ennis Manufacturing Company, at present, has the image of a low-end, "promotion"-type manufacturer. It has the image of a company with lots of different items, so many items that buyers think that they are bound to find a good deal. The Ennis lines all originated from earlier acquisitions, so that even within Ennis we had several brand names.

Quite often the products were sold with no trademark or identifying number at all. But people have been buying because Ennis has been low-priced. Even at that, we need better-quality products, better service information, and better deliveries.

Dreier Manufacturing Company has a limited line of hacksaw frames only. It has traditionally sold on a manufacture-for-resale basis; that is, Dreier sold to some 30-odd private label manufacturers or distributors who sold the products under their own names. Consequently, the Dreier name was relatively unknown, but those who were aware of the name associated an image of high quality with it. For the most part, the actual tool users have never heard of Dreier, but as you get further back in the distribution system, the name and quality image are better and better known. So Dreier does have some small consumer equity.

The Hillsboro Manufacturing Company is really a new entity in the hand tools business. It is our intention to use the facility as an original equipment manufacturer of automobile parts, pry bars, pliers, and other hand tool products. Primarily, then, Hillsboro is a manufacturing plant only.

DISTRIBUTION

Dillard was also concerned about the distribution under the old organization. He had been hired originally to accomplish the reorganization of the sales force and to manage the new national sales group. However, he was assigned additional duties as director of marketing, and the three sales forces of Dreier, Ennis, and Hillsboro were, as a result, still more or less distinct. However, the process of consolidation was progressing and was planned for completion by the national sales meeting to be held just prior to the hardware show in August. Beyond his concerns about the effects of reorganization on the sales force, Dillard was also uncomfortable about its effect upon current customers. As he put it:

> We have no distribution. Oh, we have some 2,000 active accounts, but most of these are the wrong kind. Dreier, for instance, has been selling to Proto, J. C. Penney, and Snap-On for resale under these customers' brand names. Under the Easco name these customers will be our direct competition. On the Ennis side, we have been selling in many instances direct to retailers, even small "mom and pop" hardware stores that were using our hammers as promotional items. In other words, what we have in distribution is in some ways worse than no distribution. How do you tell someone you won't sell to him anymore?

BRAND NAME

The Easco name was also a source of concern to Dillard. The decision had been made to use one consolidated brand name early in Easco Tool's existence. According to Dillard,

The first step in our strategy was to form our own marketing and distribution administration for Ennis, Dreier, and Hillsboro marketing management. Our second step was to further consolidate into one brand, and to steamline and upgrade our product offerings. It was a big decision to drop the names of the existing lines and go with a totally new name, Easco. We could very well have gone the same way as one of our competitors, Cooper Industries. They advertise and promote the individual brand names of their component companies separately. You undoubtedly know their products: Crescent wrenches, Nicholson files, and Lufkin Measuring Tools. But Cooper was in a different situation than we were. They had a very powerful consumer franchise for each of their lines, while we had only a little loyalty for our operating companies, and even that was probably lost with our new name.

We spent a lot of time, effort, and money on the development of a new name and new graphics. Our alternatives included Benchmark and Pridemark as well as Easco. The president of Easco Tools, David St. Clair, made the final selection of Easco. According to our research, it rated high in graphic potential on the tools themselves and it tied in well with the name of the company. There are some problems, though, and the name is certainly not perfect. You'd be amazed at the number of pronunciations we get. As a result, and because the name has no actual meaning, there is no particular reason for a person to remember the name readily.

PRODUCT

The management of Easco Corporation was very conscious of the need for quality in the hand tools group. In 1973 Easco began a capital improvement program for hand tools, and by the end of 1974 it had spent nearly $8 million to expand capacity, increase productivity, and improve environmental controls. As part of this program, the hand tool management improved manufacturing processes, cut costs, and increased product quality. Dillard commented:

> Our products are competitive with the top consumer names in hand tools. They are top-quality products with a moderate to low price. They are not the absolute best tools you can buy, for the most part, but they are the best value. We really have no new product characteristics up our sleeves, but we do have some innovations in merchandising. While we have tried to streamline our product offerings, we still have over 300 products and we are expanding our lines into new areas.

CUSTOMERS

On the basis of the report by Mason, Nagel & Osborne and his own evaluation of the sales force and account structure, Dillard made several observations about the customers Easco would be serving and about their needs and wants:

Our primary customers should be the large retail hardware chains, such as Ace Hardware and Cotter, and mass merchandise or discount store feeders, as well as the 28,000 or so retail hardware dealers, to be sold to through some 300 or more hardware distributors. In order to get this type of distribution and hold on to it, we will have to have more than good quality and good price. These types of customers are interested in high return on investment, gross margins, and rapid product turnover. The average yearly product turn for one of these outfits is about 2.75 times. Most, however, target their purchasing for a turnover of about 4 times. In other words, they must have an extremely fine-tuned product line which they carry, and, as a result, they are very sophisticated in their buying. A successful manufacturer must be aware of their needs and be sophisticated to deal with them. We have divided

Exhibit 4
Publication evaluation form: Circulation by job function

Publication	Total circulation	Retailers	Hardware wholesalers	Manufacturer's sales and representatives	Manufacturers
Hardware Retailing	53,177	38,789	7,021	3,216	1,999
Hardware Age	48,226	35,701	7,730	2,773	1,488
Hardware Merchandiser	53,119	45,539*	6,743	827	
American Building Supplies	32,775	24,604	5,949		2,222
Building Supply News	32,435	28,543	5,836		56
Home Center	28,727	22,040	4,673	471	1,386
National Home Center News	Not audited 25,000	Not audited	Not audited	Not audited	Not audited
American Paint & Wallcoverings Dealer	33,650	29,809	3,841		
Wallcoverings	8,463	5,008 1,001	498	507	25
Hardlines Wholesaling	11,966		11,966		
Southern Hardware	16,550	14,008	1,575	726	
Discount Merchandiser	35,041	29,908	1,470		
Discount Store News	27,669	16,060	1,282	8,376	
The Carpenter	447,970				
Masonry	Not audited				
Masonry Industry	17,009	Not audited	Not audited	Not audited	Not audited
Flooring	20,067	16,406	1,461	1,356	

*Includes Retail Hardware Stores of 23,199.
Source: Company records.

our products into two categories: regular items which will have a fast turnover, and "service items" which are slower moving but necessary. On the regular items we offer a standard 33⅓ percent markup, but on the "service items" we offer a 40 percent markup, so our margins are better than most of the industry.

You see, we don't sell like a normal consumer good. Our products are something like consumer durables. For the nonprofessional like you or me, a hammer or other tool is expected to be durable. It should last forever and be handed down from generation to generation. But a carpenter or builder will literally *wear out* three top-quality hammers in a year. So, the end user of a tool, depending on his point of view, expects different things, and the seller of tools must have a selection to meet different demands. That's where Easco comes in: we want to function as

Miscellaneous	Cost per page	Cost per thousand	Frequency of issue	Type of audit	Comments
2,152	$1,350	$25.39	Monthly	ABC AIA	NRHA publication
534	1,355	28.10	Monthly	ABC AIA	
	1,640	30.87		BPA	
	2,290	43.11	Monthly	AIA	Tabloid size
	1,760	53.70	Monthly	BPA AIA	Building materials oriented
	1,660	51.18	Monthly	ABC AIA	Building materials oriented
157	1,645	57.27	Monthly	BPA AIA	Formerly *Building Materials Merchant*
Not audited	1,204	48.16		ABC	Tabloid—new publication from
	1,814	72.56		Applied for	Lebhar-Friedman
	955	28.38	Monthly	BPA AIA	
573	660	78.01	Monthly		
498					
26					
51					
286					
	660	55.18	Feb., April, June, Aug., Sept., Oct.	Not audited	Wholesalers only Not audited
241	720	43.50	Monthly	BPA AIA	Regional
1,472				BPA	
1,230	1,750	58.52	Montly	AIA	
961					
1,786	1,646	59.48	Alternate	ABC	
195	2,480	89.62	weeks	AIA	Tabloid size
447,970	1,500	3.34	Monthly	Not audited	Extending low CPM
				Not audited	
	458	26.94	Monthly	Not audited	Primarily Pacific state association related
Bal.	1,060	53.00	Monthly	ABC/AIA	16,406 *Dealer and contractors*

marketers to help our customers sell a good program, to help pull through products. Our purpose is *not* just to write an order.

MEDIA

Dillard was fairly comfortable about the media to be used in promoting the new Easco brand. His major concerns were about the weight to be given each medium. Further, he felt that certain media were required, but he wondered whether there might not be some more unorthodox medium which would be more effective or efficient.

> The first thing that we must do is get out a new catalog using the Easco name and showing the modified lines. New price lists showing distributor, dealer, and list prices and terms will be needed as well. We estimate a cost of $1 per catalog.
>
> Another *must* is a booth at the annual Hardware Show in Chicago. To give you some idea of the importance of the August Hardware Show, we sort of use the show as the start of our fiscal year. As a bare minimum cost for the show we estimate $1,500, but we expect to spend $5,000 to $10,000.
>
> The trade magazines are important too, both as an advertising medium and as a public relations vehicle. The specific magazines to be used have yet to be decided, but some commitment will have to be made to the trade magazines. Everybody in the industry *reads* the trade magazines; they don't just glance through or let them stack up in a corner—they read them.

Dillard was also considering the use of direct mail, pamphlets, special information packets for customers, sales aids, and promotional packages. While he could recognize advantages to the use of such vehicles, he still wondered about how they would fit into an overall advertising program and about how much effort he should concentrate on them relative to his "required" media. (For a comparison of costs and circulation by magazine, see Exhibit 4.)

CONCLUSION

Dillard felt that he was quite familiar with the factors which should bear upon his decisions but that he was having difficulty coming to grips with an overall structure. He wondered how he could organize his thoughts into explicit statements of advertising objectives and strategy.

He knew that the introduction of the new Easco brand was not going to be easy, given limited resources and vigorous competition in the field, but he was convinced that a properly planned program would succeed. As he put it:

> When you try to change a brand, it's like pushing at a great amorphous mass. Customers' buying habits show up in their speech patterns,

and their speech patterns reinforce their buying habits. It's a vicious circle which is very difficult to break into when your competition is able to spend more money than you can. But when you are fighting with spitballs against elephant guns, I guess it is just a question of using the right color spitballs.

APPENDIX: EXCERPTS FROM REPORT ON HAND TOOLS MARKETS (MASON, NAGEL & OSBORNE)

EXECUTIVE SUMMARY

Primary market: Distributors

Secondary markets: Hardware retailers, home centers, building supply dealers, mass merchandisers

Tertiary markets: Paint/decorator and wall covering dealers, department stores, auto supply stores, catalog showrooms, drug and grocery chains, chain and variety stores, farm co-ops, military exchanges, schools, and premium and industrial distributors.

MARKET: PRIMARY

The primary market is the hardware distributor. Within this group there has been in recent years a tremendous growth of groups and chains. For example, in the area of "wholesaler alliances," Sentry Hardware has 4,000 stores; Pro-Hardware, 2,700; and Liberty, 1,600. Among "voluntary chains," Cotter claims 4,800; Ace, 2,900; American, 2,300; and Coast-to-Coast, 1,200.

There are approximately 7,000 executives and salesmen within this primary distribution. The three major hardware publications list their wholesaler circulations to this group from 6,743 to 7,730. *Hardware Retailing* magazine publishes the *Hardware Wholesaler Directory,* which lists all the important wholesalers. This is a must for every Easco representative.

The trend seems to be toward retailers buying from more wholesalers. They are relying less on single sources. For example, in 1969, 12 percent of the retailers purchased from one wholesaler. In 1973, only 2 percent purchased from a single wholesaler. Those buying from two or three wholesalers went from 41 percent in 1969 to 25% in 1973 (*Hardware Age,* October 1973).

Another factor to consider in the importance of the primary distribution to manufacturers such as Easco in government pressure on imports, particularly the "less expensive" Japanese tools. This pressure has caused so-called cheap imports to come within 15 percent in price of domestic tools, according to *Discount Store News* (September 1974). The following list indicates sources of supply for the ever-growing home center retailer (per *Home Center* magazine).

Home centers' sources of supply

79.1%	Direct from manufacturer
46.9	Co-op buying groups
85.0	Building material distributors
87.0	Hardware wholesalers
64.4	Paint sundries wholesalers
11.6	Other wholesalers

Note: These figures indicate that these home centers do some buying from these sources for *some* or *all* of their products.

MARKET: RETAIL

Hardware retailers

The number of hardware retailers varies from source to source. The National Retail Hardware Association (NRHA) claims there are 24,500. They refer to these outlets as "primary" hardware retailers.

According to *Hardware Retailing* magazine, sales volume through

Table 1
Selected product categories (sales percentages by type of outlet)

Product category	Hardware stores ($3,600 million)	Home centers ($3,797 million)	Building materials dealers ($1,306 million)
Large tools	9.0%	7.4%	3.6%
Paint and sundries	12.0	9.8	8.2
Hand tools	4.5	3.0	1.8

Table 2
Selected hand tool sales (percentages by type of outlet)

Hand tool	Hardware stores ($162 million)	Home centers ($114 million)	Building materials dealers ($24 million)
Axes, hatchets	12.1%	9.9%	0.6%
Chisels	2.4	1.3	0.4
Crowbars, etc.	1.1	1.6	0.4
Hacksaw frames and blades	3.0	2.5	0.4
Hammers	14.9	8.6	2.6
Knives, utility	4.4	1.8	0.6
Levels	3.6	2.9	0.9
Screwdrivers	11.3	4.0	0.7

Note: An update of this study is in process and should be ready for distribution later in 1975.

hardware stores is $4.7 billion; building materials dealers, $2.0 billion; and home centers, $5.9 billion. These figures indicate the continued improvement of the traditional hardware store as well as the burgeoning retail outlet called the "home center."

Tables 1 and 2 from the "Product Sales Study," conducted by *Hardware Retailing*, show a fairly accurate breakdown of tools through the three outlets previously referred to.

Home centers

The following marketing figures and projections will tend to point out, by some of their contradictions, the problem of definition of home centers. However, one can conclude that these stores are now, and will continue to be, extremely important.

According to Frost & Sullivan, Inc.'s 1974 study, there are now between 4,000 and 6,000 home centers. They enjoy an average of 3.44 percent return on sales. Of the 25 largest home center chains, 16 reported that 50 percent or more of their sales were to the "do-it-yourselfer."

Frost & Sullivan predicts that by 1984 home centers will supply 48 percent of the market in hardware goods. The total sales through home centers in 1984 is predicted to be $65 billion. Again, according to Frost & Sullivan, lumber and wood products will account for $7.9 billion; decorator products, $5.6 billion; hardware, $4.6 billion; and paint, $3.3 billion.

Building Supply News (March 1975) predicts a 20 percent increase in home centers by next year. *BSN* logically assumes that the bulk of this growth will occur in the older, high-density population areas such as New England and the East North Central states.

From another perspective, albeit biased, *Home Center* magazine, in a 1975 study, shows 11,000 to 12,000 home centers now in existence, with 90 percent of these single-unit operations. *Home Center* projects sales through home centers at $23.9 billion (56 percent to consumers)—12½ percent, of these dollars, or $3 billion, in hardware, hand, or power tools.

National Home Center News, in a study of "hardware/home improvement products manufacturers," indicated a change in importance for home centers from sixth to second between 1970 and 1973, in type of retail outlet. This same source predicts that home centers will be the number one hardlines retail seller in 1976.

National Home Center News claims that its circulation includes 600 chains operating 5,500 stores plus 13,500 "super" hardware stores plus 3,000 home center departments in mass merchandisers and general merchandising stores. Among the largest is Rickel, which in 1973 did $58.2 million worth of business through 15 units alone.

Of more specific interest for Easco Tools is the following information:

91.5 percent of the home centers stock hand tools.

75 percent of the home centers stock masonry tools.

82 percent of the home centers stock carpenter tools.

This same source (*Home Center* magazine, July 1973) predicted the following annual percentage increases through these same outlets:

Lawn and garden tools	8.2%
Hand tools	9.6
Power tools	9.7
Housewares	7.4

Building supply dealers

Called "lumber and building materials dealers" by *Hardware Retailing* magazine, this contractor/customer sales outlet is of importance to manufacturers of hand tools.

Trends in recent years have seen this traditional retailer selling more to the consumer and, because of the recent building slump, selling less to contractors.

Building Supply News (March 1975), which of course has a vested interest, reflects the optimism and hope of all of us that the construction business, and housing in particular, will turn around soon, which will, of course, be a boon to the building supply dealer as well as to the manufacturers of his products. It is predicted (*Discount Store News*) that total sales through mass merchandisers will be $50 billion in 1980, with a total of 7,200 store units. Presently, the hardware, tools, plumbing, lawn and garden, and electrical categories account for sales of $1.5 billion.

A number of people and functions throughout this complex retailer must be reached for the typical sale. At headquarters, depending upon the company, any or all of the following may have to be influenced for selling: the president, general merchandising manager, sales manager, division manager, buyer, and advertising manager. At the local level, again depending upon the organizational structure of the chain, the following have some influence in the decision: the regional merchandise manager, regional manager, store manager, and department manager.

The mass merchandiser has traditionally bought on price, but this, along with his image, has changed rapidly in recent years. The following, in addition to price, are important to him:

Brand name.

Self-sell packaging.

Good point of purchase.

Stock control help.

Plan-o-Grams.

Preticketing.

Personnel training, etc.

In other words, the program with the product.

Paint/decorator and wall covering dealers

It is not easy to define from available sources the exact market for hand tools through these retailers. However, a recent study conducted by Mason, Nagel & Osborne indicates a market of $20 million to $25 million. There exists very aggressive merchandise-oriented and well-entrenched competition. It includes Hyde, Red Devil, and Warner, to name a few.

There appears to be no real brand loyalty here. For example, *Hardware Merchandiser* magazine (March 1975) quotes a dealer: "The dealer is influential in that the consumer relies largely upon his recommendation." This means that among these dealers national brand name tends to sell the product to a much lesser degree than the dealer himself.

Not to be ignored are the paint contractors and paperhangers who buy at the PD&WC store for three basic reasons:

They have a line of credit.

All their needs are in one spot.

Very often the dealer will supply them with new business leads.

Just as in the other categories, the importance of groups and chains is not to be ignored. A significant factor in this market is Sherwin Williams. There seems to be a developing trend whereby manufacturers sell directly to consumers.

MARKET: CONSUMER

According to Maurice Grossman, president of Evan's Retail Group, the do-it-yourselfer (DIY) is the "hottest business in America." Grossman's stores are a clear example of what a home center is. There are now over 250 of them, and they were the first in America to hold in-store clinics for the DIY. The home center handyman is, of course, the brightest fire, flamed by today's economy. The following chart taken from the "Dealer Advertising Audit," *Building Supply News* (1974), indicates specifically this change toward homeowner sales from 1965 to 1973.

	1973	1970	1968	1965	Percent change, 1965–1973
Builders	40.8%	41.3%	42.4%	43.3%	− 5.8%
Homeowners	38.6	35.2	32.6	31.8	+21.4
Industrial	10.1	11.2	11.3	10.3	− 2.0
Farm	10.5	12.3	13.7	14.6	−28.1
	100.0%	100.0%	100.0%	100.0%	

With carpenters making an average of $12.68 per hour and painters making $10.40 per hour, it is not difficult to see that the homeowner will be doing more and more of the repairs, alterations, and additions around the house.

Again referring to Frost & Sullivan's study, residential alterations are growing at a rate of 8 percent to 9 percent yearly (50 percent of this DIY). The total market for products and equipment only is $12 billion. The Department of Commerce reports $22 billion, which includes the professional craftsman.

Home Center magazine reports the following profile of its audience:

> 69 percent make over $10,000 income a year.
>
> Those over 55 years old buy most ($13.20 average purchase).
>
> The 25–44 age group does 66 percent of the home center business in total.

Another demographic factor not to be overlooked is the importance of the female hard goods buyer. According to the National Retail Hardware Association (NRHA), seven studies made for hardware stores showed that:

1. Thirty percent of purchases are decided by the female or by the female in conjunction with the husband.
2. The female is a 33 percent factor in terms of total dollar sales.

Even more dramatic is the fact that among 17 studies conducted for home centers, 51 percent of the purchases were decided by the female alone or with her husband, representing 49 percent in sales dollars.

Heavy tool user

Tables 3 and 4 are from a study which was instigated by Stanley and conducted by *Popular Mechanics* a few years ago. The specific hand tool ownership information should be valuable to Easco Tool's marketing efforts.

Table 3
Hand tools: Personal use

	Own one or more	Total number owned	Number owned						
			1	2	3	4	5–7	8–10	11+
Hammer	94.1%	9,343,139	14.0%	19.9%	20.6%	15.5%	17.8%	4.3%	2.0%
Screwdriver	92.6	12,804,453	7.6	1.7	1.2	3.2	19.3	26.7	32.8
Handsaw	90.7	4,264,710	22.8	26.2	18.8	12.9	8.4	1.1	0.4
Hacksaw	88.7	2,527,172	47.9	31.2	6.5	1.5	1.4	0.3	—
Pliers	92.4	7,689,897	9.4	9.7	13.8	18.5	25.4	10.6	5.0
Files	89.9	9,190,030	9.8	10.1	8.5	9.1	20.0	14.3	17.6
Chain wrench	16.3	319,982	14.6	1.5	0.2	0.1	—	—	—
Monkey wrench	60.1	1,844,199	35.0	14.7	4.9	3.3	2.0	0.2	0.1
Pipe wrench	77.8	3,593,780	24.1	20.1	14.3	10.0	7.7	1.6	0.1
Adjustable wrench	83.8	4,194,177	22.4	22.1	14.3	12.2	10.2	2.7	—
Socket wrench	81.7	3,967,093	34.4	21.4	11.9	3.2	2.1	1.7	7.0
Torque wrench	18.0	354,389	16.0	1.4	0.6	—	—	—	—
Surform	14.8	321,703	11.1	3.2	0.4	—	—	—	—
Folding wood rule	66.0	1,892,369	39.3	17.8	5.2	1.8	1.6	0.3	—
Level	85.5	2,638,994	38.8	31.3	11.4	3.2	0.5	0.1	0.1
No answer	5.6								

Base: 967

Source: *Popular Mechanics Study*, 1973.

Table 4
Hand tools: Use on job

	Own one or more	Total number owned	Number owned						
			1	2	3	4	5–7	8–10	11+
Hammer	12.4%	655,448	3.2%	3.0%	2.5%	1.1%	2.2%	0.3%	0.1%
Screwdriver	12.0	1,310,895	0.8	1.2	1.9	0.9	2.1	2.5	2.6
Handsaw	5.3	215,042	2.0	1.8	0.7	0.4	0.2	0.2	—
Hacksaw	8.7	242,567	5.7	2.0	0.3	0.5	0.1	0.1	—
Pliers	12.0	765,549	2.3	3.2	1.7	1.4	2.2	0.6	0.6
Files	8.7	770,710	1.4	1.2	1.1	1.0	1.7	0.9	1.4
Chain wrench	2.9	92,898	2.1	0.4	—	0.2	0.1	—	0.1
Monkey wrench	3.4	94,618	2.3	0.5	0.2	0.4	—	—	—
Pipe wrench	6.3	309,660	2.0	1.5	0.8	1.0	0.8	0.2	—
Adjustable wrench	10.0	486,855	2.9	3.2	1.7	0.7	1.0	0.2	0.3
Socket wrench	8.8	452,448	3.7	1.9	1.1	0.6	0.6	0.2	0.7
Torque wrench	1.7	32,686	1.5	0.2	—	—	—	—	—
Surform	1.0	49,890	0.4	0.2	0.2	0.1	—	—	0.1
Folding wood rule	4.6	115,262	2.9	1.4	0.2	0.1	—	—	—
Level	6.0	178,915	3.1	1.6	1.1	0.2	—	—	—
No answer	86.5								

Base 967

Source: *Popular Mechanics Study*, 1973.

MARKET: PROFESSIONAL CONSUMER

By professional consumer, we mean the carpenter, the mason, and other contractors who buy hand tools for personal and/or at-home use.

Although new construction is down considerably, according to *Building Supply News,* sales to builders and contractors are still a large portion of the total building materials market (40 percent). Thirty-six percent of home center sales are to builders and contractors (*Home Center* study, 1974).

COMPETITIVE ADVERTISING ACTIVITY

Table 5 is a representative but not inclusive listing of advertising expenditures by some of the competing tool manufacturers.

Table 5
Competitive advertising strategy

	*Trade advertising only, 1972**	*Trade advertising only, 1973**	*Consumer advertising only, 1973 (000)†*	*Trade advertising, January–June 1974**
Ames (garden tools)	$94,854	$71,334	$ 153.9	$64,524
Arrow (stapler)	66,443	93,651	110.2	41,446
Channel Lock	32,775	43,367	114.2	19,452
Cooper Group	87,563	97,202	45.5	1,000
Cotter (wholesaler)	30,006	19,577	3,940.4	2,506
Estwing (hammers)	6,312	14,183	n.a.	6,426
Goldblatt (trowels)	0	3,043	452.2	6,306
Great Neck§	9	0	n.a.	0
Hyde	51,718	72,733	n.a.	14,149
Marshalltown (trowels)	6,510	8,377	n.a.	4,186
Red Devil	46,637	59,508	165.5	34,068
Sandvik (saws)	1,098	4,155	n.a.	8,178
Stanley	71,188	42,346	1,404.2	28,170
Vaco (low-cost line)	4,823	26,224	60.0‡	4,386
Vaughn (hammers)	21,018	24,577	n.a.	8,064

* Source: Rome report.
† Source: *Leading National Advertisers,* 1973.
‡ Estimated trade magazine only.
§ Has begun to advertise in 1975.

Case 4–6

National Beauty Supply, Ltd.

National Beauty Supply (NBS) was the largest distributor of beauty products in Canada. However, for the past two years the firm had operated at a loss (Exhibits 1 and 2). To help improve profits, the president and the board of directors hired a management consultant by the name of Mary King. King's job was to examine the operations of the company and prepare a report on needed changes.

HISTORY OF THE COMPANY

NBS was established in 1927 in Hamilton, Ontario, as a distributor organization to sell beauty supplies directly to beauty salons on a wholesale basis. NBS expanded over the years to the point where it presently maintains 10 fully stocked branches serving most areas of Canada with the exception of Quebec and British Columbia. The Montreal branch was closed in March 1980, and the Quebec City branch was closed and sold in June 1980. Present operations serve approximately 5,000 beauty shops through a permanent staff of 18 salespeople. The products are the lines of better-known brands of merchandise that are used and sold in beauty salons.

This industry is characterized by:

1. Small regional distributors which offer intensive sales coverage and operate on a low overhead. They offer the same basic product line as the larger companies in the industry.
2. A trend toward an increased emphasis on pricing and volume considerations, particularly in the large metropolitan areas. Some distributors are reducing prices, and thus margins, to actively compete in the high-volume areas.
3. An increase in product volume as well as sales volume in dollars.
4. A high rate of new product introduction and thus relatively high product obsolescence.
5. Very liberal credit terms. This situation can be attributed to the number of distributors offering products to the salon, their willingness to accept business knowing that the extended credit will be taken, and finally the inability of the salon operators to manage their finances properly.
6. The beauty salons are generally owned and operated by women who are considered poor managers.

This case was prepared by P. R. MacPherson of the University of Guelph, Ontario, Canada.

Exhibit 1

NATIONAL BEAUTY SUPPLY, LTD.
Comparative Balance Sheet
December 31, 1976 to 1979

	1976	*1977*	*1978*	*1979*
Assets				
Current assets:				
Cash.	$ 1,360	$ 1,510	$ 1,640	$ 1,640
Accounts receivable (net)	292,289	343,778	380,319	331,481
Inventory (lower of cost or market)	279,282	343,983	343,148	315,125
Prepaid expenses.	7,458	3,598	6,847	7,627
Federal and provincial taxes recoverable . . .				
Total current assets	580,389	692,869	731,954	655,873
Fixed assets:				
Office and warehouse equipment.	36,027	43,550	58,091	58,869
Less Accumulated depreciation	(25,196)	(26,211)	(29,640)	(33,297)
Goodwill	1	1	1	1
Total assets.	$591,221	$710,209	$760,406	$681,446
Liabilities				
Current liabilities:*				
Bank advances (secured)†	$ 57,791	$ 77,253	$158,140	$ 89,803
Accounts payable and accrued expenses .	133,540	183,560	156,852	196,655
Salespeople's interest-bearing balances‡ .	56,510	72,362	90,289	58,237
Federal and provincial taxes.	1,118	8,966	—	—
Total current liabilities	248,959	342,141	405,281	344,695
Net worth:				
Issued and fully paid				
Preferred, 14,725 shares	29,450	29,450	29,450	29,450
Common, 60,000 shares	10,000	10,000	10,000	10,000
Reserve for future decline in inventory				
value.	15,000	15,000	15,000	15,000
Retained earnings	287,812	313,618	300,675	282,301
Total liabilities	$591,221	$710,209	$760,406	$681,446
Ratio analysis:				
Current ratio	2.3	2.0	2.0	1.8
Net working capital ($).	331,430	360,728	326,673	321,178
Acid test.	1.20	1.04	.96	1.01
Receivable turnover (days)	62	69	71	67
Inventory turnover (days).	93	112	109	105
Gross operating profit to net worth (percent)	8	14	(.05)	(.05)
Net profit to net worth (percent).	6	9	(.025)	(.05)
Accounts payable (days)	46	58	49	67

  * Exclusive of contingent liabilities. On August 31, 1980, these were: customers notes under discount—$221,255; and arrears on preferred dividends—$139,887.

  † The company retained $10,000 in a cash discount to conform with the loan requirements. This amount was subtracted from the bank advance liability.

  ‡ Demand deposits loaned to the company by 13 of the salespeople at 6 percent per annum. Balances varied from $800 to $13,000 for individual salespeople.

Exhibit 2

NATIONAL BEAUTY SUPPLY, LTD.
Comparative Income Statements
1976 to 1979

	1976		1977		1978		1979	
Sales (less freight)	$1,683,160	100%	$1,793,281	100%	$1,827,690	100%	$1,736,336	100%
Cost of sales:								
Inventory January 1	295,957		279,282		340,448		343,148	
Purchases	1,055,316		1,135,177		1,126,920		1,051,253	
Cost of goods manufactured	27,046		28,493		6,153			
	1,379,320		1,442,952		1,473,521		1,394,401	
Less inventory December 31	279,291		340,448		343,148		315,125	
Cost of goods sold	1,100,038	65.3%	1,102,504	61.4%	1,130,373	61.9%	1,079,276	62.1%
Gross profit	583,122	34.7%	690,777	38.6%	697,317	38.1%	657,060	37.9%
Selling expenses:								
Salaries, commissions, and travel	238,393	14.1%	221,046	12.3%	224,494	12.2%	217,617	12.5%
General selling	23,265	1.3%	25,291	1.3%	22,147	1.2%	28,997	1.6%
Advertisement	20,854	1.1%	50,737	2.7%	50,797	2.7%	26,560	1.5%
General administration:								
Branch operating expense*	130,212	7.7%	160,550	9.0%	183,489	10.0%	179,608	10.3%
Freight out	39,441	2.1%	43,094	2.4%	50,280	2.5%	43,946	2.5%
Administration expense	134,144	7.9%	166,968	9.3%	205,370	11.2%	183,949	10.5%
Total administration and selling	586,310	34.8%	667,686	37.2%	736,574	40.3%	680,677	39.9%
Operating profit	(3,189)		23,091		(39,257)		(23,617)	
Other income:								
Purchase discounts	17,371		17,786		8,957		4,165	
Finance charges	13,211		11,761		10,406		292	
Common sales tax	354		530		632		786	
Total other income	30,936		30,077		19,995		5,243	
Profit before tax	27,747	1.6%	53,168	2.9%	(19,262)	(2.2%)	(18,374)	(2.0%)
Taxes	6,500		20,000					
Net profit	$ 21,247	1.3%	$ 33,168	1.8%	$ (19,262)	(2.2%)	$ (18,374)	(2.0%)

* Represents actual branch office expense: rent, salaries, etc. (excludes promotion, bad debts expense, and advertising).
Source: Company records.

7. Generally there is a close relationship between the salesperson and the beauty salon owner/manager.
8. The salespeople are usually paid on a commission basis rather than a salary basis.
9. Deal selling is an industry-wide sales promotion technique.

SALES ORGANIZATION

The sales department, headed by Mike Stone, is outlined in Exhibit 3. The branch offices are run by branch managers who operate,

Exhibit 3
NBA organizational chart

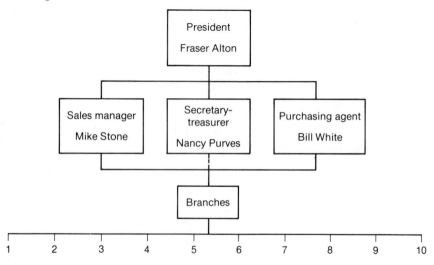

generally, as full-time salespeople. In addition to the branch managers, there are 11 salespeople located as shown in Exhibit 4.

Fraser Alton, the president of NBS, was asked by Mary King what type of function he thought the sales manager should perform. He replied that he expected him to be out policing the sales territories personally, concentrating on the weak branches. He did not want the sales manager to spend too much time in the profitable areas like the Maritimes and the Alberta branches, but rather to direct his attention to such branches as Winnipeg, Hamilton, Regina, Toronto, and Sudbury, which were relatively unprofitable areas.

Mike Stone, the sales manager, had a different concept of his function. He believed that he should devote the largest portion of his time to the strong areas because NBS had to maintain its strength in the existing strong areas, or else it would fail.

Exhibit 4
Branch locations and staff

Branch	Location	Manager	Serving	Personnel
1	Halifax	Mike Kavenaugh	Nova Scotia	1 clerk, 1 shipper
2	Moncton	C. D. Bodig	New Brunswick, Prince Edward Island	2 salespeople, 2 clerks, 2 shippers
3	Ottawa	Fred Wilkenson	Ottawa City, eastern Ontario, western Quebec	1 salesperson, 1 clerk, 1 shipper
4	Sudbury	Albany Smith	Northern Ontario, Quebec	1 clerk, 1 shipper
5	Toronto	Russell Reid	Metro Toronto and sections of Ontario	3 salespeople, 2 clerks, 1 shipper
6	Hamilton	Harland Jones	Hamilton and Niagara Peninsula	1 salesperson, 2 clerks, 1 shipper
7	Winnipeg	Jerry Milne	Metro Winnipeg, Manitoba, and Northwestern Ontario	2 salespeople, 2 clerks, 1 shipper
8	Regina	Ted Kaine	Saskatchewan	1 clerk, 1 shipper
9	Calgary	James Fairbairn	Southern Alberta	2 clerks, 1 shipper
10	Edmonton	Andrew Bendus	Northern Alberta	2 salespeople, 2 clerks, 1 shipper

INTERVIEW WITH SALES MANAGER

Mary King arranged to meet Mike Stone in his office to discuss the sales operation. The following is part of that conversation:

Stone: I have been out of this office doing shows for the last two weeks, so if you don't mind, I will take a minute and catch up with the emergencies.

He phoned Toronto to order 10 wigs for one of the warehouses. Then he turned to Mary.

Stone: That clears everything up, so where do you want to start? You know about the wigs—they are a good deal, except we are late getting them out—competitors have beaten us. I am so busy that I can never seem to catch up. I do all the work for the shows, and they take a lot of time.

King: Mr. Stone, what are all your responsibilities?

Stone: I try to get new product lines, and I work with the branch managers. I spend a lot of time in the west because I want to keep my strong areas strong, or else NBS will fail. I also figure out the NBS deal sheets.

King: You do look after the hiring and pay for the salespeople?

Stone: Yes, but I don't have time to work with the salespeople. They need counseling and better equipment. I get their daily reports [Exhibit 5], at least the ones that make them out, and I look at them and I get a feeling of how the person is doing.

Exhibit 5
Salesperson's daily report sheet

| Salesperson's name _____ |
| Salesperson's territory _____ |
| Date _____ |

Time	Customer	Location	Comments
8:00			
9:00			
10:00			
11:00			
12:00			
1:00			
2:00			
3:00			
4:00			
5:00			
6:00			

Salesperson's signature   Supervisor's signature

Date   Date

King: What if they can't send them in?

Stone: My secretary sends them an automatic reminder.

King: What are you doing about the inventory control and collections?

Stone: The inventory records are useless, and the inventory isn't nearly as high as reported. As for collections, I am concerned about that—do you have any ideas?

Later on, Stone and Nancy Purves provided more information on the sales force. The salespeople call on 12 to 16 accounts per day and work on a milk run covering their areas every three weeks. Typically they are on the road most of the five working days. During the course of an average 20-minute sales call, the salesperson solicits the requirements of the dispensable products of the salon. Nearly all of this business can be solicited on a deal basis.

Any orders taken are written up in the order book, and these are sent to the nearby warehouse daily for delivery. After the shipment is made, the warehouse mails the customer a copy of the invoice. The sale now is completed, except for collection.

During the past three years the salespeople received the wages outlined in Exhibit 6 for their efforts. Up to the end of 1978, the wages were determined on a commission basis. This schedule is shown in Exhibit 7. Part of the commission was paid at the time of sale for AA

Exhibit 6
Gross sales and wages by salespeople, 1977 to 1979 (000)

| | | 1977 | | 1978 | | 1979 | Wages | |
| | | | | | | | | |
Salespeople	Location	Sales	Wages	Sales	Wages	Sales	Salary	Total
Jones	Hamilton	$105	$14.9	$106	$13.8	$ 82	$ 9.6	$13.5
Johnson	Hamilton	88	11.0	88	11.7	64	8.1	9.5
Smith	Sudbury	81	11.9	62	7.5	84	6.0	7.1
Robertson	Toronto	18	2.8	43	6.5	42	5.8	6.5
Skinner	Toronto	15	1.9	42	5.2	42	4.8	5.2
Wilkenson, Sr.	Ottawa	57	8.3	52	7.9	61	4.8	5.8
Wilkenson, Jr.	Ottawa	57	8.3	52	7.9	61	4.8	5.8
Kennedy	Ottawa	69	8.4	72	10.0	66	6.0	7.3
Hicks	Moncton	158	20.4	162	22.8	150	13.8	17.4
Franks	Moncton	76	9.8	90	12.9	87	7.8	9.6
Kavenaugh	Halifax	95	12.1	108	15.6	114	9.6	12.4
Milne	Winnipeg	116	15.4	108	14.7	108	9.6	11.1
Fairbairn	Calgary	187	23.6	179	21.6	190	15.6	18.0
Bendus	Edmonton	116	14.2	137	17.4	122	11.4	12.8

Exhibit 7
Product sales by selected salespeople (000)

| | 1977 | | | 1978 | | | 1979 | | |
| | AA products | A products | Equipment | AA products | A products | Equipment | AA products | A products | Equipment |
Salespeople									
Jones	$26	$ 53	$26	$23	$ 57	$26	$12	$ 53	$16
Johnson	19	35	28	25	36	27	15	43	5
Smith	17	34	30	7	37	10	8	46	29
Robertson	7	9	2	16	21	6	10	24	8
Skinner	2	9	4	5	20	17	5	25	10
Wilkenson, Sr.	10	27	20	11	28	13	8	30	22
Wilkenson, Jr.	10	27	20	11	28	13	8	30	22
Kennedy	16	28	25	22	31	19	13	35	16
Hicks	55	72	31	64	78	20	49	82	14
Bodig	28	48	10	37	53	18	32	59	19
Milne	30	41	45	30	43	35	19	44	44
Bendus	29	65	22	35	79	23	22	80	16
Fairbairn	26	105	56	33	112	34	23	127	33

Commission structure

Product	Company markup	Commission total	Commission paid at sale	Commission paid at collection
AA	50%	15%	5%	10%
A	40	10	0	10
Equipment	Various	15	5	10

and A items, while a consistent 10 percent was paid at the time for collection. The salespeople met all regular operating expenses out of their own pockets.

Alton and Stone became alarmed at the low profits made by the firm and sought to cut operating expenses. Their awareness of a few high sales force salaries caused them to start cutting expenses there. Effective January 1, 1979, all salespeople were paid a monthly salary plus a 5 percent bonus on sales in excess of their respective bonus base. For example, Bill Hicks of Moncton sold $161,639 in total in 1978. Stone then arbitrarily set his 1979 objective at $170,000 and his bonus base at $140,000. Hicks was to receive $1,150 per month salary, and if he was "on objective" he would receive a $1,500 bonus. To further supplement his income, Hicks would receive approximately $2,450 as cash bonuses for selling certain cash bonus deals. Thus, Hicks's 1979 income would be $17,750 compared with his 1978 income of $22,800. (Refer to Exhibit 8 for a more detailed summary.).

Exhibit 8
Determination of salary for Bill Hicks

Estimated total 1978 sales	$160,000
Therefore bonus base of 1979 sales	140,000
Salary (10 percent of bonus base approximately)	13,800
Sales objective 1979	170,000
Possible bonus for objective 0.05 × 30,000	1,500
Estimate of cash bonus from deal sales	2,450
Total estimate income for 1979	17,750
Monthly rate	1,475

Summary of Bill Hicks's sales performance and income

	1977	1978	1979 (estimated)	1979 (actual results)
Total sales	$158,000	$162,000	$170,000	$150,000
Income	20,400	22,800	17,750	17,400

Alton recognized that he could lose his sales force with this austerity program. He had each salesperson endorse a contract to the effect that if he left NBS he would not engage in the same business in his sales area for a period of 12 months (Exhibit 9). The salespeople were also made responsible for collections in the new system even though they felt that there was no incentive to collect.

Since this new system was introduced, the salespeople have expressed serious concern over the fixed-salary approach and the pay cuts they took. Stone is considering the reintroduction of an incentive pay system to overcome this problem.

Exhibit 9
Employment contract

I hereby agree to work for the sole benefit of the National Beauty Supply, Ltd. (NBS), from the date inscribed below to such time as the company (NBS) sees fit to terminate my employment or to such date as I, Fred Wilkenson, desire to leave the employ of NBS. I have read and understand all sections of the company's (NBS) handbook, and I am fully aware that I cannot indulge in any employment whatsoever that is similar to the business of this company (NBS) for a period of one (1) year after my departure from this company (NBS).

July 3, 1979   For National Beauty Supply, Ltd.

Employee   Fraser Alton, President

SPECIAL PROMOTIONS

Annually, NBS cosponsors three or four hairstyling shows. These shows are held in Halifax, Montreal, Toronto, Winnipeg, Calgary, or Edmonton. The highlight of the shows is a showing of the latest hairstyles and an individual style competition. Manufacturers and suppliers operate merchandising booths displaying their complete lines. Salespeople are on hand throughout the entire show to solicit orders. In addition, NBS sponsors its own shows with a select group of manufacturers.

An admission fee is charged, and this revenue usually makes the shows self-supporting. If expenses exceed revenue, the differences are made up by the companies participating. Generally the shows are well attended.

ADVERTISING AND SALES PROMOTION

NBS advertises its brand products nationally with a full-page ad in *Canadian Hairdresser* every month. This advertising on an annual basis costs $4,000. Direct sales promotion is in the form of deal selling. This represents an industry sales promotion technique where the total amount paid for a deal includes the regular price plus an additional amount to cover the premium. Stone's pricing strategy is to have all premium deals self-liquidating.

The initial selling price of a product is developed by adding the desired markup plus a 10 percent markup to the original cost. For example, a $25 product includes a reserve markup of $2.50. Now in order to finance the premium in a future deal, Stone adds $3 to the original price. Using this extra $3 plus the $2.50 reserve markup, he can buy a premium, that is, a picnic bag or cutting knife, at wholesale for $5.50.

He would sell this deal for $28, pointing out to customers that they are receiving merchandise worth $25 plus a premium which would retail at $8, all for the $28. In addition to its own brand deals, NBS handles most of the deals offered by the manufacturers. Every two months the manufacturers forward to NBS a new deal sheet featuring major products.

Generally all distributors have exactly the same national brand deals, provided, however, that the brand is not exclusive to any one supplier in a specific geographic area. These deals are for products that the salon consumes as opposed to a product sold over the counter. Usually the first sales person in the salon with a new deal makes the sale.

INTERVIEWS WITH THE BRANCH SALESPEOPLE

Salesperson A

King: I understand that until three months ago you were a stock clerk. How hard did you find your job as a stock clerk?

Salesperson A: It wasn't bad at all. The manager was out most of the time, so no one did any work. The girls even went to get their hair done. If I worked hard, I could do my job in two hours.

King: With the system used in the branches for inventory control, is there any problem of out-of-stock or dead stock?

Salesperson A: There are certain items that we often are out of. For example, we often run out of Clairol Colour. When I was a stock clerk, I used to move dead stock upstairs and try to peddle it over the counter by cutting its price. This was quite effective. At times we have to order more than we really need, because of minimum shipment size.

King: When you started in sales, what instruction did you receive?

Salesperson A: Very little. If I was unable to get a sale after two or three times of trying to get to know the operator, I would stop calling and try somewhere else. I have a very large area, and only call on a few of the shops. We never have pep talks like the other distributors' salespeople. I haven't been to a meeting since becoming a salesperson.

King: How useful is your branch manager to you?

Salesperson A: I hardly ever see him. He never makes calls with me. However, he does answer any questions I ask him.

King: How useful do you find Head Office?

Salesperson A: They arrange deals, as you know. They seem to be awfully slow up there with their paperwork. One of the competitors was offering a manufacturer's deal several weeks before we got around to having it. This kind of thing puts you in a poor position with your customers.

King: I understand you pay your own expenses. How much does this amount to?

Salesperson A: I am in the city, so it amounts to $20 per week.

Salesperson B

King: We have been looking at the accounts receivable problem. Do you have any comments on what should be done in this area?

Salesperson B: Collecting is a very delicate problem when it comes to hairdressers. You have to approach it properly. I think the salesperson is in the best position to judge the situation; often when I make calls, the operators are out. Since I cannot wait around, I may miss them, and thereby not see them for six weeks at a time. You can see how it would not be difficult to accumulate 60 days' accounts receivable. Nancy Purves, when passing through one of the towns I service, called on one of my customers without letting me know. I first heard about it on my next call. At any rate she embarrassed the client in front of the customers. I subsequently lost the account.

King: How many calls can you make a week, and what are your expenses?

Salesperson B: Of course I spend a lot of time on the road between towns, but I still make 15 calls per day. My expenses are $60 per week.

King: How much does Head Office help you?

Salesperson B: They do not know what is going on in our branch. I do not think much of the deals they come up with. I usually try to talk the customer out of it. I would rather promote our private brands by offering them free with orders for our other lines. Promotion of this type would be more useful in the long run. I have been selling for over two years but have never been to a sales meeting.

Salesperson C

King: What do you think of the premium deals NBS offers?

Salesperson C: The premiums are good. They make my selling much easier. I like them better than giving away merchandise. Because beauticians can only use so much in the way of supplies, any quantity you give away is an automatic decrease in what you are going to be able to sell.

King: What does your branch manager do for you?

Salesperson C: The manager is of no use to me because he is never in when I am. The branch office could do some useful selling for me. That is, over the telephone or over the counter. Unfortunately, the opposite is often the case. Customers are often antagonized by the treatment they get when they deal with the branch office.

King: What delivery do your out-of-town customers receive?

Salesperson C: They get their goods in three days generally. None of my competitors can offer better delivery than that.

King: What do you think of NBS product lines?

Salesperson C: We could use mòre popular brands, but our private lines will always be our bread and butter. Ninety percent of my sales are private lines with high margins.

King: We have heard that if one jobber starts putting pressure on customers, they will switch to a competitor, where they can get more credit. Is this common?

Salesperson C: Yes. It is possible for a beautician to be owing several jobbers at one time. One operator in my area borrowed to finance equipment and operated for four months without paying a bill. Of course she pocketed all the money. Finally she declared bankruptcy, leaving several jobbers holding the bag. Large operators know the situation and will play one jobber against another for both credits and deals.

Interview with Branch Manager A

King: Why do you concentrate on equipment sales?

Branch Manager A: Well, I'm forced to sell equipment because we don't have the right lines. We need nationally advertised lines, such as Realistic, L'Oreal, and Zoto. Back in 1977 our president turned down Realistic because he could not get it for all of Canada. Mind you, selling equipment is time consuming. For example, last November when I was concentrating on a $5,000 equipment deal, which incidentally fell through, I missed selling a lot of cosmetics.

King: Does concentrating on equipment sales interfere with your milk run?

Branch Manager A: Oh, I don't run my sales area on that basis—a lot of my customers phone into the office because they have known me for years. However, I do have a few customers that I try to get around to every two weeks to sell and collect the accounts. If I don't, I miss a sale and their account goes behind further.

King: Do your duties as branch manager interfere with your sales work?

Branch Manager A: Oh, not too much, really. My staff usually look after things.

King: What does Head Office do for you?

Branch Manager A: Nothing but increase fixed office expense. In the last three years Head Office expenses have increased by $50,000, and $20,000 is for leased cars and traveling expenses.

King: Who would you say is your main contact at Head Office?

Branch Manager A: Well, I'm usually in contact with the purchasing agent. He is relatively new in the business and sometimes wants me to order too much, and I'm always trying to keep my inventory down. Sometimes it is better to buy small quantities at a higher cost rather than end up with idle inventory.

King: What do you think of the Head Office setup?

Branch Manager A: I feel that top management engineered the move to the new executive office location because they felt that the old offices were not modern enough to properly carry on the company's business. The Head Office location is sort of a sore point with me, because all it did is greatly increase the overhead. As far as I am concerned, they are deliberately increasing overhead and they cut my income back in order to do it.

King: You are situated near the Head Office. Does Head Office do anything for you?

Branch Manager A: Nothing.

Interview with Branch Manager B

King: What are some of the competitive disadvantages you encounter?

Branch Manager B: Our products are third class compared with the competitor's in our area. We need some more brand names like Realistic and L'Oreal, and heavier promotion for our private brands. However, even if we had these lines, we couldn't compete adequately because of price cutting. We can't sell and make a profit with only a 20 percent margin. The secret would be central buying, because then we could afford to buy a year's supply when deals are available from manufacturers. If this were the case, I could continue to sell the deal after others have run out. I should think it would be possible to obtain 60 percent of our volume on deals averaging 10 percent off regular price.

King: I understand back orders can be a problem?

Branch Manager B: Yes, we probably have 10 to 20 per month. The problem is that when we do not have an item in stock and therefore have to ship an incomplete order, our customer relations are strained. When the item finally is shipped (an extra $1.25 for shipping) the customer probably has obtained the goods elsewhere, and therefore has no use for it, and hence sends it back. Our customers definitely want a reliable source of supply. Normally we ship on a two-day delivery in the city, but a manufacturer delivery may be four to five weeks. Our inventory is too small. We don't even have the range carried in other branches. NBS is the largest company in Canada, but it does not have lines equivalent to others, the stock of others, or the purchasing advantage of others.

King: We have been looking at the accounts receivable problem. Do you have any ideas on how the company could improve its position in this area?

Branch Manager B: We should have more leniency. Only the salespeople know the true situation, that is, operator illness, a bad month, etc. We've got too much interference from Head Office.

King: If we could digress, you were mentioning promotion for products. What do you think of the premiums that are offered?

Branch Manager C: They are effective, because customers are what they are. Some of the premiums are OK; others are not. I personally would rather sell at discount.

King: How many calls should a salesperson make a day in the city?

Branch Manager C: A hardworking salesperson can make up to 30. The shops are open two evenings a week, so we can sell to them. However, since we came off incentive pay, the salespeople are not doing too much night work.

INTERVIEW WITH SALES MANAGER CONCERNING THE PRODUCT LINE

After discussing the competitive situation of NBS in the Toronto-Hamilton area with company salespeople and branch managers, Mary King discussed the product line problem with the sales manager. He stated that 10 years ago NBS had control of all the major lines in Canada. At that time the company was by far the largest and strongest jobber. When NBS was approached by Rayette, Realistic, and Zoto, NBS turned them down for fear of antagonizing manufacturers that had given them exclusive rights. These relatively new manufacturers then had to get their own jobbers. Extensive promotion accompanied this development. In certain main areas (Toronto, Montreal) these manufacturers were weak.

> It would be possible to bring in these lines under the counter and accept a low margin. Alton has instructed me not to undertake this rather unethical approach. You see, I could get the supplies from other jobbers in the U.S. or through a Montreal jobber who does not distribute in the Toronto-Hamilton area. We are working a deal with Realistic to handle their line in the Maritimes with the hope that if we do well, they will let us handle it in Ontario.

INTERVIEW WITH SALESPERSON D AND BRANCH MANAGER C

The following is a part of the conversation recorded between the interviewer and the top salesperson and branch manager from Halifax.

King: Are you having any problems with prices in your area?

Salesperson D: No, we've been lucky, we've never had to cut prices down here. You see, most of my customers are women, and they don't think about price too much. In fact, in a lot of cases I will sell a deal and the women won't even ask me the price. I think that the competition won't bother us too much. We have to do a lot of traveling, and our expenses are quite high.

King: Just how do you cover your big area?

Salesperson D: I have a schedule that I follow exactly. Sometimes I will be a little off it and the customer will remark that I am 10 minutes late today. They have thought a bit about what they need, and they will hold the order for me even though a competitor may have called in the meantime. You see, the exclusive line is the big thing with me. They want it, and then I pick up the little things besides.

King: How do you sell to your customers?

Salesperson D: I know pretty well what they will need since I know what products they use. If they don't ask first, I start with the exclusive—colors, shampoos, and then perms."

King: What about premiums?

Salesperson D: If it's a wash basket or something like that, I never mention it. I sell them on merchandise. Say, a deal was 4 free waves with a purchase of 12. I figure how many they might take and then say 16 free with 48. They will cut me down, but I always end up with at least one deal. I tell them to take the product. It is a lot of trouble for me and the branch personnel to order and ship a premium.

King: I gather that you don't want premiums?

Salesperson D: Yes I do! Some buyers will ask for them, and you have to have them for these people. What I would like is to have the product as a premium, using another of the company's brand products as the premium. This gives us more products of our own at the shops.

King: What does Head Office do for you?

Salesperson D: Stone prepares the deal sheet; that is all. Where is he most of the time—out west? We don't need a Head Office; a good branch manager is the best. Of course, Head Office should do the buying—big volume and better prices. The branch manager can hire and train the salespeople. You can't have a sales manager with a national firm. He is running all over the place and is no good to anyone.

King: Do you have the right products?

Salesperson D: Yes, I don't have any kick about that.

King: How fast do your customers want products? Could we have a central warehouse?

Salesperson D: That is one thing we have to offer—service. It is very important. I think we moved into Halifax pretty fast.

King: What are your major problems?

Salesperson D: I took a bad cut in pay when I went off commission.

   [*Branch Manager C arrives on the scene.*]

King: What do you think of premiums?

Branch Manager C: I don't like quotas as a way to figure salary. Why, my quota is too high for the amount of business I can get from my area. Then too, I can't get anything for being branch manager. You can't be a good branch manager and a salesperson too. When you're out selling, how are you supposed to run a branch?

Salesperson D: I agree with you, I think our pay should be based on how much profit the branch makes. That is the only fair way. Then too, we should be running the collections out of the branch—one clerk could do the Maritimes. Nancy Purves is some help, but what we need is a good buyer and a good deal sheet; that is all we want a sales manager for.

King: How are your collections coming along?

Branch Manager C: They could be better. However, Head Office is always three weeks late with billings.

King: What do you think about central warehousing in the Maritimes?

Branch Manager C: We could work out of Moncton, I guess. However, we would still have to stock colors in Halifax. You know a branch can be too close, the disadvantage being that our customers phone in exclusives and give the other business to the competitors.

King: How often does your sales manager contact you?

Branch Manager C: Not too often. Actually, I can only remember seeing his signature on correspondence three times in three years.

King: Well, do you see President Alton often?

Branch Manager C: No, you can never get him at Head Office. . . . Apparently he is away . . . !

INTERVIEWS WITH WESTERN BRANCH MANAGERS

The general opinions expressed by the western managers were similar to those expressed by the Ontario and Maritime managers with the exception of the following points:

King: Mr. Bendus, what are you doing about accounts receivable?

Branch Manager: At the present time we are doing our utmost to reduce accounts receivable even to the extent of getting together with our competitors.

King: Mr. Bendus, what do you think of NBS's national pricing policy? Especially the fact that you are not to cut price?

Branch Manager: If I have to compete, I compete. I don't stop to ask anyone.

King: Mr. Bendus, could you handle your own local sales promotion, that is, run your own shows?

Branch Manager: Oh, yes, we could run our own shows, even though we haven't had one since 1975. Somehow NBS seems to have them all in Calgary.

King: Mr. Fairbairn, what assistance do you get from Head Office?

Branch Manager: We don't feel that we get the assistance from the sales manager that we should. Also, we don't need a president—we could save that much money and get more for ourselves. Alton said we would see Nancy Purves and Mike Stone two or three times a year. However, this isn't so.

King: Mr. Fairbairn, just what has Mike Stone [sales manager] done for you, and what do you feel he should be doing?

Branch Manager: In all fairness to Stone, he had experience in the retail selling field and his thinking is along that line. That's the reason for the combs. [Stone, in 1979, purchased several hundred dozen combs to be sold by all branches to salons. At the present time most of these combs are dead stock in inventory.] It's a different type of selling—a salon versus a drugstore. I believe the sales manager should be inside more instead of running around the country. You know, my main contact at Head Office is the purchasing agent, and I contact him to get things done.

J. Milne felt that the sales manager's job should be one of procuring new products and forwarding new product information. He also stated that the purchasing agent was a liar, "always holding up stuff."

The western branch managers felt that they could conduct their own marketing strategy far better than Head Office because of the nature of regional business. If the branch managers were paid on a new scheme of remuneration, such as profit sharing, they would spend more time conducting the affairs of the branch, that is, hiring, supervising, and training salespeople, controlling inventory, accounts receivable, etc., since the present method of compensation was in conflict with their responsibilities as managers. Currently, they were placing more emphasis on sales than on sales management and administration.

THE FUTURE

Alton visualised a need for more control over the existing sales force. "We have to have better administrative control over the salespeople." "Hell on earth is responsibility without authority." The biggest problem facing NBS, according to Alton, was:

> There are three facts to this business: inventory, receivables, and sales. They are all giving us problems. Receivables are an industry-wide problem. You have some companies in this business giving virtually unlimited credit. Anytime I get too tough with collections they can cut me out and go to a competitor. It is really rough! You ask me if I think anybody in the industry is making money; if you look at Dun and Bradstreet, you would have to say no.

Alton was asked who had the responsibility of running the company while he was involved with Amcan (his medical supply company). "No one. I have felt that either Purves or Stone should be general manager. I would be interested in your recommendation. You see—I have been weak on feedback." Alton was then asked, "Who is actually going to improve NBS's situation. Whose nose is at the grindstone?"

He replied, "It should be mine, shouldn't it?"

Case 4–7 ——————————————

Green Acres Seed Company

Green Acres Seed Company began operations in 1929. Originally, it was a family operation located on the farm of the father and operated by the son. Green Acres' main business was the production and sale of seed corn. In 1935, the opportunity arose to purchase a small seed processing plant in a nearby town. At this time, two other brothers

---

This case was prepared by Professor T. F. Funk of the University of Guelph, Ontario, Canada.

joined the business to form the nucleus of the present organization. In 1956, the partnership was transformed into a corporation.

The years following 1935 were years of rapid growth for Green Acres. In 1936, a modest research program was established and a dealer organization was set up consisting of many farm store accounts. In 1939, Green Acres experienced a serious setback. The industry was changing, and this change was not immediately recognized by the management of Green Acres. Farm stores, the traditional retailing agent for seed corn, were passing out of the picture in favor of farmer dealers. Since Green Acres had not established a farmer-dealer organization, it realized a substantial decline in sales. Work was immediately started on an organization of farmer dealers, and sales picked up again the next year.

In the early 1940s, Green Acres embarked upon an expansion program. A new plant was constructed to have an eventual annual capacity of over 300,000 bushels of processed seed. This is the present facility utilized by the firm.

Sales of seed corn in 1971 amounted to $1.78 million for 110,983 bushels of seed (Tables 1 and 2). Of this total, approximately 70 per-

Table 1

GREEN ACRES SEED COMPANY
Statement of Income and Expenses
1967–1971
(000)

	1971	*1970*	*1969*	*1968*	*1967*
Sales of seed corn	$1,782	$1,608	$1,367	$1,292	$1,211
Cost of sales....................	998	833	691	635	618
Gross margin	784	775	676	657	593
Expenses:					
Selling expenses..............	509	497	414	308	315
Administrative expenses	195	185	113	162	163
Net profit.....................	$ 80	$ 93	$ 149	$ 187	$ 115

Table 2
Unit sales of seed corn

Year	*Single cross (bushels)*	*Double cross (bushels)*	*Total sales (bushels)*
1971	77,688	33,295	110,983
1970	62,485	41,658	104,143
1969	45,808	46,372	92,180
1968	36,280	54,421	90,701
1967	26,502	61,840	88,342

cent consisted of single cross varieties and the remaining 30 percent consisted of double crosses. Although pretax profits had been declining since 1968, management became concerned about this situation only after it learned that profits in 1971 were $13,000 below those of 1970. In attempting to isolate the problem, management observed that all of its costs had been increasing over the period 1967 to 1971. The cost of sales per unit sold had increased from approximately $7 a bushel in 1967 to over $9 a bushel in 1971. This, however, was to be expected because the proportion of single crosses was increasing and producing single crosses was known to cost considerably more than producing double crosses.[1]

Administrative costs had also increased since 1967, but the absolute increase had been relatively small. On a bushel basis these costs had actually declined. Marketing costs, on the other hand, had increased substantially in terms of both absolute dollars and dollars per bushel sold. In 1967, total selling costs were $3.56 per ton compared with $4.59 in 1971. The current financial position of the company is described in Table 3.

On the basis of this analysis, management felt that the real problem it faced was in marketing. It thought that it was simply spending too

Table 3

GREEN ACRES SEED COMPANY
Balance Sheet
August 31, 1971

Assets		*Liabilities and Net Worth*	
Current assets:		Current liabilities:	
Cash.................	$ 190,450	Accounts payable......	$ 82,000
Accounts receivable....	372,500	Obligations due within	
Inventories...........	155,600	the year	380,000
Work in process.......	49,700	Accrued expenses	52,000
Total current assets	768,250	Total current liabilities.............	514,000
Investments:		Long-term liabilities:	
Common stock........	185,600	Mortgages payable.....	79,600
Fixed assets:		Net worth:	
Cost.................	1,137,500	Capital stock	240,000
Less reserve for		Earned surplus........	585,150
depreciation.....	672,600	Total net worth	825,150
Total fixed assets ..	464,900	Total liabilities	
Total assets.............	$1,418,750	and net worth	$1,418,750

---

[1] Single and double cross varieties are the major classifications of hybrid seed corn. Single cross hybrids result from the combination of two inbred lines or use of closely related inbred lines on one or both sides of the hybrid pedigree. They offer the highest uniformity and yield potential to the farmer, but may also have a great deal of performance variability under different environments. Double crosses arise from the combination of four relatively unrelated inbred lines. These have a wider genetic base and therefore are more variable and adaptable to varying environmental conditions.

much money on a marketing program which wasn't effective. To remedy this situation, management felt that a major change was needed. As a result, it immediately began to search for a new marketing manager. In October 1971, Peter Jenkins was hired to direct the company's marketing program.

Jenkins came to Green Acres from Topco, a regional feed manufacturing firm in Illinois, where he was a sales manager. He had been in this position for the past six years. As sales manager for Topco, he was responsible for supervising the activities of 25 salespeople selling feed direct to farmers. In addition, he had worked closely with the marketing manager in the development of the total feed marketing program. Management at Green Acres was delighted to obtain his services and felt that he was just the right person to get its marketing program moving again.

Because Jenkins arrived at Green Acres in October, it was too late to make major changes in the marketing program for 1971–72. The program for 1971–72 had been developed months earlier and was in full swing in October. Jenkins thus decided that the best thing he could do would be to spend his time becoming familiar with the seed industry in general and the situation at Green Acres in particular. Once he had done this, he felt he would be in a position to develop a new marketing approach for Green Acres in 1972–73.

PRODUCT LINE

Green Acres sold 25 different varieties of seed corn, of which 18 were double crosses and 7 were single crosses (Table 4). The varieties

Table 4
Current product line

Short season			Medium season			Full season		
Variety	Type of cross	Days to maturity	Variety	Type of cross	Days to maturity	Variety	Type of cross	Days to maturity
263	DX	87	S33	SX	105	8535	DX	116
22	DX	88	S35	SX	105	678	DX	116
31A	DX	91	2570	DX	106	5907	DX	117
S19	SX	93	S30A	SX	107	603	DX	117
201	DX	95	3340	DX	111	S69	SX	117
2610	DX	97	593	DX	113	S75	SX	118
224	DX	99	5900	DX	114	706	DX	119
233	DX	101				891	DX	121
S27	SX	103						
214	DX	104						

were grouped into three categories—short season, medium season, and full season—depending upon their relative maturities. The short season varieties were well adapted and most popular in the northern corn belt, the medium season in the central corn belt, and the full season in the southern corn belt. However, many farmers would schedule their planting dates in such a manner that they could plant some varieties in each of the three maturity categories.

The product line of Green Acres was similar to that of other seed corn firms. Of the 25 varieties in the product line, only 2 were considered by management as being truly outstanding. These were S27 and 5900. For the past three years, they had shown up extremely well in state yield trials and in commercial applications. Most farmers who had tried them were anxious to use them again.

PRICING POLICY

The overall pricing policy at Green Acres had been to price double cross varieties at approximately the same level as competitive firms but to price single cross varieties substantially lower than competition. In 1971, the price of double crosses was set at $13.50 a bushel for the medium flat kernel size. This was slightly lower than the average price charged by major competitors (Table 5). Single cross varieties

Table 5
Current industry prices

Company	Double cross price	Single cross price
P.A.G.	$13.80	$26.00
Pride	13.70	19.80
Jacques	13.70	20.00
Weathermaster	13.70	19.80
Haapala	13.70	20.00
N.K.	13.75	23.50
Trojan	13.90	22.00
Acco	13.60	21.00
United	13.75	25.00
Pioneer	13.70	24.00
Moews	13.50	21.00
DeKalb	13.90	19.80
Pfister	13.20	25.90
Green Acres	13.50	19.75
Lowe	12.95	25.25

were sold at $19.75 a bushel in 1971. This represented the lowest price for single cross varieties in the industry in 1971.

In 1970, several seed corn firms adopted the practice of grouping varieties for pricing purposes. The idea was to develop a group of outstanding varieties for which demand was high and to sell these at a premium over other varieties. Usually the premium was from $1 to $3 per bushel. Green Acres was aware of this practice but decided not to follow it. It felt that farmers would not buy the higher price varieties in sufficient volume.

RESEARCH AND DEVELOPMENT

Research and development is an important function for Green Acres Seed Company. Since 1936, Green Acres has been actively engaged in seed research. Beginning in 1965, Green Acres also began some basic genetic research. Of primary importance in research is the development of new and improved varieties. The policy of Green Acres in this respect is to develop as many new varieties as possible for further testing in the 20 test plots maintained by the company throughout the corn belt.

In addition to its research and testing responsibilities, the research department also has primary responsibility for quality control. This involves checking on the performance of all other departments involved in producing and processing the seed to ensure that quality standards are continually maintained. At the present time, the research department employs four full-time professional plant breeders. The research and development budget is approximately $100,000 per year.

SALES AREA

In 1971, Green Acres sold seed in 13 states (Table 6). Although seed corn is used to some extent in all 48 continental states, over 80

Table 6
Green Acres' marketing area

	Seeding rate (bushels/acre)	Acres planted— to corn	Industry sales	Company sales	Market share
Eastern states	0.19	2,018,000	$ 383,420	$ 4,908	1.3%
Wisconsin	0.22	2,726,000	599,720	4,822	0.8
Indiana	0.20	5,134,000	1,026,800	20,513	2.0
Missouri	0.18	3,379,000	608,220	1,522	0.2
Ohio	0.21	3,185,000	668,850	16,822	2.5
Michigan	0.20	2,024,000	404,800	18,987	4.7
Iowa	0.20	10,467,000	2,093,400	11,170	0.5
Illinois	0.20	9,993,000	1,998,600	32,239	1.6
Total	0.20	38,926,000	$7,783,810	$110,983	1.4%

percent is used in the 13 states comprising Green Acres's marketing area. In total, Green Acres seed accounts for approximately 1.4 percent of the total market in the 13-state area. This varies from a high of nearly 5 percent in Michigan to a low of only 0.2 percent in Missouri. The Missouri market was opened in 1970.

MARKETING PROGRAM

The marketing program of Green Acres is similar to that of other seed companies its size. The basic philosophy is to build up a large organization of farmer dealers and to push as much seed through these dealers as possible. Thus, the major marketing effort is directed through personal selling. The total marketing expenditures of Green Acres over the period 1967–71 are shown in Table 7.

Table 7
Marketing expenditures

	1971	1970	1969	1968	1967
Advertising					
Publications	$ 2,700	$ 8,600	$ 10,400	$ 3,800	$ 5,400
Signs	14,800	24,800	11,400	16,300	15,500
Literature	10,500	5,500	6,300	2,600	3,200
Total	28,000	38,900	28,100	22,700	24,100
Promotion					
Exhibits	14,100	11,100	3,900	2,700	2,900
Premiums	22,200	33,400	20,200	34,000	48,900
Discounts	172,000	126,000	91,400	76,900	70,100
Free seed	17,000	19,800	36,000	—	—
Total	225,300	190,300	151,500	113,600	121,900
Salespeople	245,400	258,300	221,800	162,700	161,100
Sales training	10,500	9,400	12,600	8,900	8,500
Total	$509,200	$496,900	$414,000	$307,900	$315,600

Advertising

Green Acres has never relied heavily on advertising. In 1971, total advertising expenditures amounted to only $28,000. Of this total, approximately one half was spent on roadside signs and field markers. The other half was devoted to company literature and advertising in farm magazines. Company literature, for the most part, consisted of a seed catalog describing all of the varieties the company offered for sale and a monthly house organ sent to all the company's dealers. The expenditure of $2,700 for publications advertising represented the cost of a one-half-page ad in the July issue of the Indiana and Illinois edition of the *Prairie Farmer* plus other miscellaneous ads in local newspapers.

Promotion

Promotional expenditures accounted for approximately 40 percent of Green Acres' marketing expenses in 1971. A total of $14,100 was spent on exhibits at farm shows, county fairs, etc. An additional $22,200 was spent on various types of sales premiums. These premiums varied from year to year, and in 1971 consisted of jackets and caps with the company emblem, ball-point pens, and electric frying pans. The jackets and caps were given to all dealers selling in excess of 25 bushels of seed corn. The electric frying pans were given to dealers selling 50 or more bushels. It was felt that these frying pans would appeal to the dealers' wives and that they would encourage their husbands to sell more so they could receive one.

The largest promotional expense was discounts. The most significant were quantity discounts, early order discounts, and cash discounts. The quantity discount used by Green Acres was similar to that used by most other seed companies. The quantity schedule is shown in Table 8. In addition to the discounts, the company also had a policy

Table 8
Quantity discounts

Total bushels customer orders	Number of bushels customer pays for
1 through 4	All
5 through 9	½ bushel less than ordered
10 through 18	1 bushel less than ordered
19 through 27	2 bushels less than ordered
28 through 36	3 bushels less than ordered
37 through 45	4 bushels less than ordered
46 through 54	5 bushels less than ordered
55 through 63	6 bushels less than ordered

of giving away free seed. In most cases, this seed was used as payment to dealers for erecting and maintaining field signs.

Personal Selling

The largest marketing expenditure incurred by Green Acres was for salespeople, or as they are called in the seed industry, district sales managers. In 1971, Green Acres employed 15 full-time district sales managers in eight sales regions. In a few cases, these district sales managers would hire part-time assistants to aid in the delivery of seed prior to planting.

Table 9 provides some information on the sales force in 1971. The average age of Green Acres' salespeople was 44 years. Many of the salespeople above the average age were retired farmers who had previously been successful seed corn dealers. A few of the younger salespeople were university-trained agronomists. The number of years with Green Acres varied from a high of 18 to a low of 1, with an average number of 7. The average cost per salesperson, including salary, bonus, and expenses was $17,891 in 1971, or $2.42 per bushel sold.

Table 9
Sales force data

Area/sales	Age	Years with company	Number of dealers	Total sales	Total salary bonus and expenses	Sales-person cost per bushel
Eastern states						
Dietrich	41	4	110	$ 4,908	$14,878	$3.03
Wisconsin						
Thedens	32	5	103	4,822	13,649	2.83
Indiana						
Williams	43	1	128	9,445	20,001	2.11
Briggs	45	13	160	7,604	21,378	2.81
Findlay	42	16	160	3,464	9,006	2.60
Missouri						
Vanderkamp	58	2	85	1,522	7,245	4.76
Ohio						
Heiserman	48	4	135	8,294	17,946	2.16
Hanusik	36	9	122	8,528	21,197	2.48
Michigan						
Smith	60	18	250	18,987	38,406	2.02
Iowa						
Pieper	33	9	200	8,142	19,385	2.38
Larson	25	2	71	3,028	11,765	3.88
Illinois						
East	33	9	210	9,046	22,152	2.48
Brown	56	2	100	3,763	9,118	2.42
Mefford	58	1	125	3,927	15,918	4.05
Rieker	52	12	250	15,503	27,684	1.78
Average	44	7	147	$ 7,398	$17,891	$2.42

The major job of district sales managers was to service their existing dealer organization. This involved several calls each year to ensure that dealers were properly equipped and informed to carry out their selling function. It also involved arranging and conducting dealer meeting in local areas at least once each selling season. Whenever time permitted, district sales managers were instructed to accompany dealers on sales calls. The purpose of this activity was to give the district sales manager the opportunity to observe the sales approach used by the dealer and to make suggestions for improvement. It was also intended to get the dealer started making sales calls. Green Acres' management felt that most of its dealers were not aggressive enough.

Another task performed by district sales managers was establishing new dealerships. Because dealer turnover was high (10 to 20 percent each year), it was necessary to get at least this many new dealers each year to avoid losing sales.

Although most seed was shipped directly from the main processing plant to the dealers following receipt of farmers' signed orders, a certain amount of each variety was also shipped to area warehouses. The additional seed was intended to meet last-minute orders when it would be impossible to fill these orders from the main warehouse. The area warehouses were operated by the district sales managers, who would attempt to fill these orders from their available inventory. If this were not possible, they would check with other dealers, who, because of canceled orders, might have a surplus of the variety needed elsewhere. In addition to handling the paperwork involved in these transfers, the district manager would also handle the actual movement of the seed.

Because all dealers handled Green Acres seed on a consignment basis, frequently it was necessary for the district sales managers to pick up unsold seed at the conclusion of the selling season. This seed would be returned to the area warehouses, where it was assembled and returned to the main company warehouse to be rebagged or sold as market corn. All district sales managers at Green Acres were required to account for their activities by filling out daily activity summaries and sending these to the sales manager every week. A summary of the activities of each district manager in 1971 is shown in Table 10.

Table 10
Activities of district sales managers

Area/sales manager	Setting up new dealers (weeks)	Servicing old dealers (weeks)	Selling with dealers (weeks)	Direct selling (weeks)	Seed delivery (weeks)	Seed pickup (weeks)	Collections (weeks)
Eastern states							
Dietrich	7.5	12.5	2.5	2.5	12.5	5.0	7.5
Wisconsin							
Thedens	6.0	24.0	4.0	4.0	5.0	5.0	2.0
Indiana							
Williams	15.0	20.0	10.0	0.0	2.5	1.5	1.0
Briggs	2.5	25.0	5.0	7.5	7.5	1.0	1.5
Findlay	7.5	19.5	0.5	2.5	7.5	5.0	7.5
Missouri							
Vanderkamp	17.5	10.0	5.0	2.5	7.5	5.0	2.5
Ohio							
Heiserman	6.0	24.0	4.0	4.0	5.0	5.0	2.0
Hanusik	2.5	31.5	2.5	0.5	5.0	4.0	4.0
Michigan							
Smith	5.0	20.0	1.0	1.5	10.0	2.5	10.0
Iowa							
Pieper	5.0	35.0	1.0	1.0	4.0	2.5	1.5
Larson	6.0	24.0	4.0	4.0	5.0	5.0	2.0
Illinois							
East	3.5	27.5	2.5	5.0	7.5	1.5	2.5
Brown	12.5	17.5	2.5	2.5	7.5	5.0	2.5
Mefford	15.0	17.5	2.5	0.0	2.5	5.0	5.0
Rieker	5.0	35.0	1.5	1.0	4.0	2.5	1.0
Average	7.7	22.9	3.2	2.6	6.2	3.7	3.5

Dealer organization

All the seed sold by Green Acres was sold through the company's dealer organization. Green Acres employed two basic types of dealers—farmer dealers and store dealers. The farmer dealers were farmers who agreed to sell Green Acres seed to their neighbors. For their efforts they received a commission based upon the number of bushels sold. In 1971, the commission schedule was:

Type of seed	Number of bushels	Commission
Double cross	1 to 99	$1.50
	100 to 249	2.00
	250 or more	2.50
Single cross	1 to 99	2.00
	100 to 249	2.50
	250 or more	3.60

Store dealers were local farm supply outlets such as feed stores and grain elevators, which operated on the same commission schedule as the farmer dealers. In 1971, Green Acres had 2,029 farmer dealers and 180 store dealers. Their distribution and size are shown in Table 11.

Table 11
Location and size of current dealers

Sales territory	Number of farmer dealers	Bushels sold by farmer dealers	Average farmer dealer size (bushels)	Number of store dealers	Bushels sold by store dealers	Average store dealer size (bushels)
Eastern states	101	4,315	42.7	9	593	65.8
Wisconsin	96	4,758	49.6	7	64	9.1
Indiana	376	18,450	49.7	72	2,063	28.6
Missouri	85	1,522	17.9	—	—	—
Ohio	219	14,799	67.7	38	2,023	53.2
Michigan	236	17,919	75.9	14	1,068	76.2
Iowa	266	10,954	41.2	5	211	42.2
Illinois	650	31,291	48.1	35	948	27.1
Total	2,029	104,008	51.2	180	6,970	38.7

A breakdown of dealers by size is shown in Table 12. This shows that approximately one half of Green Acres dealers sell less than 25 bushels per year. Management suspects that most of these small dealers do not in fact sell seed, but rather become dealers so that they can get the larger discount for their own requirements. This may be true to some extent for the 26–50-bushel dealers also. Probably only 51-bushel-and-greater dealers actually sell to their neighbors and friends.

In addition to the information in Tables 1 through 12, Jenkins had access to a market research study which had been run on 700 corn farmers (Appendix A). He also found some figures in a university publication showing recent trends in the seed corn industry (Appendix B). After reviewing all the available data, Jenkins began preparing

Table 12
Dealer size distribution, 1965

Bushels sold	Number of dealers
0–25	1,012
26–50	530
51–100	417
101–200	227
200 and greater	60
Total	2,246

a report to present to the Executive Committee of the Green Acres Seed Company. Jenkins knew he would be in for some sharp questions from the committee, and he wanted to be sure to cover all elements of the marketing mix in his new program for the 1972–73 year.

APPENDIX A: RESULTS OF MARKETING RESEARCH SURVEY

How many acres of corn did you have this past year?

Acres		Number of farmers	Percent
A	1–59	177	25.3
B	60–119	249	35.6
C	120–249	210	30.0
D	250 or more	64	9.1
		700	100.0

From how many different companies did you buy seed last year?

	A	B	C	D	Total
No answer	12.4%	12.0%	12.4%	12.5%	12.3%
One	28.8	16.5	11.4	18.8	18.3
Two	23.2	24.1	17.1	15.6	21.0
Three	20.9	27.3	23.3	20.3	23.9
Four	10.7	12.4	18.6	14.1	14.0
Five	2.3	5.6	9.5	7.8	6.1
Six or more	1.7	2.0	7.6	10.9	4.4

Where did you purchase seed corn last year?

	A	B	C	D	Total
No answer	0.0%	0.8%	0.0%	0.0%	0.3%
Seed store	11.3	9.2	9.0	10.9	9.9
Farmer dealer	79.7	81.1	83.3	76.6	81.0
Company salesman	19.2	25.3	29.0	29.7	25.3
Combined order	0.0	2.4	2.4	6.3	2.1
Elevator	4.5	3.6	3.3	3.1	3.7
Co-op	2.8	5.6	3.3	3.1	4.0
I am a dealer	9.0	7.2	7.6	20.3	9.0

Appendix A (*continued*)

When you want more information about seed corn, where do you get this information?

	A	B	C	D	Total
No answer	5.1%	5.6%	6.2%	7.8%	5.9%
Retail store	2.8	3.2	1.9	1.6	2.6
Farmer dealer	61.6	61.0	67.1	57.8	62.7
Agricultural college	11.9	19.3	21.0	25.0	18.4
Magazine articles	26.6	24.1	21.0	25.0	23.9
Seed corn ads	16.4	18.1	12.4	15.6	15.7
County agents	6.8	11.2	17.1	14.1	12.1

The seed corn you planted last year, where have you seen this seed corn advertised?

	A	B	C	D	Total
No answer	5.6%	7.6%	3.3%	9.4%	6.0%
Billboards	20.3	14.5	18.6	26.6	18.3
Field signs	61.0	63.1	70.0	75.0	65.7
Newspaper ads	26.6	22.5	29.5	37.5	27.0
Farm magazine ads	79.7	74.3	81.4	75.0	77.9
Radio program	27.7	30.9	33.3	28.1	30.6
TV commercials	14.7	15.7	16.2	4.7	14.6

How would you rank the following reasons in terms of importance to you in deciding on the seed you planted last fall?

A. Used this variety before.

Ranking	A	B	C	D	Total
First	15.8%	23.3%	25.2%	20.6%	22.3%
Second	4.5	4.0	5.7	4.7	4.7
Third	1.1	1.6	1.4	3.1	1.6
Fourth	0.6	1.6	2.4	0.0	1.4
Fifth	0.0	0.8	0.0	0.0	0.3
Sixth	0.0	0.0	0.0	0.0	0.0
Seventh	0.6	0.0	0.0	0.0	0.1

B. A neighbor used this brand and recommended it to me.

Ranking	A	B	C	D	Total
First	0.6%	2.8%	2.4%	1.6%	2.0%
Second	7.3	9.6	7.6	9.4	8.4
Third	5.1	6.4	6.7	9.4	6.4
Fourth	1.7	3.6	3.8	1.6	3.0
Fifth	0.6	1.2	1.9	1.6	1.3
Sixth	0.6	2.0	0.0	0.0	0.9
Seventh	0.6	0.0	0.0	0.0	0.1

C. A salesperson or dealer called on me and wrote my order.

Ranking	A	B	C	D	Total
First	5.6%	6.4%	5.2%	4.7%	5.7%
Second	4.5	7.2	6.7	3.1	6.0
Third	2.3	6.4	10.8	6.3	6.4
Fourth	3.4	2.8	3.8	4.7	3.4
Fifth	0.0	1.2	1.9	0.0	1.0
Sixth	1.7	1.6	1.0	3.1	1.6
Seventh	0.6	0.8	0.0	0.0	0.4

Appendix A (*concluded*)

D. I saw official state yield test results.

Ranking	A	B	C	D	Total
First	1.1%	2.0%	3.3%	3.1%	2.3%
Second	3.4	4.4	6.7	10.9	5.4
Third	3.4	3.6	5.7	4.7	4.3
Fourth	4.5	4.4	3.3	1.6	3.9
Fifth	0.0	2.0	1.9	3.1	1.6
Sixth	1.1	0.0	1.0	3.1	0.9
Seventh	0.0	1.2	1.0	0.0	0.7

E. I saw a field marked by a seed corn company sign.

Ranking	A	B	C	D	Total
First	0.0%	0.8%	1.4%	1.6%	0.9%
Second	1.7	4.0	3.3	3.1	3.1
Third	2.8	4.4	5.2	4.7	4.3
Fourth	2.3	5.2	3.3	6.3	4.0
Fifth	3.4	0.8	1.0	1.6	1.6
Sixth	0.0	3.2	2.9	0.0	2.0
Seventh	0.0	1.6	0.0	0.0	0.6

F. I saw or heard an advertisement.

Ranking	A	B	C	D	Total
First	0.6%	0.0%	0.0%	0.0%	0.1%
Second	0.6	2.4	1.0	0.0	1.3
Third	1.7	2.4	2.4	1.6	2.1
Fourth	0.6	2.4	3.8	1.6	2.3
Fifth	1.7	2.8	2.4	1.6	2.3
Sixth	0.6	2.8	2.4	1.6	2.0
Seventh	1.7	2.8	1.9	3.1	2.3

APPENDIX B: TRENDS IN SEED CORN MARKETING

The data in Tables 13 and 14 are taken from a university publication and show the marketing mix allocations and detailed advertising and promotion breakdowns. The principal retailing agent of hybrid seed corn is the farmer dealer. In 1970, farmer dealers handled 76 percent of the seed corn sold, and the other channels—store dealers, direct sales, and farm supply centers—accounted for the remainder.

Table 13
Marketing expenditures for seed corn firms

	Small			Medium			Large		
	1960	1965	1970	1960	1965	1970	1960	1965	1970
Advertising									
Dollar expenditure	9,279	13,409	21,919	57,408	87,620	100,782	295,350	349,288	429,126
Percent	11.8	9.3	10.8	26.9	22.5	21.5	40.9	30.6	27.6
Promotion									
Dollar expenditure	3,669	7,370	9,760	41,967	71,223	75,549	174,240	198,410	354,639
Percent	4.7	5.1	4.8	19.6	18.3	16.2	24.1	17.4	22.6
Personal selling									
Dollar expenditure	52,010	109,899	148,576	88,640	186,253	217,695	73,952	317,534	444,847
Percent	66.4	76.1	73.4	41.5	47.8	46.5	10.3	27.8	28.4
Research									
Dollar expenditure	13,348	13,645	22,206	25,453	44,532	73,682	177,750	276,500	339,767
Percent	17.1	9.5	11.0	12.0	11.4	15.8	24.7	24.2	21.4
Total dollar expenditure	78,306	144,332	202,461	213,468	389,628	467,708	721,292	1,141,732	1,568,379

Table 14
Advertising and promotional allocations for seed corn firms

	Small			Medium			Large		
	1960	1965	1970	1960	1965	1970	1960	1965	1970
Advertising expenditures for seed (as percent of total advertising)									
Outdoor signs	33%	14%	12%	28%	32%	16%	22%	21%	17%
Store displays	—	—	—	1	—	—	—	—	—
Farm magazines	25	22	33	26	39	48	29	28	32
Newspapers	10	5	5	4	2	1	7	7	8
Radio and TV	4	40	35	23	15	8	13	14	14
Direct mail	19	11	12	4	1	10	16	18	17
Other	9	8	3	14	11	17	13	12	12
	100%	100%	100%	100%	100%	100%	100%	100%	100%
Promotional expenditures for seed (as percent of total promotion)									
Fair and farm shows	5%	4%	6%	6%	4%	7%	7%	6%	5%
Dealer meetings	3	8	14	14	12	16	28	30	19
Company field days	—	5	8	3	4	4	2	2	1
Dealer incentives	74	53	45	73	62	63	60	58	37
Customer incentives	18	23	23	1	4	3	1	1	35
Other	—	7	4	3	14	7	2	3	3
	100%	100%	100%	100%	100%	100%	100%	100%	100%

Case 4–8

A&W Drive-Ins (Fundy), Ltd.

"It is all psychological—when he picks up that burger, it feels pretty good. The merchandising appeal of that larger hamburger and the weight in comparison to McDonald's is significant—it is noticed by the customer. A&W isn't strong enough in the market that we can afford to tinker with the portioning, which is definitely one of our strong points." These thoughts passed through Mr. Ed Drayson's mind in 1973 as he sat preparing a set of recommendations for the company's board of directors. The company was facing rapidly rising food and operating costs in its A&W outlets in the Atlantic Provinces of Canada. These rising costs were threatening to drastically cut the contribution these outlets made to company overhead and profit.

The cost pressures were particularly severe in A&W's hamburger line, where meat costs were expected to be 40 percent higher in the summer of 1973 than they had been in the fall of 1972. The company's problems were compounded by the increasing competition posed by McDonald's and other fast-food operators, which were aggressively expanding in the A&W (Fundy) market area.

THE COMPANY

Mr. Drayson was the president of A&W Drive-Ins (Fundy), Ltd., and was directly responsible for the firm's A&W operations. Mr. Drayson's office was located in Moncton, New Brunswick, although the company's head office staff, whose main function was to provide accounting services for the company, was located in Toronto. All the managers of A&W outlets in the Atlantic Provinces reported directly to Mr. Drayson. The company was also involved in a number of non-A&W activities. Mr. Harry Brathwaite, the chairman of the board, spent much of his time supervising these activities.

A&W Drive-Ins (Fundy) was a franchisee of A&W Food Services of Canada, Ltd., which held the A&W franchise for Canada. A&W (Fundy) operated eight A&W outlets in the Atlantic Provinces and five outlets in Ontario. There were also a number of other A&W operators in the Atlantic Provinces, but none had franchises in the cities served by A&W (Fundy). The locations of the eight outlets in New Brunswick, Nova Scotia, and Prince Edward Island are shown in Exhibit 1. Monthly sales by outlet for 1971, 1972, and the first three months of 1973 are shown in Exhibit 2. All outlets in the Atlantic Provinces,

---

Prepared by Adrian B. Ryans of the University of Western Ontario.

Exhibit 1
Location of A&W (Fundy) Units

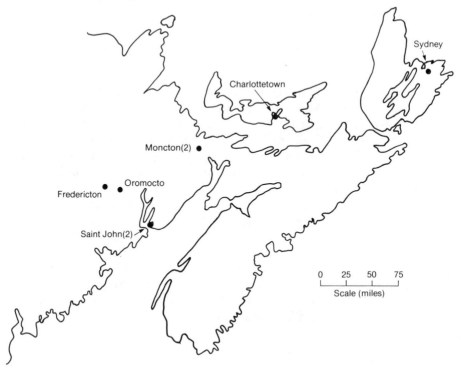

except Oromocto, were drive-in restaurants. The Oromocto restaurant provided inside seating in a shopping center.

For each unit A&W (Fundy) had opened, it had entered into a license agreement with A&W Food Services of Canada. Basically each franchise agreement granted the franchisee a license to operate a drive-in restaurant and to use the A&W trademarks in advertising and on menus, packaging, and signs in the preparation and sale of A&W beverages, products, and approved menu items. The license agreement remained in effect for a 20-year term, provided the franchisee met the terms of the agreement—the major ones being:

☐ The franchisee was to pay an initial fee of $2,500 and an annual service fee of approximately 1 percent of gross sales.

☐ The restaurant was to be constructed, at the franchisee's expense, in accordance with plans and specifications provided by A&W Food Services of Canada.

☐ The equipment for the restaurant had to be purchased from the franchisor.

☐ The operator of the restaurant was required to attend an A&W restaurant management training course.

☐ The franchisee was required to purchase all uniforms, packaging materials, and special A&W concentrates, syrups, bases, and spices from the franchisor.

☐ The recent agreements required the franchisee to contribute 1.50 percent of his gross sales to a national advertising and promotional fund. Some of the agreements required contributions to a regional advertising fund. Most agreements also specified a minimum percentage of gross sales that must be spent on local promotion and advertising.

☐ Unlike a number of other fast-food franchisors, A&W Food Services of Canada did allow the franchisee some latitude in the selection of his menu. He was required to serve certain products, such as the "Burger Family," but he was also allowed to select items from a list of optional products and could, if authorized by A&W Food Services of Canada, offer specialty items. Fried clams was one such item on the menu of the A&W (Fundy) outlets. The menu in use in the A&W (Fundy) outlets in April 1973 is shown in Exhibit 3.

Commenting on the terms of the franchise agreement, Mr. Drayson noted that the costs of supplies, while marked up by the franchisor, were not greatly different from the prices A&W (Fundy) would have to pay in the market, given its smaller purchasing power. With regard to the requirement for local advertising and promotion, Mr. Drayson noted that it was not constraining, since A&W (Fundy) typically allocated a much higher percentage of sales to local advertising and promotion. In summarizing, Mr. Drayson pointed out that the value of a franchise and the reasonableness of the terms depend ultimately on the attention to, and the skill of the national firm in, building the A&W image, creating effective national advertising and promotion, and providing operating and menu suggestions. He indicated that he felt that the national advertising and promotion program of A&W Food Services of Canada could be improved.

THE COMPETITION

Most of the A&W outlets operated in a highly competitive environment, with competition ranging from local takeouts to such national chains as McDonald's, Harvey's, and Kentucky Fried Chicken.[1] Some

---

[1] Traditionally one of the factors that had distinguished A&W from most of its competitors was its use of carhops at its drive-ins. The carhops came to the automobile to take the customer's order, and when the order was ready, they delivered it to the automobile on a special tray that could be attached to the car window ledge. When the customer had finished his or her food, the tray was removed by the carhop. By 1973, at many A&W outlets the customers could place their orders by means of an intercom system with a speaker located at each parking space. A menu with prices was permanently mounted next to each speaker.

Exhibit 2
Monthly sales by unit—1971–1973

1971 sales	January	February	March	April	May	June
Charlottetown	$ 17,503	$ 18,740	$ 21,594	$ 27,139	$ 29,235	$ 28,806
Fredericton	20,405	18,706	24,182	32,027	36,675	29,639
Sydney	22,196	21,594	26,534	31,785	34,851	34,709
Saint John No. 1	20,157	19,928	24,548	28,563	31,432	30,338
Saint John No. 2	—	—	—	—	—	—
Moncton No. 1	11,787	12,268	13,782	18,096	21,074	20,433
Moncton No. 2	9,380	9,956	11,573	15,006	17,959	18,267
Oromocto	16,408	14,006	15,886	16,182	16,710	18,042
	$117,836	$115,198	$138,099	$168,798	$187,936	$180,234
1972 sales						
Charlottetown	$ 20,702	$ 21,728	$ 25,690	$ 34,638	$ 34,776	$ 40,496
Fredericton	19,091	18,890	23,569	35,592	36,048	38,181
Sydney	21,176	17,739	25,025	30,202	35,998	39,816
Saint John No. 1	21,067	19,975	24,655	33,339	36,497	35,001
Saint John No. 2	22,523	19,712	24,090	32,407	35,425	34,725
Moncton No. 1	14,942	13,559	16,764	24,350	26,673	28,319
Moncton No. 2	12,572	11,246	14,197	20,314	22,611	25,765
Oromocto	13,875	13,399	15,950	16,255	16,953	20,531
	$145,948	$136,248	$169,940	$227,097	$244,801	$262,204
1973 sales						
Charlottetown	$ 30,390	$ 28,243	$ 42,264			
Fredericton	21,754	23,534	34,311			
Sydney	26,636	20,719	30,095			
Saint John No. 1	24,860	23,245	28,031			
Saint John No. 2	23,473	22,369	29,970			
Moncton No. 1	17,737	16,878	23,578			
Moncton No. 2	15,898	14,257	22,830			
Oromocto	14,825	14,528	19,482			
	$175,573	$163,773	$230,561			

of the local chains, such as Deluxe French Fries in Moncton, were well established, with good local reputations.

The toughest competitive environment existed in Moncton, where there were two A&Ws, two McDonald's, and one Harvey's, two Kentucky Fried Chicken stores, and three Deluxe French Fries outlets. A&W (Fundy) had opened its first drive-in in the Atlantic Provinces in Moncton in July 1965. Harvey's had been the first national competitor to follow A&W into Moncton, which it did in 1968. The second A&W drive-in was opened in 1969 and was located about two miles from the first one. The opening of the second outlet had a significant impact on the sales of the first one. McDonald's entered Moncton with two outlets in 1970. The McDonald's were both located within one-quarter mile of the two A&W outlets. In fact, every major competitor in Moncton had a store located within about one-half mile of A&W's Moncton

July	August	September	October	November	December	Total
$ 43,320	$ 43,435	$ 31,357	$ 31,965	$ 29,879	$ 23,387	$ 346,360
38,810	38,230	35,954	37,354	37,144	25,553	374,679
36,242	35,535	29,139	29,923	29,244	24,853	356,605
34,766	34,562	31,062	34,545	34,390	24,836	349,127
—	—	—	—	—	26,295	26,295
24,587	24,895	21,757	22,366	20,635	17,074	228,754
24,518	24,164	19,634	20,095	18,926	14,818	204,296
25,307	23,465	17,665	21,212	16,818	16,833	281,534
$227,550	$224,286	$186,568	$197,460	$187,036	$173,649	$2,104,650
$ 61,649	$ 58,361	$ 38,499	$ 36,301	$ 33,877	$ 33,707	$ 440,424
43,070	40,555	38,478	33,413	28,789	24,639	380,315
43,082	43,353	33,848	30,096	31,167	31,329	382,201
40,783	37,660	31,339	31,543	28,687	25,957	366,503
36,994	36,164	30,128	28,956	27,123	25,384	353,451
32,738	31,598	27,013	24,540	21,266	19,620	281,382
31,822	31,520	24,857	21,693	18,864	16,976	252,437
24,951	22,573	17,253	17,224	16,903	16,424	212,291
$315,089	$301,784	$241,415	$223,766	$206,676	$194,036	$2,669,004

No. 1 drive-in. Until McDonald's entered Moncton, the sales in the two A&W drive-ins had been expanding steadily. After the opening, A&W's sales in Moncton dropped and then gradually began to rise again. The impact of the opening was such that A&W's sales in the year following the opening were about equal to those in the previous year.

In April 1973 there were approximately 300 A&W outlets in Canada. By comparison, there were less than 100 McDonald's units, although McDonald's had announced that by the end of 1973 it planned to have 140 units in operation. Mr. Drayson knew that the McDonald's operation was in many ways different from his own A&W operation. He felt that some of these differences were reflected in two McDonald's pro forma income statements (shown in Exhibit 4). These income statements were from 1972 material provided by McDonald's

Exhibit 3
April 1973 menu

BURGERS

PAPA BURGER 64
2 Patties Meat

MAMA BURGER 44
Single Patty

BABY BURGER .24
(Cheese on above 5¢. Bacon 5¢)

TEEN BURGER .59
    SINGLE PATTY LETTUCE TOMATO
    BACON MAYONNAISE CHEESE
    TOASTED SESAME SEED BUN

ALL SERVED WITH YOUR CHOICE OF
MUSTARD, KETCHUP, PICKLES
and ONIONS

BEVERAGES

A & W ROOT BEER 20   .15
Baby Root Beer free to children under 6

A & W ORANGE 20   .15

ICE CREAM FLOAT . . . . .10 extra

MILK SHAKES .35

MILK 30   .20

COFFEE 15

TEA 15

HOT CHOCOLATE 15

	Gal.	½ Gal.	Qt.
Root Beer	95	60	35
Orange	1 00	80	50

Plus Deposit

SIDE ORDERS

COLE SLAW, side order 15

HOT DOG 34

WHISTLE DOG 49
With bacon, cheese & relish

FRENCH FRIES, side order 19   .29

ONION RINGS .35

FISH & CHIPS .65

FRIED CLAMS (When available) 75

FRIED CLAMS & CHIPS 95

CONEY SAUCE, on Hot Dogs
Burgers and Fries 15

STRAWBERRY SHORTCAKE 39

APPLE TURNOVER 20

SUNDAE 25
Chocolate or Strawberry

ICE CREAM 15

CHICKEN

CHUBBY DINNER 1.19
3 Pcs Chicken, French Fries

CHUBBY JUNIOR 89
2 Pcs Chicken, French Fries

CHUBBY "6" 1.79
6 Pcs Chicken

CHUBBY "12" 2.99
12 Pcs Chicken

CHUBBY "18" 4.49
18 Pcs Chicken

FAMILY PAK FRENCH FRIES 95

COLE SLAW
½ pint 30   1 pint 50

ALL ORDERS CAN BE PREPARED
FOR TAKE OUT

A & W DRIVE-INS (FUNDY) LIMITED

(See List of Maritime Locations on Back)

---

to prospective franchisees and were said to represent typical pro forma statements for McDonald's units in Canada.

In April 1973 McDonald's had one outlet in Fredericton, which had opened in June 1971, and one in Saint John that had only been open about two weeks. The McDonald's unit in Saint John was located within a quarter mile of A&W's Saint John No. 1 drive-in. In the two

Exhibit 4
Typical Canadian McDonald's pro forma statement

		Percent		*Percent*
Net sales	$400,000	100.0%	$600,000	100.0%
Food	134,000	33.5	201,000	33.5
Paper	20,000	5.0	30,000	5.0
Total cost	154,000	38.5	231,000	38.5
Gross profit	246,000	61.5	369,000	61.5
Controllable expenses:				
Crew labor	69,200	17.3	94,200	15.7
Management labor	19,200	4.8	19,200	3.2
Payroll deductions	5,500	1.4	6,500	1.1
Travel expenses	750	0.2	750	0.1
Advertising	16,000	4.0	24,000	4.0
Promotion	4,000	1.0	6,000	1.0
Outside services	2,800	0.7	2,900	0.5
Linen	2,000	0.5	2,200	0.4
Operating supplies	3,500	0.9	4,000	0.7
Maintenance and repairs	4,000	1.0	4,500	0.7
Utilities	8,000	2.0	8,500	1.4
Office and telephone expenses	900	0.2	1,000	0.2
Miscellaneous	750	0.2	850	0.1
Total controllables	136,600	34.2	174,600	29.1
Noncontrollable expenses:				
Rent*	34,000	8.5	51,000	8.5
Service fee	12,000	3.0	18,000	3.0
Legal and accounting	700	0.2	700	0.1
Insurance	1,600	0.4	1,600	0.3
Taxes and licenses	4,800	1.2	4,800	0.8
Equipment lease	720	0.2	720	0.1
Depreciation and amortization†	9,625	2.4	9,625	1.6
Total noncontrollables	63,445	15.9	86,445	14.4
Total operating expenses	200,045	50.0	261,045	43.5
Net operating income	45,955	11.5	107,955	18.0
Cash flow	$ 55,580	13.9%	$117,580	19.6%

All of the above figures are estimates and can change due to many factors.
* Note that McDonald's owns the land and building.
† Based over 10 years on assets, 20 years on fees.

weeks since the McDonald's unit had opened, sales in the Saint John No. 1 outlet had been about 20 percent lower than in the corresponding period in 1972. Mr. Drayson had heard rumors that a second McDonald's was soon to be built in Saint John. Mr. Drayson had also just learned that McDonald's had purchased a site in Sydney directly across the street from the A&W drive-in. This store was expected to open in October 1973. McDonald's was also reported to be looking for a site in Charlottetown. Again, it seemed quite likely that the McDonald's would be close to the A&W.

McDonald's April 1973 prices and those for the most nearly comparable A&W products were as shown in the accompanying table.

McDonald's		A&W	
Hamburger		Happy Burger	
(one ⅒-pound patty)*	$0.25	(one ⅒-pound patty)	$0.24
Cheeseburger		Happy Burger with	
(one ⅒-pound patty)*	$0.30	cheese	
		(one ⅒-pound patty)*	$0.29
¼ lb. Burger		Papa Burger	
(one ¼-pound patty)	$0.60	(two ⅐-pound patties)	$0.64
¼ lb. Cheeseburger		Papa Burger with cheese	
(one ¼-pound patty)	$0.70	(two ⅐-pound patties)	$0.69
Big Mac		Teen Burger	
(two ⅒-pound patties)	$0.65	(one ⅐-pound patty)	$0.59
Fries	$0.23 and $0.39	Fries	$0.19 and $0.29
Milk shakes	$0.30	Milk shakes	$0.35
Drinks	$0.15 and $0.20	Drinks	$0.15 and $0.20

* All weights are uncooked weight.

The competitive situation in each of the six cities is summarized in Exhibit 5.

Mr. Drayson had received in 1971 a report conducted for A&W's national advertising agency by a firm of consultants. A total of 1,200 people had been interviewed by telephone, with equal sample sizes in Moncton, Montreal, Toronto, Edmonton, Kamloops, and Vancouver. Quota sampling had been used in each city to ensure that 50 married adult males, 50 married adult females, 50 males 16 to 20 years old, and 50 females 16 to 20 years old would be interviewed. The research had been undertaken to determine the awareness, trial, and usage of various drive-in eating places. Some results from this study are reported in Exhibit 6.

A&W (Fundy) and other A&W operators in the Maritimes spent more than $150,000 in media advertising in the Maritimes, using materials produced and made available by A&W's national advertising agency. The advertising featured two fictional characters, Albert and Walter, who were used to promote the high quality of A&W's products and particular items on the A&W menu. The overall theme was "Two great ideas are better than one"—which referred to the root beer and burger combinations. Little was known about McDonald's spending plans except that McDonald's provided heavy advertising support when it opened new units. McDonald's advertising and promotion was generally regarded by those in the fast food trade as being of the highest quality, with its varied emphasis on children's promotions and the overall theme of "You deserve a break today."

Each A&W (Fundy) outlet completed a daily report of operations. Hour-by-hour sales and customer count were two of the items included in these reports. Summaries of two of these reports for different outlets and different days are included in Exhibit 7.

Exhibit 5
Major A&W competitors (in operation and expected—March 31, 1973)

Moncton, N.B.

McDonald's—two units (1970)
Harvey's (1968)
Kentucky Fried Chicken—two units
Deluxe French Fries—three units
Independents

Saint John, N.B.

McDonald's (March 1973, second unit expected)
Deluxe French Fries—two units
Kentucky Fried Chicken—two units
Independents

Fredericton, N.B.

McDonald's (June 1971)
Kentucky Fried Chicken—two units
Dixie Lee Fried Chicken
Independents

Sydney

Kentucky Fried Chicken
Independents
McDonald's (expected October 1973)

Charlottetown

Kentucky Fried Chicken
Independents
McDonald's (expected)

Oromocto

None

"We feel that we have done the best job of any A&W operator in competing with McDonald's," Mr. Drayson had remarked. "We reduced our prices substantially in 1971, and we were successful in building volume." He noted that other A&W operators had retained their historical pricing policies, which resulted in many units charging 75 cents for a Teen Burger in April 1973, versus the 59 cents charged by A&W (Fundy).

A&W (Fundy) had extensively publicized its price reductions in 1971. The publicity had included a small card, which had been distributed to customers. A sample is included as Exhibit 8. In Mr. Drayson's opinion, A&W (Fundy) had not been entirely successful in dispelling the high-price image.

Prices had stayed relatively constant from 1971 to late in 1972. In September 1972 the company had conducted an extensive cost of sales study for each item on its menu for each outlet to estimate the

Exhibit 6
Excerpts from consultant's report

A. Reasons for preferring favorite eating place

	A&W	Deluxe	McDonald's	Harvey's	All other burgers	All chicken	All pizza	All other	Total
Number of respondents	451	46	118	78	209	111	38	87	1,138
Food									
Quantity of	16%	11%	3%	4%	3%	5%	3%	3%	5%
Variety of	5	4	1	5	5	—	8	2	4
Type of	15	—	8	8	4	10	21	7	10
Quality/taste of	54	28	20	42	42	34	26	56	44
Other specific	2	—	—	1	1	5	3	1	2
Other nonspecific	—	—	10	—	10	1	—	3	3
Service									
Speed of	6	13	19	9	10	13	13	14	10
Efficiency	16	7	8	4	4	10	5	6	10
Other specific	1	—	2	—	3	2	—	2	2
Other nonspecific	*	—	3	—	4	2	—	—	1

Premises							
Clean	4	2	3	3	7	5	—	4
Decor/atmosphere	2	—	1	3	8	2	8	3
Facilities/seating/fixtures, etc.	13	—	2	3	9	2	16	8
Parking/parking lot	1	—	2	1	*	3	—	1
Other specific	1	—	1	—	*	1	3	1
Other nonspecific	—	—	—	—	*	2	—	*
Location							
Convenience of/number of/location	28	33	36	31	35	41	24	33
Other specific	1	—	—	—	—	—	—	*
Other nonspecific	*	—	—	—	—	—	—	*
Price/value, etc./all mentions:	6	30	52	10	15	13	5	15
Other							
Opportunity	*	—	2	—	—	2	—	1
Desire	*	—	—	—	*	—	—	*
Availability of transportation	1	—	—	—	*	1	8	1
Usual spot/place	6	2	3	1	1	—	2	3
Where friends go	15	7	10	14	8	1	1	11
Staff of eating place	6	—	3	4	4	5	8	4
Other comments	5	—	5	4	3	—	8	4
Nothing	*	—	—	—	—	—	—	*
Don't know	1	—	1	3	—	—	—	1
No answer	3	2	2	5	2	2	3	3

Note: Column percentages may add to more than 100 percent due to multiple responses by some respondents.
* Less than 0.5 percent.

Exhibit 6 (*continued*)

B. Things disliked about A&W by those who do not visit A&W most frequently, by municipality

	Monc-ton	Mon-treal	To-ronto	Edmon-ton	Kam-loops	Van-couver
Number of respondents	121	117	142	69	72	166
Food						
Quantity of	4%	2%	1%	—	8%	4%
Variety of	3	3	2	—	3	5
Type of	2	5	—	10%	1	3
Quality/taste of	15	8	15	22	18	16
Other specific	—	2	1	—	—	5
Other nonspecific	—	—	—	—	—	3
Service						
Speed of	3	—	10	14	17	13
Efficiency	7	—	2	7	3	5
Other specific	1	1	1	3	—	4
Other nonspecific	—	—	—	—	—	1
Premises						
Clean	—	—	1	1	—	2
Decor/atmosphere	1	2	1	3	4	4
Facilities/seating/fixtures, etc.	5	3	12	6	6	10
Parking/parking lot	2	1	—	3	1	1
Other specific	—	—	3	1	—	—
Other nonspecific	—	—	—	—	—	—
Location						
Convenience of/number of/location	4	20	8	10	1	2
Other specific	—	—	—	—	—	—
Other nonspecific	—	—	—	—	—	—
Price/value, etc./all mentions	31	4	12	7	29	20
Other						
Opportunity	—	—	—	—	—	—
Desire	—	3	—	—	—	—
Availability of transportation	4	2	2	6	1	—
Usual spot/place	—	2	1	—	—	1
Where friends go	—	—	—	—	4	—
Staff of eating place	—	3	2	1	1	5
Other comments	1	3	3	16	1	2
Nothing	25	24	25	22	13	14
Don't know	2	10	19	1	—	11
No answer	7	15	5	6	12	3

Note: Percentages may add to more than 100 percent as some respondents gave more than one answer.

theoretical food and packaging cost as a percentage of sales. Portions of this report for the Saint John's drive-ins are as shown in Exhibit 9.

In late 1972 prices, especially meat prices, began to rise across Canada, and a number of A&W franchisees in Canada began to lobby for a move to smaller hamburger patties. A&W had always had a standard of six hamburger patties to the pound (uncooked weight) in Canada. By January 1973, however, several of the largest A&W operators

Exhibit 6 (*concluded*)

C. Things liked about A&W by those who do not visit A&W most frequently, by municipality

	Monc-ton	Mon-treal	To-ronto	Edmon-ton	Kam-loops	Van-couver
Number of respondents	121	117	142	69	72	166
Food						
Quantity of	2%	—	—	6%	1%	1%
Variety of	2	4%	5%	4	6	2
Type of	—	8	13	9	4	25
Quality/taste of	45	18	19	49	54	23
Other specific	1	3	4	4	1	1
Other nonspecific	—	—	—	—	—	—
Service						
Speed of	19	4	4	10	15	6
Efficiency	7	1	8	25	11	4
Other specific	1	3	1	—	—	5
Other nonspecific	1	—	—	—	—	2
Premises						
Clean	6	—	3	3	3	2
Decor/atmosphere	—	—	1	1	3	—
Facilities/seating/fixtures	17	23	8	4	6	3
Parking/parking lot	—	4	1	3	3	1
Other specific	—	—	—	1	1	—
Other nonspecific	—	—	—	—	—	—
Location						
Convenience of/number of/location	4	—	4	4	8	4
Other specific	—	—	—	—	—	—
Other nonspecific	—	—	—	—	—	—
Price/value, etc./all mentions	2	1	2	7	8	1
Other						
Opportunity	—	—	—	—	1	—
Desire	—	—	—	—	—	—
Availability of transportation	2	—	—	—	—	—
Usual spot/place	—	—	—	—	—	—
Where friends go	1	—	—	3	—	—
Staff of eating place	10	1	2	10	13	4
Other comments	1	4	3	4	—	4
Nothing	10	3	18	10	4	12
Don't know	5	9	21	9	—	9
No answer	9	32	11	1	8	5

Note: Percentages may add to more than 100 percent as some respondents gave more than one answer.

in Canada, including A&W (Fundy), had moved to seven patties to the pound.

THE SITUATION IN APRIL 1973

By March 1973 the cost situation had deteriorated further. In a March 21 memo to senior executives in the company and members of

Exhibit 7
Summary of selected data from daily operations reports

Ending hour	Unit A (Sunday)		Unit B (Friday)	
	Hourly sales	Hourly customer count	Hourly sales	Hourly customer count
Noon	$ 23.92	13	$ 10.19	6
1 P.M.	92.02	34	84.94	41
2 P.M.	71.63	27	26.65	15
3 P.M.	64.15	33	16.75	12
4 P.M.	100.10	41	19.33	20
5 P.M.	137.72	51	20.53	13
6 P.M.	220.57	70	91.38	34
7 P.M.	221.68	77	86.80	33
8 P.M.	127.67	47	55.78	25
9 P.M.	125.71	50	34.96	17
10 P.M.	174.70	70	52.46	34
11 P.M.	155.03	60	76.85	40
Midnight	139.13	57	92.98	50
1 A.M.	83.56	32	104.36	57
2 A.M.	56.68	28	105.08	53
Totals	$1,794.27	690	$879.04	450

the board of directors, Mr. Drayson noted: "Our meat prices from suppliers have increased from approximately 61 cents per pound last September to the current 70 cents in New Brunswick and 81½ cents in Charlottetown. Sydney is the only unit with any kind of a break at the present time and is paying 61 cents per pound, but I am sure this will not last long. All indications are that beef will cost us 85 cents per pound in all units before the summer is over. Therefore, I feel any changes we make should be based on the assumption we will be paying 85 cents per pound shortly, and this will probably not decrease very much by the end of the year. If we are to meet our profit objectives, I feel we must move our cost of sales percentages back to last September's level. To do this, there appear to be at least three options: (1) raise prices, (2) decrease the patty size by moving to eight patties per pound, or (3) decrease the patty size as well as increasing prices."

Later in the memo Mr. Drayson added: "I think we must also bear in mind the fact that we have had to absorb increases not only in food costs but also in all other operating costs." Mr. Drayson was particularly conscious of the rise in labor costs. He had pointed out: "If you look back to 1965, when we first opened up, wages in our stores on an annual basis amounted to 17 to 18 percent of gross sales, exclusive of the manager's salary. Today we are looking at wage percentages any-

Exhibit 8
1971 price reduction announcement

A & W's New Look of "Total Value" for 1971!

At first glance our new menu may not seem much different. But take a second look, because there's a story to tell. Many of our prices are down. Why have we done this? Well, some people think when costs go up the only thing to do is raise prices. Sometimes that's true, but at A & W we think the best way to overcome our own rising costs is to do more business, and we think the best way to do more business is to increase the value to our customer. We refuse to compromise on quality, the size of our portions, or our service. So, as you look over the menu on the reverse side you will note we have lowered some of our prices—at first glance they may not appear large, but when your bill is totalled you will be pleasantly surprised. So that's the story, the same high standards of quality and service but greater value to you.

A & W DRIVE-INS (FUNDY) LIMITED

The BURGER FAMILY

PAPA BURGER	.64
2 Patties Meat	
MAMA BURGER	.44
Single Patty	
BABY BURGER	.24
(Cheese on above 5¢, Bacon 5¢)	
TEEN BURGER	.59

(Single Patty with Cheese, Bacon, Lettuce, Tomato, Mayonnaise, Toasted Sesame Seed Bun)

All served with your choice of Mustard, Ketchup, Pickles and Onions

CHUBBY CHICKEN

CHUBBY DINNER	1.35
3 Pcs. Chicken, French Fries, Cole Slaw	
CHUBBY JUNIOR	.90
2 Pcs. Chicken, French Fries	
CHUBBY NINE	2.75
9 Pcs. Chicken	
CHUBBY FIFTEEN	3.75
15 Pcs. Chicken	
CHUBBY TWENTY-ONE	4.95
21 Pcs. Chicken	
FAMILY PAK FRENCH FRIES	1.00
Cole Slaw, 4 oz. 15¢, ½ pint 30¢, 1 pint 50¢	

OTHER A & W FEATURES

Hot Dog	.34
Whistle Dog, Bacon, Cheese & Relish	.49
French Fries	.25
Onion Rings	.35
Fish and Chips	.65
Fish on a Bun	.15
Fried Clams (When Available)	.75
Fried Clams and Chips	1.00

BEVERAGES — DESSERTS

A & W ROOT BEER	.25 - .15
A & W ORANGE	.25 - .15
Baby root beer free to children under 6	
ICE CREAM FLOAT	.35 - .25
MILKSHAKES	.35
MILK	.30 - .20
COFFEE	.15
TEA	.15
HOT CHOCOLATE	.15
APPLE TURNOVER	.25
(With cheese or ice cream 10¢ extra)	
SUNDAE	
Chocolate or Strawberry	.20
ICE CREAM	.10

Exhibit 9
Cost of sales (Saint John), September 1972

Teenburger—59¢	
Meat	10.33¢
Bun	3.25
Seasoning	0.10
Onion	1.46
Mustard	0.15
Catsup	0.33
Pickles (2)	0.66
Bacon	1.76
Cheese	2.00
Mayonnaise	0.86
Lettuce	0.60
Tomato	0.90
Bag	1.71
	24.11¢—40.8%
Chubby dinner—$1.19	
3 pieces chicken	42.90¢
3 ounces fries	5.22
Catsup	0.66
Portion cup	0.20
Plastic fork	0.35
Salt	0.01
Greaseproof paper	0.41
Box	4.47
	54.22¢—45.6%
Jumbo root beer—mug (15¢)	3.72¢—18.6%
Jumbo root beer—take out (20¢)	6.21¢—31.0%
Baby burger—24¢	
Meat	6.20¢
Bun	2.83
Seasoning	0.02
Mustard	0.08
Catsup	0.17
Pickle	0.33
Onion	0.73
Bag	1.24
	11.60¢—48.3%

where from 20 to 24 percent, with the average being 22 to 23 percent."
He remarked that the increases were mainly due to increases in the minimum wage. The 1973 and the planned 1974 minimum wages in the Atlantic Province are noted in Exhibit 10. A&W (Fundy) paid on the average about 30 cents per hour higher than the minimum wage.

Mr. Drayson also attached to the memo a photocopy of a sales mix study done on one of the Moncton A&W drive-ins on a Saturday earlier in March. A copy of the study is contained in Exhibit 11. Mr.

Exhibit 10
Past and planned minimum hourly wage rate in New Brunswick, Nova Scotia, and Prince Edward Island

	New Brunswick	Nova Scotia	Prince Edward Island
April 1, 1972	$1.40	$1.35 ($1.20)*	$1.25 ($0.95)
April 1, 1973	1.50	1.55	1.24 (1.10)
July 1, 1973	1.50	1.65	1.65 (1.40)
January 1, 1974 (planned)	1.75	1.65	1.65

* Hourly rate in parentheses is for females, where this differs from the male hourly rate.

Exhibit 11
Analysis of sales, Moncton No. 1, March 1973 (Saturday)

Item	Selling price	Units	Sales
Pa	$0.64	107	$ 68.48
Pa Ch*	0.69	17	11.73
Grandpa	0.94	4	3.76
Pa Ch Bac†	0.79	6	4.74
Ma	0.44	77	33.88
Ma Ch	0.49	20	9.80
Ma Ch Bac	0.59	2	1.18
Teen	0.59	312	184.08
Pa Teen	0.89	5	4.45
Grandpa Teen	1.19	1	1.19
Happy	0.25	135	33.75
Happy Ch	0.30	9	2.70
Hot Dog	0.39	17	6.63
Whistle Dog	0.49	34	16.66
French fries	0.19 & 0.29	115	30.16
Onion rings	0.39	118	46.02
Fish and chips	0.69	40	27.60
Fried clams	0.85	14	11.90
Fried clams and french fries	1.05	17	17.85
Burger platters‡	Various	139	116.91
Chicken	Various	—	82.38
Drinks	Various	—	176.83
Other	Various	—	18.25
			$910.93

* Ch—with cheese.
† Bac—with bacon.
‡ Consists of a burger, fries, and coleslaw.

Drayson felt that the sales mix was quite representative of the sales mix in the company as a whole.

Mr. Drayson had already discussed the options at some length with Mr. Brathwaite, and he knew that Mr. Brathwaite had some strong opinions about what should be done. Mr. Brathwaite believed that A&W (Fundy) should try to position itself very close to McDonald's, by reducing the portions, if this was necessary to keep prices roughly comparable. Mr. Brathwaite felt that the customer didn't notice small differences in hamburger sizes. He pointed out, for example, that no customer appeared to have noticed A&W's switch from six to the pound to seven to the pound. Mr. Brathwaite felt that A&W could move quite easily to eight to the pound without the customer knowing, since it was a common practice in the fast-food trade to scale down the bun size by a proportional amount. Mr. Drayson disagreed with this. He felt that eight patties to the pound would be sufficiently different from six patties to the pound that many customers would notice.

As he once again reviewed the options, Mr. Drayson turned to the 1973 profit plan for one of the Saint John's units (Exhibit 12), which had been prepared in November 1972, based on the food cost data

Exhibit 12
1973 profit plan—Saint John No. 1

Net sales	$330,000
Food (including paper)	123,100
Gross profit.	206,900
Controllable expenses:	
Wages and fringe benefits.	83,900
Management salaries	16,600
Advertising and promotion	
National (1.5%)	5,000
Local.	19,800
Uniforms	1,200
Utilities.	4,400
Miscellaneous unit expenses*.	17,100
Total controllables.	148,000
Noncontrollable expenses:	
Lease of land and building	18,800
Franchise fee (1.5%).	5,000
Accounting services.	3,000
Insurance and taxes.	1,400
Equipment depreciation.	5,400
Administration†.	8,900
Total noncontrollables	42,500
Total operating expenses	190,500
Unit contribution	$ 16,400

  * Includes cleaning supplies, maintenance, snow removal, refuse collection, telephone, and so on.
   † Allocated by head office.

prepared in September 1972. He knew that it was a reasonably representative outlet, and he realized that if the company were to meet its profit objectives for 1973, he would have to obtain approximately the same contribution from this outlet irrespective of the rising costs. He realized that the board of directors would expect him to have a concrete set of recommendations.

Part 5

Strategic Marketing in Action

The real test of a successful corporate and marketing strategy is how it performs in a tough economic environment. The year 1981 was one of the worst experienced by producers of farm and construction equipment. Yet Deere & Co.'s performance during this period was impressive, particularly when compared to that of the troubled International Harvestor. The role of strategic planning in Deere's success is described:

> This enviable position is due largely to the solid but imaginative long-range planning of Hewitt, who has guided Deere as chief executive officer since 1955. When Hewitt took over the CEO reins, Deere was the country's second-ranking farm equipment maker, with no other business, and he quickly realized that the company would have to expand internationally and diversify if it was to grow and prosper.[1]

One of the company's real strengths is its dealer network, which helped Deere to increase its market share in farm equipment by as much as 35 percent in 1981.[2] Its independent dealer organization, a strong financial position, and excellent products place the firm in a leading position for the 1980s.

The cases in Part 5 are concerned with (1) preparing strategic marketing plans and (2) evaluating and controlling plans that have been implemented. Our objectives in this introduction are to examine strategic marketing planning and control and to illustrate the contents of a marketing plan.

---

[1] "Deere: Payoff From Planning," *Dun's Business Month*, December 1981, p. 64.

[2] Ibid., p. 64.

THE STRATEGIC MARKETING PLAN

In Chapter 1, we outlined a 10-step approach to building and implementing a strategic marketing plan. Exhibit 1 provides an overview of these steps, with the shaded areas highlighting the strategic marketing plan and evaluation of its results after implementation.

Exhibit 1
Strategic marketing in action

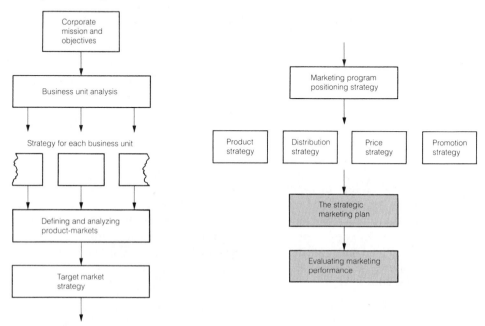

Source: David W. Cravens, *Strategic Marketing* (Homewood, Ill.: Richard D. Irwin, 1982), p. 359.

When analyzing cases in Part 5 that require the development of a strategic marketing plan, the 10-step approach serves as a useful checklist for preparing such a plan.

New Horizons Travel, Inc. (Case 5–1), offers an interesting example of how two entrepreneurs developed a business plan for a proposed new venture. A review of this case will give you an example of the scope and contents of a strategic marketing plan.

Some planning guidelines

One of the most important aspects of planning is determining the opportunities and problems underlying the plan. The situation analysis should identify the problems and opportunities that are to be specifically addressed in the strategic marketing plan. A guide to the situation analysis is provided in Exhibit 1–5 (Chapter 1). The dangers of a faulty situation analysis are illustrated in the case described in Exhibit 2. Note the use of the Profit Impact of Marketing Strategy (PIMS) analysis in problem identification.

One real danger in marketing planning is placing too much detail in the written plan. Simplicity is clearly the best rule to follow. The plan should be used as an active management guide rather than as a refer-

Exhibit 2
The case of the crumb business

The possible danger of jumping to conclusions on product strategies too quickly is illustrated by one business unit of a packaged foods company. (While the reported experience is true, certain figures and the nature of the product itself have been disguised.)

As the tale is told, this unit is in the prosaic business of producing and selling bread crumbs. During the late 1970s the unit was generating a sales volume of some $30 million a year, and it operated in a stable market environment against three major competitors. While the product was judged by consumers to be of high quality, and sales volume per employee was also high, the unit's 4.3 percent return on investment was deemed unacceptably low. (Indeed, comparison with a PIMS "Par Report" suggested that the return on investment for a business of this kind should normally be expected to be in the vicinity of 14.1 percent.)

Investigation showed three major weaknesses: plant capacity for the company's brand was about double the volume of sales; working capital was high; and marketing effectiveness was low. In a word, the crumb business looked "crummy"; and the marketing plan in the year of review contained these unequivocal words: "The number one strategic priority is to divest ourselves of this plant."

In a search for a less drastic remedy, the company's corporate staff considered boosting sales by aggressive marketing tactics or by employing idle capacity to supply private-label accounts. It was soon found, however, that neither course could provide much relief—nor could the alternative of selling the company's plant and obtaining the required crumbs from a copacker.

With further guidance from "par" ratios in the PIMS data base, it was discovered that the amount of working capital in the business was far above standard levels. Delving further, the staff investigation found that working capital had sharply increased during the previous two years as a result of overly optimistic sales forecasts, which had in turn led to excessive inventories of both raw materials and finished goods.

The outcome following this appraisal: The bread crumb plant was not sold, and an improved forecasting and inventory control system restored the business to a satisfactory range of profitability. And, for the company executives involved, there was not only respect for PIMS in helping to ensure the asking of relevant questions but also a chastened awareness of the need to avoid being too hasty in categorizing a problem business as unredeemable.

Source: David S. Hopkins, *The Marketing Plan*, Report no. 801 (New York: Conference Board, 1981), p. 41.

ence book. Below are excerpts from a critique of a manufacturer's strategic plan. The names are disguised for competitive reasons:

☐ The market opportunity analysis is weak and incomplete. Throughout the plan more attention should be given to *analysis* and *implications,* and less to description.

☐ Not surprisingly for this company, there is a heavy emphasis on production and operations, with limited coverage of markets, competition, end users, market size, and customer characteristics.

☐ The plan does not highlight strategic gaps, threats, and critical issues. For example, what does "the demise of independent fabricators in some areas" indicate—a declining market, new forms of distribution, or what?

☐ The plan does not indicate specific market targets where this company has strengths over competition and where it has the best chances of strategically positioning itself favorably against competition.

☐ After reading the plan, one gains no real sense of priorities or of what critical actions will move the firm toward improved performance.

☐ Finally, the plan is probably longer than is necessary. It should be used as an active management guide rather than as a reference book.

This is not a diversified firm, and it is operating in only a few product-markets. While the business plan was over 50 pages in length, it failed to focus on the above points. Clearly, the key to successful planning is to achieve relevance rather than quantity of paper.

A final guideline concerning planning is to recognize that planning is decision making. The focus of a strategic plan is a coordinated set of decisions for executing the strategies selected by management. Thus, it is crucial that the plan move beyond description and analysis to indicate actions to be taken. Along with actions and their priorities, responsibility should be indicated for carrying out the plan.

Implementation

One shortcoming of using cases in the classroom is that you cannot implement your recommendations and thus determine how successful they are in meeting objectives. Nevertheless, we encourage you to carefully consider implementation in your recommendations. There is often more than one possible course of action that can be taken in a case solution, although, for certain of the cases, the results of actions taken by management can be useful in showing the consequences of one course of action. Also, class discussion can provide additional insights concerning the strengths and limitations of different implementation strategies.

In part to facilitate implementation, the Norton Company of Worchester, Massachusetts, has eliminated its central planning group and instead has decentralized planning responsibility to line management, as described by Donald Melville, president:

> Planning, . . . Melville is convinced, is best done in the field. "This is not a company that creates plans, puts them in big thick binders, and then files them in a drawer," he says. "We have eliminated our planning division. Line management does the planning."
>
> What Melville watches like a hawk is how well his group vice presidents in abrasives, petroleum and mining, and diversified products fare against their competitors in the field.[3]

This hands-on approach to planning clearly facilitates implementation, since the planners are the doers.

STRATEGIC EVALUATION AND CONTROL

The relationship between strategic planning and control is shown in Exhibit 3. Strategic planning is an ongoing process of making plans,

Exhibit 3
Strategic planning and control process

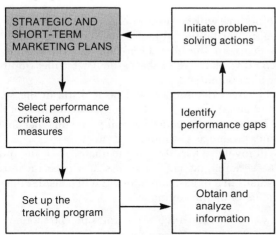

Source: David W. Cravens, *Strategic Marketing* (Homewood, Ill.: Richard D. Irwin, 1982), p. 413.

implementing them, tracking performance, identifying performance gaps, and initiating problem-solving actions to close the gap between desired and actual results. Management must establish performance criteria and measures so that information can be obtained for use in tracking performance.

---

[3] Paul Brown, "See Spot Run," *Forbes*, May 10, 1982, p. 140.

Exhibit 4
Illustrative strategic audit guide

Marketing planning audit program

For each major business unit/product   Time period: 1, 3, 5 plus years.

Objective

Assess the short-, intermediate-, and long-term marketing outlook for each major business unit (profit center and major product). The emphasis of this assessment is an "outside in" appraisal of conditions and trends occurring in the external business arenas that will create significant opportunities and/or problems for our respective business units. The assessment will (1) provide a context for developing and testing the needs for, likely value, and success of proposed alternative innovative programs; (2) focus the creative inputs of all business functions on significant short- and long-term needs; and (3) ensure necessary line/staff interaction and accountability.

These audits and resultant resource allocation planning efforts determine requirements and means to ensure profitability of operations in the short, intermediate, and long term.

This marketing-oriented audit and resource planning are intended to position operations effectively with respect to product line, market coverage, distribution, sales, and merchandising approach.

Approach

A marketing plan outline will be used to classify, collect, organize, analyze, and present the information required for the Marketing Audit Program. The approach will focus on the short-term outlook and seek to exploit strengths and overcome weaknesses of the particular business units with a view to their longer-term potential.

The marketing objectives determined will be realistic in the sense that they are attainable but ambitious enough to stretch the abilities of the company to meet them. They will be specific and call for results that are definite in expectation and measurable as to timing and effect.

The evaluation will involve a harshly realistic quantitative and qualitative appraisal of the relative strengths and weaknesses of each business unit's marketing position versus that of its competitors. It will consider the separate and combined elements of the marketing mix:

1. Product.   4. Advertising and sales promotion.
2. Distribution structure.   5. Sales effort.
3. Pricing system.   6. Customer service.

From this evaluation will emerge a limited priority ranking of critical factors essential to the progress and/or improvement in the outlook for each business unit considering:

1. Protection and/or maintenance of favorable position.
2. Overcoming competitive or unfavorable position.
3. Creating favorable competitive advantage in the marketplace.

Exhibit 4 (*concluded*)

The criteria utilized in the evaluation will be judgmental assessment as to relative importance, practical manageability in terms of limited resources of manpower, cost, time, capital, etc., and high probability of yielding sufficient incremental profit improvement to offset the incremental cost in the short and intermediate term.

Control

A management review of the audit program outlined above includes:

1. Definitive statements of what is necessary to develop and/or translate the respective marketing plans into action programs.
2. Schedules for completion of critical program elements.
3. Assignment of accountability for program execution.
4. Methods for practically evaluating program progress.
5. Procedures and criteria for measuring effectiveness of results.

Source: David S. Hopkins, *The Marketing Plan*, Report no. 801 (New York: Conference Board, 1981), p. 67.

The day-to-day management of a strategy can divert executive attention from overall evaluation of the adequacy of the strategy. Once a strategy is implemented, management should periodically analyze whether the strategy is appropriate for the current market and competitive environment. An example will illustrate the importance of an ongoing program of strategic evaluation and control. Safeway Stores is the largest supermarket chain in the United States, having gained this position from A&P in the early 1970s. Nearly a decade later Safeway was experiencing problems due, in part, to not adjusting its marketing strategy to changing conditions:

> "They've just never been innovators," explains Barry Scher of Giant Food. Safeway, for example, was late to spot the trend toward cavernous "superstores" that offer higher-margined nonfood items. The big chain also got caught in the middle of a market that was moving in two directions at once. Safeway didn't go for discount, no-frills stores; but it didn't upgrade either, refusing to open pharmacies and specialty departments. Even optical scanners, which save time and money, were usually introduced by the competition.[4]

One way to help prevent problems like those confronting Safeway is to conduct strategic marketing audits at regular intervals (three–five years). Such an audit can be used as a starting point in developing a strategic marketing planning program, and then it can be repeated at intervals suitable for a particular firm's planning environment. An example of a company's strategic audit guide is shown in Exhibit 4. A

---

[4] Jeff Blyskal, "A&P West?" *Forbes*, April 12, 1982, p. 63.

comprehensive checklist for conducting a strategic marketing audit is provided in the companion text to this casebook.[5]

To conclude our discussion of strategic planning and control, you may find a review of the marketing plan outline shown in Exhibit 5 useful in illustrating how a marketing plan is prepared in a particular company.

Exhibit 5
Topic outline for a product line marketing plan for a home furnishing products company

I. **Product policy statement**

State briefly but explicitly the price range, quality level, distribution policy and brand strategy being used to reach the line's intended consumer markets.

II. **Marketing background**

1. *Definition of consumer markets*

Describe the consumer markets in which each product line has been sold.

   a. Characteristics of significant consumer groups

Show population and per capita purchases by:

Intended use of purchase (own use, gift, etc.)
Family status and size
Family income
Geographic region
Other significant consumer characteristics

   b. Known or assumed consumer preferences and buying habits
Product feature preferences
Shopping habits
Motivations for purchases (rank by importance)
Product features
Brand awareness
Price
Advertising
Promotion
Packaging
Display
Sales assistance
Other

   c. Significant consumer market trends: Size, characteristics, and buying habits
Recent trends
Expected changes

---

[5] See David W. Cravens, *Strategic Marketing* (Homewood, Ill.: Richard D. Irwin, 1982), pp. 415–17.

Exhibit 5 (*continued*)

---

2. *Market size and sales statistics*
    a. Market trends (past five years)
        Industry sales
        Product-type sales
        Price index
    b. Distribution trends
        Industry sales by type of outlet (i.e., retail, premium, and institutional) and further by major types of outlets within each broad area (i.e., department store, chain store, specialty store, etc.)
        Product-type sales by type of outlet
        Product-type sales by method of distribution (direct or wholesale)
    c. Product line sales trends
        Sales dollars
        Sales dollars by type of outlet
        Share of total market
        Share of product-type market
        Share of key outlet distribution
        Sales dollars by method of distribution
        Price index

3. *Product line profit and cost history (five years)*
    a. Profit history
        Net profit dollars
        Net profit as percent of sales
        Return on investment
    b. Manufacturing cost history
        Gross profit dollars
        Gross profit as percent of sales
    c. Marketing cost history (five years)
        Show how marketing money has been spent and with what results
        Advertising cost
            Dollars by type (i.e., national, cooperative, and trade)
            Percent of sales
            Share of advertising versus share of market
        Promotion, display, and fixturing cost
            Dollars
            Percent of sales
            Fixture placements versus potential
        Distribution cost (includes distributor discount, transportation, warehousing, inventory carrying costs, and the cost of distributor selling aids)
            Dollars
            Percent of sales

Exhibit 5 (*continued*)

Distribution coverage versus potential
    Kinds of accounts
    Number of accounts
    Sales potential of accounts
Field selling costs
    Dollars
    Percent of sales
    Direct account coverage versus potential

4. *Competitive comparison*

Highlight significant differences between this company and its competition.

    Product line composition and acceptance
    Distribution methods and coverage
    Field selling methods
    Consumer marketing programs

5. *Conclusions*

Summarize the major problems and opportunities requiring action based on analysis of background information. Consider:

    Consumer and trade market penetration
    Distribution coverage
    Product line needs
    Price revisions
    Cost reductions
    New market and product opportunities

III. **Primary marketing and profit objectives**

1. *Marketing objectives*

    Sales dollars
    Market share by major type of outlet

2. *Profit objectives*

    Gross profit dollars
    Gross profit as percent of sales
    Net profit dollars
    Net profit as percent of sales
    Return on investment

Note external qualifying assumptions such as business cycle trends, industry trends, changes in size and characteristics of consumer market segments, distribution trends, competitive activity, price levels, import quotas, and factory capacity.

IV. **Overall marketing strategy**

State the strategic direction to be followed in order to achieve primary product line marketing and profit objectives.

1. *Consumer and trade market emphasis*

2. *Trademark and product feature emphasis*

Exhibit 5 (*continued*)

---

   3. *Marketing mix emphasis*

   4. *Functional objectives*

      Establish the contribution needed from each functional area in order to implement the overall strategy and to achieve primary objectives.

     a. Field selling

        Distribution objectives expressed in number, size, quality, and type of wholesale, retail, premium, and institutional accounts needed to meet sales volume objectives

     b. Product development

        New product objectives expressed in numbers, types, introductory dates, sales volume, and profit contributions from new products

     c. Advertising

        Identify markets to be reached

        Communication objectives (nature of message and retention level sought by consumers and trade customers)

        Trade participation objectives in cooperative advertising programs

     d. Promotion and fixturing

        Sales objectives for major promotions

        Fixture placement and sales volume objectives

     e. Merchandising

        Objectives for the number and types of new merchandising programs and for trade participation in the company's programmed merchandising

     f. Business operation

        Customer delivery service objectives

        Inventory turnover objectives

        Product line composition and size objectives

        Pricing objectives

V. Pro forma financial statements and budgets

   1. *Marketing budgets*

        Field selling expense

        Advertising expense

          National

          Cooperative

          Trade

        Promotion expense

          Consumer

          Trade

        Fixturing and display expense

        Product development expense

        Market research expense

        Distribution expense

        Administrative and allocated expense

Exhibit 5 (*continued*)

2. *Pro forma financial statements*
   a. Annual profit and loss statement (expense detail as shown above)
      Next year pro forma by quarter
      Current year budget by quarter
      Last year actual by quarter
   b. Annual revision of five-year pro forma
      Profit and loss statement (expense detail for broad categories)

VI. **Action plans**
   1. *Product line plans*
      a. New product objectives
      b. New product positioning versus identified product needs of consumers
      c. New product specifications
         Style, weight, size, finish, etc.
         Manufacturing cost
         Selling price
      d. New product budgets
         Exploration and screening
         Development
         Market introduction
      e. New product event schedule
         Design releases
         Designs complete
         Market tests complete
         Production releases
         Advertising planned and scheduled
         Selling aids complete
         Distribution achieved
         Commencement of consumer advertising, promotion, and selling
      f. Planned deletions and accompanying phaseout programs
   2. *Advertising plans*
      a. National advertising (by individual campaign)
         Definition of consumers and their buying motivations
         Message theme and objectives
         Reach and frequency objectives
         Budgets
         Preparation and execution schedules
         Creative plans
         Media plans
      b. Cooperative advertising programs
         Trade participation objectives
         Budget

Exhibit 5 (*concluded*)

> Relationships to other marketing programs
> Preparation and execution schedule

    c. Trade advertising (by individual campaign)
>   Message and audience objectives
>   Budgets
>   Preparation and execution schedules
>   Creative plans
>   Media plans

    d. Trademark changes

3. *Sales promotion and display plans*
   a. Consumer and trade promotion objectives
   b. General description of promotion programs, budgets, and calendar
   c. Fixturing programs and budgets

4. *Major packaging plans*

5. *Trade selling plans*
   a. Description of significant changes in distribution policy
   >   Approved outlets
   >   Distribution methods
   b. Distribution coverage objectives
   c. Account coverage objectives
   d. Selling expense budgets
   e. Specific new account targets
   f. Special trade merchandising programs and calendar
   g. Field selling programs and calendar
   h. New services for trade customers
   >   Delivery service
   >   Inventory backup
   >   Selling support or the like
   i. Sales quotas for each representative by product line

6. *Special market research projects*
   Include a general description of each project, its objectives, budget, and timetable.

7. *Pricing recommendations*

8. *Special cost reduction programs*
   Include a general description of each program, its expected dollar savings, and an assignment of responsibilities.

Source: Reproduced by permission from David S. Hopkins, *The Marketing Plan*, Report no. 801 (New York: Conference Board, 1981), pp. 113–18.

Case 5–1

New Horizons Travel, Inc.

As her plane for Raleigh took off from Logan Airport on July 5, 1977, Sara Wade thought about events of the last four days. She and her partner, Ellen Wolfe, had made progress in planning the August 1978 start-up of their New Horizons Travel agency. Sara regretted that she had had so little free time just to enjoy Boston's sights. She smiled remembering Ellen's toast, "To independence!" and the accompanying cheers of friends at the Boston Pops Esplanade concert on the Fourth of July. Sara found the idea of independence in the context of starting a new business exhilarating but a bit scary.

Sara's basic optimism about the new venture seemed well founded. After all, Ellen had had four years' experience as a travel agent and was now in charge of a major division of a recognized Boston travel agency. Sara herself was about to enter the second year of the MBA program at the University of North Carolina at Chapel Hill and had had several years' experience at the same agency. Both young women were mobile, energetic, and enthusiastic about travel and starting their own business.

That morning Sara and Ellen had agreed that they were ready to go to potential investors: their fathers, some relatives, and an investor in Winston-Salem who had already approached them. Because their ability to move to their target city was so important to the venture, Sara and Ellen, both single, had given New Horizons Travel priority over any developments in their personal lives that might jeopardize their mobility. Now that they were ready to present their plan to potential investors, this understanding had become even more crucial.

For the rest of the flight, Sara reviewed their business plan as any potential investor might.

This case was prepared by Mary Ellen Templeton and Professor Richard I. Levin of the University of North Carolina at Chapel Hill. Copyright © 1978 by the School of Business Administration, University of North Carolina at Chapel Hill.

449

NEW HORIZONS TRAVEL, INC.
ELLEN WOLFE AND SARA WADE, FOUNDERS

New Horizons Travel, Inc., is an innovative concept strategically designed to maximize profits and growth in the retail and/or wholesale travel business. The management team is well suited to this endeavor: Ms. Wolfe has four years of practical experience at the retail travel level and is now in a position of authority at the well-known Colonial Travel Agency in Boston; Ms. Wade will have just completed her MBA degree at the University of North Carolina at Chapel Hill and brings to the team experience in sales, advertising, and marketing as well as business expertise. The proposed business plan for a travel agency requires relatively low initial investment and working capital, while affording excellent prospects for long-term growth and profitability. In this report we have attempted to make a realistic assessment of the market, its environment, and the product types to develop a comprehensive marketing strategy outlining the growth of one or more retail travel agencies.

OVERVIEW OF THE TRAVEL SERVICE INDUSTRY

The travel agency acts as an intermediary between the traveling public and transportation companies. It is similar to an independent distributor or retail outlet selling a standard wholesale travel package to the consumer. The product it sells has the same price and the same characteristics as the product of the agency down the street. To make matters worse, there is no need for the consumer to go through a travel agency to obtain his required travel package. He can simply deal directly with the transportation company.

The travel agency must not only sell the customer on the benefits of its services and conveniences, but it must also convince him that its own unique dispensation of these services deserves his patronage. Differentiation is the key to a successful operation: the agency must market a package of services that is sufficiently distinctive from the service packages of other agencies to win the customer as a loyal client.

MARKET ANALYSIS

1. *The environment.* The travel service industry is closely linked to the government-regulated transportation industry. It is thus subject to unforeseeable market fluctuations imposed from such external sources as government regulatory agencies, technological change, economic factors, and changing consumer preferences. The greatest risk the travel agent faces is the fact that he cannot control his end product. He can control only the way he delivers and promotes the

product to his customer. The travel agency, in effect, does not sell "travel" but sells the "service" of obtaining travel for the customer. There is a wide variety of substitutable services to compete with the travel agency. Furthermore, a potential customer can simply telephone his order directly to the airline rather than telephoning his travel agency.

2. *Major product types.* *Wholesale travel* is a package put together by an agency and sold directly to the customer. A major advantage is price control—the wholesaler can set his own prices and markups and at the same time enjoy quantity discounts. He has total control over the travel product. The operation is riskier than retail because the liability rests with the wholesaler (he must guarantee his product to the retailer) and much more capital is required to be at stake.

Retail travel sells the packages put together by the wholesaler and is required by law to accept the prices as given. Control over the travel product is practically nonexistent. About 30 percent of all retail agencies sell wholesale tours on a limited basis, usually to give special service and protection to good customers. The motive here is good customer relations, not profitability.

Corporate business travel provides the major source of business for the retail agency. It is stable, steady, and does not fluctuate with economic conditions.

Vacation travel is often profitable but is extremely volatile and fluctuates with seasonal and economic influences.

Commission schedules vary with the different product types:

International air fare	8%
Domestic air fare	7
Hotels and car rentals	5–10*
Tours	11†
Amtrak	10

*These are usually incidentals, part of a package.
†The highest profit item.

The commissions of an agency usually average 7.5 percent because the majority of travel sold is domestic air fare.

3. *Demand analysis.* Travel agencies usually have three sources of customer demand:

Walk-ins respond to an agency's promotion—an advertisement, a newsletter, or often the Yellow Pages.

Established customers are the mainstay of the business and are valued for their contact potential.

Reference customers are the key to successful growth; they come to an agency because an established customer recommended it. These contacts play a major role in the growth of the agency.

The volume of business coming from these demand sources depends upon the location of the agency, how long it has been in operation, the types of business it has built up in the past, and its methods of advertising and promotion.

It is difficult to overemphasize the importance of the "word of mouth" reference: an agency often guards its contacts like cherished jewels. Contacts spur demand growth. Once a customer's loyalty is won, he will refer his friends and acquaintances to the agency, and business increases exponentially.

Contacts are the primary means of entering a market. New agencies have historically used several strategies to obtain the crucial contacts necessary to break into a market:

1. Buying an existing agency that already has contacts.
2. Moving into a town with a dying agency and stealing its contacts.
3. Finding an area with fast-growing businesses and cultivating these new untapped contacts.
4. Hiring employees away from competing agencies and hoping that contacts will follow the employees to the new business.

4. *Identifying the target customer.*   Many types of people travel: families, businesspeople, retired couples, the affluent, students, honeymooners, singles, specialty groups. The successful travel agency must find the customer types who are most likely to contribute to the growth and profitability of the agency.

An agency should use these criteria for selecting the target customer:

a. Potential for developing contacts.
b. Variety of travel products that the customer may want. (A doctor may go on professional group trips and also want a vacation.)
c. Stability of demand volume. (The agency prefers steady corporate business to volatile vacation business.)

New Horizons will focus on two categories of travel customers.

1. *The professional:* Will do steady volume of business travel; has the time and money for a vacation trip; has access to a large pool of potential contacts.
2. *The affluent:* Will do steady business of vacations—even during recessions; have ample time and money for travel; have access to a large pool of potential contacts.

5. *Promotion strategies.*   An optimal promotion strategy is designed not only to sell the specific travel product but also to sell the agency's unique brand of service. Promotions are the means of making potential customers aware that the agency is available, helpful, and free of charge. The strategy should be designed to appeal specifically to the more profitable segments.

An aggressive promotion strategy is necessary in inverse proportion to the length of time the agency has been operating and the number of contacts it has. The fledgling agency with no contacts is forced to rely on promotion strategy as the only means of cultivating a clientele.

Types of promotions can vary widely. Word of mouth, of course, is the most reliable and successful method and the least expensive. Control of this valuable tool is, unfortunately, out of the agency's hands.

The desirability and effectiveness of promotions are questioned by many agencies. Agencies that do little or no advertising usually have been in business long enough to develop a stable clientele.

The following types of promotions, however, are used successfully by a number of agencies.

a. Newspaper advertising is usually limited to the travel section of the newspaper and often promotes a specific tour package.

b. Yellow Pages advertising has proven invaluable for many agencies, particularly those just starting out. It is an excellent way to develop cold contacts.

c. Radio advertising is sometimes used to promote a special tour package or to promote a contest.

d. Direct mail promotions have become more popular in recent years. Newsletters full of lavish descriptions of exotic places are sent to present and potential clients.

e. Travel parties are also useful. The agency throws a free "theme" party such as a luau and invites all of its clients. Travel films are usually shown at such events to tickle the customer's travel fantasies.

MARKET RESEARCH

1. *Evaluating a potential market.* Our market research is focused on the selection of a location for our business. There must be market development potential. The town or community chosen is therefore a crucial factor in the success of the agency. A location will be examined against a set of criteria covering the community, competition, and future customers.

a. Evaluating the town and community:

Carefully analyze the demographic makeup of the area. Check income, age groups, and professions to find the number of people in the target customer segment.

Evaluate possible sources of travel demand: university, schools, industry. Is there a dominant organization with which to ally?

Evaluate accessibility of travel: near an airport? trains?

Evaluate economic characteristics. Is there a rapidly growing business sector whose business can be captured? Is the town's economy expanding or contracting? The new business growth will be a good indicator of growth potential for our market.

b.   Evaluating the competition:

Does the competition have more business than it can handle?

Are the competing agencies "Mom and Pop" outfits that are being run lackadaisically?

Check the competing agencies' advertising and promotion strategies. Are they in the Yellow Pages?

Are they serving their customers well?

Are their locations convenient?

How effectively have they saturated the market?

How long have they been in existence?

Find out prices, market shares, services offered, size of sales force.

c.   Evaluating potential customers:

Identify traffic patterns within the community, and find a location that will attract walk-in traffic.

Check on specialized travel requirements in the community.

Is the consumer purchasing behavior stable or fluctuating?

What amounts of business can be expected from groups, vacations, businesses? What is the development potential in these areas?

2.   *The create versus buy decision.*   The market can be entered by creating an agency or buying out an existing one. An existing agency has the advantage of established, developed contacts, but it also locks us into an already established reputation and image and perhaps even a dying situation.

These areas must be examined if we decide to buy into an existing business:

Net worth, income potential, growth potential.

The agency's types of contacts and customers.

Goodwill, physical assets, momentum.

Who are the customers, and why do they come to this agency?

Breakdown of business sources: walk-ins, vacations, tours, business.

Volume linked to previous owner's skills, reputation, contacts?

What is the agency's reputation in the industry and in the community?

Evaluate location of agency for future growth trends.

Determine why the present owner wants to sell.

Evaluate the development potential of the agency as well as the current sales level.

THE MARKETING PLAN

Our marketing plan will focus on four elements that we have identified as critical to the success of our agency:

a. *Differentiation:* Delivering the service in a way different from that of similar agencies by emphasizing *service* and *convenience*.
b. *Promotion:* Creating the image that the product is better than, or different from, its competitors.
c. *Location:* Establishing the agency in an economically healthy community and in a visible, convenient location.
d. *Service:* Ensuring a knowledgeable, friendly agent at the point of sale.

The marketing strategy is designed to create differentiation through promotion, location, and a carefully developed personal selling strategy and to reach target customers through promotion, contacts, and location. Since the product is a standard one, differentiation is the key. By packaging the product differently with a different image, we can achieve a "brand" identity and compete effectively for the customer's business.

1. *Location.* We will search for an optimum location in the "Sun Belt" region of the Southeast because that area is growing at a fast rate and its people are becoming increasingly cosmopolitan and well traveled. Within the area we will select a community that affords very good market development potential, preferably near an educational institution or a major business area.

Location within the city or community is crucial. It must be both convenient and visible. A location in a well-populated business area will bring important walk-in traffic from potential high-volume customers, help introduce the new agency to new clients, and establish the agency's reputation as accessible and convenient.

2. *Personal selling strategy.* The personal selling strategy is designed to develop and keep a loyal clientele. Our unique package of the travel service will center on service, knowledge, and friendliness to convince the customer that we are better than our competitors.

Our sales agents will be very knowledgeable in all areas of the travel business. We plan to send them to seminars and agent schools whenever possible to ensure that they are well versed in the complex changing rules and regulations of the industry. The agent with the latest information usually can give the best price on a travel package. Since our product is actually information, we consider it most important to be fast, efficient, and accurate.

At the point of sale, we insist that our agents be pleasant and friendly. We particularly value politeness, patience, and friendliness because these are necessary to win and keep customers. Since we feel that an important part of the product we sell is us, we must always present the most pleasant view to the public and maintain high product quality.

3. *Target customers.*   Our promotion package is designed to develop long-term relationships with target customers: the affluent who regularly travel and business and professional people who will give us steady business volume as well as seasonal vacation business. These people are very useful in developing contacts among their friends, and their demand will not fluctuate widely with changing economic conditions.

4. *Promotion strategy.*   Advertising is very important at first to establish the agency's reputation, image, and name. Our advertising will convey the image of a knowledgeable, efficient, and energetic agency. Its tone will be pleasant, relaxed, in good taste, and not commercial or hard sell. It will be directed to target customers first and the general public second.

The name of our agency, New Horizons, implies adventure, the future, and newness, and it has good advertising value.

The advertising budget will be $200 a month the first year and will gradually decrease over the next four years as we rely more heavily on contacts for new business.

We will use a newsletter to promote travel ideas to our clients and to encourage a sense of service to the clientele, and we will immediately begin to develop a mailing list.

A large Yellow Pages advertisement is a crucial component of our plan to develop new business.

We may use travel parties in years 4 and 5 after we are well established.

Promotion budget

Year	1	2	3	4	5
Newspaper	$1,100	$ 900	$ 600		
Radio	700	500	100		
Yellow Pages	600	600	600	600	600
Direct mail			100	100	100
Travel parties				100	100
Total	$2,400	$2,000	$1,400	$800	$800

---

5. *Product strategy.*   Our product strategy is designed to promote the high profit travel items when possible. We will carefully cultivate the business travel to ensure a steady demand level. We will also promote and specialize in group tours for maximum profit and will market ourselves as "the place for groups" by year two. By year three we plan to begin putting together our own group tours and going into the wholesale end of the business. This will happen only after we are satisfactorily established in the retail trade and have a good financial position.

6. Sales forecast

Year 1

Month	Income source			
	Business	**Vacation**	**Groups/tours**	**Total**
1	$ 2,500	$ 1,500		$ 4,000
2	3,800	2,200		6,000
3	5,700	3,300		9,000
4	8,200	4,800		13,000
5	11,600	5,400	$ 1,000	18,000
6	13,500	8,500	3,000	25,000
7	16,000	9,000	5,000	30,000
8	19,900	11,100	6,000	37,000
9	24,300	12,700	8,000	45,000
10	27,000	15,000	8,000	50,000
11	32,400	18,600	9,000	60,000
12	33,000	22,000	10,000	70,000
Total	$202,900	$114,100	$50,000	$367,000

Note: The percentage of income from each product category will change as the agency becomes more established.

Years 1 and 2

Business	54%	Business	50%
Vacations	30	Vacations	27
Groups/tours	16	Groups/tours	23

Note: Group tours, the highest profit item at 11 percent commission, will contribute an increasing share of gross sales, commissions, and net profit.

Years 1–5

Year	Gross sales	Commission income
1	$ 367,000	$ 27,525
2	700,000	52,500
3	1,500,000	112,500
4	2,000,000	160,000
5	2,500,000	212,500

Years 1–3, commissions at average of 7.5 percent of sales.

Year 4, commissions at 8 percent of sales.

Year 5, commissions at 8.5 percent of sales resulting from increased groups/tours at 11 percent commission rate.

FINANCIAL ISSUES

1. *Expense schedule*

Start-up costs

Capitalized:
Leasehold improvements for office	$3,000
Electricity and phone installation................	300
Incorporation legal fees.........................	350
Licenses.......................................	400
Equipment: Typewriters.........................	600
	4,650

Other:
Printing costs	$ 200
Insurance......................................	1,000
Introductory advertising........................	600
Supplies.......................................	400
	2,200
Total..	$6,850

Monthly overhead costs

Rent	$ 600
Equipment rental	175
Salaries	2,000
Advertising.......................	200
Utilities.........................	150
Phone............................	120
Legal/CPA	75
Postage and supplies..............	10
Miscellaneous	65
Interest..........................	400*
	$4,400

---

*On $5,000 note at 8 percent interest.

2. *Pro forma profit and loss*

Year	1	2	3	4	5
Gross sales	$ 367,000	$700,000	$1,500,000	$2,000,000	$2,500,000
Due to carriers	(339,475)	(647,500)	(1,387,500)	(1,840,000)	(2,287,500)
Commission income....	27,525	52,500	112,500	160,000	212,500
Operating expenses	(52,800)	(52,800)	(61,000)	(69,000)	(78,800)
Net income/loss	(25,275)	(300)	51,500	91,000	133,700
Expenses/start-up costs.	(2,200)				
First-year loss	(27,475)				
Tax	(6,044.5)	(66)	(24,720)	(43,680)	(64,176)
Profit/loss after tax.....	$ (21,430.5)	$ (233)	$ 24,720*	$ 47,320	$ 69,524

*Operating losses in the first two years will be carried forward to offset taxes in the third year.

3. Balance sheet

Beginning of Year 1

Assets

Current assets:

Cash	$31,050	
Prepaid insurance	1,000	
Prepaid expenses	1,200	
Total current assets		$33,250

Other assets:

Incorporation and licenses	750	
Leasehold improvements	3,300	
Typewriters	600	
Total other assets		4,650
Total assets		$37,900

Liabilities and Owners' Equity

Liabilities:

Three-year note payable, bank	$ 5,000	
Four-year note payable, grandfather	5,000	
Total Liabilities		$10,000

Owners' equity:

Founder Wade	9,300	
Founder Wolfe	9,300	
Investor Y	9,300	
Total equity		27,900
Total liabilities and owners' equity		$37,900

4. Cash flow: Year 1

	Month					
	1	**2**	**3**	**4**	**5**	**6**
Sales..........	$ 4,000	$ 6,000	$ 9,000	$13,000	$18,000	$25,000
Commissions earned but not received*......	300	450	675	975	1,350	1,875
Expenses........	4,400	4,400	4,400	4,400	4,400	4,400
Over/short......	(4,400)	(4,400)	(4,400)	(4,400)	(4,400)	(4,400)
Cumulative credit needed......	11,250†	15,650	20,050	24,450	28,850	33,250

	Month					
	7	**8**	**9**	**10**	**11**	**12**
Sales..........	$25,000	$30,000	$45,000	$50,000	$60,000	$70,000
Commissions earned......	2,250	2,775	3,375	3,750	4,500	5,250
Expenses........	4,400	4,400	4,400	4,400	4,400	4,400
Over/short......	(2,150)	(1,625)	(1,025)	(650)	100	850
First six months' commissions..........	5,625					
Cumulative credit needed......	29,775	31,400	32,425	33,075	32,975	32,125

*The Air Traffic Conference of America withholds commissions earned for the first six months while it examines your financial structure. At the end of this time period, if the conference is assured that you are solvent and legitimate, it will license you and send you a check for the commissions earned.
†Cash needed for start-up costs: $6,850.

RETURN ON INVESTMENT

The long-term growth opportunities of this plan afford the investor a very high return on investment. For an initial investment of only $9,300, the investor obtains a one-third interest in the future earnings and growth of the agency. Using the five-year planning horizon, here is a calculation of the present value of the one-third interest in the agency's earnings, using a *40 percent return rate*.

Year	Agency earnings	One-third interest $\times$	Present value factor at 40 percent
1			
2			
3	$24,700	$ 8,150 $\times$ 0.364	= $ 2,966
4	43,300	14,289 $\times$ 0.260	= 3,715
5	69,500	22,900 $\times$ 0.186	= 4,259
			$10,940

These earnings will be reinvested in the business, of course, instead of being distributed, but the calculations do give a good indication of the growth and profitability potential of the business and what the investor's original investment will be worth in only five years.

ORGANIZATION

1. *General organization. The two founders* have divided responsibilities as follows: Wolfe will be in charge of all product-related matters, employee training, hiring and firing, and operating systems. Wade will be responsible for all financial matters, marketing, advertising, taxes, and general administration. The founders are a talented and cohesive team blending practical experience with technical knowhow.

Employees will be hired in accordance with the following schedule, depending on the gross sales volume.

The board of directors will be composed of major investors and respected, experienced people in the field and in business.

2. Employee policy. We consider good people to be one of the secrets of success in the travel service business, and we will pay more to have them.

Our requirements for employees:

1. Experience working in an agency in the town.
2. Contacts in the town and community.
3. Good motivation and willingness to work.

4. Participation in agent training schools when necessary.
5. Willingness to go on agency- or carrier-sponsored trips to develop knowledge of the product.

We estimate that we can get a good person fulfilling these requirements for $700 a month, or $8,400 a year.

Our hiring policy will be on the basis of gross sales with an emphasis on high productivity:

Gross sales*	Average agency employs	Our agency employs
$ 500,000	4 people	3 people
700,000	6	4
1,000,000	7	6
2,000,000	11	8

*This information is from *Travel Weekly,* March 9, 1977, the Harris Survey of Travel Agencies.

Our hiring timetable will be:

Year 1: The two founders and one employee.
Year 2: One additional employee.
Year 3: Two additional employees.
Year 4: One additional employee.
Year 5: As needed.

We will use part-time help to cover peak demand periods.

Case 5–2

The Undercroft Montessori School

GENERAL BACKGROUND INFORMATION

The following case deals with the marketing of a social service. The principal decision makers in the case are concerned parents who have volunteered to manage the affairs of a private school of modest size located in a residential area of the city of Tulsa. Management of the school has been conservative, concentrating upon enhancing the overall quality of the existing program. Enrollment at the school has been at near full-capacity levels for the past five years, and the present Board of Trustees is considering the possibilities of expansion. There is some uncertainty among the members about which direction expansion should proceed, if at all, and little agreement has been reached.

THE UNDERCROFT MONTESSORI SCHOOL PROGRAM

Objectives and strategy

Administration of the school. Business management of the school is currently conducted by a Board of Trustees composed of 15 members. Board members are elected for three-year terms by the school corporation, which consists of all the parents of children enrolled. The members are assigned to one of six standing committees which are responsible for planning financial, educational, facilities, volunteers and hospitality, public relations, and scholarship activities. There is also an Executive Committee consisting of the president, vice president, assistant vice president, treasurer, and secretary. The purpose of the latter committee is to coordinate planning decisions between the six standing committees and to execute routine transactions related to the business activities of the school.

Objectives. There are two primary institutional objectives with which the board is most concerned as a body. These are educational quality and financial viability. The following objective statement is an excerpt from the *General Information and School Policy* manual provided for parents:

> The Undercroft Montessori School is dedicated to the Montessori philosophy and method of education through the senses. A child attending Undercroft will be exposed to a method which should facilitate the growth of inner discipline and later complex reasoning through the free choice and organized use of didactic materials within an atmosphere conducive to these ends.

Specific educational objectives related to the child's developmental process in the general areas of motor, sensory, and language (symbols) development are embodied in the comprehensive directress training program; these objectives are not at issue in this case. In addition, detailed professional and staff objectives are defined in *Staff Manual for Undercroft Montessori School.*

The second primary objective is to ensure the routine financial integrity of the school. That is, a major goal of the board is to establish and maintain an adequate flow of funds to compensate staff, provide and maintain educational materials and facilities, and provide scholarships. The major source of funds has been internal through tuition payments. Although modest surpluses have been recognized as desirable, breaking even in any given year has been considered satisfactory. Exhibit 1 is a summary of financial performance over the past several years of school operation.

Exhibit 1

THE UNDERCROFT MONTESSORI SCHOOL, INC.
Comparative Income Statement
Period July 1 through June 30, 1974–1978

	1978	1977	1976	1975	1974
Revenue from operations and contributions:					
Interview fees	$ 590	$ 560	$ 460	$ 560	$ 490
Tuition	62,172	62,020	62,148	53,768	51,181
Interest	1,057	1,225	913	534	67
Contributions	2,121	1,395	1,255	2,340	500
Total revenue and contributions	65,940	65,200	64,776	57,202	52,238
Operating expenses and overhead:					
Salaries	44,945	39,679	42,649	38,591	33,356
Payroll taxes	3,228	3,148	3,289	3,159	3,964
Insurance, health	2,914	2,373	1,871	1,384	872
Office supplies	1,646	1,789	1,402	1,268	924
Office telephone	420	400	466	562	369
Teacher training	193	608	38	582	441
Travel expenses				1,194	497
Classroom supplies	1,142	1,500	1,183	1,677	1,541
Classroom snacks	294	158	236	236	181
Classroom expendables	202	1,268	949	158	45
Building, custodial	1,835	1,571	1,275	1,406	849
Building, maintenance	497	701	498	829	2,722
Building, supplies	422	437	428	166	341
Building, utilities	1,124	1,083	953	767	717
Building, security	737	827			
Insurance, property	906	655	435	410	1,048
Grounds, maintenance	49	431		15	
Grounds, landscaping	475	405	445	740	562
Grounds, lighting	265	209	204	187	
Interest, mortgage	324	378	421	425	504
Interest, land contract	774	778	783	786	790
Dues and subscriptions	478	801	399	525	461
Advertising	435	394	238	204	149
Depreciation	2,835	2,788	2,571	2,185	1,415
Miscellaneous	658	1,346	1,793	1,766	2,041
Total expenses and overhead	66,598	63,727	62,526	59,222	53,588
Net income	$ (658)	$ 1,473	$ 2,250	$ (2,020)	$ (1,350)

Strategy. Educational quality is partly provided through affiliation with the American Montessori Society and a system for internal
staff development and review. The AMS provides a current file of
certified directresses, regional workshops, and observers to review
and evaluate school programs. Promotion of the school to stimulate
enrollment has been largely through word of mouth. Some advertising
has also been employed in local Tulsa newspapers at a modest level.
This advertising is usually planned to coincide with the annual fall

open house, for interested parents. Allocation of funds for advertising has been a somewhat controversial issue among members of the board. The argument against advertising has centered upon previous enrollment, which has been near full-capacity levels for the past several years. Some members have asked the question, "Why advertise when classes are full?" The question has been unresolved.

THE JANUARY MEETING OF THE EXECUTIVE COMMITTEE

An Executive Committee meeting was held at the beginning of the year to review the current financial situation and long-term plans for the program. The school had an opening for an assistant directress, and during the process of hiring it was learned that salaries had increased substantially due to rising demand for qualified Montessori staff. A recent report by the treasurer had indicated that a deficit was incurred during operations in 1977–78. Tuition had been increased at the beginning of the previous year from $625 to $675 for the half-day program and from $1,150 to $1,250 for the all-day program. However, a number of routine expenses had increased significantly beyond expectations. Although a tuition increase in the 1979 budget seems indicated, several members of the board have expressed concern about the possible adverse effects upon current prospective new parents.

The growth issue

During the meeting it became apparent that aspirations held by members of the committee for future school development varied considerably. The focus of the debate centered largely upon direction of growth. Three alternatives were perceived as feasible: (1) vertical expansion to include a program for older children, (2) horizontal expansion in the form of enhancement to the existing program, or (3) deferment of proposed program changes until financial stability was permanently assured.

The present ratio of children to directress was considered nearly ideal, and any form of expansion or enhancement would require additional facilities, equipment, and staff.

Another topic of discussion arose among board members about the relative merits of a full-time professional school administrator. His or her role in the organization would be similar to that of a principal in a regular public elementary school.

Nancy Martin. Nancy Martin has served one full school year as president of the school corporation and chairperson of the Board of Trustees. Before assuming her present position, she was responsible for the activities of the Hospitality and Arrangement Committee. Despite the fact that the unanimous opinion of the board is that she has done an outstanding job, Nancy is not entirely satisfied with her accomplishments as president. At the beginning of the meeting Nancy expressed her opinion that the school has a number of significant strengths, such as private facilities, reputation in the community, and an exceptional head directress. However, in Nancy's view, there are crucial weaknesses as well. Among these are considerable uncertainty about enrollment from semester to semester. Nancy candidly admitted having experienced considerable anxiety about the possibility of being unable to open the school in the fall of 1977 due to slow pre-enrollment during the previous spring. A sufficient number of parents eventually reserved positions, but Nancy recalled a few anxious moments. The school presently does not have sufficient cash reserves to support essential operations without outside contributions if enrollment should fall below about 65 students. Nancy said that she is aware of the general interest of many board members and parents in vertical expansion of the school's program, but frankly she does not agree that this objective is realistic in view of the more or less continuous tight financial situation and other more immediate administrative difficulties. In Nancy's words, "How can we even think about expansion when we barely have enough money to meet our day-to-day expenses? Before we consider expanding, which would necessarily mean an additional classroom, staff, and materials, I would rather hire a professional school administrator first and quit trying to run the school by committees."

Don Keele.   Don Keele has the greatest longevity on the board of any active member, having served approximately five years both as president and treasurer of the corporation. Don agreed with Nancy in terms of the present strengths of the school organization and program but said that he did not agree with her problem priorities. Don believes strongly that the curriculum should expand to include 7- through 12-year-olds. That is, the program should be comprehensive from the traditional preschool through the equivalent of a sixth grade. Don admitted that there would be problems involved in securing additional qualified staff (two directresses and assistants) and classrooms (two) plus meeting routine accreditation requirements of the state. But the return would be considerable. In Don's opinion, a comprehensive program would be very worthwhile from the parent's point of view in that it would solve the planning problem of where to continue the child's education after kindergarten. Don acknowledged that funding the expansion would be the most difficult task and pointed out that fund-raising efforts in the past had met with modest success at best. These had been directed toward parents of children both currently and previously enrolled and had been in the form of garage sales, carnivals, and direct solicitations.

Betty Kaylor.   Betty Kaylor, chairperson of the Education Committee, was not entirely in agreement with the president or treasurer in terms of problems and goals. Betty argued that staffing instability and lack of physical space, in her opinion, were the two most pressing issues confronting the board. Betty pointed out that since April 1974 10 directresses and/or assistants had retired or resigned for various reasons. Continuity from one class to the next had been difficult to maintain, and Betty acknowledged the fact that the school had been almost totally dependent upon the head directress. She had been invaluable in smoothing the transition periods and minimizing any overall reduction in classroom effectiveness.

Betty was also concerned with lack of adequate indoor space to develop motor skills during inclement weather. The school had a very attractive outdoor playground area and a fair complement of equipment adjacent to the classrooms. But in Betty's opinion, this alternative was not as convenient for a planned and supervised set of activities compatible with the recommended Montessorian methodology. In short, Betty believed that another classroom was needed that would serve as a gymnasium and also relieve some of the congestion in the art room. The latter was also housing the musical instruments and instruction.

Richard Carroll.   At the close of the meeting, Nancy expressed her appreciation to the members of the committee for their contributions but said that she was disappointed that a decision couldn't be reached on fall tuitions and the growth question. Don said that the tuition decision must be rendered soon in order to complete the 1979 budget and report to the parents. In Don's opinion, the tuition and growth issues were related in some way, but a firm informational base did not presently exist to guide decision making. Nancy agreed with Don, and admitted that she probably couldn't decide how to vote if motions were made on either issue that evening. She said that the arguments had been appealing but not entirely persuasive. Clearly, more information was needed before decisions of such crucial importance could be reached. Don moved that a special committee be appointed to study the economic aspects of a tuition increase and the broader growth issue, and make recommendations to the Executive Committee at the next meeting, in February. Don's motion carried, and a new member, Richard Carroll, was appointed chairman.

Richard had been serving in the capacity of assistant treasurer since the beginning of the previous fall term. He had recently completed graduate study in business at the University of Tulsa and was employed as a market analyst by a local petroleum firm. For the next several weeks after the meeting, Richard investigated school files and references at the public library. Summary tables from his investigation are presented in Appendix B of the case. After reviewing the data, Richard was uncertain as to what conclusions should be drawn. Richard believed that the committee expectations of the results of his study were high and that considerable weight would be placed upon his personal recommendations. He also recognized that the opportunity costs of any decision taken by the board would be very large and, therefore, that he must choose his recommended course carefully.

APPENDIX A

HISTORICAL INFORMATION

Brief history of the Montessori method

Early history of the movement.   The Montessori method of early childhood education was developed by a remarkable Italian woman physician, who was also a mathematician, anthropologist, lecturer, and writer. Maria Montessori (1870–1952) held the distinction of being the first woman in Italian history to graduate from a school of medicine, receiving double honors in medicine and surgery.[1] After her internship, she was appointed assistant doctor at the Psychiatric Clinic at the University of Rome, where she specialized in childhood diseases and mental disorders. Many retarded children at that time were committed to asylums with the adult insane and denied educational benefits. Through her experiences and research at the clinic, Dr. Montessori became convinced that childhood mental disorders could often be traced to educational as well as medical problems. Her writings on the subject gained the attention of the state administrators, and in 1898 she was appointed director of the state Orthophrenic School for retarded children. While supervising the other teachers at the institution, Dr. Montessori was able to test many of her theories in her classes. It was at the institution that the framework for her unique teaching method was developed.

The results of the method with retarded children were gratifying, and it became obvious to Dr. Montessori that many of the methodological elements could be generalized and applied to the task of educating normal children. An opportunity to extend the new method occurred in 1907. A Roman building association offered Dr. Montessori facilities to organize a child day-care center in a slum area of the city for the purpose of reducing a vandalism problem. The opportunity to work with normal children was appealing, and the first Casa dei Bambini (Children's House) was opened with 60 students ranging from three to six years in age. The results were immediately successful, and five additional houses were opened by the end of the following year.

Montessori in the United States.   Recognition of the merits of the method spread rapidly throughout Europe and eventually became institutionalized in some countries. The first American Children's House was opened in Tarrytown, New York, in 1912, and soon thereafter a number of public schools and private schools from coast to

---

[1] R. C. Orem, "Maria Montessori," *Encyclopedia of Education* (New York: Macmillan, 1971), pp. 388–93.

coast claimed adoption of Montessori ideas and concepts.[2] In 1960 the American Montessori Society was formed. There are currently about 1,800 affiliated Montessori schools in the United States, and new ones are opening at the rate of 75 per year.[3]

The Montessori method

Learning how to learn. The basic Montessorian thesis commonly shared is that the child carries within the unseen potentialities of the person that she or he will eventually become. Development of these potentialities begins at a very early age, during which time the child's mental set is particularly absorbent. The period from 2½–6 years is believed to be of crucial importance. The method recognizes and employs the normal physiological development of the motor, sensory, and intellectual capabilities. Carefully designed didactic materials and an observer/counselor called a directress are included in the method. Children are believed to be the best teachers, however, and emphasis is placed upon self-actualization.

The ultimate objectives of the early childhood phase are to develop self-confidence, discipline, and preparedness to deal with an expanding environment. During this phase, the child in a meaningful sense learns how to learn. The directress assumes a supporting role by providing a comprehensive but controlled environment, enhanced by alternative sets of physical, intellectual, emotional, and social stimuli. But the child is largely free to explore or pursue things of personal interest and learns by observing, comparing, classifying, and reasoning. That is, the child is allowed to freely encounter, in a natural way, environmental phenomena. Learning occurs by discovery and positive reward enjoyed through accomplishment.[4]

History of the Undercroft Montessori School

Fifteen years "under the croft." In February 1963, a group of interested Tulsa mothers formed a study group to discuss the Montessori approach to learning. The study group aroused further interest and led to the formation of the Tulsa Montessori Educational Association. This association sponsored a series of lectures by Miss Lena Wichramaratne of Sri Lanka, a close associate of Dr. Maria Montessori and a teacher-trainer of the Association Montessori Internationale.

The lectures stimulated enough interest among parents to establish Tulsa's first Montessori school. A directress was obtained, and space

----

[2] Anne E. George, *The Montessori Method: Scientific Pedagogy as Applied to Child Education in the Children's Houses*, 3d ed. (New York: Stokes, 1912).

[3] R. C. Orem, *Montessori: Her Method and the Movement* (New York: G. P. Putnam's Sons, 1974), p. 47.

[4] Ibid., pp. 95–124.

was located in the basement of the Trinity Episcopal Church in downtown Tulsa. In honor of its original location under the croft of the church, the school was named Undercroft Montessori School. In 1966, the school was able to move to its present location at 3745 South Hudson Avenue. Expanded facilities permitted an expansion of the staff, curriculum, and enrollment. At present, the staff includes two fully certified Montessori directresses, a specialized arts and crafts teacher, a music teacher, and two assistants. Children are offered a full range of Montessori activities in practical life and sensorial experiences, language, mathematics, science, geography, music, art, crafts, cooking, in-school demonstrations, and field trips.

The Undercroft Montessori School was formed as and remains a private, nonsectarian, nonprofit, parent-run corporation working with preschool and kindergarten children between the ages of 2½ and 6. Undercroft affiliated with the American Montessori Society in 1965, and it has continued this affiliation by meeting the high standards of this group.

Undercroft has grown from an opening enrollment of 30 children in September 1964 to an enrollment of approximately 90 children in 1978 (see Exhibit 2). The school now offers the regular half-day pro-

Exhibit 2
Levels of September enrollment at Undercroft Montessori School, 1974–78

Session	1978	1977	1976	1975	1974
Morning session	34	36	33	39	49
Afternoon session	30	29	25	31	50
All-day session	26	21	23	16	—
Total enrollment	90	86	82	86	99

gram and an all-day program for children four years of age and kindergarten age. Classes are currently housed in a 3½-room, single-floor, frame structure which is owned by the school. There is an outstanding mortgage of approximately $24,000 on the land and building.

APPENDIX B: SUMMARY DATA FROM RICHARD CARROLL'S PRELIMINARY INVESTIGATION

Table 1
National preprimary school enrollment of children three to five
years old, 1965–1976

Year	Total three–five population (000)	Number three–five enrollment (000)	Number as percentage of total
1965	12,549	3,407	27.1
1968	11,905	3,928	33.0
1969	11,424	3,949	34.6
1970	10,949	4,104	37.5
1971	10,610	4,148	39.1
1972	10,166	4,231	41.6
1973	10,344	4,234	40.9
1974	10,393	4,699	45.2
1975	10,186	4,958	48.7
1976	9,726	4,790	49.2

Source: U.S. Bureau of the Census, Current Population Reports.

Table 2
Estimated national enrollment in independent nursery schools and kindergartens,
1978–1985 (000)

	1975	1978	1979	1980	1981	1982	1983	1984	1985
Public	489	464	474	497	526	559	593	626	657
Nonpublic	1531	1594	1714	1869	2043	2229	2421	2609	2779
Total enrollment, all levels									
Public	54163	53436	52862	52353	52056	51855	51895	52125	52485
Nonpublic	9181	9348	9478	9636	9808	9975	10132	10258	10369

Source: U.S. Department of Health, Education, and Welfare, National Center for Education Statistics, Preprimary Enrollment, 1975.

Table 3
Projected allocation of total population by county in Tulsa
Standard Metropolitan Statistical Area, 1976–2000 (000)

County	1976	1980	1985	1990	1995	2000
Creek	50.6	53.2	58.8	66.2	74.8	84.0
Mayes	27.9	30.1	34.7	41.2	49.2	58.2
Osage	32.6	32.0	33.6	36.8	41.3	45.7
Rogers	34.3	38.3	45.6	54.9	66.0	78.2
Tulsa	422.8	441.4	471.3	503.8	533.1	564.1
Wagoner	27.4	31.0	37.8	46.5	57.2	69.0
Tulsa SMSA	595.6	626.0	681.8	779.4	821.6	899.2

Source: Population and Employment: Methods, Procedures, and Projections, Economic Planning Group, Tulsa Metropolitan Area Planning Group and Metropolitan Tulsa Chamber of Commerce, January 1978.

Table 4
Projected allocation of total population by age group in Tulsa
Standard Metropolitan Statistical Area, 1978–2000 (000)

Age range	1978	1980	1985	1990	1995	2000
0–4	46.4	46.7	53.9	57.8	60.4	63.8
5–9	50.1	50.9	54.1	63.4	68.7	71.8
10–14	54.4	53.2	56.2	60.9	71.1	76.8
Total all ages	610.8	626.1	681.9	749.4	821.7	899.3

Source: "Detailed Demographic Projections: Tulsa SMSA (1980–2000),"
Economic Development Planning Group, Tulsa Metropolitan Area Planning
Commission and Metropolitan Tulsa Chamber of Commerce, March 1978.

Table 5
Forecast of school enrollment in Tulsa Standard Metropolitan Statistical Area, 1975–2000
(000)

Level	1975	1980	1985	1990	1995	2000
Nursery	2.9	2.9	3.4	3.8	4.1	4.4
Kindergarten	8.7	9.0	9.6	11.3	12.3	12.9
Elementary	87.5	85.8	91.1	102.9	116.5	124.8
Total all levels, including high school	160.0	160.8	146.0	180.8	200.9	220.6

Source: "Detailed Demographic Projections: Tulsa SMSA (1980–2000)," Economic Development Planning Group, Tulsa Metropolitan Area Planning Commission and Metropolitan Tulsa Chamber of Commerce,
March 1980.

Table 6
Preprimary enrollment and population of children three–five years old by family
income and occupation of head of household, October 1975 (000)

	Total three–five-year-old population	Enrollment
Family income		
Less than $3,000	607	246
$3,000–$4,999	947	370
$5,000–$7,499	1,350	556
$7,500 or over	6,627	3,449
Total in four income groups	9,531	4,621
Occupation		
White collar	3,455	2,080
Manual/services	4,473	1,922
Farm	286	92
Unemployed	1,626	703
Total in four occupation groups	9,840	4,797

Source: *Standard Education Almanac, 1977–78*, Marquis Academic Media.

Table 7
Preprimary enrollment of children three–five years old by metropolitan status and age,
October 1975 (000)

Age group	Total three–five population	Metro central enrollment	Metro other enrollment	Nonmetro enrollment
Three years	3,177	260	1,158	1,028
Four years	3,499	451	1,304	1,146
Five years	3,509	810	1,368	1,128
Total three–five years	10,185	1,521	3,830	3,302

Source: *Standard Education Almanac, 1977–78*, Marquis Academic Media.

Table 8
Tabulation of private nonsectarian and parochial schools in Tulsa
County with academic offerings, 1977

	Nonsectarian	Parochial	Total schools
Preschool and kindergarten	12	8	20
Elementary K–6	4	17	21
Total schools	16	25	41

Note: Schools listed do not include trade, professional, or remedial schools.
Source: Tulsa telephone directory, 1977.

Table 9
Competitive Tulsa institutions offering early childhood development programs, August 1978

	Ages/grades	Previous enrollment	Number of teachers	Approximate tuition per semester
Representative nonsectarian private schools				
Undercroft Montessori 3745 S. Hudson	2½–6 years Prekindergarten to kindergarten Half-day and all-day sessions	90	6	$ 338 (½ day) 625 (all day)
Montessori Child Development School 4803 South Lewis	2½–6 years Prekindergarten to kindergarten Half-day sessions	40	2	350 (½ day)
Betty Rowland Nursery School and Kindergarten 2505 East Skelly Drive	3–5 years Prekindergarten to kindergarten Half-day sessions	42	2	338 (½ day)
Helen's Private Kindergarten 3416 East 33 Street	2½–5 years Prekindergarten to kindergarten Half-day and all-day sessions	38	4	284 (½ day) 518 (all day)
Anne Simpson's New School for Elementary Education 230 East 18 Street	Prekindergarten through grade 6	31 prekindergarten and kindergarten (100–120 in grades 1–6)	2 (6 for grades 1–6)	264 (½ day) 340 (all day)
Representative parochial private schools				
Holland Hall 5666 East 81 Street	Prekindergarten through grade 12	60 prekindergarten and kindergarten (800 grades 1–12)	20	875 (½ day) 1,295 (all day)

Villa Teresa Kindergarten and Preschool 1861 East 15 Street	Prekindergarten through kindergarten	n.a.	4	360 (all day)
Southpark Christian School 10811 East 41 Street	Prekindergarten through grade 4 Half days and all day	40	3	225 (half day) 473 (all day)
New Haven Methodist Preschool 5603 South New Haven	Prekindergarten Half days	135	7	225 (half day)

Representative day-care centers with partial academic offering

LaPetite Day Care and Preschool 6287 East 38 Street (three locations)	Ages 2–6 years Hourly, half day, all day	100	11	332 (half day) 585 (all day)
National Child Care Center 11633 East 31 Street (four locations)	1½–12 years Hourly, half day, all day	100	10	448 (half day) 644 (all day)
Southside Child Care 5544 South Peoria	Infant through kindergarten All day	45	4	750 (all day)

Approximate number of private preschool and kindergarten institutions (nonsectarian and parochial) with academic offerings	20
Approximate number of day-care institutions with partial academic offerings	40
Approximate number of parochial preschools	8

Case 5–3

Quincy Brothers Hardware

Quincy Brothers Hardware, founded in 1879, was the classic example of the American hardware store. Located in Zanesville, Ohio, the business was housed in a massive brick structure three stories high, a city block long, with a full basement. The inside contained a chaotic but fascinating assortment of sporting goods, tools of all kinds, bins filled with nails and other small items, and miscellaneous hardware scattered about the sales area. An impression of immensity was created by tiers of wooden drawers and cubbyholes lining the long walls and extending up to the 20-foot ceiling. Periodically one of the salesmen, none of whom appeared to be under 60 years old, would slide the rolling ladders installed along either wall and painstakingly climb to retrieve an item requested by a customer, frequently a three-cent brass screw or an equally trivial item.

The 19th-century cracker-barrel atmosphere was clearly an attraction for many of its customers. Quincy Brothers had a reputation for being the major, if not exclusive, supplier of premium quality hardware and tools for the trade in the city and outlying area. It was also known as a favorite meeting place among those in the trade. In 1974, the manager stated that 80 percent of the store's business was with contractors or other retailers. Among retail customers the store had a reputation of being a place where you could get anything you could not find anywhere else. Customers were believed to be loyal; by one estimate, 75 percent of the people in the store at any given time had shopped there several times before.

Despite its inviting surroundings and enviable reputation, the fortunes of the business began to wane in the 1960s. Sales rose to about $1,500,000 and remained at that level, but expenses continued to increase. By 1970, profits had dipped to $1,700.

In addition to mounting expenses, another problem Quincy Brothers faced was that it did not have enough space to display the 24,000 different items carried in inventory; only 15 percent of the merchandise could be displayed at any one time in the 15,000 square feet of selling space. And there was no inventory control system; many of the products had accumulated for years or had been specially ordered but not sold. On the other hand, the store was plagued by frequent stockouts on some fast-moving items.

The board of directors employed new management in 1970 in an

This case was prepared by Andrea D. Levin, research assistant, under the supervision of Associate Professor Eleanor G. May. Names, places, and figures have been disguised. Copyright © 1977 by the University of Virginia, The Colgate Darden Graduate School Sponsors.

attempt to respond to these problems and to try to turn the business around. The new management considered that one of its priorities was to expand the store selling space. A study was made in 1973 in which the main recommendation was that the best way to acquire sufficient space was to relocate the business. To accomplish this, the entire trading area was inspected for a suitable location. A plot of land was selected approximately two miles west of the city in an area where a number of other retailers had moved. Quincy Brothers acquired the land, and a building was constructed on it. The building cost had been estimated to be $400,000, but it turned out to be $870,000, which, with the cost of the land, brought the total new investment to well over $1 million. The land and building were sold and then leased under a sale-and-leaseback agreement. The store moved into the new building in August 1975.

To tighten its control over inventory, the new management installed an NCR 280 Retail System, an on-line data processing system which required electronic cash registers to transmit sales information directly to NCR's processing facility in Columbus. All cash register transactions were recorded on a tape in the store in the event of a breakdown in communications with the Columbus facility. Once a month the store received a sales analysis report from NCR (see Exhibit 1.) The system cost Quincy Brothers approximately $12,000 a year, plus an initial installation charge. Other reports were available from NCR, such as aging of receivables, detailed inventory reports, and financial statements. However, Quincy Brothers chose to subscribe only to the basic service at first because of cost considerations. The system was installed in the old store and moved to the new location when it opened.

Sales rose to a high of $1,800,000 in 1972 but declined each year after that. In 1976, revenue was at roughly the same dollar level as in 1968; but earnings had been extremely adversely affected both in dollars and in proportion to sales. Quincy Brothers experienced its first loss in its history in 1976. (See Exhibits 2 and 3 for financial data on the company.)

Even before the results for the year ending June 30, 1976, were known, the directors had begun looking for another manager. In April 1976, one of them met Jim Henderson, who at that time was managing his newly organized lawn and garden business. Impressed with Mr. Henderson's credentials and his initiative in setting up his own business shortly after receiving his MBA from a well-known southern business school, the board offered him the position of store manager. The terms of the agreement were that Quincy Brothers would buy the lawn and garden business and merge it with the hardware store. In return, Mr. Henderson would be given roughly 6 percent of the stock in Quincy Brothers with the option to acquire more in five years if he wished. Mr. Henderson agreed and started work in June 1976.

Exhibit 1
NCR sales analysis information for Hardware Department

Quincy Brothers Hardware		Sales analysis								
		Current				Year to date: June 30, 1976				
Class	Description	Net units	Net sales	Percent sales /total	Percent returns /sales	Net units	Net sales	Percent sales /total	Percent returns /sales	Percent difference of unit
3740	Glass	46	106	49.1	7.8	904	1686	67.1	4.8	77.1
3741	Mirrors	0	0	0.0	0.0	10	85	3.4	1.9	80.0
3742	Glaz compd putty	51	85	39.3	15.0	327	417	16.6	8.2	52.9
3743	Glaz tol pt clip	14	25	11.6	0.0	214	282	11.2	39.8	29.0
3744	Class cut mch hl	0	0	0.0	0.0	17	44	1.7	.0	28.6
	Department 374 total	111	216	3.5	9.9	1472	2514	3.5	11.0	60.1
	Division 9 total	2864	6251	7.7	9.8	30352	70962	8.1	39.6	168.7

Notes: Percent sales/total = Class sales as percentage of department sales; department or division sales as percentage of total store sales.

Percent returns/sales = Returned sales for class, division, or department as a percentage of class, department, or division sales.

Percent difference of unit = Index of change in sales, this year to last year.

Department = A subunit of a division.

Division = There are 13 NCR divisions; hence the Quincy Brothers divisions are not the same as the NCR divisions.

Exhibit 2

QUINCY BROTHERS HARDWARE
Comparative Income Statements
Year Ending June 30
(000)

	1972	*1973*	*1974*	*1975*	*1976*
Net sales	$1,815	$1,688	$1,683	$1,419	$1,375
Cost of goods sold	1,407	1,275	1,148	989	932
Gross margin	408	413	535	430	443
Operating expenses:					
Advertising	14	15	14	15	43
Bad debts	15	5	37	19	19
Data processing	6	9	9	11	14
Depreciation	7	9	9	10	10
Interest	19	24	39	38	33
Rent	—	—	—	5	130
Salaries	233	249	262	262	293
Miscellaneous	90	89	93	93	97
Total operating expenses	384	400	463	453	639
Operating profit (loss)	24	13	72	(23)	(196)
Other income	11	17	19	44	120
Income before taxes	35	30	91	21	(76)
Income taxes	10	8	39	6	—
Loss carry-back	—	—	—	—	16
Extraordinary gain (loss)	(7)	—	—	—	—
Net income	$ 18	$ 22	$ 52	$ 15	$ (60)

THE HARDWARE INDUSTRY

On a national scale the hardware industry was booming. In 1975, industry sales for retail outlets specializing in hardware and related items were approximately $15.9 billion (see Exhibit 4). The National Retail Hardware Association (NRHA) projected sales for these types of outlets to be $19.6 billion in 1976. The term *hardware*, used loosely, refers to a broad range of merchandise, including tools, fasteners, housewares, paint, sporting goods, and some building materials. Technically, however, the term refers to a more limited class of products, including fasteners (nails, screws, and bolts), wire, chain, locks, and miscellaneous metal fixtures (e.g., doorknobs, plates, and knockers).

The major categories of retailers who sold the majority of the hardware in the United States were traditional hardware stores, home centers, lumber and building materials suppliers, general merchandise chains (e.g., Sears, Wards, Penney's), and discounters (e.g., K mart, Woolco). Exhibit 5 summarizes the significant differences among the various types of hardware retailers. The two principal types of outlets handling hardware items, in terms of share of market, were the traditional hardware stores and the home centers. Chains

Exhibit 3

QUINCY BROTHERS HARDWARE
Comparative Balance Sheets
Year Ending June 30
(000)

	1972	1973	1974	1975	1976
Assets					
Cash.........................	$ 14	$ 17	$ 10	$ 17	$ 20
Receivables....................	269	226	175	148	190
Inventory	641	583	692	675	570
Prepaid expenses and other current assets.......................	4	3	3	35	31
Total current assets.........	928	829	880	875	811
Land..........................	21	282	282	278	275
Property, plant, and equipment	59	70	137	56	55
Other assets	1	2	3	7	9
Total assets....................	$1,009	$1,183	$1,302	$1,216	$1,150
Liabilities					
Notes payable..................	$ 74	$ 74	$ 103	$ 154	$ 250
Accounts payable...............	280	176	218	167	240
Accrued salaries (bonuses)........	5	6	19	8	6
Sales tax payable...............	5	6	6	5	3
Long-term debt (due within one year).........................	14	54	58	60	46
Interest payable	0	5	5	3	3
Accrued taxes..................	3	1	32	1	1
Total current liabilities...........	381	322	441	398	549
Long-term debt.................	126	334	282	224	67
Total liabilities	507	656	723	622	616
Capital					
Common stock (less treasury stock).......................	61	64	64	64	64
Retained earnings	441	463	515	530	470
Net capital.....................	502	527	579	594	534
Total liabilities and capital	$1,009	$1,183	$1,302	$1,216	$1,150

Exhibit 4
1975 hardware sales by type of outlet ($ millions)

	Sales
Outlets specializing in hardware and related items	
Hardware stores	$ 5,600
Home centers	7,900
Lumber and building materials suppliers	2,400
Other outlets distributing hardware	
General merchandise chains	5,000
Discounters	1,900
Other miscellaneous outlets	1,500
Total	$24,300

Exhibit 5
Descriptive data on typical hardware outlet types

	Hardware	Home centers	Lumber and building supply	Chains	Discounters
Location	Traditionally urban, but moving to suburbs or shopping centers	Suburbs, on major highways	Traditionally urban, moving to suburbs	Urban, but moving to suburbs, major highways	Suburban, in shopping centers
Selling area (square feet)	5,000	10,000 to 75,000	5,000 to 10,000	5,000 to 15,000	5,000 to 15,000
Annual hardware sales	$330,000	$1,700,000	?	?	?
Stockturn	2.5	4.3	?	?	?
Customers	Primarily retail, some wholesale	Retail	Primarily wholesale and contractor	Retail	Retail
Customer service	Emphasized	Self-service	Emphasized	Usually not emphasized	Self-service
Store hours	9 to 6 weekdays, half day Saturday	9 to 6 Monday–Saturday, half day Sunday	6 to 5 weekdays, half day Saturday	9 to 9 Monday–Saturday	9 to 6 Monday–Saturday, half day Sunday
Pricing	Higher	Slightly lower	Higher	Slightly lower	Lower
Geographic market	5-mile radius or less	25-mile radius	?	?	?

Source: National Retail Hardware Association.

and discounters, however, were making increasing inroads into the market, a cause for concern to conventional retailers in the industry.

According to the NRHA, hardware stores, whose origins dated back to the 18th century in the United States, generally were small, independent owner-operated businesses. They were community service stores located in urban areas and usually serving customers within a three-mile radius. Along with other retailers, an increasing number of hardware stores were relocating in the suburbs, often in shopping centers, where they could attract customers from a greater distance.

Traditional hardware stores usually had built their business on nationally advertised brands, backed by helpful salespeople and dependable service. Most of these stores had a mix of retail to wholesale and contractor business of about 60 percent retail to 40 percent wholesale or contractor. (The term *wholesale* here includes sales to contractors and builders. Retail sales were to end users or customers.) To meet the diverse needs of both its retail and wholesale customers, the typical store sold a wide variety of branded goods in many different product categories such as tools, plumbing and heating, hardware, housewares, automotive, and lawn and garden. Most stores were departmentalized by these categories.

Customer service had always been an important element in the success of hardware stores. Such service included not only prompt sales assistance but also help in selecting products and advice on how to use them, because most retail customers were relatively uninformed in such matters. For the trade customers, service included deliveries, volume discounts, and repair service on equipment purchased at the store.

In order to compete more effectively with the chains, discounters, and home centers, traditional hardware stores began lengthening store hours (adding Sunday hours in some cases) and lowering prices somewhat, thereby moving toward a higher percentage of consumer business.

Home centers, on the other hand, were relatively new to the industry, spawned by the growth of the do-it-yourself (DIY) market after World War II. Most were owned and operated by large conglomerates or chains or had become chain operations in their own right. Confusingly, the term *home center* often was applied loosely to describe a host of different types of outlets, ranging from hardware stores that had installed DIY and hobby departments to building supply companies that had branched into consumer business. In theory, however, the home center was a hybrid of the traditional hardware store and the building supply company, offering the tools and materials required for DIY home improvement and maintenance. But unlike the hardware store, the home center catered almost exclusively to retail customers. Exhibit 6 contrasts characteristics of home center customers and hardware store customers.

Because home centers were a relatively new phenomenon, they did not have the problem of moving out of the city. Generally they already were located in suburban areas, usually not in shopping centers, but in freestanding sites. Freestanding sites were chosen because customers required easy access to the loading docks at which they picked up their purchases. The centers also typically were located near major highways, making them accessible to neighboring communities. The trade area for a home center could extend up to a radius of 25 miles.

Home centers usually resembled supermarkets with plywood, two-by-fours, paint, and a limited selection of tools and hardware stacked on the floor in much the same manner as grocery items. Customers served themselves using shopping carts specially designed to handle the bulky merchandise. To accommodate the average do-it-yourselfer, stores were open at night and all day on Saturdays and Sundays.

The traditional middlemen in the hardware industry had been independent wholesalers, but their numbers were dwindling. As discounters and chains entered the market, they offered lower retail prices because they were able to purchase directly from the manufacturers. In order to compete, the independent retailers had to look for lower wholesale prices so they could cut retail prices. These changes at the retail level resulted in the development of three patterns in the wholesaling of hardware.

1. Wholesalers formed cooperatives (sometimes called wholesaler alliances) that often were in part publicly owned. The cooperatives achieved economies of scale and took advantage of volume discounts from manufacturers. Then they could offer merchandise to the retailer for substantially less than the independent wholesaler charged. Retailer customers who purchased from the alliances generally were not franchised and thus maintained their "independent" image to their patrons. Sentry, Allied Hardware Services, and Associated Hardware Buyers were examples of these cooperatives.

2. Retailers formed their own wholesaling cooperative with efficiencies resulting similar to those available through the wholesaler-organized cooperatives. These retailers usually were franchised by their cooperative and often carried its name. Ace and True Value hardware stores were better-known examples. One advantage of being affiliated with such an organization was the goodwill of the franchised name, which, in the opinion of many retailers, had considerable drawing power over customers. The cost of a franchise, however, was beyond the means of many small retailers.

3. Those wholesalers who remained independent tended to increase services to retailers in order to be competitive. The services they offered included automatic data processing, cooperative advertising funds, preparation of catalogs and fliers which retailers could distribute to their customers, and so forth.

Exhibit 6
Consumer profiles

	Hardware stores (7 studies, 1,130 interviews)			Home centers (17 studies, 3,600 interviews)		
	Percent of customers	Percent of dollar volume	Average amount spent per transaction	Percent of customers	Percent of dollar volume	Average amount spent per transaction
Sex						
Male adult	70%	67%	$ 6.03	49%	51%	$15.28
Female adult	24	23	6.03	29	24	12.41
Couple or family	6	10	10.06	22	25	14.30
	100%	100%		100%	100%	
Family income						
Less than $5,000	11%	4%	2.50	5%	4%	11.39
$5,000 to $10,000	22	12	3.27	26	31	15.20
$10,000 to $15,000	28	29	6.43	33	28	14.72
$15,000 or more	39	55	8.89	36	37	18.18
	100%	100%		100%	100%	

Age of household head						
Under 25 years	7%	6%	6.39	15%	11%	10.41
25 to 35 years	16	15	6.60	28	30	15.20
35 to 45 years	21	26	8.23	27	30	15.77
45 to 55 years	22	30	7.96	17	14	11.69
55 years or over	34	23	3.36	13	15	16.35
	100%	100%		100%	100%	
Shopping frequency						
First time	3%	2%	5.03	9%	15%	20.51
At least once a week	37	38	6.35	41	26	10.73
Once every two or three weeks	21	21	6.34	21	18	16.05
Once a month	21	20	5.89	20	32	22.18
Less than once a month	18	19	6.66	9	9	13.49
	100%	100%		100%	100%	
Length of patronage						
First time	3%	2%	5.03	9%	15%	20.51
Less than one year	17	16	5.90	20	17	9.41
One to two years }				14	12	12.77
Two to five years				16	14	12.48
Five years or more	80	82	6.43	41	42	14.68
	100%	100%		100%	100%	

Source: National Retail Hardware Association.

THE HARDWARE MARKET IN ZANESVILLE AND THE SURROUNDING AREA

From 1965 to 1975, the Zanesville area experienced considerable economic stimulation as a result of the expansion of manufacturing facilities located in Zanesville. The population of the area grew from under 132,000 in 1970 to 149,000 in 1975. Exhibit 7 contains selected

Exhibit 7
Zanesville: City, county, and trading area demographic statistics

Population

	4/1/70	7/1/73	7/1/74	7/1/75	1975/1970
Zanesville	44,500	46,900	47,200	46,200	+3.8%
Muskingum County (including Zanesville)	84,700	85,300	97,600	99,600	+17.6
Zanesville trading area	131,800	142,400	145,700	149,400	+13.4

Housing starts

	1970	1971	1972	1973	1974
Zanesville	504	516	272	222	226
Muskingum County (including Zanesville)	1,055	1,276	1,992	1,443	1,277
Zanesville trading area	1,377	2,354	2,536	2,200	2,038

Distribution of families by 1975 income

Family income	Muskingum County	Ohio	United States
Under $4,000	8%	8%	8%
$4,000 to $8,000	15	13	17
$8,000 to $12,000	16	16	17
$12,000 to $15,000	14	14	13
$15,000 to $25,000	34	32	33
$25,000 and over	13	17	12
	100%	100%	100%
Median income	$14,300	$14,800	$13,700

demographic information on the city and suburban areas. The most rapid rate of growth occurred in the outlying areas, particularly west of the city along Route 40, which led to Columbus. By the end of 1975, however, there were indications that while the growth would continue, the annual population growth rate could drop back to about 1½ percent.

There were 13 major retailers in the area that sold hardware and related items. Exhibit 8 provides selected data on these outlets. One additional hardware store in the planning stage was to be located in a new shopping center scheduled for construction in 1977. While the developers of the new center were interested in locating behind the Gold Circle Plaza along the 40 West corridor (see Exhibit 9 for a diagram), approval from the city had not yet been obtained.

QUINCY BROTHERS IN 1976

Exhibit 9 contains a map showing the new location of Quincy Brothers as well as the adjacent competition. Quincy Brothers was situated on North Texas Boulevard, approximately two miles west of the city limits and a quarter of a mile south of Route 40. This site was roughly five miles from the old store. Unlike the other retailers along Route 40, Quincy Brothers did not have frontage on the highway and therefore could not post a highway sign to indicate the location of the new store. When the decision was made to purchase the plot, the management of the store believed that the benefits of frontage property were not worth the additional $60,000 required to purchase it. Moreover, they were confident that, in view of the store's established reputation and loyal customers, frontage and visibility from Route 40 were less important than they would be for a new business.

The store was housed in a two-story building with 18,000 square feet of selling space on the first floor and almost 3,000 square feet (of which only half was utilized when the store opened) on the second floor. The 18,000 square feet in the basement were used for warehousing and opened onto a loading dock which could accommodate as many as six delivery trucks or vans at one time.

The atmosphere of the new building was a radical departure from that of the old store. The first contrast was piped-in music that played continuously throughout the day. Another contrast was the overwhelming presence of inventory, often stacked six or seven feet up from the floor. Bright cloth banners were suspended from the ceiling to describe the classes of products below.

The added space of the new building allowed for several new displays. For example, the lawn and garden center was enclosed in an open-ended shed constructed of light wooden slats. There was also a furniture refinishing section where a customer could view a videotape on the use of the refinishing products for sale. The video equipment was provided by the manufacturer and could be played by the customers themselves. It was not uncommon to see two or three people watching the videotape at any given time.

There were still a few vestiges of the old store. There was an arrangement of woodburning stoves in one of the large center aisles. One of the old rolling ladders and a brass cash register were on display but not usable. Overall, however, the store had been greatly

Exhibit 8
Characteristics of Zanesville Hardware Market

Name of outlet	Location	Type of outlet	Products carried						
			Hard-ware	Paint	House-wares	Tools	Lawn, garden	Sporting goods	Fire-arms
Anderson's	Mid-city	Lumber, building materials	x	x		x			
The Barn	Mid-city	Hardware, feed	x	x	x	x	x		
Billings & Co.	Mid-city	Lumber, building materials	x	x		x			
Brand Names	Route 40	Catalog-showroom			x			x	
Buckeye Supply Company	Route 75 North	Home center	x	x	x	x			
City Hardware	Mid-city	Hardware	x	x		x			
Gold Circle	Route 40	Discount	x	x	x	x	x	x	x
The Home Center	Route 75 South	Home center	x	x	x	x			
Quincy Brothers	North Texas Boulevard	Hardware	x	x	x	x	x	x	x
Samson's	Mid-city	Hardware	x	x	x	x			
T. R. Smith's Lumber Town	North	Lumber, building materials	x	x	x	x			
Montgomery Ward	Mid-city	Mass merchandiser	x	x	x	x	x	x	x
Zayre	Route 40	Discount	x	x	x	x	x	x	x

altered. Because of the high ceiling, the wide aisles, and the lights, the atmosphere of the store was brighter, though somewhat harsher and more antiseptic than before.

Immediately after the move to the new site, the store was reorganized from two divisions (Hardware and Housewares) into seven: Hardware, Housewares, Tools, Paints, Sporting Goods, Lawn and Garden, and the John Deere Division, which sold light tractors, mowers, and other John Deere power equipment. Each division, except John Deere, was headed by a manager who was in charge of scheduling sales personnel, ordering new merchandise, and setting prices. Because the John Deere Division had relatively low unit sales, it was

Lumber, etc.	Appliances	Feed	Floor coverings	Quality level of		Store hours			Selling area (sq. ft.)	Credit plans used
				Merchandising advice	Selling service	Mon.–Fri.	Sat.	Sun.		
				High	High	7:30 to 5:00	8:30 to noon	None	1,150	BankAmericard Master Charge Anderson's
	x	x		High	High	8:00 to 6:00	8:00 to 6:00	None	7,000	BankAmericard Master Charge
			x	High	High	7:30 to 5:00	8:30 to 12:30	None	6,200	BankAmericard Master Charge Billings
	x			Medium	Low	10:00 to 9:00	10:00 to 6:00	None	6,000	None
x			x	Low	Low	8:00 to 6:00	8:00 to 5:30	10:00 to 2:00	12,600	BankAmericard Master Charge Buckeye
				High	High	8:00 to 5:00	8:00 to noon	None	4,800	BankAmericard Master Charge City Hardware
				Low	Low	10:00 to 10:00	10:00 to 10:00	Noon to 6:00	6,000	BankAmericard Master Charge
x	x		x	Low	Medium	8:00 to 5:30	8:00 to 4:00	None	25,000	BankAmericard Master Charge Home Center
x				Medium	High	7:30 to 9:00	7:30 to 6:00	Noon to 6:00	19,500	BankAmericard Master Charge Quincy's
				High	High	7:30 to 5:00	7:30 to 1:00	None	4,000	BankAmericard Master Charge Samson's
x	x			High	High	7:00 to 5:00	7:00 to noon	None	10,000	BankAmericard Master Charge Smith's
	x		x	Low	Medium	9:00 to 9:00	9:00 to 9:00	None	6,700	Ward's
				Low	Low	10:00 to 10:00	10:00 to 10:00	Noon to 6:00	14,000	BankAmericard Master Charge Zayre's

placed under the supervision of the Tools Division. The six division managers reported directly to Mr. Henderson.

Neither gross margin nor overhead by division was available; therefore, divisions were not profit centers. Division sales could be derived from the monthly NCR sales analysis report, but this computation was time consuming and had been undertaken only once, for fiscal 1976.

Pricing was done by division heads who used as guidelines both recommended list prices provided by manufacturers and internally determined markups. Also, they had to take into consideration Mr. Henderson's target of 38 percent for total store gross margin. Exhibit

Exhibit 9
Map of Route 40 West Area, Zanesville, Ohio*

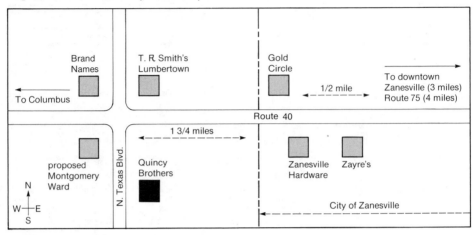

* Not drawn to scale.

Exhibit 10
Selected divisional information for year ending June 30, 1976

Division	Sales	Markup	Closing inventory	Purchases
Housewares	$ 208,000	35%	$ 63,000	$156,000
Sporting Goods	245,000	33	196,000	144,000
Lawn and Garden	137,000	50	30,000	76,000
Hardware	393,000	50	181,000	251,000
Paint	109,000	25	36,000	68,000
Tools	238,000	40 ⎫	64,000	134,000
John Deere	45,000	22 ⎭		
Total	$1,375,000		$570,000	$829,000

10 shows markups and related information by division for fiscal year
1976.

Ordering usually was based on visual checks of inventory levels,
coupled with the experience of the division managers in determining
the turnover of various items. For some products displayed on wall
racks, there were painted markings on the racks which indicated the
reorder points. Mr. Henderson planned to apply this system to as
many types of merchandise as possible in the hope that it would
reduce stockouts.

Orders were placed on a weekly basis by each division manager. In
July 1976, the store began purchasing substantial quantities of goods
from Sentry (after considering and rejecting an option to buy a True
Value franchise for $5,000). By November, approximately 40 percent

of all merchandise was being purchased through Sentry, while the rest of the purchases were about evenly divided between direct factory orders and independent wholesalers. Mr. Henderson estimated that buying from Sentry usually resulted in a 10 percent to 15 percent savings; in the case of pooled or drop shipments the savings could be 5 percent higher. (Pooled shipments were those in which the wholesaler consolidated orders from many retail accounts and then transshipped goods received from the manufacturer directly to each retailer, thus eliminating the wholesaler's warehousing. Drop shipments were those in which the wholesaler merely acted as an agent, coordinating shipments from the factory directly to the retailer.)

One of the things which had bothered Mr. Henderson when he took over as manager of Quincy Brothers was the complacent attitude of many of the employees. Regardless of what their attitudes had been once, it was apparent that many of the older employees regarded their positions as sinecures. As Mr. Henderson later expressed it, "The focus had shifted away from the customer and toward the employees." His response was immediate, and perhaps draconian. Within two weeks, 6 of the store's 28 employees were replaced, and by early fall the turnover among the personnel had exceeded 100 percent. Overall the number of employees remained the same. The new workers, however, generally were young and inexperienced, but Mr. Henderson reported that they were enthusiastic.

By the end of the summer, Mr. Henderson believed he knew the business well enough to formulate a turnaround strategy for the store. His priorities were, first, to produce a profit instead of a loss and, second, to increase sales by 70 percent during fiscal year 1977. These goals were reflected in the written objectives he presented to the board of directors in September (see Exhibit 11). To boost profits, he proposed a cost-reduction program consisting of controlling inventory and receivables, increasing margins, and eliminating unnecessary job positions. While he still retained 28 employees, he converted many of the positions to part-time jobs to give the store more flexibility to meet peak needs. He planned to achieve the sales increase by attracting more customers to the store through additional advertising, better service, and longer store hours.

One of Mr. Henderson's first steps to implement his program was to expand inventories by $100,000, most of which was financed by credit secured against receivables. He not only increased the stock of premium quality items the store had always carried but also added new products which he thought had a potential for high markups and turnover.

At the same time, certain low-turnover items such as solid brass fixtures, some of which had been in stock since the 1920s, were discontinued and sold out through advertised specials. And except for the scheduled specials, discounts were largely eliminated, especially

Exhibit 11
Company objectives, September 1976

I. Control cash
    A. Generate profit.
    B. Control inventory.
    C. Use dating plans and floor financing arrangements.
    D. Control accounts receivable.

II. Increase volume
    A. Advertise.
    B. Improve customer service.
    C. Open longer hours.
        1. Until 9:00 P.M. on weekdays.
        2. Sundays.
    E. Implement incentive plans for department heads and sales personnel.
    F. Bid government business.
    G. Put salesmen outside store to call on contractors.

III. Increase margin
    A. Buy more through Sentry.
    B. Sell more high-margin products.
    C. Control markdowns.

IV. Reduce expenses
    A. Reduce salary costs.
        1. Control overtime better.
        2. Replace overpaid people.
        3. Put department managers on salary.
        4. Cut out one to two people.
        5. Use part-time people.

V. Keys to success
    A. Tight financial control.
    B. An organization.
    C. Promotion and merchandising.

Projected income statements by month for year ending June 30, 1977

Month	Sales	Gross margin	Expenses	Operating profit
July 1976	$ 82,000	$ 26,000	$ 60,000	$(34,000)
August	112,000	35,000	61,000	(26,000)
September	166,000	55,000	66,000	(11,000)
October	175,000	60,000	67,000	(7,000)
November	227,000	79,000	70,000	9,000
December	299,000	108,000	73,000	35,000
January 1977	215,000	82,000	69,000	13,000
February	154,000	59,000	65,000	(6,000)
March	208,000	79,000	68,000	11,000
April	227,000	86,000	68,000	18,000
May	227,000	86,000	68,000	18,000
June	248,000	94,000	69,000	25,000
Total	$2,340,000	$849,000	$804,000	$ 45,000

on price-inelastic items which were not available anywhere else in the area. Lower-price products, formerly sold in bulk (such as screws, washers, and picture hangers), were now sold prepackaged from wall racks.

Mr. Henderson's changes were also directed toward increasing the proportion of the retail business done by Quincy Brothers. (The markup on wholesale sales was 20 percent, while the margin was 38 percent on retail sales.) Both the Lawn and Garden Division and the John Deere line extended the business to new customer groups. Also, the Housewares Division was expanded to include Sunbeam small appliances, which, Mr. Henderson contended, were price competitive with those sold at the Brand Names store (a catalog-showroom store). The Sporting Goods Division added Smith and Wesson handguns, considered to be top of the line, to its firearms inventory. The markup for most firearms was about 22 percent, but it was over 30 percent for Smith and Wesson handguns. The guns sold so quickly that the store had difficulty keeping them in stock. Also, Mr. Henderson was considering converting a section of the Housewares area into an enclosed "China Shop" with an expanded inventory to cater specifically to women customers.

Furthermore, he wanted to develop what he saw as the unlimited potential of the DIY market. The furniture refinishing section was a step in this direction. Another DIY project under consideration was a "Decorator Center" which would stock a selection of paint, wallpaper, fixtures, and picture frame molding. The center would not carry any furniture, fabrics, or carpeting. Perhaps the most promising opportunity appeared to be in lumber and building products, merchandise which reportedly had a high turnover. Customers had asked for these items, and Mr. Henderson was seriously thinking about establishing a separate department for building supplies. He even was toying with the idea of setting up a customer woodworking shop, under the full-time supervision of a store employee, which could promote the sale of DIY products.

Sales fell off again in the year ending June 30, 1976, and were lower than they had been in any of the prior eight years. Mr. Henderson believed that this was primarily the result of the previous management's overestimating the loyalty of its customers and underestimating the disruptive effects the move would have on established buying habits. While precise figures on the lost customers were not available, it was estimated that at least 50 percent of the customers entering the new store had never shopped there before. The mix of sales had shifted dramatically in the new location until Mr. Henderson estimated that it was about 80 percent to consumers and the remaining 20 percent to the trade.

To build up a new and consistent clientele, Mr. Henderson launched a twofold campaign of improving customer service and promoting the store to the public. In July, store hours were extended. The new hours were from 7:30 A.M. to 9 P.M. during the week, to 6 P.M. on Saturdays, and from noon to 6 P.M. on Sundays. This move was intended not only to tap the DIY market but also to compete more effectively with the nearby building supply company, which still maintained the traditional hours preferred by the trade (7 A.M. to 5 P.M. weekdays and Saturday mornings). Furthermore, Zayre, Brand Names, and Gold Circle, all located on 40 West, kept the later hours but did not open as early as Quincy Brothers.

Another method of improving customer service was to provide customers with prompter assistance and more advice. In this respect, however, the store was at a disadvantage because many of the salespeople were relatively inexperienced in selling and also unfamiliar with the merchandise and the policies of the store.

A third step to improve customer service was the liberalization of the store's credit policies. Charge accounts which had not been used for at least two years were made inactive, while a program was developed to establish new charge accounts. The store also began accepting BankAmericard and Master Charge. These credit policies were adopted in an attempt to provide a convenience to customers not available at some of the competing stores.

The store's advertising and promotional campaigns were designed "to put Quincy Brothers back on the map." In one week-long promotion 1,200 hot dogs and an equal number of Pepsis were given away at a cost to the store of $750. Mr. Henderson estimated that this promotion resulted in an increase in sales of $5,000 during that week.

An advertising campaign was built around "We are wearing the yellow rose of Texas" to make people aware of the new location on North Texas Boulevard. Starting in September, the store began daily newspaper advertising incorporating the theme and designating certain items of the week as "yellow rose specials," although it was too expensive to use yellow in the advertisements. In each of the departments which had a "yellow rose special" for the week, the sales personnel wore yellow roses pinned to their lapels. Also, the music of the song was utilized in the store and in radio advertisements when the weekly specials were announced in six daily spots.

Advertised items included regular inventory products and items specifically purchased for promotion. Sometimes the latter were "truckload specials," sold from a van or trailer in the parking lot in front of the store. Truckload specials were run during the fall on ladders, paint, and bicycles. Judging from the rate at which the merchandise was sold, Mr. Henderson believed the promotions were a success. His only disappointment in this respect was the store's performance during a week-long back-to-school special scheduled for the first week of school. A number of other retailers in town ran similar specials, with the effect that Quincy Brothers had its thunder stolen.

Once some of the internal difficulties of the store had been reme-
died, Mr. Henderson was concerned primarily with the future and
following through on his objectives. Although it was still too early to
measure the success of the new policies, by early October Mr. Henderson was sure that the store was on its way to recovery. Sales were
up in comparison with those for the previous year (see Exhibit 12),

Exhibit 12
Comparative sales figures for first
quarters of fiscal years 1976 and 1977

	1976	*1977*
July	$ 92,300	$107,600
August	75,600	131,600
September	210,200	185,400
Total	$378,100	$424,600

and he believed that the attitude among the employees had changed
dramatically for the better. The focus of the business had been shifted
back to where it belonged, according to Mr. Henderson, to the customer.

Mr. Henderson's most important consideration was what strategy
the store should adopt. Should it plunge headlong into competition
with The Barn, Anderson's, and Montgomery Ward? How could it
differentiate itself from these stores? Perhaps the best alternative was
to be a first-rate hardware store, but then this would be turning back
the clock, especially when looking at the direction in which the industry seemed to be moving.

Case 5-4

Bavaria Manufacturing International (BMI)

In April 1976, the president of Bavaria Manufacturing International
(BMI) met with members of the company's new products task force at
the firm's Munich head office. The purpose of the meeting was to
discuss the European market introduction of the company's newest
product line (see Exhibit 1). Present were BMI's marketing, produc-

This case was written by Lawrence M. Rumble, research associate, under the supervision of Professor Christopher Gale. Copyright © 1978 by IMEDE (Institut pour
l'Étude des Méthodes de Direction de l'Entreprise), Lausanne, Switzerland.

Exhibit 1
Titan

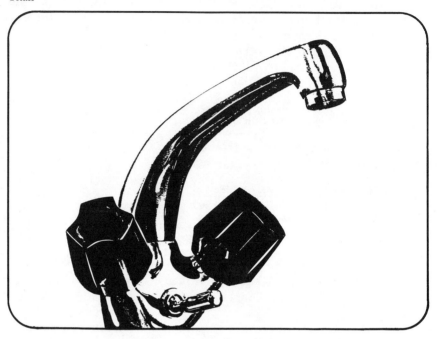

tion, sales, and engineering managers. At the meeting the president made the following statement:

> BMI has traditionally been one of the most profitable companies in the Winchester group. Winchester is looking for big things from us this year, and we are staring down at red figures on our income statement. They are pressing us to introduce the Titan faucet line now. As there is no immediate end in sight to the recession in the construction industry across Europe, we must find new ways of increasing sales. Accordingly, I am moving the Titan introduction date up from January 1977 to September 1976. I think we all believe in this product and we must make every effort to get it to market as soon as possible. Our objective is to sell DM 25 million worth of Titan in the first 12 months. . . .[1] Karl, I must have your final marketing plan by the end of next week.

This last statement was addressed to Karl Schonfeld, BMI's marketing manager. Schonfeld, a recent MBA graduate from an internationally known Swiss business school, felt all eyes on him. He sensed that the successful introduction of this economy faucet line at this time of need for the company was an opportunity for him to make his mark at BMI.

---

[1] The average exchange rate during 1976 was US$ 1 = DM 2.48.

After the meeting Schonfeld retired to his office to begin work on the plan. He began by reviewing materials on the company, the industry, and the market. He then set about examining aspects of the new business that BMI was about to enter.

THE COMPANY

BMI was one of the major water faucet manufacturers in Europe. Begun as Bavaria Manufacturing in 1924 by two brothers, Hans and Otto Weidemann, the company started producing faucets for consumer and commercial use and never significantly diversified. It grew as a family business, survived World War II, and by the 1970s was considered to be one of the "big five" faucet manufacturers in Europe. In 1976, BMI marketed a full line of classical faucets, as well as lines of "one-hand mixers," thermostatically controlled faucets for use in homes, institutions and hospitals, bathtubs, and other accessories for the bathroom (see Exhibit 2).[2] Faucets comprised 96 percent of its sales.

BMI's head office was in Munich, and all its factories were located in West Germany. The company distributed its products through marketing subsidiaries in Europe and through agents around the world. In 1958, the Weidemann family sold 60 percent of the company to Winchester Holdings of London, England, and it was renamed Bavaria Manufacturing International. The Weidemanns retired from active management in 1961.

BMI had built its business on the basis of a high-quality product backed up by good service. Over the years its faucets had gained a reputation for their ease of installation and their durability. Many plumbers tended to use BMI faucets because they had apprenticed on them. Among plumbers it was commonly said, "If it's BMI, it's *quality.*"

The Company had traditionally been an innovator. For example, it had pioneered faucets which used fewer connections than older products, to facilitate installation. However, in recent years the industry had matured, and BMI's competitors had matched the company's innovations. By the 1970s BMI manufactured products for the upper and middle segments of the faucet market, stringently maintained its reputation for quality, and sold its products at premium prices. It held 14 percent of the European market for faucets.

---

[2] There were two general classifications in the faucet industry: classical faucets and one-hand mixers. Classical faucets had two separate mounts for hot and cold water controls, and either two separate spouts or a common spout into which both hot and cold water were fed. One-hand mixers were single-spout faucets in which hot and cold water were mixed in preset amounts selected by turning a single faucet handle. These were a recent innovation, and represented a rapid growth segment of the market.

Exhibit 2
BMI products and parts diagram

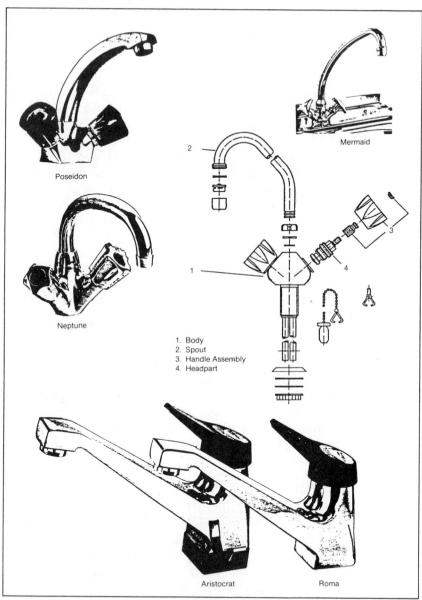

1. Body
2. Spout
3. Handle Assembly
4. Headpart

Poseidon

Mermaid

Neptune

Aristocrat

Roma

Source: Company Publications

THE FAUCET INDUSTRY: THE BIG FIVE ET AL.

The faucet industry in Europe was not highly concentrated, with the five largest producers controlling only 50 percent of the market. (See Exhibit 3 for data on sales and industry structure. Exhibit 4 presents data on market share held in selected markets by major competitors). Aside from BMI the major producers were as follows:

Grohe

Grohe was unquestionably the industry leader. A full-line German producer specializing in high-quality faucets for the upper end of the market, it was a family concern which had been in the faucet business for 50 years. Grohe, like BMI, was an innovator; its one-hand mixer had been one of the first marketed in Europe. The company's 1975 sales were estimated at DM 150 million. Grohe was strong in classical faucets, one-hand mixers, and hospital fittings. It maintained an in-house sales force and subsidiary sales and service organizations in Great Britain, Spain, France, Italy, Holland, Japan, and the United States.

Hansa

Hansa was a full-line, family-owned German producer of high-quality faucets with a particular strength in one-hand mixers and medium-priced classical faucets. It maintained its own sales force. Hansa exported faucets all over Europe, but the firm had no really dominant position in any country other than Germany. Its sales were estimated to be DM 62 million.

Pangaud

Pangaud was a privately held full-line French producer. This firm had its own sales force but was a strong factor primarily in France, particularly in the low-medium-quality segment of the classical faucet market. Its sales in 1975 were DM 60 million.

CEC

CEC was a union of several French producers which offered a full range of faucets from low-priced classical faucets up to thermostats. This group was a major factor in the French market but had no significant position outside that country. It maintained a small sales force. Its sales were DM 52 million in 1975.

One German manufacturer, Ideal Standard, a subsidiary of the US giant American Standard, was a fast growing firm which had recently introduced a popular one-hand mixer. All of these firms concentrated almost exclusively on the production of water faucets for the European and export markets.

The remainder of the market was supplied by some 200 smaller manufacturers, many of which operated on a regional basis. In Italy alone, there were more than 100 faucet manufacturers, many of them low-overhead operations catering to local markets. These manufactur-

Exhibit 3
1975 sales of major faucet manufacturers

Company	Base	Total sales (million DM)	Sales of standard faucets (million DM)	Relative price index	Unit sales (standard faucets)
Grohe	Germany	DM 150	DM 42	100*	1,300,000
BMI	Germany	125	30	100	1,000,000
Hansa	Germany	62	19	100	550,000
Pangaud	France	60	28	70	1,000,000
CEC	France	52	20	75	750,000
Ideal Standard	Germany	32	10	100	300,000
Mamoli	Italy	24	12	70	700,000
Kludi	Germany	23	18	70	800,000
Damixa	France	22	0	0	0
Porcher	France	19	12	70	600,000
Venlo	Holland	15	5	85	200,000
Buades	Spain	13	8	65	400,000
SGF	France	12	5	70	200,000
Zuchetti	Italy	12	5	70	200,000
Rocca	Italy	10	5	70	200,000
Rapetti	Italy	10	5	70	200,000
Seidl	Austria	8	3	90	100,000
Schmidl	Germany	7	12	90	100,000
Others		214	86	70	4,000,000
Total		DM 870	DM 325	80	12,600,000

* Note: This column represented management's judgement of the relative price levels for similar faucets where the most expensive product in the market was assigned a value of 100.
  Source: Company records.

Exhibit 4
Market shares of manufacturers in major European markets

		West Germany	France	Italy	Spain	Total Europe
Grohe	Standard	22%	4%	2%	7%	13%
BMI	Standard	19	4	1	2	9
Hansa	Standard	6	.5	—	4	6
Pangaud	Standard	1	5	1	18	9
	Substandard	—	2	—	4	3
CEC	Standard	—	5	—	14	6
	Substandard	—	1	—	3	2
Ideal Standard	Standard	2.5	0.5	0.5	5	3
Mamoli	Standard	—	0.5	12	1	3
	Substandard	—	—	3	6	3
Kludi	Standard	4	—	—	—	5
Porcher	Standard	—	7	—	—	4
	Substandard	—	2	—	—	2
Venlo	Standard	0.5	—	—	—	—
Buades	Standard	—	—	—	12	2
	Substandard	—	—	—	36	11
Total	Standard	55%	26.5%	16.5%	63%	61%
	Substandard	0	5	3	49	21

Source: Company estimates.

ers specialized in cheaper-quality products and supplied much of the "substandard" segment of the market.

THE MARKET FOR FAUCETS

Faucets were a DM 870 million business in Europe in 1976.[3] The market could be divided up according to the following price segments:

Medium- and high-price segment	DM 130,000,000
Thermostats and hospital fittings	225,000,000
Standard products	325,000,000
Substandard products	90,000,000
Accessories and spare parts	100,000,000
Total	DM 870,000,000

The "standard" segment was defined by BMI management as that part of the market where function and price were the main factors affecting the brand decision and where quality (durability) and service were important considerations. Style and general appearance were less important than in the medium- and high-price sector. Management defined the "substandard" segment as that part of the market where products were below normal German government standards with respect to noise and flow control and where price was a major consideration and quality and service were less important. However, these segments were not clearly distinct from each other. Certain products could be considered to be in the standard sector in one European country and in the substandard sector in another, because different countries had different accepted norms with regard to sanitary fitting installations.

Markets could also be classified according to whether they were residential or institutional. Approximately 90 percent of faucets were sold for residential buildings, while the remaining 10 percent went to the institutional market (hospitals, offices, hotels, etc.). On average a residential dwelling unit had five faucets, while the number of faucets in an institutional building varied according to its function. In the residential sector approximately 45 percent of the fittings were purchased for new construction and 55 percent for the repair and replacement (R&R) market. Of those fittings purchased for new construction, 50 percent were for individual units and 50 percent were for collective residences (apartments and condominiums). These estimates represented averages, as the rate and type of construction in individual countries varied according to economic structures and domestic government policies (e.g., with regard to social housing projects).

There was an increasing trend in the wealthier countries of Europe, such as Germany, for families to undertake construction of their own

---

[3] 1976 estimate at factory wholesale prices, excluding the United Kingdom.

homes. In approximately 60 percent of new private home construction a family or individual financed the project. The remainder was developer-financed. The social housing (state-financed) segment of the residential new construction market was virtually all collective housing and represented 70 percent of all collective housing construction. The remainder was financed by private sources.

In the residential repair and replacement (R&R) market half of the sales were for use in collective housing units and half for use in individual dwellings. There was a broad tendency toward upgrading the quality of the fittings used when replacement was needed, especially when the owner was also the occupant.

In the institutional market approximately 70 percent of faucets were purchased for new construction and the remainder for the R&R market. Approximately 10 percent of new construction was state-financed (hospitals, administrative buildings), and 90 percent was privately financed (hotels, offices, factories, clinics). In old institutional construction the sales of faucets were spread proportionally between state-constructed and privately constructed buildings.

During 1975 there was a near collapse of the construction market across all of Europe. In 1974, 714,000 new dwelling units were constructed in Germany; in 1975, this number dropped to 500,000, and predictions for 1976 hovered around the 400,000 mark. The recession occurred in most European countries to a comparable degree. It affected faucet manufacturers to the extent that they were tied to the construction sector and at a time when many were planning capacity expansions. The decline was attributed primarily to overspeculation in real estate during the early 1970s. This applied especially to units being built by private sources for investment purposes. Social housing was virtually unaffected.

DISTRIBUTION

Ninety-five percent of all faucets in Europe were sold through sanitary wholesalers. Normally a wholesaler would carry the complete range of products of one or two of the major faucet manufacturers, along with products of three or four local suppliers. The wholesaler did not normally enjoy an exclusive franchise from a manufacturer to sell its products in a particular area. A wholesaler stocked some 30,000 separate plumbing items, of which faucets represented between 2 percent and 8 percent of DM sales. His inventory thus represented a substantial capital investment. There were 4,000 wholesalers in the EEC. Though there was a diversity of size among companies in this trade, an average wholesaler would do a sales volume of DM 4,500,000 per year.

Wholesalers sold primarily to plumbers, installers, and building contractors. An independent plumber would generally buy a faucet for a specific application and install it directly. In making his selection, he would take into consideration the type of building requiring the faucet, the characteristics of the plumbing attachments, and the owner's wishes. In residential housing the owner might prefer an expensive and attractive unit or a cheap functional one. The plumber preferred to work with faucets which were easy to install and would not need service or repair for as long as possible.

Installers were businessmen who employed a number of plumbers and took on larger plumbing contracts. They would characteristically buy a number of faucets for a contract and would be concerned about the profit margins on these, the volume discounts, and the quality of the products themselves. The majority of the installers' business was in new residential and institutional construction. An installer would generally take into consideration the opinions of his plumbers when making purchase decisions, if he were allowed a free choice when purchasing faucets. However, the faucets to be used on a given contract would often be specified by the contractor himself.

Building contractors undertook construction projects independently, for private developers, or under government contract. On a small project a contractor/developer would commonly make purchase decisions on faucets himself or delegate it to the installer with certain guidelines. The contractor would take price, quality, and appearance into consideration, according to the type of building being constructed. On a larger project the developer would usually approve the faucets the contractor or installer selected. Occasionally an architect would specify a certain brand of faucet for his building, though these did not generally occupy a significant part of his attention because they did not represent significant construction costs.

On government contracts a government specifier would commonly select the faucets to be used by the contractor, with occasional input from an architect. Government specifiers were primarily concerned with the price and quality of a faucet. In the social housing sector it was important that a faucet meet price restrictions and the government norms in terms of noise and flow control. BMI management felt that of these two considerations price was probably more important.

While "quality" was an important consideration among many purchasers, BMI management felt that it was difficult to define precisely. BMI marketing executives believed that quality was closely related to the amount of hand polishing and brass (by volume) in a faucet but that these characteristics were not easily apparent to all users. However, plumbers and installers generally stated that they "could tell quality when they saw it and felt it."

COSTS, PRICES, AND MARGINS

Production costs of faucets varied according to how much brass was used in a given unit, the quality of the headpart (see Exhibit 2), the amount of hand shaping and polishing which was required, the types of handles used, and the quality of the chrome plating. With so many variables, production costs would fluctuate considerably according to the unit produced and the corporate structure of the company producing it. Full-line manufacturers would manufacture several faucet lines of varying qualities and market them at varying prices.

A manufacturer would generally sell to wholesalers at a price which would allow him an average contribution over variable factory costs of 33⅓ percent. In turn, a wholesaler generally priced in order to enjoy a 16⅔ percent markup on his selling price to plumbers, installers, and contractors.

The individual plumber or installer dealing with the public would sell the faucet at a price which would allow him a 26 percent markup.

As no two manufacturers produced faucets of exactly the same quality or appearance, prices for competing products could vary considerably. In this regard BMI tended to price its products high relative to the prices of its competitors.

BMI—PRODUCT LINES

BMI produced and sold three classical faucet lines in 1974—the Poseidon, Neptune, and Mermaid. In addition it produced the Aristocrat and Roma lines of one-hand mixers, a line of thermostatically controlled fixtures for home use, and another for institutional use. The classical faucet lines were differentiated as follows:

Poseidon line

This was BMI's top line and was characterized by its elegant shape, distinctive styling, and brilliant (transparent plastic) handles. The Poseidon line had been introduced three years earlier and was aimed at the luxury market for sanitary fittings. It was available in both chromium- and gold-plated editions. A representative chrome faucet in this line sold for approximately DM 60 to wholesalers. The Poseidon line comprised approximately 3 percent of BMI's sales.

Neptune line

The Neptune line was BMI's middle line, had equally distinctive styling but used slightly less brass than the Poseidon, and had attractive metal handles. A representative faucet from this line sold for DM 40 to wholesalers. The Neptune line had been introduced eight years earlier and accounted for 8 percent of BMI's sales.

Mermaid line

The Mermaid line was BMI's only entry in the standard faucet market. It was of comparably high quality but was of a more economical design than the Poseidon and Neptune. A representative faucet from the line sold for DM 30 to wholesalers. Although the Mermaid line was over 20 years old, it was still BMI's top seller, comprising 24 percent of total company sales.

Each of the product lines included, in addition to the basic faucets, spouts, and shower heads, attachments to adapt the faucets to various plumbing installations. Differing specifications in each of the countries of Europe (e.g., the distance between hot and cold water pipe centers) and abroad required that those producers that exported make available a large number of attachments with each line. Thus, although there was some commonality, BMI's product lines generally consisted of some 150 separate manufactured parts, made from 500 to 600 component parts.

THE TITAN PROJECT

The Titan line was BMI's newest line of classical faucets. It was an economic faucet line (EFL) aimed at the low-cost and public housing markets, where BMI had no market offering.

The product had been conceived as early as 1973. At that time management was becoming increasingly concerned about the number of small firms which imitated BMI designs and undersold it in the marketplace. These "copycat" producers would modify BMI's basic design, manufacture a cheaper-quality product which looked similar, and sell it for 30 percent to 40 percent less. These producers had for some time been making inroads into BMI's markets, especially into sales of the Mermaid line. The EFL was BMI's response to this threat.

The impetus to turn the EFL concept into a reality was provided by the recession in the construction industry. BMI, along with most of its competitors, had not anticipated the drop in demand and was caught with excess manufacturing capacity on its hands. The search for new market opportunities caused the company to again turn its eyes to the "low end" of the market. An internal study was done which indicated that the copycat products eating into BMI's sales generally used less brass by volume than did BMI's products. It also indicated that over 30 percent of the labor costs of BMI's faucets were in the hand-polishing operations, and 20 percent to 30 percent in the handles. The study recommended that BMI design a line which could be produced entirely by automated processes and which would use an amount of brass comparable to the amount used in the imitation products. Costs could thereby be reduced by approximately 25 percent. BMI would then be able to drop its prices so as to be competitive with the copycat products and would break into the social housing and substandard markets it had thus far been excluded from.

As originally conceived, the EFL was to have replaced the existing Mermaid line. It was to have been marketed under the BMI name as a high-quality, low-cost faucet line. Sold at prices 20 percent below the Mermaid, it would rely on BMI's reputation for quality, and BMI's service and distribution organization would assure its acceptance in the marketplace. BMI expected the EFL—now dubbed Titan—to pick up Mermaid's sales and take market share away from competitors in the low-price standard and substandard faucet markets.

PRODUCT DEVELOPMENT

Product development began in August 1975 with the formation of a task force comprised of BMI's marketing, sales, production, and engineering managers. This was BMI's first experience with such group management. The production manager, Mr. Rolf, was chosen to head the force, as it was his responsibility to bring the Titan into production and achieve necessary cost reductions. The engineering manager was instructed to design an EFL which looked distinctly different from existing BMI lines but which maintained BMI's standards of quality. He was to sacrifice design for function and economy where this became necessary. The marketing manager, Schonfeld, was to develop a detailed marketing plan for the EFL, to be approved by Winchester. The sales manager was to work with Schonfeld on marketing aspects of the line.

In September 1975, the first drawings were received from the engineering department. These were shown to the managers of various BMI subsidiaries across Europe to indicate the exact specifications and physical characteristics of the new line. Some of the managers indicated different specifications which would be required in their home markets. BMI engineering staff made it clear that lower costs had been achieved not by diminishing the quality of the product but by developing a line from standard parts. The development of a completely new line which used the smallest possible number of standard parts would enable the company to achieve economies of scale on long production runs.

By October models were produced for costing, and by November the first prototypes were ready. These deadlines were all met in record time for BMI product development. Among the members of the task force there was a shared commitment to the project which was manifested in a strong feeling of confidence about the future of the line.

CONSUMER TESTING

Once the prototypes were received from engineering, in November, two consumer surveys were conducted. Schonfeld wished to use these to pinpoint any problems with public acceptance of the Titan. Any alterations in the product would have to be incorporated in the near future if the EFL was to meet its target introductory date.

In the first test, 150 people selected at random were invited into BMI's factory showroom in Munich to examine the prototypes. The

Titan line was displayed alongside similar lines of French, Austrian, and Spanish manufacture. All lines were unmarked. After allowing each respondent time to view and test the faucets, BMI staff interviewed him or her in order to record perceptions of the products. Each interview took up to one-half hour, and the results were recorded on survey sheets.

The results of the first consumer test did not reveal any particular bias for or against the Titan line. It was noted that the consumer apparently judged the quality of a faucet by the handles and that his or her overall response to the appearance was also clearly related to perception of the appearance and feel of the handles. The only notable finding in the report was that respondents commonly indicated a preference for one line over another based on color. Since the handles on most, but not all, faucet sets were chrome and not colored, and since the hose and head of the shower sets were either black or white, it was not altogether clear what this meant. The problem was further compounded by the fact that Titan had plastic handles which were of a dark green color but which could easily be mistaken for black.

The BMI board of directors discussed the research results and could not come to any firm conclusion. Since it was known from experience in past consumer tests that the characteristics of the faucet handles strongly influenced consumer perception, it was decided to remove the variable from the test data. Accordingly, a second consumer survey was run, only this time all the faucets tested were supplied with identical chrome handles. Thus the only color differences were in the hose and head of the shower sets.

The results from the second survey were again inconclusive. Although there seemed to be some preference for shower sets with a white hose over those with a black hose, there was still no clearly stated consumer preference for the Titan line (with black hose) over its competitors, or for any of the competitors over Titan. From this, Schonfeld and the task force felt that the only reasonable conclusion they could draw was that there was no particular feature of the Titan which would incline the consumer to select another faucet in preference to it when the consumer was presented with an alternative choice. Armed with this information, and mindful of the approaching introductory date, Schonfeld set about making up his marketing plan.

SIZE-UP

Schonfeld began by accumulating relevant data on the countries of Western Europe (see Exhibit 5). He quickly eliminated Britain from the list of available markets because he knew its plumbing installations were so different from those of continental Europe as to make that market totally inaccessible to continental manufacturers. In order to account for differing European faucet standards he divided pro-

Exhibit 5
Statistics on European market, 1975

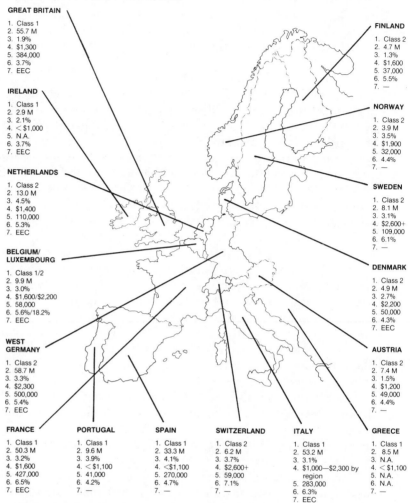

GREAT BRITAIN
1. Class 1
2. 55.7 M
3. 1.9%
4. $1,300
5. 384,000
6. 3.7%
7. EEC

IRELAND
1. Class 1
2. 2.9 M
3. 2.1%
4. < $1,000
5. N.A.
6. 3.7%
7. EEC

NETHERLANDS
1. Class 2
2. 13.0 M
3. 4.5%
4. $1,400
5. 110,000
6. 5.3%
7. EEC

BELGIUM/ LUXEMBOURG
1. Class 1/2
2. 9.9 M
3. 3.0%
4. $1,600/$2,200
5. 58,000
6. 5.6%/18.2%
7. EEC

WEST GERMANY
1. Class 2
2. 58.7 M
3. 3.3%
4. $2,300
5. 500,000
6. 5.4%
7. EEC

FINLAND
1. Class 2
2. 4.7 M
3. 1.3%
4. $1,600
5. 37,000
6. 5.5%
7. —

NORWAY
1. Class 2
2. 3.9 M
3. 3.5%
4. $1,900
5. 32,000
6. 4.4%
7. —

SWEDEN
1. Class 2
2. 8.1 M
3. 3.1%
4. $2,600+
5. 109,000
6. 6.1%
7. —

DENMARK
1. Class 2
2. 4.9 M
3. 2.7%
4. $2,200
5. 50,000
6. 4.3%
7. EEC

AUSTRIA
1. Class 2
2. 7.4 M
3. 1.5%
4. $1,200
5. 49,000
6. 4.4%
7. —

FRANCE
1. Class 1
2. 50.3 M
3. 3.2%
4. $1,600
5. 427,000
6. 6.5%
7. EEC

PORTUGAL
1. Class 1
2. 9.6 M
3. 3.9%
4. < $1,100
5. 41,000
6. 4.2%
7. —

SPAIN
1. Class 1
2. 33.3 M
3. 4.1%
4. <$1,100
5. 270,000
6. 4.7%
7. —

SWITZERLAND
1. Class 2
2. 6.2 M
3. 3.7%
4. $2,600+
5. 59,000
6. 7.1%
7. —

ITALY
1. Class 1
2. 53.2 M
3. 3.1%
4. $1,000—$2,300 by region
5. 283,000
6. 6.3%
7. EEC

GREECE
1. Class 1
2. 8.5 M
3. N.A.
4. < $1,100
5. N.A.
6. N.A.
7. —

Legend:

1. BMI's market classification.
2. Population.
3. Growth in population over five years.
4. Per capita income.
5. Housing completions in 1975.
6. Housing as a percentage of GNP.
7. EEC member or not.

Note: There were no tariffs on faucets in the EEC. Tariffs in other countries averaged 5 percent.
Source: *Business Atlas of Western Europe, 1975.*

spective countries where the Titan could be sold into class 1, 2, and 3 markets. These classifications he outlined in a memo:

Class 1

Class 1 countries include France, Italy, Spain, Portugal, and Greece. These are countries where there is a substantial market for substandard faucets. In total volume the substandard market represents DM 84,000,000 and the standard market DM 52 million at factory prices. BMI's sales in the standard sector of class 1 countries amounted to some DM 12.4 million in 1975.

Class 2

Class 2 markets are those in which few, if any, substandard products are sold, and include Germany, Austria, Belgium, Holland, Luxembourg, and the Scandinavian countries. The total standard market size in these countries is estimated to be DM 265 million in 1976, of which DM 111 million will come from Germany. BMI's sales into this sector were DM 22.5 million in 1975.

Class 3

Class 3 countries, of which the Middle East and Eastern Europe are prime examples, are those in which all products, be they standard or substandard, are sold at roughly the same price. Total market size is estimated to be DM 100,000,000. BMI sales (Mermaid only) amounted to DM 5 million in 1975. Large portions of this market are protected by government policies or trade treaties and are therefore inaccessible to BMI.

Since the Titan line was intended to allow BMI to penetrate the substandard markets, class 1 countries were to be a major focus of the marketing effort. The Titan would be positioned as close as possible to the low-priced competition in these countries. Schonfeld was aware that the product line had to be positioned in all markets in such a way as to maximize *incremental* sales to BMI and to minimize cannibalization of other lines. The president's remarks at the task force meeting had underlined this, since overall corporate sales were slumping substantially.

However, this was a complex issue, since a management decision had recently been made not to withdraw the Mermaid line from the market. Senior management at BMI believed that since the Titan was intended to enable BMI to penetrate markets it had previously been excluded from, it could be positioned in such a way as to pick up incremental sales without cannibalizing Mermaid's sales in the market segment where it was still selling strongly. The Titan line was clearly differentiated from the Mermaid and other BMI lines on the basis of appearance alone, and it was felt that it could be priced sufficiently below Mermaid so as to be considered an addition to the BMI family of products.

The pricing issue was highly influenced by the economics of the investment, however. Schonfeld had recently received a report from the production department which stated that the target reduction of 25 percent on variable Mermaid costs was no longer attainable. He had had reports to suggest this in the past, but this latest one indicated that costs of the Titan line were unlikely to be more than 10 percent below those of the Mermaid. Schonfeld was disturbed by this. Earlier predictions of rises in costs had been based on the fact that the production department had been unable to cast two faucets in a single mold as planned (something BMI had been unsuccessful at on previous occasions), because hand-polishing operations could not be fully eliminated and because fully automatic production (i.e., the purchase of some major machinery) would not be feasible until substantial sales volume materialized. These factors had resulted in predictions of costs 17 percent below Mermaid. However, the new cost increases were based on the increased tooling, setup, operating, and working capital costs associated with increased parts requirements to meet specifications in class 1 countries such as Italy and Spain. In fact the number of product variations for the line had expanded from the 20 originally envisaged to 80 to cover French, Italian, and Spanish plumbing specifications.

Schonfeld was aware that to date DM 2,975,000 had been invested in the Titan project. Of this DM 1,740,000 had been spent on product development, DM 750,000 on production machinery, and DM 485,000 on tooling. One thousand prototype Titan faucet sets had been produced for test market purposes. The expected costs per unit submitted in the latest report were based on assumed unit sales of 1 million to 2,500,000 faucets per year. If sales were 10 percent below the 1 million mark, costs per unit could be expected to rise 5 percent. This trend would continue down to a sales level of 500,000 units, after which per unit costs would escalate rapidly. If sales were only 800,000 units, therefore, costs would be equal to those of the Mermaid line.

The basic faucet from the Titan line would have to be sold to wholesalers at DM 24 in order to be 20 percent below Mermaid in price. However, in light of the new cost figures variable manufacturing cost at this price increased from the originally projected 69 percent to 75 percent. This was before expected variable packaging and shipping costs of some DM 2.5 per unit. Schonfeld was thus caught in a cost-price squeeze and had to decide whether or not to risk raising the price of the Titan. If he did raise the price, he wondered by how much this should be done and in what markets. He estimated that at DM 24 Titan sales would be 1 million units and that Mermaid sales would drop from 1 million to 800,000 units. He estimated that Mermaid sales would drop by 4 percent below 800,000 for every 5 percent decrease in Titan prices below DM 24 and that Titan sales would increase by 7.5 percent for every 5 percent drop in price. If he raised the price of Titan, he estimated that sales would decrease by 10 percent for each 5 percent increase over DM 24 but that Mermaid sales would remain virtually unaffected. This was due to his belief that

Titan and Mermaid would be perceived as different brands. Finally, Schonfeld did not believe that the market would accept a price increase on Mermaid.

He also had to wonder if cost reduction strategies might be employed. The most obvious one would be to recommend full automation immediately. However, this would take time and would require a further capital outlay of DM 1 million. The degree to which costs would be further reduced was uncertain. From the data available to him, he estimated that full automation might reduce Titan's costs by 3 to 4 percent. Another alternative would be to reduce the number of countries the Titan would be introduced in, in order to curb the proliferation of variations (estimated at an incremental 20 for each of Spain, France, and Italy).[4] A further option involved implementing a cost-reduction program on the handles of the Titan line. He believed that by moving to a plain handle, costs on this item could be reduced by 5 percent to 8 percent. However, he believed that the plain handles would be less attractive to end consumers than the existing plastic Titan handles.

Because of the cost-price issue and the positioning issue the countries in which Titan was to be distributed assumed paramount importance. From the beginning it had been intended that the line would be targeted at the social housing sectors of the French and Italian markets. However, Schonfeld had to consider how many additional markets would be required to enable BMI to reach its sales target. Germany itself was BMI's stronghold where it held the greatest market share and had the best distribution, highest reputation, and best relations with the trade. Spain was the other market for which parts were already available. However, Spain and Austria were not EEC members, and wholesalers would have to pay a tariff of 5 percent of the landed cost of the faucet in these countries. (There were no tariffs on faucets in the EEC. Tariffs in class 3 countries averaged 10 percent of the landed cost of the units.) Schonfeld knew that BMI's distributors provided good market coverage in all European countries with the exception of Great Britain and Ireland. He also had to consider the possibility of selling Titan through innovative marketing channels such as "do-it-yourself" retail outlets. These were expanding rapidly in some countries such as Germany and Switzerland.

Branding was also an important issue. Schonfeld had considered selling the Titan under a brand name other than BMI in order to avoid cannibalization of Mermaid sales. It would thus be clearly differentiated in the eyes of BMI's traditional customers and could be marketed to the substandard, standard, and social housing sectors of European countries, perhaps at a price higher than the price at which it could be

---

[4] There would be few incremental product variations required if Titan were sold in more class 2 countries.

sold under the BMI name. If, on the other hand, the BMI name were used, customers would be assured of the quality of the product. Schonfeld considered some compromise positioning, where Titan would be sold as a "subsidiary brand" to the BMI family of products.

SCHONFELD'S MARKETING PLAN

Schonfeld decided to recommend to the production department that cost-reduction measures be investigated, but knew he would have to work with the figures presently available to him. He took one last look at the results of an attitude survey which had been conducted by BMI in Germany the previous year (Exhibit 6) and proceeded with

Exhibit 6
Company assessment of target groups and factors they consider in selecting standard faucets

| Concerns | Potential customer | | | | | | |
	Whole-saler	Plumber	Installer	Developer/ contractor	End user	Government specifier	Architect
Quality	X	X		X		X	X
Price			X	X	X	X	
Function		X	X	X	X	X	X
Appearance				X	X		X
Profit	X	X	X				
Ease of installation		X	X				
Brand	X	X					

Source: Derived from company records.

his task. With time pressures mounting he did not have available to him the results of the Titan test market, which had been under way for several weeks in Vienna.

After a week he felt he had a workable proposal. Titan would be sold as a BMI line, using the BMI sales force, and would be backed up by the BMI service organization. It would be positioned at the low end of the BMI product range and distributed through wholesale channels exclusively. The EFL would be sold in Germany, France, Italy, and Spain in the introductory 12 months. Schonfeld decided to add Austria to the list of introductory markets, as there was already a full test market being conducted there.

After much deliberation he had elected to raise the factory price of the Titan by an average of 15 percent in order to assure the profitability of the line. However, he concluded from talks with salesmen in the field that buyers were more price sensitive in class 1 markets than in class 2, where the name BMI on Titan would probably be perceived as a genuine opportunity to buy BMI quality at a lower price than Mermaid. Accordingly he decided on a three-tier pricing scheme, whereby Titan prices were raised by 10 percent in class 1 markets, to DM 26.50, and by 17 percent in class 2 markets, to DM 28; on average, class 3 price (excluding tariffs) was to be DM 30. This would optimize the overall margin for the product (see Exhibit 7 for Schonfeld's sales

Exhibit 7
Titan's projected sales and cannibalization of Mermaid if Titan is sold for an average price of DM 27.6/unit (DM millions)

	1976	1977 (1st year of Titan)		1978 (2nd year of Titan)	
	Mermaid	Mermaid	Titan	Mermaid	Titan
France	2.1	2.0	6.1	1.6	9.7
Italy	1.5	1.1	3.0	0.8	5.5
Spain	0.9	0.5	2.3	0	2.8
Austria	0	0	0.7	0	0.9
Germany	16.4	14.6	8.4	7.0	18.1
Other	4.6	3.8	0	2.6	0
Class 3	5	0	4.5	0	5
Product total	30	23	25	12	42
Total sales	30	48		54	

Source: Company records.

projections and expected cannibalization of Mermaid sales over the next two years).

In order to minimize cannibalization of other lines, Schonfeld decided on a direct mail campaign for promotional material, aimed at specifiers and buyers for "standard" and "low-quality" building projects. Brochures advertising the Titan line would be directed to clients who were not likely to consider purchasing another line of BMI faucets (specifically Mermaid) and would bypass those buyers who would normally purchase Mermaid. The promotional message in these brochures would be: "Titan: BMI quality at an attractive price."

The selling emphasis, in comparison with Mermaid, would be as follows:

	Titan	Mermaid
Plumbers	20%	50%
Wholesalers	20	30
Planners, architects, specifiers	60	20
	100%	100%

The total promotional budget was DM 1,250,000.

Schonfeld finished with a summary of his plan for achieving his first-year sales objectives (see Exhibit 8). After completing it, he sat back and reflected that, if his reasoning were correct, this would be one of the most successful new products in BMI's history. He noted

Exhibit 8
Summary of Schonfeld's marketing plan

1. First-year sales objective: DM 25 million.
2. Brand name: Titan—One of the BMI Family of Products.
3. Distribution channel: Sanitary wholesalers.
4. Markets

Market	Sales
France	DM 6,100,000
Italy	3,000,000
Spain	2,300,000
Austria	700,000
Germany	8,400,000
Class 3	4,500,000
Total	DM 25,000,000

5. Pricing

Class of market price

1.	DM 26.50
2.	28
3.	30

6. Positioning: social housing and substandard and low end of standard markets.
7. Promotion: Printed material (leaflets) aimed primarily at architects, specifiers, and wholesalers; specially trained sales support—total budget DM 1.25 million.
8. Message: "Titan: BMI quality at an attractive price."

that the first test results had come in from Vienna. The report stated that there had been no complaints whatever with any of the Titan faucets which had been installed in the two months since the test began. It also reported that Titan was selling well in the test market area. Schonfeld was pleased by this, but did not wish to be overly optimistic.

Before turning in his plan, Schonfeld decided to go over it one more time. He knew that it would be scrutinized carefully by executives at Winchester House, in addition to BMI top management in Munich. He would have to explain why he had elected to proceed as he had, and what alternatives he had considered. If he were called to London, he knew he would have to defend his proposal in front of the Winchester senior management committee.

Case 5–5

FAFCO, Inc.

In September 1976, John O'Lear had just accepted the position of executive vice president and general manager in charge of operations for FAFCO, Inc., a small but rapidly growing firm manufacturing solar heating systems for swimming pools. Freeman Ford, the founder and majority owner of FAFCO, had hired O'Lear as he completed the Sloan Program (a nine-month executive education program) at the Stanford Business School. O'Lear had had several years of experience in marketing and line operations management prior to his year at Stanford (see Exhibit 1). He was hired by Ford to handle the day-to-day operations of the business so that Ford could devote more time to product development and advancing the concept of solar energy. O'Lear was attracted to FAFCO by the prospect of immediate responsibility for the running of a small, high-potential business, as well as by the opportunity for a long-term financial reward through a substantial stock option granted to him when he accepted the position.

At the time of his hiring, O'Lear and Ford agreed that FAFCO was entering into a critical phase of its development. The company had enjoyed rapid growth in sales and profitability over the previous year, establishing early dominance in the swimming pool heater market. The energy crisis caused by the oil embargo of 1974 had created a very lively market opportunity in solar energy. However, the company had reached the limit of its capacity and further significant sales increases would, in their opinion, require a major restructuring of the company. Key decisions would have to be made in the areas of marketing programs, production processes, personnel additions, and financing. To maintain and exploit the early market dominance FAFCO had achieved, O'Lear felt that these decisions had to be made quickly, given the increasingly competitive nature of the solar industry. Many smaller companies had similar products on the market or were in the process of developing them. Also, larger corporations, such as EXXON, Grumman, PPG Industries, and Reynolds Metals, were contemplating entry into the solar field.

COMPANY BACKGROUND

After a tour of duty in Vietnam as a naval aviator, Freeman Ford took a position in 1968 with a high-technology manufacturer of semi-

This case was prepared by Greg Sessler under the supervision of Professor Henry E. Riggs. Reprinted from *Stanford Business Cases 1978* with permission of the publishers, Stanford University Graduate School of Business, © 1978 by the Board of Trustees of the Leland Stanford Junior University.

Exhibit 1

Stanford University
Graduate School of Business

John O'Lear

Address: Home Address:

3345 Kenneth Drive   400 15th Street
Palo Alto, California 94303   Spirit Lake, Iowa 51360
415—493-8974

Job objective: General management. Will consider marketing or corporate planning position which would lead to general management.

Education:

1974–76 *Stanford Graduate School of Business*
Candidate for MBA degree in June 1976. Concentration in accounting/finance and general management. Stanford Sloan Fellow, 1974–75.

1958–61 *University of Northern Colorado,* Greeley, Colorado
Major in education.

Business experience:

Berkley & Co., Spirit Lake, Iowa

1972–74 Director Product Management. Responsible for marketing strategy, financial projection, and manufacturing policy for three product lines. Appointed to long-range planning committee.

1970–72 Product Manager. Responsible for profitability of one product line. Major change in marketing strategy resulted in a two-year sales increase of 75 percent and a profitability increase of 125 percent.

1967–70 Corporate Quality Control Manager. Responsible for all quality control activities of three manufacturing plants.

1965–67 Sales Service Manager. Responsible for all clerical functions of sales office, including traffic management, purchasing of pass-through products, and customer complaints. Reduced order processing time from five days to two days and cut shipping time by 50 percent.

1962–64 Quality Control Engineer. Responsible for quality evaluation of products going into manufacturing from design and development. Supervised quality control laboratory. Designed and installed statistical quality control program.

Summer 1975 *FAFCO, Inc.,* Menlo Park, California
Prepared annual business plan. Established plan for national distribution by designing dealership program. Installed internal reporting system, including cost accounting and production control system. Invited to join board of directors.

Military: A/1C U.S. Air Force. Air and sea rescue. Named Airman of the Month for 3,000-man installation.

References: Personal references are on file with the Placement Office and will be forwarded upon request.

conductor processing equipment, capitalizing on his Dartmouth undergraduate training in economics and engineering. During this time, he became familiar with the potential of solar energy and convinced of the future need for alternative energy sources. In 1970, he and a college friend formed a partnership dedicated to developing a low-cost solar heating mechanism for swimming pools. Ford invested the "seed money" for product development and worked full time with the company without compensation. Ford could do this as well as pursue his two favorite hobbies—piloting his Piper Comanche to his Lake Tahoe cabin and playing tennis on his backyard court—because he had substantial personal net worth.

The early years of FAFCO were spent testing various system configurations, using Ford's home pool or pools owned by friends and relatives in the Bay Area. At the time, prior to the crisis year of 1973, the demand for solar energy was nonexistent; moreover, the costs of producing most solar devices were prohibitive.

By 1972, FAFCO had reduced the costs of production and introduced solar systems to the market. Sales that year amounted to only $13,000. However, Ford believed in his product and felt certain that the supplies of gas and oil would dwindle, causing higher prices.

During the following phase of explosive growth, FAFCO took on some of the characteristics of a "counterculture" business operation. Working out of a garage in Redwood City and later in a small plant in Menlo Park, the company attracted "free spirit" individuals and students willing to work for relatively low wages. The atmosphere was extremely informal, and most standard business practices were ignored. Early production records were scarce, and accounting data were "collected" by means of a manual system supervised by two inexperienced bookkeepers. Budgets and annual operating plans were unheard of. The company's auditors, Price Waterhouse & Co., struggled with their first audit of FAFCO during 1975.

The key to the company's success in the early years was Ford's personality. He was a man of vision and perseverance who also had the ability to relate well with workers at all levels of the organization. His enthusiasm and idealism were a source of motivation for the employees who, despite their inexperience and unconventional ways, were highly committed and loyal to the company. Ford also had the charisma needed to generate free publicity in *Sunset, Fortune,* and *Business Week* magazines.

After three years of losses, FAFCO turned a modest profit in 1975, as sales exceeded $1.5 million. By mid-1976, when O'Lear became general manager, the company was in high gear. Sales had doubled over the comparable period of the previous year. Profits before taxes were expected to be in the range of 14 percent on sales, and a cash surplus was beginning to build (see Exhibits 2, 3, and 4).

Exhibit 2

FAFCO, Inc.
Balance Sheet
September 30, 1976
Unaudited

Assets

Current assets:

Cash..........................		$ 78,482.91
Accounts receivable—trade	$308,914.05	
Accounts receivable—other	4,950.96	
Total	313,865.01	
Less: Allowance for bad debts	23,337.53	290,527.48
Intercompany accounts receivable...		284,666.83*
Accounts receivable—employees....		399.53
Commission advances.............		20,000.00
Inventory		164,807.51
Prepaid expenses................		18,648.81
Total current assets		$857,533.07

Property and equipment:

Machinery and equipment..........	157,412.31	
Furniture and fixtures	13,397.69	
Trucks	9,475.74	
Leasehold improvements	20,658.31	
Total	200,944.05	
Less: Accumulated depreciation and amortization	71,380.59	129,563.46
Total property and equipment...		129,563.46

Other assets:

Refundable deposits	2,060.00	
Organization expense	788.81	
Total other assets		2,848.81
Total assets......................		$989,945.34

Liabilities

Current liabilities:

Current portion of notes payable....	$ 2,059.01	
Accounts payable—trade	196,522.53	
Accrued expenses	70,258.29	
Accrued payroll payable	(1,000.00)	
Warranty reserve	(9,786.47)†	
Income taxes payable	196,213.34	
Customer deposits................	42,887.94	
Total current liabilities		$497,154.64

Long-term debt:

Installment notes payable	1,697.68	
Notes payable stockholder	125,000.00	
Total long-term debt...........		126,697.68

Stockholders' equity

Capital stock....................	$189,096.00	
Paid-in capital in excess of par	23,256.00	212,352.00
Retained earnings		153,741.02
Total stockholders' equity.........		366,093.02
Total liabilities and equity............		$989,945.34

*Investment in company-owned retail outlet in Sunnyvale, commenced in February 1976.
†Warranty was accrued at year-end only.

Exhibit 3

FAFCO, Inc.
Statement of Income (Loss)
(Unaudited)
($000)

	Year ended December 31				Nine months ended September 30	
				(Audited)		
	1972	1973	1974	1975	1975	1976*
Net sales	$ 13.8	$ 75.2	$373.4	$1,520.2	$1,137.1	$2,232.9
Cost of sales	19.9	35.7	318.2	879.6	640.8	1,150.5
Gross profit (loss)	(6.1)	39.5	55.2	640.6	496.3	1,082.4
Operating expenses:						
Research and development	11.0	55.5	11.2	32.6	17.3	72.6
Marketing	7.4	18.0	59.9	340.2	172.6	380.0
General and administrative	8.7	21.3	39.4	160.1	66.2	199.3
Interest	—	—	6	11.5	11.0	5.4
Total operating expenses . .	27.1	94.8	116.5	544.3	267.1	657.3
Income before tax	(33.2)	(55.2)	(61.3)	96.1	229.2	425.1
Income taxes	—	—	—	32.3	96.0	192.6
Net income (loss)	$(33.2)	$(55.2)	$ (61.3)	$ 63.8	$ 133.2	$ 232.5

*Excludes operations of Sunnyvale retail outlet, which commenced in February 1976.

Exhibit 4
Copy of letter from Price Waterhouse & Co.

April 23, 1976

To the Board of Directors
and Shareholders of
FAFCO, Inc.

We have examined the balance sheet of FAFCO, Inc., as of December 31, 1975, and the related statements of income and accumulated deficit and of changes in financial position for the year. Our examination was made in accordance with generally accepted auditing standards and accordingly included such tests of the accounting records and such other auditing procedures as we considered necessary in the circumstances.

Our engagement as auditors was as of December 23, 1975. Therefore, we were not present to observe physical inventories taken prior to that date, the amounts of which entered into the determination of cost of goods sold for the year ended December 31, 1975. However, we tested records relating to inventory quantities at December 31, 1974, tested unit pricing, performed an inventory quantity reconciliation for the year, and performed such other procedures as we deemed appropriate.

Exhibit 4 (*continued*)

As described in Note 9, a breach of contract action has been filed against the Company. The Company is in the process of litigating this action, but the ultimate outcome is uncertain.

In our opinion, subject to the effects of such adjustments, if any, as might have been required had the outcome of the uncertainty referred to in the preceding paragraph been known, the financial statements examined by us present fairly the financial position of FAFCO, Inc., at December 31, 1975, and the results of its operations and the changes in its financial position for the year, in conformity with generally accepted accounting principles applied on a basis consistent with that of the preceding year.

Price Waterhouse & Co.

FAFCO, Inc.
Statement of Income and Accumulated Deficit
For the Year Ended December 31, 1975

Net sales	$1,517,984
Other income	2,188
	1,520,172
Cost of goods sold	879,640
Selling expenses	340,225
General and administrative expenses	204,201
	1,424,066
Income before income taxes	96,106
Provision for income taxes (Note 1):	
Currently payable	36,000
Prepaid	(3,700)
	32,300
Net income for the year	63,806
Accumulated deficit at beginning of year	(170,939)
Accumulated deficit at end of year	(107,133)
Primary earnings per share (Note 6)	0.34
Fully diluted earnings per share (Note 6)	$ 0.33

FAFCO, Inc.
Balance Sheet
December 31, 1975

Assets

Current assets:	
Cash	$ 48,596
Certificates of deposit	80,000
Accounts receivable, less allowance for doubtful accounts of $4,326	89,290
Inventories (Notes 1 and 2)	142,723
Prepaid expenses	10,011
Total current assets	370,620
Plant and equipment, at cost, less accumulated depreciation of $42,799 (Notes 1 and 3)	56,408
Other assets	789
	$ 427,817

Exhibit 4 (*continued*)

The $75,000, 10 percent
ther of the Company's pre
redeem the convertible not
prepayment premium equal
deemed. The holders of the
or in part, into capital stock
the Company notifies the ho
extent the principal of the
above, it may be converted
maturity. The conversion pr
sion are subject to adjustme
interest in the Company. Th
the payment of all indebtedr
a maturity of less than one y

Note 5. Capital stocks

At December 31, 1975, 1
reserved for issuance under
employees. At that date, the
chase 9,852 shares at $1 pe
value at the date the option
granted, exercised, or cance

Note 6. Earnings per share

Primary earnings per sha
average number of shares ou
tive effect of shares issuable
Fully diluted earnings pe
average number of shares ou
increased by the number of
vertible notes as if conversio
Net income was adjusted to
on the convertible notes pay

Note 7. Commitments

The Company's rental ex
and manufacturing facility, w
$2,600 for equipment lease
owned by the Company's p
minimum lease commitment

1976	$21,700
1977	21,100
1978	21,000
1979	3,500

The Company's principal
erty taxes, utilities, and insu

Exhibit 4 (*continued*)

Liabilities and Shareholders' Equity

Current liabilities:	
Accounts payable and accrued expenses	$ 171,432
Current portion of notes payable (Note 4)	792
Estimated income taxes (Note 1)	35,800
Other current liabilities.	3,398
Total current liabilities	211,422
Notes payable, less current portion (Note 4)	125,528
Shareholders' equity (Notes 4 and 5):	
Capital stock—authorized 250,000 shares of $1 par value, issued and outstanding—178,344 shares.	178,344
Capital contributed in excess of par.	19,656
Accumulated deficit	(107,133)
	90,867
Commitments and contingencies (Notes 7 and 9)	
	$ 427,817

FAFCO, Inc.
Notes to Financial Statements
December 31, 1975

Note 1. Business and summary of significant accounting policies

The Company is engaged in the design, manufacture, sale, and installation of solar heating panels and related automatic controls for swimming pools.

A summary of the Company's significant accounting policies follows:

Inventories

Inventories are priced at the lower of cost or market, cost being determined on the first-in, first-out method.

Plant and equipment

Plant and equipment additions and betterments are included in the asset accounts at cost. Maintenance and repairs are charged to expense when incurred.

Depreciation is computed primarily by using accelerated methods and the estimated useful life of the asset.

Assets retired or otherwise disposed of are eliminated from the asset accounts, and the related amounts of accumulated depreciation are eliminated from the accumulated depreciation accounts. Gains and losses from disposals are included in earnings.

Income taxes

Prepaid income taxes are provided for the timing differences resulting from reporting certain warranty expense in different periods for financial reporting and tax purposes.

Prior to 1975, the Company elected to be treated as a Subchapter S Corporation, under IRC Section 1371–1379, which allows for a pass-through of income or loss to shareholders on a pro rata basis. Accordingly, there is no operating loss carry-forward available for tax purposes.

Exhibit 4 (*continued*)

Investment tax cre...
the amount allowable

Research and develo|

Research and dev...
curred.

Warranties

In the normal cours...
to workmanship and ...
accrued at the time of ...
ties are reviewed and ...
reflect the most up-to-...

Note 2. Inventories

Inventories consist ...

Raw materials . . . .
Finished goods . . . .

Note 3. Plant and equi...

Plant and equipme...
rized as follows:

Machinery and equipmen...
Leasehold improvements ...
Office equipment. . . . . . .
Automobiles. . . . .

Less: Accumulated dep...

Office equipment w...
installment note payab...

Note 4. Notes payable

Notes payable consi...

7% unsecured convertible ...
    shareholder, due in 1...
10% unsecured convertibl...
    payable semiannually ...
18% installment note pay...
    including interest, to ...

Less: Current portion . .

Exhibit 4 (*concluded*)

Note 8. Subsequent event

During February 1976, the Company obtained a commitment for a $100,000 unsecured line of credit with a bank. Borrowings against the line of credit, if any, will bear interest at the bank's prime rate plus 1¾ percent.

Note 9. Legal action

The Company has been named defendant in a suit initiated by Murray Marine Corporation in the State of Florida. The suit alleges a breach of contract and is currently being litigated; however, the outcome is uncertain at this time.

THE PRODUCT

The technology for the FAFCO solar system was quite simple. Black plastic panels (10 feet by 4 feet) resembling corrugated paperboard material were used as collectors for the sun's radiant energy. They were connected to the pool's pump and filter system by a series of manifolds and pipes. As the water was forced through the panels by the pump pressure, it was heated to the desired temperature (see Exhibit 5). The system was designed to supplement the owner's gas

Exhibit 5
Product specifications

FAFCO, Inc.
Bohannon Industrial Park   **138 Jefferson Drive**   **Menlo Park, CA 94025**
Manufacturers of Solar Heat Exchangers

Panel requirements. A minimum of one half to three quarters of the pool's surface area in solar panels is the recommended "rule of thumb" for sizing a swimming pool solar heating system. (Example: 800 sq. ft. pool needs 400 to 600 sq. ft. of panel area.) Particularly in Florida, the solar panel area frequently equals the surface area of the pool to provide adequate heating throughout the entire year.

System performance. The performance of the system is directly proportional to the number of panels installed. More than the minimum requirements will increase the ability of the system to heat a swimming pool under marginal weather or orientation conditions. *Always consider increases* of panel area on a diminishing percentage basis. For example, 4-panel system plus one panel = 20 percent increase; 10-panel system plus one panel = 9 percent increase.

Ideal orientation. The panels should be facing true south, with the inclination adjusted as follows for the northern hemisphere:

Exhibit 5 (*continued*)

---

1. For year-round heating—inclination equal to latitude of installation.
2. For summer heating—inclination equal to latitude minus 10–15°.
3. For winter heating—inclination equal to latitude plus 10–15°.

Site selection.   For convenience and ease of installation, the ideal location for the solar panels is a *south-facing pitched roof*, near the pool, with enough space for mounting the required number of panels. However, an installation on a flat or west-facing roof is acceptable if the panel area is increased. Northern exposures are not acceptable, and eastern exposures tend to be about 50 percent effective and, therefore, marginally economical. Fortunately, the modular nature of the solar panel makes it easy to deal with these conditions and tailor the system to the specific site.

> *All south facing*
> Minimum of 50 percent of pool area
> *All west facing*
> Minimum of 75 percent of pool area
> *Flat roof*
> Minimum of 75 percent of pool area

Ordering

The accessories and components necessary to complete the installation of the FAFCO solar swimming pool heater have been prepackaged to facilitate ordering and handling. *Carefully check your site plan before ordering.*

The FAFCO solar panels come in 10-foot and 8-foot lengths. Both are 51⅜ inches wide. When computing the actual installed dimensions of the entire system, allow an extra 12 inches around the perimeter of the bank to accommodate mounting apparatus, plumbing fittings, and system accessories. If the panels are to be mounted on a custom-made structure, send for FAFCO Applications Sheet (Simple Rack Designs).

Required

Panel pack.   Coupling and mounting accessories needed for each panel (included with each panel).

System pack.   Special components and accessories needed for complete installation of entire system.

Optional

Split pack.   Special accessories needed each time panels split to accommodate obstructions on mounting surface.

Bank pack.   Special accessories needed for each bank of panels in multi-bank systems.

Automatic control.   Solar sensing unit that automatically causes water to be diverted through solar panels when there is enough radiant energy to heat water.

Exhibit 5 (*concluded*)

(One and one-half-inch valving standard, specify for two inches; 240 VAC transformer standard, specify for 120 VAC.)

Tropicana special.   Automatic control with two pinch valves used in systems mounted below level of pool or whenever water has tendency to circulate through panels when control valve is open.

Panel specifications

Pressure, flow, and temperature.   The FAFCO panels are designed to take a very high flow for maximum efficiency. Pressures of 4.5 psi will result in a flow of approximately 8 gpm per panel, which is maximum recommended flow. Minimum recommended flow is 2 gpm/panel, below which excessive losses occur due to overheating of the panel. Maximum design pressure at 80° F is in excess of 30 psi, and average working pressures for pool heaters are approximately 8 psi. Dynamic testing of over 100,000 cycles from 5 to 25 psi at temperatures of up to 220° F has been accomplished without failure. At temperatures above 100° F the pressure should be limited to that dynamic pressure required to achieve the flow required.

Absorptivity.   0.92 or greater to 50 microns.

Emissivity.   Same.

Corrosion resistance.   Completely inert to virtually all materials.

Freezing resistance.   Not affected.

Weatherability.   Extensive tests suggest minimum 10-year life.

Weight: 10-foot panel—16 lbs.: full of water—58 lbs.

Loading factor: 1.5 lb. per sq. ft.

For additional information:

---

heater or to be the sole source of heat for a pool. An automatic control sensor activated the solar system during periods of sufficient sunlight. On cloudy days or in winter, the pool could be heated by gas.

In developing this product, Ford made three innovations. First, he worked with a plastics company in developing the correct compound of raw materials for the panels. Second, he developed the manufacturing process by which the panels were "thermo-formed" to the manifolds. Finally, he developed an automatic control mechanism that activated the system during periods of sunlight. FAFCO was issued four patents on fabrication of the panels, the system accessories, and the automatic control unit.

THE MARKET

In 1976, there were over 1,500,000 inground swimming pools in the United States, with nearly 40 percent located in California, Arizona, and Florida. Approximately 80,000 new pools were constructed annually; approximately 80 percent of these were residential pools, and the balance were commercial. Ford estimated that one fourth of these pools could be adapted to solar heating.

In recent years, approximately 40 percent of new pools were equipped with water heaters. A majority of the heated swimming pools in the United States were heated with natural gas, the most limited of the country's fossil fuels. Natural gas was experiencing shortages and rapid price increases so that, at the 1976 price of natural gas, a solar heating system in northern California could be amortized in approximately five years; but scheduled natural gas price increases were expected to shorten this amortization period. In addition, the California Public Utilities Commission had followed the precedent of New York, Maryland, and several other states in contemplating the ban of natural gas for heating swimming pools. In Ford's opinion, given undeniable shortages and increasing demands, end-use allocation of natural gas was inevitable. He felt that, increasingly, natural gas would be directed to the production of fertilizers, chemicals, and medicines, in preference to heating applications, especially those of a luxury nature.

Swimming pools provided an ideal market for FAFCO because of the size and nature of the market. The market was well defined regionally by climate, and consisted of affluent homeowners. Swimming pool heating was an ideal application of solar energy: relatively low temperatures were required, and swimming pools provided their own storage and circulation.

PROBLEM AREAS

Product failure

Despite its recent success, the company was by no means free of problems. The major difficulty was a high incidence of product failure, the primary cause of which was deterioration of the panel material, particularly in warmer areas such as Florida and southern California. Failures caused leaks in the system, and since patching was an ineffective remedy, leaky panels had to be replaced with new panels. Ford's desire to run a "model company" resulted in the company's policy of fully guaranteeing the product; leaky panels were replaced at no charge. By 1975, 60 percent of the panels installed two years previously, and 90 percent of those installed three years previously, had been replaced. A recent change in the raw materials, to make the panel more durable, was expected to reduce the failure rate. However, even some of the panels fabricated from the new material had failed in tests, although at a much lower rate than previously.

Exact failure rates could not be determined because early production, sales, and warranty data were fragmentary. FAFCO had been able to absorb these warranty expenses for two reasons: (1) the panel could be manufactured at a relatively low cost; and (2) the sales base in the early years was so small that the extensive increase in volume financed the replacement costs. However, as sales expanded, the potential replacement liability was becoming a major concern.

The panel itself was supplied by Hercules Corporation, a major chemical and manufacturing company with annual sales in excess of $1.5 billion. Hercules' Polymer Division had the only facility in the United States to extrude a four-foot-wide plastic panel that was compatible with the FAFCO system. Engineers from Hercules had worked with Ford and FAFCO's staff engineers in developing a panel material that would have optimal thermal and mechanical capabilities. Over the previous four years, five major product changes had been made to improve panel performance.

FAFCO's volume of business was relatively insignificant to Hercules (about $250,000 in 1975). Deliveries from Hercules were often late. Some shipments had a very high rejection rate; Hercules tolerances were not stringent, as the company's purpose in developing the extrusion process was to make a product to replace heavy-duty corrugated paperboard. Hercules had looked for other uses of its process when the anticipated shortage in paperboard never developed and the oil embargo increased the cost of polypropylene resin.

FAFCO had no alternative source of supply for the panel material. As field failures increased, FAFCO complained in vain to Hercules management. Requests for refunds for defective material were rarely granted. O'Lear was also concerned about a possible price increase; his estimates of costs of extrusion indicated that the current selling price of $0.245/square foot to FAFCO could not result in a profit to Hercules. FAFCO could respond to this problem in one of three ways: (1) try to negotiate a better deal with Hercules; (2) seek a new supplier; or (3) vertically integrate by extruding panel material in-house.

The first option was the only alternative for the short term; but, as sales continued to expand, a single source of supply presented a strategic liability, especially given Hercules' past performance with FAFCO. On the other hand, Hercules' expertise in the polymer field was unsurpassed, and as FAFCO's volume expanded, Hercules might take more of an interest.

Finding new suppliers would be difficult and time consuming. Ford continuously tried to generate interest among other producers of plastics material to extrude panels, but the limited potential volume discouraged companies from making the required capital investment.

(Hercules' investment was estimated at $750,000.) In addition, much of the development work with Hercules was proprietary; thus similar efforts would be required with new suppliers who might not have the resources or capabilities of Hercules.

Vertical integration involved substantial risk. It required moving into a larger manufacturing facility (24,000 square feet versus the 14,000 square feet FAFCO currently occupied) and the investment of an estimated $150,000 in a single extrusion line that would have a life of 8 to 10 years. The extrusion of polymers was a very delicate process requiring great expertise. Ford considered it more an art than a science. Over the previous six months, he had worked with staff engineers and outside consultants to apply techniques developed in Italy. To date they had been successful in making prototypes, but there was no assurance that this process could be successfully scaled up to mass production. Also, once FAFCO converted to in-house extrusion, there would be no turning back; Hercules indicated that it would discontinue manufacturing panel material if FAFCO's order volume dropped.

O'Lear estimated that the 4-foot by 10-foot panel board required about 14 pounds of resin at $0.375 per pound and 2 pounds of other raw material averaging $1.58 per pound. He also estimated that one extruder operator employed at $6 per hour could produce 60 panels in one eight-hour shift. Finally, O'Lear figured that the overhead allocation (excluding depreciation of the extruder) would be about $0.82 per panel.[1] O'Lear wondered how much importance to give to the additional control over product quality and supply that vertical integration would bring.

Manufacturing Organization

In addition to defective raw materials, the other cause of FAFCO's product problems appeared to be inconsistent quality in the manufacturing process. The production manager, prior to joining FAFCO, had worked as a machine shop foreman and a purchasing agent, in between periods of voluntary unemployment. When he first joined the production line at FAFCO, he thrived on the informal atmosphere. He enjoyed working in the "no hassle" environment and was happy to accept relatively lower pay and longer hours to work at FAFCO. As he proved capable of handling additional responsibility and demonstrated good rapport with his fellow workers, he was put in charge of the manufacturing operations in 1974.

The production manager, as well as most of the factory employees, exhibited a "free spirit." They resisted the discipline and inflexibility

---

[1] Overhead was based on occupancy of a larger facility operating two shifts per day, five days per week.

of standard assembly line factory operations. For the most part, the workers were conscientious, punctual, and hardworking, but the lack of organization resulted in relatively few formal procedures or production methods. The result was inconsistent product quality, particularly as the production demands accelerated to meet the higher sales volume and the required buildup in inventory. O'Lear wondered if this was the proper time to look for professional production management, or perhaps to develop a production engineering department that would standardize methods and procedures and trouble-shoot quality problems as they arose.

Marketing

Although it was estimated that the 8,000 systems installed by FAFCO represented at least a 65 percent market share of the solar swimming pool heater market, O'Lear anticipated stiffer competition in the future. Two key questions surrounded FAFCO's marketing program: (1) how to structure the distribution organization and (2) how to sell the product. FAFCO's early sales were made direct from the factory to swimming pool owners in the local area. As FAFCO grew, however, more extensive forms of distribution were explored.

The traditional distribution network available to FAFCO was composed of swimming pool equipment wholesalers and dealers. The dealers were primarily pool builders and/or pool maintenance and service companies. The pool dealers bought supplies and accessory equipment for pools from the wholesalers. In a major swimming pool market such as California, there were a large number of dealers. At a recent National Swimming Pool Institute convention in San Francisco, there were over 1,100 dealers and 460 wholesalers from California alone.

Very low merchandising skills existed at the wholesaler level, and almost no merchandising or sales expertise existed at the dealer level. Products marketed through this channel tended to be commodity supply items requiring little sales expertise. Wholesalers and dealers were typically undercapitalized, not very profitable, and slow to pay their suppliers. Consequently, frequent failures occurred and the network of wholesalers and dealers was in a constant state of flux.

Except for a small number of pool supply wholesalers in the Pacific Northwest, FAFCO decided to abandon this distribution channel. As a replacement, FAFCO began setting up a network of independent distributors, primarily in California and the southwestern states, who would concentrate largely on the FAFCO line.

These distributors were typically specialized, small firms whose primary business involved FAFCO solar heating system sales and installations. These distributors had limited financial strength and required substantial assistance from FAFCO in organizing their sales and installation departments. However, all of the distributors had a great amount of enthusiasm for the FAFCO product and felt that the solar industry represented a significant opportunity for those individuals who established their businesses while the industry was still in its infancy.

The distributors were also attracted to the FAFCO product because of its ample margin, as shown below for a typical system.

	Quantity	Distributor price	List price
Solar panels	9	$495	$1,035
System pack	1	24	50
Automatic control	1	104	199
		$623	1,284
Installation materials (purchased independently) by distributor			200
Installation labor			310
Typical installed price for swimming pool owner			$1,794

To gain further marketing knowledge and to test the concept of company-owned distributorships, FAFCO, in March 1976, started a pilot company-owned sales and installation outlet in Sunnyvale, California, covering the western San Francisco Bay Area. This outlet appeared to be successful, with sales for 1976 headed toward an annual rate of $750,000.

It was in the operation of the company-owned outlet that the question of how to structure the sales operation arose. Sales leads were generated primarily through direct mail advertising. Appointments were then secured by telephone contact with the identified prospect. The telephone contact consisted of a prepared presentation with the objective of setting up a personal appointment.

Once the appointment was secured, a distributor salesperson was assigned to it. Selling a FAFCO system was complex. FAFCO's marketing program assumed that the primary selling effort would occur at in-home presentations; however, unlike most products sold in the home, the FAFCO unit required certain technical expertise to tailor the system to the customers' needs and to answer questions about the product. The configuration of each system depended upon the orientation of the house (a southern roof exposure was best), the desired temperature of the water, the size and depth of the pool, and the condition of the pool's pump and filter. Prior to the sales presentation, the salesperson prepared a solar survey with the pertinent data from which the specifications for the system could be developed. A miscalculation such as too few panels or insufficient pump flow resulted in the system not performing to expectations. Once the specifications were determined, the salesperson then attempted to sell the benefits of solar heating. Typically, one or two follow-up calls were necessary to close a sale, although occasionally sales were made on the first call.

The salesperson had to overcome two principal objections by the consumer. First, a homeowner resisted covering his or her roof with black panels, especially if the best exposure was in the front of the house or if the roof was white shingle. Second, and more important, was the cost. Early FAFCO customers were innovators and environmentalists, usually in the affluent suburbs, to whom price was not a major factor. However, as penetration increased, price became a major obstacle. The economics of a FAFCO system, of course, depended upon the configuration of the system and the heating habits of the customer. In the San Francisco Bay Area, a typical $1,800 system provided heat from April through October in the temperature range of 78°–84°. Comparable water temperatures during the period using a gas heater would require an average of $65/month at existing utility rates, or $455 a season. Consumers, especially with middle-class incomes, resisted investing $1,800 to save $455 per year commencing with the next swimming season.

This type of sales presentation required that the distributor's salespersons combine the skills of an applications engineer with the "closing" ability of a good Fuller Brush man or Avon lady. O'Lear pondered the dilemma: should technical expertise or selling skills be emphasized when recruiting and training the salespeople? O'Lear was giving some thought to using a two-person team approach. The technical expert would "spec" the job, and the salesperson would follow later to close the deal. However, it was not clear whether this approach would be effective enough to support its added costs.

Seasonality also posed a difficult problem. O'Lear preferred to keep the sales expense variable by compensating the sales force by commission; but he was concerned that such a compensation plan might cause the sales force to drift away during the winter months when sales were inevitably slow.

O'Lear wondered whether these problems of the company-owned outlet were easily solved and whether forward integration into distribution was an option worth pursuing. O'Lear was aware that some of FAFCO's independent distributors were having financial difficulties (as evidenced by past-due accounts owed to FAFCO) and that others were not meeting FAFCO's standards for quality installations. O'Lear also believed, based on the record of the company-owned outlet, that the sales performance of the independent distributors was far below the potential of their territories. However, he wondered what implications forward integration into distribution would have for the FAFCO organization and whether financial resources would be better spent in other areas. If forward integration were not pursued, O'Lear wondered how much marketing and technical support would be necessary to improve the distribution network to an acceptable level.

Financing

O'Lear had accepted his position with the understanding that equity financing would be sought to support the growth that FAFCO was experiencing. After thinking through the production and marketing questions, he now considered the capital requirements of the next year, and what sources were available. He knew that the bank's line of credit had been extended to the practical limit. Was a private placement of equity possible, given the constraint that Ford wanted to retain majority ownership and, hence, control? In late 1976 the distribution of share ownership at FAFCO was:

	Number of shares
Shares outstanding:	
Freeman Ford	157,920
Other officers and directors	14,704
Other stockholders	16,472
Total outstanding shares	189,096
Shares reserved for:	
Employee stock options	19,000
Convertible notes payable (held by Ford and his father)	25,000
Total shares outstanding and reserved	233,096

O'Lear was aware that the venture capital community in the Bay Area was well developed and particularly attracted to high-technology, high-growth ventures. How would it view the future prospects of FAFCO? He remembered how companies as small as FAFCO "went public" in the late 1960s, but he knew that only "seasoned" companies had access to the public market in the mid 1970s.

Decisions

As O'Lear contemplated these production, marketing, personnel, and financial issues, he knew that an overall company strategy would have to be agreed upon. He and Ford must make some major decisions that would set the direction of the company for years to come. Could FAFCO survive so much change so quickly?

Case 5–6 —————————————————————————————

Mirco Games

Mirco Games, a division of Mirco, Inc., designs, develops, and markets table soccer, electronic video, and pinball games for the coin-operated and home entertainment industries. Located in Phoenix, Arizona, the firm has experienced rapid growth in the sales of its games. Although Mirco Games was enjoying an increase in demand for its product lines, John Walsh, chairman of the board of Mirco, Inc., was concerned about what strategies the Games Division should employ over the next few years.

HISTORY OF MIRCO, INC.

Mirco, Inc. (the company), was incorporated in Arizona on November 11, 1971, to succeed and to acquire the assets of a partnership known as John L. Walsh & Associates, which was composed of Messrs. John L. Walsh, Bruce E. Kinkner, and Robert M. Kessler, who were the founders of the company. As of January 1, 1976, the company consisted of the parent company, Mirco, Inc., and five divisions: (1) Mirco Electronic Distributors, (2) Mirco Systems, (3) Mirco Games, (4) Mirco Games Australia Pty., Ltd., and (5) Mirco Games of Europe.

At its founding, the company's business was to design, develop, and market computer software for automatic testing systems used in high-volume production maintenance, depot, and field testing facilities for electronic equipment. The Mirco Electronic Distributors division was established on December 15, 1972, to engage in business as a distributor of component parts to electronic equipment manufacturers. On December 18, 1973, another division, Mirco Systems, was formed to carry on the electronic test business through the continued design and marketing of the company's software and to design and market test equipment. On December 26, 1973, the company acquired the assets and business of Arizona Automation, Inc., which was merged into another division called Mirco Games. The business of Mirco Games is to design, manufacture, and market table soccer, pinball, and electronic video games. Each segment of the company's business is more fully described below.

Generally, the parent company provides planning, accounting, legal, and financial services to each of the divisions. As of March 1976, corporate headquarters had 35 employees: the chairman of the board,

This case was written by Robert B. Kaiser, director of marketing, Mirco Games; Lonnie L. Ostrom, associate professor of marketing, Arizona State University; and William E. Rief, professor of management, Arizona State University. Used with permission.

president, vice president—operations, vice president—controller, an accountant, an office manager, 4 bookkeepers, 2 secretaries, 1 personnel specialist, and 22 purchasing, maintenance, quality control, and warehouse personnel.

In fiscal year 1976, ending January 31, 1976, the company achieved sales of more than $9 million, which represented an outstanding record of growth. Exhibit 1 contains consolidated income statements for

Exhibit 1

MIRCO, INC., AND SUBSIDIARIES
Consolidated Statement of Income
For the years Ended January 31, 1973–1976

	1976	1975	1974	1973 (*unaudited*)
Net sales...............	$9,394,397	$5,033,717	$2,078,266	$1,156,319
Cost of sales	6,045,170	3,286,400	1,383,670	601,782
Gross profit	3,349,227	1,747,317	694,596	554,537
Operating expenses:				
Engineering	897,407	268,207	255,130	85,924
Selling................	1,218,905	775,188	164,411	54,934
General and administrative........	891,822	525,256	327,723	293,988
Total operating expenses	3,008,134	1,568,651	747,264	434,846
Income from operations...........	341,093	178,666	(52,668)	119,691
Interest expense	84,995	68,390	17,648	4,168
Income before income taxes and extraordinary item	256,098	110,276	(70,316)	115,523
Provision for income taxes	123,000	48,625	31,048	55,145
Income before extraordinary item....	133,098	61,651	(101,364)	60,378
Extraordinary item—income tax reduction resulting from loss carry-forward benefits..........	—	48,625	—	15,708
Net income.....................	133,098	110,276	(101,364)	76,086
Income per capital and equivalent share:				
Before extraordinary item........	0.08	0.04	(0.08)	0.05
Extraordinary item..............	—	0.04	—	0.02
	$ 0.08	$ 0.08	$ (0.08)	$ 0.07
Average number of capital and equivalent shares outstanding during the year...............	1,575,939	1,450,112	1,232,623	1,114,173

the years 1973–76, and Exhibit 2 contains consolidated balance sheets for 1975 and 1976.

The distribution business

Mirco Electronic Distributors supplies component parts such as semiconductors, capacitors, connectors, and resistors to (1) manufac-

Exhibit 2

MIRCO, INC., AND SUBSIDIARIES
Consolidated Balance Sheet
For the Years Ended January 31, 1976 and 1975

	1976	1975
Assets		
Current assets:		
Cash and certificates of deposit	$ 129,556	$ 17,700
Accounts receivable, less allowance of $45,000 at		
January 31, 1976, and $181,500 at January 31, 1975,		
for doubtful acccounts	839,730	813,473
Account receivable from Membrain, Ltd.		
(a stockholder)	27,148	—
Notes receivable	14,586	—
Inventories	1,573,684	1,223,169
Prepaid expenses and other assets.	27,497	5,986
Total current assets	2,612,201	2,060,328
Leasehold improvements.	47,812	38,117
Machinery and equipment	300,197	178,902
Automobiles.	13,028	14,324
Furniture and fixtures.	56,627	26,579
Total leasehold improvements and equipment.	417,664	257,922
Less: Accumulated depreciation	112,782	53,603
	304,882	204,319
	$2,917,083	$2,264,647
Liabilities and Stockholders' Investment		
Current liabilities:		
Notes payable	$ 610,000	$ 445,503
Current portion of long-term debt.	15,213	12,923
Accounts payable	709,032	713,102
Accrued payroll	37,570	6,221
Accrued interest	6,702	8,727
Other accrued expenses.	73,113	23,790
Income taxes currently payable.	104,000	—
Total current liabilities	1,555,630	1,210,266
Long-term debt, less current portion	33,838	49,051
Stockholders' investment:		
Capital stock; no par value; 5 million shares author-		
ized; 1,607,423 shares outstanding at January 31,		
1976, and 1,391,880 shares outstanding at January		
31, 1975.	1,270,037	947,863
Note receivable taken as consideration on sale of		
capital stock	(132,987)	—
Retained earnings	190,565	57,467
	1,327,615	1,005,330
	$2,917,083	$2,264,647

turers of electronic equipment and (2) users of the equipment for modification, replacement, or spare parts. This division performs an economic role by purchasing components from manufacturers (and sometimes from other distributors), maintaining an inventory, filling orders on demand, and providing quick delivery. In addition, it complements the other Mirco divisions by providing them with accurate information about the status of parts and equipment in the industry and supplying them with component parts and equipment at a reduced cost.

The distribution business is highly competitive. To meet competition, one must be able to obtain representation of lines of components, anticipate customers' future needs, and maintain inventories accordingly. If Mirco Electronic Distributors stocks components for which demand fails to develop, it will tie up working capital in unprofitable inventories that may have to be disposed of at or below cost.

Mirco Electronic Distributors is a regional distributor. Its market area includes Arizona; the Albuquerque, Las Cruces, and Roswell areas of New Mexico; the Denver and Henderson areas of Colorado; Los Angeles, California; Las Vegas, Nevada; and Salt Lake City, Utah.

The test business

Micro Systems designs, develops, manufactures, and markets hardware and computer software for the automatic testing of commercial and military digital electronic equipment. *Software* is a term generally used to describe computer programs, that is, a set of instructions which cause a computer to perform desired operations. The term *hardware* is used to describe the actual equipment.

Electronic equipment generally consists of numerous integrated circuit boards. Each circuit board contains approximately 10 to 300 components. These boards are tested for defects by the manufacturer at the completion of the manufacturing and assembly process. Circuit boards also are tested after the equipment has been put into use, as part of preventive or remedial maintenance programs.

Recent advances in technology have led to the development of computer systems to perform such testing automatically. These automatic test systems determine and identify faulty components in circuit boards. Automatic test systems are used primarily in high-volume production and maintenance testing facilities. The users of such systems include both the manufacturers and the owners of equipment using semiconductor components. It is possible to test circuit boards manually, but it is becoming increasingly more difficult and costly to do so because of advanced technology and the time required to test the more complex boards.

At present, Mirco Systems markets its proprietary Fault Logic and Simulation Hybrid (FLASH) program. The FLASH program aids in the development of software for logic card testers, including the simulation of complex test patterns and the generation of a fault directory for logic components on printed circuit boards. It also is used to develop testing programs for specific circuit boards.

Mirco Systems also manufactures and markets automatic test equipment (hardware). In addition, it purchases test equipment from Membrain Limited, a United Kingdom corporation, for sale in the United States. Such equipment is usually sold in conjunction with the sale of software products generated by Mirco Systems. Although FLASH is considered a proprietary product, in reality the program has little protection from competition. Because there is a constant risk of obsolescence in the test business, the firm's long-run success may ultimately depend on the success of its research and development program.

Test Programming Services is a group that creates software and specific test programs for customers. It functions primarily in support of hardware sales. This capability is considered to be critical to the test business as it enables Mirco Systems to offer complete test systems. Mirco Systems has had no difficulty in recruiting suitable people to write test programs and expects to have no difficulty in the future.

Management believes that competition in the test business is based on quality, product performance, price, and postdelivery support. There are several other companies in the test business, most of which are larger, well-financed, diversified electronics firms. Each competitor has its own systems.

The games business

On December 26, 1973, Mirco, Inc., acquired the business of Arizona Automation, Inc., which had existed since 1970. The company issued 174,000 shares of its capital stock, without par value, to Richard N. Raymond and Virginia A. Raymond, his wife, who were the sole shareholders of Arizona Automation. The shares were valued, for the purposes of that transaction, at $3.50 per share. Arizona Automation was merged into Mirco, Inc., and became Mirco Games. Of the 174,000 shares, 30,000 shares were escrowed for a period of one year. The escrowed shares were to be available to the company in case any claims were to arise against the former shareholders in Arizona Automation on account of any breach of warranty made in connection with the transaction. The purpose of the acquisition was to acquire an existing marketing organization for the distribution of electronic games and to acquire the know-how in the games business possessed by Mr. Raymond.

Of approximately 150 employees in Mirco, Inc., about half are in the Games Division. The company has two main product lines: (1) table soccer, marketed under the name "Champion Soccer," which comes in a variety of models; and (2) video games, which consist of two versions of electronic ping-pong and come in either an upright cabinet or a cocktail table cabinet. Exhibit 3 provides a display of the basic models offered by Mirco Games.

Of the $9.4 million total sales in fiscal year 1976, about $7.3 million

Exhibit 3

were from the Games Division. Of the $7.3 million games sales, $1.2 million were from the table soccer and $6.1 million from video games. The breakdown geographically was: $6.5 million in U.S. games sales, $200,000 in German games sales, and $600,000 in Australian games sales. This compares with games sales of just under $1 million in both fiscal year 1973 and fiscal year 1974.

The company believed that competition in the games business was based upon playability, price, and quality. Contrary to soccer games, which have been marketed in Europe for over 50 years and have more recently established a strong market in the United States, it is difficult to predict whether electronic games will continue over time to have consumer appeal.

Mirco Games has several competitors in soccer and video games. The major competitors in soccer are Dynamo, Tournament Soccer, Garlando, and Deutsch Meister, while in video games they are Atari and Ramtek. There is also a risk that a major, well-financed firm will enter the video games market, in which case the industry would be faced with much stiffer competition.

Australia and Europe were perceived to be good potential markets for video games. In order to avoid high import duties, Mirco began to assemble video games in Australia in April 1975 and in Germany in September 1975.

THE AMUSEMENT GAMES INDUSTRY

The term *coin industry* is often applied to the manufacturers and distributors of coin-operated equipment for consumer use. The two main segments in this industry are vending machines (food, drink, cigarettes, and so on) and amusement machines.

Amusement machines consist of coin-operated phonographs (jukeboxes) and amusement games, such as pool tables, pinball machines, table soccer, and video games. The principal manufacturers of pinball machines are Gottlieb, Balley, Chicago Coin, and Williams. Coin-operated phonographs are manufactured by Seeburg, Rock-ola, and Rowe. The newest development, video games, has been spawned by new companies outside the traditional industry network.

Sales are seasonal in nature. New products are introduced in the fall and generally available in the following first quarter (February, March, and April). New product introductions are geared to the Music Operators of America trade show, which is held annually in late October or early November.

The present structure of the amusement games industry was developed in the 1930s. At that time, the need for the distributor came into being with the introduction of coin-operated phonograph and pinball machines. The primary purpose of the distributor was to provide electrical and mechanical servicing. Distributors were either owned by the manufacturers or were independent. They, in turn, helped set up the operator, who was responsible for locating the game equipment and sharing revenues with the location owner. This distribution network remains virtually intact today.

The operator is the owner of the equipment. In addition to seeking out new locations, he is responsible for routine servicing. The operator typically has a route which he maintains, making periodic collections from the cash boxes attached to the equipment and dividing the earnings with the location owner (typically 50–50). The specific functions associated with each member of the conventional channel are identified in Exhibit 4.

Exhibit 4
Channels of distribution for the amusement games industry

A. Conventional distribution network for coin-operated equipment

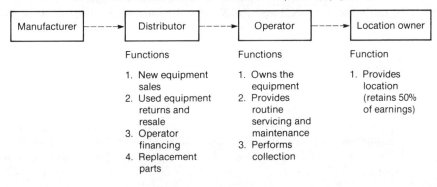

B. Primary distribution network for the home market

TABLE SOCCER

Table soccer appears to have originated in Germany in the late 1920s or early 1930s. Soccer is known as football in many European countries, and the German word for football, *fussball*, is the alternative name used for table soccer in the United States (under a variety of spellings). Presently, European versions of the game are manufactured in West Germany, France, and Italy.

The first soccer games that were exported to the United States in the mid-1950s were not readily accepted. In 1962, L. T. Patterson Distributors of Cincinnati made the first major commitment to distribute a German-produced table called "Foosball." Because it was a relatively unknown sport in America and required a high skill level, the acceptance was slow for many years and it was not until the late 1960s that table soccer became a significant factor in the games industry. One of the contributing factors to its growth in popularity in the United States was the demand created by servicemen who had been introduced to the game while stationed in Europe.

In 1967, Dick Raymond and John Walsh, while working for General Electric in Germany, became interested in table soccer. Soccer tables were found in many of the bars and taverns of France, Germany, and Italy and were avidly played by Europeans as well as by American servicemen and businessmen. Raymond and Walsh saw the potential for such a game and made plans to export tables to the United States.

When Raymond and Walsh returned to Phoenix in 1970, they formed Arizona Automation. Within a year following incorporation, Raymond purchased Walsh's share and became sole owner of Arizona Automation. In 1971, Arizona Automation began building a soccer table known as Champion Soccer. In four years, annual sales climbed from $15,000 to approximately $1 million.

Manufacturing

The component parts for Champion Soccer are purchased from outside vendors, and the game is assembled by Mirco Games. There are presently alternative sources for all of the components except the figurines. Should that source fail, it is estimated that production would be delayed for approximately two months while a new source was found.

Patents, trademarks, and licensing

The company has registered Champion Soccer as a trademark in the United States and in Canada. An application for trademark registration has been filed with respect to the design of figurines for the soccer game, and a patent has been granted for the "two-point ball control" figurine. There are no other patents or other protection for the table soccer products.

Competition

Due to the high quality of its soccer tables, Mirco has been a dominant force in the U.S. market, with about $1.2 million in sales out of an industry total of $12 million. Recently, however, Mirco has experienced increased competition from a number of firms that have entered the market, especially Dynamo and Tournament Soccer. In order to maintain its leadership in the soccer table market, Mirco was forced to significantly redesign its soccer tables to improve their appearance, playability, and durability. Dynamo's approach to the market is similar to Mirco's in that it cultivates a high-quality image and has introduced several technical innovations into its product; among them are the textured tempered glass playfield, the massive table to prevent table movement during play, the balanced figurine, and precision-ground steel rods. Mirco subsequently incorporated some of these innovations to maintain its market position. Tournament Soccer has pursued the market through an active and expensive program utilizing table soccer tournaments throughout the United States. Its current tournament program offers prize money in excess of $250,000 per year.

Marketing

Mirco markets its coin-operated soccer games through approximately 50 distributors that are located for the most part in the United States and Canada (see Exhibit 4). As is typical of the industry, there are no binding contractual arrangements with any of these distributors. They are free to deal in competitive products or to discontinue distribution of Mirco's products at any time. Home table soccer games are distributed through major retail chains, sporting goods and department stores, and the American Express catalog. In addition, a small amount of government business is handled via the General Services Administration.

Pricing. Pricing is consistent with Mirco's image as a quality producer of soccer games. There is only one distributor price regardless of quantity. A typical selling price to the operator for a high-quality coin-operated table soccer game is around $675. The channel markup is approximately 35 percent.

Promotion. Mirco Games advertises in the coin-operated equipment trade journals, such as *Cashbox, Playmeter,* and *Replay,* and in sporting goods magazines. It also promotes its products at trade shows such as those of the National Sporting Goods Association and the Music Operators of America. Bob Seagren, Olympic gold medal winner and superstar champion, is used extensively in advertisements and trade show displays.

Mirco also has engaged in a series of promotional events, mainly in the form of statewide tournaments in key metropolitan cities. In 1973 and 1974, it sponsored the Louisiana State Soccer tournaments, both of which were $2,000 events. In 1975, Mirco tournaments were held in Detroit, Minneapolis, Omaha, and Kansas City, with total prize money exceeding $16,000. The 1976 schedule includes St. Louis, Rochester, and Detroit.

Market research. Market information is obtained from three principal sources: the distributors, operators, and location owners. At times, games are "test-marketed" by placing them in selected locations and analyzing their earning power over a given period of time.

ELECTRONIC (VIDEO AND PINBALL) GAMES

Atari was the first company to successfully market a video game. It was called "Pong" and was a two-player tennis-type game operated with electronic paddles and a ball. The acceptance of this product was phenomenal, and before long more than 30 producers of video games were in the market, from the large established companies to the newly formed "garage-type" operations. Although it is relatively easy for a new company to enter the video games market, the failure rate of new entrants is extremely high, due primarily to a lack of adequate testing capability, poor service, high operating costs, limited financing, and little marketing expertise. According to one financial analyst who observed 24 games companies during 1974, 20 went out of business, 2 were marginal in nature, and the remaining 2 were Mirco and Atari.

Mirco Games entered the market in 1973 with its two-player video game, Champion Ping Pong, at a time when competitors were introducing a great variety of more sophisticated games. It was felt that the company's expertise in the area of electronic testing equipment would provide it with two immediate advantages over its major competitors: quick turnaround in servicing (24 hours) and a more reliable product. Unfortunately, these two advantages were not sufficient to offset Champion Ping Pong's lack of playability, which is the primary competitive factor in video games. The urgent need to develop new products was recognized by Mirco at that time; however, an extremely tight cash flow position prevented major R&D expenditures for video games. In 1973, the Mirco Systems Division had invested heavily in R&D to develop its computer-controlled test equipment, which was not yet ready for production, and it had severely drained the company's finances.

In March 1974, Mirco Games introduced the Challenge upright four-player video game, which featured one free game in the event that one or two players beat the machine in the player versus machine mode. Unfortunately, this innovative feature was not sufficient to offset the fact that competition had introduced four-player games 12 months earlier and the market was now saturated. In July 1974, the Challenge cocktail table version was introduced. The major advantage of this game was its appeal to sophisticated locations, such as Holiday Inns, Playboy clubs, and country clubs, which previously had not been a viable market for video games. Unfortunately, the conventional distribution network was ill equipped to implement a marketing strategy to take advantage of this new and rapidly expanding market.

Distributor

In order to exploit this new market for cocktail table models, Bob Kaiser, marketing manager, decided to set up an entirely new channel of distribution, which became known as the nonconventional distribution network (see Exhibit 5). He sought out individual entrepreneurs,

Exhibit 5
Nonconventional distribution network for video games

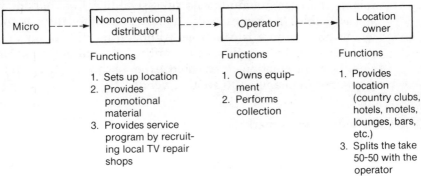

Micro	Nonconventional distributor	Operator	Location owner
	Functions	Functions	Functions
	1. Sets up location	1. Owns equip-ment	1. Provides location (country clubs, hotels, motels, lounges, bars, etc.)
	2. Provides promotional material	2. Performs collection	
	3. Provides service program by recruiting local TV repair shops		3. Splits the take 50-50 with the operator

such as real estate people and stocks and bonds salespersons, who, due to the recession, were without a product to market but had sufficient capital to invest in a new venture. This strategy proved to be very successful and, in fact, helped stimulate sales of the tabletop video game through conventional distributors and operators. One major advantage of the nonconventional channel is that terms are cash, whereas in the conventional channel they are net 30 and the manufacturer is frequently forced to extend credit for 60 to 90 days.

Innovation

Innovation is a requirement for survival in the games industry. Mirco's achievements in this area have not been spectacular. However, a Mirco processor pinball machine, which was a first in the industry, was introduced in late 1975. Management felt that this product would successfully lead Mirco into a new segment of the coin-operated market.

Pricing

Two pricing constraints are active in the marketplace. In the segment of the market dominated by innovative games, particularly video, pricing is determined primarily by the earning power of the machine, that is, its ability to sit in a location and, without being promoted, attract players. (The location life of a video game is less than 90 days as a rule.) In that segment of the market where the products are stable and have a long life in a specific location, such as pool tables and table soccer, pricing is solely a function of competition.

Manufacturing

With respect to electronic games, Mirco purchases all components, such as television monitors and subassemblies, from outside vendors and assembles the games itself. At the present time, the sole source for television monitors is Motorola. Although no difficulties are anticipated in obtaining sufficient quantities of monitors from Motorola, significant production delays and expenses probably would be encountered in changing to another vendor.

The home video games market

Along with coin-operated electronic games, video and pinball games for the home promise to have a great future: projections go as high as $1 billion by 1980. In 1972, Magnavox brought out the first home video game, Odyssey, for the price of over $100. Several new entrants are now active in this area, including Atari, which introduced its home model version of Pong in 1975. One of the obstacles in this new market is that FCC approval is required for any games that hook up to a TV antenna.

Brisk sales were reported by both Magnavox and Atari during the 1975 Christmas season. Atari's version of Pong was sold by Sears, which stated that it could sell all it could get. Magnavox, which had introduced an improved version of Odyssey a few months earlier, marketed its products through its vast network of approximately 2,500 dealers throughout the United States.

It is anticipated that home video games will soon be available for $30–$40 retail. Most products will include multiple games, color, sound, and remote controls. On-screen score display and variable difficulty are possible features.

In January 1976, Mirco entered into an agreement with Fairchild Camera and Instrument to jointly develop and produce home video games. Christmas of 1976 was targeted for a major promotional effort for creating a new consumer mass market.

Computerized pinball

In 1975, Mirco was the first on the market with a microcomputer pinball machine in which one printed circuit board handles all electronic functions. The game featured an electronic semiconductor memory, LED (digital display) readouts, and a self-diagnostic capability for quick troubleshooting. Although it was the hit of the annual Music Operators of America trade show, it was too early to tell what impact it would have on the traditional coin-operated pinball market. One concern is that because of Mirco's lack of expertise in backglass and playfield design, both strong competitive features in pinball machines because of their association with playability in the minds of players, it may not be able to take full advantage of being first in the microcomputer pinball market.

THE FUTURE OF THE GAMES BUSINESS

In 1976, the electronic games market was still in its infancy. Atari was the leader in video sales, with about $18 million in 1975 and "close to $30 million" projected for 1976. Although sales information is difficult to obtain about other firms in this industry, it was believed that Mirco Games was number two. Whereas Atari produces many different types of video games, Mirco has concentrated its efforts on producing a few models of one basic game. During the period in which Mirco successfully marketed the Challenge tabletop video game, Atari introduced 50 new game designs.

It is expected that semiconductor companies will play a major role in the games business. In early 1976, research was under way at General Instrument, Texas Instruments, and National Semiconductor to develop video products. With the possibility of many companies invading the territory of the traditional manufacturer of coin-operated games, the long-run outcome is somewhat uncertain. The traditional companies are likely to react strongly to protect their existing markets.

Table soccer appears to have a good 15 to 20 percent per year growth potential. In contrast to the video market, this market appears to be extremely stable.

Another uncertainty is the extent to which the expanding home game market will affect the sales of coin-operated games. The traditional companies feel that home games will stimulate rather than take away from their business, and they predict a steady growth in the next few years.

Strategies in the home games market are difficult to determine because of rapid technological changes. Games with their own video displays are likely to evolve, and they may be tied in with the computer terminal that one day will be installed in most homes. One definite advantage for new companies entering this market is that because home electronics games (video and pinball) are so new, no strong brand loyalty currently exists.

Case 5–7 ———————————————————————

The Clorox Company

As a part of his regular procedure for reviewing the health of the company's marketing operation, John S. Hanson, group vice president, the Clorox Company, decided to take a look at the brand management system through the eyes of an impartial outsider. How, in other words, would a nonmarketing, nonconsumer product observer see the Clorox system? How would the observations be interpreted, and what were the implications of these observations in respect to the selection of new brand managers?

To this end, an engineering manager enrolled in the Stanford Sloan Program was given permission during the spring of 1977 to interview throughout the company and to write up his impressions.

HISTORY OF THE COMPANY

SELF LIFE
7 1 YEAR

The Electro-Alkaline Company of Oakland, California, began commercial production of liquid chlorine bleach in 1913. The initial markets for this new product were limited to laundries, breweries, walnut wood bleachers, and municipal water companies. These companies used the product for bleaching, stain removing, deodorizing, and disinfecting. The original form of the product was a much more concentrated solution than is currently available on the retail market. In *1994* 1941 the "Clorox" brand name was registered; the company's diamond trademark was registered the following year; and in 1922, the firm changed its name to Clorox Chemical Corporation. During its first eight years of business, the company achieved distribution in the Pacific Coast states and Nevada and initiated eastern U.S. distribution with the appointment of a distributor in Philadelphia. Advertising was begun in 1925 in 20 western newspapers and four farm journals. In 1928, the company was reorganized as Clorox Chemical Company and common stock was issued for the first time. By 1939, the company operated production facilities in Oakland, Chicago, and Jersey City. By 1955, 10 additional plants were in operation around the country. In 1953, the Clorox Company initiated spot television advertising.

In 1957, the Procter & Gamble Company acquired Clorox Chemical Company, but within three months the FTC charged Procter & Gamble with attempting to lessen competition among household bleach manufacturers. Shortly thereafter, the FTC ruled that Procter & Gamble had to divest itself of Clorox. Litigation continued until

---

This case was written by Jack Moorman and Stephen A. Snow. © 1978 by the Leland Stanford Junior University, Graduate School of Business.

1968, when the Supreme Court upheld the FTC ruling. Directly after the Supreme Court ruling, the Purex Corporation, manufacturer of the principal competitor of Clorox liquid bleach, filed suit against Procter & Gamble, charging that the company's acquisition of Clorox violated antitrust laws.

During 1968, Procter & Gamble divested itself of Clorox by offering for sale 15 percent of Clorox stock and subsequently offering the remaining 85 percent to Procter & Gamble shareholders on the basis of 3.85 shares of Clorox stock for each share of Procter & Gamble stock. The stock was listed on the New York Stock Exchange in August, and in January 1969 Clorox began operation as an independent company. (See Exhibit 1 for relevant data regarding Clorox's operations during the period 1968 to 1977.)

PRODUCT EXPANSION

Until 1969, the Clorox Company made and sold only one product, Clorox liquid bleach. With the exception of one unsuccessful introduction of a general-purpose household cleaning solution, Boon, in 1946, the company's new product introductions consisted of minor variations of its basic brand of liquid bleach or of package modifications.[1]

After the divestiture by Procter & Gamble, however, Clorox management began to implement a previously adopted program of growth which called for the development of: (1) a line of nonfood household products, (2) a line of specialty food products, and (3) a line of food and nonfood products for the food service industry.

The company planned to seek acquisitions to accelerate its sales and earnings growth. At the same time, it would strengthen existing brands and, over the long term, expand its business through internal development of new products.

The first step toward a broadened line of retail consumer products was the acquisition of Jiffee Chemical Corporation, manufacturer of Liquid-plumr drain opener. This was closely followed by the Acquisition of Formula 409 Spray Cleaner from Harrell International. Exhibit 2 presents the proliferation of Clorox-owned brands which are marketed by Clorox.

The expansion into the food service line began several years later. In 1972, Clorox acquired the Martin-Brower Company, a distributor of disposable packaging items, food and nonfood products, and restaurant supplies to fast-food restaurants and institutions. The Clorox Company also established the Clorox Food Service Products Division to market institutional versions of its retail brands. (See Exhibit 3 for Clorox performance on the three basic groups.)

---

[1] The basic product was never changed, although changes in the strength of the bleach solution were attempted.

Exhibit 1
Clorox Company performance, 1968–1977

	Year ending June 30									
	1977	1976	1975	1974	1973	1972	1971	1970	1969	1968
Net sales*	$872,817	$822,101	$721,505	$537,601	$412,631	$188,203	$145,866	$98,212	$85,365	$85,854
Net income*	32,265	27,262	21,150	19,656	26,922	19,252	15,031	12,010	11,173	11,411
Earnings per share (primary)	1.44	1.22	0.95	0.88	1.23†	2.15	1.68	1.48	1.40	1.43

* In thousands of dollars.
† Reflects two-for-one stock split effective November 1972.

Exhibit 2
Product expansion, Clorox Company 1969–1977

Brand name	Description	Source of development	Year acquired or marketed
Liquid-plumr	Drain opener	Acquisition	1969
Clorox 2	Nonchlorine, dry oxygen bleach	Internally developed	1969
Formula 409	General-purpose household cleaner	Acquisition	1970
Formula 409	Disinfectant bathroom cleaner	Acquisition	1970
Litter Green	Cat box filler	Acquisition*	1971
BinB Mushrooms	Canned mushrooms, broiled in butter	Acquisition	1971
Kitchen Bouquet	Flavoring sauce	Acquisition	1971
Cream of Rice	Hot cereal	Acquisition	1971
Hidden Valley Ranch	Salad dressing mixes	Acquisition	1972
Kingsford	Charcoal briquettes and barbecue products	Acquisition	1973
Prime Choice	Steak sauce	Internally developed	1973
Mr. Mushroom	Mushrooms in natural cooking juices	Internally developed	1973
Cooking Ease	Natural vegetable cooking spray	Acquisition	1974
Salad Crispins	Seasoned croutons	Acquisition	1974
Soft Scrub	Mild-abrasive liquid cleanser	Internally developed	1977

* Patents and concepts for institutional products were purchased, and these were subsequently developed into consumer products.

Exhibit 3
Clorox performance, 1972–1977, by basic lines of business ($ millions)

	Year ending June 30					
	1977	1976	1975	1974	1973	1972
Net sales:						
Retail consumer products						
Nonfood products	$342.5	$308.7	$268.1	$223.8	$225.8	$167.6
Specialty food products	63.7	59.7	56.7	44.0	25.8	20.6
Subtotal	406.2	368.4	324.8	267.8	251.6	188.2
Food service industries	466.6	453.7	396.7	269.8	161.0	—
Total	$872.8	$822.1	$721.5	$537.6	$412.6	$188.2
Income:*						
Retail consumer products	$ 74.6	$ 55.0	$ 43.4	$ 32.8	$ 46.9	$ 41.5
Food service industries	3.6	5.8	7.5	7.2	5.5	—
Total	$ 78.2	$ 60.8	$ 50.9	$ 40.0†	$ 52.4	$ 41.5

* Income before taxes on income and before allocation of corporate expenses not directly attributable to a specific line of business.
† Does not reflect one-time loss from discontinued operations.

As new companies were acquired, they often maintained their organizational integrity within the Clorox corporate structure. Indeed, in several instances newly acquired companies were treated as separate profit centers. The corporate organization underwent various revisions during the first few years after the Clorox divestiture from Procter & Gamble. (See Exhibit 4 for the current organization of the Clorox Company.)

In the 1973 annual report, Clorox President Robert Shetterly informed stockholders that he was de-emphasizing acquisitions as a means of further product expansion during the short term and that

Exhibit 4
Clorox Company organizational diagram

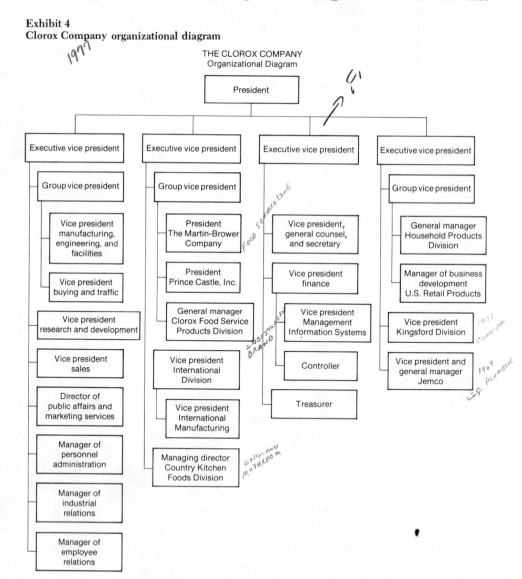

THE CLOROX COMPANY
Organizational Diagram

emphasis would be placed on utilizing internal resources for new product development. As a step toward this objective, the company moved to supplement its R&D capabilities by signing a 10-year agreement with Henkel KGaA of West Germany in 1974. Henkel is the second-largest European producer of detergents, cleaners, and related products. It subsequently acquired a minority equity position in Clorox by purchasing 20 percent of the company's outstanding shares. Under the terms of the agreement, Clorox is licensed to market Henkel-developed products on a royalty basis in the United States, Canada, and Puerto Rico and has access to Henkel technology for developing new products. Clorox agreed to pay Henkel minimum royalties of $1 million per year, beginning in 1976. These payments will be credited against future royalties earned by Henkel on products marketed by Clorox.

In the 1977 annual report, Shetterly announced that Clorox once again was looking for suitable acquisitions to build the company's business. At the same time, he said, Clorox would seek opportunities to expand its liquid bleach market internationally.

Clorox ventured into the international sphere in 1973, when it set up a Canadian marketing operation that eventually would sell most of the company's retail products as well as a line of household cleaners and personal products marketed in Canada under the French Maid brand name. That same year, Clorox acquired Country Kitchen Foods, England's leading mushroom-growing and -marketing company. In 1975, the company began bleach production in its first offshore plant, in Puerto Rico. In addition, in the period between divestiture from P&G and 1975, the company had developed export markets for liquid bleach in about 30 countries and had licenses that produced Clorox in Latin America and the Middle East.

THE BRAND MANAGEMENT SYSTEM

Clorox has been a strong supporter of brand management. In 1977, the marketing operation in the Household Products Division was organized as shown in Exhibit 5.

Although a bit unusual from an orthodox organization point of view, it is useful for the reader to think in terms of two subdivisions below general manager—"Brand" and "all other." The significance of this dichotomy, which will be explained shortly, underlies the heart of the Clorox system.

There were five job levels in the brand system: brand assistant (BA), assistant brand manager (ABM), brand manager (BM), associate advertising manager (AAM), and advertising manager (AM). The focus of this case is on the brand manager and lower levels, i.e., assistant brand manager and brand assistant. (See Exhibits 6, 7, and 8 for relevant job descriptions.)

Exhibit 5

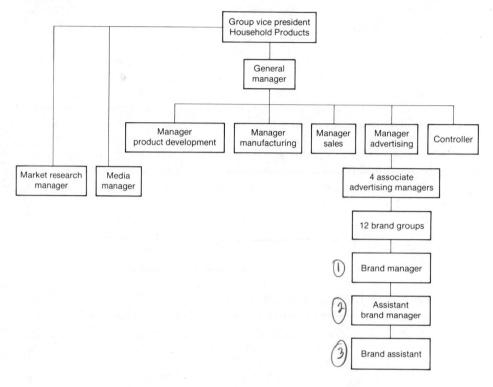

Exhibit 6
Job description: Clorox brand manager

Function.   To contribute to the overall growth of Clorox through develop-ment, recommendation, and implementation of effective marketing programs capable of building brand volume, share, and profit for assigned brands. The brand manager is charged to:

a. Provide management with relevant data regarding the state of the busi-ness, serving as management's antennae in the category to identify prob-lems and opportunities.
b. Develop recommendations which are designed to stimulate brand growth.
c. See that all programs are coordinated and run properly, serving as the focal point for all brand-related activity.
d. Ensure that brand personnel learn the skills to handle multifaceted re-sponsibilities of the job.

The brand manager's specific marketing responsibilities are as follows:

1. *Product.* Ensure that the product and package are superior to competition within cost constraints demanded by the marketplace and profit consider-ations. Requires consumer usage/attitude and product research, establish-

Exhibit 6 (*concluded*)

ment of product improvement objectives, and periodic review of progress toward these objectives.

2. *Positioning.* Position the product to maximize volume within the existing consumer and competitive environments. Periodically review marketing strategy in light of changing consumer needs, wants, and attitudes and competitive product positionings and sales. Develop and test alternative copy and promotion strategies attuned to the marketing strategy to improve the brand's overall positioning.

3. *Copy.* Ensure that copy provides the optimum selling power. Demands an ongoing effort in development and testing of new copy pools, different executional formats, and alternative copy strategies.

4. *Media.* Ensure that media plans are designed to deliver advertising in the most effective and efficient manner against the brand's target audience. Requires periodic review of target audience criterion and testing of alternative mixes of media vehicles within budget constraints, as well as testing of different media weights.

5. *Promotion.* Plan, execute, and evaluate, with the assistance of the Sales Department, consumer and trade promotions which are cost effective in increasing brand volume. Demands testing of a variety of promotions each fiscal year and testing, on a periodic basis, alternative annual promotion levels and/or alternative consumer/trade promotion splits within existing budgets.

6. *Volume control.* Make adjustments as necessary in fiscal year plans to deliver volume base.

The brand manager's specific management information responsibilities are as follows:

1. *Volume.* If fiscal year overshipment or undershipment seems obvious, inform management and recommend action.

2. *Competitive developments.* Report significant competitive activity and recommend defensive action.

3. *Product problems.* Analyze and recommend action on any product or package problems which threaten volume.

4. *Problem markets.* Identify, analyze, and propose remedial action.

5. *Schedule changes.* Advise promptly when delays from expected test market or expansion dates are encountered, and explain reason for delay.

6. *Costs/P&A.* Report significant shifts and recommend action (e.g., price increase).

7. *Governmental actions.* Report on any legislative or regulatory activities that could affect the business and recommend action.

Although this case does not deal extensively with the AM and AAM levels of management, it is useful to know the overall roles these managers play. The AM manages all aspects of marketing, except sales execution, for the division. This manager's key objectives are not only achievement of short-term volume and profit goals but also develop-

Exhibit 7
Job description: Clorox assistant brand manager

Marketing responsibilities:

1. *Business building plans.* Develop, recommend, and execute those key projects which, long term, will have a major effect on the shipments/consumption of the brand. Examples of these are the introduction of new sizes/products, major distribution building programs, or major trial-generating promotions.
2. *Copy.* Work with the brand manager in providing direction to the advertising agency in the development of new executional formats (based on current strategy) and the testing of new copy strategies/executions. Also, work with Technical and Legal to obtain copy clearance/claim/support.
3. *Media.* In conjunction with the brand manager, provide the agency with direction on new ways to more efficiently reach the brand's target audience. This may take the form of media mix tests or testing of different media levels.
4. *Product.* Ensure that a product which fulfills consumer needs and wants is marketed within cost constraints.
5. *Market research planning and analysis.* Initiate and analyze those market research projects which will yield information upon which the brand may act to improve current market position or correct an ongoing problem.
6. *Package design.* Ensure that the package in the marketplace is appealing, eye-catching, and connotes those attributes of the product most important to consumers.

Management information:

1. *Market research.* Analyzes research and recommends next steps to correct any problems or capitalize on any opportunities.
2. *Media.* Analyzes results of media testing and recommends action to be taken.
3. *Schedule changes.* Informs brand manager of delays in the progress of key projects in order that management may be apprised of the delay and the reason why.

---

ment, testing, and expansion of new products, improved products, and line extensions. These latter goals are heavily emphasized by top management because they ensure continued corporate growth. The AAMs largely serve coordinating, controlling, training, and strategic overview roles between the AMs and the BMs. They also have final decision-making authority on promotion activities within existing budgets, and they handle many of the administrative jobs in the Advertising Department.

The entry-level job was that of BA. The BA was primarily responsible for monitoring the product budget, developing sales promotion, and analyzing market information (e.g., sales data from the company's

Exhibit 8
Job description: Clorox brand assistant

Marketing responsibilities:

1. *Sales promotion.* Plans, in consultation with other Brand group members and the Sales Department, national and test promotions. Writes promotion recommendations and issues related feasibility requests and production orders. Implements consumer-oriented portions of promotions (coupon copy and media, sample drops, etc.) and oversees and/or cooperates with Sales Department in implementing trade-oriented portions of promotions (preparation of organizers, selection of salesman's incentives, etc., etc.). Controls all budgeting for promotions. Evaluates promotions.

2. *Budget administration and control.* Reviews and codes invoices. Reconciles the budget with Accounting on quarterly basis. Closes out budget with Accounting at the end of the fiscal year.

3. *Market analysis.* Analyzes Nielsen data and writes bimonthly Nielsen reports. Audits other sources of market information (monthly shipment reports, SAMI's, etc.) and writes analytical reports as necessary.

4. *Shipment estimates.* In consultation with assistant brand manager and/or brand manager, prepares monthly shipment estimate which forecasts next three months' shipments with supporting rationale.

5. *Competitive activity.* Monitors competitive activity reported by Sales (promotion and pricing activity), agency (competitive media spending), and other sources (periodicals, etc.). Writes reports on significant developments.

6. *Public relations.* Cooperates with Consumer Services in handling special consumer-oriented problems which fall outside normal Consumer Services activities. Works with Research Services (home economists) and Public Affairs on brand-related consumer information projects.

Other areas where brand assistants may contribute, depending upon individual brand assignments, are as follows:

1. *Package design.* Development of design objectives. Interfaces with package designers, marketing services, and technical staff on development, consumer testing, and feasibility determination on design. Recommendation, implementation, and evaluation of any test market.

2. *Business-building tests.* Works with assistant brand manager and/or brand manager on one or more of the following aspects of business-building tests—planning, recommendation, implementation, and evaluation.

Management information—reports to brand manager on:

1. *Competitive activity.* Significant competitive developments.
2. *Budget variance.* Any variations from budget forecasts.
3. *Promotion problems.* Any problems with implementation of promotions.
4. *Consumer relations.* Any product problems which threaten volume.

management information system, consumption data from the A. C. Nielsen Company, and additional data from other outside market research services). New projects were added as competence was gained until the BA was sent out for "sales training," a 12-week field sales assignment.

Promotion to ABM followed this selling experience. Emphasis was placed upon learning advertising copy and media, developing long-term business-building programs, and assisting and helping train the BA in the area of sales promotion. ABM was a transition job which could last from 1 to 2½ years, depending on the capabilities of the ABM and the needs of the company.

When the ABM was promoted to BM, he[2] was given overall marketing responsibility for one or more products, including planning, forecasting, and controlling volume and spending for these products. He also supervised ABMs and BAs. Due to rotation and normal turnover, not all Brand groups were fully staffed with a BA and an ABM.

In terms of day-by-day operations, the Brand Management Group considered the other Clorox functions as "staff" to it. Hence, the earlier reference to "Brand" and "all other." Nonetheless, it must be recognized that Brand had no direct authority over sales, manufacturing, market research, and product development. But it did have the responsibility to obtain from staff the inputs necessary to successful marketing. Each functional group, for this purpose, had a representative designated to deal with the brand manager. An integral part of this system of "responsibility without direct authority" was the fact that Brand controlled budgets for areas such as market research and package design and represented staff's channel to top management. For example, a departmental request for information or specific action was typically directed to the brand manager who not only had to concur but was the interface with top management. Communication to top management, in other words, was generally through the Brand groups.

Perhaps the best summary of the brand manager's role is contained in Exhibit 9.

CLIMATE

Clorox had been a Procter & Gamble subsidiary from 1957 until separated by government order in 1969. The P&G influence pervaded Clorox. A number of top- and middle-management people had either stayed with Clorox after divestiture or had joined Clorox from Procter & Gamble. The P&G style of memo writing, job titles, and organization continued.

---

[2] Although we use the masculine gender throughout this text rather than both masculine and feminine (e.g., he/she) to improve readability, the reader should assume that this refers to both female and male brand personnel.

The brand management system had been very strong at P&G and continued to be strong at Clorox. The brand managers played a "line management" role within the marketing function at Clorox. The reasoning for this was that the BM had direct responsibility for the most critical marketing factor—advertising—and had the broadest exposure to the operations of the company and the best overall perspective on his product and markets.

The BM was able to accomplish his goals through other people by using his control over the product budget, his position as the coordinator of all information, and his interpersonal skills. He had to be successful "at getting others to do the job."

But there was even more to the essential nature of the brand manager's job, a perspective that can only be expressed by senior management. These men looked upon brand managers as people who could be expected to ask the type of questions a top manager might ask, gather the facts necessary to make a decision, and then recommend a course of action in a very succinct memo. The net effect was that top management's job of managing the marketing of a large number of diverse brands in diverse categories became easier and more effective. The system assured that all brands, even those with small sales, were given attention and that a variety of marketing approaches designed to stimulate growth would at least be explored and recommended.

The power of the brand manager rested largely in his authority to ask questions anywhere in the company and demand carefully thought-out, responsible answers, as long as the questions and answers were limited to matters which either directly affected the consumer of his product or affected his brand's contribution margin (revenue less manufacturing and shipping costs and brokerage commission). In addition, the successful brand manager had informal authority arising from his superior knowledge vis-à-vis any functional specialist in the company of all consumer aspects of his product, and he had the power to discuss his recommendations (in writing, usually) with top management.

SELECTION AND SCREENING

no real work experience

Typically, brand assistants were recent MBAs from such schools as Stanford, Berkeley, Columbia, Northwestern, and Wharton, with minimum work experience, particularly in brand management. In recent years, Clorox had hired some graduates with advertising experience as well as some transferees from other Clorox departments, but these were exceptions. Brand managers were almost always promoted from within.

During the initial hiring process, Clorox sought individuals who were intelligent, trainable, competitive, aggressive, and hardworking.

* how do you recognize this without work experience

Exhibit 9
Interface matrix

Brand manager responsibilities	Work with these departments	Brand role
1. Product or package improvement	Sales, R&D, Market Research, Manufacturing, and Controller	a. Develop objectives for product or package development. b. Approve aesthetics. c. Develop consumer research objectives, fund research, and summarize results. d. Determine unit profit potential and return on investment. e. Recommend test market to management. f. Write manufacturing production orders for test market production of product. g. Analyze test market results and recommend national expansion.
2. Positioning	Advertising agency, Market Research, and Legal	a. Develop alternative positionings. b. Develop consumer research objectives and fund research. c. Analyze research results and recommend test market. d. Analyze test market results and recommend national expansion.

3.	Copy	Advertising agency, Market Research, and Legal	*a.* Review agency copy submissions and select copy to be presented to management. *b.* Approve final production for on-air copy testing. *c.* Analyze copy test results. *d.* Recommend national airing of copy.
4.	Media	Advertising agency and Media Services	*a.* Review agency media objectives and strategies and recommend alternatives. *b.* Review and modify agency media plans with help of Media Services. *c.* Forward agency media plan to management. *d.* With help of Media Services, monitor implementation of media plan.
5.	Sales promotion	Sales, Manufacturing, Promotion Development, and Legal	*a.* Develop national promotion plan with help of Sales Department. *b.* Recommend plan to management. *c.* Write manufacturing production order for production of sales promotion product. *d.* Implement consumer portion of promotion (i.e., coupons, samples, etc.) and fund all trade allowances and consumer promotions.
6.	Volume control	Sales	*a.* Monitor shipments. *b.* If undershipment of objectives seems possible, recommend remedial marketing efforts.

Ideal candidate qualities were generalized as: analytical ability; communication skills; the ability to plan, organize, and follow through; the ability to work well with others; leadership; resourcefulness and ingenuity; decision-making skill; drive and determination; and maturity.

How able confidence

TRAINING

The introduction of the new brand assistant was strenuous. Although the initial jobs might range from planning promotions to writing market research summaries (see Exhibit 1), there was a lot of arduous "number crunching." Hours were long, often including weekends. There were no shortcuts or special courses and readings that could bypass this breaking-in period. Nor was there much sympathy for the neophyte. Everyone in Brand had been through the same experience, recognized its necessity, and knew the work could be done. "Help" was mainly in the form of providing initial direction, pointing out errors, and suggesting new projects as competence increased. The newer projects were invariably more interesting and challenging, which provided additional incentive to master the earlier tasks. And as the new BAs were hired, the more mundane jobs could be passed down.

The purpose of this training was to internalize certain "first principles" which were considered necessary to maintain the brand management system:

lot of this could look good people because did not try unorthodox approach to their work mature

1. *All information can be derived from numerical data.*

    Brand people have minimal contact with either customers or suppliers. Customers are normally represented by market research findings and sales results. Suppliers are represented by specific liaison people. Thus it follows that there must always be an analytic justification for a project or program. The results need to be reduced to cases of product and P&A (revenue minus all costs except advertising).

2. *Concern for mistakes.*

    Brand people are trained to be detail oriented and are concerned about not making errors. No mistake, particularly in a memo, was too small to be noticed. The feedback was intensive since memos were commented on in writing as they were passed up and down the distribution chain. If anyone found a mistake, then everyone who missed it was embarrassed.

3. *The budget is a critical device by which the brand manager exercises some basic control.*

    This first principle is a bit deceptive, however. It is true that some staff groups—Market Research, Sales Merchandising, and Package Design—are dependent upon Brand for funding of projects, but it would be erroneous to conclude that Brand uses the budget as a club. The range of interrelationships between Brand and staff is too involved to be reduced to the single lever of money control.

4. *Career success requires the "Clorox Style."*

The Clorox Style contributes to the climate and mystique which make Brand management successful. This style includes dress, memo, format, job concept, and attitude. Memos conform to a particular writing style and format and are not supposed to exceed two pages without an attached summary. Brand people must be the resident experts on everything affecting their products. The BM thinks of himself as the general manager of a very small company. Nonetheless, Brand people must maintain their aggressive, competitive attitude without hurting their relations with staff. The BA may achieve a basic competence in one to two years. This competence is recognized by the addition of more complex assignments. As his credibility and influence increase with the staff, the BA conforms more and more to the Brand "image."

BMs estimate that they spend as much as 25 percent of their time training BAs and ABMs. In fact, the entire brand management system is a training program. There is no such thing as an old BM; there is no place for the person who doesn't want to be promoted.

MANAGEMENT INFORMATION SYSTEMS

The BM used current data almost exclusively, even though comprehensive historical files were maintained. Meetings were usually frequent and short, with only a few people present. Telephone calls were also frequent and short. Memos were passed through for comment and review by the BM. Magazines might be scanned for ideas, but they were seldom read. For many BMs, only the Nielsen chart books, the product fact book, and project folders were kept within easy reach.

Tests were used extensively to determine the accuracy of the information routinely received so that results could be optimized and problems avoided. Brand people went out into the field infrequently, yet they had a strong perception about what was happening through their tests and the management information system.

Emphasis had to be placed on the management information system because the BM changed products about every 18 months to two years and thus lost all of his personal contacts in the agency and staff groups who tended to remain with the products.

RELATIONSHIP WITH THE "BIG FIVE"

The five groups which Brand dealt with regularly were the advertising agency, Sales, Market Research, Manufacturing, and Product Development. With each group, there were conflicts which the BM had to resolve. These conflicts might include work priorities, differences of opinion about strategy or objectives, and disagreements over project timing. Brand argued that it had the responsibility for volume and spending without explicit authority to force staff compliance.

These other departments, however, saw Brand as more in control due to its final authority to make recommendations to top management as well as its role in setting initial objectives. The other departments would have preferred a better understanding (by Brand) of their role and problems, yet essentially believed in the brand system as the best way to run Clorox.

ROTATION AND PROMOTION

Brand people were expected to shift products about every two years. Due to attrition, new hires, and promotions, the time could vary, but it seldom exceeded 2½ years. It took a BM several months to become familiar with a new assignment and perhaps a year to implement a major strategy. Thus, the typical BM was working on his predecessor's strategy for much of his tenure.

Performance was judged on a number of bases:

1. How well did he train?
2. Did he prepare a sound annual marketing plan, and was he able to sell it to management?
3. How well did his product perform against volume objectives in the marketplace (regardless of who prepared the budget)?
4. What sort of major improvements or line extensions were proposed (though not necessarily implemented)?
5. How well did he master the Clorox Style?

This last criterion referred to the fact that Clorox used an evaluation sheet which included such factors as communication, analysis, thoroughness, prioritization, productivity, organization, leadership, work with others, responsibility, ability to accept criticism, motivation, maturity, capacity, judgment, and attitude.

SUMMARY

Brand management at Clorox was a total system. The climate, selection, training, and promotion all tended to encourage the "best and brightest" people to dedicate themselves to making a product successful.

The people were supported by a management information system and organizational structure that allowed them to be trained on the job and to rotate from product to product at frequent intervals. The products were all marketed in a similar enough way, i.e., advertising, sales promotions, grocery store outlets, etc., that the system and organization were the same for each.

The strength of the system lay in the fact that each product had a "champion" who attempted to achieve volume and share objectives, as predicted in an annual plan. The short term was not sacrificed for the long term, since the long term generally represented the incumbent's proposed strategy and ongoing business-building tests and the short term represented his predecessor's strategy. In addition, a pool of potential general management talent was being established and utilized as managers moved up.

THE INTERVIEWS

Although the general outline of the system was essentially as depicted, individual managers saw reality in slightly different ways. Therefore, it may be insightful to add depth to the description by noting a number of remarks gathered by the interviewer. Needless to say, these remarks are personal interpretations—meant to put some meat on the bones. The danger, of course, is that the reader might accept each at its face value or fail to recognize that they may appear out of context. In the writer's view, however, they are consistent with his interpretation of the "true environment." The remarks are presented in question and answer format.

Question 1: You typically hire MBAs with a small amount of work experience. What do you look for, and how would you describe their jobs as BAs?

Brand Manager No. 1: I find it takes several months for a BA to become acclimated. He is usually too theoretically oriented; at this level, pragmatic application of judgment to problems is more important.

The most important thing for a BA to learn is to pay attention to details. Even typos have a dollar impact. The BA should learn to think things through comprehensively.

The BA begins working about 10 hours per day plus homework, but the time goes down as he learns his job.

All marketers are pretty much alike—aggressive, detail-minded—and that's what we look for.

Brand Manager No. 2: The biggest problem a new BA has is to learn how to juggle projects and determine priorities. Business schools teach sequential problem solving, but Brand requires juggling 15 trivial things and one major one. The BA's initial problem is establishing credibility. Brand requires a mixture of talents, but no one specific personality is appropriate. Brand people do consider themselves prima donnas.

Brand Manager No. 3: The BA's problem is simply a lack of experience with the Clorox system. The system relies on numbers, and the numbers come from the BA. The BA is constantly calculating and must think in analytic terms.

The BA must work very hard, develop rapidly, and learn what Brand is all about. It takes two to six months for the BA to have a good grasp of the job and become acclimated to the system. All training is on-the-job.

The BA is responsible for sales promotions and the budget. It is important for the BA to develop creative ways to solve problems.

The BA must determine what motivates people and use it. → *better if more experience*

Question 2: What is the relationship between "Brand" and the "other departments"?

Brand Manager No. 1: Brand is considered with respect by the advertising agency, but Brand is committed to the agency because the BM can't fire them.

Most of the people in other departments do not want to move as fast as Brand. It is a problem conveying the urgency and importance of timing.

The BM is responsible for planning, and the other departments for advice and/or execution.

Knowledge is power, and the BM is the resident expert on his products.

Brand Manager No. 2: Brand is more a line than a staff function.

Brand has responsibility for achieving volume objectives and keeping profit/case close to target level, but Brand has no direct authority over many other departments which impact his ability to achieve objectives. Management recognizes that sometimes performance is beyond the control of Brand.

Brand doesn't have to be nice to suppliers and sometimes becomes a tyrant due to the pressure.

Brand Manager No. 3: Brand controls the money. Many other departments must rely upon Brand for direction and project funding.

The advertising agency has account executives who deal with Brand and the agency's creative and media departments. The agency presents a national media plan once a year. Since the budget is mainly advertising, Brand and the agency write the request.

Sales promotions are originated by Brand and proposed to Sales.

Brand recommends and analyzes market research and test markets. The purpose of these is to avoid "national blunders," although the risk is relatively small with ongoing products.

Question 3: What common characteristics do brand managers have?

Brand Manager No. 1: The important attributes are aggressiveness and attention to detail.

Brand Manager No. 2: The BM must have an aggressive outlook toward life, be competitive, like to win, and be action oriented.

It's important to learn to do a thorough analysis of all inputs.

Question 4: How does a brand manager spend his time?

Brand Manager No. 1: Daily activities are coordination, short questions and answers on the telephone, and commenting on memos passing through. Wide variation exists, but a day might have one hour for thinking and strategy, one hour for standard reports, one hour for the "in/out basket," two hours on the phone, one hour with subordinates, and two hours in meetings.

Dealings are mainly with the "Big Five": the account executive at the advertising agency; Sales; the Manufacturing coordinator; Market Research; and the Product Development specialists.

On the average, the BM flies to the field once every three months.

Brand's job is to study the product, determine what is needed, and prioritize projects. The budget for this is set once a year.

Brand Manager No. 2: The most important job of Brand is the budget request and appropriation. Once each year, a two- to three-hour meeting is held which lays out how and why money is to be spent for the next year. During the period preceding this meeting, much of a BM's time may be spent with the agency. During the remainder of the year, the time falls off with the time spent in once-a-week meetings and telephone calls.

The second major job is the Brand Improvement Objectives meeting, which is also held once a year. Brand works with R&D to develop both short-term and long-term product development plans.

Brand strategies require 1½ to 2 years to implement. Long-range planning is important because few changes can be made in the short term due to long lead times in production and media planning.

Most of the BM's time is spent on specific projects.

Heavy use is made of the telephone, and many short meetings are held, usually with six people or less.

Brand has a meeting with the Product Development Center every two weeks.

Question 5: How often does a brand manager change brands?

Brand Manager No. 1: All Brand people are interchangeable, although it takes about two to four months to become the most knowledgeable. You spend one to two years on a brand.

Brand Manager No. 2: Rotation is caused by promotions and departures and occurs every 1½ to 2 years. Continuity is provided by the staggered rotation of BAs, ABMs, and BMs. Once you rotate, you usually don't have time to find out how your old product is doing.

Case 5–8

Blueprint Building, Inc.

In the spring of 1979, Mr. John Mason, one of the principals of Blueprint Building, was enthusiastic over the future of the organization. He explained that the present operations of his firm were in good shape and that the "sky was the limit" as far as the future was concerned. He was quick to point out how busy Blueprint was at the moment and that being busy was a sure indication of a successful, profitable operation.

BACKGROUND

Blueprint Building, Inc., is a small firm located near Clear Lake City, of the Houston, Texas, metroplex. Its business is the construction of equipment shelters which are used by two primary industrial customers, the railroads and oil companies, for the purpose of protecting expensive communication equipment. The communication hardware requires strict monitoring of its environment to prevent damage to sensitive electrical components from a variety of climatic conditions that range from hot to cold and from dusty to wet weather. The shelters that Blueprint manufactures are engineered to control the interior climate.

The demand for the product has risen over the past decade with the advance of electronics technology. The rapid rate of technical knowledge has resulted in reliable, yet small, components with wide application, such as microwave message transmission. Blueprint's clients use microwave hardware to provide a low-cost method to structure a communication network where facilities for sending and receiving messages do not exist. A microwave is a high-frequency radio signal which ranges from one millimeter to a meter in length and travels only in line of sight between a sender signal and a detector. The length of the transmission is 60 to 70 miles; thus, relay stations requiring durable equipment shelters are positioned at fixed intervals to assure lucid reception and reproduction of the microwave. Thus, especially with the recent increase of oil drilling activities, a contemporary enterprise operating in diverse areas requires networks of relay stations to expedite information.

A CLOSED CORPORATION

It was late in 1969 when Mr. Joe Lance saw that the time was ripe for entering the business of producing equipment shelters. As president of DX Tower Company in Houston, his firm was engaged in providing the antennas and other related products used for transmitting microwave signals. He noticed a need for supplying shelters and decided to start a new company for this purpose. However, because of the demands of his job, Joe Lance did not have the necessary time to put this project on its feet.

During February 1970, Lance formed a partnership with Jim Barber. Under the partnership agreement, Jim became president of Blueprint and Joe Lance assumed the role of a silent partner, providing financial assistance for the firm. Prior to becoming president of the new firm, Jim worked from 1941 to 1944 as a foreman in the electrical, hydraulic, and bombing equipment section for aircraft being built by North American Aviation. From 1944 to 1969 he was involved in various employment that was not related to the technical phase of Blueprint's operations. When Blueprint was organized, he was the prime mover of organization, and he presently supervises the firm's operations. Jim Barber's primary responsibilities are all production tasks and manpower assignments. He supervises up to 30 employees when business is booming, and a core of 10 during slack periods.

The physical plant for operations is currently five times the size of the 40 by 40 building in which the firm began. Further expansion of the plant is restricted, however, as the land behind the plant has a contour that declines too sharply to be leveled. Jim Barber considers the plant clean and well organized in its work-in-process flow. Jim takes pride in this fact, stating, "There's no one here who could run this place half as good as I can." Although the plant's operation ran smoothly from 1970 through 1972, the firm was continually showing a loss, as can be seen in Exhibit 1. Because of the recurring losses, the

Exhibit 1
Net profit to sales

Year	Sales	Gross profit		Operating expenses		Profit (loss)	
		Amount	Percent	Amount	Percent	Amount	Percent
1970	$ 87,341	$ 26,976	31%	$ 27,062	31%	$ (86)	−0.09%
1971	80,303	18,380	23	28,902	36	(10,522)	−0.13
1972	218,799	44,625	20	53,710	25	(9,155)	−0.04
1973	379,117	86,885	23	81,084	21	5,802	1.53
1974	416,629	118,647	28	105,709	25	12,937	3.10
1975	518,259	161,912	31	139,118	27	22,795	4.40
1976	928,260	304,696	33	221,835	24	55,431	5.9
1977	1,099,641	305,908	28	218,326	20	58,094	5.3
1978	756,882	325,782	43	236,028	31	59,533	7.8

Source: Company records.

two partners decided to incorporate and to seek a third stockholder to aid in administrative processes and additional financing. The search resulted in John Mason joining the firm; John is 52 years old and holds the title of secretary-treasurer. He came to Blueprint after spending 21 years with Schlumberger Well Services, in Houston, Texas. With Schlumberger he held various positions, including field engineer and location manager for the Texas Gulf Division. As he explains, "My electrical engineering degree has been useless, except that it got me my first job in 1950. Most of my work involved training new engineers in methods of utilizing our products. I also spent some time managing field locations."

For John, joining Blueprint was a dream come true, as he possessed the entrepreneurial spirit. He did not have experience in the product line, nor was he familiar with policies concerning marketing, pricing, and cost accounting. His simple philosophy is, "The good Lord takes care of those who are honest. All we try to do is make our products with the highest standards of quality and then deliver them at a fair price."

At the office Mason handles the phone calls with clients, oversees financing and credit arrangements with the bank and suppliers, and provides advice and consent when key decisions are made. He knows only the rudiments of the plant operations as he and Jim Barber divide their responsibilities between duties of administration and operations.

In 1973, Blueprint showed its first profit; however, growth of sales and income was not as rapid as the owners desired. The corporate officers decided that they needed to bring in a consultant to inspect Blueprint operations.

Bruce Burns was retained as the consultant in 1974. Mr. Burns, who describes himself as a "peddler and a pretty fair accountant," had been marketing communication products for nearly 30 years. To aid Blueprint, he established a cost accounting system and a method for pricing and set up a system of quality control in the plant.

Burns, now 63, had made a career of helping struggling firms through initiating pricing and marketing policies which ordinarily put the companies back on their feet. "I usually stay with them for three or four years, giving them the assistance they need, and then I drop them," he said. For Blueprint, his assistance was obvious: income and sales have increased dramatically since 1974 due to his efforts, although he is slowly decreasing his sales activities. He currently is Blueprint's sole agent for marketing its product. He operates on a "handshake" contract which provides him with 4 percent of gross sales, whether he makes the sale or not. Both Jim Barber and John Mason feel greatly indebted to him as he made Blueprint into a profitable business enterprise. Exhibit 2 shows Blueprint's organization chart.

THE MARKET

The market served by Blueprint's product is limited to users of microwave equipment, primarily in the oil industry. Bruce Burns, besides handling equipment shelters, represents several other related product lines through his firm, Burns Sales. His technique for marketing his line of products is to acquire "grass roots" information about companies that will be establishing operations in outlying areas; then he makes his sales calls stressing the need for microwave equipment as a means for transmitting information. He then offers a package that includes the equipment shelter, the tower for sending and receiving the signal, and support services, such as laying the foundation and repairing damaged equipment.

Much of Blueprint's current sales volume is from customers of

Exhibit 2
Organization chart
BLUEPRINT BUILDING COMPANY

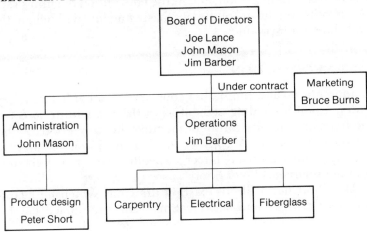

long standing. The firm's main strength lies in its production of top-quality shelters; this is recognized by Blueprint's customers, which include Exxon Company, U.S.A., the Shell Pipe Line Company, Texas Instruments, and Southern Pacific Transportation Company. A map at Blueprint has flags denoting the placement of its product across the country. Although the map has not been updated since 1972, it indicates that the shelters are primarily located along the Gulf coast and in the southwestern United States.

COMPETITION

Blueprint's competition is located in Denver, Colorado, and Houston and Tyler, Texas. Many of its competitors are small businesses like Blueprint, although Porta-Kamp in Tyler is able to produce 1,000 equipment shelters in 30 days. At Blueprint, production from start to finish of one unit can take up to 15 days. When asked about the prices competitors received for their equipment shelters, Mason stated: "We're a highly ethical company, and we do not attempt to find out what other companies charge for their product. Besides, what good would it do us anyway?"

SALES PROMOTION

Advertising has consisted of a four-page ad run in a single issue of a trade publication. Mr. Mason explains why only one attempt has been made so far: "Sales did not seem to increase as a result of our advertising, and it seemed like a waste of money to me."

The firm's main promotional device is to bring its equipment shelter to the annual convention of the Petroleum Electrical Suppliers and Users Association in Houston. At the convention the firm's representatives "press the flesh" of the purchasing agents with whom they deal, and show their product.

CONTRACT NEGOTIATION

John Mason and Jim Barber consult each other before accepting an order. Upon mutual agreement as to the availability of construction facilities and the feasibility of meeting the delivery date, the formal negotiations begin. A copy of the list of options desired from the estimate sheet and the buyer's specifications are delivered to the drafting engineer, Peter Short.

Mr. Short has a file of existing drawings which he adapts to the buyer's drawings and specifications. His experience has been that most shelters are of common sizes and are readily adaptable by simply moving door openings and fixtures. Occasionally exotic designs are ordered, but he is equally capable of drawing the structures from scratch. Peter doesn't really know why customers order such differing designs, but feels that this results from the individual efforts of the buyer's engineering department.

The finished drawings are sent to Mason and Barber for approval. Before being forwarded to the buyer, the costs are tallied and a price is put on the quote. Sometimes it may take several additions or modifications before the designs are finally approved by the buyer.

PRICING POLICIES

Pricing policy is made by Bruce Burns, the firm's marketing agent. To compute costs per unit he has taken historical data on the amounts of direct labor and materials, per square foot, which go into shelters of various sizes. After determining the cost for direct labor and material for a shelter, the figure is multiplied by 1.5 to cover operating expenses, and the price per unit is complete. The multiplier allows for a 30 percent gross profit, which, after covering operating expenses, is planned to provide Blueprint with an 8 percent rate of return on sales. Pricing lists for direct labor and material are updated every year or so by Burns. Appendix 1 shows examples of the estimate sheets which Blueprint uses in pricing.

Neither John Mason nor Jim Barber is involved in the mechanics of the firm's pricing policy; instead they have devout faith in their agent's ability to quote prices. For quotations taken over the phone by John Mason, a pricing list developed by Bruce Burns is used. Recently, Burns told Mason, "We ought to increase prices by 6 percent this year since I'm sure our competitors are doing it. Besides, those oil companies don't care what they pay for a shelter as long as it conforms to their technical specs." John Mason, however, feels that they are already receiving a fair 8 percent. He said, in fact, that any more would be dishonest. Upon receipt of the buyer approval, Jim Barber and John Mason decided when to begin production.

PRODUCTION

Exhibit 3 shows the production flow in terms of production processes and their relative order of occurrence. The flowchart shows that

Exhibit 3
Blueprint Building, Inc., production flowchart

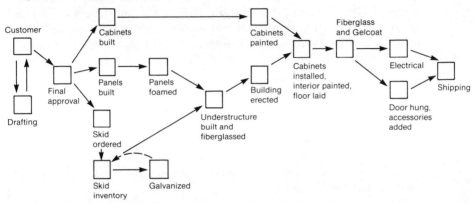

some steps in the process must be completed before the next step in construction can begin. Production is initiated when Jim Barber or John Mason hands the specifications and blueprints to the shop foreman, Ed Smith. Ed draws the necessary construction materials from stock and supervises all carpentry work. Except for the electrical work the structures are built to completion one at a time.

SKID CONSTRUCTION

Heavy-gauge steel beams, angle iron, and tubing are welded together in the back lot of Blueprint by George Jones, who is also Barber's brother-in-law. Although he is not an employee of the company, he has a verbal agreement with Blueprint to weld skids when needed. The skids are welded to the buyer specifications, though they can be divided into two classes: standard and custom. *Standard* skids can be stockpiled and built by Jones when he has the time. *Custom* skids are built only on customer demand or when odd-sized shelters are ordered. In this case, Jones must be called in from his regular job in

Houston—40 miles away—to weld the skid. All skids are shipped by company truck to Houston, a distance of approximately 30 miles, for a hot-dip galvanizing which usually takes a week to 10 days. Then the skids must be picked up by a company truck.

PANEL FABRICATION

Panel fabrication is done completely in-house by members of the carpentry trade and supervised by Ed Smith. The panel operation is conducted in the panel room, which is located next to the materials inventory storage space (Exhibit 4). Three carpenters lay out the plywood sheets, blocks, studs, etc., and staple the frame together, forming the hollow walls and roofs. Only the panels required in one shelter are built. Upon completion, the shop foreman inspects the panels for accuracy and squareness. Not all wall panels are the same since the door frames require more stability and the heights of the buildings vary, but most are of a common size. The panels for the understructure are made of heavier material, and the roof is slightly crowned for water drainage. Peter Short, the drafting engineer, says that most wall, roof, and understructure panels are the same size, "but we build these shelters to order: one at a time." No documentation is made for materials drawn from inventory or actually used. The high-quality particle board must be cut to size to reflect specifications. Upon final inspection, the finished panels are moved to the foam room, which is located next to the panel room.

The foam room is an environmentally controlled enclosure which is kept at a temperature range of 70°–80° F. For the chemicals to react predictably this temperature range must be maintained. The panels are stacked on a large vise-type structure, with ridged plywood separating each panel, and chained tightly in the vise. The foam is then shot through holes drilled in the edges of the panel and allowed to cure for 15 minutes. The panels are then taken from the vise and checked for hollow spots by sounding with a hammer. Finally the panels are stacked just outside the foam room in the assembly area.

ASSEMBLY

When the understructure panels are drawn from the finished panel stack, a skid is drawn from the outside skid inventory and moved to the assembly area. The understructure is then bolted to the skid frame and moved to the fiberglass area for spraying; then the product is moved back to the assembly area. At this time the shop foreman checks the blueprint for cutouts and door locations. Upon final inspection the structure is moved back to the fiberglass area.

The fiberglass man sprays the chopped fiberglass and gel coat. The shelter is then moved to an area along the wall with other buildings of

Exhibit 4
Blueprint Building, Inc., plant layout

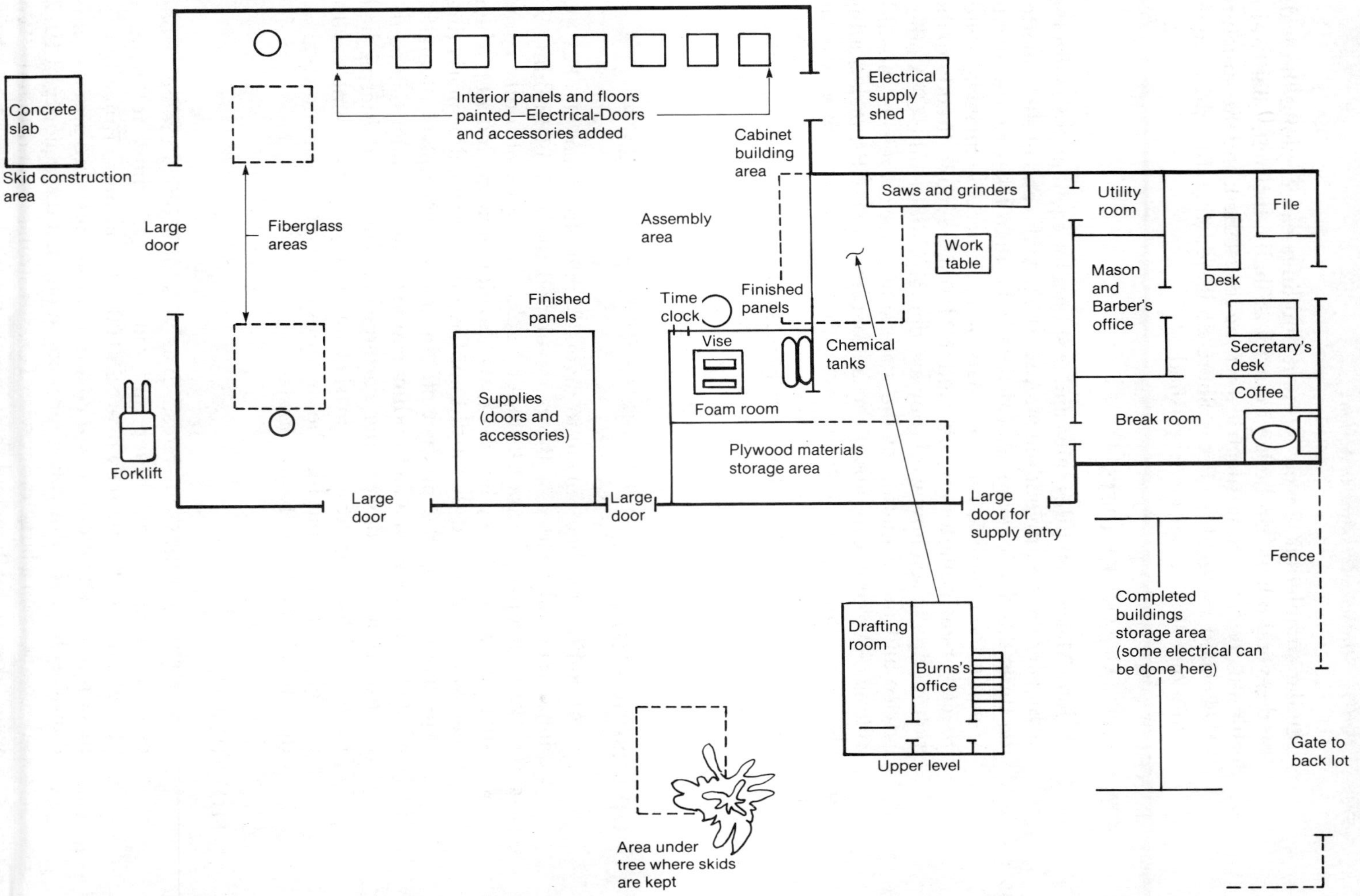

similar completion. Seven or eight buildings can fit along the wall, and several others can be kept outside. Finally, the high-quality aluminum doors are hung, electrical wiring is installed, and the structure is checked for quality. Peter Short explained that Blueprint could build one shelter per day if pushed.

FINANCIAL ARRANGEMENTS

John Mason compiles sales and cost data for each quarter, with the fiscal year for the firm ending on August 31. At the end of each quarter he turns the data over to a local CPA, who then takes two weeks to compile the data into financial statements. Once the financial statements for each quarter are returned to Mason, he looks directly to the bottom line to see how well they are doing. Although the CPA offers advice and interpretation of the statements, Mason rejects this aid, stating, "We only care about the bottom line. The CPA makes a big deal about some form which supposedly tells where the money came from and where it went. I don't know whether it does or not. All I know is that when we're busy, we're making money. Besides, with the loan from the SBA for our plant expansion in 1977, we're audited once a year anyway. If we're in any trouble it will show up then." Appendix 2 shows Blueprint's income statement and balance sheet.

DIVERSIFICATION

Attempts have been made to diversify into other markets. For example, several years ago Burns developed the idea of building fiberglass sleepers for tractor-trailer trucks. Six thousand dollars was spent on a prototype; however, its development fizzled out when management realized that it did not have the technical or marketing expertise to bring the product off. In another attempt to diversify, $20,000 was spent on a fact-finding trip to Guatemala after that country experienced a devastating earthquake. Burns and Mason had hoped that they could find a market for supplying the country with temporary housing, but like the previous foray into an unknown area, this attempt to diversify also fizzled.

THE FUTURE

As a Chinese proverb states, "It is very difficult to predict especially about the future." Blueprint is currently quite busy, following a year when sales dropped by over $250,000. According to Bruce Burns, this drop was attributed to the government not opening up more microwave channels. Burns further pointed out that the majority of 1977 sales came from a large order with Texas Instruments and stated, "We were taken in by them and their learning curve business. It may look good on paper, but our production costs did not measure up to the standards we expected."

As a result of this incident management is wary of entering into any more large contracts. Still, management wonders, "What can we do to make our business more profitable?

APPENDIX 1

Options Estimate Sheet

Quote no. <u>1177-7</u> Date <u>11/7/77</u>

DX COMMUNICATIONS
Customer's name

NEW YORK AREA
Project or rfq number

Code:

B—Building vendor furnish and/or install
O—Others furnish and/or install

F—Field installation and/or purchase
TQR—total quantity required (per unit)

F/I		Option packages	TQR	Fab./hrs. Fa.	Fab./hrs. Tot.	Materials Ea.	Materials Ext.
BB	17.	A.C. serv. entrance—1½″ CH, LB 57	1	1	1	6	6
		With power mast and weather head	1	3	3	36	36
		With explosion-proof materials		1		38	
BB	18.	Main breaker panel—100 amps. w/bkrs., single phase	1	3	3	70	70
		—100 amps. w/bkrs., three phase		3		113	
		—200 amps. w/bkrs. (20)		3		110	
		—200 amps. w/bkrs. (30)		3		145	
BB	19.	Convenience outlets—duplex	2	1	2	5	10
BB	20.	Interior lights—40 watts, 48-inch Fluorescent		1		14	
		—100 watts, incandescent	4	1	4	5	28
BB	21.	Exterior lights—weatherproof—incandescent		1		18	
		—explosion proof	1		130		
BB	22.	Interior light switch	1	1	1	8	8
BB	23.	Joslyn secondary arrester no. 1250–02		1		42	
		Joslyn secondary arrester no. 1250–03		1		62	

Appendix 1 (*continued*)

		Joslyn Surgitron arrester no. 1230–01		1		195	
		Joslyn Surgitron arrester no. 1235–01		1		295	
BB	24.	Grounding—12″ copper bus bar, drilled	1	1	1	25	25
BB	25.	Air conditioner: GE ATCIO D Btu: 9100	1	1	1		210
BB	26.	Environmental control system—for 110 v.a.c.		3		107	
		Environmental control system—for 220 v.a.c.		3		114	
BB	27.	Heater—electric, wall-mounted, forced-air	1	1	1	67	67
BB.	28.	Hi/low-temperature alarm	1	1	1	37	37
BB	29.	Illegal entry alarm swtich, Admenco 39–2	1	1	1	9	9
BB	30.	AC/DC wireway or six (6″) cable ladder P/lft		.2		7	
OB	31.	Battery charger installation		4			
OB	32.	Battery rack installation		1			
OB	33.	Automatic dehydrator installation		1			
OB	34.	Tower light control installation		6		3	
OB	35.	Engine generator installed with shock mounting frame, thimble, and hot-air exhaust duct	20			150	
BB	36.	Exhaust fan with motor, thermostate, hood, and fresh air intake vent filtered	1	4	4	98	98
BB	37.	DC pnl. 24/48—8 bkrs. Q08–16DC (AC-rated)		4		73	
BB	38.	DC pnl. 24/48—8 bkrs. Q08–16DS (DC-rated)		4		396	
BB	39.	Convenience outlet for air conditioner	1	1	1	6	6
BB	40.	_____					
BB	41.	_____					
BB	42.	_____					
BB	43.	_____					
BB	44.	_____					
BB	45.	_____					
BB	46.	_____					
		Totals				24	602

Appendix 1 (*continued*)

Estimate Sheet

Quote No. <u>1177-7</u>   Date <u>11/7/77</u>

DX CCOMMUNICATIONS

Customer's name | Contact's name
Box 358

Mailing address | Telephone number
Granbury, TX 76048 | TEL

City, state, and zip code number | Rfq number

Project and Location: <u>NEW YORK AREA</u>   Req. Del.

F/I Standard construction: Series 100 Equipment Shelters

BB   *Roof*—¼" FG, ¼" PW, 1½" poured urethane insul., ¼" PW, w/painted interior
BB   *Walls*—⅛" FG, ¼" PW, 1½" poured urethane insul., ¼" PW, painted or prefinished interior
BB   *Floor*—⅛" FG, ¾" PW, ⅛ " vinyl asbestos tile
BB   *Exterior finish*—FG/white gel coat
BB   *Door*—Aluminum, mill finish, recessed two inches below floor level, equipped with three (3) stainless steel hinges, welded pins, Kason 879 latch with spring and chain door check—"Z" bar frame to match, door size 3070
BB   *Threshold*—aluminum to match door and frame with neoprene bulb for complete seal
BB   *Dripcap*—2" fiberglass over door—forty (40) inches wide
BB   *Skid*—six (6") inch—twelve and one-half (12.5) pound I beam—galvanized

Codes:
  PW—Plywood or Blandex
  FG—Fiberglass

SIZE: <u>8'</u> wide × <u>8'</u> long × <u>8'</u> Ch. <u>1</u> room(s)

		Fab./hrs.		Materials	
	TQR	Ea.	Tot.	Ea.	Ext.
SIZE line	1		93		1107

F/I Option packages

			TQR	Ea.	Tot.	Ea.	Ext.
BB	1.	Inside partition w/aluminum exterior door		10		315	
		Inside partition w/interior 2068 wood door		10		87	
BB	2.	Extended skid with or without mesh—p/sq. ft.				5	
BB	3.	Lifting eyes and cable guides				91	
BB	4.	Insulated floor—per square foot	64	.05	3	.60	38
BB	5.	Brass Kason latch in lieu of Kasonized		1		24	
BB	6.	_____ " PW in lieu of ¼" on _____ p/sf					
BB	7.	Heavy-duty door closer		1		50	
BB	8.	Dead bolt lock set with key				20	
BB	9.	Wave guide port opening with PVC liner		1		1	
BB	10.	Air conditioner opening	1	2	2	3	3
BB	11.	Battery box w/FG pan, vent, and opening— p/lin. ft.		2		20	

Appendix 1 (*concluded*)

BB 12. Air conditioner steel galv. bracket		2		20	
BB 13. _____					
BB 14. _____					
BB 15. Subtotal		98		1148
16. Other options—See attached sheet		24		602
Material cost				1750
Fabrication cost		122	825	1007
Cost of sales				2757
Gross profit				1375
Selling price—FOB plant				4132
Hauling and off-loading via our truck				391
Price—FOB site				4523

Hauling and off-loading per truckload: <u>1565</u> miles @ <u>100</u> per mile equals <u>1,565</u> per truckload divided by <u>4</u> qty. = <u>391</u> per unit.

Prepared by: _____

APPENDIX 2

BLUEPRINT BUILDING, INC.
Income Statement
For the 12 Months Ended August 31, 1977
(Unaudited)

Sales:

Building sales	$695,710.33
Hauling	28,083.50
Field work	20,521.79
Miscellaneous material sales	10,256.15
Gain on sale of assets	2,310.32
Total sales	756,882.09

Cost of sales:

Beginning inventory	67,346.30
Labor	142,765.49
Materials	342,871.84
Workmen's compensation insurance	6,190.00
Subcontract	20,106.17
Depreciation	1,988,95
Shop expense and small tools	7,202.13
Equipment rental	423.67
Less work in process	(157,794.98)
Total cost of sales	431,099.57
Gross profit	325,782.52

Operating expenses

Salaries—officer	65,640.00
Travel	9,333.44
Utilities	5,074.97
Telephone	8,163.33
Equipment repair	846.33
Insurance—general	9,389.53
Interest	20,442.02
Office supplies	5,711.93
Group insurance	3,445.46
Depreciation	19,286.00
Auto Repair	5,058.14
Advertising	2,636.01
Legal and accounting	3,115.00
Freight-in	3,872.55
Payroll taxes	10,199.27
Taxes—other	4,000.65
Gas and Oil	7,660.31
Commissions	30,211.07
Entertainment expenses	886.19
Officers—medical fees	3,531.81
Truck expense	9,589.43
Miscellaneous	1,526.85
Freight—out	407.60
Permits	2,224.82
Rent	200.00
Officer's life insurance	3,575.64
Total operating expenses	236,028.35
Net income before tax	89,754.17
Federal income tax	30,220.81
Net income	$ 59,533.36

BLUEPRINT BUILDING, INC.
Balance Sheet
August 31, 1977
(Unaudited)

Assets

Current assets:

Cash on hand	$ 100.00	
Cash in bank—Denton	9,497.22	
Cash in bank—savings.	61,732.20	
Total cash.		$ 71,329.42
Accounts receivable—trade.	124,737.78	
Accounts receivable—employees	3,333.46	
Advances	12,242.00	
Total accounts receivable.		140,313.24
Inventory		157,794.98
Prepaid insurance.	7,697.20	
Prepaid interest.	2,027.62	
Total other		9,724.82
Total current assets.		379,162.46

Fixed assets at cost:

Land		3,000.00
Warehouse building	$103,708.99	
Accumulated depreciation.	(15,233.27)	88,475.72
Automotive.	53,335.55	
Accumulated depreciation.	(32,000.97)	21,334.58
Machinery and equipment	18,946.68	
Accumulated depreciation.	(11,598.40)	7,348.28
Office equipment	1,875.55	
Accumulated depreciation.	(1,045.47)	830.08
Fixed assets—net.		120,988.66
Goodwill.		6,599.66
Total other assets		6,599.66
Total assets		$506,750.78

Liabilities and Stockholders' Equity

Current liabilities:

Accounts payable—trade.	$ 88,394.72	
FUE taxes payable	71.21	
SUE taxes payable	61.03	
Sales tax payable	2,075.12	
Accrued salaries	5,951.44	
Note payable—FSB—autos.	6,516.38	
Federal income tax payable.	25,220.81	
Total current liabilities		$128,290.71
Note payable—FSB—truck	6,775.31	
Note payable—Mrs. Lance.	50,000.00	
Note payable—FSB—SBA	139,452.11	
Total other liabilities		196,227.42

Shareholders' equity:

Capital stock	3,000.00	
Retained earnings.	119,699.29	
Current earnings.	59,533.36	
Total shareholders' equity		182,232.65
Total liabilities and shareholders' equity		$506,750.78

Part 6

Marketing Research Planning and Analysis

Surprisingly, Planning Research Corporation, one of the nation's largest professional service firms, first launched a strategic planning program in 1981.[1] Suffering from losses due to poorly performing business units, management decided to use the planning expertise it had been marketing to others. The strategic role of marketing research is clear in this statement by Planning Research's chairman and CEO, John M. Toups:

> To remedy such shortcomings, the company last year established a seven-member strategic-planning committee to formulate and refine corporate objectives, and also to review proposed acquisitions, divestitures and major capital commitments. It also established a market research unit at the corporate level to serve the committee, separate from such activities conducted by each operating group. "They don't guarantee we don't ever stub our toes again," says Toups, "but they should impart some protection against that likelihood."[2]

We shall consider three important aspects of marketing research planning and analysis: (1) problem definition and determination of information needs, (2) strategies for obtaining information, and (3) estimating the costs and benefits of proposed marketing research projects. The discussion is not intended to be a complete examination of marketing research methodology. There are several good marketing research books that offer a comprehensive treatment of marketing research concepts and methods.

---

[1] Michell Gordon, "New Strategy: Planning Research Is Counting on It for a Sizable Rebound," *Barron's*, April 5, 1982, p. 44.

[2] Ibid., p. 44.

PROBLEM DEFINITION AND INFORMATION NEEDS

How information is used

There are three situations for which decision makers may need marketing information. The first is a situation requiring choice among two or more alternatives. For example, should we test-market product X before introducing it on a national scale? The second situation involves selecting information needed to track the performance of strategies that have been implemented. Market share information on a new product is illustrative of performance monitoring information. The third situation consists of the use of marketing information to uncover opportunities and problems. For example, in the early 1960s the toothpaste market was heavily oriented toward cavity prevention. In 1964 Colgate-Palmolive found from an ongoing consumer research program that a need existed for a toothpaste with cosmetic benefits.[3] This identification of a potential market opportunity led to the national introduction of Ultra Brite toothpaste in 1967.

Opportunity/problem identification presents the greatest difficulty in deciding what information is needed. Unless a situation requires a choice among two or more alternatives, problem definition is often far from obvious. One of the most challenging marketing research tasks is to be sure that the problem for which marketing information is needed, is clearly defined. As we noted in Chapter 3, managers often confuse a symptom with a problem. For example, a substantial drop in market share may be due to one or more of several possible causes such as faulty products, changes in customer requirements, price reductions by competition, and aggressive promotion by a major competitor. In this instance exploratory research may be needed to identify possible problems. This could be followed with research aimed at deciding how to solve the problems.

After the situation requiring marketing information has been determined, specific information needs must be specified. For example, if management requires repeat purchase information to assist in tracking new product performance, then this is an information need.

A case illustration[4]

A case illustration will be useful to show how required information is identified. The marketing manager of a manufacturing company is concerned because sales of a major product line (portable power tools for home and professional use) have declined steadily for the past six

---

[3] *1967 Annual Report*, Colgate-Palmolive Company, pp. 12–13.

[4] This illustration is drawn from David W. Cravens, Gerald E. Hills, and Robert B. Woodruff, *Marketing Decision Making: Concepts and Strategy*, rev. ed. (Homewood, Ill.: Richard D. Irwin, 1980), pp. 465–66.

months. Possible causes must be identified, and then information must be specified which will aid the manager in pinpointing the nature and extent of the causes of the sales decline. Possible causes include:

☐ Environmental changes, such as economic conditions, technological advances, and governmental requirements which might cause a decline in buyer preferences for the product.

☐ Changes in the marketing strategies of competitors, such as the introduction of an improved product, price reduction, and increased advertising.

☐ Weaknesses in the firm's marketing strategy (market targets, objectives, product, price, advertising, sales force, and distribution).

Obtaining extensive information in the three areas would be prohibitive in terms of time and cost. The marketing manager must identify the most probable causes of the sales decline and the information needed to investigate them. The decision maker should have some knowledge about the problem confronting him or her. Suppose, for example, that the marketing manager for the portable power tool firm is able to pinpoint the cause of the sales drop as a weakness in the firm's marketing strategy. Information regularly received from trade sources and market and competitive intelligence from the company sales force have helped eliminate the other possible causes. He or she is now in a position to identify the aspects of the marketing strategy that may be responsible for the problem. The marketing manager decides to review customer sales (available by computer analysis on a monthly and year-to-date basis) over the past six months compared to the same period in the previous year and finds that sales have fallen off to dealers who sell to professional users of power tools. This suggests that a shift in preferences or an overall decline in purchases is occurring in this target market. The manager also recalls that several complaints have been received from the field concerning delays in servicing power tools (serviced by either the factory or the dealer, depending on the type of servicing required) and that there have been some unusually long delays in shipping tools to dealers.

The marketing manager is reasonably certain that his or her products compare very favorably with those of the competition based on regular factory tests of competitive tools. Confident that the pricing structure is competitive and that the advertising program is sound, the manager is able to tie the problem to the professional market for power tools and has identified possible problems with the servicing and distribution of the firm's products. These factors could be of major significance to professional users, causing them to purchase competitive products. Trade association reports received each month indicate no overall reduction in power tool purchases by professional users.

The marketing manager is now ready to specify information needs. He or she has identified the information listed below after consultation with the marketing staff:

1. Attitudes and preferences of professional users toward the firm's products.
2. Brand preferences of professional users.
3. Factors most important to purchasers of power tools.
4. Types and frequency of service problems.
5. Needed improvements in service operations.
6. Service practices of competitors.
7. Possible improvements which would reduce service problems.
8. Reasons for increased delivery time.
9. Particular products involved in slow delivery.
10. Distributors' opinions concerning service and delivery.

The marketing manager must now consider how the information will help solve the problem. He or she will undoubtedly identify additional information needs and eliminate some of the items listed initially. When this has been completed, priorities must be established as to the importance of the information to guide cost-benefits analysis and planning for obtaining the information.

While the list of 10 information needs is extensive, consider how long it would have been if information were collected on all the possible causes of the sales decline (environmental, markets, competition, and marketing strategy). By using a combination of experience and review of available information, the marketing manager was able to substantially reduce the necessary information requirements.

STRATEGIES FOR OBTAINING INFORMATION

There are several possible strategies for obtaining needed information, as shown in Exhibit 1. An overview of each information category is provided below:

□ *Existing information.* The main distinction between this category and the other two is that the information exists prior to its use for a particular marketing problem. A wide variety of published information and company information is available for use by marketing managers. Included in the first group are census data, industry publications, and many other publications. The latter group covers information generated internally such as income statements, sales analyses, and product test reports.

□ *Standardized information services.* Several information services are available from information suppliers on a subscription or one-time purchase basis. The information provided from these services

Exhibit 1
Information strategies

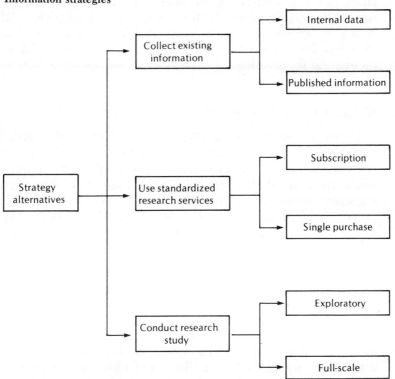

Source: This illustration is drawn from David W. Cravens, Gerald E. Hills, and Robert B. Woodruff, *Marketing Decision Making: Concepts and Strategy,* rev. ed. (Homewood, Ill.: Richard D. Irwin, 1980), p. 468.

is intended to meet the needs of a variety of users. The main distinction between this information category and research studies is that the information can be used by more than one company. A study of the fast-food industry available for purchase by any firm is illustrative of a standardized research study.

☐ *Customized research studies.* A specific research study initiated on a problem represents this category. These studies are planned and conducted to obtain information on a particular problem. For example, a survey of a sample of consumers on brand preferences for a product, conducted by a manufacturer, is illustrative of a customized research study.

There are clearly overlaps among the three categories. For example, a customized research study may draw from existing information. A standardized information service may utilize the same research methodology as would be used for a customized study.

You will have an opportunity to use information from all three categories when analyzing the cases in this book, although existing information will typically be the category provided. For certain cases it may be appropriate to recommend that additional information be obtained. If you do so, you should still make recommendations based on existing information.

ESTIMATING COSTS AND BENEFITS

Unlike expenditures for advertising or salespeople, marketing research does not directly generate sales and profits. The primary purpose of marketing research is to help executives make better decisions. Because of this, estimating the benefits to be gained from acquiring additional information is often difficult. One popular approach to deciding whether research should be conducted is to estimate costs and then proceed if the costs are acceptable to management. Let us discuss costs first, followed by benefit estimation.

Information acquisition costs

It is difficult to generalize about the cost of marketing information. A research study may cost from a few hundred dollars up to several thousand dollars or more. The cost of developing extensive marketing data banks can exceed $1 million. For example, conducting a test market for a new product often exceeds $1 million. Because of the wide variation in the costs of information acquisition, it is more appropriate to discuss several factors that affect costs.

The difficulty of obtaining information and the amount of information collected have an impact on costs. Contrast, for example, the time needed for searching through a wide variety of published information sources covering a 10-year period with the time needed to obtain the average household income in the United States for a particular year from a U.S. Census publication. In addition, such factors as sample size and length of questionnaire will affect costs. Another influence on costs is the method used to obtain information. Personal interviews are more expensive than telephone interviews due to the time involved in making contact with the respondent. Other factors may affect costs such as interviewer qualifications, complexity of study design, type of analysis, and the difficulty of interpreting results.

To give you an illustration of costs, a study involving 600–800 respondents using a short questionnaire administered by telephone or mall interview can be conducted by a research firm at a cost in the range of $14,000. Personal interviews held in the home will expand costs substantially above those required for telephone interviews.

Estimating benefits

In most instances good estimates of the costs of obtaining information can be obtained. In contrast, the benefits of new information are very difficult to quantify. Often this is not necessary since the real issue confronting management is whether or not to acquire additional information. The costs of the proposed research can be evaluated in terms of the importance of the decision being considered. Potential risks and uncertainties weigh heavily upon the go, no-go decision regarding information acquisition.

Estimates of the benefits of new information draw heavily upon past experience. For example, companies such as General Mills, Procter & Gamble, and McDonald's have learned through experience of the value and importance of marketing research. Companies conducting test markets have developed guidelines for estimating the value of tests.[5] Given an estimate of the costs of information acquisition, management can evaluate the risks and uncertainties along with the possible contribution of the research. If there is a favorable cost-and-benefit situation, then the research should be conducted.

CONCLUDING NOTE

The cases in Part 6 examine several situations involving marketing information planning. You will be asked to review and critique purposed research studies involving different products and situations. While the cases included do not offer an exhaustive coverage of marketing research, they provide an illustrative coverage with particular emphasis on research planning. In addition, certain of the cases found earlier in the book involve the use of marketing research studies and the analysis of internal data and published information.

---

[5] An interesting discussion of test markets by a CEO is provided in N. D. Cadbury, "When, Where, and How To Test Market," *Harvard Business Review,* May–June 1975, pp. 97–98.

Case 6–1

TLT (A)

"What this town needs is a reliable source of transportation between here and the Memphis airport," said Jim Newman. "I've been in the travel business with Braniff for over 10 years, and I never had a sorrier time getting in or out of here on that blessed plane they call an airline."

This conversation took place on January 11, 1979, as Jim Newman, Bill Ranford, and Knox Gary sat over lunch and tried to explore various business opportunities in Oxford, Mississippi. Newman, a former sales manager for Braniff Airlines, was now a managing partner of the largest Thoroughbred horse breeding farm in Mississippi, his first love. Bill Ranford was a marketing professor at the University of Mississippi, located in the town of Oxford. Knox Gary, a retired U.S. Air Force colonel, was presently involved as a real estate broker and also dabbled in the horse breeding business. All three had experienced difficulties with Republic Airlines in trying to make connecting flight to Memphis, Tennessee, some 80 miles northwest of Oxford.

"It seems to me," continued Newman, "that if we put together a limousine service between Oxford and Memphis, we could have a viable business which would provide us with some additional income and give the people of Oxford something which is really needed."

"I agree," said Ranford. "I am sick and tired of running up to Memphis to pick up relatives, faculty recruits for the university, and for my own traveling that I do to conferences." "I have had my share of problems in bringing people into Oxford to look at real estate," added Gary. "Only two days ago, I was to meet a couple at the local airport who were interested in moving to Oxford, and Republic canceled the flight. I had to drive up to Memphis and pick them up. In addition to that, there's the time I left my car at the Memphis airport and somebody ripped off my hubcaps. I just hate the thought of making that drive."

All three agreed to think about the idea of a limousine service and to get in touch next week to further consider what they would have to do to initiate such a service. In the meantime, they also discussed the possibilities of a full-service car wash, a janitorial service, and a health club as other businesses that could be established. They were certain that any of these new ventures could be and should be profitable in a town such as Oxford.

BACKGROUND

The city of Oxford

Many people consider Oxford to be atypical of the many rural towns that exist in the state of Mississippi. While Mississippi is known to have the lowest per capita income of any state in the United States, this generalization does not hold true for Oxford. Located 80 miles from Memphis, it represents a combination of culture, industry, and agriculture found in few other cities. Known as having been the home of William Faulkner, it attracts many visitors for the Faulkner Festival, various cultural events, and the annual spring pilgrimage through antebellum homes.

The population of Oxford and the immediate surrounding area is approximately 25,000 inhabitants (not including students). A large proportion of these people are professionals and skilled workers who are employed by local industries and firms or by the university. The figures also include a number of wealthy retired people who have returned to Oxford to spend their remaining days. Residents are served by the Tennessee Valley Authority for electric power and by South Central Bell for telephone service (over 90 percent of the homes have telephones). Since Oxford has a very low crime rate and a high police-to-resident ratio, the use of unlisted phone numbers is almost unheard of in the town.

INDUSTRY

The University

The University of Mississippi, affectionately called "Ole Miss," is the largest employer in the area. The university has 505 faculty members, 225 professional staff members, and 1,020 clerical and blue-collar workers on its payroll. In addition, the student body is composed of some 9,600 students who come from predominantly middle- to upper-class family backgrounds. The university is known somewhat as a "good time" institution, and its students frequently party in other parts of the state or country.

Since the university places emphasis on research and publishing, faculty members receive encouragement to engage in these activities. The results of their research productivity were frequently presented at academic conferences throughout the United States. This required faculty to travel to these conferences by either car or plane. This type of travel was only part of the university's travel plans. Faculty recruiting was constantly going on to replace existing faculty or to fill new positions on campus. Additional travel was done by the administration and professional staff to attend seminars, give briefings, and carry out a myriad of other duties. For the majority of these people, Memphis represented the gateway to Oxford.

Light industry

Oxford was not simply a university town. There were several divisions of major corporations that engaged in light industry and were headquartered in the city. Emerson Electric's Small Motor Division was the largest single employer (over 500 people) in town other than the university. Also located in Oxford were Chambers Corporation, manufacturing drop-in stoves and oven units for Sears; Champion Building Product's Novaply Division, making particle board; and Kellwood Manufacturing, producing clothing. These firms had a number of executives who traveled quite extensively to their headquarters or other regional operations. Infrequently, corporate jets were seen at the local airport, but due to lack of space, runway length, and ILS (instrument landing systems), this was not the most frequently used form of transportation.

Government

Not only the university and light industry, but also a number of state and federal agencies, were present in and around Oxford. The U.S. government had located the U.S. district court in a new building just off the town square. The federal government had the Department of Agriculture's Sedimentation Research Laboratory, Hydrology Laboratory, and Soil Conservation Service, as well as the Southern Forest Service, in Oxford. The state of Mississippi chose Oxford as the site for the Regional Rehabilitation Center and Regional Mental Retardation Center. Employees of these state and federal agencies did extensive traveling throughout the state and to Washington, D.C.

In short, Oxford was a unique city for such a rural setting. There were a number of diverse professionals who had to travel in their work. This travel was in addition to the pleasure and business travel of these and other people residing in Oxford. (The city has a high proportion of medical doctors, lawyers, and small business owners.)

TRAVEL MARKET AND COMPETITION

Travel market

The out-traveler from.Oxford was typified as a businessperson representing the university, local business firms, and federal or state agencies. Also, the pleasure market consisted of the occasional family trip during Christmas, spring, or the summer holidays. There was some student travel for the purpose of recreation and recruiting trips, but it was not a significant proportion of the total travel market.

The in-traveler to Oxford consisted of people calling on firms, governmental agencies, or corporate recruiters. University business included visits by athletic recruits, visiting lecturers, performers, and people attending continuing education programs on campus. Other in-travelers were visiting relatives and those coming for various lengths of stay, especially during the holiday season.

Travel information and reservations could be obtained through two sources. The first was a toll-free call to any of the major airlines serving the Memphis International Airport. The second source was World Travel Agency, the only active full-service travel agency in town that could handle all aspects of travel—airline reservations, rental cars, and hotels. World Travel handled the major portion of reservations made going out of Oxford and was well respected in the vicinity for its travel advice.

Travel competition

There were four ways that a person could travel from Oxford to Memphis and eventually arrive at the Memphis International Airport. These four modes of transportation were a Continental Trailways bus plus a taxi, a privately chartered airplane, Republic Airlines, and private automobile.

Continental Trailways made two daily trips from Oxford to Memphis with four stops en route. (See Exhibit 1 for a schedule and fares.) The buses did not stop at the Memphis airport but went to a central, downtown terminal located some 20 miles from the airport. A passenger would then have to get a taxi from downtown Memphis to the airport to make a flight. The cost of the taxi ride was between $6 and $10, depending on the time of day.

An alternative means of transportation was to charter a private plane at the local Oxford airport. This service ran on prior request and could only carry three passengers with limited luggage per trip. The service was available if the weather was good but could be canceled on short notice. The cost to the traveler was $48.50 per person for a one-way trip to the Memphis airport.

Scheduled airline service was available to Memphis and back on

Exhibit 1
Continental Trailways bus and fare schedule

Oxford to Memphis

Lv 10:05 A.M.	Ar Batesville 10:40 A.M.	Lv 6:00 P.M.	Ar Batesville 6:35 P.M.
Lv 10:45 A.M.	Ar Sardis 11:00 A.M.	Lv 6:40 P.M.	Ar Senatobia 7:20 P.M.
Lv 11:05 A.M.	Ar Senatobia 11:25 A.M.	Lv 7:25 P.M.	Ar Memphis 8:00 P.M.
Lv 11:30 A.M.	Ar Memphis 12:10 P.M.		

Memphis to Oxford

Lv 6:40 A.M.	Ar Senatobia 7:15 A.M.	Lv 5:30 P.M.	Ar Senatobia 6:05 P.M.
Lv 7:20 A.M.	Ar Sardis 7:40 A.M.	Lv 6:10 P.M.	Ar Sardis 6:30 P.M.
Lv 7:45 A.M.	Ar Batesville 7:55 A.M.	Lv 6:35 P.M.	Ar Batesville 6:50 P.M.
Lv 8:00 A.M.	Ar Oxford 8:35 A.M.	Lv 6:55 P.M.	Ar Oxford 7:30 P.M.

Fares

One-way $10.40
Round trip 19.80

the newly formed Republic Airlines. Republic was the result of a merger between the regional carriers North Central Airlines and Southern Airways. Republic's two daily departures and returns did not coincide well with connections in and out of Memphis and would typically result in layovers of from two to four hours in Memphis. (See Exhibit 2 for schedule and fares.) These layovers would be experienced only *if* Republic flew to or from Oxford. It was not uncommon for Republic to cancel a flight in Oxford or Memphis for one of two

Exhibit 2
Republic Airlines flight and fare schedule

Oxford to Memphis

| Lv 10:13 A.M. | Ar 10:43 A.M. |
| Lv 5:05 P.M. | Ar 5:35 P.M. |

Memphis to Oxford

| Lv 8:00 A.M. | Ar 8:30 A.M. |
| Lv 3:05 P.M. | Ar 3:35 P.M. |

Fares

One-way with Republic connection $13
Round trip with Republic connection   26
One-way no Republic connection   42
Round trip no Republic connection.   84

reasons. The first reason was mechanical failure of the aircraft. Since the merger, Republic flew to 153 cities—more than any other domestic airline. Coverage of such an extensive market brought on an equipment shortage, so if one plane could not fly, another could not be found to replace it in enough time to make the flight. Second the Oxford airport did not have an instrument landing system to guide aircraft during inclement weather. Therefore, a ceiling of 2,000 feet and visibility of one mile was required for a plane to land. After a period of time, Oxford residents became disenchanted with the service and began using their automobiles to get to the Memphis airport.

Driving one's own car to Memphis was the most common means of getting to the airport if one wanted to be sure to arrive on schedule. However, the rising cost of gasoline was starting to take hold and people thought twice about driving someone to the airport and returning home. This would cost approximately $20–$30 in gasoline if a trip back and forth had to be made. Alternatively, a person could drive to the airport and park the car for the period of the trip. Parking was currently $4 per day for long-term parking or $10 per day for short-term parking. Hertz recently calculated that it cost an individual $0.384 per mile to operate a mid-size car when all costs of operation were included.

THE JANUARY 18TH MEETING

"Well, what do you guys still think of the limousine business?" asked Newman. "Do you still think it is a worthwhile idea after you've had a week to mull it over?"

"I mentioned the concept to several different people," volunteered Ranford, "and the majority of them think it's a great idea. They had several questions though that I couldn't answer at the time. These involved the frequency of service, times of the day it would run, how much it would cost, and so on. These are definitely questions we're going to have to address before we can initiate service."

Knox Gary chimed in, "The initial reaction I have had from folks on the square has been quite good. They think the idea has merit, but they asked some of the same questions Bill was asked. Do we have any idea of how much this little venture is going to cost us?"

"Funny you should mention that," said Newman. "I've done a little snooping around and talked to a few people. I ran an estimate of the start-up costs, and here they are. [See Exhibit 3.]

"First of all, we must decide on the concept of the service we want to offer because that will determine the type of vehicle we will purchase or lease. If we decide to go with a customized van and executive comfort as we originally proposed, then we are looking at an $11,000 vehicle."

"Let's stay with that idea, Jim, since it is an hour and 30 minutes

Exhibit 3
Estimated cost of operating limousine service

	Per year	Per month
Fixed costs:		
Vehicle $11,000 ÷ 2 (two-year life)	$5,500.00	$ 458.33
License—ICC	450.00	37.50
Attorney fees	1,100.00	91.66
State tags	200.00	16.67
Advertising (prestart)	500.00	41.67
Total	$7,750.00	$ 645.83
Variable costs		
(two trips/day—30-day month):		
Driver salaries		$ 900.00
Fuel		900.00
Maintenance		100.00
Advertising		50.00
Printing		50.00
Commissions to travel agency		100.00
Total		$2,100.00

trip," said Ranford. "Your bottom can get pretty sore riding on one of those hard benches for that long."

"Right," echoed Gary.

"OK," Newman continued. "Second, since we are crossing state lines we need to have an ICC [Interstate Commerce Commission] permit to operate. Zab, the attorney, knows a specialist over in Greentown who does this type of thing, and he believes it should be no sweat to obtain it. Our other start-up costs will be for insurance, state licensing, commercial tags for the vehicle, and advertising.

"Variable costs will involve gasoline, drivers' wages, and maintenance of the vehicle. These costs will all depend on how many trips per day we plan to make between Oxford and Memphis. I made a preliminary estimate based on two round trips per day. So as you can see, the estimated break-even costs for the operation are $2,745.83 per month."

"Let's see those figures again," asked Ranford. "I have my calculator here, and I'll run the figures based on what we think we will charge each passenger. If we charge $25 round trip, the break-even is roughly 3.6 passengers per trip. At $30, it is three passengers per trip for the first year."

"That last figure sounds better," said Gary.

"Right," added Newman. "That corresponds to a 50 percent load factor, which is slightly less than the airlines have to have to break even. Let's go!"

"Wait a minute, guys," Ranford interrupted. "I have seen this situation before in my consulting experience, and it is contrary to what I preach in the classroom. Before we jump into this venture, we should determine what the demand is for the service, who our market will be, what times we should run, and how many trips to make, among other things. With this information, we should be able to make a more intelligent decision. Now, let's get down to brass tacks and decide how we are going to do this feasibility study."

Case 6–2

Boltronics Corporation

On April 1, 1976, Bob McAfee left his position as a manufacturing manager for W. R. Grace, a large industrial company, to devote his full efforts to Boltronics Corporation, a "panel shop" company he had founded. Presently, Boltronics was primarily an assembler of electrical control panels which started, stopped, or regulated machinery. (Exhibit 1 shows control panels for a piece of production equipment.) Boltronics' production facilities were now located in the basement of McAfee's home; a spare bedroom served as the president's office. Boltronics had been incorporated six months before, and until April 1 it had been treated as a nighttime and weekend enterprise by Mr. McAfee and several others involved. Sales so far totaled about $12,000.

McAfee wanted to reassess how to make Boltronics grow to a sales level of well over $100,000 annually.[1] Boltronics had already filled or booked several orders, but additional orders would have to be booked soon and, moreover, possibly a whole new marketing strategy developed to provide desired sales. It was possible that the company should move away from serving mainly as an assembly subcontractor for control panels. For example, Boltronics could try to deal more directly with final buyers rather than as a subcontractor for some other supplier. And there were many other possible ways to "grow" Boltronics. McAfee was considering initiating some type of market research project to assess alternative strategies possibly available to Boltronics.

© 1977 Dan T. Dunn, Jr., Northeastern University.

[1] McAfee's basement production facility could handle such a sales level. The maximum level was probably $200,000 annually.

Exhibit 1
Control panels for a piece of production equipment

GENESIS OF THE BOLTRONICS ENTERPRISE

For at least 10 years McAfee had wanted to start his own company. His dream was someday to own a series of small companies, each with sales probably under $1 million, so that the total operations would be substantial. This desire began while he served as an electrical engineer and afterward as a nuclear engineer for the Navy (1960–70) and extended through his years at W. R. Grace. (McAfee had graduated from the Naval Academy and later had completed two electrical engineering degrees at the Massachusetts Institute of Technology.)

McAfee had joined a W. R. Grace plant in Lexington, Massachusetts, in 1970 as a project engineer, where he defined his initial responsibilities as follows:

> Once the decision to build a plant was made, then all responsibilities regarding plant construction and operation were the project engineer's. The function was multifaceted. Areas of responsibility included finance, construction, engineering, and continual contact with all suppliers involved in the operation. In fact, there was as much or more contact with outside suppliers as inside contact with other Grace affiliates.

In 1971 McAfee was promoted to manufacturing manager of the Letterflex Systems Group, which was a part of the company's Polyfibron Division. The Letterflex Systems Group, with sales of about $20 million, was involved primarily in the design of machines used for printing newspapers and commercial products (textbooks, etc.) and the manufacture of the chemicals used in the machine process. Specifically, the Letterflex System developed a Letterflex Plate for printing which utilized a liquid photopolymer curable with photoelectric light. The actual assembly of Letterflex machines was contracted to outside companies, while the chemicals were made by Grace.

At Letterflex, McAfee had supervised 30 people and managed over $750,000 in overhead. Primarily, McAfee said he was accountable for getting "the parts in, the people in, and the production out on schedule." He frequently dealt with outside contractors. Concerning control panels, he managed a group of engineers who designed various pieces of production equipment, many relying upon such controls. Most of this equipment was designed by McAfee and his staff and built by outside electrical-mechanical contractors (subcontractors).

In one instance, he had been responsible for designing and later debugging a new machine built by outside contractors. When the new machine was completed under budget and in one half the time predicted, McAfee said he developed a reputation as "something of an expert with regard to project engineering and research and development."

In addition, experience with this project crystallized some of McAfee's feelings about contracting electrical-mechanical equipment to outside suppliers, Specifically, as a customer, he was distressed that he could not find a reliable supplier to provide a complete "machine controls package." Typically, what happened was that an outside machine shop, in turn, had to subcontract the design and/or assembly of associated control panels. This procedure, according to McAfee, slowed deliveries of the equipment and at least raised the possibility that the control panels were more expensive than necessary and/or of rather unknown quality. However, he had no idea whether buyers at other firms shared these feelings.

In late 1975, W. R. Grace told McAfee to expect a transfer to Baltimore due to "the recession's effect on Letterflex orders." Considering the transfer a lateral shift in his career and not anxious to leave New England, McAfee began to seriously consider starting his own business. The problems he personally had experienced with suppliers seemed an obvious area for further investigation.

MARKET INFORMATION GATHERED PRIOR TO APRIL 1976

By April 1976, McAfee already knew something about a number of companies which he considered Boltronics' competitors since he had dealt with them as Grace suppliers. It was common for Grace to let several outside contractors compete for a job, and part of the screening process involved asking questions about supplier products, operations, personnel, financial strength, etc. For example, he knew that three or four panel shops had sales of almost $500,000 in the New England area.

McAfee had tried to organize his thoughts about these suppliers-turned-competitors. Depending upon how he defined Boltronics' business, McAfee thought that there could be several categories of potential competitors, performing one or more of the following functions:

1. *Parts distribution.* According to the Yellow Pages, at least 100 small and medium-sized Greater Boston concerns were parts distributors (manufacturer's representatives) for component parts manufacturers (among electrical parts manufacturers were such well-known companies as General Electric and Westinghouse and a host of other companies). Parts distributors carried a variety of parts made by different companies. (See Exhibit 2 for the products of one "full-line" distributor.)

Electrical parts were used in a wide variety of applications, including control panels. Parts might find themselves in control panels in several ways. McAfee offered the following framework:

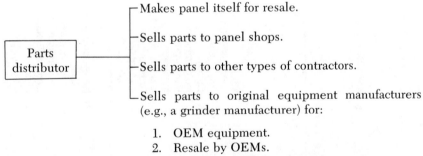

Parts distributors usually received discounts of 49 percent off "list" prices; those who bought "at wholesale" (e.g., panel shops, contractors, certain OEMs) from such distributors received 41 percent off list. (Final users/buyers were normally billed at list prices.)

Some distributors had large parts sales to panel shops, while others concentrated on self-manufacture, he thought. Parts sales to other contractors and OEMs could also vary substantially between distributors, McAfee noted, although he was not sure of the actual variation among the parts distributors in his area.

2. *Control panel assembly.* According to McAfee, many parts distributors also assembled parts into finished control panels, having initially added this operation to support parts sales to certain cus-

Exhibit 2
Product brochure of a parts distributor

Mount Electric Company
Electrical Distributor
Worcester, Massachusetts

Ballasts
  Advance
  General Electric
  Jefferson

Batteries—flashlights
  Ray-O-Vac
  Union Carbide (Eveready)

*Bells—buzzers—signals
  Edwards
  Federal
  General Electric

*Blocks—terminal
  Buchanan
  Connectron
  Cutler-Hammer
  General Electric

*Boxes—enclosures
  Appleton
  Hoffman
  Lee
  Raco
  Red Dot
  Steel City

Fixtures
  Compakett (Photo-Sw)
  Day-O-Lite
  Dazor
  Holophane
  Litecontrol
  Miller
  Stocker & Yale
  Stonco
  Swivelier
  Sylvania
  O. C. White

*Fuses—accessories
  Buss
  Chase-Shawmut
  Connecticut
  General Electric
  Ideal
  Littelfuse
  Marathon
  Mini-Breaker

Greenfield
  American Flexible Conduit

Tape
  General Electric
  Minnesota Mining & Manufacturing Co. (3M)
  Plymouth

Testing equipment
  General Electric
  Ideal
  Mueller
  Sperry Instruments

*Transformers
  Acme
  Edwards
  General Electric
  Hevi-Duty
  Jefferson

*Wire
  American Electric Cable
  American Flexible Conduit (Bx)
  Brand Rex
  Carol
  Cornish
  Excel
  General Electric
  PWC

Cable grips
  Kellems
Conduit—accessories
  Greenlee
*Conduit—emt
  E.T.P.
  Kaiser
  Republic
*Controls—motor and distribution
  Cutler-Hammer
  General Electric
  Micro Farmer
  Micro Switch
Emergency lighting
  Chloride
  Dual-Lite
  Litecor
Fans
  Airmaster (Diehl)
*Fittings
  Appleton
  Briscon
  Efcor
  O.Z. Gedney
  Russell & Stoll
  Thomas & Betts
  Victor

*Heating devices
  Chromalox
  General Electric
Lamps
  General Electric
  Sylvania
Meter equipment
  Anchor
Proximity switches
  Cutler-Hammer
  General Electric
  Micro Farmer
  Micro Switch
  Tann Controls
Sealtite
  Anaconda
Solder
  M. W. Dunton
*Switches
  Cutler-Hammer
  General Electric
  Linemaster
  Micro Farmer
  Micro Switch
  McGill
  Tann Controls

Rome
United States Steel
Wire clamps, staples, etc.
  Briscon
  Victor
*Wire connectors—lugs
  Atlas-Rattan (Marr)
  Burndy
  Ideal
  Ilsco
  Minnesota Mining & Manufacturing Co. (3M)
  Thomas & Betts
*Wire markers
  W. H. Brady Co.
  Stranco
  T&B (E-Z Line)
Wireway-racks
  ECP Corp.
  Hoffman
  Kindorf (Steel City)
  Power Strut (Power Eng.)
  Taylor
  Wiremold
Wiring devices
  General Electric
  Harvey Hubbell
  McGill
  Daniel Woodhead

Established 1885

Call us for your electrical needs

Manufacturers' catalogs available on request

* Types of parts bought by Boltronics and other panel shops.

tomers who also demanded assembly. McAfee felt sure that such assembly was much less important to the shops than parts sales, in terms of both revenue and profit. He guessed that control panel assembly accounted for less than 15 percent of most concerns' total sales. Since most concerns were not specialists in assembling control panels, McAfee thought that they were not always the most efficient. For example, he had "priced out" one control panel done by a Grace supplier, and figured that the components cost could have been lowered 20 percent by substituting completely adequate but less expensive components.

There were also an undetermined number of panel assembly operations not owned by a parts distributor, although many assemblers sought to establish some type of long-term relationship with distributors in order to seek price concessions, get referrals, etc.

3. *Control panel design.*   According to McAfee, the design work for control panels done by parts distributors and/or assemblers ranged from "very good to homemade and unnecessarily expensive." Few of these concerns employed degreed engineers, and much of the design work was "based on experience with similar designs or was drawn from information supplied by the components manufacturers." It should be noted that many assemblers used designs supplied by customers (for example, at W. R. Grace, McAfee himself had done the design for many control panels that were then assembled by outside companies). McAfee also thought that, regardless of the design source, many control panels also were "not designed with human engineering in mind" and that placement of control buttons, switches, etc., was important to plant workers using them. McAfee believed that most designers, as well as many manufacturing managers, thought too little of such operator needs.

Most of the Boston-area concerns with one or more of the above functions (1–3) were local companies, according to McAfee. There was one notable exception, however—the Foxboro Company. Foxboro, a $300 million company with headquarters in New England, made and sold parts and designed and assembled control panels, in addition to other operations.[2] McAfee said, "Maybe I could become a Foxboro."

---

[2] The Foxboro Company is a leading worldwide supplier of instruments and systems for process management and control. Its worldwide customers include the chemical, oil and gas, pulp and paper, power, food, metals, minerals, textile, and marine industries. The company's products range from control instruments and accessories to computer-based process management and control systems. The products are used to measure, indicate, record, control, and monitor such process variables as flow temperature, pressure, and liquid level. The company also provides extensive engineering, training, and field service support to its customers.

4. *Contractors.* According to McAfee, competition could also come from certain other concerns:

A. *Electrical-mechanical contractors* (sometimes called machine builders). A few large shops apparently provided a complete machine controls package without subcontracting out any part of the job. A piece of production equipment which automatically blended paint was one example McAfee knew of. The contractor had assembled and fabricated metal and plastic parts and supplied as well the electrical drive and associated control systems. The Greater Boston Yellow Pages listed about 30 companies calling themselves electrical-mechanical contractors. (The Yellow Pages had no separate electrical-mechanical contractor heading; rather, the company names were found under such headings as machine shops and electrical contractors.)

B. *Machine shops* (mechanical contractors). The Yellow Pages listed over 300 shops which designed, assembled, and/or fabricated parts, finished items, installations, etc. McAfee believed that the great majority of shops had to subcontract electrical control systems, if needed, to electrical contractors, control panel shops, etc. An undetermined number of shops had ties with a parts or panel business.

C. *Electrical contractors.* The Yellow Pages also listed over 375 electrical contractors ranging from residential electricians to larger companies in the commercial market with a broad line of products and/or services. An unknown number designed and assembled control panels or had subcontractors.

D. *Controls, control systems, and regulator companies.* The Yellow Pages also listed over 135 concerns under this heading. (Some were also listed under electrical contractors.) The companies ranged from Digital Equipment, Foxboro, Honeywell, and General Electric to local panel shops and parts distributors. McAfee thought that at least 11 of these concerns would be direct competitors of Boltronics in the eastern Massachusetts area (see Exhibit 3). There might be others, but he was fairly confident that his list of 11 was complete.

Most of the companies involved in the above activities (1–4) relied heavily on previous customer relations as a method of securing sales. Beyond such direct sales activity, the Yellow Pages and catalogs were also considered important. McAfee could not recall any other major forms of promotion used within the controls business.

5. *Indirect competition.* Many user companies themselves had the capability "in house," if they chose, to design and assemble control panels. Some of these panels controlled production equipment; other panels were incorporated into OEM items (such as the Letterflex System) which were sold to customers. McAfee could not hazard a guess as to the overall size of this market were it to be placed with outside suppliers. (At Grace's Letterflex operation, about $75,000

Exhibit 3
List of competitors

Company name	Panel designer	Panel assembler	Parts dealer	Other known information as of April, 1976
Control, Inc.			X	Close ties to Componapart; uses Componapart almost exclusively for its customers who need panels
Control Design, Ltd.	X	X	X	Has excellent engineering capabilities, but fortunately for Boltronics, does not use them well
Rustin & Co.		X	X	
Beta Controls	X	X		Formerly an electrician, turned panel builder
Efficiency Controls				—
Systems Service and Controls, Inc.				—
Bell Company, Ltd.	X	X		
Componapart	X	X		Close ties to Control, Inc.; uses Control, Inc., as a parts dealer and a major source for its designer and assembly business
Wyatt Engineering		X	X	Boltronics buys parts from and also competes, in terms of assembly operations, with Wyatt Engineering
Industrionics	?	?	?	Uncertain as to whether a competitor or not
Mekontrol	?	?	?	Uncertain as to whether a competitor or not

of panel business per year was given to outsider suppliers.)

McAfee had also thought about potential customers for Boltronics. Given his present understanding of the market, he chose to place them in several categories:

1. *Machine shops wanting to become electrical-mechanical contractors.* One way for some machine shops to expand their sales was by also supplying associated controls. Boltronics could possibly seek business from these shops, serving as their subcontractor.

2. *Overflow business of other contractors.* Shops supplying controls could at times, and maybe frequently, McAfee speculated, become overloaded with orders. Rather than turn away business, such shops might take the business and subcontract panels to Boltronics.

3. *Chemical companies.* Process-oriented manufacturing companies such as chemical companies (e.g., W. R. Grace) needed various pieces of production equipment requiring controls. According to

McAfee, "The chemical companies are always changing their manufacturing processes and thus need to change or add controls. However, the chemical companies are full of chemical engineers, not electrical engineers who can do the control panel design." There were at least 25 large chemical plants in New England, according to McAfee.

4. *Other manufacturing companies needing machine controls panels.* McAfee thought that food, pulp, textile, and paper, rubber, and perhaps other companies could use Boltronics when they needed control panels for production equipment or OEM items.

For chemical and other types of companies, McAfee viewed the design and assembly of machines and/or controls as an important "make-or-buy" decision. However, he was not sure that many companies were very analytical about the economic and quality trade-offs involved, particularly in the design stage. "Design engineers themselves routinely are responsible for the make-or-buy decision, and they like their own in-house designs unless the project is clearly beyond their field of expertise or they're swamped with work," he said.

In an attempt to gain some understanding of the needs of various customers, McAfee had conducted a mail survey of 100 companies in early 1976. The companies, all located in Greater Boston, included machine shops and industrial companies in the chemical, food, textile, paper, and rubber industries. Specific company names had been selected from a list provided by the state of Massachusetts to anyone interested. The survey was addressed to the "Chief Design Engineer" at each company since people's names were not given in the state report.

The survey is shown in Exhibit 4. Four replies were received. Three said "no interest"; a fourth requested a visit by a Boltronics representative.

Exhibit 4
McAfee's mail survey

Boltronics Corporation is a newly formed company organized to provide a unique combination of service and product. There are many engineering firms that design electrical control systems for a fee, and there are many electrical shops that build to your design. Boltronics Corp. has the capability to both design and build control systems to meet your requirements. Our design costs you nothing—all you pay for is the control system itself, which is guaranteed to work in your application. The control system will be manufactured in strict accordance with all applicable codes and designed to keep costs to an absolute minimum. We will not proliferate parts at your expense.

Boltronics Corp. employs two graduate electrical engineers with a total of 23 years in the design and manufacture of control systems. Rather than hire full-time talent like this, we offer you the alternative of utilizing our expertise when the need arises.

Exhibit 4 (*concluded*)

Boltronics Corp. is anxious to give you the chance to use our design and manufacturing capabilities while expanding your own business base in the process. In the past you may have had to turn down attractive OEM contracts because of the lack of necessary electrical capability. No longer—Boltronics Corp. will completely relieve you of all your electrical headaches. We will design the controls, build them in our own shop, wire your machine, and thoroughly test to demonstrate suitability. We do the work, you control the job. Let us become your electrical design engineers and electrical production shop all in one.

Please. . . .

take a few minutes of your time to read our advertisement and give us your response. Thank you!

Sincerely,
Boltronics Corp.

1. Is the service described in our advertising flyer of interest to you?   ☐ Yes   ☐ No

2. Could our service expand your business?   ☐ Yes   ☐ No

3. Have you turned down jobs because electrical design and/or assembly were required?   ☐ Yes   ☐ No

4. Would you be able to bid on OEM machines and equipment if you had access to our electrical skills?   ☐ Yes   ☐ No

5. Would you like more information about us or our service?   ☐ Yes   ☐ No

6. Would you like our sales engineer to contact you?   ☐ Yes   ☐ No

If you checked either 5 or 6 yes, please give us your company name and address

_____

_____

_____

BOLTRONICS AS OF APRIL 1976

In April 1976, Boltronics was, according to McAfee, merely a skeleton of the company he anticipated. Presently he employed only a few part-time assemblers, in addition to his wife, who served as a part-time secretary-bookkeeper, and his teenage son, a part-time assembler.

By April, Boltronics had finished $12,000 in orders and was working on a $11,000 order, a $1,500 order, and a small order or two. The largest order had come from a company that McAfee had known while at Grace. This machine shop, Wicker, Inc., had subcontracted to Boltronics the assembly of several control panels which were part of a Grace order. The $1,500 order came from P. B. Hinkle Company, a machine shop which McAfee had "cold-called." A few small orders ($200–$300 each) had come from a small contractor who was a personal friend of McAfee. It also seemed that Wicker, Inc., might give Boltronics a second order for similar equipment, but Wicker, Inc., wanted it at 3 percent below the price on the first order. All of these orders would absorb present production capacity through the early summer. At the present level of operations, the $11,000 order represented about two months' work.

The first order for Wicker, Inc., according to McAfee, had been priced "at the market," although he could have chosen to "cut price, possibly cut costs by redesign, or have done both." For planning purposes, McAfee tried to estimate his gross margin on the order:

Sales		$11,000
Cost of goods sold:		
Components		5,200
Estimated labor at $5 per hour		1,050
Total cost of goods sold		6,250
Gross margin		$ 4,750

Again, for planning purposes, McAfee made a guess at some probable *minimum fixed manufacturing and delivery costs* for Boltronics for the first year:

Truck depreciation and operation	$1,600
Depreciation on tools	200
Salaried personnel: secretarial	2,000
Total	$3,800

Also, McAfee noted that he had placed a $20,000 loss limit for himself on the Boltronics venture should it turn sour. This amount represented his assets other than his house. As of April, he had invested about $2,000 in tools, equipment, and supplies and in trading in one of his cars for a pickup truck.

POSSIBLE MARKETING STRATEGY ALTERNATIVES

McAfee wanted to generate an overall marketing strategy that would make Boltronics more stable and prosperous. He knew he was going to have to greatly expand his customer base, possibly changing the basic concept of Boltronics in the process. Most important, he would have to concentrate on new customers. Personal contacts from his W. R. Grace days were exhausted, it appeared, and Boltronics would have to seek business from people who knew neither him nor Boltronics.

As for customer groups, the initial thinking was that they could be one or more of the groups previously discussed. How to turn them into actual buyers was basically unresolved, although McAfee said it was time "to brainstorm about various ways of reaching them, selling them, and keeping them sold." Also unresolved was whether Boltronics should be a control panel designer, a control panel assembler, a parts distributor, or some combination of these. Another issue was, Should Bontronics deal at arm's length with other contractors and parts distributors, or should it try to formalize some kind of relationship, as many other panel shops had done? Finally, McAfee could deemphasize panel assembly, concentrating on design and becoming a general design consultant.

POSSIBLE MARKET RESEARCH ALTERNATIVES

Within the New England–based control panel industry, McAfee knew of no company that conducted "formal" market research such as a mail, telephone, or personal survey of customers. McAfee, though, had taken a marketing course during a night MBA program where market research had been discussed, and wondered if market research was appropriate for Boltronics. About five classes had been spent on the topic. The discussions had focused more on the "managerial aspects" of research (purpose of the research, value of the information, and general research methodology) than on "technical aspects" (specific research sample designs, advanced quantitative data analysis techniques, etc.). McAfee was hopeful that his exposure to market research in school would be helpful in picking an appropriate market research strategy for Boltronics.

At a minimum, McAfee knew that he had several possible research alternatives. First, he had already spoken with the professor for the marketing course he had taken concerning the possibility of retaining the professor on a consulting basis. In his files, he had a letter from the professor outlining a possible research project and some very preliminary estimates of costs (see Exhibit 5).

Exhibit 5
Consultant's research proposal

February 4, 1976

Mr. Robert McAfee
Whitcomb Road
Bolton, Massachusetts 01740

Dear Bob,

I have enjoyed hearing about Boltronics and believe you have made the right decision to leave W. R. Grace at the end of March to devote your full efforts to this enterprise. As requested, I am outlining a possible market research plan for Boltronics based on our very brief discussion of what you have told me you are trying to do. The project can be initiated immediately, or we can wait until the spring after you have left Grace. Please understand that this is a preliminary proposal that reflects what you told me was your most serious problem—lack of detailed information concerning the market and its various segments and competitors.

What I am proposing is a multistage research project that will begin with an exploratory field survey of customers and competitors. Afterward I would be willing to supervise or conduct additional "library" research of the industry, public data available about competitors, trade association files, government reports and data, etc.

The basic purpose of the customer survey would be to probe the buying motives and habits of various customer groups and their perception of suppliers. If you decide to initiate the project with me, we'll sit down and generate a series of research hypotheses concerning market and competitive behavior that can be tested through the survey.

The library research stage should probably begin with further investigation of competition. There must be public data about them available somewhere in state government files. We'll find it. Or we can get some very basic information from financial rating services.

The survey research part of the project would basically be divided into design and implementation phases. I would be responsible for research design. As for implementation, I suggest a methodology based on personal interviews with potential customers. A less costly approach would be telephone interviews. And of course the total cost of the project will be largely dependent upon how many people you want to interview or call. We'll have to discuss this further.

My fees in relation to designing the survey project would be $150 per day. The library-type research is $80 per day if I do it myself or $40 if I subcontract it. As for someone to actually conduct the personal or phone interviews, I can contract to hire people at $10 per hour for personal interviews, or $3.50 per hour for telephoning (all expenses included). The agencies I have in mind, however, tend to concentrate on consumer products, although they will also research industrial products. An alternative is to use one of my MBA students.

He has a bachelor's degree in mechanical engineering and has taken several of our MBA marketing courses. He said he is available for $5 per hour, plus expenses if he has to travel or call long distance.

I hope this very tentative proposal meets your expectations at this stage. If you decide to proceed, we will have to sharpen the general research plan discussed herein. Please call if you have any questions.

Yours truly,

Greg Parker

Second, the professor had introduced him to an undergraduate Marketing major at the school who needed a project as part of a course requirement. Several weeks ago, McAfee had spoken with the student, Arthur Marshall, about it. Based on a three-hour meeting with McAfee, Marshall had proposed a research strategy for Boltronics. McAfee would pay for Marshall's out-of-pocket expenses in relation to the project, estimated at $50. The basic elements of the proposed research, scheduled for May and June 1976 and to be conducted by the student under McAfee's supervision, were as follows:

1. Telephone survey of sample of 25 potential customers

    Using a list of a sample of companies provided by McAfee, Marshall proposed to telephone either the company's purchasing agent or the design engineer responsible for controls. The companies would be drawn from SIC (Standard Industrial Classification) groups thought to be prime candidates for Boltronics business (i.e., food, textiles, fibers, pulp, paper, chemicals, rubber, and nonelectrical production machinery).[3]

Marshall proposed a methodology consisting of a few closed-end questions and a series of open-end questions. Closed-end questions

---

[3] *Major Group 20,* Processed Foods—foods and beverages and certain related products such as vegetable and animal fats and oils, and prepared feeds for animals and fowls. *Major Group 22,* Textiles and Fiber—(1) manufacturing of yarn, thread, braids, twine, and cordage; (2) manufacturing broad woven fabrics, knit fabrics, and carpets and rugs from yarn; (3) dyeing and finishing fiber; (4) the integrated manufacture of knit apparel and other finished articles from yarn; (5) coating, waterproofing, or otherwise treating fabric; (6) the manufacture of felt goods, lace goods, nonwoven fabrics, and miscellaneous textiles. *Major Group 26,* Pulp and Paper—the manufacture of pulps, paper, and paperboard as well as converted products such as paper bags, paper boxes, and envelopes. *Major Group 28,* Chemicals—(1) basic chemicals, (2) chemical products to be used in further manufacture, and (3) finished chemical products to be used for ultimate consumption. *Major Group 30,* Rubber—rubber products such as tires, rubber footwear, mechanical rubber goods, hats, soles, and flooring. *Major Group 35,* Nonelectrical production machinery; also, machines powered by built-in or detachable motors, and portable tools, both electrical and pneumatic.

required the respondent to pick among several answers supplied by the researcher. Open-end questions did not limit the respondent to any set answer, but required more conversational answers. Marshall said that the open-ended questions could be used for "in-depth probing of customer needs and wants, in addition to their perception of competition, since the objective would be to determine what the buyers would like to see when they consider process controls."

2. Reports available from the state of Massachusetts

    Several types of secondary (published) data were also anticipated. First, McAfee knew that the state government collected at least some information about companies operating in Massachusetts for tax and legal purposes, although he was not sure of the exact nature and amount of the information available. Marshall's plan here was to visit the statehouse and "fish around for interesting information." Second, Marshall proposed to assemble statistics on industrial growth and capital expenditures for Massachusetts and New England industry since he believed that industrial growth or decline in the area would be a prime indicator of Boltronics' prospects. Finally, Marshall wanted to collect basic demographic and economic information on the major manufacturing cities in Massachusetts.

3. Background information

    Since the research would be part of a class project, for his term paper Marshall would be required by the professor to gather additional information from McAfee concerning Boltronics—its history, corporate objectives, product line, production plan, financial capabilities, employees, marketing policies, etc. Marshall also planned to interview McAfee to record in as much detail as possible McAfee's understanding of the market and competition prior to the research.

4. Recommendations

    Marshall planned to conclude his report with a set of action recommendations for Boltronics.

5. Final report

    Marshall expected the final report to be "about 100 pages." About one quarter would be comments on the data collected, while the rest would be photocopies of government reports, completed survey forms, and other data. Marshall proposed to submit the finished report to McAfee in late June, the deadline set by his professor.

Marshall had asked permission to "pilot-test" one part of the plan (telephone interviews), and McAfee had agreed, giving him a few names to call. The answers from one pilot respondent to the *closed-end* questions only are shown in Exhibit 6. Also in Exhibit 7 is a letter from the professor to McAfee concerning Marshall.

McAfee knew that other research strategies were possible. For example, the sales calls he had already made to a limited number of

Exhibit 6
Responses in pilot test of Marshall's survey (closed-end questions only)*

---

1. Name [a textile mill]
2. Address Worcester, Massachusetts
3. Phone number 965-5099

4. Purchasing agent Ben Hill
5. SIC number 84 041

6. Do you use process controls in your manufacturing?
   Yes_____ No_____

7. What do you manufacture? Textiles

8. What type of controls do you use presently? Electronic X
   Mechanical_____ Computerized _____ Other _____

9. Do you use or have you ever used outside sources to develop and/or
   implement your process controls? No_____ Yes X

10. The following rating system will be used to evaluate the answers to the
    following questions:
    1. Not important.
    2. Very little importance.
    3. Secondary importance.
    4. Very important.
    5. Determining factor, of greatest importance.

11. I would purchase new process controls because:
    1. It would make my operation more efficient. 4
    2. It would increase my production. 5
    3. It's the trend in sophisticated manufacturing. 1
    4. I would have a need for it in the expansion of my operation. 1
    5. Other reasons._____

12. The following are how important to you in purchase determination of
    process controls? Price 4   Quality of the system 5
    Sophistication of the system 1   Company that makes the
    system 2   Principle in the company 1   Salesman 3
    Amount of time the company is in business 2   Company's
    reputation 2

13. When and if my company purchases process controls:
    1. We develop it and produce it ourselves._____
    2. We develop it and have an outside source produce it._____
    3. We have an outside source develop it and we produce it._____
    4. We let an outside source handle the whole thing; we just let him
       know what our needs are, and he takes care of the rest. X
    5. Other._____

14. When I have an outside source involved, my selection process in giving
    out the job would be by:
    1. A competitive bidding process. X
    2. Referral._____
    3. Picking the one I like the best._____
    4. Just going to the Yellow Pages and picking one._____
    5. Other._____

15. What is the time span of planning, purchase, and implementation of the
    process controls? 72 weeks

Exhibit 6 (*concluded*)

---

16. Are you using an outside source presently? If so, whom?__No__
17. What does he do for you? _____
18. Do you want your salesman to be:
    1. Highly educated and trained in the field?__Yes__
    2. Somewhat educated and trained? _____
    3. Makes no difference. _____

Company Classification

19. Sales__$26.5__million
20. Number of factory workers__120__
21. Number of management people other than engineers__4__
22. Number of engineers__0__
23. Have you had any expansion recently in the company, or do you expect to have expansion in the near future?__Yes__
24. How much have you spent on process controls in the past two years?__$10,000__
25. How much will you spend in the next two years?__$30,000__
26. How long has your company been in business?__6__years
27. Any additional comments: _____

---

* Marshall also took rough notes on the answers to the open-end questions he raised; he would discuss these with McAfee during a face-to-face meeting.

---

companies had generated considerable information that was already a part of his understanding of the market. Thus it was possible that McAfee himself could continue such informal research in conjunction with sales calls or perhaps without trying to push for an order during a "research" visit.

Also, McAfee knew that he himself might undertake some or most of the research steps proposed by either the professor or the student. And he knew that there were numerous other survey research possibilities concerning his customers and competition. Finally, he could also consider using the test market approach or the observational research method. Possibly, test marketing could be used on a limited number of customers to assess various marketing strategies. In the observational method, market behavior was generally observed without directly questioning the respondent. For example, from the MBA program he remembered how one of the large tire companies had sent an employee into the field to pose as a customer at competitive tire stores.

McAfee also remembered from his class how the professor had concluded one session citing the principle that "good decisions are based on good information about the market." Intuitively, that guideline seemed to make sense, and he wondered to what extent and how the guideline should be applied to Boltronics.

Exhibit 7
Letter concerning student

March 20, 1976

Mr. Robert McAfee
Whitcomb Road
Bolton, Massachusetts 01740

Dear Bob,

   I am pleased to respond to your request for further information on the student we discussed. As I said, I had him in one of my undergraduate marketing management classes, where he was an able performer and earned the grade of B. He was aggressive in class discussions and also did well on tests on the textbook and notes; his papers were less impressive, although still in the top half of the class.

   Other than grades, I will add that the student is known by the faculty as a hard worker. Also, he has told me that he was a "star" on his co-op job, where he worked several quarters for a silverware manufacturer selling to discount jewelry outlets. He says that the company wants to hire him permanently, starting August, for a pile of money but that he wants to go on to graduate business school.

   Hope this helps.

Yours truly,

Greg Parker

Case 6–3

Bay-Madison, Inc.

In January 1980, Mr. George Roberts, research director of Bay-Madison, Inc., a large advertising agency, was faced with the problem of how best to conduct a study on Rill, a product of the Ellis Company, one of the agency's clients.

Rill, a powdered cleanser, was first introduced by the Ellis Company in 1923. Its original use was as a heavy-duty cleansing agent for removing dirt and stains from porcelain, metal, and ceramic tile surfaces. A unique bleaching property of the product eliminated the necessity for scrubbing, and it contained no abrasive material. In 1936, the company's research department developed and added to the product an ingredient which imparted a light, fluffy texture to textile products washed in a mild solution of Rill. Recognizing the problem of keeping such articles as baby clothes, towels, and blankets soft through repeated washings, the company had promoted Rill both as a cleanser and as a laundry wash water additive since 1937. Over the years, about 50 percent of the company's advertising had featured the product solely as a cleanser, 30 percent as a laundry additive, and 20 percent as a dual-purpose product.

Rill was nationally distributed in a concentrated form in three can sizes—4 ounces, 8 ounces, and 1 pound. Six other nationally distributed cleansers and two nationally distributed laundry additives posed formidable competition.

The product had sold well during the earlier years, but during the past five years unit sales had declined considerably apparently because of competition, although dollar volume over this period had remained fairly constant.

Company and agency personnel were in basic disagreement as to whether the product should be promoted as a cleanser, a laundry additive, or a dual-purpose product. In order to formulate marketing and advertising strategy for the coming year, the agency personnel believed it was necessary to supplement the quantitative information they had on unit sales, outlets, margins, and distribution with information of a more qualitative nature on consumer attitudes toward the product, usage patterns, and opinions on different product characteristics such as strength or concentration, odor, and package size.

This case was written by C. B. Johnston, dean and professor of marketing, University of Western Ontario. Used with permission.

In November 1979, Mr. Roberts and his staff had drawn up a research proposal which they had forwarded to six marketing research
firms for detailed information regarding the following:

1. An appraisal of the proposal and suggestions for any changes.
2. A price quotation on the project (*a*) as outlined and (*b*) including
   any suggested changes.
3. A brief description of the staff who would handle the project.
4. Time required for preparation, implementation, tabulation, and
   final presentation.
5. Pilot testing suggested.
6. Detailed explanation of suggested sample size.
7. Information on the firm's executive personnel, interviewing staff,
   and the projects handled over the preceding two years.

The research proposal contained a description of the product's marketing problems, the objectives of the proposed research, broad suggestions regarding research methodology, and a proposed questionnaire.

In his proposal, Mr. Roberts outlined the major marketing problems
as follows:

1. We really want to know how many people would buy Rill because
   (*a*) it is a cleanser, (*b*) it is a laundry additive, or (*c*) it is a dual-
   purpose product.
2. How do people buy products like Rill? Is it better to have a strong
   product or a weaker one? What size package should we have?
   Should it smell like soap or like perfume? At what price should it
   be retailing?
3. Do people see Rill as being a good, averge, or poor product? What
   do they like about it? What don't they like about it?
4. Do people want a one-use product or a multi-use product?

By early in January, Mr. Roberts had received the submission of all
six marketing research firms requested to bid on the job.

Three of these firms were eliminated after preliminary consideration of their submissions revealed either inadequate staffs, superfi-
cial recommendations, or excessively high costs.

In considering the three remaining firms, Mr. Roberts felt that he
was hampered by his lack of knowledge of the techniques proposed
by two of the firms and by his inability to decide whether it was
reasonable to expect that a detailed plan could be drawn up from the
information he had provided in his proposal.

Two of the firms under consideration, National Research Associates
and The Progressive Research Group, had outlined quite comprehensive plans for the research. The third, H. J. Clifford Research, had
merely stated that it would not attempt to formulate any research
plans from what it considered inadequate information. It believed that
the only way a detailed plan could be formulated was "through a

continuing cooperation, based on mutual confidence, between the research firm, the advertising agency, and the client."

Mr. Roberts knew that many marketing research executives considered the third firm to be the outstanding marketing research company in the country and because of this, he did not believe it could be overlooked.

SUBMISSION OF NATIONAL RESEARCH ASSOCIATES

INTRODUCTION

The present research proposal is based upon the assumption that it is crucial to obtain answers to the following marketing problems:

1. Is it advisable to continue to promote Rill as a multipurpose product?
2. If it is, should its various uses be promoted simultaneously or separately, and what are the promotional approaches which would be most effective?
3. If it is not advisable to continue its promotion as a multipurpose product, for what uses could Rill be most successfully promoted?
4. What would be the most effective promotional approaches for the uses decided upon?
5. Would it be advisable to launch another product, or possibly the same product under a different name, for either of its uses?
6. What are the ways in which Rill distribution, packaging, pricing, and merchandising could be improved?

RESEARCH OBJECTIVES

To be able to plan a sound and effective marketing policy for Rill it will be essential to know:

1. The present market position of Rill in relation to its competitors in each of the fields in which it is used.
2. The reasons why Rill is in its present position in each of these markets.

I. Consumer habits and practices

The study will provide as complete a description as possible of the cleanser and laundry additive markets. Data will be provided in regard to (1) users and nonusers, (2) brand usage, (3) purchasing habits, and (4) usage habits.

This information will be cross-analyzed by age, socioeconomic status, community size, and level of education of the respondent.

II. Consumer attitudes, opinions, and motivations

The study will thoroughly explore the underlying reasons for the market strengths and weaknesses of Rill in each of the usage categories as completely as possible under the broad headings of:

1. The underlying attractions or resistances to using any product for each of the purposes with which Rill is concerned.
2. The comparative strength of attractions to using Rill and to using competing brands for each of these purposes.
3. The comparative strength of resistances to using Rill relative to competing brands.

Some of the specific topics which will be investigated under these general headings are discussed below:

1. The perceived uses of Rill and its major competitors.
2. Factors affecting the perception of Rill, i.e., confusion regarding usage, incompatibility of uses, one use more efficient than the other, and where the attitudes toward the product originated.
3. Attributes of the most desirable product for each of the uses.
4. Common knowledge of the attributes of various brands now on the market.
5. Associations evoked by the brand name Rill and the brand names of competing products.

III. Consumer knowledge of and attitudes toward relevant advertising

1. How far the terms and phrases currently used in promoting Rill and competing brands are seen as (*a*) meaningful, and (*b*) appropriate to the product and its uses.
2. What copy points and adjectives might be most effective for the promotion of each use.

IV. An evaluation of the advertising themes and approaches used by Rill

The research will attempt to determine whether the themes and approaches used in past and present Rill advertising are likely to operate toward overcoming resistances to Rill and capitalizing on sources of attraction.

V. An assessment of the Rill package

The Rill package will be tested to determine:

1. Its visual effectiveness as evidenced by its attention-getting ability, its legibility, its memorability, and its apparent size.
2. Its psychological effect on the consumer's perception of the brand.

METHODOLOGY

Market survey. Face-to-face interviews will be conducted with 2,275 homemakers who will be asked to give factual information about the products they use for each purpose. This survey will show the competitive position of Rill but will not attempt to provide "reasons why."

Intensive interview study. The "reasons why" Rill is in its present position will be explored in 200 1½- to 2-hour depth interviews which will attempt to discover attitudes, perceptions, and feelings toward the product and its uses.

The depth interview is designed to prompt the revelation of true attitudes and reasons for them by employing projective techniques which, instead of emphasizing personal behavior, invite comment on the behavior of others.

In-depth interviewing takes place in a relaxed, informal atmosphere. Interviews are usually conducted in the respondent's home, and her verbatim responses to questions are noted.

The interview schedule contains a large number of open-ended and close-ended queries.

In addition, it employs a variety of techniques, most of which are taken from or patterned after standard psychological tests. A description of some of these techniques is given below.

1. *The Personification Test.* This is essentially an extension of the projective technique employed in psychological testing. It involves an attempt on the part of the respondent to describe certain products in human terms. Such an approach provides an opportunity for the expression of attitudes and opinions not otherwise easily obtainable.

2. *The Thematic Apperception Test (TAT).* Like the Personification Test, this test is similar to the TAT in psychological projective testing. It consists of presenting to the respondent an unstructured drawing of a particular situation and asking him to "make up a story" of what is happening.

3. *Word-association tests.* Respondents are asked to relate what comes to mind when a given word or phrase is read to them. This technique aids in throwing light on areas which may warrant fuller investigation.

4. *The Semantic Differential Test.* This method, developed by us, has been designed to provide insights and information in regard to the perception of company and product attributes.

Fundamentally, the test consists of having the respondent rate a series of products on specially designed scales. The scales are so designed as to provide an extremely sensitive measure in regard to many dimensions as applied to the various products.

The manner in which these data (along with the data obtained through the use of other techniques) are analyzed makes it possible to determine:

A. The extent to which a given product's image is correlated with the perceived "ideal" product.
B. The desirable direction of change in the perceived product attributes, if such change is found necessary.

Other techniques which may be employed include: (*a*) rank-ordering tests, (*b*) sentence completion tests, (*c*) forced choice tests, (*d*) paired comparison tests, and (*e*) true-false tests.

Laboratory study. Our visual laboratory is equipped to evaluate the relative effectiveness of various merchandising and advertising stimuli. By means of specially designed instruments it will be possible to evaluate the relative effectiveness of the Rill package and label in comparison with those of major competitors.

The various tests which will be conducted include:

1. Attention-getting tests.
2. Product recognition tests.
3. Brand identification tests.
4. Visibility and legibility tests.
5. Memorability tests.
6. Apparent size tests.
7. Color preference and association tests.

SAMPLE

Market survey. For the purposes of economy it is suggested that a quota-controlled, weighted, national sample of 2,275 housewives be employed. The accompanying table presents an unweighted sample in proportion to household figures and the proposed weighted sample (see Exhibit 1).

Exhibit 1

| | Rural | | | | Urban | | Total | |
| | Farm | | Nonfarm | | | | | |
	Unweighted	Weighted	Unweighted	Weighted	Unweighted	Weighted	Unweighted	Weighted
Southeast	44	44	76	76	132	132	252	252
Northeast	101	101	110	110	614	614	825	825
Midwest	126	63	139	70	837	436	1,102	569
West	179	90	107	53	324	162	610	305
South Central	22	22	60	60	242	242	324	324
Total	472	320	492	369	2,149	1,586	3,113	2,275

The unweighted sample exceeds the number of interviews necessary to ensure reasonable reliability.

However, to allow for a cross analysis of white and black and urban and rural respondents, a total of 3,113 interviews would be required. The weighted sample cuts by 50 percent the number of interviews in the Midwest and the West. The data from these areas will be mathematically converted to representative proportions in the final tabulation.

Intensive study. Quota-controlled samples of 450 white and 150 black homemakers will be used.

Laboratory study. The number of respondents varies from test to test, but the samples will be designed to ensure statistical reliability.

FIELD STAFF

Market survey. Our field staff of 455 interviewers located across the country will conduct the interviews and will be specially briefed and trained for this survey.

Intensive study. Our staff of 88 university-trained depth interviewers will conduct an average of seven interviews each.

BRIEF DESCRIPTION OF FIRM

National Research Associates has conducted almost 400 separate and varied research projects since its establishment in 1954. The success of the organization is portrayed by its rapid growth from a small unknown company to a recognized leader in the field in the United States. Further attestation has been the establishment of "continuing relationships" with many clients. The company is an "official training ground" for graduate students in the Department of Social Psychology at a prominent university.

The following individuals will be involved in this project:

R. J. Morrison, Ph.D., research coordinator and major client and agency contact; academic training—B.Sc., M.Sc., and Ph.D., 1944 to 1959, major universities; research experience—wide experience in research as study director, consultant, and research associate in four U.S. universities from 1944 to 1956; teaching experience—seven years of lecturing in psychology at two American universities.

A. Milton, study director; graduate in economics with 10 years' experience in the research field, including 3 years with a prominent United Kingdom research firm and a number of years with other English companies.

H. W. Rolland, associate study director; senior staff psychologist who will coordinate the intensive study phases of the research; M.Sc. working on Ph.D.

R. W. Brown, associate study director; university graduate in sociology and statistics—10 years' experience in research—will handle tabulation and statistical analysis.

(Four additional staff members were listed, all of whom were university graduates.)

TIME AND COST ESTIMATES

The research can be completed in 12 weeks after finalization of the research design. The cost is estimated at $62,000, 50 percent payable upon initiation of the study and 50 percent upon completion.

SUBMISSION OF THE PROGRESSIVE RESEARCH GROUP

NATURE OF THE PROBLEM

It is possible that the two major uses of Rill may, in combination, affect the market negatively. Women may think of it primarily in one sense or the other, and those who regard it as a cleanser may not be willing to use it as a laundry additive, or vice versa.

In addition to this possible overall problem, there are certain marketing specifics which may also be important.

1. Is the product right?
2. What about its physical characteristics (strength or concentration, odor, physical form)?
3. What about its psychological connotations?
4. What about the packaging (size of package, nature of package, labeling, and package)?

We propose a consumer study covering the major areas of behavior and attitude, including:

1. Brand personality and image for each of several cleansers (including Rill).
2. Brand personality and image for each of several laundry additive products (including Rill).
3. Habit pattern on home cleaning (including products used).
4. Habit pattern on laundry additives (including products used).

SCOPE OF THE STUDY

We see this as a national study, as it is entirely possible that varying areas may display differing habits and attitudes.

The section of this proposal dealing with the sample will show the reasons underlying our recommendations. We suggest a total of 750 interviews in this consumer study, and the sample will be of a "tight" nature.

THE SAMPLE

Type of sample.   The sample will be of such a nature that it properly represents the homemaker population in terms of region, socioeconomic group, urban-rural, and the like.

The sample design will be a known probability sample. Primary sampling units will be selected proportionately across the country, and randomly selected starting points will be chosen from which a predetermined path of interviewing will be followed.

Size of sample.   We recommend a total sample of 750 housewives.

There are several reasons. The first concerns our belief that no subsample on which results are based should have fewer than 150 cases.

The other reason concerns overall accuracy with a sample of 750 cases. Better than 9 times out of 10, results based on this total sample should be accurate within some 2.4 percent; this level of sampling accuracy on an overall basis seems highly acceptable for the purposes of this particular study.

The numerical distribution of interviews is indicated in the accompanying table (Exhibit 2).

Exhibit 2

	Natural proportional distribution of sample	Proposed sample distribution	Weighting factor	Weighted cases
Southeast	77	125	2	250
Northeast	211	211	3	633
Midwest	265	177	5	885
West	130	130	3	390
South Central	67	107	2	214
Total	750	750		2,372

FIELDWORK

Our field staff is of highest quality. It has been built over a 10-year period, and we spend a sizable amount of money each year on maintenance and development of this staff.

The field staff totals 723 workers, and all states and community sizes are represented.

SUPERVISION

We maintain a staff of 20 salaried regional supervisors across the country. With the exception of a few small, remote areas, this means that every interviewer works under the direct control of a regional supervisor.

QUALIFICATIONS OF INTERVIEWERS

The average interviewer on our staff has been working for the firm for approximately four years. For our consumer work, we make use of women who, on the average, have the following characteristics: (1) they fall between the upper middle and lower middle socioeconomic group; (2) they have completed some or all of high school; (3) they are extroverted; and (4) they are above the average in intelligence.

THE QUESTIONNAIRE

It is difficult to evaluate your questionnaire without considerable field testing. In the present case, there has been no effort at all to do so. We would save our "criticism" for (*a*) detailed discussion with the agency and (*b*) considerable field testing.

We have conducted a group interview with the subject matter pretty much in its present sequence, though the questions asked were more of an open-minded variety than contained in the questionnaire draft submitted with your specifications.

We do know that the sequence of questions will work. We also know that women can and will answer these questions, despite their nature, if the right approach is used. We further know that while the questionnaire form is quite lengthy, it is still feasible in terms of its length. So it is not as if we know nothing about feasibility of the instrument.

FIELD TESTING

As a result of the group interview, it will be possible—though we have not taken the time to utilize it in such a manner—to study the consumer response to the interview so carefully as to make sure that the phrasings used in the questionnaire follow the words and phrases used in the consumer's actual thinking. The group interview thus means that we are that much further ahead in the phrasings of this questionnaire, even though it so far has not been utilized for such a purpose.

We plan a field test—or perhaps several—with a total of 100 homemakers distributed among people of varying socioeconomic groups, largely concentrated (for efficiency of handling) in the Chicago Metropolitan Area to make sure that the sequence and phrasing are of such a nature as to be understandable, to get cooperation, and to obtain unbiased replies.

DESCRIPTION OF THE FIRM

The Progressive Research Group began operations in 1948 and, as such, is one of the oldest marketing research companies. Over the years the company has handled a large number of projects and has among its clients many of the largest consumer goods manufacturers.

The company possesses the most advanced computer equipment in the country, and constant improvements are being adopted to speed up and make more economical, complete, and detailed client reports.

The following persons will direct the project:

A. W. Willis, B.A., overall project coordinator; president of The Progressive Research Group and a graduate in economics from a large university.

B. K. Walker, M.B.A., project director and client contact; vice president and a graduate in business administration from a major univerity.

R. C. Moffatt, Ph.D., project adviser; major in sociology—five years' research experience as project director with large U.S. advertising agency before joining The Progressive Research Group in 1957; three years spent as lecturer and consultant at two large American universities

TIME AND COST

Our report should be available 12 weeks after the finalizing of the project details. Our estimate of the cost of this project is $38,900 plus or minus 10 percent. It is our practice to bill one half of the estimated cost at the time of authorization, with the final half billed on delivery of the report.

In discussing these proposals with his assistant, Mr. Jacks, Mr. Roberts wondered whether his own staff could not answer some of the questions if a thorough study of past consumer panel reports were conducted. For some 10 years Bay-Madison had received full reports from an independent research company which ran a consumer panel, but these had only been used for day-to-day planning. Never, for instance, had a long-term, thorough study of the trends in Rill sales been compared with the various advertising and promotional campaigns the company had used or with the various price levels that had existed from time to time. Mr. Jacks was particularly enthusiastic about the idea as he had long maintained that the agency was not getting full value from the panel data. He said that he would personally like to work on such a project.

Mr. Roberts, in considering the idea further, estimated that such an analysis could be done for approximately $9,000. He had checked with the research company and found that all past reports were kept on automatic data processing cards. The company was most interested in the idea as an experiment and estimated that all the data required by the agency could be compiled for about $2,500. Mr. Roberts thought he could release Mr. Jacks from his other duties for a period of two months and that the cost of Mr. Jacks' salary, statistical and secretarial help, and other expenses would not exceed $5,500.

It was at this point that Mr. Roberts found himself in January 1980. He knew a decision had to be made quickly as the client was very anxious to get the Rill situation straightened away.

Case 6–4

Morning Treat Coffee Bags

William Brandt, marketing manager to the Morning Treat Coffee Company, was trying to decide if the company's newest product was ready for a test market. The product—real, fresh coffee in a bag similar to a tea bag—had been tested by a consumer panel for several months. The results were encouraging, and suggested that the product would have appeal because it offered the convenience of instant coffee combined with the aroma and flavor of fresh coffee. Mr. Brandt was concerned about going into test marketing without a better understanding of the types of coffee drinkers most likely to use the new coffee bag.

BACKGROUND

Approximately 2 billion pounds of coffee were sold annually through food stores in the United States. About 35–40 percent of total

From Harper W. Boyd, Jr., Ralph Westfall, and Stanley F. Stasch, *Marketing Research: Text and Cases,* 5th ed. (Homewood, Ill.: Richard D. Irwin, 1981), pp. 576–80.
© 1981 by Richard D. Irwin, Inc.

coffee sales were in the instant or freeze-dried form, which was a growing segment of the coffee market. This growth in instant and freeze-dried coffee was due to the increased popularity of convenience foods. The demand for convenience in beverages was reflected in the fact that over 90 percent of the loose tea sold in the United States was packaged in individual bags.

It had taken more than 20 years to develop a process for packaging coffee in individual bags. Tea can be packaged in a cellulose fiber bag placed inside an individual paper bag because it is an organic material that is relatively unaffected by exposure to air. However, coffee is a more complex substance, consisting of oils, solids, and gases that are affected by oxygen. Because of its complex chemical composition, freshly ground coffee cannot be packaged in a tea bag. The newly developed coffee bagging process used a specially developed synthetic fabric which sealed freshly ground coffee in a bag containing no oxygen. The shelf life of the coffee in the new bag was in excess of one year.

ISSUES

Mr. Brandt and other members of the marketing staff believed that Morning Treat Coffee Bags would appeal to convenience-oriented consumers. It was felt that heavy drinkers of fresh coffee were not likely to be included in this group because of the ingrained habit of brewing a large pot of coffee. The target groups were thought to be moderate and light drinkers of fresh coffee and all drinkers of instant and freeze-dried coffee. The marketing staff believed that many users of instant and freeze-dried coffee liked the convenience but that they were less than satisfied with the flavor, taste, and aroma of that beverage. Heavy users of instant and freeze-dried coffee were considered to be the main market for the new product. Some staff members were concerned, however, that the coffee bags might appeal most to a relatively unimportant market segment—households of only one, two, or three individuals who consumed small quantities of fresh coffee.

Identifying the best market segments for coffee bags and the reasons why some segments would be attracted to coffee bags were thought to be critical issues which had to be resolved before going into test markets. The J. M. South Company, a marketing research firm, was invited to propose the research that would clarify these issues. An abbreviated version of its proposal is shown in Exhibit 1.

Exhibit 1
Proposal

Purpose

The purpose is to identify the market segment or segments which include the most potential users of the new coffee bags and also to identify the basic reasons for the product's appeal to those segments. Specific measures of respondent identification will include whether they drink fresh or instant/freeze-dried coffee, and the amount of coffee consumed. Because of the convenience aspect, coffee bags may appeal most to single persons and families with two working parents. Therefore, potential users will also be identified relative,to the number of adults in the household and their employment status.

Design

The following four-point research design is proposed.

1. Use the U.S. Postal Service to distribute free packages containing three coffee bags to households on selected blocks in selected zip code areas in the same city or cities to be used as test markets. Each package of sample coffee bags will include a cover letter explaining that the product is new, the samples are free, and the respondents are invited to try them at their convenience.
2. Follow-up personal interviews will be made three to six weeks after the sample mailing. Persons selected as respondents will be adults who received and tried the new coffee bags.
3. Respondents will be identified as potential users or potential nonusers, depending upon how they score on the product-attitude rating scale to be used in the proposed questionnaire. (That scale is described below.)
4. All respondents (both potential users and potential nonusers) will be classified according to three descriptive measures: (*a*) amount of coffee consumed—three or more cups daily (heavy) or less than three cups daily (light); (*b*) form of coffee consumed—fresh only, instant/freeze-dried only, or both; and (*c*) number of working adults in the household—single adult, one working parent, two working parents, or others. Thus, respondents will be classified according to amount and form of coffee consumed and number of adults in the household and their employment status. Tabulation will consist of counting the number of respondents falling into each category and calculating the percentage of potential coffee bag users in each category. These findings will identify the most important market segments for coffee bags.

Questionnaire

A four-part questionnaire will be used during the personal interview.

1. Questions will measure the type and amount of coffee consumed and necessary demographic information.
2. Respondents will rate their regular coffee drink on each of the following seven traits. (Figures shown in parentheses are the weights to be given to each rating. The weights are used in the analysis discussed below.)

Exhibit 1 (*continued*)

Coffee trait	Very important (+3)	Important (+2)	Slightly important (+1)	Not important (0)
Aroma	_____	_____	_____	_____
Convenience	_____	_____	_____	_____
Flavor/taste	_____	_____	_____	_____
Freshness	_____	_____	_____	_____
No messy cleanup	_____	_____	_____	_____
Price	_____	_____	_____	_____
Strength	_____	_____	_____	_____

3. Respondents who tried coffee bags will compare them with their regular coffee drink on each of the above seven traits, using the five-point scale shown in the following table.

	Coffee bags are definitely better (+2)	Coffee bags are slightly better (+1)	Coffee bags are neither better nor worse (+0)	Regular drink is slightly better (−1)	Regular drink is definitely better (−2)
Aroma	_____	_____	_____	_____	_____
Convenience	_____	_____	_____	_____	_____
Flavor/taste	_____	_____	_____	_____	_____
Freshness	_____	_____	_____	_____	_____
No messy cleanup	_____	_____	_____	_____	_____
Price	_____	_____	_____	_____	_____
Strength	_____	_____	_____	_____	_____

4. Respondents will be asked their "intentions to buy" coffee bags on a five-point scale: very likely to buy, likely to buy, don't know, not likely to buy, will not buy.

Analysis

1. *For each of the seven traits* measured in questionnaire items 2 and 3, the following weighting system will be used to determine a "score" for each *respondent* relative to each trait. The respondent's "score" is the figure shown at the intersection of the appropriate row and column.

Exhibit 1 (*continued*)

The respondent indicated in questionnaire item 2 that the trait is:	In questionnaire item 3 the respondent rates coffee bags on this trait as:				
	Definitely better (+2)	**Slightly better** (+1)	**Neither** (0)	**Slightly worse** (−1)	**Definitely worse** (−2)
Very important (+3)	+6	+3	0	−3	−6
Important (+2)	+4	+2	0	−2	−4
Slightly important (+1)	+2	+1	0	−1	−2
Not important (0)	0	0	0	0	0

Thus, if a respondent indicates freshness is "very important" in questionnaire item 2 (weight of +3) and that coffee bags rate "definitely better" than his/her regular coffee drink (+2), the respondent is given a score of +6 (+3 times +2) on freshness. If aroma is "important" (+2) and the respondent rates coffee bags as "slightly worse" (−1), the respondent is given a score of −2.

2. Respondents will be given a score on each trait. These seven scores will be summed to determine "total score," which will lie somewhere between +42 and −42.
3. The respondent's "total score" and "intention to buy" coffee bags (from questionnaire item 4) will classify her/him as a potential user or not a potential user, according to the following rules.

Potential user	**Not potential user**
a. Total "score" is > +12 and respondent *answers* "very likely to buy" or "likely to buy" coffee bags.	c. "Score" is > +12 and respondent *does not answer* "very likely to buy" or "likely to buy" coffee bags.
b. Total "score" is between +6 and +12 and respondent *answers* "very likely to buy" coffee bags.	d. "Score" is between +6 and +12 and respondent *does not answer* "very likely to buy" coffee bags.
	e. "Score" is +5 or less.

Exhibit 1 (*concluded*)

4. All respondents who tried coffee bags will be classified into one (and only one) of the following cells.

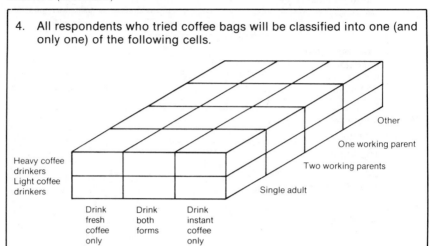

5. Each cell will have a total *number* of respondents and the *percentage* who have been classified as "potential users" of coffee bags. This information will identify the more important market segments which find the new coffee bags appealing.
6. Answers from respondents *in the more important market segments* will then be reanalyzed to identify that aspect, or those aspects, of coffee bags which they find most appealing. This reanalysis will identify the coffee traits which these respondents consider important or very important *and* for which they rated coffee bags as better than their regular coffee drink. Those are the product characteristics which potential users find most appealing.

Case 6–5

TLT (B)

In April 1979, the future officers of TLT (Tender Loving Transport) met to discuss the feasibility study conducted for the proposed limousine service. Present were Bill Ranford, marketing professor, Knox Gary, realtor and Jim Newman, Thoroughbred breeder. This unlikely group meeting in Oxford, Mississippi, was seriously contemplating a limousine service to run from Oxford to Memphis International Airport. At this juncture, they were discussing the questions that were answered by the feasibility study and with new information, deciding whether the limousine service was a viable concept.

BACKGROUND

Last January, these three potential entrepreneurs had agreed upon the need for a limousine service from Oxford to Memphis International Airport. All three had suffered from the poor airline service offered by Republic Airlines and believed that the community could support another public carrier to make connections at Memphis, which was a regional hub airport. Since Oxford was some 80 miles from the Memphis airport, private automobile use provided the major form of transportation and the major competition to such a service. Although a major bus line, Continental Trailways, also served Oxford, it did not stop at the airport but went directly to the central downtown terminal, from which there was a $10 cab ride to the airport. With the rising cost of gasoline and parking at the airport, the time seemed right for an additional public carrier.

As mentioned before, Oxford was 80 miles southeast of the Memphis airport. Although a university town with a population of 25,000 persons in the immediate metropolitan area, Oxford was not totally dependent on the University of Mississippi for employment. There were several industrial plants in the area which employed over 1,500 people. The federal government had its regional headquarters for the state in Oxford and had a Soil Conservation Service lab and Forest Service installation in the town. There were also a disproportionately large number of doctors serving the regional medical center and a large number of attorneys serving federal, state, and local governments. All in all, Oxford was a unique environment with its mixture of professionals, as well as the many small business owners and retirees that it attracted.

It was in this setting that Ranford, Newman, and Gary had proposed initiating a limousine service for residents and visitors alike. The concept was to have comfortable and convenient service (a customized van with captain's chairs and a couch) between Oxford and the Memphis airport. A preliminary cost estimate was developed (see Exhibit 1), and they decided (or Ranford did) that they needed to have a feasibility study done on the demand-side factor.

THE APRIL 10TH MEETING

"Well, here it is," said Ranford, as he dropped three copies of the feasibility study on the desk. "My marketing class spent over two months working on this project, and I think it gives us the information we have been looking for."

Exhibit 1
Estimated cost of operating limousine service

	Per year	Per month
Fixed costs:		
Vehicle $11,000 ÷ 2 (two-year life)	$5,500.00	$ 458.33
License—ICC	450.00	37.50
Attorney fees	1,100.00	91.66
State tags	200.00	16.67
Advertising (prestart)	500.00	41.67
Total	$7,750.00	$ 645.83
Variable costs		
(two trips/day—30-day month):		
Driver salaries		$ 900.00
Fuel		900.00
Maintenance		100.00
Advertising		50.00
Printing		50.00
Commissions to travel agency		100.00
Total		$2,100.00

"I am not well versed in marketing research," responded Gary. "Could you go over how the study was done and who the people were that were interviewed to get the results?"

"I'd be glad to if you really want to know," said Ranford. "The project was fairly straightforward and really didn't involve anything very sophisticated. I'll be as brief as possible, and then we can look at the results together."

Ranford went on and summarized the research methodology involved in the feasibility study as best he could to his uninitiated listeners.

Methodology

A questionnaire was developed that would hopefully hit on the major questions which needed to be answered (see Exhibit 2). The questionnaire was a structured instrument and designed to be used for either personal or telephone interviewing. The questions probed the level of satisfaction with present service, frequency of use, time of departures and arrivals, usage of a limousine service, prices for fares, and pertinent demographic characteristics.

The survey was conducted by telephone on three sample populations: (1) professors, (2) professionals, and (3) students. These groups were believed to make up the bulk of travelers between Oxford and the Memphis airport. Sequential sampling was used to reach the university population, the names having been drawn from the univer-

Exhibit 4
Plane travelers' responses

	No	Yes
Are you satisfied with the airline's dependability between Oxford and Memphis?		
Professionals	55%	45%
Students	100	0
Professors	100	0
Are the airline's flight times convenient for making your connecting flights?		
Professionals	73	27
Students	50	50
Professors	100	0
Do you feel that the airline's prices are reasonable between Oxford and Memphis?		
Professionals	100	0
Students	50	50
Professors	72	28

Exhibit 5
Frequency of travel

How many times per year do you fly out of Memphis?	
Professors	6–8
Students	2–3
Professionals	3–4
What percentage of your trips are business-related?	
Professors	90%
Students	7
Professionals	78
Do you normally travel alone?	
Yes	63%
No	37%
How many people normally travel with you?	
Professors	2.3 average
Students	4.7
Professionals	1.2

Exhibit 6
Time of flight departures

	12 A.M.– 9 A.M.	9 A.M.– 12 P.M.	12 P.M.– 2 P.M.	2 P.M.– 5 A.M.	5 P.M.– 12 A.M.
Students	29%	25%	8%	29%	8%
Professionals	18	36	0	9	0
Professors	11	30	11	18	5
Total	58%	91%	19%	56%	13%

What times of the day do
  your flights normally
  arrive in Memphis:					

Students	0%	17%	8%	58%	16%
Professionals	0	18	9	18	18
Professors	0	2	7	43	21
Total	0%	37%	24%	119%	55%

Exhibit 7
Airline departures and arrivals in Memphis

	12 A.M.– 9 A.M.–	9 A.M.– 12 P.M.–	12 P.M.– 2 P.M.–	2 P.M.– 5 P.M.–	5 P.M.– 12 A.M.–
Frequency of flight departures from Memphis per week*					
Delta	82	73	39	62	93
Braniff	23	25	8	16	31
Allegheny	13	41	0	32	17
Piedmont	21	6	0	5	4
Republic	27	29	21	51	82
Frequency of flight arrivals into Memphis per week*					
Delta	68	41	48	60	126
Braniff	3	35	18	31	40
Allegheny	0	39	0	36	20
Piedmont	0	8	0	5	10
Republic	48	31	27	42	98

* This information has been taken from published airline schedules.

"That's a nice report," began Newman, "but my previous experience with Braniff does not give me a lot of faith in marketing research. Our research staff was wrong as many times as they were right. How much confidence do we put in these figures since our money is riding on the outcome?"

"Jim's got a point, Bill," chimed in Gary. "What does this mean in terms of starting our business? Should we or shouldn't we make the 'go' decision?"

Exhibit 8
Days of Departure and arrival

	Mon.–Wed.	Thurs.–Fri.	Sat.–Sun.	Varies
What is your usual day of departure from Memphis?				
Students	8%	75%	21%	21%
Professionals	27	0	0	64
Professors	9	27	5	59
Total	44%	102%	26%	144%
What is your usual day of arrival in Memphis?				
Students	13%	8%	58%	21%
Professionals	2	9	9	64
Professors	0	9	32	59
Total	15%	26%	99%	144%

Exhibit 9
Use and cost of proposed service

Would you consider using a limousine service between Oxford and Memphis?				
Yes	76%			
No	24%			

	$30	$25	$20	Under
Would you pay $30, $25, $20 or under for round-trip service?				
Professors	43%	34%	19%	4%
Students	66	7	7	20
Professionals	66	0	11	23

Case 6–6

Pacific Coastal Federal Savings and Loan

Pacific Coastal Federal Savings and Loan Association is one of the largest savings and loan associations in the United States. Headquartered in San Francisco, it has 56 offices throughout California. In 1980, Pacific Coastal Federal's management was making preparations for offering NOW account service. NOW accounts are basically checking accounts which pay interest on the account balance. Pacific Coastal Federal's management knew that the federal government would shortly authorize banks and savings and loans to offer such accounts. Previously, Pacific Coastal (and all other California S&Ls) had been prohibited from offering any form of consumer checking accounts.

Although Pacific Coastal Federal's annual advertising budget was about $4 million, its management had historically spent little on marketing or advertising research. When research was conducted, it was usually directed by a staff person in either the marketing or advertising department. Lisa McClean, an assistant to the vice president of marketing, was given the task of developing a consumer research project to study the area of NOW accounts. After a week's work she submitted the following research proposal.

NOW Account Research

I. *Problem situation*
   1. *Definition*
       NOW accounts are interest paying transaction accounts. The public views them as simply interest-paying checking accounts.
   2. *National situation*
       It is believed that sometime in 1980 Congress will allow NOW accounts to be offered by savings and loans throughout the United States, including California. If legislated, the tentative date for allowed offering will be January 1, 1981. Presently NOW accounts are authorized only in New York, New Jersey, and the New England states.
   3. *California public*
       The greatest problem surrounding NOW accounts is that much of the general California public does not know what NOW accounts are. To motivate consumers to open NOW accounts at Pacific Coastal Federal, the association must first build awareness, educate, show advantages of NOW accounts over other types of traditional checking accounts or telephone-transfer savings accounts, and show advantages of Pacific Coastal Federal's NOW accounts over other local financial institutions' NOW accounts.

4. *Secondary research*
    a. *Demographics*

    A January 1979 survey of persons in 1,714 locations outside of New England, New York, and New Jersey revealed that the idea of a savings and loan checking account appealed to younger, more educated, higher-income customers. Six in 10 with family income of more than $30,000 preferred an interest-bearing checking account to transferring funds back and forth between checking and savings. White-collar workers and professionals found the interest-bearing checking accounts more attractive than did blue-collar workers or retired persons. Those in cities with populations over 500,000 found NOW accounts more attractive than did those living in towns under 15,000—with the percentage of appeal growing in relation to size of the city. In a survey by the U.S. League of Savings Associations, data showed that savings and loan association savings customers are heavier users of most types of financial services than are other Americans. For instance, only 58 percent of all adult Americans have checking accounts as compared with 88 percent of association savers. Twenty percent of Americans have stocks or bonds compared with 60 percent of association savers. Savers are heavier purchasers of mutual fund shares (20 percent versus 3 percent), U.S. Savings bonds (40 percent versus 23 percent), and life insurance (81 percent versus 51 percent). According to the league's survey, the income difference between Americans and American savers at savings and loans is not large enough to explain the much heavier usage of checking accounts, etc. The league attributes this greater usage to personal factors, such as greater financial sophistication, more commitment to investment, or more concern with financial security. Along with other demographic information, this leads us to believe that our own customers will be a good market and we can hypothesize that savings and loan customers' awareness levels of NOW accounts will be higher than those of noncustomers.

    Do the UNIDEX demographics of persons interested in NOW accounts differ from those of checking account users? In a U.S. League survey of savings and loan customers who have checking accounts, the highest percentage of persons with checking accounts were persons between the ages of 25 and 65 who held professional, executive, managerial, supervisory, or self-employed jobs. The percentage of persons holding checking accounts increased directly with age (for example, 88 percent with incomes $5,000–9,999, 94 percent with income $15,000–19,999, and 97 percent with incomes over $25,000).

    Pacific Coastal Federal's California research may be able to determine any specific demographic differences between current checking account holders and persons interested in NOW accounts.

    b. *Competition*

    Research in existing NOW markets (by the Federal Reserve Bank, the Federal Home Loan Bank, the Federal Deposit Insurance Corporation, and "local" institutions such as the New York Reserve Bank) show that savings and loans are holding smaller market shares on NOW's than banks, and smaller average account balances.

However, according to a 1979 survey done by Anita Miller, a recently resigned member of the Federal Home Loan Bank Board, the savings and loans currently offering NOWs are relatively small in terms of both asset size and market share. She felt that California savings and loans would get a much larger share of the market (in comparison with banks) than the current savings and loans.

In addition to local banking competition, Pacific Coastal Federal will receive competition from other savings and loans. Because the start-up costs of NOW accounts are predicted to be substantial, and because 1980 is not expected to be a very profitable year for the savings and loan industry in general, only the larger savings and loans in the state will provide strong competition in the battle for NOW account market shares.

II. *Research objectives*
  1. Evaluate high potential markets for NOW accounts.
  2. Determine consumer awareness levels of NOW accounts to estimate amount of consumer education needed in advertising, promotion, and publicity.
  3. Determine characteristics of California consumers most receptive to NOW accounts (age, income, sex, profession, and residence).
  4. Determine competitive pricing strategy for NOW accounts and consumer preferences for NOW account features.
  5. Determine nature of trade-offs consumers will make in selection of NOW accounts.
  6. Determine best "image" of NOW accounts to be promoted.

Information needs
  1. Determine inadequacies of checking accounts.
  2. Determine popular types of checking accounts.
  3. Determine whether NOW accounts represent improvement over inadequacies of checking accounts.
  4. Determine whether other types of accounts are competitive. Determine what may affect use of the account.
  5. Determine important features of NOW accounts and rank of importance.
  6. Determine demographic profile of respondents interested in NOW accounts.
  7. Determine what percentage of persons are aware of NOW accounts.
  8. Determine awareness levels toward NOW accounts.
  9. Determine differences between customers and noncustomers in views toward NOW accounts.

III. *Sampling*
    Telephone surveys allow each of the three major sampling groups to be surveyed in the same way, because sampling units for each one include phone numbers. The three major sampling frames are: (*a*) Pa-

cific Coastal Federal customers, (*b*) other savings and loan customers, and (*c*) non–savings and loan customers.

Categories *a* and *b* must be broken down into *loan* customers and *savings* customers because exploratory research showed that the two groups are often mutually exclusive. Two hundred persons from each group will be interviewed, with the first two groups being broken down further into 100 savings customer interviews and 100 loan customer interviews. This is more simply explained by the diagram:

Pacific Coastal Federal customers	Other S&L customers	Non S&L customers
Random sample from savings list: quota—100	Random sample digit dialing—100 savings	Random sample digit dialing—200
Random sample from loan list: quota—100	Random sample digit dialing—100 loan	

1. Because some savings list customers have loans, and *vice versa,* any savings list customer who also has (a) loan(s) is a valid interviewee. This is true of the opposite circumstance as well.
2. Because savings and loan customers in general may have both savings accounts and loans at savings and loans, up to 35 persons in each category may be interviewed if they have both savings accounts and loans at a savings and loan.
3. The third category is limited to persons who do not, at *the time of the interview,* have an account or a loan at a savings and loan.

Six hundred persons were decided upon because this allows a large enough number of interviews in each category breakdown for purposes of comparison. Precision in sample size is not needed here because this is a general survey of attitudes toward NOW accounts as opposed to a projection of number of persons intending to purchase, etc.

The sampling plan is basically a stratified sampling of each group, accomplished through random sampling of a list of loan customers and savings customers (until quota is reached) and random digit dialing to get a quota of other savings and loan customers and non–savings and loan customers. (See Exhibit 1 for the proposed data collection form.)

IV. *Time schedule and budget*
1. *Budget*
     Six hundred interviews at $12 each totals $7,200. This cost includes staff costs, research time, computer time costs, coding costs, secretarial costs, and printing of code manuals and surveys. Any sophisticated training tools (such as an audiovisual presentation on telephone interviewing, etc.) would be an extra incurred cost.
2. *Time schedule*
     Two telephone interviewers working three 40-hour weeks should be able to complete the quota of 600 surveys. (Approximately 10 to 20 extra surveys in each of the five sampling categories will be completed to use as replacement surveys where needed.) This esti-

mate is based on three completed surveys per hour, allowing extra time per hour for no response, wrong numbers, etc.

Prior to that, the interviewers should be given a one-day seminar in data collection training, including training in telephone interview techniques and specific background about NOW accounts and what this survey is attempting to accomplish. The interviewer should be provided with an easy-to-read manual on NOW accounts, so that any respondent questions about NOW accounts may be answered.

Exhibit 1
Proposed data collection form*

HELLO, THIS IS M_____OF THE FINANCIAL SURVEY COMPANY. I AM DOING A CONSUMER SURVEY ON A NEW FINANCIAL SERVICE THAT THE FEDERAL GOVERNMENT MAY ALLOW TO BE OFFERED IN CALIFORNIA WITHIN THE NEXT YEAR. HAVE YOU BEEN APPROACHED IN THE LAST THREE WEEKS BY ANYONE DOING A SIMILAR SURVEY? WOULD YOU CONSENT TO ANSWERING A FEW QUESTIONS FOR ME ABOUT BANKING SERVICES? THIS SURVEY IS DESIGNED TO TAKE ONLY A FEW MINUTES OF YOUR TIME AND WILL GIVE YOU AN OPPORTUNITY TO EXPRESS YOUR OPINIONS OF CURRENT BANKING SERVICES.

Screening:

1.   DO YOU HAVE A SAVINGS ACCOUNT AT A SAVINGS AND LOAN ASSOCIATION?
   _____Yes
   _____No
   _____More than one account
   _____Don't know
2.   DO YOU HAVE A LOAN AT A SAVINGS AND LOAN ASSOCIATION?
   _____Yes
   _____No
   _____Don't know

Interviewer: If on Pacific Coastal Federal list, category A.
   If answer to any question is *yes,* category B.
   If answer is *no,* then category C.

		(Possible)	
Interviewer check one	1–100	0–70	1–100
Category A_____	Loan_____	Both_____	Savings_____
Category B_____	Loan_____	Both_____	Savings_____
Category C_____			

Questions:

1.   CURRENTLY, SAVINGS AND LOANS ARE NOT AUTHORIZED TO OFFER CHECKING ACCOUNTS. DO YOU HAVE A CHECKING ACCOUNT AT ANOTHER FINANCIAL INSTITUTION?
   _____No (skip to Q12)
   _____Don't know (skip to Q12)
   _____Says has one at S&L (skip to Q12)
   _____Yes (continue)

---

* Material printed in capital letters is to be read out loud by the interviewer to the interviewee.

Exhibit 1 (*continued*)

2. (If yes) DO YOU KNOW AT WHAT TYPE OF FINANCIAL INSTITUTION IT IS?

    _____Bank   _____Don't know   _____Other

    _____Credit union

3. (If no) HAVE YOU HAD A CHECKING ACCOUNT IN THE PAST?

    If no, continue to question 13

    If yes, WHY DID YOU CLOSE IT?

    _____Not used enough   _____No response/don't

    _____Charges too much   know

    _____Minimum too much

    _____Didn't like the bank (or credit un-
    ion)

4. DO YOU HAVE A TYPE OF CHECKING ACCOUNT FOR WHICH, WHEN MINIMUM BALANCE IS MAINTAINED, NO MONTHLY SERVICE CHARGE OR OTHER FEE IS CHARGED?

    _____No   _____Don't know

    _____Yes

If yes,

5. WHAT IS THE MINIMUM BALANCE REQUIRED?

    _____Less than $100   _____$1,500–$2,000

    _____$100–$499   _____More than $2,000

    _____$500–$999   _____Don't know

    _____$1,000–$1,499

If no,

6. DO YOU HAVE A CHECKING ACCOUNT WITH A MONTHLY SERVICE CHARGE OR OTHER FEE?

    _____No   _____Don't know

    _____Yes

If yes,

7. IS IT A SET FEE PER MONTH, OR IS IT DETERMINED BY THE NUMBER OF CHECKS YOU WRITE?

    _____Set fee

    _____Number of checks

    _____Other

    _____Don't know

If set fee,

8. HOW MUCH IS THE FEE?

    _____$0–$3   _____Don't know

    _____$3.01–$5

    _____$5.01–$10

    _____More than $10

If number of checks,

9. IF IT IS CALCULATED BY THE NUMBER OF CHECKS YOU WRITE, WHAT IS THE CHARGE PER CHECK?

    _____0–5¢

    _____6¢–10¢

    _____11¢–15¢   _____Don't know

    _____16¢–20¢

    _____More than 20¢

If don't know,

Exhibit 1 (*continued*)

10.   WELL, CAN YOU ESTIMATE WHAT THE AVERAGE MONTHLY SERVICE
        CHARGE HAS BEEN DURING THE LAST TWO OR THREE MONTHS ON
        YOUR CHECKING ACCOUNT?
        _____0–$3 per month
        _____$3.01–$5 per month   _____Don't know
        _____$5.01–$10 per month
        _____More than $10 per month

11.   IF YOU COULD CHANGE ANYTHING ABOUT YOUR CHECKING
        ACCOUNT, WHAT WOULD YOU LIKE TO SEE CHANGED?
        Interviewer: Write in comments or check._____
        _____
        _____
        _____Make it free
        _____Pay interest on it
        _____Change cosmetically (shape/color of checks)
        _____Change monthly statement to bimonthly, semimonthly, etc.

        AT THIS POINT, I WOULD LIKE TO ASK YOU A FEW SHORT QUESTIONS
        ABOUT NOW ACCOUNTS. NOW ACCOUNTS ARE CURRENTLY OFFERED IN
        BANKS, SAVINGS BANKS, AND SAVINGS AND LOAN ASSOCIATIONS IN
        NEW YORK, NEW JERSEY, AND THE NEW ENGLAND STATES. CONGRESS
        IS CONSIDERING MAKING THEM LEGAL FOR ALL FINANCIAL INSTITU-
        TIONS IN THE UNITED STATES INCLUDING CALIFORNIA. BASICALLY, NOW
        ACCOUNTS ARE LIKE CHECKING ACCOUNTS, EXCEPT THAT THE CUS-
        TOMER ALSO RECEIVES INTEREST PAYMENTS—AS YOU DO ON A SAV-
        INGS ACCOUNT—RANGING FROM 3 PERCENT TO 6 PERCENT.
        Interviewer: Write any comments made:_____
        _____
        _____

12.   DO YOU THINK MOST PEOPLE HAVE HEARD OF NOW ACCOUNTS?
        _____Yes
        _____Don't know
        _____No
        _____Not sure

13.   HOW ATTRACTIVE DO NOW ACCOUNTS SEEM TO YOU?
        _____VERY ATTRACTIVE
        _____SOMEWHAT ATTRACTIVE
        _____SOMEWHAT UNATTRACTIVE
        _____VERY ATTRACTIVE
        _____Not sure/don't know

14.   WHICH WOULD YOU PREFER? (1) A NOW ACCOUNT WITH THE MAXI-
        MUM INTEREST ALLOWED PAID, SAY, 5 PERCENT, AND A MINIMUM
        BALANCE REQUIREMENT OR (2) A SMALLER AMOUNT OF INTEREST
        PAID, SAY, 3 PERCENT, AND NO MINIMUM BALANCE.
        _____(1)
        _____(2)
        _____No preference

15.   IF YOUR NOW ACCOUNT PAID 5 PERCENT INTEREST, WOULD YOU
        BE WILLING TO KEEP IN IT . . . .
        _____A $500 MINIMUM BALANCE
        _____A $1,000 MINIMUM BALANCE
        _____A $2,000 MINIMUM BALANCE
        _____A $2,500 MINIMUM BALANCE
        _____No minimum balance
        _____Don't know/unsure

Exhibit 1 (*continued*)

16. IF YOUR NOW ACCOUNT PAID 5 PERCENT INTEREST, WHICH OF THESE, IF ANY, WOULD YOU BE WILLING TO PAY IN CHECK CHARGES?
    _____10¢ PER CHECK   _____Don't know
    _____15¢ PER CHECK
    _____20¢ PER CHECK

17. AN ALTERNATIVE TO PAYING PER CHECK, OR TO MINIMUM BALANCES, WOULD BE TO PAY A MONTHLY FEE. WHICH OF THESE, IF ANY, WOULD YOU BE WILLING TO PAY?
    _____$2 PER MONTH
    _____$3.50 PER MONTH
    _____$5 PER MONTH
    _____None
    _____Don't know

18. IN GENERAL, WHICH OF THESE THREE WOULD YOU PREFER ON A NOW ACCOUNT PAYING 5 PERCENT?
    _____FEE PER CHECK
    _____SET MONTHLY FEE
    _____MINIMUM BALANCE
    _____All would be same
    _____Not sure/don't know

19. IF NOW ACCOUNTS WERE OFFERED IN YOUR BANK OR SAVINGS AND LOAN, WOULD YOU BE INTERESTED IN OPENING ONE?
    _____Yes   Why?_____
    _____No

20. IF A SAVINGS AND LOAN NOW ACCOUNT PAID HIGHER INTEREST OR HAD LOWER OR NO MINIMUM BALANCE REQUIREMENTS COMPARED TO BANKS, WOULD YOU OPEN A NOW ACCOUNT AT A SAVINGS AND LOAN?
    _____Yes   Why?_____
    _____No
    _____Don't know

21. DO YOU THINK YOU WOULD CHANGE FINANCIAL INSTITUTIONS TO DO SO?
    _____Yes
    _____No
    _____Don't know

22. IF YOU HAD A TRADITIONAL CHECKING ACCOUNT, WOULD YOU CLOSE IT TO OPEN A NOW ACCOUNT?
    _____Yes
    _____No
    _____Don't know

THANK YOU. THE FOLLOWING QUESTIONS ARE FOR STATISTICAL PURPOSES ONLY. THEY ARE SOLELY TO HELP US ANALYZE THE DATA FROM THE SURVEY AND WILL NOT BE IDENTIFIED WITH YOUR ANSWERS.

1. WHERE DO YOU GET MOST OF YOUR INFORMATION ABOUT BANKING SERVICES?
    _____Newspaper and magazines
    _____Radio and/or TV
    _____Word of mouth
    _____Professional consultation (lawyer, accountant)

2. WHAT IS YOUR MARITAL STATUS?
    _____Married   _____Separated
    _____Widowed   _____Other
    _____Divorced
    _____Single

Exhibit 1 (*concluded*)

3. DO YOU HAVE ANY CHILDREN?   _____Yes _____No
4. WHAT IS THE HIGHEST GRADE OF SCHOOL OR COLLEGE YOU HAVE COMPLETED?

_____Grade school   _____Some college, technical, or trade school
_____Some high school   _____College graduate
_____High school   _____Postgraduate

5. PLEASE TELL ME WHICH OF THESE AGE GROUPS YOU ARE IN.

_____18–24   _____45–54
_____25–34   _____44–64
_____34–44   _____65 or OVER

6. WHICK ONE OF THESE INCOME GROUPS DOES YOUR TOTAL FAMILY INCOME FALL INTO?

_____LESS THAN $5,000
_____$5,000–$9,999
_____$10,000–$14,999
_____$15,000–$19,999
_____$20,000–$24,999
_____$25,000–$30,000
_____OVER $30,000

The Strategic Marketing Planning Process

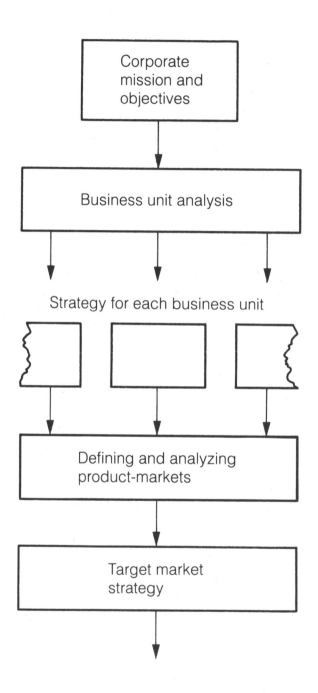